D1613417

THE TYPHOON OF WAR

Lin Poyer • Suzanne Falgout • Laurence Marshall Carucci

THE TYPHOON OF WAR

Micronesian Experiences of the Pacific War

University of Hawai'i Press
Honolulu

06   05   04   03   02   01   5   4   3   2   1

Library of Congress Cataloging-in-Publication Data
Poyer, Lin, 1953–
    The typhoon of war : Micronesian experiences of the
Pacific war / Lin Poyer, Suzanne Falgout, Laurence
Marshall Carucci.
      p.   cm.
    Includes bibliographical references and index.
    ISBN 0-8248-2168-8 (cloth : alk. paper)
    1. World War, 1939–1945—Campaigns—
Micronesia (Federated States).   2. Micronesia
(Federated States)—History.   3. World War, 1939–
1945—Naval operations, American.   I. Falgout,
Suzanne.   II. Carucci, Laurence Marshall, 1949–
III. Title.
D767.99 M53 P69 2001
940.54'26—dc21   00-029875

Designed by Jean Lee Cole

Printed by The Maple-Vail Book Manufacturing Group

CONTENTS

ILLUSTRATIONS

ISLAND NAMES

PACIFIC ISLAND names exhibit a bewildering variety of spellings. Islanders often prefer a different spelling or form than that recognized as "official" by the national government. This table lists names and spellings that have been applied to individual islands and island groups mentioned in the text. The first column is the spelling used in this book. The second column is the spelling normally used in U.S. documents during World War II. The third column lists other variant spellings, including the official standard name if different from the first two columns. Asterisks (*) indicate currently accepted official spellings.

Text Spelling	World War II–Era Spelling	Variant Spellings
Ailinglablab	Ailinglapalap	Ailinglaplap*
Banaba*	Ocean Island	
Chuuk*	Truk	
Enewetak*	Eniwetok	Brown's Range
Eten (Chuuk)	Eten (Truk)	Etten*
Ifaluk	Ifaluk	Ifalik*
Jaluij	Jaluit*	
Kiribati*	Gilbert Islands	
Kosrae*	Kusaie	
Mili*	Mille	
Mokil	Mokil	Mwokil*, Mwoakilloa
Parem* (Chuuk)	Param (Truk)	

Text Spelling	World War II–Era Spelling	Variant Spellings
Pohnpei*	Ponape	
Puluwat*	Enderby Island	
Ronglap	Rongelap*	
Rongrik*	Rongerik	
Sapwuahfik	Ngatik	Ngetik*
Toloas (Chuuk)	Dublon Island (Truk)	Tonoas*
Tuvalu*	Ellice Islands	
Weno* (Chuuk)	Moen Island (Truk)	

Note: We use the English spelling of Palau and its islands. The local name is Belau, and each of the islands has a different Belauan spelling. Original spellings are retained in quotations.

PREFACE

OUR GREATEST resource has been the interviews granted to us by the participants in our oral history collection project of 1990–1991, funded by the National Endowment for the Humanities (those who wished their names known are listed in Appendix A). It is obvious that this book could not have been written without their help. What is less obvious from the written word is the passion, generosity, warmth, nostalgia, and commitment to remembering history that characterized their interaction with us. In using interview material in the text, we have identified speakers by name only where we used more than a phrase of direct quotation. In a few cases, we have masked identities of contributors to protect their privacy.

Laurence Carucci gathered accounts in the Marshall Islands; Suzanne Falgout in Pohnpei and Kosrae; Lin Poyer in Chuuk and Yap. In each area, the authors worked with Micronesian assistants, whose names are also listed in Appendix A. The daily work of these assistants and their help with local arrangements made the project possible. The assistance of local historic preservation officers in each area—also listed—was vital to our success. Each of us has our own memories of people who gave special aid and encouragement; we offer them our thanks, and include their names also in Appendix A. Finally, we are indebted to our two historical consultants, Dr. David Purcell and Fr. Francis X. Hezel. At the University of Hawai'i Press, we thank editor Pamela Kelley and two readers who reviewed and commented on our manuscript. We also thank David Poyer and Joseph Foster for reading and commenting on the manuscript, and Masako Ikeda, Lee Motteler, Dee Spock, Robert Kelly, and

Lela Goodell for their work in the production of this book. All errors are, of course, our own responsibility.

Our coverage of Guam, the Northern Marianas, and the Republic of Palau—where we did not ourselves conduct interviews—depends on existing literature and oral history sources, especially holdings at the Micronesian Area Research Center at the University of Guam (in particular, work by Wakako Higuchi and Dirk Ballendorf) and the Hamilton Library at the University of Hawai'i. We have greatly benefited from recent work on Micronesian history, especially that of the Japanese colonial era, which we cite throughout this book. Our understanding of the Micronesian war experience has been aided by research into U.S. military archives, published and unpublished writings of anthropologists working in the area, and interviews with American veterans of that time and place. Our thanks go to the historians, archivists, anthropologists, military veterans, colleagues, and student assistants who have made it possible to manage (insofar as we have been able to do so) the vast store of written information available on the war. One caution: our access to Japanese attitudes and intentions toward Micronesians was limited to information published in English. The result may be skewed, especially since all three coauthors are Americans. A large number of elderly Micronesians speak Japanese, and we hope there will be a chance for more Japanese-speaking researchers to pursue the ethnohistory of the Pacific war, as Goh Abe, Wakako Higuchi, and Hisafumi Saito have done.

We are fortunate to have begun our work during a period of multidisciplinary reassessment of the Pacific war, as new information and interpretive approaches supplement the standard military, journalistic, and memoir sources. Historians adopting cultural and critical approaches outline the wider context of the conflict in which Islanders were usually powerless participants (e.g., Dower 1986; Iriye 1981; Spector 1985). This widespread rethinking of the war in the Pacific signals an opportune time for anthropological contribution to the scholarly dialogue. In addition to adding to our knowledge of Micronesia during this era, the careful study of Islanders' oral histories contributes to the comparative framework within which scholars seek to understand the significance of global conflict. Our task has been immeasurably aided by the work of Geoffrey White and Lamont Lindstrom both in exploring the war in Melanesia and in stimulating the ethnohistorical study of the impact of the war throughout the Pacific (White and Lindstrom 1989 [developed from a series of Association for Social Anthropology in Oceania conferences]; Lindstrom and White 1990; Lindstrom 1996; White et al. 1988; and the 1988 East-West Center Conference, "Cultural Encounters in the Pacific War" [White 1991]).

Funding for the field collection of oral histories was provided by the National Endowment for the Humanities, RO-22103-90, "World War II in Micronesia: Islander Recollections and Representations." The East-West Center provided an opportunity for us to meet following fieldwork. Additional funding for Poyer's travel to archives and research support was provided by the Taft Memorial Fund of the University of Cincinnati. We are grateful for the support of institutions and individuals both in the islands and in the United States, many of whom are named in Appendix A, but of course we take responsibility for the interpretations presented in this work.

We hope this book will be in some measure a tangible thank-you to all those who helped in our work and a tangible memorial to the Micronesians who suffered through—and especially to those who did not survive—the stormy winds and waves of war.

Chapter 1

WAR IN THE JAPANESE MANDATED
ISLANDS OF MICRONESIA

An Introduction

MICRONESIA—the "little islands"—consists of some twenty-five hundred islands with a total land area of only 1,000 square miles tossed across a swath of ocean larger than the continental United States. What was less likely than that these tiny islands should be the scene of a great global conflict? How unexpected was it that, for those critical months and years, their tides and reefs, their harbors and landscapes, and the circumstances and attitudes of their inhabitants should be studied by the world's most powerful nations with an attentiveness they have never received before or since?

The Pacific war brought major, rapid, and dramatic changes to Micronesian life and transformed Islanders' understandings of the world. Experiences varied greatly, with some islands suffering violent invasion while others saw no military action. Yet, like a typhoon, the war swept away a former life. Throughout the region, the Pacific war is remembered as "the greatest hardship" endured by recent generations.[1] As on other World War II battlegrounds, the passage of half a century has not erased memories. The telling of war stories continues to bond elders of the disparate cultures of Micronesia and to educate younger generations. The lessons taught through war stories guide Micronesian leaders as they plan the futures of their nations.

This book provides the first complete overview of Islanders' lives during the war. It situates Micronesian experiences by outlining the prewar context of Japanese colonial rule, military expansion, and the shift to a defensive posture as American forces advanced through the Central Pacific, and American attack, invasion, and occupation. Our work intentionally focuses on the islands of the former Japanese mandate—the Marshall, Caroline, and North-

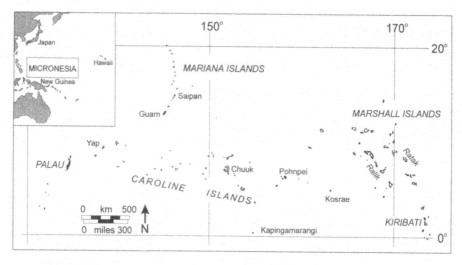

Map 1. Micronesia

ern Mariana Islands—with only brief treatment of the war in Guam, Kiribati (formerly the Gilbert Islands), Banaba (Ocean Island), and Nauru. (Sources for war history in these areas—which have unique colonial histories as well as very different prewar and postwar circumstances—are cited in context.) Our effort has been to foreground Micronesian voices, while putting them in the context of historical information from documentary sources. At the close of the book, we discuss the legacy of the war for Micronesians and for Micronesian nations.

Our study of Micronesian experiences of the war era relies on personal accounts, supplemented by archival and bibliographic research. (The chronology in Appendix B facilitates correlation of oral and documentary information.) In 1990–1991, funding from the National Endowment for the Humanities enabled us to conduct more than three hundred interviews with people who lived through the war in the Marshall Islands, Kosrae (then Kusaie), Pohnpei (Ponape), Chuuk (Truk), and Yap.[2] Micronesian accounts contain a wealth of detail about wartime activities, local conditions, and social change. In addition, they embody culturally significant interpretations of these experiences, as they were felt during the war and as they are understood today.

TOWARD A MICRONESIAN HISTORY OF THE WAR

While American, European, and Japanese historians have produced voluminous documentation of military experiences and interpretations of the war in the Pacific, they seldom describe the effects of wartime operations on indigenous populations. Equally important, little is known of the local view of the conflict, largely because Pacific Islander representations of history have been primarily oral and performative, recorded in narrative, dance, drama, and song. Research in the Southwest Pacific and our own and others' work in Micronesia indicates the historical richness of Islander recollections of the war years.[3]

As anthropologists, we found ourselves interested in the war because of its critical effects on Micronesian life. This is true in the obvious sense, as the physical remains and political and economic arrangements shaped in the context of war mold Micronesia today. But the war is also a cultural and psychological factor in modern life, as people make decisions about cooperating with Japanese or American businesses, enlisting in the U.S. Armed Forces, voting on international affiliations, or responding to news of U.S. military action abroad. Studies of the role of history in society from throughout the Pacific Islands and the world show the complexity of the links between images of the past and everyday life. In Micronesia, where war history remains largely at the level of personal memory rather than public history, writers must join these memories together into a tapestry that will display, as much as possible, a broad history of the war years.

Micronesians are fully literate, but they seldom record historical accounts. In speaking of their islands' recent past, they usually distinguish the sequence of colonial orders, describing Spanish, German, Japanese, and American eras. (Another major temporal marker is the shift from pre- to postmissionary times.) The war is not usually marked as a separate historical period, but it signals the transition from Japanese to American rule. Unlike earlier transitions, this one was in the form of conquest, a significant distinction in cultures where conquest was traditionally a way to gain control over new land. The Pacific war is spoken of as a watershed historical event, coming at the end of a long period of increasing Japanese presence in the islands: "Trukese tend to divide the Japanese period into phases during which there were 'few Japanese in Truk' (until the early 1920s and the establishment of the civil government), when there were 'many Japanese, but they lived on Dublon' (early 1920s until about 1930), when there were 'many Japanese who lived on Dublon and in }our villages' (1930 until about 1937) and 'wartime' (ca. 1937–1945)" (King and Parker 1984:91).

The war is spoken of more freely than many other historical and traditional matters. Most Micronesians, certainly those east of the Marianas, regard information about the past as intellectual property, valuable for arguing claims to leadership, status, and land or other rights. Accounts of clan history, former owners of land, myths, or other important topics are commonly told only under special circumstances. Those lacking kin links conferring rights to such information are unlikely to get more than an incomplete and perhaps intentionally garbled account. We were fortunate, then, in seeking to inquire about a topic on which older Micronesians were not only able, but usually eager, to speak openly.

To say that people speak openly about their experiences of war is not to say that oral history of this era is unproblematic. Though war history is for the most part unlikely to be subjected to the subtle management that characterizes more sacred and pragmatically consequential histories (e.g., Falgout 1984), it is, like all history, subject both to the vagaries of memory and to numerous intentionalities of representation. Zeleneitz and Saito (1986, 1989) demonstrated the most obvious researcher effect when they compared wartime accounts given by Melanesians to an American and a Japanese interviewer, respectively. Like other Americans in Micronesia, we found that people were at times reluctant to speak to us too positively of the Japanese, or, on the other hand, that they spoke of Japanese virtue so as to make a point of some shortcoming of American rule. Representations of American actions during and immediately after the war were also governed by these concerns of politeness or politics (Carucci 1995). Even more clearly, legacies of war with current practical implications proved to be very challenging interview topics: claims for compensation from Japan and the United States for wartime and postwar damages, land rights tangled in wartime confiscation, the modern roles of the U.S. military and Japanese business. Because our main goal is to grasp a general understanding of Micronesians' recollections of their war experience, the use of the war for present-day political purposes does not form a part of this book.

Sometimes the least politicized topics led in emotionally complex directions because they were so personal. As elderly people recalled the deaths of kin and friends, the kindness of long-deceased neighbors, the hardships of struggling to survive under the worst of attack and scarcity, their thoughts and emotions drew their memories in valuable personal directions that had not been foreseen in our interview questions.[4] Our goal was always to let people speak and to allow them to choose their most significant memories. The content and expressive form of their memories took its shape from their personal and communal circumstances during the war years and in the current day. Gender, rank in the social order, status in the Japanese colonial structure, education, and place of origin and residence all contributed to the content of memory and to the depth of the interview.

The age of each storyteller and the circumstances in which they spent the war years are crucial to differences in personal accounts. Some people we spoke with lived nearly half of their lives during Japanese times, while others were eight or ten years old when the Americans arrived. Each recollection is inherently comparative, but some people are old enough that, when thinking back, elements of the Japanese arrival during the First World War merge with recollections of the coming of the Japanese military during the Second World War. Those born in the first years of Japanese colonial rule are able to describe aspects of the Japanese era in its developmental perspective. Those born nearer to the time of the war recall the Japanese era almost entirely from accounts they have heard from others and begin their own story with memories of hardship and destruction.

Whether they spent the war in bomb shelters, in sweet potato fields under the guns of Japanese military guards, or in their own homes on atolls sheltered from the winds of war, Micronesians who survived those years know that their peoples passed through a major historical transformation. Their memories of the Pacific war recount the personal, but their representations of that war, and war itself, reflect Micronesian worldviews and engage modern political and philosophical issues facing Islanders. Students of culture and history know that all representations of the past, however nearly they approach an accurate record, have a cultural meaning that rewards close study. We hope in the future to complete such a work with the rich material shared by those we interviewed. In this volume, however, we seek only to make a first pass at assembling a broad and comprehensive account of what Micronesians experienced before, during, and immediately after the war and what those experiences have meant for their islands.

BACKGROUND OF MICRONESIAN GEOGRAPHY AND HISTORY

For more than four centuries of contact with Islanders, foreign interest in Micronesia has been primarily economic. The larger islands of Melanesia and Polynesia have been the more prized jewels in Western empires, offering greater natural bounty and larger populations to colonial exploitation. The small, scattered islands of Micronesia held comparatively little in the way of commercial resources. These geographic factors made most of Micronesia a relatively late and neglected colony in the history of European-American contact with the Pacific.[5]

Some Micronesian islands became stopovers for cross-Pacific travelers where whalers, trading schooners, or warships could rest and replenish supplies. Guam served as a port of call for Spanish galleons crossing from the Philippines to Mexico. This important trade route persisted for two centuries and led to Spanish control of Guam and later of the other Marianas, but Spanish galleons brought little contact to other islands along the route. In the early nineteenth century, Pohnpei became a favored rest stop for whalers and traders en route to China. From this, a limited trade in turtle shell, pearl shell, and coconut oil developed in the Marshalls and Carolines, accompanied by small expatriate settlements and missionization.

Only in the late nineteenth century did European countries express serious colonial interest in Micronesia, when British phosphate concerns led to the colonization of Kiribati. Spain and Germany contested colonial rights to the rest of the area. Spanish efforts in the Carolines (1885–1899) focused on missionization; German efforts in the Marshalls (1885–1914) and later in the Carolines and Northern Marianas centered on economic production. But overall, Western interests were limited and the colonial presence meager.

Micronesia held a different potential for Japan. Resource-hungry and over-populated, Japan saw these islands lying close to home as valuable possessions for an expanding empire. Fueled by romantic notions of the South Seas as a tropical paradise, the Japanese eagerly claimed German-held Micronesia at the outbreak of World War I. Japan's priorities in its new League of Nations mandate were emigration and economic development to aid the home islands. Administrative policies and activities thus centered on Japanese nationals.

Like earlier colonial governors, the Japanese South Seas Bureau targeted some areas of indigenous Micronesian life for acculturation and ignored others. Japanese colonial policy affected mandate islands differentially, forming a west-east gradient. Enormous sugarcane plantations worked by immigrant laborers spread over the large islands of Saipan, Tinian, and Rota in the Marianas; relatively few Japanese reached the small, sandy atolls of the Marshalls, where economic development was limited largely to stimulating the copra trade and commercial fishing. While Japanese penetration into Micronesian life during the years of the mandate varied greatly across the region, Micronesians under Japanese rule experienced the closest contact they had ever had with foreigners, resulting in significant social and economic change. And, more than in previous colonial administrations, Japanese Micronesia shared regional and global connections. Living for the most part in kin-centered, subsistence-based communities, largely segregated from the Japanese colonists, Micronesians nonetheless gained access to a wage economy, grew familiar with Japanese goods and services, and internalized features of Japanese customs and attitudes in their own social practices.

Micronesia became a successful colonial segment of Japan's expanding empire. In the late 1930s, the Japanese military capitalized on the islands' strategic location, with plans to make them a springboard for expansion into the Central and Southwest Pacific. The Japanese launched the early air and sea attacks of their Pacific campaign from Micronesia. Later they moved troops and supplies through the area in support of embattled and occupied regions to the east and south.

As the Allies resisted the Japanese expansion and then turned to the defeat of Japan, Micronesia emerged as a key battleground. Because the Japanese were well entrenched there and because the islands lay along the road to the Japanese homeland, Allied forces brought the war to Micronesia as they combined Admiral Ernest King's Central Pacific "Road to Tokyo" with General Douglas MacArthur's advance through the Southwest Pacific. Before the war, Micronesia had been virtually unknown and of no great interest to Americans other than missionaries. But once the United States conquered the region, it maintained its hold for nearly half a century, with the goal of denying any other power the opportunity to occupy what had been, for the United States, such a strategically damaging enemy possession.

OVERVIEW OF THE WARTIME ERA IN MICRONESIA

Micronesians must be seen as active participants in the Pacific conflict. Their contributions were crucial to Japanese—and later American—successes. But in the end, as at the beginning, it was not their war. Micronesians were quite literally caught in the middle of a bitter struggle for control of the Pacific. Their fate lay in the hands of the major combatants, their fortunes determined by changing Japanese and Allied strategic plans.

Japan had expended considerable effort to engage Micronesians as loyal members of the empire and, by the start of the war, had achieved some success. As members of chiefly societies where warfare had been culturally valued, Micronesians took note of the hard work and competence of the Japanese as they prepared for war, garrisoning troops and introducing sophisticated military technology to the islands. The Japanese seemed prepared for anything. In contrast to Japanese propaganda branding Allies as racist, stupid, disorderly, and weak, Micronesians were impressed by Japanese devotion to the emperor's cause. Ichios Eas of Chuuk remembers a wartime event that confirmed this impression:

Japanese ships experienced many losses and much damage . . . in the open seas. When I was in Nampo [the main dock on Toloas (Dublon)], damaged ships and submarines came in. One time we went out to bring water to a damaged submarine near Eten. They had to immediately cut off our rope from the submarine as it completely sank. . . . When it was about to sink, all of the crew members went back inside the submarine and closed it and went down with it. No one was left.

That is the code that the Japanese live by: Go all the way! They do not worry about losing their lives, rather than turning back. . . . The submarine is still there today. They [the crew] could have gone to Eten, which was not far at all. Instead, they cut off our anchor and pushed us away as the submarine was quickly sinking. And everyone got in and went down with it.

At the outbreak of war, few Micronesians doubted that such strong-willed Japanese would win, and many gladly joined the war effort, some volunteering for hazardous missions. In addition to immediate prestige and extra pay, they anticipated rewards for their hard work and loyalty at war's end. But nothing in prior Micronesian experience could prepare them for the nature of the conflict that was about to take place in their homelands. The stunning force and suddenness of the first air and sea attacks shocked Islanders who had been reassured by Japanese confidence and apparent strength.

For most Micronesians, "the war" began when violence actually reached their island. Thus the time frame of war experiences varied dramatically throughout the area. For the people of the few Allied possessions in Micronesia (Kiribati, Banaba, Nauru, Guam), the war began when they were seized by the Japanese in December 1941. The Marshalls and Kiribati received light retaliatory American attacks beginning on February 1, 1942. But throughout that year, Allied forces concentrated on the defense of Hawai'i and Midway, then shifted to the Southwest Pacific to protect Australia and New Zealand while plans proceeded for a Central Pacific offense. For most Micronesians, the war arrived, or returned, during the American push toward Japan in late 1943 and early 1944.

The Allies knew little about the islands or about the nature of Japanese defenses there when the decision was taken for a Micronesia campaign. At first, Allied plans called for seizure of important Japanese bases throughout the region. But lessons learned early in the Pacific campaign taught the advantage of a less direct strategy. Called by such innocuous terms as blockading, neutralizing, leapfrogging, and bypassing, it meant that Americans invaded only a few islands to be used as bases from which to launch the next stage of attacks, with the goal of reaching the Japanese home islands as soon as possible. Bypassed islands—the largest number of Micronesian islands—were isolated by Allied control of sea lanes, rendered ineffective by continual bombing, and left to endure and starve until surrender.

The Micronesian history of the war is distinct from that of the Japanese and Americans in this theater. The militarization and regimentation of indigenous life caused by war preparations accelerated changes in island lifeways that had begun under colonial rule. Under Japanese military direction, most Micronesians spent the war years working on construction, agricultural, and manufacturing projects. Micronesians were pressed into hard labor, often without relief or compensation. Many were forced to relocate, their property subjected to confiscation. Families were disrupted, churches and schools closed. Food became scarce, imported clothing and luxuries nonexistent. As the Allies took control of sea lanes, Japanese troops were stranded, their supplies cut off. Military rule became harsher as the war continued and food shortages grew dangerous. Micronesian affection and admiration for Japanese turned to distress, doubt, apathy, resentment, and resistance. By the war's end, relationships between Japanese soldiers and Islanders were severely strained. Mistrust and brutality, if not commonplace, were not rare. Toward the end of the war, Micronesians everywhere suspected that the Japanese planned to exterminate them—perhaps to alleviate the critical food shortage, in retaliation for disloyalty, to cheat the enemy of his prize, or as a final attempt to achieve honor in a lost war.

Meanwhile, at the hands of American forces, Micronesians were subjected to every sort of attack, from invasions on the scale of Kwajalein and Saipan to the regular, unremitting bombing raids that hit Chuuk almost daily for nearly one and a half years to the occasional strafing run that targeted fishing canoes in the lagoon of a tiny unfortified atoll. The Japanese warned Micronesians that American victory would mean their annihilation as enemy collaborators. This proved false; Americans decided to regard Micronesians as friendly neutrals liberated by Allied forces. This official policy did not prevent the damage to Micronesian lives and property that accompanied attack and invasion, though there is evidence that Japanese commanders made efforts to remove Islanders from harm's way, and American forces tried to avoid targeting them.

Today Micronesians are remarkably generous in their judgment of both Japanese and Americans. They acknowledge the extreme circumstances that led some Japanese soldiers to resort to harsh measures yet cannot forget those kindly Japanese officers and enlisted men who made daily life more tolerable, as well as those who protected them from danger. And they speak with genuine affection of their old friendships with Japanese civilians. The Allies and their motives for war were, of course, less well known. Nevertheless, elderly Micronesians often point out that the Americans were at war only with the Japanese, not them, and that harm caused to them was unintentional. And they recall fondly the liberality and kindness of American soldiers and sailors who came ashore as the Japanese left. Profoundly impressed by the speed of American victory and the scale of their supply train, Micronesians formed consequential understandings of American wealth, generosity, and military might.

COMPARISON OF MELANESIAN AND MICRONESIAN
THEATERS OF WAR

Geographic differences in the islands of Melanesia and Micronesia, their history of colonial occupation, the wartime strategies used by the major combatants, and the timing of the war's arrival resulted in quite different wartime experiences for indigenous peoples in these regions. Yet American approaches to invading and governing Micronesia were in part based on their military experiences in the Southwest Pacific.

The islands of Micronesia received some of the first action of the war, with the quick Japanese capture of Kiribati and Guam and brief American return strikes against the Marshalls. But it was the relatively large and more closely spaced islands of Melanesia that saw the first major land battles in the Pacific theater, where the Japanese and Allies met face-to-face and also came into direct contact with Islanders, as the Southwest Pacific was contested in battles fought close to indigenous population centers. It was also in Melanesia that new wartime equipment and strategies were first tested in an island-by-island campaign.

Melanesians, ambivalent about centuries of governance under various Allied nations, had nevertheless been surprised at the colonists' hasty retreat at the start of war. In some places, the Japanese were initially greeted as the liberators they claimed to be. Then, as hardships increased under the Japanese, relations with these new foreigners began to sour as well. Local people were often caught in the middle as captured areas seesawed between the opposing forces. Melanesians aided soldiers on both sides and suffered and died for their loyalty, their charity to the sick and wounded, or simply their presence. The complexity of the situation in Melanesia was further increased by the presence of Polynesians loyal to various Allies and Micronesians owing allegiance to the Japanese.[6]

As the contest closed in major engagements, massive amounts of equipment, supplies, and personnel flowed into the Southwest Pacific. The attitude with which Allied troops—Americans in particular—shared these goods and worked with Islanders gave Melanesians a dramatic sample of Western democracy. These troops implied, or even stated outright, promises of enhanced status or equality with colonials after the war. The shattering of this dream, when at war's end Melanesia was again divided among the colonial powers who conducted business as usual, played an important role in independence movements and cargo cults in the postwar period.

By the time war came in earnest to Micronesia, much of the framework of Japanese-American military encounters had been worked out in the Melanesian theater. Allied experiences in the Southwest Pacific, the enormous expanse of ocean to cover, and American military politics put the U.S. Navy in control of the Micronesian campaigns. Although the Japanese had prepared for and constantly awaited the invasion of these islands, considered part of the empire, in the end there were few actual battlegrounds in Micronesia. Land battles waged in the Marshalls, Saipan, Guam, and Palau focused on Japanese military targets, with most Islanders evacuated from battle zones by the Japanese.

The Allied strategy of blockading, neutralizing, and bypassing islands had a direct effect on a much larger number of Micronesians and lent an eerie impersonality to the war. Some Micronesians had an acquaintance with Americans, gained either by listening to stories about the times of whalers and traders or from their knowledge of a few missionaries, educators, or expatriate merchants in their midst. But for most, Americans—who remained offshore, underwater, or in the air, bombarding or bombing from a distance—were recognized as a dangerous force, an entity much speculated about but largely unknown until the war's end.

The very timing of the Micronesian campaign contributed to the harshness of the war in this arena. Coming when the Japanese were on the defensive and when they lacked reinforcements of troops or supplies, the Allied strategy meant that each island met the later phases of war largely in isolation. People's ability to survive depended on each island's resources, less the destruction sustained during bombing. It also depended on the quality of local leadership and relations among the various peoples thrown together for the duration.

Like Islanders in the Southwest Pacific, Micronesians were caught in the middle of a foreign war. The two enemies—one known and one unknown (the nationalities reversed for Micronesians and Melanesians)—surrounded them and contested their lands and waters. Micronesians were rarely forced to choose sides as rapidly and at such cost as many Melanesians were, yet the issue of loyalty and the weighing of Japanese and American resources, propaganda claims, and behavior was vital to the survival of both.

DIVERSITY IN MICRONESIAN EXPERIENCES

The geographic term *Micronesia* obscures the sociocultural, linguistic, and historical diversity of these island groups, as the diminutive size of the islands belies the great geographic and cultural complexity of the region. Micronesia consists of islands of both continental and volcanic origin, varying from large and verdant high islands to sandy atolls awash at high tide. Guam (209 square miles) is the largest; many islands are too small to be inhabited. The overwhelming presence of the sea and the diversity of individual islands and island groups are keys to the variability in wartime experiences in Micronesia. One of the challenges in writing a general history of the war has been to describe life on the high islands, with their large populations and major military fortifications, as well as on small atolls of little interest to either Japanese or Allied strategists. Micronesian experiences of war varied not only by location but also as a result of the differential treatment accorded by the Japanese (and later by Americans) to people of different ethnic backgrounds, social statuses, wartime roles, ages, and genders.

The conflict itself, because of geography, strategy, and chance, affected islands variously. The Marshall Islands, critical to the U.S. Navy's "island-hopping" plan, received the full force of American power in the eastern Pacific after Kiribati was retaken. Some atolls came under American control with the first invasions; Majuro, Enewetak (formerly Eniwetok), and Kwajalein became U.S. bases supporting attacks farther west. Other atolls were leapfrogged by U.S. forces, leaving Japanese and Micronesians isolated together until surrender. The Caroline Islands were bypassed by U.S. strategy but suffered aerial bombing, bombardment, and blockade. Still, Japanese submarine and air attacks were launched from Chuuk and Yap as late as June 1944. Palau, Saipan, and Tinian were heavily defended by Japanese forces and experienced major land battles, as well as the common danger of bombardment and increasing pressure on food resources in the final months of the war.

Finally, Micronesians had varied experiences with the victorious occupying forces. Americans were first and longest in certain of the Marshall Islands; they were in greatest numbers in the Marianas; they were fewer and later but still extremely visible and the subject of intense interest in the Carolines. We see the result in later trajectories of the relationship of Islanders and Americans. Because of their military histories, Enewetak, Kwajalein, and Bikini have become key points in U.S.–Marshallese relations. The Mariana Islands became the administrative center for the U.S. Trust Territory of the Pacific Islands and are today the most "Americanized" of the former Japanese mandate islands in economic and social life. Questions about U.S. military interests, the nuclear-free Pacific movement, American responsibility for island economies, immigration and customs policies, and other issues suggest the contemporary significance of local ideas about Americans, American power, and Micronesia's role in global geopolitics—ideas that have their origin in the experiences of Islanders who witnessed the transfer of power from Japan to the United States in 1944–1945.

The Pacific war profoundly altered Micronesia. Wartime encounters with Japanese and Americans were unlike Islanders' past experience with the people of these two Pacific powers. The peaceful domestic character of Japanese colonial administrators or businessmen and American missionaries was replaced by professional soldiers, willing to expend all the natural and human resources of the islands in pursuit of their goal, ultimately careless of civilian bystanders. During these years, Micronesians stretched to the utmost their personal and cultural capacity to survive. But they perceived in the midst of war novel opportunities to develop skills and enhance their status in old and new social worlds. The war forced a rethinking of cultural values, and it expanded Islanders' knowledge of global military, political, and economic realities. World War II in Micronesia meant, in short, both terrible suffering and momentous change. Nothing would ever be the same again.

Chapter 2

BEFORE THE WAR

Islander Life in the Japanese Mandate

PURSUING a long-standing economic and strategic interest in the South Seas, Japan took possession of Germany's Micronesian colonies in 1914, formalizing control in a League of Nations mandate at the end of World War I. Aided by entrepreneurs already living in the islands, the Japanese Navy administered the area from 1914 to 1922 with an active program of public works, surveys, education, and hygiene. Even in its early stages, Japanese administration was more intensive than previous Spanish and German regimes. In 1922, the establishment of the civilian South Seas Government (Nan'yō-chō) inaugurated the framework that shaped the lives of Micronesians and Japanese immigrants alike until the war years returned the mandate to military control. This chapter describes Micronesia in the 1930s, a decade of economic growth, administrative stability, and a restricted but productive and in many ways satisfying way of life for the fifty thousand Micronesians under Japanese rule.[1]

The South Seas Government had two goals: to develop Micronesia as a productive part of the empire, and to demonstrate that Japan, like European powers, was a capable and "civilizing" ruler of colonial peoples. The mandate was a colony of lesser value to Japan than Korea or Taiwan, but it nonetheless held its share of bureaucracy. The Nan'yō-chō governor, who reported to the prime minister, was headquartered in Koror, Palau, and directed branch governors of the Marianas, Yap, the central Carolines, the eastern Carolines, and the Marshall Islands. The trained staff was aided by the socializing influence of increasing numbers of Japanese immigrants and of the dual Micronesian elite—traditional leaders, and youth educated in Japanese schools and hired by the colonial government.

In reflecting on the civil administration, Mark Peattie comments on the relative autonomy of officials of the South Seas Government, who operated "untroubled in the daily exercise of their authority by indigenous resistance, domestic complaint, or foreign criticism" (1988:77). Apart from Palau's *Modekngei* movement and perhaps some activities of Pohnpei's Typhoon Society, no organized resistance to Japanese colonial civilian rule took shape, and Japanese and Okinawan immigrants cooperated in pursuit of economic opportunities. Of course, this vision of an untroubled colony reflects the rulers' perspective. The Japanese government limited opportunities for foreign visitors to evaluate colonial policy. Peattie's study concludes that despite Japan's early commitment to League of Nations ideals for mandated territories, Micronesian interests were eventually overshadowed by Japanese priorities. Rule of the islands became, increasingly after 1930, an effort to create an outlet for Japanese emigration and a profitable element of the imperial economy (Peattie 1988:81–117). It is difficult to discern contemporary Islanders' attitudes toward the colonial order from the historical record. In hindsight, these years take on a rosy tint in the recollections of survivors of war.

EVERYDAY LIFE BEFORE THE WAR

Micronesians' memories of prewar life are shaded by nostalgia for a time when young people were respectful and imported goods were cheap. Even if we take some of the shine off those golden years, we receive nonetheless a vision of a life that was, for many Micronesians, more pleasant than it is today in some respects—and infinitely better than the hardships of the war years.

In stark contrast to later deprivations, the 1930s were a time of material prosperity and apparent stability. It was a time when Islanders made plans for their families' futures based on ample wage work, public education limited in scope but open to many talented young men and some women, and a social life active in the familiar forms of chiefly feasts and Christian church events, but increasingly enjoying sumo, tennis, baseball, and young people's clubs. Micronesians saw themselves as low-ranked but integral members of an expanding Japanese empire, and while most people's lives centered on family and traditional affairs, access to news and rumor brought them into the ever more tense global conversation.

Every island of Japanese Micronesia was linked with a colonial system providing basic schooling and health care. As the mandate's economy gained momentum, Micronesian men and many women had access to wage labor and markets for farm and marine products and handicrafts. Imported goods were plentiful and affordable. Islanders adopted rice as a regular part of their diet, along with new vegetables and fruits introduced by agricultural experiment stations and demonstration farms. Wealthier Islanders and those in towns built Japanese-style wooden houses with tin roofs. Electricity was available in parts of Palau, Chuuk, and Jaluij (Jaluit) as early as 1922, and the government subsidized wells, cisterns, and water tanks. The level of imports used in daily life was higher before the war than it would be for years afterward in most places. In Pohnpei, for example, every family owned china, glassware, and cutlery, important status markers. Japanese-made furniture was common, and some households owned phonographs (Bascom 1965:84).

Micronesians living in town—and everyone else, who visited when they could—grew accustomed to movies, ice cream, postal savings accounts, and newspapers. Indeed, as the region's small cities grew, they came to be quite attractive. Even though few Micronesians lived there—or if they did, they lived in only one section of town—urban excitement came to be part of life. Young people especially felt a sense of freedom when a youth went to work for a Japanese storekeeper or a young woman gained an income by doing laundry for Japanese. Social activities surrounding church and school, clubs, and sports all contributed to a sense of pleasure and activity and of being part of a large and exciting world. It is true that when elderly Micronesians remember the fun and excitement of this time, they are also recalling their own youth. But the sheer range of activities in which Micronesians engaged—partly segregated from Japanese life as they were—indicates that Islanders were growing up in a system that gave them regional and global connections, while they remained rooted in familiar life at home.

At the same time, Micronesians recall that the pleasures of colonial administration were tempered by Japanese ideals of obedience. Racial segregation and discrimination limited Micronesians' lives. Acculturative pressure in some areas, such as Yap, gallingly restricted indigenous religious and customary practice. In particular, the discipline of the Japanese administration made an indelible impression on Islanders. "The law was enforced strictly even before the war started," recalls Marcus Alempia (from Pohnpei), indicating that wartime regulation was seen as a tightening of general Japanese discipline, which itself differed from traditional means of social control.

Japanese regulations governing Islander life were shaped by League of Nations policies and by the Japanese desire, which increased in the 1930s, to integrate the islands into the empire. For Islanders, the law focused on a few key prohibitions on drinking alcohol, theft, gambling, and sex with Japanese women. Micronesians recall beatings with rubber straps or a thick rope and policemen hoisting a person upside down and beating him on the feet; or being forced to stare into the sun, to sit on a board put behind the knees, or to lift a biscuit tin filled with water for half a day. The police also used shaming punishments, shaving prisoners' heads and exposing their nakedness.

The agent enforcing the petty regulations of daily life—and the first line of investigation for criminal accusations—was the policeman. Japanese policemen manned a station in each branch capital, with substations in larger villages and main islands. These were the primary and sometimes almost the only link between rural Micronesians and the Japanese administration.[2] The police force included Micronesian constables *(junkei),* who became important local sources of guidance in dealing with colonial authorities. The police force, assisted by appointed Micronesian leaders, provided the grassroots network for control of local life—a system that later proved effective in mobilizing labor and production for the war effort. Micronesian police continued their role as interlocutors and enforcers throughout the war years, and also received special consideration from their Japanese superiors.

Under Japanese rule, traditional leaders (who had been largely supported by the preceding German administration) were incorporated into colonial bureaucracy by receiving assignments as village chiefs or headmen *(sosonchō* and *sonchō)*—or, if they proved uncooperative, were set aside in favor of more Japan-oriented appointees. As early as 1922, traditional chiefs' functions were separated from those of village head and administrator. The colonial staff handled criminal cases and land tenure decisions but appointed indigenous leaders who organized labor, conducted censuses, collected taxes, and acted as liaison between administration and local people. At the same time, multifaceted pressure toward acculturation lessened Islanders' attention to traditional obligations. In the Marshall Islands, new rules altered the division of copra income, guaranteeing a percentage for chiefs but often restricting the amount they could obtain from commoners. In Pohnpei, Japanese regulations limited duties owed to high title holders, while ensuring them a minimum of honor feasts. In Palau, Nan'yō-chō headquarters and the most intensively acculturated area, limits on using traditional currency in marriage exchanges joined with other changes to reduce the power of high-status castes, dramatically decreasing their power by the late 1930s. Even outer islands felt the effects of acculturation, as respect gifts to clan chiefs in the Mortlocks declined in the 1930s and nearly disappeared in the 1940s. On Namoluk, an atoll chief was appointed following Japanese patrilineal custom rather than local matrilineal ideas. And, as Islanders became integrated into the Japanese economy, leadership became increasingly linked to financial standing.[3]

ECONOMIC DEVELOPMENT

Germany had not made the islands an economic success, and it was not until a combination of government support and private initiative set to work in the late 1920s that the mandate began to turn a profit for Japan. By 1932, Nan'yō-chō was financially independent of the home government. Peattie (1988:118–152) describes the development of four main industries: sugar (by far the most important export) in the Marianas and to some extent on Pohnpei, phosphate on Angaur and Fais, copra throughout the islands, and fishing. The two major private companies, given much government encouragement, were NBK (Nan'yō Bōeki Kaisha, the South Seas Trading Company, locally called "Nambō," or in the Marshalls "BK"), which monopolized interisland shipping and the copra trade; and NKK (Nan'yō Kōhatsu Kaisha, the South Seas Development Company, locally called "Nankō"), which ran the sugar business in the Marianas along with numerous other enterprises throughout the Carolines. These industries—and additional projects in agriculture and small-scale manufacturing—were supported by a surge of immigration of Japanese and especially Okinawan laborers, farmers, and fishermen.[4]

After 1930, whole families (not just male workers) arrived, and "the society of immigrants took on a settled, permanent character" (Hatanaka 1973–1974:7). In 1936 the government began a five-year immigration plan, part of an economic push that included establishment of the Nan'yō Takushoku, the South Seas Colonization Corporation (locally called "Nantaku"), which took over phosphate mines and funded new industries from pearl diving to pineapple packing. The plan encouraged immigrants as small farmers and businessmen and as fishermen, traders, and factory workers employed by the expanding corporations. The majority of immigrants in 1937 were poor farmers from Okinawa and the southern Japanese islands. Okinawans would work for half the wages of Japanese in Tokyo, or less; immigrants also received company houses, gardens, low-cost medical care, and a small bonus at the end of their contract.[5] As immigrants flooded into the larger islands, those areas underwent intensive urbanization, agricultural intensification, and market development.

Nan'yō-chō became in essence an economic development agency to profit Japanese, but it also provided what many Micronesians saw as benefits, such as an assured market for their products (many of which were in demand in the Japanese empire—fish, copra, sugar, fibers [Peoples 1977:146]), shipping and travel opportunities, and useful infrastructure. The Islander elite, both traditional and Japanese-educated, served as office workers and labor foremen. Cooperative work groups *(kumiai),* patriotic organizations, youth groups, and volunteer community labor *(kinrōhōshi)* strengthened with the growing economy and denser population of expanded urban areas. At the same time that these new forms of cooperation emerged, life in extended family and village became more individualistic. Especially in the Marianas and Palau, ethnicity and economics began to sort people, including Micronesians, into classes.

Japan's war in China stimulated production throughout the empire. In Pohnpei, for example, new pharmaceutical, fiber, and tannin industries greatly increased income from exports between 1936 and 1940. As a result, "Just before Pearl Harbor, Ponapeans experienced their greatest period of prosperity and their highest standard of living" (Bascom 1950:144). Even the community life of small islands was affected by trade in raw materials and handicrafts, resident Japanese merchants and police, men leaving home for contract labor, and children attending school in urban areas.

The economic boom was accompanied by a "boom" in bureaucratic regulation of daily life. Islanders lived under 10 P.M. curfews; rules about clothing, alcohol use, and gambling; travel restrictions; fishing permits; requirements for planting food crops; control of leases on public lands for farming; and labor recruiting for government and private companies. Such regulation primarily affected population centers, though people from smaller islands encountered them when they traveled, and Japanese policemen on some outlying islands gave residents the experience of living under tight constraints. The regulation of life as immigration peaked was to intensify further as the mandate shifted toward military government.

ISLAND ECONOMIES

As the pace of the colonial economy picked up, it affected Islanders in three ways that presaged wartime events. People were relocated to make way for Japanese projects; land was transferred from local to Japanese control; and ever-larger numbers of Islanders were encouraged and then obliged to work in Japanese-directed activities. Official land surveys and changes in Nan'yō law increasingly moved land out of Micronesian hands. As early as 1933, some 73 percent of Micronesia's total land area came under government control—ranging from small plots in the Marshalls to nearly all of Tinian—most of it subsequently leased to Japanese settlers or corporations (McGrath and Wilson 1971:183). It should be noted that the geographic distribution of these impacts during the 1930s, governed by economic strategy, did not match later wartime patterns of relocation, confiscation, and labor recruitment, which were governed by military strategy. The greatest effects of economic development in the 1930s were in the Marianas, Palau, and Pohnpei, which colonial officials judged most likely to return profit.

The Northern Marianas became a major sugarcane producer, supported by large-scale immigration. First Saipan, then Tinian and Rota were intensively developed as sugar plantations. Of the more than fifty thousand Japanese in Micronesia in 1935, forty thousand were in the Marianas. Chamorro land was protected from alienation until 1931, when it became possible for Japanese citizens to purchase it with government permission. Saipan, Tinian, and Rota were among the first islands the Nan'yō-chō surveyed in the mid-1930s effort to inventory private land in the mandate, though it is not clear whether titles were legally registered. Many Chamorros found it more remunerative to sell or lease land for sugarcane production than to farm it. Despite pressure to turn land to sugarcane, the Japanese respected certain types of local land rights, with the important later exception of land taken for wartime military installations. Economically driven relocation meant that Micronesians now lived at the edges of the Japanese city of Garapan in Saipan, and Chamorros and Carolinians in Rota were moved off their land and out of Songsong village to make way for Japanese families growing sugarcane. Development reworked the human geography of these islands, altering settlement patterns, roads, flora, and fauna. By 1937, of a total of 46,708 residents in the Japanese Marianas, only 4,145 were Micronesians.[6]

The people of Palau were more involved with Japanese economic development plans than any other Micronesian population, except perhaps Chamorros. Although Palau saw immigration of Japanese farmers to the island of Babelthuap beginning in the 1920s, Palauans themselves also entered actively into production, marketing, and service occupations. The prewar economy included commercial production of copra, tapioca, pineapple, bananas, papaya, yams, breadfruit, citrus, taro, hibiscus, pandanus, coffee, cocoa, domestic animals, trepang, trochus (shellfish for buttons), mangrove charcoal, firewood, sawmills, and tuna and bonito fishing. Though Japan's rural immigration program on Palau was not a success, Koror in the mid-1930s was a boomtown built on its role as the Nan'yō capital, fruit and vegetable farming, and, after 1937, the dramatic growth of the pearl and mother-of-pearl industry. Yet only about sixteen hundred of the twenty thousand residents of Koror were Palauan (of only four thousand Palauans in all).[7] Palauans "were not, on the whole, participants in the Japanese development of their islands" (McKnight 1978:10)—though they felt they were, to an extent, among its beneficiaries.

Pohnpei ranked third in Japanese immigration, with many fewer settlers than the Marianas and Palau. Commercial agriculture included cattle, pineapple, tapioca, cassava, copra, and tobacco. Factories processing copra, tapioca, and fish, along with lumber, cotton weaving, and the manufacture of soap, ice, paper, cigarettes, starch from cassava, and alcohol from sugarcane stimulated the urban center at Kolonia, which is recalled as a bustling, pretty town in the 1920s and 1930s. Its Japanese population was about four thousand; another three thousand Japanese made a small town at Sapwalap. Infrastructure kept pace, with an airport, wharves, roads, docks, dams, and electric generating stations. Here too, the goal was Japanese investment and employment, but Micronesians felt they also benefited. Wage labor in plantations and industry drew both Pohnpeians and workers from nearby atolls, Kosrae, and Chuuk.[8]

By 1939 Pohnpeians were outnumbered, and throughout the 1930s land moved from local to foreign control. The 1940 census counted 5,866 Pohnpeians and 7,803 Japanese. Changes in land law facilitated commercial agriculture, beginning with 1931 revisions allowing sale, lease, and mortgaging of Pohnpeian land. As government control over resources increased and freshwater swamps became wet-rice fields, Pohnpeians' own agriculture was restricted to existing farmsteads, exhausting the soil more quickly. Some Japanese spoke of taking the entire island from Pohnpeians and removing them elsewhere.[9]

Other areas, though affected by the strong economy, were less targeted for growth. In 1935, only 25 Japanese lived among 1,189 Kosraeans. The slow pace of five to six steamer visits to Kosrae per year before 1920 increased to twenty-eight in 1932 and thirty-three in 1937. Later, as war construction began in the Marshalls, Kosrae's agricultural development accelerated to supply those garrisons. Once begun, intensification hit the island hard. Exports of copra, rope, coconut husk and hibiscus bark fiber, machinery, boats, and vehicles increased throughout the 1930s, as did imports of food, textiles, and metal products, especially as the Japanese population grew dramatically in the immediate prewar years and Lelu became a town. Steady wages from public works, carpentry, stevedoring, domestic service, administration, and private enterprise increased Kosraean consumption of imports.[10]

Although Kosrae's mission-based Christian society was not congenial to the Japanese colonial order, "one feature of the Japanese regime, its prosperity, was popular" (Lewis 1948a:45). German-planted coconut groves matured so well that people were able to buy imported food by the case, wristwatches, outboard motors, and bicycles, as well as imported lumber for new houses. Such prosperity, however, did not offset the opposition produced by a 1932 survey of Kosrae alienating most land not in actual cultivation and later land purchases by Japanese. Lewis indicates that Kosrae people "offered passive, but definite resistance" to Japanese development, disobeying orders as to how coconut trees should be planted, establishing garden plots on government-appropriated land, avoiding the court system and maintaining "a general secretiveness in Kusaiean affairs" (93). This plus a strong church organization allowed Kosraeans, like Yapese, to offer a certain amount of passive resistance to military occupation in later years.

Chuuk, which was to be an important Japanese naval base and military garrison during the war, was not a focus of immigration and development in the 1930s, though it shared in the mandate-wide economic growth. Chuuk lagoon held more than seven hundred Okinawan fishermen and traders by 1935, concentrated on Toloas (Dublon) and Tol—mostly men, who often took Chuukese wives. Economic development in Chuuk included large fishing fleets with drying and refrigeration plants, trochus beds, and manioc cultivation. The district capital at Toloas was a small town of perhaps eight hundred Japanese in the mid-1930s, and it did not see its boom until the immediate prewar period when the Japanese navy's arrival escalated population and construction activities.[11]

Of all the high islands of the mandate, least attention was paid to Yap's economic development. Yap had few resident Nan'yō-chō officials, and those were unsympathetic to local culture. It was at the tail end of the colonial supply line in the western mandate, getting supplies—and perhaps officials— only after Palau and Saipan had taken the best. Yap's urban center, Colonia, held only 275 Japanese in 1931, and fewer than 600 in 1935; the number grew to over 1,400 early in the war. Yapese avoided involvement in economic initiatives, leaving such roles largely to the several hundred immigrant Chamorros who worked as Japanese employees and as entrepreneurs and middlemen. "The Japanese did not hide the fact that they felt the Yapese were vastly inferior, and they gave little consideration to the local culture" (Labby 1976:5). For their part, Yapese developed a society "geared to resisting Japanese control" (Useem 1946a:54). They participated in the market economy but were less involved in wage labor and trade than most other Micronesians. Despite urging by Yap's leaders, the government set no regulations on land transactions or the use of land by foreigners. Before or early in the war, the Japanese confiscated, rented, or forced sale of land, turning some over to the South Seas Development Company.[12]

Least affected by the immigration and development boom were the Marshall Islands and the outlying atolls of the Carolines. As late as 1940 there were only 680 Japanese in the Marshalls; the number of other foreigners dropped from 17 (in 1931) to 4 (in 1940). Preparations for war, then, were less foreshadowed by economic and demographic changes here, although Marshallese benefited from increased trade in the 1930s. We see the same general conditions as throughout the mandate: colonial policy intended to benefit Japan through immigration and economic development, "Japanization" of Islanders through education and cultural policy, gains to Islanders from increased handicraft and copra trade, and foreign-staffed fishing and sponge enterprises. The Marshalls became the mandate's leading copra producer, and local handicraft expertise was so well recognized that the Japanese sent Marshallese women to teach mat weaving on Pohnpei and Kosrae. While Marshallese chiefs had seen their rights in land maintained and possibly enhanced through most of the mandate era, in the late 1930s the government "proposed to abolish chiefly rights and to give full title to individual occupants," compensating chiefs for their losses, a plan interrupted by war (McGrath and Wilson 1971:184). The government held most of Jabwor islet (on Jaluij) and parts of other islands but did not systematically survey Marshall Islands land until 1939.[13] In contrast to their relative quietude in the prewar years, the Marshall Islands were to become an early site for military construction.

Although physically distant from urban centers, by the late 1930s even the smallest and most isolated atoll communities were firmly in the matrix of the colonial economy. Atolls exported jack and tuna (caught by Okinawan fishermen), sea slugs, coconut fiber, pandanus leaves, coconut twine, and mats. Each island group had a hierarchy of Japanese-appointed leaders, and regular visits by Japanese officials on copra boats conveyed orders and information. (That this system remained operational during the early part of the war can be deduced from the number of men called up for military labor. The position of native policeman on Satawan in the Mortlock Islands, for example, continued from the late 1920s to the early 1940s.) Outer Islanders also shared in developments on high islands through their emigrant communities. For example, the Kapingamarangi community on Pohnpei was led by a Japanese-speaking chief, and its members engaged in wage work, copra production, schooling, and selling fish, handicrafts, and local foods to Japanese. They patronized Japanese restaurants, stores, pool halls, and theaters.[14] Outer island men were drawn from home by the demand for contract laborers at plantations and mines and expanding wage-labor opportunities in urban centers.

LABOR

Wage work, whether off-island or at home, had touched island communities since the nineteenth century. During the 1930s, Islanders performed three types of government-organized labor: public projects, local volunteer work organized by village officials, and paid labor for large companies (Peattie 1988:82–83).

Obligatory public labor was instituted perhaps in the late 1920s to early

1930s, with only light demands early in the Japanese era. People recall working on roads and other projects for the several days per month required of each adult. From the 1930s until 1944, the Pohnpei government required two six-month shifts for road building and construction from a quota of men aged twenty to forty. In the Mortlocks, an energetic administrator named Fukuyama conducted an extensive program of civic labor from the late 1930s through the war years. Fukuyama organized work teams on each island to level land and build seawalls, docks, meetinghouses, garden paths, and roads (Borthwick 1977:54–57; Tolerton and Rauch 1949). On Etal, with most men gone for contract labor in the late 1930s, the largely female workforce built seawalls and coral-block enclosures for pigs and worked taro gardens (traditionally a male task). Etal people "detested" this community labor, especially when it was forced on women (Nason 1970:218).

Military labor conscription must be seen in the context of this obligatory public labor and of the long-established habit of contract labor. Over 70 percent of the adult men of the small atoll of Etal traveled for wage work in Chuuk, Pohnpei, or Angaur during the prewar decades (Nason 1970:213). Contract workers from the Mortlocks built roads, mined phosphate on Angaur, worked in copra on Pohnpei, as laborers in Chuuk, and crewed ships; one man clerked in a Japanese office in Chuuk. They were paid a salary, but "most recall the work as being very hard and not very enjoyable" (Nason 1970:217; Reafsnyder 1984:102, n.36). On Pohnpei and nearby islands, Nambō was a major recruiter for its copra plantations, and Pohnpeians also worked at tapioca and pineapple farms and processing plants. As wage labor attracted the region's young men, family relations were altered. Men's clubs disintegrated, and some areas, for example on Yap, even experienced food shortages without young men's subsistence work (Kodama n.d.:32–33). Contract labor intensified in the years preceding and initiating the war; in many areas it evolved gradually into unpaid pressed labor.

Phosphate mining, which involved the most intensive use of Micronesian contract labor, followed the German pattern of recruiting. This was "in effect, a compulsory recruitment system" in which the mining office sent a requested hiring quota to district headquarters, who passed it on to village officials, who were obliged to produce the required number of laborers (Hatanaka 1973–1974:5–6).[15] By the late 1930s, village headmen selected workers when volunteers fell short. Islanders took pride in their role as workers, and developed a sense of self-worth that was retained well into the much harsher wartime conditions.

Voluntary associations were a rationalized form of labor that presaged wartime organization. Cooperative work groups *(kumi* or *kumiai)* paved the way for large-scale management of military labor. Kosrae's *kumi* were organized in the 1930s to stimulate public works. Prewar *kumiai* on Palau were voluntary groups of Islander entrepreneurs that fixed prices and set standards, led by two high chiefs and including farmers, barbers, charcoal makers, trepang dealers, and workers in copra, lumber, ferries, and construction. *Kumiai* were introduced to Yap in 1939–1940 as cooperative produce farms which, consonant with Yapese culture, were worked by women, but they were not popular.[16]

Other voluntary associations, modeled on Japanese village forms, were established by immigrants and sometimes took root among Micronesians. A national civic organization headquartered in Tokyo had branches on Palau and Saipan. During the war it organized food and clothes rations for blocks of houses and supervised civil defense on Saipan (Sheeks 1945:110). This was probably restricted to Japanese, but Islanders took part in similar groups, such as age-graded clubs, which later became part of organizing the work of war. The most widespread were young men's groups *(seinendan)*, which engaged in community work, sports competitions, and other recreation and service activities.

EDUCATION, RELIGION, AND LOYALTY

By December 1941, Islanders' attitudes toward the Japanese had been shaped by decades of colonial effort to socialize them as loyal members of the empire. The program's success was limited by the official ethnic hierarchy, which ranked Japanese first, then Korean and Okinawan immigrants, and lastly Islanders *(tōmin)*, who were rarely imperial subjects (this was possible by marriage or naturalization only). Peattie (1988:112) states that Japanese colonial policy further ranked Islanders within the category of "third-class people," with Marianas Chamorros at the top, followed by Carolinians and Marshallese. Yapese, difficult for the colonial administration to govern to their satisfaction, anchored the ethnic ranking.[17]

Japanese ethnocentrism and administrative preoccupation with a profitable colonial economy hampered encouragement of Micronesian loyalty.

Nonetheless an effort was made, and to some extent succeeded, to imbue Islanders with a Japanese sensibility, devotion to the emperor, and obedience to authority. The effort was largely indirect, through the restructuring of economic, social, and political life, but was supported by official policies: familiarization trips to Japan, cultivation of local leaders, and ideological instruction through schooling and regulation of religion. Islanders also grew fond of Japanese culture as they adopted its clothing, food, etiquette, house styles, songs, and games.[18]

Education for Islanders consisted of a three-year primary school, with a two-year course in a district school for promising students. More than half of Micronesia's children were enrolled by the 1930s, studying Japanese language, moral instruction, and the basics of "practical education."[19] Advanced work for a few young men was available at the Koror carpentry and manual arts school and in agriculture. Children of immigrants attended separate schools, consonant with the ethnic hierarchy and with a different set of expectations for adult status. (Islanders were aware of the differential educational outcomes. Matsuko Soram of Chuuk remembers that she attended the Japanese kindergarten on Toloas for awhile [her father was a policeman], before being directed to attend the Islander school.)

School reinforced discipline for several generations of Micronesians. Those educated in the 1920s and 1930s describe being beaten, running laps around the building for tardiness, or being shamed by wearing costumes and signs proclaiming their errors. Children were punished for theft, for lying, for smoking, for having long hair. Thaddeus Sampson (Marshall Islands) recalls: "The way they would school you was that they would beat you on the head until blood would come out of your nose. And then you would say to yourself, 'Did they not tell you that this was a bad thing?'" (He lowers his voice to a whisper.) "'Well, I will never do it again.'"

Along with discipline, Island schoolchildren learned spoken and some written Japanese (even mission schools were required to use Japanese in the mid-1930s) and a sketchy patriotism. In the late 1930s, school indoctrination was intensified, with students learning patriotic songs and parading to celebrate Japanese victories in China.[20] Peattie (1988:90–96) doubts whether this moral education had the intended effect, given the segregation and inequities in schooling, daily life, and future opportunities that Micronesian youth experienced firsthand. Although Islanders who achieved success under the Japanese system recall their schooling with affection and their teachers with respect, those who attended only a year or two dwell on the harsh discipline and unpredictable anger of instructors. Except for the Islander elite, the cultivated loyalty of Micronesian youth to Japan proved insufficient to withstand the stress of the war years.

Administrative policy also governed religion. The South Seas Government began by supporting—even subsidizing—Christian missionary and church work. On Lukunor, cooperation among mission, colonial, and traditional island leadership persisted through transitions from German to Japanese to American eras. In Yap, the first Japanese officials discouraged traditional religion, prohibiting rites, destroying meeting sites of traditional councils, and restricting men's club activities, all of which contributed to widespread adherence to Catholicism after 1925. And the government subsidized the Congregational Church of Japan's Christian mission in the islands, Nan'yō Dendō Dan.[21]

Yet as time went on, Japanese were hopeful of a shift toward more wholly Japanese attitudes. Norman William and his wife (from Pohnpei) recall that the Japanese permitted people to worship as they chose, "But, really, the Japanese religions were Shinto and Buddhist. And they objected to Christianity because it was an imported religion in Pohnpei." In Kosrae, the powerful island church covertly resisted Japanese rule by refusing to recognize marriages performed by the police sergeant and punished women who married Japanese men by dismissing them and their parents from the church. The church continued to regulate both the personal lives and social problems of Kosraeans—including such things as land tenure disputes, which were officially colonial concerns (Lewis 1948a:44–45).

Growing nationalist sentiment strengthened official desires for Islander loyalty, and the government eventually sought to neutralize religion as a provoker of foreign sympathies by constraining mission (and later all church) activities. Despite discouragement of Christianity, little direct effort was made to foster conversion to Buddhism or Shinto, which perhaps were considered inappropriate for Islanders and in any case are not evangelical religions. (Though with schoolchildren participating in processions and services at the Shinto temples by the 1930s, conversion may have been envisioned for the future.) A very few Micronesians accepted Japanese religion; among those mentioned was Pohnpei's *Nahnmwarki* (paramount chief) Iriarte, and this may have been true of elites elsewhere. Their conversions may have been as much political as spiritual.[22]

Most Islanders were unfamiliar with the doctrines of the Asian religions, and in some places they were not allowed to attend worship services. Asked what kind of religion the Japanese had, Daisey Lojkar (from the Marshalls) says, "Well, I do not know. We had no idea. They prayed only to the emperor." While some recognized Japanese religions as having their own theology and calendar, many Micronesians did not understand Japanese beliefs, visible to them only as ritual obeisance and prayer to revered objects. Nathan Tartios (Marshall Islands) recalls that the Japanese "worshiped some things that were on top of a table . . . images, caricatures," but the Japanese religion was "for themselves only," not the Marshallese; "They said they worshiped, perhaps, the spirits that were powerful in Japan, but I do not know. Only they did this, they did not tell us to do it." Others learned enough to take advantage of Japanese devotion: Andon Quele from the Mortlocks recalls that he shamed his Japanese boss in Chuuk into letting him return home by calling on the sacred name of the emperor.

On public occasions, Islanders joined in the forms of civic religion, respecting the emperor, Tennō Heika, and celebrating his birthday. At school, at work, and on public holidays, Micronesians joined Japanese in patriotic displays. People recall lining up behind Japanese leaders, facing Japan, listening to prayers, and singing songs dedicated to the emperor, though Islanders' participation was not necessarily wholehearted. As Saito Rewein (Chuuk) said of the rituals: "This doesn't mean that we joined their religion, but we did this because we were very scared of them. Because if we didn't bow with them, they hit us." Christianity had a strong presence in most of Micronesia, and such ritual duties troubled devout Islanders. Swingly Gallen (Pohnpei) spoke feelingly of the obligation to bow toward Japan before going into church for services: "This was the thing that was very important to me, because it presented a hardship to everyone who worshiped. I can never forget it."

Palau, the site of greatest acculturative activity and of the mandate's major Shinto shrine, also fostered the most organized ideological resistance to Japanese colonialism in the form of the Modekngei movement, a revitalization of Palauan religion and custom, beginning in 1914 and emerging powerfully in 1938. Peattie (1988:78) concludes that this organized movement had little influence until the final year of the war, but Hatanaka describes it as a strong form of resistance spurred by Japanese immigration, which "resulted in much agitation among the people by starting a rumor that an army from Heaven would come to save them from the Japanese" (Hatanaka 1973–1974:14). Modekngei did provide an alternative to acculturation for Palauans under Japanese rule, but that it was not exclusively an "anti-Japanese cult" is demonstrated by its continued vigor. Though suppressed by the Japanese before and during the war, it reemerged, although less powerfully, under U.S. rule and continues today.[23]

RELATIONS WITH JAPANESE

Despite the marginalization of Micronesians in some of their home islands, the relationship among peoples in the mandate during the 1920s and 1930s was more complex than a simple economic and technological overwhelming of small-scale Micronesian society by Japan. For one thing, "Japanese" immigrants themselves varied, including Okinawans and Koreans, well-educated administrators and uneducated farmers, entrepreneurial fishermen and unambitious manual laborers (Peattie 1988:198–229 describes Japanese colonial life). For another, although Japanese and Okinawans in urban centers were likely to regard Islanders with "complacent indifference" once the Japanese population became the majority (217), the Japanese also approached the Nan'yō with a romantic sentiment toward the South Seas. As the number of Japanese-educated Islanders and of immigrants increased in the late 1930s and early 1940s, relationships between Islanders and Japanese expanded at the local level, creating an abundance of close personal ties. This is in marked contrast to earlier and later Islander relations with Europeans or Americans: "Today [1960s] local residents over forty years old can still speak perfect Japanese and still consider Japanese as their brothers" (Hatanaka 1973–1974:3).

Our interviews agree with Peattie's conclusion that, apart from the Japanese-educated elite, most Micronesians "seem to have been ambivalent in their feelings" toward Japanese (1988:219), though memories are much colored both by the horrors of war and by comparison with American colonial life. Japanese assumptions of superiority resulted in discrimination both official and unofficial: in limits on schooling and employment, in segregated living and working arrangements and even brothels, and in marriage, permitted only between Japanese or Okinawan men and Islander women, not vice versa.

Yet Islanders who had close personal contacts with Japanese employers or relatives were at ease with them, enjoying the opportunity to improve their language skills and vicariously share the privileges of "first-" and "second-class" peoples.[24] Those unlucky enough to deal with less virtuous employers or the police were confirmed in their ideas of harsh and unreasonable Japanese demands and discipline. In Yap, Kosrae, the outlying atolls of the Marshalls, or the outer Caroline atolls, people saw few immigrants other than traders and had relatively little experience with Japanese before the war. But on Pohnpei, urban Chuuk, Palau, and the Marianas, the comfort and practical ease of life depended on a network of personal relationships that encompassed Japanese friends as well as Micronesian family. Both elements—the strength and usefulness of personal ties with Japanese immigrants, and fear and caution about the strictness and potential cruelty of officials—played a role in how Micronesians managed relations with Japanese during the war. McKnight (1978: 8–9) summed it up:

> Palauans I have asked about it remember the Japanese not as a stereotyped group, but as individuals: stern school-teachers stopping you as a child in the street and exacting a politely correct greeting; benefactors 'fronting' a commercial enterprise, while illegally permitting Palauan friends to manage and profit from it; "geisha" secretly welcoming Palauan sweethearts when business through the front door was slow. Unskilled Japanese migrants and Palauan laborers worked along side one another, developing a rapport unlike that between administrators and colonial subjects—there were friends and there were lovers.

Chapter 3

THE FIRST PHASE
OF WAR PREPARATIONS

Springboards for Japanese Expansion

THE ECONOMIC program of the Nan'yō-chō built up harbor, fuel, air, and communications facilities throughout the region by the mid-1930s. Late in the decade, imminent war spurred further construction—this time of offensive airbases and military infrastructure. Japanese attacks on Dutch, French, American, and British islands in the Central and Western Pacific at the end of 1941 sortied in part from installations in the Marshalls, Chuuk, Palau, and Saipan (Peattie 1988:257).

This chapter and the next describe Japanese military preparations in the mandate, first using the region as a springboard for expansion and then (in chapter 4) as a defensive buffer for the homeland. This chapter also addresses how the Japanese prepared Islanders for war, as Micronesians' lives turned increasingly away from their own concerns toward military priorities. Although the intensity and form of war preparations varied widely, we stress the similar experiences of Micronesians as offensive strategy drew them into activities supporting Japan's advance and, later, as defensive preparations put them in the front lines.

Rather than being a decade grimly foreshadowed by war, the 1930s in Micronesia held a sense of excitement and opportunity. While busy with new projects, Japanese citizens and urban Micronesians followed world events through radio and newspapers. Islanders who visited Japan on familiarization trips or for medical care returned with news. Japanese victories in Asia were celebrated in Nan'yō schools and towns, and a few Micronesian-Japanese men, such as the sons of the Mori family in Chuuk, served with the army in China. The Asian situation seemed most immediate in the western mandate. Saipan's

predominantly Japanese populace followed the mainland war through two local newspapers, radios, and newsreels and obeyed orders to build bomb shelters after the start of the Sino-Japanese conflict in 1937 (Sheeks 1945). Less
privileged Islanders, especially in rural areas or outlying islands, knew little of
current events. Even now, many have only a slight understanding of the geopolitics behind the war in the Pacific.

Few Micronesians at first connected news of growing international tensions with local activity. In Chuuk, workers dynamited Eten's cliffs into a flat
plain, but people accepted the explanation that this was to be used for drying
fishnets. Chuukese contributed to a tinfoil collection drive, said to be for new
currency. One Catholic missionary on Chuuk suspected signs of war mobilization by 1940 in labor conscription, higher prices for imported rice, and
declining enrollment in the Catholic girls' school as students took up family
work needs (Hezel n.d.:22). But most Islanders did not read such activities
as danger signals. Mandatory public work and contract labor were already familiar; increased labor demands did not necessarily presage anything other
than continuing economic growth. Sachuo Siwi, son of the Chuukese chief of
Toloas who worked in the Japanese administration, recalls: "We asked them
why they were building all these things and some of the *kumpu* [premilitary
construction workers] told us that Chuuk was going to improve. They said
they were building the road because big businesses from Japan were coming
to Chuuk. They also said big, big buildings ten stories high that we had never
seen were going to be built for the Japanese businesses that were going to come
to Chuuk. But that wasn't it. They were preparing for the war."

Perhaps the increasing regulation of daily life by local police had put Micronesians in a frame of mind that allowed the first phases of military preparation to occur with little questioning. Anko Billy recalls seeing land surveys
and new construction in the Marshall Islands as a boy, but he did not realize
what they meant. "I am just becoming aware of the sorts of activity they were
engaging in to prepare for the battle, but I did not know it was a battle, I
thought it was a development activity." Government actions that might have
seemed threatening were for many Micronesians easily offset by the greater
opportunities for education, employment, higher wages, plentiful consumer
goods, and a bustling regional economy.

Prewar changes appear, in hindsight, as habituation for the overwhelming
social and economic reorganization needed to launch and then to survive the

war. The imperial philosophy taught in Islander elementary schools segued into nationalistic propaganda. Friendships with immigrants merged into relations with the influx of civilian construction laborers, itself a prelude to the arrival of troops. Recruitment of young men for contract labor away from home prefigured the massive conscription of Islanders for military construction. Community labor for expanding taro gardens or building seawalls shifted to labor for military-controlled food production. Years before the war, then, stepped-up economic activity and labor requirements had begun to alter the pattern of Islander society in the direction of greater regulation of daily life and obedience to Japanese law in ways that would later prove crucial. It was not until war erupted that the military implications of the emerging patterns were realized.

THE WAR BEGINS

December 8, 1941, was a big event here.

Whatever rumors or signs of war appeared at the close of the 1930s, at last doubt was removed. Clanton Abija was at school on Jaluij (Marshall Islands) when the news of the attack on Pearl Harbor was greeted with fireworks so loud and bright, "Well, you could not sleep that night, you walked around and drank sake. You were happy and the stores were open. On this day all the stores were open and you could purchase anything." After Pearl Harbor, Micronesian students at Palau's carpentry school were told they might soon emigrate as colonists to Southeast Asia (Shuster 1982b:62). The Japanese on Pohnpei declared a holiday, with a parade, flags, and songs. Yvette Etscheit, the teenage daughter of Belgian planters, recalls the celebration in Kolonia:

> December 8, 1941, was a big event here.[1] The Japanese knew right away. In the morning they blew a loud whistle, which they used to call mail. Everyone woke up. Then a car went by, announcing America had declared war on Japan and everyone had to go to a shrine. . . . There was a hill with a shrine; it was like a lovely park with flowers and trees, a Japanese-style garden. Everyone ran there and it was announced that Japan was at war with the United States. We all had to pray so that Japan could win the war. The whole town was there. A Japanese Buddhist priest said a prayer. They explained that the war was on and asked everyone for their help. We prayed, clapped hands. Then we bowed for a minute in silence and prayed that Ja-

pan would win the war. That week the [Japanese] school changed the curriculum to include more exercise, more training, more farming. For us it was more fun! The day of the announcement, there was no school. Afterwards, there was a parade of flags, marching, and singing of Japanese military songs. That night, the same, but with the addition of Japanese paper lanterns. It was fun! This went on for three or four days.

In every Japanese town, the day was marked by banzais, marches, official celebrations, and unofficial parties. In Jaluij, Marshallese were called to a meeting on Jabwor, where they joined in banzais. Joseph Jibon recalls celebrating with the Japanese:

> That entire day, people were drunk, really drinking. It was a time of happiness. They ate and danced and were drinking all sorts of things. They had already brought out all the alcohol under the awnings in front of all the stores and put it on tables. You would drink here and then go off and walk over to another building and then drink over there and in this way they "conquered" all of the stores on the islet. Well, as for us schoolchildren, we could not drink, but we ate *manjū* and swam in the lagoon, and they brought a lot of food to the place we were staying because our teacher said, "Bring in food so we can eat. There is no school on this day. Happiness only," for they said the Japanese had won.

THE FIRST MICRONESIAN ISLANDS ON THE FRONT LINES: JAPANESE CONQUEST OF THE ALLIED COLONIES

Japan's Pacific offensive of December 1941 brought the first experience of war to Micronesians—those living in the Central and Western Pacific Islands under British and American rule. The Japanese South Seas Force attacked Wake Island, Makin, Tarawa, and Guam simultaneously and later invaded Nauru and Banaba (Ocean Island). Micronesians in these areas were culturally related to the peoples of the Japanese mandate, but as legal subjects of Allied nations they were considered enemies by the Japanese.[2]

Kiribati (Gilbert Islands)

Occupation of Kiribati was strategically important for establishing Japanese forward bases to protect the occupation of Indonesia and to facilitate air patrols of the Central Pacific. Sam Highland (1991:110) recounts the initial Japanese landing on Betio islet in Tarawa Atoll, when the village was asleep:

> Everybody was rounded up near the post office, and some of the [expatriate] captives were tied up with ropes to coconut trees. The only food store on Betio, that of Burns Philp, was taken over by the Japanese and later destroyed. The Betio villagers had depended on the . . . store for their basic needs other than traditional food. Curfews were set, and most movements were restricted. At about 4 P.M. that same day . . . the Japanese flag was hoisted and the Japanese commander declared Tarawa to be under Japanese jurisdiction. The Japanese left Tarawa that same day, leaving behind the Betio people, who were scared and worried about their lands and lives.

Makin and Butaritari were the first islands occupied. The Japanese troops confiscated merchants' stores and organized the men into work groups. While some in Butaritari stayed and "became really friendly with the Japanese," the occupiers urged others to leave the village to avoid danger of attack (Mamara and Kaiuea 1979:131–132). Kiribati was not strongly fortified until the August 1942 submarine-borne U.S. raid on Butaritari stimulated Japanese reinforcement.[3] The Japanese returned to Tarawa to build Betio into the atoll's major military site. Tarawa's people experienced the sequence of suffering that would be replayed throughout Micronesia: The Japanese destroyed vessels to prevent escape, then demolished houses and crops to make way for fortifications. Displaced Betio villagers trekked over 25 miles of reefs to wartime homes in north Tarawa. Men drafted for unpaid labor reported harsh treatment. Workers were injured and killed when they huddled into taro pits during Allied air raids that were meant to halt construction of the Betio airbase. The base was operational in late January 1943, and by July Tarawa's complex defenses were nearly complete. The island then awaited American invasion, which came in November.

Nauru and Banaba

Nauru interested Japanese strategists for its rich phosphate deposits and its potential as a transit point in the push toward the Southwest Pacific. After an initial attempt on Nauru and Banaba in May 1942, the Japanese took both at the end of August. Following the capture of Nauru, the Japanese brought in more than 4,000 troops and laborers and more than 600 Banabans to join the 1,800 residents. To relieve overcrowding, they shipped 1,200 Islanders to Chuuk lagoon in 1943, using the 600 Nauruans who remained (along with some Chinese, Marshallese, Kiribati, and Tuvalu people) as laborers. Despite the evacuations, Nauru remained crowded, and when it was bombed by Allied planes from Funafuti, blockaded, and hit with drought, residents suffered from hunger and disease. Banabans were also transported to Kosrae, Nauru, and Tarawa, though 150 young men remained as laborers for the Japanese. Nauru and Banaba remained in Japanese hands until the end of the war.

Guam

Guam had been a U.S. territory for more than four decades when the Pacific war began.[4] Surrounded by islands of the Japanese mandate and despite international tension in the Pacific, Guam was very lightly defended. Chamorros were confident there was no danger: "For one thing, they felt quite strongly that war with Japan would not last long—perhaps two weeks—certainly not over a month. . . . They were fully convinced that the U.S. Navy and Marine Corps would not permit Japan to attack Guam, not to speak of capturing the island" (Sanchez 1983:8).

Four hours after the attack on Pearl Harbor, as people prepared for the fiesta of the Immaculate Conception, Japanese planes attacked Guam. Two days later nearly six thousand soldiers invaded the island, opposed only by a small contingent of U.S. Navy and Marines and Guamanian Insular Guards.

The invasion, quickly followed by occupation, was only the first of many changes in Guam. Nearly half the population had lived in Agana. The Japanese sent these people to the countryside to farm and for a while Agana became a ghost town. During the first months, almost fourteen thousand Japanese soldiers poured into the island. They "looted stores and homes, strutted, paraded, menaced and hit the Guamanians" (Apple 1980:28–29), as Guam's life was reorganized under military control. Then, in early 1942, the army departed for other Pacific destinations, leaving fewer than five hundred Japanese, mostly civilian officials under a navy garrison.

Most Guamanians lived at their ranches during the occupation, avoiding Japanese police. This was the first and only time since European contact that Guamanian Chamorros lived a self-sufficient lifestyle—their fishing and agriculture supporting themselves and also supplying the Japanese military (Carano and Sanchez 1964:278). From mid-1942 Guamanians had to meet agricultural quotas, and residents and occupiers established a modus vivendi, bartering local food for Japanese imports. A private commercial company took over the island's economy, coercing local labor, and 455 Japanese, mostly farmers, immigrated (Hough 1947:283).

On Guam, the Japanese were faced with a population committed to the United States. Initially they attempted to win Chamorro loyalty through techniques used elsewhere in Micronesia. They established schools, brought in Japanese priests for the largely Catholic population, held parades, spread propaganda. Recognizing hostility, however, they also instituted controls. People were required to register with the new government, wear identity tags, and obey numerous regulations (including rules about bowing, which Chamorros found especially offensive). Appointed leaders formed daily work groups and assembled audiences for lectures about Japanese victories. Some fifty Chamorros from Saipan and Rota interpreted and conducted police and administrative activities for the Japanese (Rogers 1995:172)—setting Chamorros against each other in a way that has had longstanding repercussions in the relations between Guamanian and Northern Marianas peoples. Felipe Camacho Mendiola, later mayor of Tinian, was brought from Rota to translate for the Japanese on Guam and was later chosen for intelligence work.

> One obligation there on Guam was to make the Chamorros on Guam believe, and make sure that they believe, in the Japanese military. This was the most important obligation that we had.
>
> We had a Japanese Commander who was our leader, and who worked with us on the job. We wore civilian clothes and we traveled around to the villages on bicycles, to the Chamorros' houses, to find out what their feelings were. How much they believed in the Americans. We also tried to find out what they had in mind regarding the Japanese. We would take these reports to the Japanese Commander and to the Japanese Admiral. (Owings 1981)

Despite Japanese efforts, Guam's Chamorros maintained strong passive resistance throughout the war, spreading news heard on hidden radios, preserving pro-American popular culture, and protecting several Americans in hiding. They sang anti-Japanese songs and shared rumors predicting imminent American invasion. The story of how two Guamanians of the Insular Force Guard had died protecting the American flag was retold, as these "became the first heroes of the occupation for the Guamanians" (Apple 1980:27; Rogers 1995:169).

By late 1943, when the tide of war began to turn, Chamorros were conscripted to work at farming and airfield construction. Student workers "eventually became full-time labor gangs," clearing Orote airfield, gathering food for the military, and digging foxholes when U.S. bombing started (Apple 1980:33). Conditions worsened when the Japanese army returned from the Central Pacific in March 1944, and Guam's defenses were reinforced with Korean laborers and troops from Asian battle zones. The influx increased pressure on food production, and the military took control of resources and labor. Schools and churches closed; Japanese dependents were evacuated. Then Guam, like all the Micronesian islands, awaited American invasion.

TURNING ISLANDS INTO MILITARY BASES

All of the old people cried.

Although the attacks on Pearl Harbor, the Central Pacific Islands, and Guam mark the historical beginning of the war in the Pacific, its beginning for Micronesians was both earlier and later. The distinct shift from prewar to wartime, which Islanders highlight in oral recollection, did not occur as of December 8, 1941, but must be dated locally—to the confiscation of land for military installations; to the institution of forced labor; to the period of profound scarcities of food and consumer goods; to the supersession of civilian rule by the military; or to the time of actual bombing or invasion. For those who lived on land selected as sites for offensive bases, major change came long before the action of December 1941. Before turning to Islanders' memories of this time, we will briefly review the scope of Japanese military preparations throughout the mandate.

The United States and Japan had been preparing for war in theory since early in the century, when the two militaries recognized each as the other's greatest potential rival in the Pacific. In the 1930s, both nations built airfields and harbor facilities in their Pacific possessions. Japanese attempts to exclude foreign visitors from the mandate after its withdrawal from the League of Nations in 1933, the ongoing naval rivalry between the United States and Japan, Earl "Pete" Ellis' intelligence mission in the Carolines in 1923 and his "mysterious" death in Koror—even the disappearance of Amelia Earhart—were among the reasons some Americans suspected Japan of fortifying the islands. Other historians take the view that the United States was little concerned with Japan's aggressive potential in the decades before the war, and American visitors to the mandated islands "scoffed at rumors of fortifications" (Pomeroy 1948:50).[5]

The argument has continued long after the war (for example, in popular books about Earhart's disappearance, as well as professional comment, e.g. Burns 1968; Okumiya 1968; Wilds 1955). Most American historians now see Japan not as deliberately initiating military preparations in Micronesia much in advance of 1939–1940, but as building infrastructure in the islands which, in the event of war, converted readily to military use. Peattie (1988:230–256) reviews the argument in detail, concluding that the military preparation of the mandate began with civilian construction of commercial and communications facilities (1930–1934); construction of air and communications facilities in the Marianas and Carolines by the Nan'yō-chō and the navy (1934–1939); rapid base construction by the navy (1939–1940); and deployment of navy units and aircraft (1940–1941) (Peattie 1988:247–248). The situation then stabilized until late 1943, when revised Japanese strategy called for intensive construction of defenses and deployment of army troops in the Marshalls and Carolines.

Prewar Construction

During the economic expansion of the 1930s, the Nan'yō-chō began to improve transportation infrastructure, laying the groundwork for a civilian air connection across the islands (barely begun when halted by war) and improving harbors, wharves, and communication facilities. In 1934–1939, the Nan'yō-chō and the navy cooperated in a series of construction projects, the navy assisting with site selection and logistical support (Peattie 1988:249–250; Wilds 1955:403). This program caused several major land confiscations and population relocations, the largest at sites in Saipan, Palau, Pohnpei, and Eten Island in Chuuk.

Saipan and Palau, both with highly developed prewar economies, saw major projects begun (though not completed) in the mid-1930s, including Saipan's Aslito and Pagan Island airfields, a two-runway airstrip on Peleliu, and seaplane facilities, harbor improvements, and navigational aids in both areas. Chuuk's islands were similarly affected: between 1934 and 1939, roads, canals, and interisland shipping improved, oil storage tanks and an observatory were built, and Eten Island became Chuuk's first airfield.[6] Eten was completely leveled and built over in a project that pulled labor from throughout Chuuk lagoon and the Mortlocks. Workers recall that most of the construction was done by hand, with low wages and poor working conditions. Landslides caused deaths and injuries, and workers suffered from strict discipline and only two days' rest per month. Yet it was an impressive accomplishment. Keigo Ezra was a schoolteacher when the seaplane base at Eten was completed: "The school children on Dublon, both Japanese and Trukese, were told that they were going to see an airplane land on Eten. On the chosen day, Mr. Ezra's students waited in high anticipation of this event, as did he, also. 'We were very disappointed, however,' he recalls, 'the plane first landed in the *water*, then climbed out onto land. We had expected it to land on the concrete'" (Dolan 1974:87; author's emphasis).

Pohnpei and Kosrae, the other Caroline Islands population centers, also gained infrastructure during the 1930s, including an airport on Pohnpei, wharves, roads, docks, dams, and electric generating stations. The Japanese also insisted that Islanders plant more tapioca, potatoes, sugarcane and other crops, and agricultural quotas were added to contract labor demands. (Workers building the airstrip near Kolonia in 1935 or 1937 spent two weeks at government work for every week at home [Bascom 1965:161].) Even on Yap, relatively neglected by development plans, seaplane facilities were begun, along with those at Saipan and Arakabesan in Palau, in 1934 (Peattie 1988:248).

Construction of Bases, 1939–1941

As the decade closed, civilian work blended into military labor. By 1937, the Japanese navy controlled planning, though civil government remained in charge of Nan'yō (Morison 1951:74; Peattie 1988:249–251). The Fourth Fleet was organized as the naval unit assigned specifically to Micronesia in 1939; in mid-1940 it established base forces in Kwajalein, Chuuk, Koror, and Saipan. This reintroduced a military element into what had been from 1922 a civil-

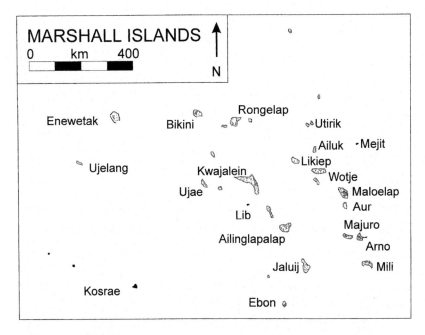

Map 2. Marshall Islands

ian colonial administration, but naval personnel were at first limited to five hundred men, a small air unit, and a communications unit in each sector. The Marshalls, however, where offensive airbases were under construction, received an additional twenty-four hundred navy personnel (Peattie 1988: 252–253).

From this point on, Micronesian experiences varied greatly depending on whether their home islands had been chosen as sites for military installations or were instead to be devoted to food production or act as labor reserves. As a result of strategic decisions, some islands were barely altered by war preparations; others were transformed overnight. When Islanders remember the hardships of the war years, those whose islands were the sites of airbases begin by speaking of the large-scale relocation or conscript labor assignments accompanying base construction in 1939–1941. Others reserve memories of "the war" for the period after the first bombs fell, or the time of intense privation after large numbers of troops were deployed to Micronesia in 1943–1944 (described in chapter 4).

We find a roughly similar sequence in military construction across the region. The first phase of work in the Marshalls, Chuuk, and the Marianas was done by Korean conscript labor and Islander wage workers under the direction of NKK; in addition, two thousand Japanese convicts labored for a year on airstrips in Wotje in the Marshalls, Weno (Moen) in Chuuk, and Tinian in the Marianas (Peattie 1988:251–252; Denfeld 1984). Paid and convict workers preceded military troops in most areas, but their large numbers, uniform clothing, and hard labor under strict discipline made it difficult for Micronesians to distinguish them from soldiers.

The Marshallese were the first victims of intensive war preparations, which began with a 1939 Imperial Navy survey of potential airfields. Of key importance at the empire's edge, both for offensive staging and as a defensive screen, the Marshall Islands differed from the large islands farther west in that they had not seen heavy immigration or development under the mandate's economic plan. With the decision for war, the Japanese compressed military construction into an urgent timetable. Laborers began to arrive in late 1939 to develop Kwajalein, Wotje, and Maloelap and, to a lesser extent, Jaluij. By December 1941 these had operational airbases, but almost no defensive capabilities. During the first year of war, these four sites were strengthened. Mili (Mille) was built into a major base in April–November 1942. When the Japanese high command modified its operations plan in mid-September 1943, drawing a new line around the "vital defensive area" of the Kuriles, Marianas, and Carolines—leaving Kiribati and the Marshalls outside the protection of the Combined Fleet—Marshalls bases were further strengthened to gain time to protect the Marianas and Bonins. Fortification of the garrisoned atolls was still underway at the time of American invasion.[7]

Military construction, compacted into a brief and intense shock to Marshallese, profoundly transformed local life. The airbases consumed entire islets, often the largest islet of an atoll (usually the site of the main village). Marshallese who lived on Maloelap, Wotje, and Mili vividly recall villages being displaced, followed by rapid construction of airstrips, defenses, and support services.[8] Nathan Tartios recalls that Maloelap Atoll's chiefs consulted with Japanese officials, after which the people of Taroa islet were called together and told that Japan was taking it for a military base. "All of the old people cried," he remembers. In talking about that time, "One elderly woman repeatedly used the poignant word *boromwij*—an untranslatable lament meaning homesick, heartsick, sad, and despairing—to express Taroa people's feelings of loss and regret when they left their island" (Poyer 1997:25). Marshallese relocated to other islets of their home atoll, even *Iroij* (paramount chief) Tomeing moving his capital to Ormej islet when people left Wotje. Some stayed on Wotje islet until the construction almost literally pushed them off; as Lele Ram puts it, they had to move "because there was no place for people to live at that time." Marshallese who worked on the Mili base construction describe felling breadfruit, coconut, and pandanus trees as the first step. After clearing the islet, workers logged throughout the atoll, ferrying lumber to build a loading dock at Mili. Next they began the airfield, filling swampy areas with rocks hauled from the ocean side. Marshallese workers commuted from the other islets to join Japanese prisoners and Korean construction workers on Mili.

We can sharply divide war preparations in the Marshalls between the fortified atolls and those that held small garrisons or no military presence at all. Major bases were at Kwajalein, Mili, Wotje, and Maloelap, with Enewetak developed late in the war as a defensive and transshipment base. Jaluij Atoll held a seaplane base and fleet anchorage, though plans for major air facilities were abandoned. Jabwor in Jaluij was the Marshalls' colonial capital, an urban center with a large Marshallese population of workers, students, and families; it was a focus of military-civilian interaction. Preparations in the months before Pearl Harbor alerted Marshallese at Jabwor—many of whom worked closely with Japanese—to the coming war.

The rest of the Marshall Islands saw little construction, though nearly all atolls eventually had a small military presence. A nearly two-year effort to build a seaplane base on Majuro was abandoned in late 1942 and the construction units dispersed. On Ebon, phosphate workers and soldiers lived together as phosphate mining continued. Weather stations for military use on Mili, Ujae, Ujelang, and Utirik supplemented prewar meteorological stations at Jaluij, Wotje, and Enewetak.

At the western end of the mandate, the first phase of war work supported Japanese operations in the Southwest Pacific. Overtly military construction in the Marianas dates to early 1941, with appropriations in September 1941 for "military barracks, baths, latrines, kitchens, infirmaries, storehouses, workshops, torpedo storage sheds and air raid shelters" on Saipan (Russell 1984: 82). In addition to Aslito airfield, two others were undertaken on Saipan, two fields were built on Tinian and a third started, and one airfield was laid out on

Rota. Barracks and administrative buildings surrounded the fields. Once war began, these islands became part of the support corridor for the Japanese advance into the Southwest Pacific, with troops shipped through the Marianas by late 1941.[9]

In Palau, limited military work began in 1938–1939 with land purchased or appropriated as "gifts to the emperor" for oil pumps and storage installations and the evacuation of two villages in southern Peleliu for airstrip construction. Koror, already a commercial and administrative center, boomed again with the arrival of military units and was transformed into a naval base by 1941. Palau played a part in December 1941 strikes on the Philippines and became a staging, replacement, and training center for troops and ships in the Southwest Pacific. Although even isolated Tobi had a small garrison at the end of 1941, intensive buildup in Palau awaited the turn to a defensive war.

Pohnpei played little direct role in Japanese offensive operations but supported the movement of troops to the Marshalls and produced supplies for the war effort. The military arrived on Pohnpei after the start of Japanese actions in China; warships and navy shore defense units entered with the general deployments after the Fourth Fleet was headquartered at Chuuk in February 1941. Pohnpeians recall construction of Nanpohnmal airstrip as the first major labor demand (built between 1935 and 1940 [Denfeld 1979:24]). When the first plane landed, Suhlet Abraham said, "We were surprised"; her mother named her newborn sister "Lamwei Japan" (Japanese Lady) in honor of the planes.

With no dramatic early fortification, recognition of a state of war came gradually to Pohnpei.[10] The Belgian Etscheit family retained "very friendly" relations with Japanese throughout the 1930s. Only in 1939, when officials continually put off plans for young Yvette Etscheit to attend boarding school in Japan, did the family realize war was approaching. "From 1939 on, we were not allowed to leave; we were like prisoners on the island," Ms. Etscheit recalls. In December 1941 they were arrested.

> Then on the 22nd of December, after school we students used to go to the nuns to have classes in entertainment, art, music, and so on, from 2 P.M. on. I was there when our maid came running in and said Father (Carlos Etscheit) wanted us home right away. My sister was very excited; my mother had been ill. When we reached home, we saw some Japanese po-

licemen in the house. Father calmed us and explained that the Japanese police had come to say that Belgium had broken relations with Japan. They had orders to put us in jail. We were told to pack our suitcases and go to prison [Yvette stayed with Mrs. Etscheit at home, while the rest waited in prison until Japanese carpenters fenced in their house.]. . . . This happened on December 31. We had four houses there with a large field in the middle; it made a small compound. We kids could play there under the trees. We were there one and a half years, until February 22, 1943, when the bombing began.

Imperial Navy headquarters on Pohnpei were at Yasarin, with barracks in Kolonia. The rest of the island was organized for production, with few military sites. In addition to airfield construction, Pohnpeians also worked on building and widening roads (a task begun around 1940 and unfinished when bombing began). Large-scale military construction did not start until after the U.S. submarine blockade. Pohnpeians then experienced uncompensated destruction of coconut trees, land confiscation, and relocation. In the more intensive phase of preparation, guns were installed at strategic points, some in very challenging sites—including one mounted atop Sokehs mountain to guard colonial headquarters in Kolonia. Fuel, ammunition, barracks, and military stores took additional sites. Pohnpeians working on defensive fortifications, barracks, and storage areas "were sworn to secrecy," according to Pensile Lawrence, with guns carried up to their mountain installations at night. A large gun guarded the channel leading to the rice and sugarcane fields at Sapwalap, Madolenihmw, which with its barracks for soldiers and field laborers later became a military target. Another important site was Nanpil (Net), where large plantations were linked by a wide road to Madolenihmw. A small airstrip was also built at Palikir.

Kosrae was never fortified for offense—an attempt to build a seaplane base was abandoned just before completion—and was barely fortified for defense. Like Pohnpei, its value lay in supplying food for troops in the Marshall Islands, as long as shipping was possible. NKK turned from its prewar experiments with sugarcane and cotton to tapioca, cassava, and other food crops. The first labor force on Kosrae was a group of Asian contractors and Banabans stationed at Malem who built barracks, a dock at Tafweyak, and a dam to supply cargo ship water tanks. New roads linked harbors and docks with food

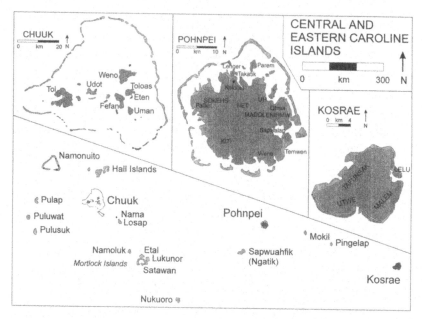

Map 3. Central and Eastern Caroline Islands

production and storage facilities. About three ships a month made the circuit between Kosrae and the Marshalls bases before the American blockade (Lewis 1948a; Peoples 1977:149).

Despite its later role as a symbol of Japanese power in the Pacific, Chuuk was not intensively developed as a military base until defense became imperative. Nonetheless, 1938–1939 saw significant expansion of infrastructure useful to the navy. In 1940, some 35,000 laborers (including 12,000 Korean conscripts, 500 prisoners, and 7,000 Micronesians) began base construction in Chuuk lagoon. Weno's airfield and seaplane bases were soon started; similar facilities on Toloas were complete by late 1942. Chuuk began the war years as a bustling, pleasant imperial outpost, rear-area headquarters for the Japanese Combined Fleet. The first Allied aerial photos of Chuuk, in January 1942, show a dozen warships, a few other ships and flying boats, and about twenty-seven bombers on Eten airfield. Chuuk served as a staging area for aircraft and troops moving to forward positions, but not until sometime in 1943 did it see major development as a naval base.[11]

Despite Chuuk's relatively inactive offensive role, early war preparations affected local communities, most dramatically in the relocation first of Eten people, then of those living where the first airstrip was built on Weno (known as "Moen #1" to American bomber crews). It was probably in 1941 that the people of Iras village on Weno began their lengthy exile, in what they call the "flight" *(su)* (Parker 1985:53). Ordered to make way for the airstrip, they dismantled and sold meeting houses and rafted family homes and goods along the coast to Tunnuk village. For many, this relocation was only the first of several. As military needs dictated, Iras villagers were moved to three successive sites on Weno during the war—then endured two postwar resettlements, the last returning them to Iras in January 1948.[12]

After the navy arrived, Chuukese were hired to haul guns and dig ammunition storage bunkers. They heard from Japanese that the guns were "to protect people," but recall no warnings about impending war. They noted the arrival of land troops and quasi-military "CAT teams" or "Seabees" as people today refer to them, using terms for U.S. military construction workers (indicating that they recognized military auxiliaries). Along with civilian and prisoner laborers (locally called *maraw*—"green," the color of their uniforms), they fixed water lines and built barracks, roads, and airfields.[13] At this point, the needs of the influx of foreigners could still be supplied by imports.

For most Chuukese, all this navy-directed activity was but a prelude to the real hardships of war. The fact that the early construction was done by civilian or prisoner labor, that local people were not told its purpose, and that shipping, travel, and food supplies continued normally all meant that for Chuuk, "the war" did not begin in local eyes until the Japanese army arrived in overwhelming numbers in late 1943 and early 1944. With the flood of army troops and Chuuk's shift from staging and supply base to defensive "fortress," ordinary life changed irrevocably, as described in the next chapter. For most Chuukese, as for Masataka Mori, "that's when the war started."

The small atolls of the eastern, central, and western Carolines were little changed by the early offensive phase of military construction. Administration by colonial agents and traditional leaders continued on small islands during these years—and, on most, throughout the war. Signs of war for atolls were the departure of copra traders recalled to Japan, stricter regulation of daily life, school-taught nationalist ideology, and the withdrawal of European missionaries (Borthwick 1977 on Lukunor; Nason 1970 on Etal; Witherspoon 1945).

More significant was the contribution to labor levies. Eastern Caroline atoll people worked on military projects on Pohnpei; Chuuk lagoon drew in central Caroline atoll dwellers; workers from Ulithi and Ifaluk (Ifalik) went to Yap. A few Carolinian atolls were fortified for defense later in the war, as described in the next chapter.[14]

At the beginning of the war, then, it was the Marshallese who experienced the greatest impact. Marshall Islands airbases supported the attacks on Hawai'i, Midway, Wake, and Kiribati. And, as the Micronesians closest to the initial Japanese offensive actions, Marshallese also became the first to suffer Allied counterattack.

RETALIATORY STRIKES ON MARSHALL ISLANDS BASES, 1942

When we saw the planes above Jabwor, we said
they were Japanese planes staging a practice.

Allied forces struck at the Marshalls early in the war with a brief attack on February 1, 1942. This morale-raising effort was considered an American success—"Pearl Harbor Avenged"—the first attack on Japanese territory (Costello 1981:211).[15] Memories of the strike remain fresh in the minds of many who lived on Kwajalein, Wotje, Maloelap, Jaluij, and Mili, as the first shocking experience of what the war could mean.

On Jaluij, people mistook the attack for an announced Japanese drill. John Ezekiel was an airplane maintenance worker on Imiej islet:

There was no expectation that they (Americans) would come. No one foresaw this thing, that many people would be hurt. Because . . . there were training exercises. That morning at 4:00 A.M., the practice on Imiej would begin. Planes from Imiej flew training flights above Jabwor. This is what people were saying. So the planes were flying as expected—that is, doing practice exercises—but then they "practiced" on the ships in the lagoon and they sank! This was an attack—that is, American planes coming at first light.

Our mother was washing rice and she looked up, but she continued to work, and my father pulled her hair and said, "Don't you see that the sky is filled with fire, don't you see that?" She repeated what she'd been told, that it was an exercise. "But it is not that sort of thing. You hurry up!" Because of their slowness, they were still seeking shelter as Tur was set afire. But if the two of them had been slow about getting into the shelters, who knows but that they might have been hit with a shell?

Ten-year-old Joseph Jibon, living on Jabwor with an uncle while he attended school, recalls:

At that time all the people were sleeping and no one knew a thing about the method that was used to destroy Tur. . . . On that morning, the planes flew over us. They flew over us from 4:00 [A.M.] until sunrise. And we Marshallese, when we saw the planes above Jabwor, we said they were Japanese planes staging a practice. At that time, everyone came outdoors and observed the planes as they strafed. . . . Then people said, "Oh, the planes from Imiej are also taking off to practice and test their abilities." When the planes were shooting, people were hit, many were hit, but people did not yet believe that these were American planes. And then when people began falling, they said, "Why are they falling? Why is this happening—don't the army people see that they are hitting them, even though they are dying?" They still did not know that these were American planes flying downwind and upwind over Jabwor and shooting, because of the darkness.

Then, as daybreak arrived—at the time when you could walk around and distinguish which person is which—they began dropping bombs and damaging Jabwor. . . . Many people from all of the various places in the Marshalls were wounded at that time also, but the most damage was done to Ebon people. Now as it was increasingly light, it was possible to look upward and see that it was American planes with the morning star on them and the American flag.

Marshallese had not been at all prepared for the possibility of attack, and most fled militarized areas after their first experiences with bombing and strafing. They escaped in boats and sailing canoes or ran along the reefs to other islets, despite the risks.[16] Marshallese who worked closely with Japanese and had more accurate information about the war remained in place.

Japanese military personnel rounded up Micronesians assigned to military labor a few weeks after the raid, and they returned to work for almost two years before the Allies attacked Japanese Micronesia in force. Throughout the mandate, the two years of labor before the Allies began their Central Pacific drive formed new ideas about the meaning of war.

LIFE AND LABOR IN EARLY WARTIME CONSTRUCTION

Myself, I believe there is no authority for throwing my life away.

During the first phase of war preparations, people were caught up in patriotic excitement and economic expansion, preoccupied with handling new labor obligations, security constraints, and the still small navy presence. Relocated populations in the Marshalls, Kosrae, and Chuuk settled into their new homes, not realizing that these were temporary. Hospitals, civilian police, and schools carried on, though the last became increasingly nationalistic. (Students on Jaluij often went to the military base "to dance for the soldiers" and tour the impressive artillery.) Blackouts and curfews were enforced with new strictness, though on Pohnpei at least, alcoholic beverages could be bought more openly after Pearl Harbor (Bascom 1965:86). And, in a change of great importance to Micronesians, Christian practice was subject to stricter regulation and even harassment.

Constraints on Religion

By the mid-1930s foreign missionaries in Saipan had already experienced restrictions, with continual Japanese disapproval of Christian church activities. Children were obliged to be at the Shinto temple for their early morning exercises at the time Mass was held; teachers spoke out against the church in school and forbade children to wear religious medals. After 1938 or 1939, missionaries were not allowed into Saipan to replace those who fell ill or died.[17] On December 9, 1941, "the Japanese prohibited all public acts of religion" on Saipan (D. F. Smith 1946:8).

Similar constraints shut down churches across the region. Mrs. Solomon Lorrin (Pohnpei/Mokil) recalls: "The change [with the coming of war] was that the Japanese did not want you to go to church. . . . The Japanese told us that if we went to church, we did not want to work for their 'president,' the emperor." As military preparation became the main activity in the islands, churches in parts of the Marshalls, Pohnpei, Kosrae, and Saipan became warehouses or barracks for construction workers. Mission schools were ordered to teach in Japanese, mission replacements were denied entry permits, and on Palau, everyone was required to visit the shrines on Shinto holidays. All foreign missionaries left the Marshalls in 1941, and meetings of the Protestant Church Association were banned. American missionaries were forced out of Kosrae in 1941, their school taken over by two Japanese Christian women. Catholic Church activity on Pohnpei was impeded by blackout regulations and harassment by Japanese soldiers. On December 8, 1941, military officers arrived at Chuuk's Catholic girls' school and marched the students away for road work (Hezel n.d.:22). In May 1942 missionary priests in Chuuk were restricted to a house on Toloas and forbidden to say Mass in public. Once troops arrived, missionaries needed permission to travel off-island, and those on outlying islands were brought to Chuuk lagoon in May 1943. On Lukunor, the largest church in the area was destroyed for military preparations—or, as the mission claimed, to erase its influence.[18] Detention of missionaries put church activity wholly in the hands of Micronesian Christians, who took up the responsibility with courage and resolution.

Increasing workloads and the denial of a Sunday free of labor also inhibited religious practice. Early in the mandate era, the Japanese government had paid double on Sundays in deference to Christians. Contract laborers from Etal in the Mortlocks were at first imprisoned when they refused Sunday work despite the financial incentive (Nason 1970:217). The double-pay program stopped with the arrival of large numbers of Okinawan workers (Hatanaka 1973–1974:6–7). At some point and in some places, Sunday work became the norm despite opposition. On Pohnpei, people worked for the Japanese two Sundays out of four, increasing later in the war to every Sunday. Mary Jane Jemes recalls Pohnpeian men making sennit and women making handicrafts on Sundays. She remembers, "Japanese told us to face and salute Japan and say 'Tennō Heika banzai' ['banzai to the emperor'] before we started to work." On Kosrae, adds Anna Brightly, "They even forced us not to do our church service on Sunday"; that was the day for air raid training.

The First Phase of Wartime Labor

Though Japanese and Okinawan contract laborers, Korean conscript workers, and Japanese civilian prisoners were the mainstay of military construction, Islanders were the nearest and easiest to assemble labor force. They participated variably: sometimes as an integral part of these other workforces, sometimes supplying food and casual labor outside the formal military organization, in some places as a separate civilian workforce. Micronesian involvement in wartime labor parallels the chronology of base construction. The first period of paid work to build and supply bases was seen as an intensification of prewar contract and levy labor. Then, in 1943, came a shift to nearly universal forced labor in a desperate effort to keep bases operational, defend against air attack and invasion, and feed thousands of troops and civilians (see next chapter).

The first phase moved men from outer islands and rural areas to construction sites, concentrating Islanders in workers' barracks or ethnic quarters where they interacted with other Micronesian and foreign laborers. Sometimes family members accompanied workers, with women taking jobs doing laundry or housecleaning. But women, old men, and children seldom traveled for labor (though this would change later in the war). As young and mature men left villages, women took on subsistence work and community maintenance to an unprecedented extent.

The prewar organization of cooperative work groups in rural areas expanded as fewer able-bodied men were left at home. At times there were fewer than twenty men between the ages of eighteen and fifty on Lukunor Atoll, as they took six-month labor assignments abroad. From 1937 to 1943, the well-organized colonial official Fukuyama and Japanese policemen rationalized Lukunor's economy for subsistence and copra production. Older women worked taro fields and cooked for the others, who were assigned to daily task groups: Monday, gather copra; Tuesday, clear underbrush; Wednesday, taro swamp work; Thursday, copra; Friday, work on breakwater and causeways; Saturday, prepare food in lineage groups. Women were supervised as they made mats, hats, baskets, and gathered weaving materials for export. With so many men gone, men and women fished together, women doing everything except diving and retrieving traps. They "said they had no time to come to church . . . the birth rate dropped" (Tolerton and Rauch 1949:158–159), but until shipping stopped, people enjoyed high levels of production and cash income.

The civilian habit of kinrōhōshi—obligatory but unpaid community work required of adult men (an obligation familiar since German times)—became a source of early military construction labor.[19] In Chuuk, one man brought to Toloas to unload supplies described it as "work without pay. We worked just to help them, but not to earn money." *Kinrōhōshi* was inadequate to the vastly increased workload, so men were recruited through the existing contract labor system. Parang Namono of Fefan in Chuuk lagoon recalls that Fefan's chief was told, by the same government agency handling civilian contract labor, to send workers to Toloas for construction and stevedoring. Called up in the usual way through village chief and secretary, he says, they "were very curious as to what was going on." Not until he was moved to Eten, when they used dynamite to flatten the cliffs for an airstrip, was he told that the rapid preparations were for a war between Japan and the United States; at that point, "we even worked at nighttime."

Work long done as ordinary contract labor—plantation agriculture on Pohnpei and phosphate mining in the western islands—intensified as war approached. Michael Faraguy of Woleai recalls working seven days a week in the Fais phosphate mines until the war "really started." Workers would have found it hard to distinguish intensified prewar labor from preceding contract stints, except that it was harder to choose not to work. On Lukunor, "The Japanese asked for 'volunteers' and those who had not served recently were assigned by their headman and the chief" (Tolerton and Rauch 1949:163–164). Rosete Hebel ironically compares the war years on Pohnpei with the modern shortage of employment: "Nowadays, they are happy (fortunate) because they are searching for jobs. But we were running away from jobs, because of the hard work and poor wages. . . . This is different from people today; they are looking for jobs, not running away from jobs." Later, under army rule, harsh conditions of wartime labor would distinguish it starkly from civilian labor obligations and opportunities.

Marshallese were among the first Micronesians heavily recruited and then conscripted for military work, joining Korean and Japanese convict laborers in construction and support services (such as maintenance and mess hall work). Daisey Lojkar, who lived on the small islets of Kwajalein during the war, recalls reports from those who worked with the Japanese there: "They say it was good, the way they fed them, and the way they stayed with them." Men recall being treated as well as Japanese and Koreans ("The things that we ate were delicious as long as you worked, the same as the things that the soldiers ate"), though the three groups lived and messed separately. Women laundered and ironed clothes, worked in offices or cleaned for remaining civilian company employees, and both men and women cleaned barracks. In this early period, wages were good and purchased food was cheap.

Nathan Tartios has some pleasant memories of his work at the Taroa, Maloelap, airbase—for example, a good diet of rice, fish, potatoes, onions, cucumbers, and watermelons, along with beer, sake, and cigarettes (Poyer 1997:26). But discipline was strict. The construction force of Marshallese, Japanese, and Koreans rose and ate before sunrise:

> And then when the hour came, you would line up for roll call. "Hey! Hey! Hey! Hey!" Afterward you wanted to say "Go to hell!" If you did not work, but you were ill, they would really watch you and if you lied, they would beat you with sticks and their hands. We worked and worked and worked and there was a time to eat between 12:00, no food at 9:00, no food to give you a little strength, and then when it was actually twelve o'clock you finally ate then. You ate right there at the place where you worked, you did not go off to the mess hall. The Japanese came and brought food to you . . . they used a pushcart and brought the food to the place where your group was located. They knew how many people worked in your group. At that time they brought food and we ate and ate and slept and then, at one o'clock—work time.

> (Interviewer asks: What did they give you to eat?)
> There were these sorts of things: rice, a meat, and then a type of liquid they called wasa—it was not sweet, it wasn't sweetened. Perhaps they still use it in Japan now, I think they use it. Then we would work, work, work and when it was quitting time at night, we went off to our camp. We would bathe for a short time, and then we rested. Oh, and we watched movies, but the movies of the Japanese were humorous [these were Kabuki movies].

> (Interviewer: After movie time, you would then—?)
> Go back and sleep and then eat first thing in the very, very early dawn.

An important dimension of wartime labor was population movement, sometimes over great distances. Islanders had always journeyed for family reasons, education, government business, and most of all for wage labor. War preparations intensified travel, then froze people in place when shipping halted. Movement of laborers had the same disturbing influence on communities as relocation to make way for military needs or, later, to escape bombing. Some people relocated voluntarily for work in the first phase of war preparations. Some moves may have been pressured by labor quotas or personal ties with Japanese. Some moved from project to project throughout one island: Pohnpeian men describe shifting from airport construction to road work to plantation agriculture to transporting military supplies. The Marshallese men who worked on the Taroa base came largely from Maloelap and Aur, but also Majuro, Ebon, Ronglap (Rongelap), and Utirik. Nauruans, Banabans, and Kiribati people were moved as prisoners of war. Next to those actually enlisted in the Japanese military, Islanders laboring far from home were those most at the mercy of circumstances and, later, of military authorities.[20]

A famous labor relocation that took place soon after the Japanese army's arrival in the eastern Carolines was a large July 1943 draft of Pohnpei men for work on Kosrae. (Ironically, before military labor began on Kosrae, groups of Kosraean men had come to Pohnpei for three-month construction tours.) All were from Kiti, the most remote and traditional of Pohnpei's chiefdoms. The 179 who left comprised virtually all remaining able-bodied Kiti men. Their tale of labor-in-exile is widely remembered on Pohnpei. Pensile Lawrence describes his experience:

> It was in July 1943. I did not know what was needed by the Japanese government or military, except that I knew that there was an army with a Japanese administration from here, Pohnpei, that went to RonKiti and got the registration book from the municipal office, and then called the names of the number of people that they wanted from that book.
>
> I remember seeing the military man carrying a rifle but not knowing why he had that rifle with him. We knew that the Japanese administration was under the governor. And they went to RonKiti and a message was passed out in the municipality calling everyone together at Pohnpwehl. We got there and there were two men, one from the administration and one from the army. They called every one of us, but excepted those who were working at Nanpohnmal and Lenger Island, those working at the warehouse by the waterfront, and they left out also the young men who were of school age. This was the main reason why every one of us who went to Kosrae, well, among us were father and son, brothers, etc.

We did not know exactly why they needed that number of men from one municipality. We were so stupid, we did not know. See, some of us were working at the rice fields in Sapwalap (Madolenihmw), and they would give us one-week contracts. People from Kiti could finish up the one week contract in four days, instead of six, Monday-Saturday. We would finish up Thursday evening and go home for the weekend, a long weekend including Thursday night. So one day, the guy from the administration went to Madolenihmw and checked up on the workers and found that many of us, the Kiti people, were not present. But people from Uh, Madolenihmw, and so on were there working. So, they gave us this kind of punishment, as we call it. They decided men from Kiti would be sent to some place for some kind of reasonable work for the government of Japan.

Some Kiti men believe their reputation as hard workers made them the obvious choice for labor selection. Others suggest that Japanese chose them all from one region to limit fighting, and only Kiti could supply enough. Still others speculate that a high-titled Kiti chief who enjoyed close relationships with the Japanese may have proudly volunteered the chiefdom's men, or that the *nahnmwarki* failed to object and allowed the Japanese to take his people. Pensile Lawrence continues:

> After we all knew that we were going to leave Pohnpei for some place and we knew who was in this 179, we left RonKiti to return home. That night we had feasts from one place to another, house to house. The next day we went back to RonKiti, our names were called, and we boarded the boat . . . straight from RonKiti to Lenger. The date we departed was July 27, and we stayed in Lenger for two weeks. We were not allowed to go to Kolonia. Our relatives were also restricted from seeing us at Lenger, even our friends. But we were so smart; we sneaked ourselves away on some of the Japanese workers' boats, especially those of the Koreans. We sneaked into Kolonia in the evenings to see our relatives; early in the morning we went down to the dock, jumped on the boat, and went back to Lenger.

One morning the men were alerted by a Japanese shore patrolman, married to a Pohnpeian woman, that they were to sail that day for an unknown destination. Just before they left, a rumor circulated that the destination was

Kosrae. Eneriko Pablo says, "They told us we were going there [Kosrae] to build a place for the planes. But nothing was said about the war."

> We stayed then until August 12; this was the date we left Pohnpei on a boat called *Sunsang Maru*. . . . There was a big gun, we thought, on the bow of the ship and it was covered. We thought this was a real gun. The night we left Pohnpei, they scheduled us, they divided us, every five men, into a group, watching, guarding the gun at night. This had been done, I think it was midnight, when we found out this was a wooden gun covered with canvas! Maybe this was just to scare the U.S. submarines. One group, when they were watching, a guy by the name of Ventura Augustine, who was a funny guy, was the one who opened the canvas just to see what kind of gun it was and he found that this was a piece of wood. He laughed and started passing the word among all of us. We started laughing. The second night, someone played around with the gun, before we reached Kosrae.

On the way to Kosrae they saw oil bubbling up as they passed a spot where the *Omi Maru* had been sunk, heading to Pohnpei with Kiribati people and Japanese aboard. Santos also recalls seeing a huge shark, which they at first mistook for a submarine: "It accompanied us all the way to Kosrae and then disappeared. I still can't figure out what it meant. Maybe it was a good luck sign, omen, or whatever. Maybe it was there to protect us."

On Kosrae, the men worked on airport construction, served as watchmen, obstructed sea channels, excavated tunnels, built bomb shelters, sharpened and distributed sticks, dove to recover sunken metal, fished, logged mangrove swamps, and manufactured zoris from hibiscus fibers. They were promised higher wages than on Pohnpei, but payment never materialized. Ignasio Paulino says they were paid only for the first six months. After that, he says, "The Japanese told us never to dream of going back to Pohnpei." At war's end, 169 survivors returned home.[21] Members of the group composed a memorial song, which begins:

> *Running there, we suddenly see Kosrae,*
> *With mountains like those of Kiti chiefdom.*
> *I begin to recall our happy chiefdom*
> *From which we were forced far away.*

At one o'clock we reached the open sea of selfishness
All of us prepared and going forth.
Myself, I believe there is no authority
For throwing my life away.[22]

Cross-Cultural Interactions

The influx of Okinawan, Korean, and Japanese construction workers (who followed the earlier immigration of farmers, factory workers, and entrepreneurs) and the travels of Micronesian laborers gave Islanders unprecedented exposure to diversity. While kinship remained the primary vehicle for social relations, common experience under difficult conditions now came to be valued as well. Asked whether the men from the various Mortlock Islands who served at Satawan's Japanese garrison were kin, Kenio Ipon replies, "Some of them were related, but some weren't. But they came to know each other while working with the soldiers." Other interactions had a different result: Parang Namono recalls that in the work crew at Eten airstrip in Chuuk, "The men from our island [Fefan] fought with men from Tol, Weno, and other islands. There was never any cooperation among us."

Micronesian attitudes toward Korean and Okinawan laborers varied from considering them Japanese to adopting derogatory Japanese attitudes toward them.[23] We have few stories of interaction between Micronesians and Okinawans or Koreans (with the important exception of the revolt of Koreans and Marshallese on Mili; see chapter 6). When asked about foreign workers, however, Micronesians remember where they worked, what work was assigned to them, and which groups were treated well or badly by the military. For example, on Kosrae, Tadasy Santos recalls that Pohnpeians were treated better than Chinese and Taiwanese, who "were sometimes punished when they failed to complete their assigned contracts." The Japanese consistently separated work, living, and mess groups by ethnicity.

Kosrae showed the greatest wartime diversity, with Koreans, Okinawans, Chinese, Pohnpeians, Nauruans, Banabans, and people from Tuvalu and Kiribati.[24] The organization of labor segregated work crews and living areas but grouped Micronesians together. Pohnpeians and Kosraeans had the most freedom and formed helpful friendships. Pernardo Lainos, who as a sixteen-year-old accompanied his father to Kosrae, recalls that "the Pohnpeians and Kosraeans respected each other because of the hardships they experienced at that time." He and Pensile Lawrence were the two Pohnpeians who became fluent in Kosraean. Despite good relations early in the war, food scarcity eventually forced Pohnpeians on Kosrae to resist sharing and even to take from local people: "If we didn't steal, we would die." Still, at the end of the war, the chief of Tafunsak asked to host Pohnpeian men until they were returned home. Okin Sarapio recalls, "Kosraeans took care of us; they gave us food and cloth. When we left Kosrae, we had already become strong and healthy." Some Pohnpeians later returned to visit Kosraeans they had known during the war.

Micronesians from British colonies that had been invaded at the end of 1941, who were relocated to Kosrae were prisoners of war, at the bottom of the ration priority list. Kiribati people were already on Kosrae when the Pohnpeian workers arrived. The two groups got along well, aided by a few men who could interpret. Dobi Kilimete of Pohnpei recalls: "I felt sorry for the Kiribati people because the Japanese didn't let them be with us. We ate only coconuts and other things, but the Kiribati people ate only potato leaves. They had many good things, but they sold them for ten coconuts . . . they didn't know how to speak Japanese. They must have been very strong because they ate only leaves, yet they were strong."

Nauruans were also held as prisoners of war, with most of them sent to Chuuk.[25] At first, Nauruans seemed strange to Chuukese. Their skin color identified them as Islanders, but their language was unintelligible, their clothing was different, and they ate local food only half-heartedly. Manuel Hartman recalls no advance warning about Nauruans being brought to Tatiw: "No, they didn't even inform us! And all of a sudden we saw them there, and we were confused, we didn't know who they were, where they were from. But there were some Chuukese who had been on Nauru, working there. They heard them talk and that's when they recognized them as Nauruans." In Chuuk, Nauruans worked at airport construction, agriculture, and fishing for the Japanese. They suffered from poor living conditions and unfamiliar food, then a meager diet as food became scarce. By the end of the war more than four hundred had died and many were weak and ill. On Weno and Tol, Chuukese and Nauruans became friendly. Chuukese brought Nauruans home and fed them, and they recall watching Nauruans dance, though interaction was restricted once the Allied offensive began. Repeated postwar visits from Nauru prove the strength of wartime friendships between Nauruans and people in several areas of Chuuk.

ENGAGING ISLANDER LOYALTIES

Everyone thought that the Japanese would win.

Islanders observing the unprecedented scale of Japanese military preparations were profoundly impressed. Seeing weapons, planes, and supplies brought ashore, workers and soldiers mobilized, islets cleared and mountains leveled for airbases, tunnels dug through basalt cliffs, reinforced concrete buildings rise and underground complexes deepen, Micronesians from every region of our study had similar comments: "I didn't ever suspect that they would lose"; "Everyone thought that the Japanese would win"; "They told us that the Japanese did not know how to lose."

The few sources of international news confirmed such confidence. Thaddeus Sampson, who worked in the Marshalls as an interpreter, recalls hearing war news by radio: "And it was from there that they told us all about the movements throughout the Pacific 'Oh, we have completed taking Singapore, we have finished taking Colonia, we have finished taking the Philippines, we are coming toward you there on Tarawa.'" Living on Jaluij, he also knew a great deal about the disposition of Japanese military units. Even those living at the tiny weather station and garrison on Ronglap got news: "Yes, messages would come to Ronglap all the time and say, 'Well, the Japanese have conquered the Philippines,' 'Well, they have already landed in the Solomons.'" Illium Tartios (Marshalls) got American souvenirs from a Japanese serviceman who had participated in the Wake Island victory (Poyer 1997:26). On Yap, Raphael Gisog not only heard about the war, but saw a film of the attack on Pearl Harbor. Those who worked for the military picked up news from servicemen (as Bwirre Lejmen heard of an attack on Kiribati later in the war when he ferried the farewell party of four kamikaze pilots at a Marshall Islands base). As troops were transferred about the theater, Islanders were able to assemble bits of war news—predominantly good news for the Japanese. "The Japanese said that it was they who had won, and their news was 'They had won!' and in the pictures that they showed us they won" (Luke Lantir, Marshalls). Augustine Mauricio of Pohnpei comments: "At that time I thought the Japanese were the strongest, that they could not lose. This was because I couldn't see what the other side was doing."

Bwirre Lejmen was asked: "When you first saw the readiness of the Japanese on Jaluij, did you have any thoughts that the Americans might win?" He replied:

> Well, my thought was that Japan was going to win, because everything was ready, they had brought in everything, all the buildings were so close together there was no space in between, line after line, and we said, "*Urrur!* Japan has already won." Everything was ready, the guns and swords of these people [soldiers], and the foods needed for them to eat. And on the island, planes were ready on Imiej and cannon and all things were ready, machine guns were ready. . . . And ships, there were also many. Sea vehicles, land vehicles, there were an abundance of these. So we said, "Japan is never going to lose." We did not have any way to know that America would win because we had not seen the methods that they would use.

Along with guarantees of victory, Micronesians also recall Japanese promising a change in status after the war was won. Okinawans would move up to join the Japanese class, and Islanders would move up to the status held by Okinawans. As Keigo Ezra (familiar with Japanese philosophy as a student and then as a teacher) said, the Chuukese had learned the racial ranking system—Japanese at the top, then Okinawans, Koreans, Formosans, and Micronesians—that would encompass the Pacific after Japanese victory (Dolan 1974:112–113). A step up in this hierarchy could be expected to bring tangible rewards.

Chiefs and Commoners

By the 1930s, the Nan'yō-chō had reshaped local government to suit its needs. Micronesian leaders entered the war years with different degrees of traditional legitimacy and Japanese-supported authority—and different degrees of loyalty to Japan. As the first effects of war reached island communities, Micronesians found that the pressures of land alienation, labor conscription, relocation, and security regulations forced local leaders to a new level of dealing with Japanese requests.

We cannot speak of "traditional" and "appointed" leaders as clear-cut categories. Colonial administrators sought forms suitable both to local social organization and to Japanese goals. On outer islands such as Ifaluk, Ulithi, and Puluwat, indigenous leaders were encased in but not superseded by colonial administration. In Chuuk, appointed leaders were often acknowledged heads of lineages or other important men. In Pohnpei and the Marshalls, the Japanese affirmed traditional leaders, joining administrative roles to respected statuses. Japanese officials on Pohnpei called in men of high traditional rank for consultation at the start of the war. Pohnpeians thought of Japanese as people who were, like themselves, "respectful" to traditional leaders. Other Micronesians thought that the Japanese disregarded local custom, restricting and overturning chiefly rights. Regardless of variable relationships between colonial rulers and traditional leaders, the Japanese worked constantly to acculturate young men who would cast their lot with Japan and to engender the kind of loyalty that would carry the Micronesian population through the war without threatening Japanese security.

Local elites who maintained special ties with the administration, and later with the military, benefited from those links. Elites included traditional leaders, Micronesian-Japanese families (such as the Moris on Chuuk), foreign business families (such as the Etscheits on Pohnpei), and the new elite of Japanese-educated young men who worked in offices, as labor foremen, and as policemen. Language skills and personal ties enabled the elite not only to gain wealth in an expanding economy, but also to navigate the colonial bureaucracy. (Yap was the exception; here Chamorros filled the role of Islander elite, and few Yapese cultivated connections with Japanese.) Elites had seen their positions affirmed in privileges awarded during the peacetime years. For example, William Prens (a Pohnpeian policeman) said that drinking alcohol, smoking, and visiting geisha houses was usually limited to Japanese over twenty-one years of age and "policemen, *nahnmwarki, nahnken* [talking chiefs], section chiefs, teachers—only those who worked for the government."

Islanders lacking family advantages could join the elite through education—especially by learning the Japanese language—and personal ties. The government encouraged the new elite through school activities, young people's associations, trips to Japan, and even schooling in Japan for a few. As the labor force became more tightly organized, these men served as foremen and translators. Sinio Peter (Mokil) was appointed leader of Mokilese workers on Pohnpei based on his prewar work—first as a babysitter for his sister and her Japanese businessman husband, who took him to Pohnpei, then as a janitor for NBK, a waiter, and a messenger—all by the age of nine. "At that time all Japanese knew me," he says. Wendolin Gomez of Pohnpei, who worked as a supervisor for a Japanese businessman doing "mostly translation and office work," was recruited to work at the Kolonia hospital (his seventeen years of medical experience later got him a job with the Americans). During our interview with Erwin Leopold of Pohnpei, his friend Anso Seiola said, "This man was important to the Japanese at that time so they took really good care of him." Schooled in Kolonia, Mr. Leopold worked as a policeman and made two lengthy trips to Japan, one for medical care that required special wartime travel permission. On that trip he began to work for a pharmaceutical company. On his return he worked for that company on Pohnpei, "responsible for three hundred men—Okinawans, Japanese, and Pohnpeians."

In turn, their involvement with the Japanese system had already partly committed these men to loyalty in the war effort. Marcus Alempia (Pohnpei) says: "During the war, I was on the Japanese side because I did not know about Americans and their country. I had not yet seen an American, but I had already seen the Japanese and knew the language a little." Young Islanders who had staked their careers on the Japanese administration worked to understand and reflect Japanese ideas, and they expected to benefit by their efforts. Damian Primo of Pohnpei recounts his experience: "Japanese treated the emperor as their God. When they were about to die, they would say, 'Tennō Heika banzai'—that was the end of the war for their life. We Pohnpeians also did that so the Japanese would think we acted or thought like Japanese. Working with Japanese was good and they were very kind to me because I was one of their students, and I also understood how to speak the Japanese language."

Thaddeus Sampson, an interpreter for Japanese officials in the Marshalls, recalls: "They said, 'If Japan wins, you will go to school in Japan.' If Japan had won, I would have gone to school in Japan, to the high-ranked schools in Tokyo. This is what they told me." And Sampson believed them (and still does): "For the Japanese . . . once they came to understand how to love you, then everything could be possible: They would sleep with you and they would eat with you and everything. And then, if you went to Japan, you see, you would be just like a Japanese. They would stuff you and feed you and everything would be free."

Patriots and Volunteers

By 1941, a generation of Islanders had grown up under a policy of patriotic education. Many—predominantly those in urban areas, members of elite families, and those with more than elementary schooling—felt themselves part of the Japanese Empire, although not "Japanese" (Dolan 1974: 112–113). Leban Jorju (Marshalls) describes the power of the Japanese model:

> They prayed, bowed their heads to the flag, and faced the north and they said they faced then toward the emperor. They said that the emperor is one of their highest leaders, and deserving the highest honor for their lives. Some said, "You die for Tennō Heika [the emperor]; you die for your country." If you do not want to die, you just stay put, but then they will kill you anyway, because you have not chosen to die for Tennō Heika. Their tendency to elevate this religion of theirs was very great, elevate it to the highest degree.

Education and public display were important means of integrating Micronesians into this ethos. Celebrations of Japan's victories in China made a big impression. Sontak Kansou (Chuuk) still recalls the names of three Japanese brothers who sacrificed themselves in China—learned from a story told half a century ago at such a celebration. Patriotic military songs became popular and were sung during war training and wartime labor. Military displays and parades also built patriotism. Japanese in charge of Islanders' labor spoke to them in terms of "helping the emperor." In Palau, where Micronesians were more acculturated than in islands farther east, young men were active in Tōmin Seinendan (Young Islanders' Association), which joined with the Japanese Shōbō-dan (Fire-Fighting Association) and Keibō-dan (voluntary guards preparing for air attacks) (Peattie 1988:108; Higuchi 1991). Palauan women were also organized, sometimes joining Japanese associations to be with their friends. Six Palauan women on Angaur joined a Japanese women's group supporting the troops in China and performing Palauan dances and songs for the Japanese (Higuchi 1991). Pro-Japanese Palauans more directly implemented Japanese policy with the increased tempo of war after 1939, recruiting Palauan labor, increasing production, and maintaining civil order (Vidich 1980:260–261).

All the efforts at acculturation were put to the test when Micronesians were asked to work hard and with little recompense in the war effort. Julio Vallazon (Pohnpei) describes the role of patriotism in the incredible task of winching an artillery piece to the top of Sokehs Rock: "The big gun could only be moved two feet per day, using a winch to help pull it straight up the cliff. There was a picture of the emperor on top of the gun crate. When people saw the picture of that great leader, they worked even harder for the Japanese. They kept trying to get it up and keep the crate from being scratched, because of the importance of the picture of the emperor on top."

Yet the participation of Islanders in the war was limited by the same ethnic hierarchy that had constrained their peacetime opportunities. Not being Japanese citizens, Micronesians were not eligible for nor required to enlist in military service. "The Japanese never actually met with us and asked us to help them fight the war," Sachuo Siwi (Chuuk) says. Max Mori of Chuuk recalls, "Some of the Chuukese young men had asked if they could join the army or the navy, but they were told they could not unless they applied for Japanese citizenship" (Dolan 1974:86). Men with Japanese fathers and Micronesian mothers were considered Japanese citizens, however; among them were the young men of the Mori family, who served with Japanese forces in China, the Philippines, and Chuuk. Two died in service. Masataka Mori was in Japan when the war started. "When Yamamoto died," (April 1943) he went through considerable trouble (including leaving his wages behind and having a ship sunk under him on the way home) to get back to Chuuk, where he began a two-year stint in the Japanese army, serving on Weno to the end of the war.

Though restricted from a full citizen's participation, many Micronesian men saw their wartime labor as quasi-military and were encouraged to do so by the Japanese attitude. A few served in explicitly military roles. Several dozen men in Chuuk lagoon worked on supply ships and as pilots in the lagoon as part of a military organization. Hatanaka (1973–1974:10–11) writes: "When the Pacific war compelled Japan to mobilize all the military power it could, the members of the *seinendan* came forth as army volunteers in large numbers, indicating the effectiveness of the education they (young men) had received and their positive response toward the Japanese mainland."

The *seinendan* and similar paramilitary groups practiced military drills and sometimes had uniforms, but they were not issued weapons, and Islanders were, with few exceptions, not allowed to possess guns.[26] A few Micronesians joined the military as noncombatant volunteers (*teishintai;* Peattie 1988:301). Late in the war, the Japanese organized military training for some Palauan youths (Shuster 1982b:73).

Micronesian men served as air raid lookouts throughout the islands, but this does not necessarily mean that they willingly supported the war effort. When we asked Bwirre Lejmen whether Marshallese served as lookouts, he took the question as asking whether they were voluntarily helping the Japanese: "Yes, there were lookouts, why not, if you did not obey them, they would beat you [kill you]. On account of this, even if you knew they would shoot you while you were on that thing [the watchtower], you would go ahead [and do what they told you to do]. For if you did not go, then they would have you stand up—buuk!—and they would shoot you. In all things, we had no power over them—if you were Marshallese, you had none."

At the beginning of the war, the Japanese made a modest recruiting effort to encourage Micronesian volunteers to aid the Southwest Pacific advance. A group from Palau and one from Pohnpei are the best known of the volunteers. Early in the war, some sixty Palauans volunteered to work for Japanese surveyors in New Guinea. To a greater degree than other Micronesians, Palauans—whose home was the Nan'yō capital and host to a very large Japanese immigrant population—had accepted Japanese rule and were beginning to consider themselves part of the Japanese nation (see Higuchi 1991; Trumbull 1959:167). The spirit of adventure, patriotism, and pride felt by these volunteers is captured in song:

> *I'm leaving home and going very far,*
> *We, young Palauans, are on our way to the South*
> *There are about sixty of us*
> *We are Palauans,*
> *But what we do is for Japan.*

I just want to let you and everyone know
Our work is difficult, it's a matter of life and death
The dangers and the snakes are difficult to describe
We crossed dangerous rivers and plains. (Nero 1989:124)

According to one volunteer, Elibosang Eungel, they traveled with civilian Japanese on a six-month trip to survey New Guinea's natural resources. Mr. Eungel also made a second trip to New Guinea after war had begun in earnest. According to Yano K. Mariul, Palauan carpenters, drivers, machine operators, and cooks were chosen to aid the Japanese in New Guinea, where they moved supplies and ammunition to mountain shelters, then fished and hunted wild pigs for food. Several succumbed to malaria and were evacuated, some were injured or killed in action, six died when they drank methyl alcohol, and one was reportedly killed as a spy. It was impossible to return to Palau after the original contract, and their stay was extended another six months. But Mr. Mariul did not return to Koror until 1946 (Higuchi 1991).[27]

The story of the small group of Micronesian men from Pohnpei recruited for Melanesian service within six months after Pearl Harbor, the "Ponapean Death Band" (as it is called in a Japanese account of that title [Watakabe 1972]), is well known on Pohnpei today and remains a source of pride. The exact number in the group and whether their participation was coerced, deceptive, or entirely voluntary remains unclear. The Japanese motive for recruiting them remains obscure to Pohnpeians, but it was thought to be a test of their courage and loyalty, appropriate for a culture that respects warfare.

Benjamin Lopez, one of a handful of Pohnpeians sent for advanced education in Palau and who later worked for the administration in Kolonia, remembers:

One group went with the soldiers—men from Kiti, Sokehs, Uh, Madolenihmw, but not from Net—to New Guinea, Rabaul. I was among those chosen. I was working in the office, and the boss there was Valentine Dosilua. This man started preparing Pohnpeians and he asked me to get ready to go. A Japanese man, Osipo, worked in the office, and he heard this and said, "Please come here. I want to meet with you." He asked me, "Are you really going to go to Rabaul?" I said, "Yes, they talked to me and told me to prepare to go." He asked me if I had any siblings. I said yes, sisters. And two younger brothers, but they lived in different places; on different pieces of land from our different fathers. He asked, "If you go to Rabaul, can anyone take your place on your land?" I said, "No." So he said, "Then, you're not going." This is when I started thinking maybe if I went I would die. There was talk that those who were preparing to go would never return. I knew I wasn't going.

[In the end,] almost all of them died; only three returned—Popohn from Uh, Sohn [Alpet] from Madolenihmw, and Ludwik Alik from Sokehs.

Ludwik Alik, a Mokilese man who was the last survivor of the group, recalls the roll: "Two were from Yap; the names of these two men were Noal and Pwungieri. One man from Chuuk was Sapwuro. On Pohnpei there were six from Sokehs. Their names were Ludwik, Swinglen, Lemuel, Makis, and Oscar. From Kiti there was Ioanis, Ioakim, Isiro, Bensis, and Deodore. From Uh, there was Popohn, Ioanis, Shute, Wilson, and Valentine. From Madolenihmw was Sohn. We left under Japanese force, except for two Pingelapese volunteers, Lemuel and Swinglen."

Mitsuo Watakabe, a Japanese navy man, was on board the ship that went to collect the twenty young men. From shipboard conversations with them, Watakabe (1972) asserts that they were chosen from several dozen volunteers of superior ability who would be sent to Rabaul as supervisors of work gangs.[28] He describes their recruitment by the Japanese police officer:

The news went apace all over the island and many a young man gathered at the Japanese Administration burning with passion for joining the "Dai Toa" War.

"Now that you will sacrifice yourselves for your father country Japan, you need no longer worry about your families. All of you are just requested to accomplish your tasks holding together against the enemy."

This was a familiar expression and a matter of course as well. They took it to be the Imperial command and at the same time believed it was the assurance by the Japanese Government.

Some of them had already been married but cast away their homes, cutting off the bond of affection and making their blood boil, so that they might take part in the battle for the right. . . .

These twenty Ponapeans[29] were cheered up with most stirring remarks and admiring compliments by the government and the people of the whole island, and a special farewell party was held at a restaurant of the flourishing place in Colonia [*sic*], the only one town of Ponape.

In those days it was prohibited to sell alcohol to the natives, but at that banquet drinking continued two days and two nights. . . .

Those young men, who had steeped in liquor for the first time in their lives, felt as if they had been let free from their class and become true Japanese soldiers. (Watakabe 1972:4–5)

But, as Watakabe says, "It was really the merry-making to the grave." They left Pohnpei on June 14, 1942, arriving via Chuuk in Rabaul on August 20. Fighting was already underway, and Ludwik Alik recalls seeing aerial dogfights and Japanese busy loading ships. After the first night, the group was split up.

Sixteen of us went to New Guinea, and two got sick; that's why they didn't go with us to Kiriwa [on the south coast of New Guinea]. We stayed there [in Kiriwa] during September, October, November, and December. In December we learned that some of us had died. The one from Yap died. We stayed in New Guinea until January 8. Times were difficult, because the Americans had begun to help the Australians, so many Japanese died at that time.

Beginning on January 19, the Japanese told us that each of us had to find his own way to reach his home. On February 7 we took planes to Kumwus, because there was a boat waiting for us there. When we landed in Kumwus, we started running, looking for a way to save our lives. We arrived in Rabaul on August 3, 1943.

On board ship, Ludwik Alik was reunited with his compatriots, Sohn and Popohn, who had been hospitalized in Rabaul. Together they made their way back to Pohnpei aboard a steamer. The details of the trip home, via Palau and Chuuk, are forever etched in his memory (and in that of others, such as Klemete Actouka of Chuuk, who met them when he was working on the ship that brought the three survivors home.) They arrived on October 16, 1943: "We were carrying some dead bodies on that ship, the bodies of some of our group. When we arrived in Pohnpei, the Japanese who lived in Pohnpei greeted us, and they honored us."

The grief of family and friends of those who died in New Guinea is captured in a song composed on the return of their remains (cited by Ludwik Alik):

News has surfaced that really breaks my heart.
They selected my sweetheart and took him to the land of death.
Left every family in a hard place, crying, because the country is far away
All the families are crying because they returned only for their funeral
Greetings, Mina-san, I am leaving
Greetings to all of you, because I am leaving
Mina-san, sayonara.

The three survivors hoped to find peace by going home, but by that time the Allies' Central Pacific drive had begun. Ludwik Alik continues: "When we returned to Pohnpei, the three of us who survived the group went to work for the Japanese. We carried food for the Japanese soldiers."

All Micronesians would soon experience the war that these volunteers had barely escaped in New Guinea.

Chapter 4

DEFENSIVE PREPARATIONS

The Japanese Military Takes Charge

ISLANDERS had some two years to adjust to the first phase of military operations when the turning tide of war spurred a reevaluation of Micronesia's strategic role. Early in the war, Japan had had little need to fortify the islands, since their primary role was as bases for offensive air activity and support services for distant fronts. But following the June 1942 defeat at Midway, losses in the Southwest Pacific, and the effective U.S. war on shipping, Japanese strategy turned from expanding the war to building a protective shield around the home islands (Peattie 1988:262–265). In September 1943, Imperial General Headquarters established a second line of defense in Micronesia.

Micronesians experienced the shift from an offensive to a defensive stance in terms of massive troop influxes, confiscation of land and food, repeated relocations, labor drafts, and shortages of food and goods. These were the hard times that contrasted so vividly with the good life and thriving economy under civilian rule. In the Marshall Islands, this change occurred after Allied bombing in early 1942. In other places life did not change dramatically until defensive fortification in 1943–1944, and in still others, not until American blockading, sustained air attack, or invasion in 1944–1945.

GARRISON TROOPS COME ASHORE

When the army arrived, that's when things changed.

The reinforcement of the islands with Japanese Imperial Army troops marked a sea change in Micronesian experience. The army's task was rapid construction of defense in depth to form an impassible barrier to Allied invasion. The army was under many pressures when it arrived in the islands in late 1943 and early 1944: much of its materiel lost to Allied submarines, imminent U.S. bombing, the threat of invasion, and the closure of supply routes. Tens of thousands of troops had to be supplied from a food base already supporting construction laborers, civilian Japanese, and Islanders (Peattie 1988:265; Spector 1985:485–487). Problems facing the military, especially the army, formed the context of Islanders' hardships during the latter years of war.

The men of the Japanese army seemed to Micronesians to be "different"— not only from civilian Japanese, but even from the more familiar navy personnel. As Masataki Mori (Chuuk) says, "When the army arrived, that's when things changed, because the army was different [from the navy]." As troops came ashore, they spread across the larger islands rapidly, confiscating land and dwellings for barracks and warehouses. Kristo Sowas (Chuuk) adds: "These soldiers came with their own laws. They didn't respect anything or anybody, not even our culture. They did whatever they had to do, never mind the local people." After supply lines were cut, soldiers' needs on Pohnpei, Kosrae, Chuuk, and garrisoned Marshall and Caroline atolls expanded until it seemed every bit of land and every able person's labor was under military control.

La'ew, a Yapese woman, explains that when soldiers first arrived people did not realize how profoundly their life was about to change. She was then around ten years old: "You see, when we saw the Japanese soldiers, we were fascinated. They were novel. So I used to go and stand at the fence, and I would bow like the Japanese. I used to bow and bow because I really enjoyed watching them when they were marching, because they wore uniforms, they wore shoes that made noise [as they marched], they held guns at their shoulders, and they wore hats. But in the end [despite the attractive novelty], they turned around and beat people."

The first two years of war, during which the Nan'yō remained well behind the front lines, had conferred a sense of security. Despite increased labor and restrictions on civilian activities, prewar life remained largely intact. The 1942 attack on the Marshalls and the tightening of supply lines later that year encouraged some Japanese civilians to leave. But after the Allied counteroffensive became a reality with the invasion of Kiribati in November 1943—allowing U.S. planes to reach Japanese Micronesia—all sense of safety dissolved. The current of immigration reversed itself as entrepreneurs and farmers left for home. Families separated as some Japanese took their Islander wives and their children, while others left them behind.

As the Allies won control of the sea lanes, transportation became uncertain. Many evacuees waited too long, such as the company people, government workers, and "all of the women from the hotel" (prostitutes) who left Jabwor (Marshall Islands) on the *Yajima Maru*, which was sunk en route to Japan. The last ship carrying civilians from Chuuk was likewise attacked. Those who missed the last boat out, or who chose to stay, came under military control. As towns and rural areas emptied of Japanese and Okinawan farmers, businessmen, and service workers, the internal economy of the mandate began to disintegrate.

DEFENSIVE PREPARATIONS: ISLANDS AS FORTRESSES

This was the time that I really believed about the war.

When strategy shifted from offense to defense, the implications of the war for each island group also changed. The first phase of war had seen a roughly similar sequence in the Marshalls, Chuuk, Pohnpei, Kosrae, and the fortified Caroline atolls, with navy personnel and construction workers arriving as local labor intensified. The shooting war approached Micronesia from east to west; Japanese strategy after autumn 1943 attempted first to strengthen the outermost bases of Kiribati and the Marshalls, then drew consecutively tighter circles within which the Imperial Navy and Army would commit to action as the geography of empire began to shrink.

Marshall Islands

Marshall Islanders had already experienced major shocks of land loss, relocation, and militarization on the fortified atolls. In late 1943 new troops flowed in to bolster the outer ring of the empire's defenses. Soldiers were for the most part assigned to existing bases, which were kept supplied as long as sea routes remained open. By the end of the year, some thirteen thousand Japanese troops were "lapping up on shore" (as one Marshallese put it) of the fortified islands.[1] The numbers include accidental as well as intentional reinforcements, with survivors of torpedoed troop transports (minus supplies and equipment) joining the nearest garrison (e.g., see Morison 1951:78). Over-crowding further displaced Marshallese still living on the garrisoned atolls. After troops arrived on Kwajalein Atoll, for example, the Islanders' school was shifted to Namu, and Marshallese lived only on three tiny islets of the atoll. Yet as troops poured into the Marshalls, the region was actually losing its strategic importance, coming to be seen only as protection for the Carolines and Marianas (Shaw, Nalty, and Turnbladh 1966:139). No new bases were developed, as defensive fortification focused on islands farther west—within Japan's own defensive perimeter.

The rapid defensive preparations in the Marshalls were incomplete at the time of the first Allied invasions of Kiribati and the Marshalls. For Islanders working on the fortified atolls, the intensity of labor increased dramatically as the threat of invasion approached. While those who labored for high-ranking Japanese typically continued to be treated well, others suffered abuses. American victories on Kwajalein, Majuro, and Enewetak soon brought an end to the defensive phase of war on these atolls. On the other fortified atolls—Mili, Maloelap, Wotje, and Jaluij—food shortages and daily bombing runs became a way of life beginning in January and February 1944. These experiences are described in detail in the coming chapters, but bear in mind that they took place at the same time that parts of western Micronesia were still engaged in defensive preparations.

Marshallese living on ungarrisoned atolls, if they had escaped labor conscription, got through the period of defensive buildup with relatively little trouble. Of Lib Atoll, Ijimura Lautoña says, "That was a fairly good place to be because there were no soldiers to create difficulties for us in our lives." Lib received visits from Japanese military ships ("They called them fishing ships, but there were machine guns on their bows"—some, at least, were mock guns made of wood). Islanders exchanged coconuts, papayas, and chickens for rice and clothing until, "after a few more months, it (the sea) closed and then there were no more ships." At the time of American invasion there was no Japanese resistance on Ailinginae, Rongrik, Ronglap, Erikub, Aur, Bikar, Namorik, Kili, Ailuk, Likiep, Lib, or Arno. Other islands held only a few soldiers (Richard 1957c:511).

Ronglap provides an example of life on the unfortified Marshall Islands. Here there had been no resident Japanese until soldiers set up a weather station. Clanton Abija and John Anjain recall fewer than ten Japanese at the station, which consisted of an observation tower, the large weather station itself, a mess hall/barracks, a cooking and shower house, a warehouse, and gardens. Despite the small military presence, Ronglap people "lived under the laws of the soldiers." Some eighteen men who spoke Japanese worked at the station. They were paid until shipping ceased, when cash became useless. The soldiers lived close to the Islanders: "It is like we surrounded them, their houses and their workplaces." John Anjain, who worked for the soldiers as a cook, in construction, and as a lookout, recalls, "in terms of the way we worked together, everything was very good."

Pohnpei and Kosrae

On the high islands of the eastern Carolines, 1943 saw major changes as the influx of troops militarized daily life. Troops had been staged through Pohnpei earlier but, compared to the Marshalls or Chuuk, relatively few foreign laborers preceded the army's arrival in force. Significant defensive construction and garrisoning came only in late 1943 and early 1944. After the buildup, soldiers and foreign civilians on Pohnpei far outnumbered the 5,900 Islanders. When the United States evacuated the island in 1945, there were nearly 8,000 military and 14,066 Japanese, Okinawan, and Korean laborers and civilians (Bascom 1950:144).

The army located units throughout the island—at Lenger, Sapwitik, Parem, Nahpali, Temwen, Metipw, Sokehs, Sapwalap, Palikir—"on land they were everywhere. They made their places all around Pohnpei"—and installed bunkers and lookouts on nearby Ant Atoll. The imposition of military discipline on civilians coincided with or soon followed the army's arrival. The military took over government buildings and used churches as barracks (Carmen Miguel says Japanese soldiers "turned the churches into dance halls"). The greatest impacts were confiscation of land for military use, relocation of local populations, and demands for Islander labor and food production.

The first airstrip at Nanpohnmal had been on public land, but the seaplane base built at Lenger Island displaced local residents. Construction moved Lenger and Sapwitik people to Palikir and Lewetik, Net; Ohwa people moved inland to the forest, taking a missionary with them, when soldiers arrived to fortify the area. Kapingamarangi people on Pohnpei were moved inland from their village of Porakiet to avoid American bombing, and some moved again in response to Japanese orders for labor (Lieber 1968:216). In Temwen, soldiers slept in vacated houses while those they displaced moved in with relatives elsewhere. Paulina Aisawa remembers that the Japanese knocked down her family's house in Temwen with a huge rock and ordered them to move to make way for arriving soldiers; but some people remember that soldiers staying in their house kept it safe while they lived elsewhere.

As the size of Pohnpei's garrison grew, material shortages led to confiscation of household goods: "Clothing and dishes were appropriated by the military, with the result that many Ponapeans buried their good china until the war was over. Some houses were invaded, and floors, walls, and furniture torn up for firewood. All district feast houses were ordered destroyed" (Bascom 1950:145). Keropin David, born during the war, heard that Japanese soldiers tried unsuccessfully to get rid of kava pounding stones that were "in their way" by burning them and breaking them with sledge hammers. Soldiers in evacuated areas ruined food crops, dug up yams, ate out taro swamps and turned them into gardens, killed pigs and chickens, and commandeered food ("You went out fishing and came back; they took all of your fish just as if they had been the ones who had gone out fishing"—Solomon Lorrin). In Dolonier they felled coconut palms to eat the hearts and young leaves. Carmen Miguel's father faced requisitions by Japanese soldiers: "They told him to give the goat. My father said he no longer had a goat, and they beat him." Suhlet Abraham and her husband had more success when the Japanese "destroyed our house and used the wood for fire. My husband and I got mad and started to argue with the Japanese, who ran away." Yet such confiscation may have been the exception, at least at first; Yasio Behris, speaking of the war, says, "Everything the Japanese wanted from Pohnpeians, they paid for it—such as yams, pigs, fish, etc." Lihna Lawrence adds: "Some soldiers were good; they objected to stealing. Some soldiers were cruel; they just came into peoples' houses and took what they wanted. Not all Japanese were bad; the bad ones gave the others a bad reputation."

Military preparations on Pohnpei aimed to make the mountainous island defensible in an invasion. Workers built roads through the forest, blocked lagoon channels with mangrove logs and barriers of sharpened sticks, erected shore defenses, and installed heavy fixed guns and searchlights. A second airstrip at Sokehs was built in sixteen days in early March 1944 with workers pulled from agricultural labor. But compared with Chuuk or the Marshalls, fewer Pohnpeians worked on military construction. Instead, they recall most their work on agricultural plantations, as food production was intensified at existing prewar farms and new fields were planted: rice in Sapwalap, Madolenihmw, at several areas in Net, and in Palikir; yams in Palikir; pineapple in Madolenihmw; tapioca in Net—all using local labor (including schoolchildren) and Okinawan and Korean workers. Crops also included potatoes, cucumbers, papaya, tobacco, sweet potatoes, and cabbage. American intelligence recognized Pohnpei's agricultural value to the Japanese, estimating that Palikir alone produced 6 tons of vegetables per week.[2]

In addition to farm labor, people worked in canneries or factories as long as these remained operational. Production of salt, soap, hibiscus sandals, mats, bark fabric, and liquor continued through most of the war. Many Pohnpeians worked gathering coconuts and pressing them for oil. Women made coconut sennit twine and roof thatch and collected leaves the Japanese used for soup; men fished for the Japanese, traveled by boat around Pohnpei collecting breadfruit for the military, or delivered food to soldiers in the mountainous interior. Although at first the work was presented and seen as wage labor, simply an increase in prewar labor obligations, Mikel Diana said wages "stopped when the war started," those who refused to work were beaten, and some pretended sickness "to avoid the hard work and punishment." Describing how her family got along with the occupying soldiers, Masako Luhk Karen says, "My father worked as a fisherman then. I'm not sure whether he was paid. People just did things then; they wanted to be helpful to the Japanese so that they could survive."

The flood of army troops was equally traumatic on Kosrae. "This was the time," Tolenna Kilafwasru says, "that I really believed about the war." Osmond Palikun comments, "We called this time when the Japanese soldiers came the 'hard time' (pel koluk)," and recalls that "everything stopped" when the soldiers came. The army took over the barracks of Japanese laborers working on the airstrip, while those men moved on to build a coal rail line at Yeseng. Most civilian Japanese on Kosrae were evacuated after the army arrived; those who remained became military workers. Troops moved across the island building roads, barracks, and gun emplacements. Otinel Eddmont recalls that "all the local Kosraean people stopped their own work and joined the Japanese in their war efforts." Anna Brightly did laundry for civilian laborers at Pilyuul until the soldiers arrived, when she and all the Lelu women began to weave thatch roofing and walls for them. Soldiers were also stationed at a lookout on Poro mountain. Later, when food grew scarce, troops were divided among locales in Welung, Tafunsak, Lelu, and Malem.

Kosrae was only lightly fortified and like Pohnpei was transformed into a factory for food and goods needed by the military. Initial war work was done by imported labor, but in 1943 Kosraeans were conscripted for agriculture, fishing, carpentry, lumbering, airport construction, domestic work for Japanese, and work at a refrigerated produce storage facility and a sawmill on a Monday-through-Sunday, no-rest schedule (Peoples 1977). The vast agricultural plantations already established under NKK and the Japanese navy were worked to feed the troops stationed there, as well as workers and prisoners brought from elsewhere, and—as long as transport was possible—to continue supplying the Marshall Islands bases. Austin Albert recalls four large military-run plantations: in Lelu (where Lelu people worked), Tofol (where Kiribati and Banaba people worked), and Tafweyak and Pilyuul (where Okinawans and Japanese worked). Later in the war, as Kosrae was cut off from both export and resupply, cultivation expanded, eventually reaching nearly 700 acres in 1944, with the largest cleared areas in Tafoyat and Pilyioul. As James Peoples notes, "Several Kusaeiens told me that one could stand on Lelu island and Langosak, beside the church buildings, and look westward to the large island and see nothing but cultivated fields between the mangrove swamps and the mountains" (1977:148–149).

Palikun Andrew recalls that Kosraeans were ordered to plant both local and fast-growing imported crops. When food shortages hit, Islanders were warned not to harvest what they had planted: "Everywhere the soldiers were watching us to keep us from climbing coconuts or picking bananas beside our house until it was time to harvest them and give them to the soldiers." After American bombing began, the Japanese formed Kosraeans into work groups for military construction and food production. As on Pohnpei, many Islanders were forced to relocate. Palikun Andrew continues:

> The soldiers went around the island for one whole day and told the people in Malem to leave their village and go to Inkoeya and the people in Utwe to move out to Koasr. The two places they forced us to go are both in Tafunsak. At that time, the governor and Isaiah Benjamin went with me to the owner of the place to ask permission before we could enter or live there.

The owner (Alik Kephas) had doubts about what we wanted and told the governor to ask his son (Palik Kumat) for what he had to say. The son said yes. Then, that was the time we went back to Utwe and told everyone to break apart their houses and to take them to Koasr.

We started to take down our house piece by piece, working day and night. We really worked hard to finish the work that month, because the governor told us to finish that month. During the day we worked on the houses and at night we transported the supplies in our canoes. The tide was not so good, so we had to drop them off along the channel and come back for the rest. During this time, some of the family stayed along the coastal strip for the time being. After we took all of the supplies and families to Koasr, Tafunsak, the governor told us that from now on no one was allowed to return to Utwe; even our own property we were not allowed to touch. That was on July 1. We stayed in Koasr for one, two, and then a third year. That was the time the bombing or air raids began. The same year they told us again that everybody should move out to the mountain, but to take what we could take with us. At that time, the people started to live by the mountain from Likinlulem all the way down to Isra.

Compared to Chuuk or Pohnpei, a fairly small number of Kosraeans moved, but for those who did, the challenges of the war years were intensified.[3]

Chuuk

In Chuuk lagoon, geographic complexity combined with military necessity to produce a jigsaw puzzle of relocations as troops poured in beginning in January 1944. Japanese businessmen and civil servants had lived mostly in urban Toloas, but the army spread throughout the lagoon islands, confiscating land, houses, and labor as it went. By the time troops arrived in force, construction workers had built barracks and other infrastructure, and soldiers moved right into Toloas, with the overflow housed in schools. Matsuko Soram was a child in downtown Toloas when the soldiers arrived. She didn't see them, but one day "there was a big noise in the house for the Japanese unmarried women. I asked, 'What is the reason for the noise?' And my dad said, 'The soldiers are arriving, and they're in that house.'"

Before January 1944, Japanese Imperial Army strength on Chuuk was only

300 officers and enlisted men, who had arrived in November 1943 to join navy units already in place. Major elements of the 52nd division began to arrive in 1944, and by April 1944 there were 14,293 troops. The army's job was to repel invasion, so it began to build defenses immediately, hampered by loss of materials to Allied attacks on shipping. The major U.S. air raid of February 1944 necessitated even greater speed as the lagoon prepared for invasion.[4]

Chuuk's islands were variously fortified, but all had at least communications centers, artillery, barracks, and supply depots. Most heavily fortified were Toloas (headquarters, combined airstrip and seaplane base, storage, barracks, support services); Weno (early airstrip, combined airstrip and seaplane base by April 1943, barracks, communication center); and Eten and Parem, with airfields completed in December 1943 and January 1944 respectively. The Faichuk islands in the western lagoon, less heavily fortified, became garrisoned farming areas. Reefs were mined and potential invasion sites blocked.[5] All this was in addition to the facilities befitting a major naval base.

It is our impression that the proportion of land confiscated for army use in Chuuk was greater than in the Marshalls, eastern or western Caroline Islands, or Palau. On some lagoon islands, such as Eten, Parem, Udot, Weno, and Toloas, it seems that every bit of land was controlled by the military for defense or food production. For Chuukese, confiscations were the beginning of war. The following is from an interview with Masataka Mori:

When the war started, the government told the people to move from the land, because the government owns the land. They came in and said: we own this land, and we decree that no one can collect breadfruit from the breadfruit trees. That's when the war started.

(Interviewer asks: Did they remove your house from the land?)
Yes, they took possession of the house. Everything on the property— trees, fruit—nobody could take anything.

(Interviewer: What was the hurry?)
Just like I said, at that time the war had already started. They (the Japanese) had no place to live.

In some cases, whole villages were evacuated. On Weno, construction cleared breadfruit and coconut trees in Mechitiw village and threw people's houses "into the sea"—this is remembered as happening suddenly, without warning. The navy had already built a communications building and a gun emplacement in Sapwuk village and restricted use of the area, but it was not until the army arrived in force that people had to leave. Iras village people had already relocated for airstrip construction; they later moved off Weno completely. Eten people, displaced to Toloas before the war to make way for the airfield, moved again to interior Toloas as construction crowded the shore, then when bombing intensified to relocation sites on other islands. Parem people evacuated their island as it was turned into another airfield. Toloas was the most developed island (and later the one most heavily bombed); Micronesians there were eventually restricted to five designated areas (the rest was reserved for Japanese use), and those not working for the Japanese were moved off-island, many to Tol. Weno, Toloas, and Fefan people were also shifted around their home islands.

Refugees lodged with family or clan relatives or friends made during previous labor trips away from home; others relied on the generosity of strangers. Says Tarup Ounuwa, "Some people lived together who were not relatives"— a striking departure for Chuukese. On Weno, Toli Jessy was among those who moved from Neuwe to Sapwuk village to make way for a seaplane base.

Oh, those Sapwuk folks were very generous people. They not only let us stay on the land but they also showed us their breadfruit trees and coconuts to eat from, or rather steal from [because of military control of food]. I think that because we had been moved there by the Japanese, that was why the Sapwuk people welcomed us. The people of Weno showed a deep feeling of working together or helping one another. Note that when we moved we didn't just get up and leave with the clothes that we had on. We had to move everything, such as our clothes, cooking pots, even our houses, we had to disassemble them and take them with us. Absolutely everything.[6]

The Japanese navy had come to Chuuk well supplied, but army units lost their supplies to American submarines en route, a reason given for taking over the housing and soon the food trees and garden areas of Chuukese. Ichios Eas remembers that the army "just came in and moved us out" of his father's nice, glass-windowed house; "We saw the guns and swords—that was it! Who was going to answer them back when they were carrying guns?" Japanese moved into local houses or renovated them to suit their needs. Asako Mateas, speaking about Tol, says: "For instance, if we were living in this house, they'd come and tell us to move. They'd take half of this house [the tin roof sheets and ply-wood walls] and use it to build something else, and they'd use the other half for storing ammunition and explosives." (On Udot, however, Piara Esirom says the soldiers took only empty houses and gave people cooking pots and other things in exchange, though not money.) Those evicted made shelters from coconut and ivory palm thatch or lived in caves, often struggling with in-adequate and unclean water. People's memory is that soldiers did not ask per-mission but simply ordered them out of their houses, took boats and canoes without payment, stored supplies on people's land without informing them, and destroyed meeting houses and land to erect their buildings. Recalls Sai-kichi Tommy: "They destroyed the resources without being concerned with the landowners. What can we say of this kind of behavior? We can say it caused suffering. But the main thing that was really important, taro, that was one of our main sources of life, it was taken by the soldiers because they said they were going to keep it for us. But it was not for us, it was for the soldiers. That happened during the time they owned the whole place."

On Tol, soldiers dug up taro and widened irrigation ditches, destroying gardens; on Uman, they replaced taro patches with watercress; on Patta they filled in the taro plots and planted corn. In Tunnuk village on Weno, Chuuk-ese lived surrounded by soldiers, who put numbered signs on coconut trees stating, "This land belongs to the soldiers." Konstantin Enik adds: "So when we came to take coconuts or breadfruit from those trees, they saw us and said they would shoot us, because those trees didn't belong to us, they belonged to them. That was one of the main things we suffered from." The army took not only land and houses; on Udot "they took away everything except clothes, what a person was wearing"—so books, photographs, and written documents were lost (Saikichi Tommy). They even confiscated air-raid shelters that Chuukese had dug. Manuel Hartman recalls: "If they liked our hole, they would move in and take it. [They'd say,] 'You go dig one over there, and we'll take this one.'"

Yap

Two major military projects mark the war on Yap. The first was the clearing and burning of a large area in southern Yap, which the Japanese said was in-

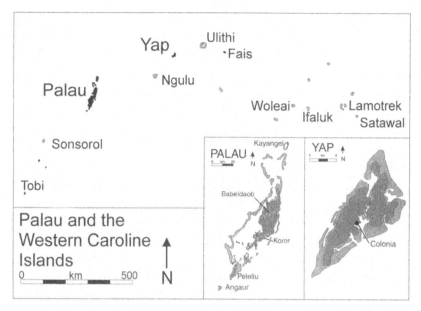

Map 4. Palau and the Western Caroline Islands

tended to raise food for soldiers (though none had yet arrived). This work was interrupted when Yapese were assigned to join Koreans, Okinawans, western Caroline outer islanders, and Japanese supervisors and heavy equipment operators in building the airport in southern Yap. The large food plantation absorbed nearly all able-bodied men of Yap; the airfield work included also men from Yap's outer islands. Even children participated, making these two activities stand out as a vivid memory of the war years.

Yap had been in the backwaters of war during the first years of conflict, but Allied progress and the retreat of the Combined Fleet to Palau in February 1944 turned the western Carolines area into a rapidly and heavily reinforced defensive line.[7] Yap was not strongly fortified until spring of 1944, but then things happened quickly—first the arrival of a construction group, building bunkers, installing guns, and bringing equipment for working on the airport already underway. "They moved fast and they worked fast"—the arrival of the laborers, population movement around Yap to support construction, completion of the airport, and the landing of Japanese planes all in rapid sequence just before the first American air attack on March 31, 1944. After this attack, Japanese civilians on the island—especially women and children—were evacuated, some on the same ships that had just landed troops. Military headquarters was established at Okaw, Weloy, and soldiers set to work digging defensive trenches over parts of Yap.

As on Chuuk, the arrival of troops initiated large-scale confiscation. In Aringel village in Dalipebinaw, soldiers occupied houses, and the women, children, and elderly left in the village (most men having gone to work on airport construction) lived together in a single house. Soldiers took over furnishings with the houses and set up tents where no houses were available. After the evacuations of vulnerable areas following the first air raid, residences and men's houses were used for storing ammunition. The Japanese used house foundations and even stone money to build fortifications and air raid shelters, razed men's houses and meetinghouses down to the stone platforms so they wouldn't draw enemy attention, broke up houses and canoes for firewood, cut down all the large trees, felled palms to eat the hearts and betel nut trees for timber; they used stone money to anchor floating strings of coconuts. Soldiers confiscated Mitag's father's new house, broke it apart, and took everything: "They took the house posts and used them for cooking fires. They took the sennit rope and used it for their houses, and other things."

After the Imperial Army arrived, a second airport was begun in Tamil, and the rest of the island was devoted to production. A good number of soldiers were concentrated in Thabeth, where salt and coconut oil were made. Yap was divided into sections, each under a military commander who took charge of the labor and resources of villages in his area. The assigned work might include theft from a neighboring command's area. Venitu Gurtmag recalls that in one area kitchen workers were required to deliver two baskets of food per day, which they were not allowed to gather from the gardens or taro patches of that village—in other words, they had to steal from other villages, whose military commands were protecting their own supplies. The workers were beaten for not providing the requisite amount of food; they were also beaten if they were caught stealing.

After air raids began, Yapese men returned to their home villages or to relocation areas, working under the military units in place. Ianguchel served as an officer's houseboy, but other men worked in gardens, in fishing parties, making salt, building houses, making coconut oil and tuba, cooking, and constructing land and shore defenses and bomb shelters, under strict discipline, supplying their own food, and without pay. Women worked on military projects, made roof thatch, and also bore the burden of intensified taro garden work, their traditional concern (Hunt et al. 1949). Gardening was particularly galling because it was for the benefit of the soldiers. As La'ew says, "When they planted a garden, they planted it as soldiers' food. When they planted dry taro—[it was] soldiers' food. And when they planted sweet potatoes—soldiers' food."

At surrender, Yap held 6,500 troops, 400 Korean and Taiwanese civilians, about 2,500 Yapese, and more than 400 Chamorros (Useem 1946a:4). More than a hundred Yapese men spent the war away from home, working in Palau, Pohnpei, Kosrae, and Saipan.

Outer Carolines

The later years of war brought military control to several outer islands. Satawan in the Mortlocks and Puluwat (Enderby Island) and Woleai to the west were developed as airbases, with local people displaced and nearby populations pressed for labor and food. The experience of Carolinians as their homes were turned into bases resembled those of Marshallese in the first phase of war construction.

In the western Carolines, the focus of Japanese attention was the atoll of Woleai, population approximately 350, located midway between Palau and Chuuk. In 1942 the Japanese navy built a small airstrip there, and a small garrison arrived the following year. When Michael Faraguy returned home to Woleai from a contract labor journey that had taken him to Palau, Fais, and Ngulu, no Japanese military were on the atoll, but he joined in the work of building bomb shelters. Later, six Japanese soldiers arrived "to watch over the place like policemen"—eventually a total of about thirteen of them—then a boat—"and then we started building houses for the military people.... When they came, they came in as if they had no regard for or questions about the place. They came in and started right away; they did not ask the chiefs, they did not explain to the people what they wanted to do. We were very confused about what was going on, and there were many of them."

As the new airstrip on Falalap islet was cleared, local people moved their houses closer and closer to shore until they were perched at the edge of the islet, and a policeman "told us to think about going to other islets" (airbase construction was in March–April 1944). The police helped with the move, leaving Japanese laborers to finish the airstrip. The Woleai base was reinforced with seven thousand Japanese troops in April 1944. Woleai men continued to commute to work from the other islets, paddling in before sunrise.

When bombing began, their living area was shifted farther and farther away, eventually to the westernmost islets of the lagoon, where they were accompanied by Japanese lookouts and military police. Then the Woleai chiefs "asked if the Japanese could help by taking us on their boats" to Ifaluk, 30 miles away. The Japanese told them it would be better if they took their own canoes, because Americans were likely to attack Japanese ships. After sending a scout to Ifaluk to be sure the same situation didn't obtain there, most Woleai people moved, using both Woleai and Ifaluk canoes (several canoes were lost in a storm, but they showed up a few weeks later). They placed themselves under the protection of the chief of Ifaluk. Kinship links allowed Woleai people to make connections, but Ifaluk was very crowded, food was tight, and some refugees subsequently sailed to Satawal.[8]

The fortification of Lukunor and Satawan in the Mortlocks and Puluwat in the central Caroline Islands also forced relocations. In March 1943, a Japanese naval vessel from Chuuk spent two weeks in Lukunor's lagoon, taking inventory of the island's size, taro swamp, and food-bearing trees, and generating rumors of displacement. (Similar rumors must have disturbed many communities during these months.) Lukunor was spared until January 1944, when 150 Japanese army troops landed, ordering residents of one half of the island to move to the other half, then directing all Lukunor people to move to nearby Piafa islet. "On February 18, 1944, the people of Lukunor left their islet and watched from the shores of Piafa as the army company readied Lukunor for combat" (Borthwick 1977:57–58). The garrison grew to 690 men; they destroyed Lukunor's taro swamp to clear lines of fire and for their gardens, dynamited the lagoon for fish, and required local people to provide food to the garrison as well.

Construction of the Satawan airbase began in 1943 and was not yet complete when the first air attacks came the next March. Residents of Satawan and Ta islets were warned to leave immediately before the arrival of the large Japanese garrison; they fled to the small islets of Kutu and Moch. The evacuation of Satawan is recalled in poignant accounts of people dragging their houses through the water along the reef to other islets. Two women who had just given birth were taken in canoes.[9]

Koko Suda of Oneop describes the complete transformation of the islet where the Satawan base was built—with electricity, an airbase, hospital, offices, stores, restaurants: "The whole island was sparkling [with electric lights], just like one of the Japanese small towns or cities." Taro gardens and food trees were destroyed. Then ships arrived with load after load of soldiers, weapons, and supplies. The Satawan base produced shock effects of relocation, conscription, and intensified agricultural production throughout the southern Mortlocks. Men were called in to work for the garrison: "Old men, young men, even our minister went to work in Satawan" (Andon Quele, Kutu). Those who stayed home supplied food and goods, such as cooking oil, soap, and lamp oil from copra. The garrison commander announced that each neighboring atoll was expected to contribute large quotas of taro. Taro patches became depleted, and people survived on copra and fish.

Eventually, Satawan's troops were distributed among nearby islets to give them access to local food supplies, a pattern seen also in the fortified atolls in the Marshalls. When Japanese were assigned to other islets in any numbers, they felled food trees for garden space. When a group went to the main islet of Moch, the local people moved to the tiny nearby islets where they felt less afraid, though some later returned. About a third of Kutu was occupied by a small detachment of soldiers. Kutu became a rest and recovery area for soldiers near starvation on Satawan.[10]

Puluwat's first experience with Japanese soldiers had been the prewar construction of a lighthouse (with labor by Puluwat and lagoon Chuuk men) after a ship went aground. But when Puluwat became part of the empire's defense, a large contingent of soldiers arrived to install artillery and machine gun emplacements and build an airfield on Alei islet; Ikefai recalls soldiers crowding the beach so you couldn't squeeze through. With both troops and Puluwat people eating from them, gardens spared by construction were soon destroyed. Japanese officials called a meeting of Puluwat people together to order relocation, despite the chief's opposition. Eventually, pressure on resources led the Japanese to order all but a few fishermen to leave. As in the case of Woleai, Puluwat people set off in their own canoes and spent the remainder of the war on Pulusuk (where the chief gave them access to land and taro gardens) and Pulap (where they outnumbered Pulapese). There were few Islanders left on Puluwat late in the war, when it was transformed into a military base (and when, after months of isolation, the Puluwat garrison suffered starvation). In Pulap Atoll, Pulap and Tamatam islets held small numbers of Japanese during the war, with Pulap serving as a rest station for Japanese troops.

Of the eastern Caroline atolls, only Kapingamarangi had a small military installation as a reprovisioning and refueling post for planes headed for the Southwest Pacific. Based on his 1947 visit to Kapingamarangi, Emory notes that the Japanese installations "disturbed the life of the natives very little" (1949:231). But the atoll was visited by navy vessels, and planes and their crews moved in and out, shifting between it and Pohnpei or Rabaul several times a month (Lieber 1968:21). Dione Hatchkarawi remembers six big Japanese airplanes that used to land on Kapingamarangi, load bombs at dawn, then travel on to Rabaul. On two islets the Japanese built barracks, an observation building and tower, a weather station, a pillbox, antiaircraft guns, a wharf, a seaplane base, and storage for bombs, weapons, and oil. As usual, the Japanese paid for cleared trees but not for land, and they confiscated houses for storage, displacing residents to other islets. About eight men served as airplane spotters at night (Lieber 32), and the Japanese hired other people for construction, cooking, cleaning, and laundry. (Wartime Kapingamarangi held few young men; most were laborers on Pohnpei.) Each family had to dig its own bomb shelters, and they enlarged their taro patches to increase production, though the fifty Japanese did not overly strain local resources. There was some exchange of rice and seafood. On the other hand, says Alwihs Amida, "Some of the soldiers were very cruel. If they wanted to get anything from you, they wouldn't ask, they would just come and get it by themselves. They said that nobody could talk to soldiers, that the soldiers could do as they liked." Nehdo Vicky recalls good relations, but also tension over labor: "The Japanese did not treat Kapinga people in a good manner. If they wanted you to work for them, they would treat you as a slave. They would never get permission from your mother and father to work for them."

Micronesians who spent the war on ungarrisoned eastern and western Caroline atolls had little contact with the Japanese military. Signs of war on these islands were travel restrictions, blackout regulations, and a ban on deep-sea fishing (and these were variously obeyed [Witherspoon 1945]). Murphy (1949) describes the outer islands of the eastern Carolines as quite unaffected by the war, except for the cessation of copra and handicraft trade with the centers. Immediately after the war, these Islanders described Japanese behavior as "generally agreeable and 'polite'" (Witherspoon 1945:11–12).[11]

The war's greatest impact on unfortified Caroline atolls and islands was the loss of labor—as men were conscripted to work at population centers—and the cessation of transport. For a small and close island community, the loss of half a hundred men meant a severe constriction in the available workforce and a real emptiness in social life. In the central Carolines, outer island men were brought to work in Chuuk lagoon (and later to Satawan); in the eastern Carolines, to Pohnpei. Most of the adult men of Pis islet in Losap and Nama (southeast of Chuuk lagoon) worked in Chuuk from the beginning of hostilities, at one point leaving only five older men with women and children on Pis (Severance 1976:57). Yap's outer islands had contributed regular work quotas to phosphate mining on Fais, a demand that increased to seven-days-a-week labor as war approached. More than three hundred Ulithians and eighty-eight Ifaluk people spent the war working on Yap; the Japanese boat that came to recruit them brought Ulithi's first news of war. The transportation embargo protected low islanders from the harsh midwar labor conscription, but of course those already on Chuuk or Satawan remained there for the duration. Often living with compatriots, they nonetheless worried about family and suffered from the lack of communication.

Palau

As elsewhere, the September 1943 change in strategy escalated the defensive fortification of Palau. The Combined Fleet withdrew to Palau from Chuuk in February 1944. Later that spring, when the Japanese began to strengthen their inner defense perimeter by moving troops from China, Palau was given priority over the Marianas. Some forty thousand Japanese troops, largely without logistical support, had to be supported locally. But after July 1944, doubting that Palau would be an Allied target and concentrating on the defense of the Philippines, Japan largely ceased supplying Palau. By the time of American invasion, most Islanders had been moved from vulnerable areas to Babelthuap, and Peleliu had been prepared with elaborate defenses. After the September 1944 American assault on Peleliu and Angaur, with the rest of Palau suffering regular bombing raids from American bases in Guam, the Japanese became preoccupied with their own survival. As time passed they lost interest in—and control of—the Palauan population. Famine and increasingly bad relations with the Japanese army modified Palauans' loyalty. In December 1944, a trickle of people began escaping to American lines.[12]

Marianas

The Marianas, which had seemed such a secure part of the empire at the beginning of the war, became a frighteningly vulnerable target with the turn to a defensive stance. The Japanese well understood the need to protect these islands within striking distance of the homeland. After the fall of the Marshalls put the Marianas in the Allies' path, the first major troop influx began in February 1944, and reinforcement continued until a few weeks before the June invasion. Civilian Japanese began to leave in 1943, and evacuations of women, children, the elderly, sugar company dependents, and government officials continued through spring of 1944 despite the danger of attack en route. Thousands of Korean, Okinawan, and Japanese civilians remained on Saipan at the time of American invasion.

The island of greatest military value was Saipan. Earlier in the war it had not been heavily fortified, serving more as a supply depot than a base. But the loss of the Marshalls and neutralization of the eastern and central Carolines put the Marianas on the front line, and the effort began in May 1944 to make Saipan an "impregnable fortress" (General Obata's words, [Peattie 1988 : 282]). "In order to accelerate the construction of fortifications and airfields, the military pressed Chamorro and Carolinian men into labor gangs. Work was hard, the hours long and there was no pay, but to refuse was unthinkable; a severe beating was the minimum consequence of such defiance. Japanese civilians, both young and old, [fared] little better and, shortly after the fall of the Marshalls, the island's schools and factories were ordered closed. Soon teachers, students and workers were devoting their full time to military preparations" (Russell 1984:86).

Two months before the invasion, the Japanese army took over Garapan and most of the coast, evacuating civilians to the interior hills. Chamorros and

Carolinians had lived in town, commuting to work in outlying fields; now they were ordered to move to their farms, and troops were billeted in their houses since construction could not keep up with military housing needs. The evacuation of Garapan came in March 1944, with Micronesians and Japanese civilians ordered to the interior. Garapan was partly dismantled as departing refugees scavenged materials; troops were quartered in remaining buildings. With the evacuation of Garapan, "virtually all civilian work was stopped" (Russell 1984:86). "Schools and the sugar company closed, most agriculture ended, and every available hand turned to constructing such works as trenches, revetments, hundreds of food and ammunition storage shelters, and a new airfield under the direction of the Japanese Island Command" (Sheeks 1945:110).

The period of intense military preparation in the Marianas was brief; the American invasion began June 15.[13]

LABOR

There were no Sundays during that time.

The defensive preparations in response to the Allied Pacific advance posed labor needs of a scale and intensity not seen in the islands before or since. On garrisoned islands, military work became a total institution. Wartime labor consisted of direct military construction, infrastructure for the needs of soldiers and laborers, meeting military quotas of food and supplies from home production, and (perhaps most extensively) large-scale agricultural labor—at first for export, then to feed the vastly increased population of islands cut off from outside supply.

At the height of war, the physical exertion, separation from home and family, harsh discipline, poor living conditions, stress of bombings, and shortages of food and goods combined to make memories of wartime labor among the most vividly recalled and deeply resented of the war years. Says Lupalik Nithan of Kosrae: "What I remember most about the wartime is that we were not free and we were really hard workers, not like today. And it looked like those Israelites under the Pharaohs. Even if we wanted to take a rest, we could not. There were no Sundays during that time."

As military and agricultural activities intensified, Islanders everywhere became part of a single vast labor pool.

Types of Labor

Simple manual labor formed the greatest part of wartime work. Our interviews elicited a long list of tasks Islanders performed. On Kosrae, for example, men farmed, fished, tended domestic animals, hunted wild pigs, made salt, made roof thatch, gathered, transported, and prepared food for the military, cut and towed logs, worked as lookouts, carried weapons, ammunition, and supplies, dug bomb shelters, and built barracks and roads. Women made copra and coconut oil, wove mats and baskets, made thatch roofing for barracks, cooked for workers, caught land crabs, fished, and worked on plantations. In Chuuk, men and women labored in endless sweet potato fields (the harvest made into miso for the troops) and shoveled human manure for fertilizer, which Chuukese thought disgusting; women grated copra for oil and cooked for soldiers. Most tasks were familiar in themselves, but they were performed in very unfamiliar circumstances.[14]

Military construction was manual labor, with only occasional use of machinery. (Some people saw bulldozers and backhoes for the first time when American forces arrived.) The airport in southern Yap was built with only a few trucks and rollers operated by Japanese. It was cleared by hand and leveled with logs by Koreans, Okinawans, and Yapese. The road to Palikir on Pohnpei was built with shovels and crowbars. At the seaplane base on Majuro, Japanese "worked with their bodies and dug holes and they crushed rock with large sledge hammers" (Manutil Lokwot). "The Japanese pulled things up with their hands and block and tackle, and then a hundred people would grab on and pull. They always used their hands" (Elson Ebel, Marshalls). Tadasy Santos helped haul the big guns to the top of Sokehs Rock on Pohnpei: "It was very hard work, pulling and pushing those big guns up that rocky mountain. We pulled up the guns on the side facing east. They told us that the guns were brought from Germany. They used some kind of winch for pulling and we did the pushing. There were about thirty of us. In a week's time we moved the guns upward about 60 meters. We were able to move them about 10 meters a day or so. We worked on this from 5:00 in the morning until dark every day. Rail, shovels, and crowbars were the kinds of tools used."

On Weno, Chuuk, "all able-bodied men were conscripted as a work force" to surface the Iras coastal flat with clay for the first airstrip, build revetments to protect planes, storage bunkers for fuel and bombs, and barracks and warehouses (King and Parker 1984:106). Men from throughout Chuuk were recruited to quarry clay and basalt from the mountains and dump it into the steel carts of a narrow-gauge rail line to be hauled by hand to the runway (King and Carucci 1984:475–476). Chipun Kom, who worked on the Weno airstrip along with Japanese and Korean laborers, recalls that every task was made laborious by the lack of machinery: felling coconut trees and hauling them to the sea by hand (they sang to make the job easier), digging and leveling the ground, layering rocks around the field, and "after that, cement. Day and night, day and night, on and on and on just like that—cement." Once air raids began, they filled bomb craters with rocks from nearby basalt cliffs (and, as attacks continued, with anything else available. Archaeologists examining bomb holes in "Moen #1" airfield found that one was "filled with basalt boulders and chunks, pieces of a wooden boat, and two wrecked wheeled vehicles" [King and Carucci 1984:476]). Besides construction, there was the constant work of unloading and moving supplies. Military labor increased until in some areas night and day shifts kept defensive preparations going full time.

Everyone living in the islands was in danger from frequent air attacks during the Allied advance and neutralization. But some jobs were more exciting—and dangerous—than the tedious and backbreaking agricultural and manual labor. Men served as air raid lookouts, signalmen, office workers, canoe chauffeurs for Japanese leaders, and helpers in plane servicing areas. A dozen Chuukese men worked as lookouts on sea patrols in the lagoon. On Kosrae, Pohnpeians and Japanese dove to recover sunken cargo. Tulenkun Waguk (Kosrae) worked with a bomb demolition squad, defusing or detonating duds. Construction work was much more dangerous under bombings, but such labor could be risky even apart from air raids, where—as on Toloas—dynamite was used in excavation. As Iteko Bisalen relates, the explosion of a munitions ship in Toloas killed many workers:

> After the explosion they went out and collected the dead and brought them ashore to burn them. The Chuukese recognized some of their relatives among those who died, and they found my uncle. . . . The corpses were like fish that you string on a line, because they tied their hands together and pulled them in on a line. Many of the Japanese soldiers who died had arms

missing and so on. My uncle must have been many miles away from that big ship [when it exploded], so that his body was intact.

The Japanese asked the Chuukese to come and see if they could find their relatives and to take their bodies. When they pulled the line of bodies in, they saw my uncle on the line; they recognized him because of his missing finger.

Fishing was one of the most dangerous jobs. Given the food scarcity, the danger of taking the few usable boats or canoes out into lagoons or open ocean, and the availability of explosives, dynamiting became common. Groups of men fished under Japanese direction or were given explosives and told to fish for the troops. Sometimes the fishermen got a portion of the catch or a share was distributed to Islanders working on military projects. On Pohnpei, men from the eastern Caroline atolls (known as expert fishermen) were often assigned to fish. Wherever explosives were used, we heard of fishermen who died, were burned, or lost limbs. Iosep Salvador (Pohnpei) recalls: "We fished with dynamite. And one time I lit a stick of dynamite; it had a very short fuse and I told the other guys to chase down the fish, but they told me to wait. And I told them that I would not hold the fuse. And, you see, I was very lucky. I was holding it up when it blew up and it cut off my arm."

Ines Etnol recalls that the Japanese on Pohnpei fished with hand grenades: "Sometimes, they would give the grenades to their best local friends." Obtaining explosives without official sanction was forbidden, however. Kalifin Kofak, who led a group of fishermen in Chuuk lagoon, says, "I had scars all over— my arms, my chest, and my legs—all over" from using dynamite. It was after Mr. Kofak was taken to a hospital that he learned fishing with dynamite was illegal—the soldiers injured with him asked him to tell his relatives that he had been hurt by a bomb (though air attacks had not yet begun). He refused to lie; the soldiers told him they could be executed for the infraction.

More conservative fishing techniques, such as line fishing on the reef at night or net fishing, held their own risks during wartime. Two Kapingamarangi men fishing on Pohnpei were killed when they took shelter from an American plane in a mangrove channel and touched off a Japanese mine. Women also occasionally ran these risks. On Tol in Chuuk lagoon, Aknes Victor says that women fished while men were away working: "But we went fishing carefully, because there were mines in the sea. We were afraid of the mines, but because of the hunger, we went."

Though all workers shared common dangers of war, policemen and Japanese-educated elites formed a privileged group. William Prens, for example, a six-year veteran of the Pohnpei police force at the start of the war, worked in the police office in Kolonia, helped train prisoners, moved the prison (including the Etscheit family) to Net, and, as he put it, "went around looking for problems to solve." Sachuo Siwi, whose father was chief of Toloas, continued his prewar administrative job, but the work itself changed when aerial attacks began; his new task was to check on Toloas people, note where they were living, and report on who died and how. A few Micronesians held supervisory positions. On Majuro, Manutil Lokwot, who worked as an explosives detonator for fishing, comments, "I was adequately high in rank during the time that I worked with the Japanese." Another privileged group was children of Japanese. Johna Melia (Pohnpei), whose father was Japanese, passed the war on his farm at Wapar, supplying food to the Japanese: "I didn't experience any hardship because the Japanese liked me. They let me have my own farm to take care of my family. I worked for the Japanese and I gave them goods for free." Other relatively privileged jobs were those in civilian hospitals and offices. Ciro Barbosa worked at Pohnpei's hospital (assisting Japanese, driving, translating, doing physical examinations and pharmacy work), but the only special treatment he got was free lunches: "They did not compliment us for all the hard work that we did. They never even thanked us."

Kalifin Kofak held one of the grimmest jobs late in the war, when he worked at the crematorium on Toloas: "This was the time the attacks were going on. The number of dead went up to fifty a day. That was my job. They brought them to my workplace, and I burned the bodies, one by one. My workplace overflowed with dead people's blood and body fluids. But that was my job, until the time I got tired of my work. I ran away."

Organization of Work

Wartime labor arrangements were based first on the preexisting system of public and contract labor, and then on military organization. Recruitment in the Marshalls was through quotas assigned to village magistrates, with service at first for a year, shortened to six months after protests about family separations (Pollock n.d.:41, citing Mason 1946:194). On Pohnpei, municipality secretary Norman William's job was to call out names and work assignments from the census roster; normally people worked only in their own municipality ("This allowed the Japanese to keep track of people"). According to Takio Williams, Pohnpeians wore numbered tags that identified the group of soldiers they worked for—"If you didn't [wear it] the other soldiers would take you." On Yap, military units controlled whole villages. In Gochlaw, for example, the local commander gathered all village inhabitants every morning to assign agricultural tasks.

In Chuuk as well, the Japanese relied first on village-level recruiting. Later, the lagoon islands experienced very tight control through work groups *(putai)* instituted when the army arrived (the army and navy ran separate *putai*). People were assigned to these groups, though some passed through several jobs or sought to avoid assignments. When Takis Taylor got a travel pass to visit relatives on Toloas, he was called in to have his papers checked. When he came in with a friend, the supervisor said, "Okay, so you have papers? Then I'll look for a job for you"—and they were assigned to a work group on Toloas. Groups were led by soldiers and local men appointed by the Japanese commander.

In the early years, moving away from family meant freedom for young men. When John Anjain went to Kwajalein, the young men who worked for the Japanese still felt themselves fairly well off. They would "go out and play around in the evenings," then sleep at 8 or 9 P.M. Each took a turn at a two-hour watch night and day. The several hundred Marshallese workers on Kwajalein lived in one area and worked for several "companies," which messed together and lived in separate buildings.

Such relatively pleasant conditions became increasingly rare. Rationalization of work was familiar to Islanders from school discipline and prewar labor. Nonetheless, the strict control of time during the war made a profound impression. Military work ran Monday through Sunday on Pohnpei and started at 6 A.M. for rice-field laborers living in dormitories. On Kosrae, Austin Albert recalls a 7 A.M. start for agricultural laborers; Anna Brightly recalls working from 8 A.M. to 4 or 5 P.M. and every other Sunday. On at least some Pohnpei plantations, workers traded off fifteen-day shifts. Workers began the day with lineup and roll call, bowing to the emperor and singing a patriotic song. Some ate and slept in workers' messes and barracks (like the separate buildings for men and women near Pohnpei's rice fields); others commuted home to do their own chores before they could rest. Paulina Aisawa recalls her parents living at their Nanpil, Pohnpei, workplace on weekdays, returning on weekends to their children at Enipos. They walked home through the forest, since the guarded roads were forbidden.

In Chuuk lagoon, land and population were reorganized for maximum production of military food needs. On Tol (at least) this was run by Nantaku, which turned the church at Foup into a warehouse and set out gardens of potatoes, corn, eggplant, papayas, and pumpkins. Wangko Wasan recalls two sorts of farms on Udot, Chuuk: military farms and prison farms worked by local people and run by a Japanese "policeman"; he dared to steal only from the latter. After regular American bombing raids began in the spring of 1944, people on some lagoon islands who were not working on construction were restricted to specific locations ("calaboosed," Akeisuk Mokok calls it on Weno, using a Spanish loanword for "jail") and assigned to *buraku* (Japanese "hamlet"), a combination of air-raid district and work region. Here they did agricultural work under combined military and NKK direction.

At first, people were usually fed at their workplaces, but after supply lines were cut, provisioning became a challenge for the authorities. During the first years of the war, workers were either paid a wage and fed by their families, or messed with Japanese workers on imported supplies. As supplies became scarce, Japanese on Pohnpei provided rations such as rice and cloth to workers, but these eventually ceased. Workers in several areas were forced to get their own food. Those who were lucky had family nearby who were not fulltime wage laborers; others had to fish or forage for themselves after work.

Workers were paid throughout the first period of military preparations and in some cases well into the war—often, it seems, as long as it was possible to continue a cash or scrip system. Marshallese laborers on Kwajalein ate with Japanese and were paid 5 yen a month. John Anjain recalls:

We didn't use it because when they went off and came back with cigarettes, and then there were things that they rationed to us, we would just go seek them out and there was no cost.

(Interviewer asks: And so you didn't purchase much?)
    No, we didn't purchase any of these things.

(Interviewer: And what about clothes?)
    Well, clothing, we ourselves found it.

(Interviewer: You did not wear uniforms or that sort of thing?)
    We did not.

People recall wages figured daily, at 50–70 "cents" or "yen," and that prices were equally low (this became irrelevant as goods disappeared from stores). At first, people made extra money from the military presence—cutting firewood, selling produce and handicrafts, "renting" their houses. In the early days after soldiers arrived in Chuuk, they paid Chuukese to do things for them, like climbing coconut trees to get drinking nuts.

Wages continued—though often they were directly deposited into savings accounts rather than handed to workers—even after the major deployment of army troops in some areas, but eventually in most places even a promise of pay went by the board. Anko Billy (Marshalls) recalls that workers on Kosrae were paid for the first two years of military labor, but then there was no money left and pay stopped. (His description suggests that the same cash kept circulating until it dwindled to the point of uselessness.) As a schoolboy on Pohnpei, Swingly Gallen and other students worked but were not paid cash "because it was our help for the country of Japan. They affixed a stamp, how much for each student, but no money was given to us. They said that this money was sent to Japan." In one large labor project, men from Chuuk lagoon and the outer islands flooded the Nambō docks on Toloas for stevedoring work, unloading coal, lumber, food, gas, oil, and military supplies. They stopped stevedoring when shipping ceased and troops arrived (almost simultaneously), and the only remaining work was that organized by soldiers and the Korean military construction workers. While the Nambō stevedoring work had been paid, later work was not. They were told, Sontak Kansou recalls, "that they would write down our names and after the Japanese won the war, they would pay us." As Likiak Benjamin (Kosrae) puts it, "I spent most of my time during the war with no wages. I worked not for wages, but out of fear."

Discipline

Before the war, Micronesian workers had been treated as civilians by civilians, and they remember that era with pleasure. Parang Namono (Chuuk) recalls the change:

> New Japanese replaced those of the previous government. They were our bosses and were very tough on us. They often beat us with metal or anything at hand. At this time, work got harder, just the opposite of our previous jobs. We were told to work hard because it was for the war, and if we didn't they would beat us because it was also for their Japanese leader, Tennō Heika, that all these things or work should be accomplished. We worked days and nights. Sometimes, lunch hour got shorter. We often looked at the clocks and saw that it was past lunch time, but we just kept working because of the Japanese demand for completion of the war works. We were also forced to eat our lunch faster, which made it seem as if we never had a lunch break.

Daily discipline was tight. Roll was called, and those who claimed sickness were checked by a doctor. Okaichy Sapwo (Chuuk) remembers: "If I was sick and couldn't go to work, the Japanese would come to my home and drag me out to go to work. Even if I was sick, I'd still have to go to work. If I didn't go, they'd beat me up." "Headache was not an illness," Oska Seiola (Pohnpei) recalls, "for it was caused by laziness." Actual working conditions varied, however, depending on security and the character of those in charge. At one extreme, workers on the inland road in Pohnpei were closely watched by armed guards. According to Pretrick Ringlen, a Pohnpeian supervisor on the project, the guards accompanied them even when they went to relieve themselves. Elper Penias, who worked on the Sapwalap, Madolehihmw, stretch of the road, adds: "We were divided into three groups; we were about five hundred, Pohnpeians, Mokilese, Kosraeans, Ngatikese. Twenty-four of us were in the open field. . . . We were twenty-four in number, and there were also twenty-four guards. Each one of us had a shovel and a crowbar. We worked with no breaks, only five minutes was allowed for smoking. We sweated all day long." Finas Bossin (Chuuk) recalls the treatment by the Japanese: "They were really noisy. They yelled all the time. They didn't want anyone to be listless, they didn't even like us to walk slowly. If they saw that you were lazy, they'd beat you up. That was why they didn't like anyone to be slow."

The temperament of supervisors was an important variable. Raphael Gisog recalls that work in the sweet potato plantations was more harshly disciplined than the (presumably harder) work on the airport in southern Yap, because of differences in personality of the Japanese in charge. On one plantation in Sokehs (Pohnpei), people speak fondly of the kindness of their supervisor, who allowed time off to those who became ill and organized periodic dances to keep up morale. But the overall experience of wartime labor was of un-relieved exhaustion, fear, and hardship, as related by Dr. Ciro Barbosa: "The Pohnpeians who worked at the airport in Palikir had a very hard time. They worked hard day and night without much rest. They were treated like slaves. The soldiers watching them carried guns. Some of the locals got so tired that they would shit and then cut open their skin and mix their shit with the blood. Then they would call over the soldiers to see the shit. The soldiers would then dismiss them, thinking that they had serious internal infections. The locals had to devise such plans, or work themselves to death."

Working at refueling on Toloas, Chuuk, Ikiuo Silluk recalls: "We were just like animals. There was no time to stop to wipe the sweat away, and we were covered with dirt. All the work before the war was done in a hurry. There was no time for a work break." People recall being beaten for not coming to work, for lateness, for resting, for refusing to obey a casual order, for talking while working; they were hit with sticks or slapped in the face by soldiers. Pohn-peians recall particular cruelty to those working on the Palikir airport, where men were beaten or poked with a sword if they stood up to take a break. Son-tak Kansou (Chuuk) was burned on the arm with a cigarette, hit on the head with a stick, stabbed in the leg with a sword—all three scars still visible—when he refused to climb a coconut palm to get drinking nuts for some sol-diers: "They told me that I wanted Japan to lose the war, and also disobeyed the soldiers."

Another vivid description of working conditions comes from Solomon Lorrin (Mokil), who worked with Japanese civilians to build Lenger airfield on Pohnpei:

This work, I considered it just like killing people. You had no rights. . . .
We started the airfield in Lenger. Pingelapese, Mokilese, and Kiti men were

their slaves at that time. It was a hardship. Our Japanese commander was very cruel. My brother Soulik was the Mokilese leader and Dan was the *nahnmwarki* of Pingelap and led the Pingelap men. Each day, we lined up rocks from the shore to the mountain. We filled the wheelbarrow with rock, but the Japanese commander would jump in the wheelbarrow and we would push. Then one day, the man Sengkin argued with the commander. Sengkin was a Pingelapese. The commander got mad and said, *"Yuhs."* Then they took Sengkin and hung him up. They hung him under the sun; his legs almost reached the ground close to the road so all the people would see. If they punished people, they liked everybody to see. The Japanese really knew how to punish people. [This story continues to describe how the *nahnmwarki* of Pingelap saw that Sengkin was in danger of dying and went with Soulik, who knew some of the Japanese soldiers, to apologize for him. The Japanese told Soulik they would have shot him had they not come to apologize. "My brother told him, 'Don't shoot him, because if you shoot him, you will run out of workers.' "]

Shaming was common in Japanese discipline, familiar from its prewar use, when prisoners' heads were shaved. On Uman, Chuuk, people were beaten, stripped naked, and hung up in public to shame them when they missed work: "That's why most people never missed their days of work," Ikiechy Edwin recalls. When asked what he will never forget about the war, Joseph Jibon had this to say:

I will tell you something that I have told others before. I said, "I want you to watch closely, the Japanese really damaged the Marshallese, beat them, shot them, placed them in jail, set them out where the planes would shoot them [he describes this earlier in the interview as one form of punishment], and treated us as if we were animals." This is the thing that I told my children, that during this period, this is the way they would treat us. If you did something slightly wrong, they beat you; if you did something wrong, they would cut off your head. This is the thing that I tell them stories about, and as for me, these were the sufferings that I encountered with the Japanese. These are the things they did in the midst of war. And as for me, I was always afraid, because if I erred, they might take me to Imiej and cut off my head and throw it away.

People feared the soldiers they worked for, and the fear took root and fed on rumors. In one story from Chuuk, when two men did not come to work on Udot and the Japanese were told they were sick, the Japanese responded, "'Oh, we're going to give them medicine.' So they gave them the medicine, and they died."

In response to the danger, Islanders sought all forms of protection. In Chuuk and the central Carolines, people used magical safeguards. Anang Samwel (Chuuk) recalls using magic to shield himself from punishment when he left work without permission:

> When I worked on Parem, they planned to beat the group I belonged to. The reason was that we had come in the morning and then returned to Oaan. So when they found out, they sent a message to me. I came to Parem and was dragged to the office and they started to investigate me. There I knew that magic worked, because they [elders] had given me *eis* [a fruit used for magic] and taught me how to use it. I bit it and blew it to the door where they were stepping out. They were ready to beat me. But when the boss came out, he only told me to take my group back, and that we should work harder. . . . I was impressed and believed in it.

Other old men specialized in chants to prevent Japanese guards from beating those who traveled without the proper papers and protective magic for relatives away from home.

While memories of war work throughout Micronesia are predominantly those of hardship and suffering, it must be repeated that no experience is uniform—not even that of suffering. The 179 Pohnpeians taken to Kosrae have vivid memories of their hard work there—but are also proud of their ability to exceed Japanese expectations. Okin Sarapio says, "The Kiti people were the best workers for the Japanese because they worked very hard and fast," and he cites the fact that only Kiti men were taken to Kosrae to build the Japanese airport.[15] Sekismwindo Sarapio, one of the Pohnpeian men who built the Kosrae airfield, describes its construction: "We cleared and dug the ground; that place was muddy, and half of the airfield was in a swampy spot. We carried earth to the swamp. That was work for youth; I don't think that people of today could do that work. Imagine standing under the sun—because the airfield was big. We constructed two miles [of it]. We cut down mangrove trees from where we worked. . . . We used a small saw and ax to clear with. . . . They gave us a work contract for a week, yet we finished the work within a day. Our guard told the Japanese about our work."

Some Micronesians labored in fortunate conditions with good bosses and enjoyed the period of war work. John Ezekiel cleaned and helped service planes at Imiej airstrip in the Marshall Islands. Asked what life was like with the Japanese soldiers, Mr. Ezekiel replied, "Well, it was good. The things that the soldiers did were good. We lived just like the soldiers." Benjamin Lopez (Pohnpei) says he doesn't remember hardship, "because I worked for the soldiers and I was being fed, given smokes, and everything. I lived okay in the war. While I was working for the Japanese, there wasn't any time I was beaten by them up until the day they left." On Chuuk, Toli Jessy recalls that he didn't have to do distasteful work such as shoveling human manure for fertilizer: "The place where I used to work wasn't like that. We never touched manure. We could also eat with the Japanese, which was rare. We could eat as much as we could. We ate the same kind of food that the Japanese ate. The place where I worked was very nice. I worked there until it was bombed by the Americans."

Women's Work

Gender roles were variably retained (as in Yap) or directly contravened (as in Pohnpei) by military labor. Regardless of the specific work assignments, Micronesian women found their lives changed by wartime labor demands. Women had done wage work in urban centers and sold farm produce and handicrafts. But they had not done contract labor and had seldom been part of public works groups outside their local community. In addition to stresses of relocation, bombing, maintaining family food production, and caring for children, the ill, and the elderly, conscription into work groups operating under strict discipline was an unforgettable part of women's war experience. Women who did not work for the military, who lived on outer islands, or who were exempted by pregnancy, family obligations, or elite status nonetheless found their world changed: with most men absent, women faced novel responsibilities and opportunities.

In central Micronesia, as defensive preparations escalated, women labored at military construction, factory production, and, most of all, agriculture.

Women on Chuuk and Pohnpei (at least) worked directly on military preparations. In Chuuk, they joined men in agriculture and military labor (people recall the women doing the lighter work, the men hauling heavy loads and doing the hardest tasks). Women broke up small rocks and hauled dirt for construction, carried supplies and ammunition up mountains, built docks, seawalls, bunkers, gun emplacements, and buildings. Marwin and Resen (Chuuk) recalled a job carrying supplies when asked whether such labor caused hardship: "Yes. That's when Mieko started to cry, because she couldn't carry the box of ammunition. . . . There were women who couldn't carry them, then they started to cry because they beat them."

Marusima Bier (Chuuk) did not work while pregnant, but otherwise "I would work and I suffered from working every day from sunup to sundown" sorting ammunition and supplies for soldiers: "We would go to work in the morning without eating. We would come home in the evening exhausted." On Pohnpei—where they were traditionally not expected to do strenuous labor—Andohn Semes remembers women carrying two-by-fours up Mount Kupwuriso; Mary Jane Jemes' hands were permanently injured when she carried four large sheets of plywood from Temwen to Ohwa for a cave the men were digging.

In Yap, where women were the primary farmers, the Japanese military retained the division of labor, pressuring them to produce large amounts of taro. But both men and women did field work on Pohnpei and Kosrae, contravening the familiar pattern there of men working in gardens and women at home. Pohnpei women worked two-week shifts on farms—some of this work later became permanent and full time—for sugarcane, rice, tobacco, and tapioca; Meruse William recalls, "I used to carry a sack full of tapioca from the field to the factory. They didn't let you rest." Some worked with their husbands, others in separate assignments. Tulpe Jackson describes agricultural work on Kosrae: "At the plantation there were no barracks or houses to stay overnight, so the women had to come all the way back to their homes. The women had a very hard time then. When the women went farming at the plantation, their lunch was a piece of breadfruit or banana or slices of coconut." After work, they went fishing for their families.

In the tapioca fields in Palikir, Pohnpei, a woman supervisor composed a song that women sang as they huddled in their tiny bunkers, too small for them to sit erect:

Our dwelling makes us really lonely.
It is worse than being in prison,
Because we have assumed the appearance of frogs,
Crawling around and looking straight ahead.

Especially for women unaccustomed to strenuous physical labor, health consequences were grave. Pohnpeian women who worked on the strictest plantations remember periods of hemorrhaging, and blame subsequent infertility on wartime hardships. Pohnpeians explained the scarcity of young children in 1947 by saying that many miscarriages were caused by the women's work in unhealthy rope-making factories (Murrill 1950:188–189).

Throughout the islands, women cooked, sewed, and laundered for Japanese soldiers. As the first Marshalls airbases were being built, women worked as domestics for Japanese troops. In Jaluij, they did hospital work and housecleaning and laundry for high-status Japanese. Humiko Mori describes joining other women in doing soldiers' laundry at her home on Fefan, Chuuk. Her mother would mend clothes for Japanese officers (this was in the context of personal friendships, rather than for wages). They also worked at the hospital and learned to make sandals from hibiscus. Mortlockese women cleaned fish and wove baskets for the Satawan garrison. Women's weaving skills were maximized on Kosrae, where they made mats and baskets (many for packaging food sent to the Marshalls), sleeping mats for troops, thatch roofing, and woven curtains for military barracks and civilian laborers' housing.

Japanese officials excused pregnant and postpartum women from work in all but the most harshly regimented circumstances. Women from Pohnpei, Kosrae, and Chuuk recall being free of obligatory labor due to pregnancy or to care for small children. Rosete Hebel (Pohnpei) had a break from work because she was caring for children and her husband's elderly parents. (It is not clear whether these women were officially excused because of domestic responsibilities, or if they successfully evaded work.) Women may have been exempt on the basis of their husbands' rank, as were, for example, some wives of Micronesian policemen.

When women did not work at military or agricultural projects, they faced familiar domestic labor exacerbated by hard times. For example, Tulpe Jackson cooked for workers on Kosrae and later wove baskets and mats for sale to soldiers, but when others left for plantation work, she stayed home with her young children: "What I did at home was just fish and look for food for my children." Since nearly all able-bodied men and many women were working at military sites, those doing domestic work struggled with a double burden. During base construction in the Marshalls, women in some areas took on a "second shift" to feed the men of their family who worked for the Japanese. On Kosrae and Pohnpei, a separate domestic economy remained operative despite the demands of war work. Kosraean women, children, and the elderly farmed, fished, made salt, built canoes and houses, cared for domestic animals, and gathered food for the soldiers, while middle-aged men worked directly for the military. In the Wene area of Kiti on Pohnpei, only children, old men, and some women remained at home. Masako Luhk Karen (Pohnpei) recalls, "At that time women worked like men. They climbed breadfruit trees, dug yams, buried the dead. There were very few men who were available to help with work then." Andonio Raidong recalls that in Net, Pohnpeian women took on the unfamiliar role of farmers, planting tapioca, potatoes, and other crops to ensure survival; Lukunor women likewise took on the usual men's task of taro gardening (Tolerton and Rauch 1949:153). On Satawan Atoll, while all the able-bodied men of Kutu islet worked at the base on Satawan islet, women, children, and the elderly struggled to provide food for themselves and a quota of supplies for the Japanese military as well.

For women at home, or in sex-segregated working conditions, the lack of men gave a peculiar flavor to daily life. Yapese remember villages bereft of mature and young men—some gone for long periods of labor service, others leaving in the morning and returning at night; in either case, the village was a place of women, children, and elderly men. In Kiti, where nearly two hundred men had been recruited for work on Kosrae, Lihna Lawrence recalls, "There were no men during the war in Kiti. One man could have three women. The ones available were no good. During the war the Pohnpeian women from Kiti stayed together in Palikir," where men occasionally came for visits by canoe.

Working Children

Because students already formed an organized group, and there was a tradition in Japanese schools of community work, Micronesian schoolchildren in many places found themselves at serious labor. (Recall Chuukese Catholic girls school classes were marched off to work on the first day of war, though boys were more often recruited.) Islander and Japanese schoolchildren participated in patriotic displays before and at the beginning of the war. When attacks reached the islands, elementary students were simply sent home when the bombs started to fall. Students from outer islands were in many cases stranded once war began, and were housed with local families or moved to safer locations. But the limitless need for labor also drew students and other children into service for the war effort. Students at the carpentry school on Palau worked on military buildings (Shuster 1982a:173). Kosrae mission school students helped in airport construction. Children cut brush for the southern airport on Yap, then when this lighter work was done, worked in village gardens planting eggplant, potatoes, corn, and tapioca. Chuukese schoolchildren, supervised by their teachers, did road work, picked bugs off potato plants at military farms, and helped with military construction on Toloas. Marusima Bier recalls Nauruan children working the gardens on Tol for Nantaku. Paulina Aisawa was in fifth grade when Kolonia was destroyed and Pohnpeians fled inland; there, she recalls students were "picked" by soldiers to work in rice and tobacco plantations. Though she says, "We lived like slaves, working without attending school," she also recalls being taught her lessons by a policeman there.

For a few young people, the Japanese practice of training selected Micronesians continued even in wartime. On Yap, a group of about thirty young men were chosen for service at Japanese headquarters. Ralph Gisog, for example, worked as a houseboy for the commander. These selected youth were called "*seito*" (students), but they worked, rather than attending school, living in a house with their own cook. In Chuuk, Wangko Wasan held a part-time job in the navy's communal bath on Toloas and continued to attend half-day classes—his teacher recommended him and five others to a friend who was a lieutenant. Besides the chance to interact with Japanese military, bath attendants had the pleasant problem of what to do with the personal belongings and money left behind without identification in the stampede to catch the 3 P.M. military shuttles. Mr. Wasan had wanted to attend high school in Palau, but the danger of traveling at the time led to this job instead. (He later worked as a policeman for the army on Udot, showing how the educated elite retained privileged positions throughout the war.) Another privileged young man, Naboyuki Suzuki, whose father was Japanese, showed entrepreneurial precocity. He recalls that he and some fifteen friends, all about ten years old, fished with dynamite for the Japanese hospital on Wonei in Chuuk. They did this as volunteers, since all they received for their donation was a meal. Later he exchanged extra fish with Okinawan and Japanese neighbors for farm produce.

Alter Bedly describes his feelings as a schoolboy at the mission school of Ohwa, Pohnpei, among those ordered to work (most students were eighteen to twenty-two years old—"Except for me, I was little"). He joined a large group of men from Pohnpei, Pingelap, Sapwuahfik (Ngatik), and Kapingamarangi to build a road in Net: "At 4 A.M. we went to work. . . . I cried as I went. The soldiers followed us, poking their swords into our backs. We had no life. We were unhappy. We were afraid of the planes, the sound of the guns."

TRAINING FOR WAR

During a bombing, you should know how to run and cover your ears.

Whatever their age or status, all Micronesians were subject to the dangers of military attack. Although Micronesians frequently say they were not warned of the reality of war, the Japanese did take steps to prepare the civilian population for air raids and invasion. They ordered civilians to relocate from areas of prime military targets and to build shelters, and they organized civil defense training.

Much of the training was done through Young Men's Associations (*seinendan*). Chuukese recall young people learning to carry messages and put out fires, and brown-uniformed *seinendan* on Uman practiced rescuing the wounded. Sachuo Siwi, a government worker on Toloas, described formal drills where Micronesian youth marched with sticks (cf. Cockrum 1970: 109–110). As war approached, training intensified: air-raid drills with water and sand set out to douse fires, invasion drills, "and even practicing taking wounded people to the hospital" (Wendolin Gomez, a Pohnpei hospital employee). Kosraeans went through air-raid, first-aid, and poison gas training every Sunday. And, Tolenna Kilafwasru recalls, "We even learned some war songs." Once Allied attacks began, *seinendan* took on new jobs, with those in the Marshalls acting as lookouts and post-attack cleanup crews. On Pohnpei, each municipality had an assigned gathering spot in case of American invasion; Yasio Behris recalls practicing that drill twice, having to walk through the forest since the road was off limits. People recall lessons on how to act in a poison gas attack (run downwind to avoid breathing the poison) and how to use lamps with colored cloth to signal plane sightings. Schoolchildren learned "how to hide from planes," to jump into ditches, and run from bombs. At a school in Chuuk, teachers explained the soldiers' drills. As Kariti Luter recalls, "They told us to watch carefully what they were doing: When the bombs fell, we were to stick our fingers in our ears, to prevent the noise from destroying our ears. 'During a bombing, you should know how to run and cover your ears.' That was really our lesson, what we learned in the classroom."

Alter Bedly was in the Ohwa mission school, where "some Pohnpeians and workers showed us how to fight with sticks to prepare for the arrival of the Americans. When they came, we could help Japan." Islanders were, in retrospect, keenly aware of the absurdity of the make-do preparations in light of the sustained bombing that was about to engulf them. Lusiana Sackryas (Pingelap/Pohnpei) says: "The Japanese soldiers told us to carry our local-style broom with us, so if the American planes dropped bombs, we would use our brooms to protect ourselves and hit the American planes. There was one Japanese soldier who really liked the Pingelapese. He told them not to listen to what they said, because they were lying [foolishly tricking]. He told us to dig a cave for shelter."

Micronesians were told to build bomb shelters and obey air-raid sirens, but the timing and effectiveness of warnings varied. Saito Rewein recalls being taught to run to shelters, but also to hurry when doing chores, such as getting firewood—"that means we would always run to get what we wanted or always run to do whatever we're supposed to do. And this is how we Chuukese realized that there would be a war." Despite the drills, Milton Timothy recalls that the warning came too late for Kosraeans—people ran outside to wave at the first American planes until they realized their mistake. On Kosrae and Chuuk, preparations were too little and too late; shelters were unfinished at the time the bombs fell. It was only because Matsuko Soram's father was a Japanese-employed policeman on Chuuk who overheard Japanese discussing the war that he built a bomb shelter, but it was forbidden and dangerous to talk openly about the possibility of attack. Robert Gallen describes Japanese military preparations on Pohnpei—new wartime laws, building defensive shelters—then adds, "I myself did nothing to prepare for the war. I was just waiting to die."

WARNINGS AND PROPHECIES

The battle just stood itself up.

People's recollections of how much warning they had about impending attack and invasion vary. There are those who profess ignorance until the moment the bombs fell, and those who say they were worried by increasing labor demands and the arrival of soldiers but that secrecy prevented them from putting a name to their worry. Lotis Seneres (Pohnpei) says, "I always knew the war was coming, I just didn't know what it would be like." People's awareness depended in large part on their access to news. Urban centers such as Kolonia on Pohnpei heard Japanese radio broadcasts, and increasingly rare ships brought newspapers and rumors. This news was communicated primarily to the Japanese living in town but was also passed on to Islanders who worked there or who had Japanese friends. Yet even Ciro Barbosa, with a relatively privileged job in Pohnpei's hospital, found it hard to follow the war's progress, though he says he suspected there was fighting elsewhere because of the bombing of Pohnpei. Ines Etnol (Pohnpei) spent her time at home caring for her children and knew practically nothing about Japanese activity; "It was when the first bombs were dropped on Kolonia that we found out about the war."

Lusios Jak, who spent a year leveling ground for barracks and digging a gun emplacement at Nanpohnmal, Pohnpei, says, "They told us about the war coming, but it was secret, just like when the war was over." Pohnpeians working on military construction "were sworn to secrecy," with guns carried up at night. "The Japanese tried to keep it [the war] a secret, but we began to suspect it" (Pensile Lawrence). Many Islanders with Japanese friends or relatives heard enough war news to suspect that their homes were in the path of Allied attack and invasion.

Even if one had news of the encircling war, as military rule settled over the islands, how could one prepare for an unknowable future? Asked how she felt when soldiers arrived on Udot, Chuuk, Nusi Niesik replies, "At that time we didn't feel anything. We just knew that maybe the war was going to start. But we didn't feel scared, because we didn't foresee how much worse it was going to be." Tarup Ounuwa (Chuuk) answers a similar question: "Before, when we had not yet heard about that word 'war,' we weren't familiar with it; we were thinking that there might be no problem with it." As Pensile Lawrence says,

"We didn't know anything. Should we be scared? We didn't know what was coming until after February 12" (the first air attack on Pohnpei). Jomle Malolo (Marshalls) was asked when he first knew there would be war: "Well, let us see, this thing was not really clear to us. I don't know about those Marshallese who knew more about it. But among people like me, well, we did not know when there was to be a battle and if there would in fact be one. But we went off and turned around and were amazed. The battle just stood itself up."

Some drew their own conclusions. A student at Ohwa mission school, Alter Bedly noted martial training at the school, saw a Japanese warship arrive at Pohnpei, and concluded that "it was easy to see war was coming." Mikel Marquez recalls when construction of the Pohnpei airstrip and emplacement of big guns got underway: "Watching and seeing all these preparations made us youngsters feel afraid. When we heard the elders talking about bad consequences of what might happen, we became more afraid. There was nothing we could do, but we braced ourselves for what might happen."

Pirisika Nukunukar recalls that the early signs of war on Toloas, Chuuk, were the blackout regulations and Japanese in uniform holding regular exercises on an open field: "We used to call them *niteyikepar* because they only wore short pants, and their shirts were red and black—that's why we called them *niteyikepar,* because they looked like the bird *niteyikepar* ["ruby-throated honey-eater" (Goodenough and Sugita 1980); or scarlet honey-eater]." She also recalls seeing soldiers having their hair shaved close; when she asked them why, they said it was because they were going to fight the Americans.

Soldiers in the Marshalls also spoke about possible invasion, according to Leban Jorju: "At that time things changed and there was a certain type of atmosphere, and that is when they began speaking about the war. The Japanese said, it would be just a little while and then the battle will begin. . . . I used to hear from the Japanese who said that very soon the Americans would come and boom, boom, boom, boom, everyone would die."

Bwirre Lejmen worked at the government boat pool on Jabwor when his civilian boss, a carpenter, told him to go home because war would start within the year. But his request to leave was denied, and when he told his boss he feared the coming war, "He said that he would take good care of me, just as if I were his own son." Mr. Lejmen's father came from Ebon to take him home, but his boss "said they would watch over me just the same as he would watch over me, and so I stayed put. If I were to go back to Ebon, it would be the same as if I were on Jabwor: I would die, and if I went back to Ebon, I would still die."

Micronesians' knowledge of the war was a function not only of their ties to Japanese, but also of island geography. The Japanese themselves, and with them the preponderance of wartime activity and news, clustered in administrative centers, where few Islanders were permitted to live. Generally speaking, the farther away one was from these centers the less one knew about the war and the more the first attacks came as a surprise. Once shipping stopped, outer islanders were at the greatest disadvantage for information. Andohn Jemes says only a rare fishing boat came to Mokil; it was on one of these trips that they learned war was imminent. Ruben Rudolph recalls, "The people of Nukuoro did not know that there was a war coming. Then, my father found a newspaper that drifted on the sea close to our beach. In the newspaper it said that the war had started on Pohnpei." Nama people saw little evidence of war except for debris floating by—until the bombs hit their island. The first Puluwat people to realize war had arrived were those sent to do contract labor on Palau, where they saw ships damaged by Americans. Similarly, many high islanders living in rural areas did not know of impending war. Meruse William of Pohnpei notes, "There was no radio at that time; it's not like today, when you can hear news of the world everyday. Before, it was just like I was living in a jug."

Late in 1943, those who learned that the Allies had begun a Pacific offensive got a head start on worrying. Lele Ram (Marshalls) heard about American victories in Kiribati, and "the Japanese said the Americans were just killing people, it did not matter if they were Japanese or Kiribati, they were killing everyone." On Kosrae, Austin Albert (who worked as a lookout), learned of the invasion of the Marshalls from the military communication station. Likiak Benjamin (Kosrae) recalls hearing about Tarawa, Pohnpei, Kwajalein, Palau, Saipan, "and all the islands. We knew about these, because the Japanese told us"—and American planes dropped informative leaflets in Japanese. Nathan Tartios said sympathetic Japanese told Marshallese about American landings in the Southwest Pacific, Kiribati, and Kwajalein, "but they said, 'Do not say anything, for if you say something, they will slit your throat.'"

Yet even those who knew that the American advance was bringing war closer were unprepared for the implications of being at the front. Chuukese working for government and businesses on Toloas were told to dig shelters, but were not told the what or when of the attack, so many were caught far from home and unprepared by the first raids. Schoolchildren knew men had been digging ditches, but didn't know until the first attack (when their teachers told them where to run) what they were for.

We cannot discuss war preparations without adding a category that many Islanders identified as a source of information and reassurance about the dramatic changes in their lives: prophecy and communication with spirits. Individuals throughout the Marshalls and Carolines (at least) experienced visions, performed divinations, or otherwise prophesied the hard times ahead. Members of Palau's Modekngei religious movement predicted future events in the war from its beginning, including U.S. involvement, the first bombing of Palau, and the end of war in August 1945 (Vidich 1980:244). An Ifaluk song is said to have foretold American victory (Burrows and Spiro 1957:204–205, 221–222). In the Mortlocks, Moch and Kutu people were warned by spirits that Japanese would arrive, to prepare for shortages, loss of their land, and interference with their lives. Moch people also relied on "our spirit" to keep abreast of the hardships of Moch men working at the Japanese base on Satawan.

Marshallese tell many prophecy stories, citing men and women from Wotje, Namorik, Majuro, Ronglap, and Ebon who predicted the arrival of Japanese, the battles, and American victory. Henry Moses describes prophecies of a woman in Majuro who foretold the future in trances. A woman on Pingelap in Jaluij predicted the evacuation of that islet, even identifying the spot where they would board the LCIs, some three weeks in advance—"we held her to be crazy, because she walked around and said, 'Get all the people ready to go'" (Joseph Jibon). Tom, a young man from Majuro, became a seer after his parents' death, and composed a song:

> They are going to come again and set afire all of the Marshalls,
> And then when the battle arrived, the battle arrived,
> The young men would be filled with apprehension,
> And the young women would be filled with apprehension,
> Because so many bombs would fall.

When invasion came, people said, "It is clear that these were predictions." Those who believed Tom's prophesies "listened to him and they sang songs to one another" (Thaddeus Sampson).

Christianity also provided glimpses of the future. Iteko Bisalen, now a Protestant missionary, recalls that it was the minister on her home island of Tol, Chuuk, who told people "to pray hard, because if the Japanese soldiers came they would control everything." Billy Anko's teacher at Kosrae mission school said Americans would return, and Chipun Kom met a priest in Chuuk in 1943 "who told me to keep to prayer because within three years, we would be free."

In retrospect, supernatural warnings seem to have been considered more valid than any administrative actions. Few people now recall official efforts by the Japanese to prepare Islanders for the coming dangers. Sachuo Siwi of Chuuk, whose father was chief of Toloas, said that the prewar civilian governor did warn people of hard times ahead once at a formal assembly of the chiefs of Chuuk held before he left: "They had the meeting and in that meeting, he told the chiefs to be ready because the war was about to begin in these islands. . . . My father was a chief and none of those chiefs or even the people knew what war is like. Would it be like the excitement of a track and field meet or a baseball game or what? That's right, the chiefs went home and told their people to get ready for war, but the people didn't know what war was like. I'll speak for myself, because I didn't know what war was like. I had only seen it in movies, but it was exciting in a movie. I didn't know and never knew that it would be miserable."

One day on Weno, Chuuk, a Japanese friend of Biloris Samor's husband came to visit from the island's communication center.

He called my husband and asked him how he was, how work was, and my husband told him that everything at work was fine and that his family was fine. The man told my husband that the war was coming. He said he couldn't tell my husband the exact time or day but that my husband should bear in mind that the war was about to begin. That was when I learned that the war was coming. The Japanese soldier told my husband to tell us to be prepared for the war. He told my husband to tell his family to sleep lightly that night so that we could easily be awakened when the attack came. Soon enough, the war began. The soldier hadn't lied to my husband, because not long after he left, we heard the sound of a plane in the sky.

Chapter 5

THE SECOND ROAD TO TOKYO

THE WAVE of the Allied front in Micronesia crested on the reefs of Kiribati (the Gilbert Islands) almost two years after Pearl Harbor and six years after Japan began fighting in China. The first Allied offensive of the Central Pacific campaign came in November 1943, with the recapture of Kiribati paving the way for invasion of the Marshalls in early 1944.

The Kiribati operation held lessons in island warfare for both Japanese and American forces. Tarawa's Japanese commander gave orders "to defend to the last man all vital areas and destroy the enemy at the water's edge" (Morison 1951:148–149). This became the standard defense throughout the islands as the Allied amphibious attack inaugurated here was repeated on other shores. By December 8, 1943, the Allies had taken all Japanese bases in Kiribati. Fortunately, most Islanders had been evacuated from the invaded islands, but damage to their homelands was severe. On Betio, an islet 3 miles long by 1/4 mile wide, bombardment and invasion further ravaged land and reefs already ruined by Japanese military construction. After the Tarawa battle, there were more corpses and war debris than crops and trees on the tiny atoll, and the lagoon and ocean were contaminated with wreckage and unexploded bombs.

During the invasion, Kiribati people assisted U.S. Marines by carrying equipment, supplying intelligence, providing canoes, and helping with first-aid and burials when Marines fought a small group of Japanese on Buariki. A day after the Japanese surrender, more than a hundred Islanders were hired to help clear dead bodies and debris on the island, and the first Gilbert and Ellice

Islands Labour Corps was established in December 1943 to aid with construction of American bases and local reconstruction. In September 1944, some four hundred corps members were sent to the Solomons for similar work (Mamara and Kaiuea 1979:143–144).

Life in Kiribati did not return to normal after Allied victory, though the British set up colonial headquarters in Tarawa by the end of 1943. American airbases were built at Tarawa, Abemama, and Makin to serve the next phase of the counteroffensive.[1] Kiribati people were the first Micronesians the American military had dealt with, apart from Guamanians.

U.S. Marines were charmed by the hospitable Kiribati people. "It was a pretty picture: the lean, unshaven Marines in their steel helmets and green coveralls trudging under coconut palms and pandanus trees with laughing, half-naked boys and girls springily keeping pace. . . . Every night, Marines and natives bivouacked at discreet distances apart and amused each other with song" (Morison 1951:177). Relations were so good—including handicraft trade and impressive amounts of American goods—that some Kiribati people petitioned for American sovereignty (Mamara and Kaiuea 1979:144–146). Military histories and memoirs of the Kiribati campaign present a stereotypical "friendly natives" image—a representation that tells us little about the people themselves, but a good deal about American ideas of Pacific Islanders at the time—ideas with significant impact on the course of life in American Micronesia after the war.[2]

THE WAR ARRIVES IN THE MANDATE: INVASION OF THE MARSHALL ISLANDS

From dawn to dusk they shot at this islet.

The Marshalls campaign was the first attack on territory held by the Japanese before the war. Early plans had called for simultaneous invasion of Kwajalein, Wotje, and Maloelap. Heeding the lessons of Tarawa, the Allies decided instead to seize strategically advantageous atolls—first Kwajalein and unfortified Majuro, then Enewetak. The other Marshall Islands bases—Maloelap, Wotje, Mili, and Jaluij—would be bypassed, neutralized by continual bombing, and isolated from resupply.

Invasion: Majuro, Kwajalein, Enewetak

Allied reconnaissance identified Kwajalein Atoll as the primary Japanese air-base in the Marshalls, with two airstrips, a lagoon anchorage, a torpedo station, a supply depot, Fourth Fleet and 6th Submarine Fleet headquarters, and a bomber strip—which the invaders could turn to their own use—under construction. Majuro was targeted for its superb lagoon anchorage, and Enewetak, a Japanese distribution center, would be captured to support American air raids on the bypassed bases.[3]

Air attacks during and after the Kiribati operation in November 1943 had alerted Japanese and Marshallese to the threat of invasion, as Allies sought to reduce Japanese air power and protect the new American bases. Kwajalein and Wotje were hit by a fast carrier strike in early December. By January 1944, with "Operation Flintlock" (the attack on Kwajalein and Majuro) planned for the end of the month, air raids had nearly destroyed bases at Mili, Maloelap, and Jaluij; attention then turned to Kwajalein, Wotje, and Enewetak.

The Marshalls invasion began with dawn air strikes on January 29 and continued the next day, followed by surface bombardment. On January 31, U.S. forces launched amphibious attacks on Majuro and Kwajalein. The reconnaissance party landing on Majuro the night before had found no Japanese troops on the island, but could not inform the task force until twenty minutes into the morning bombardment. "As the ships sailed toward the northeast corner of the atoll where the landings were to be made, some 600 natives sat under the coconut palms calmly watching this unnecessary display of naval might." The Americans walked ashore, took the few Japanese into custody, and found the local chief. "They had no language problem because one of the first natives to greet them was Michael Madison who spoke English fluently" thanks to a sojourn in San Francisco (Richard 1957a:330).

Although safe from violence, Marshallese on Majuro had an unforgettable glimpse of U.S. military power. Manutil Lokwat recalls the scene:

> When that landing first began, the [American] soldiers began landing at Delap. . . . The planes were flying overhead like this all day and on until nightfall. Perhaps they were watching the location where the guys [soldiers] were landing during sunrise. Afterwards, perhaps they saw that the place

they planned to land was okay. No, they did not shoot or anything. No one died.

They came to see me at my house, where we were living, the same house where the two of us are living now, and we walked east to the house, with Lainlañ [the chief]. . . .

They did not ask any important questions of the chief, but asked him if it would be possible for the boys [soldiers] to land for a bit in the morning and relax. This was the word: Could the boys land for a bit in the morning and rest?

Then, when the boats docked and they landed and came closer you could not see the earth, it was obscured. Thousands, thousands, thousands of ships. Battleships, and planes as well. The ships did not anchor but were strung together and floated side by side. And these [ships] were only those inside the lagoon. But those on the ocean side . . . we have no idea how many ships there were on the ocean side. There were many planes as well.

On Kwajalein, Americans found the battle they anticipated. Watching Japanese prepare, listening to their confident boasts, Micronesians on Kwajalein expected them to be the victors. Leban Jorju recalls: "They said, 'We are going to win. Tat-ta-ta-ta-tat, everyone will be killed by machine guns.' As for me, I was thinking that they would win, such was their readiness. And then the tools of those friends [the Americans], they were so powerful, and then, they landed on Kwajalein — and then there were no people. All of them died." Leban Jorju gives an account of the Kwajalein invasion:

It was just dawn. First they saw two planes up very high. The Japanese told us that these were Japanese planes, but then they looked closer and said, well there, way off there they saw two planes, and they said those were the American planes and all of us ran to the shelters. And those planes disappeared and on and on things went, and then one day, at first light, some planes flew toward us, the planes that were short and black. They kept coming toward us and set that place on fire. The admiral's house was there, and he stayed inside all through the night. At first light, the planes flew toward us and they dropped bombs and hit the admiral's headquarters setting it on fire, and some of that area, and a battleship nearby, filled with Japanese men.

The next morning, and three or four days later, the American fleet came by Kwajalein. They were everywhere, in the air as well as on the sea. You could not see the end of the fleet. You could walk on ships from here to Laura [islet], for there were that many American warships. They came ashore and when they landed, as for the tanks. . . . They came onto the sand and fired and burned the islet and you could not see the lagoon side or the ocean side. There were no people on the ocean side or the lagoon side. They ran off. And then, in the morning—no, it was still during the night—I went to see my [Japanese] friend; he also was running away. And then, the Japanese planes were not able to fly—the airport was totally damaged by the American bombs.

Morison (1951:278) called Kwajalein one of the most complicated amphibious campaigns in history: landings on thirty islets, fights on ten, lengthy battles on four. Though many Japanese troops had recently been shifted to Mili and a preinvasion bombardment left the atoll devastated and the people dazed, Americans were able to move quickly only across Roi islet, where only a small portion of the Japanese were combat troops. They had a harder fight with the trained soldiers on Namur and Ebeye. On heavily fortified Kwajalein islet, the Americans were met by about four thousand committed defenders, most from combat units.

American objectives on Kwajalein were accomplished within a week, but casualties were high. When Leban Jorju emerged after the battle he had to walk atop the bodies of the dead, they were so numerous. On Namur, no trees or buildings remained; there were only the bodies of dead Japanese soldiers (Morison 1951:250). The 41,446 American troops in the campaign suffered 372 dead and 1,582 wounded; 7,870 Japanese were killed (Richard 1957a:124).

Nearly two hundred Marshallese died in the attack on Kwajalein, perhaps the only Micronesian location where Islanders were killed while actually fighting for the Japanese. The geography of the atoll allowed no escape; their choice was either to fight alongside the Japanese or hide with them in their bunkers. They also faced a crisis of conscience. Ijimura Lautona recalls that "Nearly all of those who were with the Neinbu [Nambō?] on Kwajalein sided with the Japanese and fought with them." When they realized the extent of American power, some thought the Japanese had deceived them. Some, Thaddeus Sampson recalls, "thought that they would stand up against the Americans," but then were hurt because they had been "taken in by the kinds of thinking"

Photo 1. Enjebi Island, Enewetak Atoll, February 19, 1944, after American naval shelling and air bombardment. (U.S. Navy photo, National Archives photo no. 80-G-216031)

of the Japanese soldiers and didn't realize the "customs of warfare" under which the Americans would invade.

American control of Kwajalein by February 5 severed a Japanese supply line and restricted the power of Japan's Pacific Fleet (Broadwater 1971). Next, the conquest of Enewetak would give American air forces a base for regular strikes at the other Marshall Islands. Japan's fortification of Enewetak had come late in the war, rushed by the loss of Kiribati. Elson Ebel remembers Enewetak's defenses as so unready that troops erected tree trunks "to look like cannon protecting the airfield."

Intensive bombing of Enewetak began in February, with the land invasion scheduled for mid-month.[4] At the same time, Americans conducted a major air strike on the Caroline Islands to forestall Japanese support of Enewetak (see below). Unlike on Kwajalein, some Marshallese on Enewetak—those on Enjebi—had a chance to escape to the southern islets with the permission of the Japanese officer in charge. From relative safety, they watched a stream of American planes bomb Enjebi. Marshallese on more isolated Enewetak and Meden islets, however, had no escape route. They suffered along with the Japanese defenders, huddled in bunkers as the bombing began and the Americans came ashore.

> For those of us on Meden, perhaps we are lucky to still be speaking today because, in only another moment, we would have been gone. It was that man on Meden [the American battalion commander] who was very *lege* [ferocious and unpredictable], bad and worse yet [than bad]. His uncontrolled anger was so great that in a moment he would have killed us all. From the beginning, those of us on Meden were unfortunate. To begin with there were ships, lagoon and ocean side, and planes helping from above. From all directions the damage was inflicted. If you wanted to "go" [run], you had to dig, for there was no other place open for escape. From dawn to dusk they shot at this islet. At the finish, there was not a single coconut standing. Also on Enewetak it was almost the same, but the two were not equal [in intensity]. It was on Meden that the white men, the soldiers, exhausted their total strength. All of us were in the holes. Anything not in the holes disappeared. But even in the shelters there was damage. That man Lekomta, the reason he is damaged today [is as] a result of the holes; fragments of shells destroyed his vision. So much harm was done, he was fortunate to still be alive. And others also died in those holes, some from fragments, but almost all after the soldiers landed. You see, there was no limit to the warring instinct in that man's throat [the commander's "heart"]. In the holes it was awful. We were hungry and thirsty, but no one could go out. If you traveled outside you would disappear. So the hole was also bad because we had to pee and shit inside, even desecrate the face of close kin. Then in their coming, the warriors were not straight in their work. They came to our shelter, guns ready, and looked toward us inside. So great was our fear that we were all in a corner, like kittens. And then they yelled and threw in a hand grenade.

(Interviewer asks: Did they really see you? The thing is, they knew you were Marshallese?)

They knew! The soldiers called out to the leaders, "Kanaka! Kanaka!" and waited until they responded, and then threw in the hand grenade. Such was the measure of their damage [mental impairment].

Well, at that time we knew we were gone [dead].

(Long pause — smokes — reflects)

Perhaps it was a bad explosive. When it burst, the whole shelter was torn apart. So powerful was the thing one could never stand. Earth fragments struck us, but others in the other half, they died. All the force of the explosion went over there. *Iokwe* [love, empathy, sad recollection; uses endearing kin terms to list those who died].

Afterward, we did not move, but stayed there for awhile amidst the dirt and sand, and then they returned to check, and they took us out and stripped us with the bayonets on the fronts of their guns, like some sort of game [entertainment], and then they took all of us to the field and lined us up and prepared to shoot us. We trembled, so great was our fear, but still they pointed guns at our heads. And then they tied cloths around our heads so you could no longer see in front of you and readied us to be slaughtered. Perhaps some did not want to shoot us and told the colonel that they did not wish to, but he made them raise their rifles. They quibbled, and maybe that person [their leader] was mad because they answered [spoke back to him], and he became enraged. Then we said, "Okay, perhaps we are gone now," and some started to cry like old women at the announcement of a death, and others began to pray; but all of us trembled.

We stayed there a long time. They called the ship. We waited. They spoke again to the ship. And so on it went. Afterward, they took off the blindfolds, took us to the ship, gave us fatigues and food, all kinds of food. But for some days we did not see the others [from Enewetak and Enjebi], so we could not yet determine who was alive and who was dead.[5]

"Mopping Up" the Marshalls

Marshallese knew that Americans brought overwhelming force to the attack. But they did not at first realize that Japan was not going to respond in kind.

Photo 2. A U.S. Marine gives water to a group of Marshallese who survived the battle for Enewetak Atoll, February 22, 1944. (U.S. Navy photo, National Archives photo no. 80-G-217287)

Kiribati and the Marshalls had been excluded from the September 1943 "absolute national defense sphere." The bases had been quickly strengthened to buy time to establish the new perimeter, but they could expect no reinforcement (Peattie 1988:262–263).

Intense and brutal, the war on the first Allied targets was, nevertheless, mercifully short. American forces attained their goals in the Marshalls in just over three weeks. They moved Islanders from new U.S. bases on Kwajalein, Majuro, and Enewetak to settlements where they had their first "postwar" experiences with Americans (explored in later chapters). Then, while the front shifted to the Marianas, reconnaissance teams occupied the remaining unfortified Marshall islets and atolls throughout the spring of 1944. At Enewetak

Atoll, for example, where "friendly, cooperative" villagers had provided intelligence to the invaders, U.S. troops fanned out to nearby islets after capturing Enewetak itself. First a patrol plane made a photo flight, then if defenses looked weak, a small expedition set out, including civil affairs and medical personnel, interpreters, and Marshallese guides (Shaw, Nalty, and Turnbladh 1966:197, 216–218).

Marshallese were often recruited to deliver "surrender or die messages" to Japanese on unfortified islets, many of whom committed suicide in the name of the emperor. In a few cases, Islanders actively joined American troops in these cleanup operations (Morison 1951:310–314). On Kiejej islet, Japanese soldiers had pursued some Marshallese escaping from Ronglap. Their plan to kill the Marshallese, some say, was thwarted when Americans arrived the next morning. American troops killed most of the Japanese, but Marshallese were given guns and told to shoot survivors. (Most, however, had committed suicide.) By the end of April, the Japanese held only Wotje, Mili, Maloelap, and Jaluij; systematic air attacks on these bypassed atolls had begun the month before (Shaw, Nalty, and Turnbladh 1966:219).[6]

The Allies now controlled the double chain of the Marshall Islands. The campaign had destroyed Japanese ships and aircraft and neutralized the four uninvaded bases. Americans were now prepared to push toward the Japanese homeland far more quickly than the Japanese had anticipated. The next invasion of Japanese-held territory would be in June, thousands of miles to the west, at Saipan. The Allied decision to leapfrog intervening islands had profound implications for how those trapped there would live during the final years of war. The strategy, which isolated the unconquered Marshalls bases, the eastern, central, and most of the western Carolines, and parts of Palau and the Marianas, meant a double hardship of food shortages and constant air attacks for Micronesians as for Japanese. Saipan invasion plans included overwhelming use of carrier aircraft and bombers out of the new American bases in the Marshalls and Kiribati to prevent action by Chuuk and its neighbors.[7] The bypassed bases became regular bombing targets, by war's end serving as "milk runs" for bored pilots, training runs for inexperienced ones, and experiments in new weapons such as napalm firebombs (USSBS 1947a,b).

MARSHALLESE ON NEUTRALIZED BASES

There were people living even on islets that lacked coconut trees.

Jaluij, Mili, Maloelap, and Wotje were the first Micronesian islands to be defined as "bypassed." They were, of course, only bypassed as to invasion; they were very much in the Allied war plans. In February 1944 alone, the U.S. Army Air Force flew a thousand sorties in the bypassed Marshalls (Morison 1951:307).

Once again Islanders were disabused of the apparent invincibility of Japanese fortifications. Elson Ebel, seeing preparations on Mili, recalls, "with all this readiness, I said that the Japanese would never have been damaged as easily as they were on Mili." They also learned that their own resources were paltry protection from American weapons—for example, the bomb shelters Marshallese built on Imiej: "Some holes could hold two or three families. We made them out of coconut logs—we cut down coconuts and dug the holes and covered them with coconut logs and covered them over with sand. We spaced the coconut logs across the holes and then buried them."

After the loss of Kiribati, Japanese commanders of the bypassed bases had made "feverish preparations for an invasion which they expected momentarily"; instead they were victims of a long war of attrition, struggling to keep airfields potentially operational and strengthen defenses against continual air attacks while they fought starvation and loss of morale in a population that grossly exceeded the local resource base (USSBS 1947a:24). Mili, Elson Epel explains, was crowded with Japanese soldiers, their numbers swollen by stranded reinforcements (see Morison 1951:137; Richard 1957a):

> There were forty-some thousand soldiers on Mili. You see, there were three boats that were planning to go to Kiribati, filled with soldiers for Kiribati. An American submarine blew up the ships on the ocean side of Mili, and thus all of those soldiers [landed and added to the population of] Mili. A few died, but many survived because the rescue ship acted quickly and brought them ashore. They blew up the ships around seven o'clock in the evening. These were three . . . large transport ships for soldiers and when they were added to the soldiers on Mili, there were forty-some thousand. There were so many people on Mili, the soldiers divided them up, and

there were people living even on islets that lacked coconut trees. The forty thousand were spread out over the entire atoll. At first they were on the main islet, and then there was not enough room for people, so they divided them up throughout the atoll.

One of the first Japanese responses to the neutralization strategy was to move Micronesians away from military targets to outer islets of each atoll. Bwirre Lejmen was foreman for a Marshallese work crew of fifty on Jabwor. When Marshallese workers were moved to other islets after the battle for the Marshalls began, Mr. Lejmen stayed to operate the boat (the only other Marshallese remaining were another young man and Carl Heine, a prisoner on Jabwor; Japanese civilians were consolidated separately). Relocated Marshallese commuted to work, returning to the other islets in the evening. On Wotje, Marshallese were moved from the air base when attacks came in earnest: "They told us to move then because there was no time to work, since they were bombing and shooting nearly all the time" (Lele Ram). Marshallese workers also left Mili before the first American bombing (USSBS 1947a:233). Continual air attacks severely curtailed travel—even for subsistence activity—during the rest of the war. U.S. fighters were ordered "to destroy even dugouts and canoes" during air strikes against Mili and Jaluij (Howard and Whitley 1946:194).

As time passed and American bases in the Marshall Islands became well established, Japanese commanders increasingly feared that Marshallese would escape to the American side, perhaps furnishing them with information. While a very few Japanese officers turned a blind eye to—or even enabled—such escape, most responded by further tightening controls on the local population. Marshallese were no longer permitted to walk freely to connecting islets, and security increased.

The only serious morale problem at Jaluit was caused by the presence of large numbers of natives who were definitely anti-Japanese. All attempts to inculcate into the mind of the natives the theory that they were Japanese citizens failed miserably. There were frequent instances of raids upon warehouses by natives in search of saki and tobacco and there was apparently some serious trouble with them following bombings of Jabortown. The possibility of the natives going over to the Americans was of constant concern, and guards were kept continuously around the perimeter of the various islands to prevent their escape. (USSBS 1947a:50–51)

Threats against those left behind were used to prevent escapes. Elson Ebel of Mili recalls:

They said that if you ran off, the remainder of your family would be killed.

(Interviewer asks: Were there people that they killed?)

Many, because people ran off, and they killed those who remained. Laninlan and spouse, Leijekar, Luanbo, Teliji—well, over in the other location, her husband ran off and they killed her as well, they shot her. They shot off her ears first, to make her feel ashamed, that was what the soldiers of that time did. . . . They said, "Do you want to die?" She said, "I am not afraid of dying. If you want to take my life, take it." They sat her down on the sand and shot off her ear—and then shot off the other ear. Then they shot her in the hands [arms]. She was still alive, she did not whine or any such thing. There were ten-some bullets they fired into her before she actually died . . . such was her strength. Then finally, they fired right through her heart and placed their guns there, and that is when she died. This was done because their husbands ran off. Because the Japanese law was, "If you escape, we will kill the remainder of your family."

Those who did not escape—about a thousand Marshallese on the bypassed islands (Richard 1957a:362)—worked under worsening conditions. Americans had bypassed these four bases precisely because they contained dense troop concentrations. Now, with all shipping blocked save the occasional submarine, soldiers, remaining civilians, and Islanders relied on local foods and dwindling stores of imported rice and tinned food. Laborers struggled to repair base facilities under constant bombings.[8] Elsen Ebel continues:

There were many Marshallese who worked with the Japanese. Things were so bad, do you see, when we worked, you could never sit down. It was prohibited to sit. You had to stand all the time. You could not sit down to eat—they placed the food in your hand, and water. Five minutes, and you would grab the shovel and shovel, mixing cement or hauling the things around, or work with the trucks that went to the ocean side and were filled with rocks, for they would then come and fill all of the swampy areas and low spots.

(Interviewer asks: Was there pay?)

There was none, they only gave you food. If you were at fault in the least, if you were a minute late, they would hit you, beat you—beat you with their hands, or there were many other things to beat people with, sticks and ropes.

Those who could fled to unfortified islets. Despite strongly held ideas about land rights, during the war Marshallese lived wherever they could find greater safety and freedom. "When we ran off, we did not say, 'Well I am not going to stay here, because it is not my place of residence.' You could stay anywhere during this period, it did not matter if it was not really our place" (Clancy Makroro). On several bypassed atolls, the military maintained a presence not only in fortified positions, but also on smaller islets where Marshallese lived and food was produced. But on Maloelap and Wotje, once Islanders moved from the main islet, they were left alone. They were free of most of the danger experienced by those on Jaluij or Mili and were eventually able to leave the atoll completely. Carl Jelkan was one of the few who stayed on the main islet of Maloelap, working as a lookout. He recalls only eight Marshallese men and no women; three Marshallese had been executed there by the Japanese before the invasion. Nathan Tartios recalls that Marshallese workers on Taroa, Maloelap, escaped when bombing became intense, but the Japanese forced them to return to work. So they labored for the Japanese in two groups, working alternate days; on their off days, they fashioned canoes for their escape to the Americans.

As the motivation to flee increased, so did opportunities. The Americans were by now known to be nearby; they actively encouraged escape by alerting air patrols to watch for Islanders and detailing ships to aid evacuations. In the earliest case of former Japanese subjects helping the new rulers, a group of Marshallese "scouts" assisted with surveillance and escapes.[9] Escapes from the bypassed atolls were sometimes simple and safe, sometimes a desperate race under fire. Marshallese used their seafaring skills, knowledge of local geography, carefully gathered rumors of American movements, and understanding of the Japanese to carry out daring maneuvers.

The first U.S. Navy-assisted escape from Wotje came in early June 1944 and is an example of Marshallese-American cooperation. Learning that a few people had escaped to nearby uninhabited Erikub Atoll to search for food, the American atoll commander at Majuro organized a reconnaissance party and told those on Erikub to return to Wotje with canoes for the rest. During the nights of June 10–15, about 727 Islanders escaped to Erikub, then were transferred by LCI to Arno, where the U.S. Military Government established a refugee camp on Dudu islet. The Marshallese left behind only one family that lived too near the main Japanese base—and they captured three Japanese soldiers, whom they turned over to the U.S. officer on Erikub (Richard 1957a: 360–362).[10]

John Ezekiel planned his escape from Jaluij with compatriots after a friendly Japanese officer warned him that the Japanese planned to kill the Marshallese once they had learned their subsistence techniques. After sharing a meal, the officer said:

> "Do you see, two months hence, yes, thirty days after next month, there will be a single hole [a term used for bomb shelter, but here with the added meaning of grave] for the Marshallese." I said, "Why is this?" He thought again then and said, "Do you see these people, the Japanese, practicing making coconut toddy? When they know how to draw the sap, then there will be a single hole for the Marshallese." I said, "For what?" He said, "To throw them into." Then after two or three days, he said, "Do you remember that I said there would be a single hole?" "Yes, yes, so that there would not be any slowness in killing the Marshallese."

Although planned, John Ezekiel's escape nonetheless depended on luck. Late one night, a Japanese officer collecting food from the islets boarded the boat that the young men were using for their escape, thinking it was Japanese. Shortly afterward the group encountered another Marshallese man attempting escape. When the officer decided to execute him, the Marshallese decided to kill the officer and continue their journey. Along the way, they happened upon four more Japanese soldiers, whom they also tried to kill. These men escaped and alerted others. The Marshallese men, disavowed by relatives and friends who disapproved of their actions and feared Japanese reprisals, sailed alone to the islet of Lejron. There they tried to contact Americans by waving to planes returning from bombing runs on Imiej. One day, a plane dropped a letter, written in Marshallese, telling them to hide and await rescue. But as time passed they worried about Japanese pursuit and decided to sail on to Taruk islet. There Americans fired on them by mistake, so they took to the open sea. As a U.S. ship approached, they feared a final fatal misunderstanding. But the ship stopped alongside their canoe, and two Marshallese men working for the Americans welcomed them aboard.

On Maloelap, the Japanese eventually advised Islanders to find boats and leave, though they had to do so in secret, since they were escaping from military control. The Americans moved to aid escapees after several made their way from Maloelap to Majuro, reporting that "the starving Japanese garrison had threatened the Marshallese with mass decapitation if they did not leave the atoll" (Richard 1957a:362). An air-dropped request for a truce went unanswered. Nathan Tartios recalls the dramatic escape that followed in early January 1945:

I know only that we ran off from Maloelap because the food supplies were shrinking; they began thinking that only the Japanese would eat on Maloelap. Yes, that high-ranking [Japanese officer] on Taroa was still okay (still our friend), he would come and tell us we should find boats to go to Bwiowi from Airik. . . .

Those [Marshallese] fellows came and discussed the situation among themselves and said, "Well, we should meet here. But, should we wait up all night until morning, or go ahead [and set sail] right now, or what?" A man came and said, "The soldiers have already gotten out of bed," so the adult men and women went ahead and set sail and took on board their companions. There was no conference, for that fellow came and said the soldiers had gotten up. When the canoe I was on set sail, the fellow who was watching over the canoe said, "Wait, let us see who did not get on board."

Onward and onward things went and two women did not get on board, their sailing craft sailed away without them. He came and said, "Well, the two of you come ahead, we will go ahead and make this canoe heavy." His canoe was far too full. In order to get aboard, people had to float in the water holding onto the edge of the canoe, for it was over capacity. Now they said, "Throw off the sail" [let it go slack]—the sail was made from Marshallese pandanus matting.

We went ahead and floated downwind from the islet, and encountered another canoe that was damaged. So they again took people from that canoe and put them in the other canoe. After that, it became even more overloaded. The boat could never sail, but they said, "Well, drift with the surf to Aur." It did not go toward Aur, it just continued to float about in between Maloelap and Aur.

Things kept going and going and going for four nights as I recall. Yes, four nights that you were in the ocean, you could not sit (on the boat) like here, you were totally drenched. . . . Everyone stayed put in the water, soaking. Many children died. [They were still holding on to the canoe.] Some people became disoriented, what Marshallese refer to as having "lost all sense of direction," I do not know what it is in English. Their minds were damaged, some from their having been in the ocean for so long. There were many children who were swimming about the entire time in the ocean and sharks bit them. The sharks were not very large . . . possibly [3 to 4 feet]. Well, the canoe went ahead and turned upside down; they turned it right side up—just six people worked on it, righted it, and it was okay.

So we again stayed there with the canoe and [drifted] onward and onward and then one day, we did not get up because we had not slept, because those folks were so cold that the numbness overcame their sense of being cold. . . . The American planes came and the women waved to them but they did not see them. We then woke up from our dazed state and saw that we were close to Aur, we were drifting downwind right next to Aur. But there were no paddles and no canoe bailers. We drifted downwind, drifted downwind and then about nine o'clock or ten o'clock or so, we drifted ashore on the small islets to the north of Tabal. Next to Biken (Aur). And our canoe, it did not really turn upside down, it turned like this [outrigger down]. Now you see, the women with us, they fell downward on the outrigger and some fell down inside [between the outrigger and the canoe], but some fell down in front of it. Well, the two of us, me and a young man, we dragged up a woman who was alive as other women fell unconscious [or dead] to the north and south. Me, I walked some, but I also crawled on my hands. I could not stand and walk. I was too weak. I was so cold that my sense of being cold had disappeared. We were so hungry that hunger had disappeared. You could barely hear; you could only hear people speak in the slightest degree. Perhaps after only one more night we would have died.[11]

Photo 3. Escape of Marshallese from Japanese-held Jaluij Atoll to a U.S. Navy LCI, May 1945. (U.S. Navy photo, National Archives photo no. 80-G-323829)

The refugees reported that the other Marshallese on Maloelap were planning escape. For the next four days, the U.S. Navy conducted offshore operations while 462 Islanders, all but twenty of those on the atoll, swam or fled in canoes to an LCI (Richard 1957a:362).

On Mili, thirty-six Marshallese and a Japanese prisoner were taken off by a destroyer escort and an LCI in April 1945. During June air strikes on Mili, a plane crew reported white flags on Pigero islet, and American ships later picked up more than a hundred Micronesians and a few Japanese and Koreans. On May 6, 494 Marshallese were evacuated from Jaluij under fire, and a U.S. Military Government officer was killed as he helped Micronesians aboard. A few more escaped in May, and an August 1 effort took 203 people off the southeast reef at Jaluij.

Of an estimated 3,500 Marshallese on the four bypassed garrisoned atolls, about 2,500 escaped to American lines before the end of the war.[12] Rescued Marshallese were shuttled to camps for displaced Islanders on Majuro, Arno, and Aur or returned home if they were from atolls already under U.S. control.

THE BOMBING OF THE CAROLINES

*That was when we got really scared. . . . we had
seen what those bombs could do.*

While Japanese rapidly revised defensive strategy to protect a shrinking imperial perimeter, Allied attention turned to the Carolines, and in particular to Chuuk lagoon. The Allies saw Chuuk, equidistant from Enewetak and Rabaul, as a threat to both the Central and Southwest Pacific campaigns. A February 12 night raid on Americans at Roi-Namur (Kwajalein) by flying boats staged through Pohnpei sharpened awareness of the Caroline bases' offensive capabilities. Rather than invade any of these—Chuuk, at least, was thought to be strongly defended—the Allies decided to continue the successful strategy of neutralization. Regular air raids on the Carolines began in February 1944, preparatory to the attack on Enewetak, then continued in support of the June invasion of Saipan. Chuuk lagoon was a key target, but the massive U.S. effort included constant destructive pounding of the bypassed Marshalls bases, Kosrae, Pohnpei, and by March, the western islands of Woleai and Yap.

A lone plane flying over Pohnpei in January 1944 had been spotted by a few Pohnpeians, and people recall seeing several reconnaissance flights in early February. But the first heavy bombing of Pohnpei came in mid-February, when B-24s from Tarawa replied to the raid on Roi-Namur with nearly two weeks of attacks, dropping 118 tons of high explosives and more than six thousand incendiary bombs. The first raid targeted the Lenger Island airfield and seaplane base and the town of Kolonia. Built largely of wood, Kolonia burned quickly and almost completely. It was rumored that the port had received a shipload of ammunition just before the raid, adding to the destruction. The Japanese were unable to put protective fighters in the air; in fact, not a single

Japanese plane was encountered during any of the 176 Seventh Air Force sorties against Kosrae and Pohnpei.[13]

> The [post-raid] photos showed almost complete devastation. The first four raids had practically destroyed the town. The southern waterfront section was virtually wiped out.
> The radio station was gone. In all, more than 300 buildings of all sizes had been razed, and the seaplane base at Langor Island had been pounded into ruins. (Howard and Whitley 1946:196)

Kosrae was hit with 9 tons of bombs during the Enewetak invasion, then suffered three more raids in February 1944. After Enewetak was taken, Kosrae, like Pohnpei, Nauru, and the bypassed Marshalls bases, continued to be bombed by the Seventh Air Force. Japanese on Kosrae were apparently unprepared for the first attack. Otinel Eddmont remembers troops stationed at Utwe standing up, waving, and shouting "Banzai!" at the planes, mistaking them for their own. Austin Albert, who worked in the watchtower in Lelu Harbor, recalls B-24s arriving in formation: "They began to drop bombs at the edge of the surf and came up into Lelu. . . . They flew from the east and then passed over the island. They dropped several small bombs, about 50–100 pounds. Two Kosraeans died that day. Others were wounded. Many Japanese died on the other side [of the harbor]."

With the first bombs, Caroline Islanders realized that the war had come to them. Wendolin Gomez, who worked at the Japanese hospital, was one of the few Pohnpeians in Kolonia that day:

> On the first day of the war, a lone American plane flew over Sokehs. It flew down low and then went over to Lenger. At that point the Japanese started firing at it, but they missed. The plane then dropped a bomb on Lenger and flew away. Maybe it was only patrolling to check things out. Then others came and started dropping bombs at Sokehs, Dolonier, Kolonia. I left the hospital to check on my wife [who was at the shore in Dolonier]. I found her cooking fish. She had gotten the fish from the shore. The bombs killed the fish and when they floated close to shore, people picked them up and cooked them.
> The people, including most of the Japanese, left Kolonia for Net. But I couldn't go because we were expected to stay and wait for the wounded to

arrive. When they came in they were a mess. They had all kinds of body wounds. Some had to have their arms and legs cut off immediately. Others had big chest wounds that needed to be closed up. Those that died were taken away for burial. Others had their guts hanging out. It was a great mess. By that time, most of the Japanese had left and only the head doctor and a man from New Guinea, called Anat, and myself were left to look after things. The other doctors and nurses went to Lehdau in Nanpil to wait for the other wounded soldiers there. They [the Japanese] had a new hospital there.

As the bombing continued, Mr. Gomez drove around the island looking for victims. He aided those with minor wounds and took the more seriously injured to the hospital.

Andonio Raidong was also passing through Kolonia that day:

I almost died at the bridge at Doweneu [Net]. The planes started dropping bombs there. I was coming from Palikir to see my family. A soldier asked me where I was going. I said, "To Net." He said, "Hurry, the planes are coming." I reached Namiki [in Kolonia] and the siren in the post office went off. Everyone hid. I rushed off toward Net. This is where I met a man. I was standing by a house near the bridge when four huge planes approached. I walked under the bridge to hide, and soldiers there saw me and said, "Hey there, watch those planes; they'll kill you if they see you." I ducked down, and a man from Net joined me, just as four bombs went off. One bomb was only 6 feet from the bridge; three others landed in the water. The Americans were trying to blow up the bridge so the Japanese soldiers couldn't walk on or hide under it. So I told the other man, "Let's run."

When we started to run, a Japanese soldier told us to go back and hide under the bridge. We were more afraid of the bombs than of the Japanese soldier, so we just took off. When we were trying to climb up from under the bridge, I was wearing tabis and I kept slipping back, but the other man was barefoot and climbed out faster. We kept running to a house called pampei, a guard house. I jumped over something that I thought was a piece of wood. I realized that it was the foot of one of the soldiers. Then I jumped into a ditch and the bombs kept exploding. I reached the bridge where the Net [municipality] office was located. The people there said to stop running because the bombers had already left. But I kept running anyway.

I met other people from Net who were looking for their kids at school. School was still being held in Kolonia. I almost died.

The first, mid-February bombing of Pohnpei overlapped the major air raid on Chuuk. Chuuk held a dangerous reputation among the Allied forces and was referred to as an "impregnable bastion of the Pacific," the "Japanese Pearl Harbor," or the "Gibraltar of the Pacific." One author writes, "Truk was the object of much speculation and sinister vagueness because almost nothing substantial was known about it" (Tillman 1977:64). The Allies felt they had to deal with Chuuk before proceeding on the Central Pacific road to Tokyo, yet invasion would be difficult and costly. In fact, they overestimated Chuuk's strength, though the lagoon islands had been significantly fortified. With a garrison numbering over eight thousand and substantial defensive construction, Japanese and Chuukese may have felt secure from American attack.

> The reality was far different. While there were indeed military installations on all the main islands, several hundred planes on its airfields, and a garrison that was the largest in the central Pacific, Truk's reputation as a fortress was a sham; the aircraft were no longer the equal of the enemy, nor were those who flew them; incredibly, most of the trained pilots were quartered on Dublon while the aircraft were parked on Eten and Moen; there were only forty antiaircraft guns in the entire archipelago, and all fire-control radar had gone down with the ship carrying them to Truk; aviation fuel was so scarce that it was difficult to fly regular patrols outside the islands; indeed all supplies, ammunition, and fuel were in short supply because of the endless attrition by American submarines. (Peattie 1988:274)

Furthermore, when American planes did arrive, the heart of Chuuk's military capability—the Combined Fleet—was gone. Alerted by a reconnaissance flight in early February and alarmed by the loss of key islands of Kwajalein Atoll, the Japanese had removed major units. The Combined Fleet shifted its headquarters to Palau; the Fourth Fleet command on Chuuk was henceforth in charge only of bypassed islands. On the day of the attack, Chuuk lagoon held mostly freighters and transport ships.

"Operation Hailstone" was launched with seventy-five U.S. carrier-based fighters hitting Chuuk lagoon February 17. The dawn attack gave little warning, and Japanese pilots barracked on Toloas were minutes too far from planes on Eten. Only forty to fifty planes could be launched; most were immediately downed. At the end of the two-day attack, thirty-one merchant marine ships and ten warships had been sunk and planes, airfields, fuel oil, barracks, and an estimated 75 percent of Japanese supplies destroyed. The attack effectively ended Chuuk's air strength, demolishing or damaging 250–275 Japanese planes with relatively slight American losses.[14] Hailstone's success and fear of a difficult amphibious attack shaped the American decision not to invade Chuuk.

The arrival of the war, in the form of this massive bombing raid, shocked Chuukese. Konstantin Enik and his companions made their morning commute by canoe from Fano to Tunnuk on Weno:

> Every day, early in the morning, we paddled to Tunnuk to go to work. We had a surprise when we saw planes, but we thought they were just Japanese planes practicing. That was the first time American planes came, but at that time we didn't know it was the beginning of the war, because we really didn't know about the war. We paddled to Tunnuk and we went straight to the village at the end of the point called Upween. Then we walked down, we met the soldiers; they were all in their uniforms. Then the officer said, "Did you guys see the *teki* that came?" But we didn't know what that word *teki* meant. We didn't know that was the term for American planes.
>
> So, then we discovered that Americans had come, because we saw one of the huge Japanese planes try to leave the airfield, and those American planes chased it and strafed it, and it fell on one of the small reefs called Tawenap. We saw the plane fall. At that time, they told us to run away to the mountains, because the Americans had come. And when we started to leave, we looked out to sea and saw huge ships called *kungan* [aircraft carriers]. They were outside the reef. We saw those ships shooting at each other. At that time we knew that there was war.

Watching the fleet of bombers draw near, the noise growing impossibly loud, Chuukese did not at first understand what was about to take place. Piriska Nukunukar remembers her initial awe at seeing the American planes arrive: "We weren't scared, we were just amazed, because it was the first time we had seen that happen. Then, after a few rounds of airplanes, the bombers started to drop bombs on the land and everywhere. That was when we got really scared, because we had seen those who were already dead on the ground. Also, we had seen what those bombs could do. Everyone ran for bomb shelters."

Those who lived through that first massive raid retain indelible memories of the destruction. People on other islands stood transfixed, watching flames and smoke shoot up from Toloas as the big oil tanks were hit and the military headquarters was destroyed. Recalls Kimon Phymon: "The first bombing started on Chuuk when twelve big planes came in, and when we looked up we said, 'Oh, oh, we are going to die.' The American planes came and we believed that we were going to be hurt. When night fell, the planes started the bombing. They dropped them on the airfield, and the place was on fire. And, next, the first *kitoputai* [wave of planes attacking]. They came and dropped bombs on Toloas and on the oil tanks. It was on fire. When we looked from Winipis, there was dark smoke on Toloas from the oil tank."

Chuukese on Toloas, the key land target in that devastating raid, sought words to match their memories. Here is Sachuo Siwi's attempt:

I can't say anything that would really describe the scene at that time. Everywhere I went, I saw dead people just lying around everywhere. Sometimes I'd find an arm or a leg or even a head separated from the body—people were dying out in the open, a messy death. There were no more clusters of buildings, even the offices weren't there anymore. . . .

People were very pitiful. . . . The Japanese were to be pitied. The soldiers and civilians had no places to stay—their homes were gone. They had some trucks so they hauled the Japanese to that village [Rere on Toloas] and spread them around under the breadfruit trees. They were everywhere, under the bushes, under big trees, wherever they could make a home, for they had no more homes. That was when my father told the local people to take care of themselves. He also begged the Japanese to get out of here— that could never happen because those were soldiers and just made up their own rules to take over our lands. . . .

At that time, I remember—ooh, so this is what war is like . . . now that war has come, war kills people—I just realized what war is all about— what its consequences were—this was the time I started to suffer.

Piara Esirom was about thirty years old, mother of several children, at the time of the attack on Toloas.

I was sleeping in my house when the siren went off. I woke up and wondered, "What was that?" I woke up my children and told them, "We're going to run away. We're going to the Japanese priest." So we walked at night. While we were walking, we saw the soldiers. They stopped us and asked us where we were going. We told them that we were running away. When we looked up in the sky we saw the planes dogfighting. So we ran to the priest's house. Then we heard gunfire . . . we were very afraid. Japanese and American planes went down.

The sun was rising, and we were very hungry. My children and I were starving. One of my boys decided to go back to our house. I said to him, "What if you get hurt?" And he said, "But what can we do? We are hungry, and if we don't at least have something, then we'll die." So he went to our bomb shelter and cooked rice for us, but a soldier came and scolded him. He took the water and poured it on the fire. He didn't want the planes to see the smoke. We didn't have a kerosene stove. The Japanese soldier left.

The planes were having a dogfight. Japanese planes went down, and American planes, too. The ships in the ocean went up in flame, they were just like fires in the ocean. The American planes were dropping bombs on these ships, and all were destroyed.

Night came, and the soldiers told us to go up into the mountains. Everybody: Japanese women, men, and all Chuukese, all except the soldiers. We stayed up in the mountains, and the planes were fighting. We heard the sounds of machine guns. Planes burst into flames in the air. So we just waited for the bullets to hit us.

Then daytime came, and our hunger. We were losing our strength. We couldn't eat or drink. My boys became friends with the Japanese, so they would go with them and ask for rice. They would bring us the rice and I would give a little to everyone so that it might help us, or at least we would have something in our stomachs.

Then the oil tank went up in flames. It was at night, but what could we do? We couldn't hide, because it was like daytime when that oil tank went up in flames.

My husband asked for a boat to take us to one of the other islands—Udot.

The Japanese were surprised when such a massive attack was not followed by invasion. They set about repairing damages, and "began a belated but intensive effort to place everything possible underground" (USSBS 1947b:3). The February attack marked the start of regular air raids on Chuuk, part of the neutralization strategy. By early March, American bombers based on Kwajalein began to join attacks on Chuuk, sometimes coordinating with B-24 Liberators from the Solomons in a "one-two punch." The first night raid was a complete surprise: "The huge base was brilliantly lighted and swarming with workers, when our [U.S.] bombers droned into sight" (Howard and Whitley 1946:200, 207). A second major raid on April 6 and 7 inaugurated a month of nightly bombings. Naval planes from Enewetak dropped aerial mines into the main passages of Chuuk lagoon in April. A carrier attack at the end of April destroyed 93 planes, and photographic evidence showed 423 buildings and 6 hangars destroyed and 44 buildings damaged. This attack "virtually nullified Truk's value as a supply and air base" (USSBS 1947b:4).[15] Toloas, Weno, and Eten islands lay in ruins. Garrison and civilian workers exhausted themselves repairing airstrips that were repeatedly bombed into uselessness. Sachuo Siwi remembers this time:

They [American planes] just came to drop bombs and strafe. Some places were damaged, but mostly places where the Japanese had stored their war materials, their houses. Eeeh, as for the Chuukese people's houses, they couldn't bomb them—because what was there to bomb? Some thatch houses had half of the roof gone or sometimes there would be two coconut palms left as the roof, so I think that was why they didn't bother to bomb them. They just bombed to kill the Japanese soldiers. . . . During the second raid no Chuukese died, only Japanese soldiers, because by then there were caves for local people. Also during the second [raid] we were thankful because some of those [Japanese] leaders of our *putai* told us to go run to the caves and hide with them. So we were hiding with the Japanese in some of the caves. . . . They just bombed to kill soldiers, to destroy their war materials, houses, or offices for the soldiers; also the caves and the bunkers where they had machine guns. . . .

But the misery still continued for us, because the Americans had not only bombed the soldiers' places but they had also bombed our taro, breadfruit, coconut, and bananas, so that was why the local people continued to

Photo 4. Toloas (Dublon), Chuuk, after U.S. attack of April 30, 1944. (U.S. Navy photo, National Archives photo no. 80-G-227331)

suffer. At that time, Toloas was really cleared (of vegetation). Even the local papayas that grow wild in Chuuk were gone.

For Klemente Actouka, a Pohnpeian seaman in the Japanese merchant fleet, it seemed that the war followed as he traveled through the Carolines in early 1944.

Before the war, I was on a ship, *Nanyo Pwehki.* This ship had traveled a lot to the South Pacific before the war [during "business times"]. We went to Tinian, Rabaul, Samoa, New Caledonia, Fiji, Tonga, Vanuatu, and the Solomons . . . I was perhaps twenty years old when war started; I was in Chuuk. At that time, Yamamoto's ship was in Chuuk, too. A plane came to Chuuk at that time, and Yamamoto's ship left by sunset.

After three days we left Chuuk for Pohnpei, and when we got to Pohnpei, the bombing of Pohnpei had already begun. The first plane that went to Chuuk had been a lookout plane. We were already in Pohnpei when the bombing of Chuuk started. The day we reached Pohnpei was the same day that the bombing of Chuuk started. I heard that forty-eight ships were sunk in that bombing. They were transport ships, with goods for the soldiers.

We were in Pohnpei for one day and then we left for Kosrae. This was the last ship. We got to Kosrae . . . on March 24. At seven in the morning the ship was sunk. It was destroyed by three American planes. We swam from the [sinking] ship, and we were lucky because we were on the reef, not outside of it. Of eight soldiers, six were killed; two lived. And three passengers died.

LIFE UNDER THE BOMBS

*There's a shaking like my heartbeat when
the bombs explode right next to me.*

In addition to U.S. Navy carrier air attacks, the U.S. Army Air Force bombed bypassed islands through the end of the war, at first flying long-range missions from Kiribati and Marshalls airfields. From March to September 1944 the Seventh and Thirteenth Air Forces flew regular, almost daily raids on Carolines bases, protecting the invasion of the Marianas and New Guinea. Chuuk was "neutralized" by the end of May, but near-daily raids continued in support of the Marianas campaign until mid-June to forestall repairs. With each attack, fewer fighters rose in opposition; besides those destroyed, the Japanese had transferred planes from Chuuk to defend the Marianas. Nonetheless, work teams continued repair efforts. Chuuk's airfields were usable for Japanese raids on Saipan's harbor in late June and early July. In mid-June, a British carrier air attack on Chuuk—actually a training mission—did little damage, but caused the Japanese to burn files in expectation of invasion.

Chuuk was essentially useless to the Japanese by mid-1944, without planes for reconnaissance or defense. Allied intelligence determined that repair efforts after these devastating attacks were fruitless, but neutralization continued throughout the war—though in the end, bombing runs on Chuuk became little more than training flights. Land-based B-24s of the Seventh and Thirteenth Air Force continued to hit Chuuk through October 1944, when

B-29s from the Marianas took over. Weak defenses and high altitudes prevented much damage to U.S. planes. The "experimental" B-29 flights, for crews training for raids on Japan, kept Chuuk from rebuilding or promoting suicide missions. The last major raid on Chuuk was two weeks of B-24 attacks in April–May 1945, though B-29 flights continued. The last bombing Chuuk experienced was by British Royal Navy aircraft on June 16, 1945.[16]

Pohnpei was also regularly attacked. Between February 1944 and August 1945, an estimated 250 air strikes were mounted against it. On May 2, 1944, six U.S. battleships shelled the northern portion of Pohnpei. The attack was halted after seventy minutes, with no worthwhile targets remaining. The airfields were destroyed and an estimated 75 percent of the 940 buildings in Kolonia leveled (Denfeld 1979:30–35). Kosrae was bombed less intensively but was the usual alternate target for U.S. Army Air Force missions against Pohnpei deflected by weather (Craven and Cate 1950:30–38). The people of Lelu Island and the civilian governor's office were evacuated across the harbor after the first bombing, and soon Kosraeans abandoned their villages and moved to the hills (Schaefer 1976:37).

Enduring Neutralization

While the first experience of bombing remained an indelible memory, repeated raids soon merged into a stream of frightening images for those on the bypassed islands. Sinino Mateas of Chuuk vividly recounts the experience:

> The time the airplanes came it was at night—these were American airplanes. During the war, I was in Tol (Chuuk lagoon) and it was about two in the morning when I heard the sound of airplanes. It almost sounded like bombs on our house. Then I heard the explosion and it was very loud. The bomb had landed—maybe, say our house is here and it landed in Mechitiw [i.e., a short distance away]. It seemed like the bomb had landed beside our house. Then we heard a woman's voice. She was calling for her husband—the bomb had landed on the hill next to that family's house and it caused a landslide which buried their house. The man was knocked down by only the concussion/debris from the bomb. The house was buried with some kids under the earth. So we ran to that house to help, but the Japanese had dug them out. They [Japanese] had heard the cries of the kids be-

neath the buried house. So after the Japanese dug out the kids, we started to look for the father. We found him lying on some roots of a breadfruit tree. He was dead. A rock was near him. I don't know if the rock landed on him or what.

Wendolin Gomez endured repeated air attacks at his work in Pohnpei's hospital:

It was during one of these raids that my eardrum was broken. When the planes came, we all ran to a cave, but I stood at the entrance so I could see where the bombs were landing. We had all our wounded and sick people with us at the time. When the bombs came too close to us, I would warn the guys in the cave so they could brace themselves. But then one bomb hit too close to the cave, and I was blown away from the entrance all the way to the bottom of the cave. All I heard was this tremendous explosion and a great rush of wind lifted me and just blew me away. When I came to, I had a ringing in my ears and was very dizzy. The doctors ran over to where I was, but I felt okay by then and told them so. Later on during the war, I started to have a hard time hearing people. When the doctor checked my ear, he found the eardrum torn apart. . . .

Another day I went to . . . get another motorcycle. There were many soldiers there. All of a sudden the siren went off and we ran around looking for whatever shelter we could find. This place was close to where the nuns lived. One Japanese soldier was close by at my right, and another was to my left. When the bombs started falling, we all bent down and covered our heads. When the bombing stopped I felt relieved because no shrapnel came my way. When I looked to my right, all I could see were the intestines and other mutilated body parts of what was left of the soldiers. The guy to my left was missing his head. I stood up and ran like hell to the other soldiers and told them what happened. I never knew what they did because I left. I don't know whether I became scared, or confused. What I remember is that I had pinned inside my shirt a picture of Jesus and the Sacred Heart, and this little picture never left me. Maybe that's what brought my luck. . . .

During another air raid, the man from New Guinea and I were near the present-day Bernard's gas station. There was a small cave nearby, so we ran into it. But three soldiers came and told us to get out. So we went outside and sat down in a ditch. There was nothing to do because the bombs were already falling. We got up, ran to a fence, and stood there. The soldiers in the cave that we left were less fortunate, because they took a direct hit and died.

Chuukese suffered the greatest number of casualties in the Carolines, perhaps in the hundreds (USSBS 1947b gives Chuukese figures as sixty-three killed, sixty wounded, but this is conservative, and does not include those lost when ships sank [Denfeld 1981a:49–51; see also King and Parker 1984:108]). Only a dozen or so Pohnpeians were killed by American attack; even fewer died on Kosrae. Erwin Leopold of Pohnpei recognizes that even that much-bombed island was relatively fortunate: "The fighting here could not be called a war. It was very minor compared to what happened in Saipan, Peleliu, the Marshalls, and so forth." But repeated bombing took a psychological toll. The greatest stress was the constant need to be alert, to be aware of planes overhead and the site of the nearest shelter. Because of this, one of the most dreaded jobs on Pohnpei was fishing in the open lagoon. A Pohnpei fisherman's wartime song laments:

> There is no place we can hide.
> Those who work making salt and farming are lucky,
> Because on land there are places to hide.

People had to be ready to rush to shelter when the alarm sounded; as the frequency of raids increased, some decided to remain near bomb shelters as a general precaution. Not infrequently, women gave birth there. The former governor of Pohnpei, Rehsio Moses, was born while his parents hid in a shelter. Chuuk suffered more intensive bombing than any other area, sometimes several raids in a day. Those in targeted areas, such as Finas Bossin, were always prepared to grab their children and run for shelter:

When those Americans came, they came in airplanes. They would start dropping bombs. We were just running around at that time. Then when it was all clear, we would run to our houses and pick up some stuff and run for the caves. . . . The airplanes had left to refuel or reload their guns and they would come back again to attack. It could be two to three hours, then they'd come back again. Some people who got to their homes just stayed there, or ran for the caves. But some of us like myself never made it home. We just stayed with the Japanese in their caves. When the airplanes would go away, we'd start to work again [for three hours], then when they came back we'd run for the caves again.

By mid-1944, daily raids had become predictable. Women in the rice fields in Sokehs, Pohnpei, started work at 5 A.M., then retired to a bunker at 8 A.M. to eat breakfast when the planes arrived. When the all-clear sounded, they returned to work. Men on the interior road crew began their day at 3 A.M. in order to put in a day's work before the 8 A.M. air raid.

The choice of hiding place in an air raid meant life or death. Some turned to traditional divination or prayer for guidance. As Akeisuk Mokok (Chuuk) says, "That's why we moved to the forest, because some people used coconut leaves to divine whether we should stay here or go over there. Some used another kind of magic to call ghosts to possess them [in a trance] to tell them where they should be" to avoid bombs. Toli Jessy remembers Chuukese using magical spells to deflect an approaching attack: "Some men in our village could do things like [magic to protect themselves]. When they saw the airplanes flying toward us, they could sing to them or just sing [a magical chant] in order to make them fly away. It helped a little. We thought it worked, because the airplanes did turn away from our place."

A song from Lamotrek details the spirits' protection, saying that they "go into the planes and sit with the pilots" to ensure that the bombs are dropped where no one will be killed (Lindstrom and White 1990:169). A woman on Weno, caught in a raid with her young son, recalls that she began with Christian prayers, then appealed to the ancestors for protection.[17] Tupun Louis remembers explosions from pattern bombings approaching his shelter:

We were hiding in caves in a village [on Toloas, Chuuk]. . . . They were bombing from morning till night. The bombing was coming nearer and nearer to our cave. Then it stopped, just a few yards from our cave. Maybe he was out of bombs. Then he flew back, without dropping any bombs. He flew back and reloaded. . . .

When the plane went back to reload, Reverend Rupen was one of the leaders. Reverend Rupen called us together and said, "We will pray now, to God. If He's going to take us, He'll show us whether to stay in our cave, or to move from this place." And then he prayed—prayed, prayed, prayed. After he said "Amen," he looked up and told us: "Let's get out and move to another cave."

There were quite a number of us in that cave—old people, children, women—all together. We ran uphill, towards where the previous bombing had been, running for a cave. There were some old people with children, who were running, who were a bit slow. When the bombers came, they resumed [bombing] from where they had stopped, and continued on. And unfortunately, some members of our group died, because they were running with children, falling, slowing their speed.

In the first attacks, protection was meager. Some tried to huddle behind coconut tree trunks, under breadfruit roots, or in taro patches. Underground shelters or tunnels into Chuuk's basalt cliffs had been started but were neither plentiful nor deep enough to accommodate all Japanese, much less Chuukese. Chuukese such as Anang Samwel realized that the shelters they had prepared for themselves under Japanese instructions were completely inadequate: "The place where we hid—the Japanese taught us to do this—we dug out the ground, laid the [coconut] logs on top, and buried the logs. I thought it was really good. But when I saw the place where the bombs had dropped—it was no good at all. It would only save us from the spray of the bombs. For example, a bomb fell near where we were. Someone was killed from the shrapnel of the bombs. We were lucky that we hid in the cave. The second time the bomb dropped on the hillside, it killed four and buried the rest in the cave. After that, we were seriously worried."

It seemed to Mr. Samwel that most deaths were of Chuukese; he speculates that perhaps this was because Japanese, forewarned, had prepared cave shelters rather than foxholes. He remembers what happened after working to excavate underground areas for the Japanese military: "When they called kūshū [air raid warning] and the American planes came, I ran to the cave where the Chuukese were—but we [Chuukese] were gathered only at the entrance. The soldiers' leader was right in the middle of the cave." Akeisuk Mokok recalls how his family lived after moving near the basalt cliff at Peniyesene on Weno at the start of the bombings: "Right up next to that rocky mountain, that's where we lived, just hanging under the rock, like an animal [i.e., like a bat, curled up against the rock wall]." Sontak Kansou says that even though Chuukese had made shelters in rock cliffs, Japanese would force them out during a raid and tell them to seek another place.

Where they could, Caroline Islanders fled the most dangerous target areas, and Japanese officials did their best in many places to move "nonessential" Islanders away from hazardous sites. Both Japanese civilians and the small resident Islander population evacuated Kolonia after the first attack on Lenger in Pohnpei, leaving only a few soldiers; when the hospital was destroyed, that staff left too, for a new hospital in Net. Nearby Sokehs was also evacuated—"Everyone paddled to Madolenihmw." People were preoccupied with the problem of how to keep safe. Robert Gallen describes a meeting of Madolenihmw people: "They were trying to decide what to do [about the war], where to hide. Nothing else happened [at the meeting] but this. Each family made their own decision." Carmihter Abraham recalls Pohnpeians being told by the Japanese to "go into the forests to hide," inaugurating a period of hardship that lasted for two years.

Within the constraints of labor requirements, the Japanese organized mass evacuations from Toloas, the prime target in Chuuk. Civilians moved to five designated locales, where they assembled makeshift shelters. The civilian governor directed a general evacuation of Toloas in November 1944. Eten people, already twice displaced, were among those ordered to leave; only a few lucky families were able to stay together through repeated moves. Few Chuukese remained on Toloas: "Those who did not want to leave their jobs, whom the 'office' did not allow to leave, who did not want to leave their property, stayed behind" (James Selem). Many Chuukese who experienced the first attack on Toloas, like Ichios Eas, did not wait for formal evacuation orders: "Everybody started leaving Toloas and going home to our own islands. We all started going back to our islands, but the bad thing about it was, if we didn't have a pass or an ID, we were turned back. But then, what for? What good was it? We went to our islands, and we didn't stay at home. We just stayed in the forest, under the trees—there were no more homes. Some men would build little shacks from coconut palms. Some would just stay under the breadfruit or under the mango trees."

Evacuees were taken to less-fortified islands devoted to food production—Tol, Udot, Uman, Fefan—whose residents were told to meet them at the dock. On Tol, a Chuukese policeman walked through the crowd, assigning refugees to areas of the island as they arrived. The lucky ones stayed with relatives; others, like Take Katiw's group, were assigned to host families. Throughout Tol, people moved into the bush, bringing only what they could carry, then went into the mountains to live "under rocks" during the air raids. Some hid in the forests in hastily constructed thatch houses or simple lean-tos, crowding together sometimes ten or twenty to a house; others lived under trees or huddled in caves during the months of bombings.

At the Mori family compound on Tol in Chuuk, Echen Nakamura remembers that she and others "had no idea" what the planes were when they first flew over—but "those family members who knew about airplanes" told people to gather their supplies and move up to Nechocho mountain. Later, during a pause in the bombing, the family leader told them to go to Pwelle Island. While Chuukese generally moved from coastal villages to the sides of mountains during the bombings (where many remained until several years after American occupation), as war drew to an end the Japanese consolidated many villages to keep closer track of the population (Hall and Pelzer 1945).

Moving inland on a small island, as many did, did not bring relief from the sights and sounds of air raids. The geography of Chuuk lagoon meant that those not under direct attack could look across the water and watch the bombs fall, as did Ichios Eas: "When the American planes would come in, we would look up in the sky—they were like birds, like lots of birds in the sky. They would start dropping bombs. All we would say is, 'This is it! We are dead!' But then we were grateful, because they were not dropping bombs and shooting all over the place. They just hit the places, Parem and Toloas, where the shooting was coming from. The war was mostly on Weno, Parem, and Toloas, where they dropped the bombs." Those who lived at a distance from the attacks could be fairly safe observers, though they always felt threatened and worried constantly about the safety of relatives on the targeted islands.[18]

Imperative construction continued despite attacks. On Toloas, even after Chuukese moved to the mountains to escape the bombs and were living without houses ("At night, we slept under the mango trees, by the rocks. We just scattered around"), they returned daily to headquarters for work assignments. Airstrips were repaired regardless of danger; people ran at the air-raid warning, then were called back to continue repairs after the planes left. Koko Suda, who worked at Satawan airbase, remembers: "During the first night of the American air attack, they dropped their bombs at the air base. It was completely ruined. As for us [Islanders], we had to rush out in the middle of the night to do what they told us to do. They pushed us so hard to do the work, but we were not even eating any food. We were desperately hungry, afraid, exhausted. We planned to escape—but we didn't do it, because they were always watching us."

People did sometimes try to escape—"because they were hungry and tired of working"—but the Japanese tracked and punished runaway workers (Wangko Wasan's job as a policeman for the army in Chuuk was to check up on absentees). Resen of Chuuk recalls that when the war was about to start, the Japanese "said we couldn't go away, because we had to help them. Where they went, we had to be with them. If we escaped, they'd cut our heads off." Aitel Bisalen, with others, did flee Toloas (where he worked at Nambō) after the first air raid. He paddled home to Patta Island, only to find Japanese there searching for runaway workers. When people escaped work on Chuuk, the Japanese wrote to local officials on their home island, and police were assigned to look for the runaway, punishing him or her with a beating.

Sontak Kansou was among a group of men who fled from working on Eten, swam from Toloas to Weno, and hid for about a month until police found them. He describes his punishment:

After we were beaten, they took all our clothes off, [leaving us] like small naked children. They lined us up on the road and forced us to walk to Mapuchi, where the women worked. While we were walking to Mapuchi, there were some women from Penia village fishing in the ocean. The policemen lined us up and they called the women to come to see our naked bodies. The police forced the women to look at us. They told the women that if they refused to look at us, they would beat them, too.

After that incident, we continued our walk to Mapuchi. As we approached Mapuchi, one policeman went to see the higher official to tell him we were coming. We walked up, and the women were really astonished to see us naked. They tried to avoid us. Some of these women were our own sisters. The police lined us up again in front of the building and forced the women to look at us. The Japanese told us to go back to our assigned work, and if we disobeyed, they would do the same thing again. After that, they gave us back our clothes.

In telling of their emotions during the bombings, Chuukese speak of constant "confusion" and "suffering." The terrifying sound of the huge bombers overhead was like the noise of a ghost. Pohnpeians describe the great weight they felt, and their inability to sleep during the entire war. Many Pohnpeians say that they surrendered themselves to the inevitability of death. They no longer thought about the war or what tomorrow might bring; they just lived from day to day, following Japanese directives. Some became despondent; expecting to die, they no longer even attempted to flee when the American planes flew over. When the Japanese ordered those in target areas to evacuate, Alter Bedly (Pohnpei) says: "Some old people, seventy years or more, stayed in their houses because the soldiers couldn't move them. They told people to leave and go to the forest, because they would take over their houses. . . . We didn't prepare where people would live. They didn't care about the old people or the children. We thought we would die; we didn't think we would live."

In both Chuuk and Pohnpei, the horror of dying out in the open, perhaps alone, and in a particularly "messy" or filthy way became a preoccupation. In Pohnpeian tradition, warriors would enter battle with empty stomachs, to avoid shame should their intestines be cut. Some people killed in air raids had full stomachs, "and the filth that came out of their intestines was regarded as very shameful. . . . Many of the people took to drinking kava every night instead of eating so that if they were killed they might at least die cleanly and without shame" (Bascom 1965:86).

Physical destruction, deaths, and injuries were only the visible part of the harm caused by the bombings; psychological trauma and moral callousness were invisible changes that many survivors noted. Wangko Wasan of Udot, Chuuk, who is today a Catholic deacon, reflects:

> In the beginning, it was fascinating to watch the soldiers pouring in by the hundreds, but as time went by it became unbearable to see dead bodies being unloaded from the ships like stacks of copra. There were endless loads of corpses ferried ashore for eventual cremation. We had the feeling of the waste of human lives. There were all kinds of people: civilians, businessmen, and others, who just awhile ago had been in their various destinations in the lagoon. It was heartbreaking to hear life and death stories from survivors. There were even babies. There was one particular story about a family, I read in the papers, whose ship sank. They lost a child when the ship went down.

When bombs fell, people found themselves passing by the wounded; "We didn't even care if they were our family." The strongest ties, the most poignant bonds of pity or concern, were fragile in this environment of danger. Kintin Raphael, who was a child during the bombing of Chuuk, recalls: "Once, the planes came and they were late in giving the warning. My grandmother scooped me up so we could hide under the big rocks there. A family from Toloas who lived with us delayed us, because they were just children—their parents had gone fishing and there was no one to take them. If they had dropped bombs, we would have died, because we couldn't run and just leave them behind. An uncle of mine came and scolded my grandmother for staying behind with the children. He said she should have just left them behind and gotten me to the rocks so I wouldn't be hurt."

A well-known hymn composed during the war captures the constant anxiety of the year and a half of intensive bombing in Chuuk:

We were running from the sound of the fighter-plane under the clouds,
There's a shaking like my heartbeat when the bombs explode right
     next to me.
Oh, bombs and bomb-concussions, bring us close to a horrible death.
But we are safe only by depending on God.
Thanks to God, we are safe.

On December 8, the war started.
War on the sea and on the land
In all the nations of the world.

On January 17,[19] we are not yet awake, early in the morning, the bombing
     fleet has arrived.
We were startled, we didn't know what was going to happen to us.

The air-raid siren blew in the evening, and we heard the sound of
     firecrackers.
We zigzagged, carrying our mats and our possessions bundled up in a cloth.

Attacks on the Central and Western Carolines

American plans had included invasion of both Yap and Ulithi, but on the day after the Peleliu landing the decision was made to neutralize and bypass Yap. Here too, people recall being unprepared for the arrival of American planes.

Raphael Gisog remembers the first bombing of Yap (March 31, 1944). The night before, a Japanese plane, possibly to escape fighting in Saipan, had landed short of the runway. The next day, as Gisog's crew went out to investigate, they heard the warnings and saw planes dropping bombs, targeting the airfields and Colonia. Airfield workers initially thought these were Japanese planes trying to lighten their loads for a safe landing. Like other Caroline Islanders, Yapese tell many tales—some humorous—about startled responses to the first bombing: people who jumped into the water while still holding onto baskets; others who lost their clothing while running; one normally slow moving man who was the first to arrive at a distant village (see Poyer 1995).

After this initial raid, Japanese civilians on the island—especially women and children—were evacuated at the same time that Japanese troops arrived in force. As on Pohnpei and Chuuk, Yapese moved of their own accord after the first bombing. When raids became frequent and food scarce, the Japanese moved people in target areas—troops, Japanese civilians, and some 430 Chamorros from Tinian and Saipan—quartering them in interior villages. After bombing ended work at the airport, Yapese men returned to their own villages or, if these were in dangerous areas, to assigned locales.

The raid on Yap (along with Ulithi and Ngulu) at the end of March accompanied attacks on Palau and Woleai in support of landings at Aitape and Hollandia in the Southwest Pacific. Yap was bombed repeatedly in June, preventing its airfield from defending Guam and Saipan. After Americans built an air base on Ulithi in September 1944, Yap became a regular bombing target. Remarkably, no Yapese and only two Chamorros died of gunfire or starvation.[20]

While attention focused on airfields and seaplane bases harboring military threats, Americans also checked out each small island in the Carolines as they had in the Marshalls. Scouting planes swooped low to search for installations and draw fire from any Japanese guns. War memories on these peripheral islands take on a narrow focus but are nonetheless vivid. Often small incidents are remembered in intricate detail because of their singularity.

Most unfortified islands experienced only occasional flyovers, but American planes attacked even small Japanese garrisons and occasionally struck islands with no troops at all. Infrequently, Islanders were killed and wounded. On Mokil, southeast of Pohnpei, bombing and strafing by U.S. planes scattered people throughout the atoll's three islets (they had previously lived on only one); they paddled back to the main islet at night to get taro (Bentzen

Photo 5. One-thousand-pound bomb being prepared on Ulithi for an attack on Yap, August 1945. (U.S. Navy photo, National Archives photo no. 80-G-347493)

1949:94). Mokilese remember an American plane dropping a leaflet telling them to move away from the village. Mistranslating the message, they stayed put, and two people were killed by strafing. Mokil was probably hit fairly often because of the many flights attacking Pohnpei that were often disoriented or turned back by weather conditions.

No Japanese were stationed on Nukuoro or Sapwuahfik (Ngatik), south of Pohnpei. During the war, however, a Japanese plane was downed close to Nukuoro and the pilot was rescued by local people. Perhaps spotting the wreckage, an American plane passing over the island one day bombed and strafed it. Although no one was killed, the bombs did lasting damage to the island's freshwater lens. Sapwuahfik had wartime visitors of another sort: friendly Americans. Since the massacre of the island's aboriginal men in 1837 and its subsequent repopulation by Micronesians and Europeans, the people of Sapwuahfik have been known for their sense of affiliation with Americans and use of English pidgin. Seeing American warplanes flying overhead after bombing

Pohnpei, someone, it is said, wrote with coconut palm leaves on the beach, in English, "No Japanese on island." American planes would occasionally land in the lagoon, exchanging food, cigarettes, and clothing for local handicrafts and seashells. Sometimes they dropped large tins of corned beef. "In Ngatik people made a joke: the planes dropped food at Ngatik; they dropped bombs at Pohnpei" (Vic Edwin; see Poyer 1989). Nevertheless, a few people were hurt by strafing.

In the central Carolines, the Japanese base at Satawan was bombed heavily and repeatedly, and the unfortified Mortlock Islands were also routinely bombed and strafed. Namoluk's only encounter with Japanese military, though, was when fifty men from a ship torpedoed near Kapingamarangi reached Namoluk in two lifeboats in 1942. The only U.S. attack was in 1944, with three bombs hitting the reef and a sailing canoe strafed; there were no injuries. As on many other outer islands, the greatest impact on Namoluk was the death or injury of Namoluk men conscripted for war work elsewhere (Marshall 1972:37).

Isolated atolls farther west were seldom attacked, and then usually by accident. The only Japanese installations on the atolls of the western Carolines were at Woleai and Puluwat. Woleai was a frequent target of air raids, including an aerial mining run by Australian planes in April 1944. American B-24s bombed the Woleai airfield daily at 10 A.M. for fifteen months, and Task Force 58 ended its late March 1944 carrier attack on the western Carolines with a strike on Woleai. The few Micronesians who remained as workers, like the Japanese defenders, suffered more from disease and hunger than from the predictable bombings intended to keep the field unusable. Most Woleai people had moved to Ifaluk, which was occasionally attacked.[21] Tobi, which held a small Japanese garrison, suffered only one bombing raid (either American or British, depending on the story); and, according to Tobians, this one need not have taken place had an overzealous Japanese sergeant obeyed his superior's order to refrain from firing on the lone plane that patrolled daily from the new American base at Peleliu (Black 1977:92). The Japanese installation at Puluwat was on the American target list, but Puluwat men working for the Japanese there escaped harm (Ochs and Toarus n.d.:24). Unfortified Pulusuk, where most Puluwat people lived during the war, suffered an attack when an American bomber crew dumped its load when they found themselves lost 70 miles west of Chuuk, without enough gas to return to the planned course

Photo 6. U.S. attack on Woleai airstrip, March 29–30, 1944. (U.S. Navy photo, National Archives photo no. 80-G-045318)

(Craven and Cate 1950:681). Taken completely by surprise, twenty-four Pulusuk people were wounded or killed.

Allied bombing raids continued until the Japanese surrender.[22] In October 1944, a new phase of the "passive war" arrived with the use of high-altitude B-29s, nearly invisible to the naked eye (Denfeld 1981a:49–51). In 1945, the Allies used the islands for target practice for training and to experiment with new types of bombs. While the danger and significance of bombing to the American attackers lessened with each passing month, conditions for those on the ground steadily deteriorated.

Patriots and Volunteers

As war continued, Micronesians on the bypassed islands increasingly turned away from the Japanese cause. The store of loyalty built up during the colonial era proved insufficient in the face of military harshness, continual air raids, and severe food shortages, and in places it turned to strong resentment and hatred of the Japanese military (Peattie 1988:300–303).

Nonetheless, we must acknowledge courageous Islanders who stepped forward in response to calls to support the emperor. In retrospect (and perhaps even at the time), Micronesians are of two minds about this service. Though bitter at the suffering and loss of life and what they see as deceit in Japanese recruiting practices, still they take pride in the bravery they showed. The U.S. government has publicly honored men who served as "scouts" assisting U.S. forces during the Pacific War. Micronesians who served imperial military efforts were not honored publicly by Japan at war's end, but their lives should not be forgotten.

That their commitment was real cannot be doubted, seeing the risks that they were willing to run. When four boatloads of Marshallese left Pingelap islet in Jaluij to escape to waiting American ships, some Marshallese remained, "Because they really believed in the Japanese. They were not enthusiastic about leaving them. They really liked the Japanese" (Joseph Jibon). Micronesians served the Japanese military directly as lookouts and quasi-military servicemen of various sorts; as loyalists who passed information and enforced local security rules; or rarely and most dramatically as recruited members of the military services (described in chapter 4). Of course, the labor that Micronesians did, the foods they produced, the self-control they displayed, and the hardships they suffered were also a form of service, albeit often unwilling, to the emperor. The Japanese openly acknowledged and actively supported the metaphorical interpretation of Micronesians' work as "fighting." Netek Rewein, when asked whether Chuukese were forced to work for the Japanese or were willing to do so, answered: "It wasn't because we were willing to, but they told us, 'You must strive in your work because the war is for you.'"

Referring to his labor on potato farms and airport construction, Raphael Gisog recalls Yapese being indoctrinated with the idea that "my tools are my guns"—that work was their way of assisting the war effort. They were to approach it as fighters; their working day was to be like a day of battle; "anything that comes in front of you, goes, with your tools." When he was hurt in an explosion in Chuuk while fishing with dynamite, Kalifin Kofak remembers the Japanese boss who came to take the injured men out of the boat saying to him, "Try your best to hang on, because you are a soldier. Even though you are a laborer, today you are a soldier. If you die, where the soldiers are buried, you will be buried." When a Chuukese coworker died of his injuries, he was buried in the soldiers' cemetery, despite Kofak's request that his body be returned to his home island. The Japanese refused, saying, "If you've died as a soldier, it's not necessary for your relatives to know that you're dead."

Japanese in charge of organizing Islanders spoke to workers in terms of "helping Tennō Heika [the emperor]." Alter Bedly recalls that if you were caught traveling on Pohnpei (he had gone to see his family) instead of doing agricultural work, "you were taken to the boss. He would ask you why— didn't you care about making food for the soldiers, didn't you care about helping Tennō Heika? You had to stand at attention when talking about him. They told you not to go around without a care, but to help the soldiers, help build Tennō Heika's empire." Oska Seiola (Pohnpei) noted the line between cruelty and patriotic hard work: "During the war, some soldiers were kind and some were not. The cruel ones, if you did not say 'hai' (yes) to them, they would beat you up, but they also respected those who worked for them, for it meant that they were working for Tennō Heika."

Micronesians were quick to recognize the paradox of being "third-class citizens" expected to serve as loyally as Japanese. Ichios Eas (Chuuk) comments that he was "supposed to be a soldier" but did such unsoldierly work as digging holes and bunkers or placing guns: "They made it sound like we were soldiers, but that's what we did." Some were able to turn Japanese ideology to their advantage in securing better working conditions. Aten Niesik (then assistant chief of Udot, Chuuk) used Japanese nationalism to defend a man who had fought with a higher-ranking soldier. As munitions workers in Japan work for the emperor, he argued, so do Chuukese make their war contribution:

When I answered, I said back to them, "What about Tennō Heika's message? The one that we say every day: "We are Tennō Heika's soldiers." What about us—aren't we Tennō Heika's soldiers? Are only you Japanese people Tennō Heika's soldiers? We are the grip of Tennō Heika's gun, Tennō Heika's people. We are not English soldiers or American soldiers, but Tennō Heika's people. So why is there a separation between soldiers and us? . . . If you are at war, and you don't have the grip of the gun, you will be lost. Us, we don't make things like guns and bullets, we just farm, plant potato fields, and grow fruit.

They said, "You're right. We're the same, you and us." So, that time I won.

Aitel Bisalen also argued with his Japanese boss when he worked as a foreman on Chuuk—but with a different outcome:

One time, I was called to the office. I was a bit late after lunch—all the workers went back to work and I was putting the food away. I didn't expect the Japanese to get upset, because I was one of the bosses. I went down, and my boss [who was Japanese] scolded me: "Why are you late?" "Because I was putting the food away." I told him, "I don't care whether I'm late or not because we both work for money. You work for money, and I work for money also." And that guy said, "No, that's not the way it's supposed to be," because we work to help the Japanese so they will win the war. I said, "Do you mean the few minutes that I was late will make the Japanese lose the war?" Then my boss came and slapped my face. He grabbed me and pushed me toward the office, and we both fell down on the boat [they were on the dock at Toloas]. I was on top, and I was pushing him down into the boat. When I was on top of him, my uncle (my mother's brother) came—he saw another Japanese coming with a stick to beat me—my uncle came in time and pushed that other Japanese, and he fell down. I was lucky; if my uncle hadn't been there, they would have beaten me up. Some of the Chuukese came and stopped us all from fighting [he and his uncle were both fighting with the Japanese]. I told that Japanese I was fighting, "I could take away your life, kill you."

Mr. Bisalen was reported to the office; he was beaten by the police and his head was shaved.

Many Palauans, part of the region most fully acculturated to Japanese ideals, continued enthusiastic support of the Japanese throughout the war. Eighty young men were enlisted in the Patriotic Shock Corps, named after a Japanese squad that counterattacked American forces on Palau in late September 1944 (Higuchi 1991). Volunteer Timarong Adelbert recalls that his *sonchō* selected ten young men for the group, stating: "This is for our country. Please do your best to help the Japanese. If Palau will be occupied by the U.S., everybody will be killed. If we can win, we can take Omote-Nanyō [Pacific Islands except Micronesia]." They were given spears and trained for six months.[23]

Many Palauans who belonged to these units believe they were training to attack the Americans in Peleliu. Yet Higuchi (1987, 1991) maintains that the Japanese command did not envision Palauans actually fighting. Rather, the training was part of Japanese educational policy, meant to boost morale and maintain discipline over young Palauan men.

THE INVASION OF WESTERN MICRONESIA

The Northern Marianas first came under attack preparatory to the Enewetak invasion and again following the February 1944 raid on Chuuk. These attacks crippled Japanese air power in the area. After Allied successes in eastern Micronesia, the Marianas became the defensive frontier of the Japanese homeland, and the new imperial plan, "A-Go," sought a decisive naval battle in the western islands. But improvements in American submarine warfare made it difficult to fortify the Marianas sufficiently for the new Japanese "absolute national defense sphere" to hold. The rapid American advance through Micronesia forced the Japanese to rush reinforcements to the region, but many supply and transport ships were destroyed en route (Shaw, Nalty, and Turnbladh 1966:220–221). Evacuation of the 43,000 Japanese civilians in the islands, begun in 1943, was stepped up, but most late evacuees died when transports were torpedoed. In the end, over 10,000 Japanese, 2,300 Chamorros, 1,300 Koreans, and nearly 900 Carolinians remained to face the invasion (Peattie 1988:286).

In February 1944, troops poured into Saipan and all efforts turned to defensive fortification. Japanese civilians and Chamorros participated in military labor until nonessential workers were ordered inland. The invasion of Saipan on June 15, 1944, was the first major land battle on a Micronesian high island. Defenders fought to stop the Americans at the water's edge, then fell back to the central spine of mountains. With Japan's air support destroyed in the Battle of the Philippine Sea, defenders were squeezed into the northern part of Saipan, where they made a final counterattack—but the battle was over; there remained only the final horrifying scenes of Japanese civilian suicides at Marpi Point. By this time, the majority of Saipan's civilians had already surrendered or were still in hiding; when they were taken into U.S. custody, most suffered from hunger and disease. In addition to Japanese, Korean, and

Okinawan civilians, the Saipan invasion gave Americans their first experience in dealing with large numbers of Micronesians in conquered territory (described in chapter 7).[24]

By the time of the Marianas invasions, Guamanians no less than other Micronesians were laboring on Japanese war projects. The first air raid in February 1944 renewed their confidence in American rescue and drove Japanese to increased defensive preparations. In March, the small navy garrison that had ruled Guam since invasion was swamped by the incoming Japanese army defense force. Food and labor quotas increased. Women and children worked in fields of sweet potatoes, corn, taro, and tapioca; men worked at airstrips, roads, and military installations, where "they were slapped, kicked, punished and clubbed by Japanese and Korean supervisors. Guamanians worked side by side with hundreds of Korean laborers, who received better treatment than the Guamanians"; yet, as everywhere, some Japanese are remembered for their kindness during these times (Apple 1980:39–40; Carano and Sanchez 1964:290).

Japanese on Guam prepared for invasion as the Saipan operation brought heavy bombardment. In July, Guamanians were ordered away from the coasts to inland camps. Men continued to be called out day or night for military labor; conditions were miserable, and most Guamanians believed they had been gathered into camps to be killed by the Japanese. Perhaps the Japanese intended the camps to shield Chamorros from American bombardment, or to ensure that they did not aid the invaders. In any case, forced concentration into relatively safe areas inland guaranteed the protection of Chamorros during the invasion.

As American forces approached, Guamanians were treated as the enemy by some Japanese soldiers: "The breakdown of Japanese military morale and discipline was manifested in numerous mindless atrocities against Chamorros" (Rogers 1995:178), including unprovoked killings, rapes, and the torture and death of a Spanish priest. At Fena, some thirty Chamorros hiding in a cave were machine-gunned and then stabbed by angry Japanese. Survivors hid behind the dead. On July 15, thirty men and women from Merizo were forced into caves outside the village and attacked with hand grenades and bayonets. The next day, Japanese killed another group of Merizo men. Men from Merizo who had been removed to camps learned of the massacres and retaliated

Photo 7. U.S. Marines in urban fighting; Guam, August 1944. (U.S. Navy photo, National Archives photo no. 80-G-241223)

by attacking Japanese guards at the camp, then chasing troops from the village, "making Merizo the first village on Guam to be liberated, and the only one liberated by the Chamorros themselves" (Rogers 1995:181).[25]

The invasion of Guam took place on July 21, preceded by enormous air and naval bombardment. Chamorros remaining near the coast took refuge where they could. Peering from a cave holding about fifty relatives and friends, Joe Pangelinan said, "all I could see was fire" (Palomo 1984:197). Agana was destroyed, perhaps unnecessarily. The number of Chamorros killed or wounded during the battle is not accurately known, but it was well over six hundred (Rogers 1995:194). With many Guamanians in interior camps, U.S. Marines did not encounter them until several days after the invasion, when they met those who had overcome guards or simply walked out when guards fled. "All were eager to guide us to where others of their countrymen were held, to fight by our sides, to be of help in any way they could" (Hough 1947:284). Chamorro men joined American troops in the battle and mopping up. The

Photo 8. Native military government patrol on Guam searching for
remaining Japanese troops, early 1945. (U.S. Navy photo, National Archives
photo no. 80-G-329467)

Americans declared organized resistance on Guam ended on August 10, 1944,
though thousands of Japanese troops remained.

For Americans, victory in the Marianas opened the way to East Asia. The
U.S. Army Air Corps began preparing Marianas bases for air strikes against Japan. The navy planned invasions of Peleliu, Angaur, and Ulithi, followed by
the Philippines and Taiwan (Rogers 1995:194–195). Japan had thought since
spring of 1944 that Palau would soon be an invasion target, since the Combined Fleet had moved there from Chuuk in February, and Americans had
targeted Palau's Airiai Airfield and Malakal Harbor at the end of March 1944.
Now, the loss of Saipan and Tinian changed Japan's defensive picture once
again. Japanese high command pulled back to the Philippines, "making the
Palaus expendable" and completely isolated after the summer of 1944 (Peattie
1988:291). Americans bombed Palau again in June, in late August, and in early
September, targeting Koror and Babelthuap.

A Palauan account describes the confusion as Japanese and Micronesians fled to the Rock Islands for shelter:

> So it was early in the morning, one day in March, and then there were a lot of airplanes all over Palau, and there was a lot of confusion. And we were at the time expecting some reinforcements from Japan, from Saipan, to prepare for the United States attack, so there was a lot of confusion as to whether they were the enemy planes or Japanese planes. And then they started bombing and strafing, and my father didn't have time to come back to help us. So my mother and about eight children (I was about ten or eleven years of age at that time) we just put together some empty drums and then some belongings, some food, blankets, stuff like that. And then we just made a platform for our food, clothing, and then we drifted. We started to swim across the channel, looking for some island, some rock-island hideout. Because the bombs were falling over the place. And my father was not there, so it was the oldest son, the male in the family, who was myself. And so we sculled together under some rock-island overhang, and in the water, all night, all day, all night. (Nero 1989:125–126)

Most Palauans were well clear of the invasion of Peleliu and Angaur—though not clear of the hardships of war. Koror was evacuated after its destruction by repeated air attacks. Colonel Nakagawa, in charge of the Japanese army on Peleliu, had begun to move the five hundred or so Islanders living there north to Koror as soon as his regiment landed. They spent the next months in Ngaraard and Ngeremlengui villages on Babelthuap. Some Peleliu people remember American leaflets telling people to leave before the invasion of September 1944; they used their own vessels to get to Babelthuap. By the time of invasion, all but about three hundred Palauans were on Babelthaup, where remaining Japanese civilians also concentrated. So Peleliu, one of the most bitterly contested actions of the Pacific War, had little direct impact on Islanders. But the attack (September–November 1944) included destruction of shipping and mining of Palau's channels. In addition, the Japanese defeat and the death of Admiral Koga (who, as commander of the Combined Fleet succeeding Admiral Yamamoto, had set up his headquarters in Palau) transformed the conditions under which Micronesians in Palau lived the rest of the war.[26] The new American airfields at Peleliu and Angaur supported the regular bombings that became part of life on Palau, as on the other bypassed islands: "It became a daily ritual, kind of. . . . They were coming hourly, so we couldn't go fishing, we couldn't farm. If we did, there was the plane. So that gave us a hard time. So we farmed at nighttime, in the moonlight" (Nero 1989:129).

As elsewhere in Micronesia, starvation even more than bombing became the enemy for soldier and civilian alike. "There was no refuge; the Palauans were reduced to living like wild people in the forest, foraging for food, sheltering in huts and holes" (Nero 1989:117). Under these conditions, escape began to seem necessary and possible to some whose enthusiasm for the Japanese and their cause had begun to wane. As in the Marshall Islands, Palauans undertook, cautiously, to slip through to American-held territory. Most of the two hundred Chamorros and some Palauans on Babelthuap escaped. Perhaps the most famous escape was that of Oikawasang (Joseph Tellei), a Palauan leader highly regarded by the Japanese administration, who fled with his wife Josefa to Peleliu via Angaur.[27] Itpik Martin Ruwutei was another Palauan who escaped with some Japanese soldiers:

One month later when Oikawasang escaped to the U.S. ship, I was taking fish with the Japanese soldiers. Their names were Suzuki, Yamauchi and Araki. We discussed: "Let's go to [Peleliu] because we have no more food." "No, if we go there by ship they should attack us." "No, no, if we show a [white] flag we can do it." Only Araki refused strongly. We almost started to fight. When we were 300 m distance from Aimeliik, Araki insisted on swimming to Aimeliik and jumped into the ocean. We went to Peleliu. One small Kuchikukan (destroyer) was near [Peleliu]. We took off our Fundoshi (loincloth) and put it on a bamboo pole. We raised it and moved close to the Kuchikukan. That night there was a full moon. The sky was very clear, no clouds. It was almost 6:00 pm. We waited in the shadow of a rock island until 7:00 because we were afraid to go out until it was dark. At 7:00 the moon showed light. We waved our flag and moved close to the ship. The U.S. ship showed Sinkaito [a searchlight] to us and someone invited us by showing a white flag. We moored our boat alongside the U.S. destroyer. [Then] the U.S. sailors dropped a [ladder] and two of them came down to our boat. Many [soldiers] held guns at the ready. I was so scared. I thought I would be killed by their guns. I believed I could oppose them. They checked our naked [bodies] except Fundoshi. They gestured us to come aboard their ship. We had only glasses for fishing and piskan (spear). We didn't have guns. Three of us were disinfected by DDT and were injected in our [buttocks]. I remembered what sisters in Catholic Kindergarten said: "If we surrender, the foreign soldiers will [never] kill us." (Higuchi n.d.; bracketed words correct misspellings in unpublished typescript)

In a final expression of the American island-hopping strategy, Ulithi, Fais, and Ngulu were invaded, while the rest of the western Caroline Islands were bypassed. Ulithians had had some news of the war when men and women were conscripted for work at Yap's southern airstrip, the few civilian Japanese evacuated, and a Japanese ship sunk. The atoll had first been scouted by American planes in 1943. Mistaken about Japanese strength (Ulithi held only a lightly manned weather station), the U.S. attacked it several times in mid-1944, once strafing three Ulithi men fishing in canoes. American plans called for Ulithi to become a naval base, and it was taken in September 1944 with no opposition. On the first day, though Islanders were warned to stay out of the danger zone, the chief's daughter Klara was hit by shrapnel and died aboard a U.S. hospital ship (Cusenbery 1946:27; Lessa 1950).

American forces immediately began to move base facilities forward from Enewetak to Ulithi (USSBS 1946:275). Ulithi people were moved to the islet of Fasserai, and the Americans used the rest of the atoll for military activities and recreation. The Ulithi base launched air attacks on Yap and other western islands and housed the fleet that would invade Okinawa. Now in relative safety themselves, Ulithians continued to worry about relatives on other islands. They were also getting to know Americans for the first time, and were mutually engaged with the U.S. Navy in constructing a sentimental myth—one that would be replayed in other Micronesian theaters—about tropical paradises and high-tech warriors.

After airfields at Ulithi and Peleliu and the Ulithi naval base secured American control of the western Micronesian air and sea, and while the final stages of the battle for Peleliu still raged, the Pacific battle line moved west. The front had now left Micronesia behind—but the war remained.

Chapter 6

LIFE ON THE BYPASSED ISLANDS

BY THE END of 1944 the invasion of the Philippines was underway and the Central Pacific front had moved on toward Iwo Jima and Okinawa, leaving nearly sixty thousand Japanese military on the bypassed islands, along with thousands of Korean, Okinawan, and Japanese workers and civilians, as well as Islanders. Bases in unconquered Micronesia retained a theoretical chain of command headquartered on Chuuk. But, for these isolated islands, the Pacific command structure was impotent (Peattie 1988:303). Offensive action was impossible and defensive activity less feasible with every air raid. Japanese officers turned their attention to preserving the troops they had from despair and starvation. Micronesians faced the same challenges, and in addition, they began to reevaluate their understanding of the Japanese and of the war.

FOOD SHORTAGES AND CONSTRAINTS ON CONSUMPTION

It was as if I had closed my eyes—and when
I opened them again, everything was gone.

Military historians point to the Allied war against merchant shipping as an important factor in weakening Japanese power. Certainly life became much harder for Micronesians after "the seas closed" (as Marshallese say). As early as 1941, imports to many areas had ceased and local markets shut down. Some 17 percent of army supplies shipped from Japan were sunk in 1943, 30 percent in 1944, and 50 percent in 1945. In mid-1945 Japan stopped supplying distant ground forces, concentrating instead on defense of Japan itself—but by then many areas were receiving few if any shipments.[1] The Islanders' standard of living, "which had been gradually changing for the better since 1919, sharply declined" (Embree 1946b:62). Shortages of food and goods—next to the loss of loved ones, physical suffering, and fear—are a hallmark of this era. As Bernard Behris of Pohnpei recalls, "The Japanese didn't care for the people during the war. For example: It was as if I had closed my eyes—and when I opened them again, everything was gone—there was no more rice, clothes, kerosene."

As the Japanese military prepared for siege, they took control not only of Islanders' land and buildings, but of all crops; in places they even managed wild foods and marine products. Malnutrition and hard labor increased susceptibility to disease. The defensive preparations described in chapter 4 drew Islanders into increased military labor demands. While food grew scarce, working conditions deteriorated. "This was the time that we felt hardships," Anko Billy says of Kosrae after the first American bombing. Construction, farming, and service jobs continued, without pay and often without food. On Uman in Chuuk lagoon, Kisiuou Nua worked in a military mess, "but all the food was for the soldiers, we weren't allowed to eat it." So, he says, "We would cook food every day for the soldiers—and steal some." Eventually, Kalifin Kofak (Chuuk) recalls being given only "leaves and water" at lunchtime.

Prudent Japanese had warned people to plant extra gardens and stock up on consumer goods. Masuko Luhk Karen recalls: "Some Japanese told the Pohnpeians to prepare, for example to buy cloth. But some Pohnpeians, including myself, didn't believe them. There were a lot of clothes in the store; I wondered who would buy all of them. But when the war came, we did encounter hardship."

As goods disappeared, local economies broke down. In the Marshalls, Thaddeus Sampson continued to receive pay as an interpreter after imports became scarce. "At first, when we got paid, we used to shop for t-shirts and a little bit of food. But then things went on and we were rationed food and they said, be cautious with the rice because it will only last until it is exhausted." On Pohnpei, where people had relied on selling produce to Japanese, marketing stopped and businesses closed. On Chuuk, those who had money and lived near stores stocked up as supplies dwindled and prices rose. Store supplies may also have been set aside for military use, as Sontak Kansou suggests about cloth: "When the war began, they kept the goods for the soldiers." On Toloas, people used scrip to get cigarettes—the only thing available—at the last open store. By the time Yapese were working on military projects, village stores had shut down and those in Colonia had meager supplies of staples such as rice and cigarettes. Bombings targeting urban areas further destroyed stocks. After stores emptied, scarce goods circulated through trade, kin, and friendship links. The only other source was chance, as when boxes of C-rations or drums of kerosene floated ashore or a rare contact with an Allied submarine crew or flier brought in rations, soap, or cigarettes.

Food stores were never exhausted on the invaded Marshall Islands, Ulithi, and Angaur, because battles there were swift and decisive—and American largesse then replaced Japanese sources. In the Marianas as well, invasion came well before people faced serious shortages. Imports were scarce, and Guam saw malnutrition after a drought early in 1944, but adequate food for the Marianas was assured by turning fields from export to subsistence crops (Bowers 1950:47; Rogers 1995:176). Strict rationing and scarcity were most keenly felt in bypassed areas—from centers like Chuuk, Pohnpei, Kosrae, and Jaluij to uninvaded Rota and Pagan (Peattie 1988:304) and small outlying atolls.

Ronald Spector writes that among the less obvious horrors of the war "are the thousands of other deaths from famine and disease caused by the crushing demands of the locust-like Japanese war machine upon the fragile economies of the countries that it occupied" (1985:xv–xvi). Indeed, many Micronesians did suffer from the Japanese military presence, but Allied blockading and bombing also intensified hardships. In Chuuk, a war-era song by Michi captures this experience in its lyrics: "We survived on the leftovers of *Pishishantai*," a Japanese work group on Weno. Where "leftovers" were not enough, Micronesians died. Stories of cannibalism and threats of genocide arose in the Marshalls, Chuuk, Kosrae, and elsewhere when food scarcity peaked. The greatest disparity between human needs and local resources occurred in the bypassed Marshalls and Chuuk.

Bypassed Marshall Islands

Although atolls have more limited space and resources than high islands, only a few Micronesian atolls held excessive populations during the war. Where there were few or no troops, such as Arno and Lib, prewar subsistence remained intact, though people lacked imports and in some cases worked extra time to supply a nearby garrison. But on the crowded bases at Wotje, Mili, Ma-loelap and Jaluij, scarcity hit hard after supply lines were cut and reserves dwindled.[2] Micronesian laborers shared the soldiers' diet, increasingly short of familiar imports. "There was no rice, beware lest you even talk about rice. There was not even a single grain."

Though no large shipments reached the bypassed islands after January 1944, Imperial Headquarters had tried to supply its Micronesian garrisons with six months' to a year's worth of provisions, and three submarines reached Mili in the first months after American invasion. Rationing (begun as early as May 1943 on Jaluij) came in earnest when Kwajalein fell, disrupting the re-gional supply system. A Kiribati cook who escaped from Mili in May 1944 re-ported that the food situation was fine, with soldiers receiving three meals a day (Morison 1951:309). But this was not to remain the case. Not only did sur-veillance from new American bases block resupply, but constant air attacks napalmed gardens and prevented lagoon travel or use of marine resources. Asked whether life on Maloelap grew difficult as time went on, Nathan Tartios answered: "Well, things were difficult on account of food, but it was still okay. We ate coconut and fish, we fished every day. We ate breadfruit also. The Jap-anese on Maloelap had not yet begun to hate our eating as they did on the other atolls; we still ate breadfruit, we still made arrowroot, they did not hate us if we made these things. But we also made food for them. We helped the Japanese soldiers."

Commanders of the vulnerable bases learned from Marshallese how to make local foods and accustomed their troops to the taste. (But the Japanese disliked pungent fermented breadfruit: "If there was preserved breadfruit they would say, 'What is it? Who brought all this shit?'") Such preparation paid off for the small garrison on Ronglap. Once imports stopped, Japanese there ate from their gardens, excelled at fishing, and learned to make and appreciate Marshallese foods such as arrowroot and coconut toddy ("Sometimes they were much better at making coconut toddy than we were").

Japanese commanders also responded to shortages by dispersing soldiers and civilians throughout an atoll's islets. At Mili the bulk of the garrison was quartered on other islets after air raids destroyed half the food supply (USSBS 1947a:49). Soldiers and Marshallese sent food to the main garrison by boat or outrigger, often at night, as long as U.S. planes allowed. On Wotje, local residents fared relatively well when evacuated to outer islets to fend for themselves. The people of Jaluij, however, were organized into work groups to exploit their own resources to feed Japanese troops, who made motorboat rounds of the islets to bring supplies to their base at Imiej. "It was extraordinarily difficult to conduct life with the Japanese—it was really oppressive," Bwirre Lejmen recalls of that time, with threats of execution for failure to meet quotas.

As an example of the situation on the smaller islets of a garrisoned atoll, Pingelap islet in Jaluij was occupied by two camps of six or seven hundred Japanese soldiers, one on each side of the Marshallese: "We were in the middle of them and they watched us." The garrison controlled food production, forwarding to the main base supplies of coconut toddy and toffee, pickled clams, salt fish, dried fish, ripe coconuts, breadfruit, and fish taken by dynamiting (much of the work was done by soldiers). On the islet, says Bwirre Lejmen, meager allotments were redistributed: "Each person was rationed food, one coconut, to split open and slice into strips and combine it with a little salt and eat it along with coconut syrup. Well, they dipped it in the coconut syrup, and ate it, and drank."

Marshallese stretched their rations by scavenging, cooking a pot of anything edible—fish, leaves, fallen unripe breadfruit, hard coconut crab legs, "all sorts of stuff they kept and made soup with." Some work bosses shared the pot among Japanese and Islanders. People were permitted to fish and scavenge freely, but could not harvest food except under supervision—"It was illegal for you, personally, to climb and harvest a breadfruit or throw down a drinking coconut; they would shoot you." Eating was prohibited—"tabu"—says Elson Ebel. "The Japanese hated it if we ate. They held onto the food and kept it from us, and there were many people who were hungry and died." On Mili, food was considered Japanese property and was carefully allotted to Islanders. Elson Ebel adds: "No one could say 'eat.' If you were caught [with something, it meant] you had stolen. You had to give everything to the Japanese." Friday was food ration day, "But Monday and every other day, the foods were only for them, the Japanese. The Marshallese and the Koreans ate on Fridays, and then you would save things up during the other times."

When John Ezekiel was called in to share a meal at military headquarters in Jaluij, he learned that the commander was eating the same poor food as the Marshallese. In fact, despite (or perhaps because of) the harsh discipline, Jaluij was the safest of these atolls on which to pass these perilous months. In dramatic contrast to the thousands of deaths from malnutrition and disease among troops and foreign laborers on the other bypassed atolls, Jaluij had no starvation and adequate living conditions and medical care, largely due to effective leadership. The Japanese admiral in his dying statement "boasted that no one had starved on his atoll"—no small achievement (USSBS 1947a:50).

Under such strict rationing, explains Bwirre Lejmen, Marshallese began to steal their own crops, despite the fact that theft was a capital offense under military rule:

> The way that you would eat is to wait for night and, if you knew how to steal, you could remain alive a while longer. You would climb a coconut with a husking stick, and you would have to hide the husks up in the fronds, but you would drink the coconut and climb down and [act as if nothing had happened]. Breadfruit: You would climb the breadfruit tree, and you needed to see which breadfruit were nearby, because soldiers were on guard under the coconuts and breadfruits and pandanus. The only thing was, the Japanese were blind at night. We would see them, they would be standing there, but we would climb, climb, and seize the thing we were after.

On Pingelap islet (Jaluij), people evaded the Japanese sentries, distracting them on their scheduled rounds while confederates grabbed tree crops. People hid cooking fires or buried stolen food beneath a legitimate fire for cooking rations or husked coconuts and buried them at night to eat the next morning. "You could not just hide the sprouted coconuts under fallen coconut fronds," says Bwirre Lejmen, "you had to dig holes, for if they saw them, they would take their knife and slit your throat. Difficult, your life was difficult."

The desperate scarcity gave rise to frightening stories, like this one from Lele Ram: "Well, we do not know because we had distanced ourselves from them [Japanese soldiers], but we heard that they ate people. They ate the Koreans, they killed the Koreans and consumed them, that's how far it went; their food supplies were exhausted." Such rumors were not unfounded. The U.S. Strategic Bombing Survey (1947a:49–50) reports that on Wotje, Maloelap, and Mili, where almost four thousand soldiers and laborers died of malnutrition, the desperate turned to eating rats, grave robbing, and cannibalism.

Chuuk Lagoon

Unlike the Marshalls, where invasion relieved some islands from shortages and Islanders on others were able to escape to American lines, Chuukese lived the latter part of the war in complete isolation. The last Japanese convoy to Chuuk in May 1944 was sunk en route. The lagoon islands were made into a plantation to supply the thirty-eight thousand military and laborers who shared space with ten thousand Chuukese (Peattie 1988:304). Between air raids, boats carried food from islands devoted to agriculture to military centers. As in the bypassed Marshalls, Chuukese were forbidden to harvest their tree and garden crops; these and extensive fields of sweet potato were reserved for soldiers' use. Those who labored under military levies received rations: "If you worked [for the soldiers], you ate." Those who didn't, such as the elderly, weakened from lack of food.

Conditions on the islands of lagoon Chuuk varied from bad to intolerable.[3] The military confiscated food trees and gardens ("They just came to our house and told us not to take anything from our land because it was all theirs"). On heavily garrisoned islands, all available land was turned into potato fields. On Fefan, soldiers nailed confiscation notices to breadfruit and coconut trees. To receive a breadfruit ration, Islanders showed documents stamped by the civilian governor at distribution posts. Or, "They'd give us a small piece of plywood [with something written on it] to give to the officers to show we were permitted to climb a tree. But when we'd climb down from the tree, they'd beat us and take away the things we had gathered" (Resen). Even on lightly garrisoned Romonum, soldiers noted the owner of every bunch of bananas and rationed food strictly.

To feed themselves, Chuukese searched mangrove swamps for fallen coconuts, even if "spoiled and stinking." They turned to famine foods: grass shoots, leaves, young coconut trunks and fronds, morning glory and wild yam vines—bitter even after being boiled from morning until night: "Our excrement was like animal excrement from eating the leaves." On Uman, Ritok Ruben says, "The sign of our starvation is that we ate banana root mixed with a bit of rice. They rationed it out in a coconut shell: one person, one shellful." When bombs fell in the lagoon, Chuukese gathered the dead and stunned fish—sometimes at the cost of their lives, as in the case of the Weno man whose raft hit a mine when he went for fish after an air raid. (The Japanese forbade people to enter the water, "but because of the starvation we did not pay attention to them. We wanted to eat fish, so we thought we would survive.") Those who got rations at work were in some cases able to bring them home to share. Sometimes Japanese civilians traded potatoes with Chuukese for fish. Even after food was found, cooking was a problem, since fires were forbidden.

On Weno, Toloas, and Uman, shortages reached starvation levels for the ill, elderly, and very young; but on Fefan, Tol, and Udot, people were able to control at least some of their own food. On Udot, which seems to have had the best situation, strong chiefs cooperated with the Japanese and in turn got concessions for an organized food distribution. Chief Nero in Sapota village, Tol, organized a store of ripe coconuts before bombings began and arranged for men to gather and preserve breadfruit at night. A Tol chief traveled to petition a Japanese officer, who allotted nine breadfruits/person/day in season and a hundred fallen copra/family/week. People ate only this and the small crabs that the Japanese did not eat; but Tol people were not forced to famine foods such as the vines eaten on Weno. (Yet it is said that on Tol soldiers stopped giving the elderly their share of food "because they were useless, because they couldn't work.")

Elites had privileged access to food, and some held onto subsistence plots. The European-Chuukese Narrhun family on Uman received a small allotment of fish and rice for a time. On Tol, Echen Nakamura lived with the Mori family, whose leaders planned carefully to support them all. Ms. Nakamura says, "We were really starving, but thanks to God we weren't really starving. Why we were hungry was because the taro was spoiled. We couldn't eat it any more. It [the corms] just broke apart, so we just grated it, cooked it, and ate it. Then it is just like the banana trunk. The men made their tuba, and it came out all right. For that, we give thanks to God, because we ate grated taro with tuba."

Because of a large garrison and strict enforcement of food control, Weno experienced the worst conditions in Chuuk lagoon. Keke Tawe, then a military worker, comments that the Japanese "no longer thought that we were humans, so they treated us like animals. That's why they didn't care if we didn't eat." Here, according to Ichios Eas, there was no shared food distribution with the Japanese: "If the Chuukese got taro or breadfruit or coconuts, we were not only beaten up, but we were treated like thieves." Konstantin Enik adds: "They put up signs with numbers on them that said, 'This land belongs to the soldiers.' So when we came to take coconuts or breadfruit from those trees, they saw us and said they would shoot us, because those trees didn't belong to us, they belonged to them."

In rare cases, a Weno person could establish helpful trade relations with soldiers. Katin Nikkichiinnap recalled that even during the scarcity following the fall of the Marianas he got food from a Japanese military food storage cave, with permission of a soldier living with one of his relatives. In exchange, he provided coconut toddy for the soldiers (King and Carucci 1984:498). All of Weno became farmland, but that was not enough. Children died, and "some were divorced because of the hunger," as men abandoned their wives to feed themselves.[4]

In the end, forced by near-total confiscation of local food resources, Chuukese lived on what they stole, under threat of jail, abuse, and death. People stole at night, straightforwardly, by complex ruses, or by using magic to confuse guards; they stole from each other and from Japanese storehouses, but most of all they "stole" from their own confiscated gardens and trees. Young men tied coconut leaves to their arms to signal each other that they intended a stealing expedition. On Patta, men told to gather breadfruit for the Japanese threw it down into the brush, where they later collected it for themselves. Anang Samwel's work group had the job of guarding potato fields, so, he says, he was lucky—he was able to steal from them. Piara Esirom's husband, a policeman (away from home most of the time), would scold her: "He would tell me not to steal, for they might cut off my head if I got caught. . . . I would steal food, but I was scared, too. My children were hungry and they needed food." On Tatiw, Mieko Nipuk recalls that thieves would confess their sin to the priest, who told them that taking food from their own confiscated property was not theft. *Itang*, Chuuk's traditional leaders in war and magic, regained some of their former importance as they used their skills to plan tactics to evade food restrictions and preserve crops and fish from Japanese demands (Hall 1950:28).

As Chuukese became increasingly clever at theft, Japanese threats and punishments became more brutal. Stealing was seen as bad not only in itself, but as an act of treason: Istor Billimont says that though he was repeatedly punished for theft, he never admitted to it. He would have been killed, "because that meant I had shown disrespect to the soldiers by stealing their food." Perhaps more than on other bypassed islands, Japanese threats often became realities in Chuuk. Thieves were shamed, beaten, or imprisoned for stealing; at least four men on Weno were executed; and parents were punished for children's thefts. Osong Seleti of Romonum was one of the unfortunates caught stealing from his own gardens:

> I was going up to the mountains and tried to dig up this sweet taro of mine. Just then a Japanese soldier happened by and asked who I was, and I said I was Osong. He said, "Why are you stealing the boss' sweet taro?" I said, no, it belonged to me. Then he came and started hitting me. After awhile I ran away to town, away from the mountain. Then he hunted me down until he caught up with me. He took me up to the mountains, where he tied my hands and legs and proceeded to hang me about a foot and a half from the ground.
>
> Then the boss called his soldiers, and with a baseball bat they began taking turns hitting me ten times each. Ten hits for me from all the soldiers. I could not feel any more strength. I thought I was dying. Here, my bones were crushed to pieces. The flesh was hanging out of here. Then the boss said, "If anyone uses that latrine, then he should also hit Osong." So then, one went to the latrine and on his way he took the bat and hit me. On his way back, he did the same. At that time, I thought surely I was going to die. In the going to and from the latrine, my life was ebbing.
>
> At three o'clock I was taken down and untied. A brother of mine, Chipen, had to carry me because I was dying. A Chuukese man came and massaged me. I was vomiting blood while he was doing this! It took about three months before I could try walking in and out of our house. Then I began to get my strength back.

Mihne Mokok explained how her husband Akeisuk was punished: "That was the beginning of the time they started to make us suffer. They arrested him, tied his hands, and put him under the roosts of a chicken shed, where the chicken shit fell on his head." Mr. Mokok was imprisoned for four days and nights, beaten up, his scalp burned by cigarettes ("They used me for an ashtray"). Why? "Because when we had to harvest the potatoes, we took some and hid them so we could take them to our families." Another time, near the end of the war, he and others arrested for theft were forced to dig their own graves and were tied to a tree while the guards taunted them about the meaning of the holes they had dug.

Simako Onuson says that when a theft was discovered on Uman, the Japanese chose a woman from among the workers, tied her up, and stripped off her clothes: "And finally, they called the woman's brothers and started to beat her. But there was a fire underneath where they were hanging her up. When the brothers of the woman were in front of her, hanging there, they separated her legs apart." Ms. Onuson says she saw this happen several times: "Sometimes the women they hung up and beat, they were almost unconscious."

In the Marshall Islands, cannibalism rumors described Japanese troops eating Asian workers. In Chuuk, the widespread cannibalism story is that a Weno man named Nekiroch was killed by the Japanese and his flesh distributed in an experiment on the utility of eating human (i.e., Islander) flesh. Anisiro Aninis says, "Some of us knew that the Chuukese would be the meat with their potatoes"—that is, literally. In the story, Nekiroch was caught stealing food. The soldier who found him planned to take him to jail, but Nekiroch killed the soldier instead. Sachio Siwi, a Japanese-educated government worker, was part of the investigation, but cannot confirm the rumors of cannibalism: "Our office here [on Toloas] went there [Weno] to help investigate the case. I went there with some officials [police and military security]. So we went to investigate and there the Japanese found—they dug up the mud and they found the soldier's body. Then that was when they killed Nekiroch. I didn't know that they distributed the flesh to the soldiers to eat it. I only heard about it, but I never saw it. But I actually saw the body of the Japanese whom Nekiroch killed." A man who had been on Weno remembers: "Oh, yes, that fellow— Nekiroch. I believed that the Japanese ate his flesh, because I was in my work group when they brought us his flesh. I personally ate some, so I knew it wasn't animal meat. I tried and tried to chew on it but it was different so I threw it away. When I threw it away, those Japanese asked if I didn't like it, and I said no, because I didn't know what kind of meat that was. The Japanese said, 'It's your flesh.' They told me that it was the flesh of Nekiroch."

Other Caroline Islands

While Chuuk and isolated bases in the Marshalls suffered the most from food shortages, similar if less dramatic stories of deprivation come from other bypassed islands. Large numbers of troops, foreign laborers, and Islanders pressed hard on the resources even of the fertile island of Kosrae. Shortages were controlled by strict rationing, confiscating Kosraean farms and trees, and supervising fishing and food collecting. Kosraean families supplied quotas of food to a military collection point. Some military leaders were sensitive to the disruptions in local food production caused by land confiscation and relocation. Milton Timothy recalls that army work groups set quotas, "and whenever they ordered from us, they ordered less, because they knew that this was not our property where we were staying. So whenever they ordered, our contributions were the smallest."

As supplies ran low for Kosrae's swollen population, traditional crops were overexploited, new crops were harvested prematurely, and all became depleted. Malnutrition and disease set in, following the hierarchy of food distribution. The Japanese were fed first; the best food, including all large fish and most other protein, went to officers. Enlisted men and Korean and Okinawan laborers received less, and more of the local foods to which they were unaccustomed. Men from these ranks filled the hospital, where they are remembered as walking "stick men" who tried pathetically to perform small tasks to aid the war effort or just to stumble outside to sit in the sunshine.[5]

Other Micronesians on Kosrae had to live on less—and on less desirable rations. Lowest ranked were Kiribati people, considered prisoners of war, who labored in near isolation by the swamps. They "ate only potato leaves" cooked into a soup toward the end and were forced to sell their possessions for coconuts. Hundreds reportedly died of malnutrition and illness. The Pohnpeian men taken to Kosrae as military workers turned to famine foods, especially after the Japanese stopped workers' rations. Lusios Jak recalls: "I ate the kinds of foods on Kosrae that pigs cannot eat on Pohnpei. At that time, I ate with the soldiers. We ate potato leaves, tapioca, hibiscus leaf mixed with these things for soup. I ate a spoiled coconut; I washed it in saltwater and ate it." Another says, "During the war, we ate things that weren't meant to be eaten."

As on Chuuk, both Kosraeans and Pohnpeians on Kosrae turned to theft to compensate for inadequate rations, despite severe punishment. Okin Sarapio recalls that his fishing group persuaded the man carrying the fish to share it out: "He made *sashimi* with his spear, and we dove [underwater] to eat that *sashimi*, because there was a soldier watching us fish." Klemente Actouka describes his success as a thief when he was working with Koreans under a Japanese supervisor: "I stole taro for us. I went to the taro patch and first cut off the leaves because they make noise. Then I put the taro in a bag and took it with me. I stole one day, then rested the next. One time a guy named Ukau came to me and we went and stole coconuts. We climbed three trees and got 150 coconuts. I got 120 that night and didn't sleep until morning."

Dobi Kilimete, another Pohnpeian working on Kosrae, expresses sympathy for Kosraeans: "Life during the war was very hard. It was okay for the Pohnpeians because we were stealing for ourselves. But the Kosraeans stole for the women and children." Like Islanders elsewhere, Kosraeans "stole" from their own gardens. And the Japanese, says Kilimete, defined "stealing" very broadly: "One time when we were in Utwe, we looked through the forest and saw some breadfruit. We sent some of us to go and get them. So we hid it for us to eat, and when the soldiers found out about this, they beat those who went to the forest to get it. But why? Those breadfruit would drop, and no one would see them."

Kosraeans recall that they themselves got through this period of hardship with less difficulty than the Japanese, partly because they were used to eating local food; extreme scarcity was limited to a few locales. Anna Brightly's description makes it clear that Kosraeans did suffer, however: "We had no food, so we had to look for sliced coconut meat for our lunch when we worked at the plantation. Sometimes we took salted fish to the plantation and ate it with our sliced coconut. It's really true that we had hard times. Men climbed the trees and tied coconuts with ropes and lowered them down [because if they dropped them, soldiers might hear]. The women would get them and use them for food."

Of the bypassed high islands, Pohnpei suffered least from food shortages. The large island supported a near tripling of its population, although as Carmihter Abraham says, "The Japanese had eaten almost everything" and destroyed most gardens. People who stayed on their own farmsteads could often provide for themselves away from watchful Japanese eyes. Those working on nonfarm projects in remote locations, which were difficult to supply, faced greater challenges. Neither Japanese nor Pohnpeians starved, though there was a protein shortage, undesirable foods were consumed, and people occasionally went hungry. As Julio Vallazon recalls, "The Japanese asked us for food; there was enough. If the war had lasted a long time, perhaps we would have had this problem [a food shortage]."[6] Domestic animals and poultry were used up for food after imports ceased. Turkey and geese disappeared completely sometime before the bombings. During the period of air raids, Pohnpeians were forbidden to fish on reefs, so families sometimes had to kill twenty or more chickens in a month (Bascom 1965:258).

Pohnpeians also worked to create a reserve against invasion. The Japanese told them to establish refuges far from military locations: "People made houses and gardens in the forest with extra food supplies in case the Americans landed." This double effort—to provide daily needs for a swollen population and to lay in stores—led people to grasp every opportunity for provisioning.

Pohnpeians in some areas were obliged to supply food to the military, including bananas, tobacco, tapioca, sweet potatoes, coconuts, yams, and breadfruit. Osei Sohram says: "The Japanese soldiers really destroyed Pohnpei. They made the land their own and took their food. They dug up yams without asking; they climbed breadfruit trees without asking; they never asked permission for anything." In some areas, soldiers destroyed resources (for example, felling palms to eat the hearts); some who had planted extra food in response to Japanese warnings lost it all to soldiers when they moved inland to escape the air raids. At some point, people were prevented from harvesting breadfruit and coconut from their own land, and "people who were caught with these foods were beaten up and the foods were taken away from them." The Japanese kept strict records of supplies such as chickens and pigs; to kill one's own pigs amounted to theft. Soldiers also practiced unofficial confiscation. Lotis Seneres recalls that one couldn't carry food from place to place: "For example, if I wanted to go to Palikir, I couldn't take anything because hungry soldiers would stop and take it from me."

Food rationing on Pohnpei was never so complete as on the bypassed Marshall atolls, Chuuk, or Kosrae. Pohnpeians compensated for the loss of labor and harvests to the Japanese by extra subsistence work. Most did without the highly valued rice, though some got it from Japanese friends or in exchange for pigs. They ate less favored foods, foraged for wild foods, and worked harder to get what was available, going to the sea to fish, to the reef for clams, into the mangrove swamps for crabs. And, when necessary, Pohnpeians too stole food controlled by the Japanese.

Pohnpeians recall an additional obligation to assist civilian Japanese who evacuated Kolonia after the bombings. These refugees moved throughout

Pohnpei, building houses in the forest (some camouflaged with grass growing on the roof), eating local foods, and working to assist soldiers and supply themselves. Lacking rice, they struggled to eat unfamiliar island food. Since many Japanese women did not breast-feed, they sought cow's milk for newborns, which Catholic priests supplied. Antipathy to the military did not embitter Pohnpeians toward the refugees. Instead, they "were really helped by Pohnpeians and they got along really well," confirmed by continued contact long after the war with these civilians, who write letters, send gifts, and return to visit their old companions.

Yap, like Pohnpei and Kosrae, saw its abundant food supply stressed but not exceeded by a large military population. In some areas, soldiers dug up and destroyed taro patches; but other commanders were more careful and ordered Yapese to supply taro. Since "the Japanese did not know how to tend the taro patches," Yapese (in particular, women, who are Yap's farmers) exerted some control over food. As the Japanese consumed their stores and resupply failed, Yapese planted sweet potatoes and did other agricultural work under military control, and the military tagged and guarded food sources.

Sweet potatoes, though fast growing, had to be harvested before ripe, and even marginal foods such as small coconuts were exploited. Soldiers would steal cooked food that Yapese had prepared in the morning and left in their cooking pots when they went to assigned labor. Mitag recalls cooking for the soldiers, gathering sprouted coconuts and sweet potato tips and mixing them with fish or meat in huge pots. To fill the subsistence gap, Yapese women stole from their own taro gardens, and men stole fish. They also stole tobacco and sweet potato and tapioca leaves from Japanese gardens. Plants closer to one's residence were safer from the Japanese, so people stole banana trees at night and replanted them beside their houses. Stealing on Yap also took an additional form when the military commander of a village would send people out to forage for food—that is, to steal—from areas under another military unit. In this case, the Yapese stole from each other, and from other Japanese, *for* the Japanese.

Crowding and relocation meant that a number of Yapese customs, part of a highly structured body of tradition, were severely violated during the war. Separate living spaces for people of different social classes and genders were merged. At least, as Maria Leemed recalls, Yapese maintained familiar eating rules: "Fear was everywhere! We were afraid of the American planes and the

Japanese soldiers. But we kept our customs. The men still used one [cooking] pot and the women and children another one."

Of the two strongly garrisoned Carolinian atolls, Satawan and Woleai, the latter suffered the greatest food stress. The seven thousand troops that arrived in April 1944 to defend Woleai airfield lived a military epic of suffering. Fifteen months of bombing destroyed installations, but it was disease and starvation that killed most; fewer than sixteen hundred survived to be evacuated in September 1945 (Peattie 1988:305–307; Boyer 1967). Before they sailed to Ifaluk, Woleai people lived on resources from the small ungarrisoned islets, with men staying on even the tiniest islets to protect them from Japanese foraging. Ignacio Letalim remembers that taro patches, breadfruit trees, and preserved breadfruit pits were depleted and palms cut down for their hearts. The Japanese would sometimes walk to other islets at low tide and steal food, or sometimes people would give them food, knowing they were suffering. Higher ranking Japanese traded hoarded rice and other imports for local food; soldiers secretly bartered with blankets and sheets.

Mortlockese more actively supported the large Satawan base. As in the bypassed Marshalls, some Mortlock islands supplied taro, copra, coconut, fish, and breadfruit to the eight-hundred-man garrison after supply lines were cut. From April to October 1945, Lukunor sent at least 10 tons of taro to Satawan every three weeks; Kenio Ipon says each island in the Mortlocks was assigned quotas—"That was when we started to worry, because it was like that forever. Every other week we had to bring tons of taro to go to Satawan. . . . When we looked at our taro patches, they were almost empty." Etal had only one resident Japanese, a handicrafts trader, but people were obliged to sell (for a fair price) pigs, chickens, breadfruit, and taro to Japanese on Satawan and Lukunor, especially during the height of war. Most Islanders were relocated from Satawan itself; the few who remained had so little food that they turned to theft, and their relatives on a nearby islet would cook food and sneak it onto Satawan for them.[7]

The Japanese base at Puluwat sent military parties to Pulap where the malnourished soldiers could regain strength and grow food, which they then dispatched to Puluwat; Pulapese were detailed to feed these soldiers and work in the gardens (Flinn 1982:45). The Japanese used canoes to bring the vegetables they grew—and a quota of taro from the Pulapese—to Puluwat. John Sandy recalls the Japanese commander on Pulap as "a good man" who controlled his troops. And he recalls the condition of those who arrived from Puluwat: "They were so skinny . . . they would lie flat, and we had to carry them on a stretcher. They were like dogs—they would lie there, and if a fly came by their mouth, they would snap at it. . . . We would feed them, and when they were better, they would go back to Puluwat and more would come."

Palau

As in the Marshalls, American plenty neighbored starvation in unsurrendered areas of western Micronesia. While Islanders in American-occupied Peleliu, Angaur, and nearby small islands reveled in oversupply, crowded Koror and Babelthuap suffered scarcity until surrender.[8] Japanese soldiers and civilians and Palauans faced food shortages and tight security regulations. Agricultural and fishing projects were initiated to meet the increased demand, but more than two thousand troops died of starvation and disease (Peattie 1988:304).

Eventually, Japanese resorted to violence to obtain food and Palauans took to the woods to forage. Japanese reportedly ate their horses and dogs, then turned to lizards and snakes. Kyota Dengokl, who worked as a military messenger, described seeing food thieves imprisoned, put in wire cages, and exposed outside. As he moved around Palau, he saw Japanese, Okinawans, and Koreans dying from wounds, starvation, and disease. On his way to Ngiwal one day, he passed a group awaiting transportation, some lying down, others leaning against trees, some vomiting, some already dead (Higuchi 1986). Karen Nero describes Palauans during this "year of famine and starvation," living in the woods, suffering from inadequate food, exposure, and illness caused by poor diet and sanitation. Today, Palauans point with pride to the fact that, even during the worst times, they shared their food with each other and helped the Japanese (Nero 1989:127, 130).

Social Impacts of Food Shortages

Under the continual stress of strict discipline, hard labor, inadequate food, fear of military punishment, and enemy attack, family relations on the bypassed islands threatened to dissolve. "At that time there was a little bit of carelessness or disorganization, inattention within some families," Okaichy Sapwo of Chuuk recalls. "Before the war every family member used to do things together—like work, eat, live, and so on. When the war started, family members no longer worked together—they didn't cooperate anymore." Simako Onuson recalls a time when deaths by starvation were happening one after another, forcing families apart: "Even if we were relatives we did not eat together. You were on your own. Supposing you heard someone break open a ripe coconut, you got up and asked for some pieces. If she/he loved you, she/he shared. We would go around the Chuukese houses and sneak in and steal the food. Besides that, there were persons who stood up with their excrement running down loosely [diarrhea]. Relatives came to dislike each other."

Sontak Kansou (Chuuk), when asked whether he fed anyone besides his family during the war, says, "A long time ago I fed people, but during the starvation I did not." Each individual or family had to forage for famine foods; "Because there was no food, we did not care or we pretended not to see" those outside the family. On Pohnpei, one woman confessed, "Hunger caused me to do bad things to my brother. For example, if my brother hid his food before he went fishing, I would steal the food because I was hungry." Thaddeus Sampson (Marshalls) speaks of the dissolution of all social ties under such circumstances:

> Because there is a great deal of need. So now, I do not wish to help other people and other people do not want to help me. And so the spaces between people have become damaged because it is bad between the two of us.
>
> (*Interviewer asks: So you are saying that as long as there are no needs, everything will be fine? But if people need things . . .*)
>
> There is disruption. I hesitate to cooperate. Because if there is just a little of something, it becomes important. If I see that there is just a small amount, I will never give it to you for your own. Because it is critical.

But the same difficult conditions could also call forth superior levels of compassion and sacrifice. Chuukese like Sontak Kansou say, "There was love between families at that time because of the difficulties." And in the Marshalls, Clancy Makroro says: "During this time very great was the love [caring] the Marshallese had for one another—it did not matter what atoll you were from, if you were Marshallese, they [other Marshall Islanders] would watch over you." Kija Edison (Marshalls) adds: "During the time of the battle there was a certain sort of lifestyle. It was very different from these times because people then really knew how to watch over one another. Our life during those times was in line with the old people who were our grandmothers and grandfathers. We really knew how to share and how to live with one another and be together. We knew how to watch over one another, watch over one another, and this was the very greatest thing. It definitely was not like these times, now."

Constant relocation, hiding from air raids, and scrounging for food were doubly difficult for those caring for children or elders. Sachuo Siwi (Chuuk) states, "I admired the parents, especially the mothers, because they took extra care for their babies and children during the famine." It was no easy task, as Okaichi Sapwo (Chuuk) explains: "As for those children, it was hard to know what they were feeling within themselves, but [on] the outside we could tell that they were suffering. Parents really took care of them so they could grow in spite of the hardship we had during the war." When families were displaced by soldiers on Tol, Chuuk, Niferta Eas says, "We were very thankful because we didn't have babies. There wasn't any arrangement for babies. Had we had one, she/he would have just gone around with us, hiding." Another Chuukese woman, Aknes Bier, recalls her experience: "[My baby] was crawling at that time and hungry. He couldn't sleep, so he cried and cried. For me, a thought came into my mind that I would steal. I stole potatoes to cook for my baby. Then a Japanese soldier came and was going to shoot me, but I ran in the woods and hid. When I came back, my baby wasn't there, so I cried. He had just crawled away. I looked for him, but I couldn't find him. That was a great suffering. I was also in fear of the Japanese soldier, thinking he'd shoot me if he saw me." [9]

SHORTAGES OF OTHER GOODS

If you had a baby die, you wouldn't have
the clothes to cover him up with.

Though food shortages were most dangerous, other goods were also sorely missed. In the Marianas, as everywhere in Micronesia, consumer goods "steadily decreased in quality and quantity during the early years of the war"; by 1944 goods "had disappeared completely from the shelves of island stores" (Russell 1984:86).

Clothing

Most Micronesians were separated by decades or even generations from the time when clothing had been made from local materials and believed that being properly clothed was a moral necessity. (Yapese and western outer islanders were able to continue making and wearing fiber skirts.) Since most people owned few clothes, they had little stockpiled, so the bombing of urban areas precipitated a clothing shortage. On Kosrae, Anna Brightly recalls coming home after work and washing clothes to wear the next day. People near Japanese storehouses, for example in Kolonia and Net on Pohnpei or Toloas on Chuuk, got by with whatever cloth came to hand or modified Japanese clothing to suit local tastes. When the Japanese traded a dress "like those of women from the Japanese brothel" to Chuukese women, they "cut it and sewed it into a proper dress." Or they adopted Japanese garb, even if it was culturally inappropriate. Men working on the farms of Kosrae often wore loincloths, though they thought them immodest.

In Chuuk, men got clothing from the soldiers they worked with, but women were barely covered. In parts of Chuuk, women wore trousers and shorts. "Those women who knew how to make skirts out of hibiscus bark or coconut husks were very lucky" (Asako Mateas). Some women found that the only way to obtain clothing during the war was by trading sex. When the soldiers "came into the house and made love to a woman in that house—that was the only time they would give away a coat as a price or in exchange for what they wanted in the house. They just gave us that garment like a *kappa* [raincoat; overcoat]—we'd then remake that coat into a dress."

Where cloth was completely unavailable, people turned to creative alternatives, such as mosquito netting. Sachuo Siwi (Chuuk) comments, "Those old people decided that it was better for mosquitoes to bite us and suck our blood than for us to walk around naked." While Kosraean women made clothes from mosquito netting, men used tarpaulins and canvas, and peeled apart the soldiers' protective clothing. Humiko Mori worked at Chuuk's hospital, which gave out bandages to use for clothes. Another expedient was to employ traditional woven materials in new ways, such as wrapping sleeping mats around the waist. Marshallese on Lib used pandanus fronds and other local materials to make clothes, which "became older, older, and older and more tattered and there was nothing to stitch them with." At the extreme, people found themselves in the position of those on Namoluk's small islets: "When canoes with people would approach them, they would run for the thick bushes to hide their naked bodies."

As the months passed, the lack of clothing on Pohnpei became so serious as to be comic, at least in retrospect. Women bathed in the river, washed their one garment, hung it to dry and stayed in the water until they could get dressed again. People crafted clothes from anything available—canoe sails or parachutes or mattress covers, or they pieced stockings, bandages, or handkerchiefs into a skirt. Toward the end of the war, some clothing was manufactured in Pohnpei for Japanese soldiers, but it was insufficient to supply Islanders. Japanese planted cotton on Pohnpei during the war, but it did not mature before war's end (Bascom 1965:271). Eventually, a school was started for making cloth from ivory palm fronds. So valuable had scarce clothing become that Pohnpeians sold pigs in order to buy it. People even shared clothes. Peleng Kilimete recalls, "Some women had to go out and their daughters had to stay home naked, because they had only one set of clothing." Others rolled up in mats "and stayed inside the house all day." Kristina Sehna says, "If my mother had died, I couldn't have left the house, because I had no clothes." Men resorted to Japanese loincloths or traditional male grass skirts, and even women started making grass skirts for their own use (Bascom 1950:147). Eperiam Agripa says, "I have seen with my own eyes men and women alike wearing empty sacks for clothing. A man who died was buried in a sleeping mat because that was all there was that could be used."

Many Pohnpeians hid a few precious garments throughout the war to display in triumph at its end. Mikel Diana recalls a feast after the Americans arrived: "I found out that day how good Pohnpeian women were in storing and keeping belongings, because it was a great surprise to me when I saw people wearing good clothes: long pants and nice shirts. I thought we had all run out of good clothes."[10] Reflecting on the years of shortage, Masako Luhk Karen says, "Even today, I cannot throw away old clothes."

Despite creative responses, lack of clothing was a persistent and demoralizing problem, and it became a measure of hardship. Resen (Chuuk) thought of this when she responded to a general question about what life was like during the war: "That's when—I must just give an example—if you had a baby die, you wouldn't have the clothes to cover him up with. You'd just cover his face, dig a grave and bury him. What cloth could you cover him with? We didn't have any left. . . . We buried our dead without any covering over them."

Tobacco and Other Imports

Another shortage, that of tobacco, distressed Micronesian men. The strain of military labor and lack of food were exacerbated by loss of this familiar luxury. For workers on Maloelap, Nathan Tartios recalls: "There were no cigarettes. *(Interviewer asks: You craved them?)* Craved, and then, craving became a thing of the past, for they said, 'It is useless to crave cigarettes.'" Smokers turned to other leaves, such as papaya, when tobacco ran out. On Chuuk, a man was executed for stealing tobacco at night. Others saw a chance for profit. Naboyuki Suzuki's Japanese father had acquired a few packs of cigarettes. He sold them to the soldiers near his home in Wonei at 200 yen each and traded them to officers at one sword per pack. Some Pohnpeians planted tobacco "and sold it anywhere because cigarettes could not be found during the war and tobacco could be planted and sold easily" (Manuel Amor). Toward the end of the war, a tobacco plantation was established in Madolenihmw, entailing especially backbreaking work from Pohnpeians.

Other shortages made daily life more tiring and time consuming as local materials were substituted for the imports on which Islanders had come to depend. With gasoline and kerosene scarce, people used fires when they could or turned to coconut oil for lamp fuel; they used fireplows instead of matches, substituted plant leaves for soap and hibiscus bark fibers for thread, and stole salt when the Japanese boiled it from seawater. Piara Esirom of Chuuk had laid in a supply of needles in advance of war, but others used coconut palm midribs for sewing. When Nathan Tartios' group escaped by canoe from Maloelap to American lines, "the sail was made from Marshallese pandanus matting."

A Few Areas of Plenty

In contrast to prewar conditions, outer islanders were in many cases better off than those on high islands—both because they had relied less on imports before the war and because Japanese demands on them were less insistent. For example, Nukuoro did not suffer badly: There was "plenty of food, but not many clothes," Ruben Rudolph reports. Mokilese expanded taro gardens when the atoll was cut off from outside supplies for two or three years during the war (Murphy 1950:64), so were fairly secure. Andon Quele (Kutu) said that people in the Mortlocks didn't suffer as much as those in Chuuk's lagoon islands, though they experienced harshness from local Japanese officials. "But as for money, clothes, food, we didn't suffer on those." When ships from Satawan made the rounds of the Mortlocks to collect provisions for the Japanese garrison, a secret "basket trade"—in small goods such as soap, Japanese loincloths (to be resewn into dresses), and "thread" (really strings from cement bags)—accompanied the quota of supplies.

Once invaded islands came under U.S. administration, they experienced a dramatic—though as it turned out, temporary—increase in the availability of food and goods (see chapter 7). And on a few isolated islands, the escalation of war and the American advance also had a positive effect on conditions of daily life. On Piserach (Namonuito, Chuuk), after test strafing to determine any Japanese presence, U.S. planes dropped food and clothes, and people were left well supplied and at peace. In the Carolines, Sapwuahfik (Ngatik) was identified as friendly and received American airdrops and visitors that provided an abundance of clothing, cigarettes, and food. "The people of Ngatik were very happy during the war," Takio William (Pohnpei) says. "After the war, we went there and the men of Ngatik were wearing [American] officers' clothes."

MILITARY-CIVILIAN RELATIONS

*The soldiers stopped caring about us. Their concentration
and efforts were directed at the war.*

The civil government had played a large role in the first phase of war preparations.[11] But the mandate's bureaucracy changed in November 1943, when the navy took control of civil affairs. As we have seen, the colonial system of appointed leaders facilitated labor recruitment in the first phase of military construction, and village chiefs and secretaries played a role in the military occupation—although, far from being privileged, they were in many cases treated with the same discipline as villagers and felt more pressure. Thaddeus

Sampson describes the military commander for the eastern Marshall Islands moving into the same building as the civilian governor, "and the two of them doubled in their duties and their efforts were doubled toward the Marshallese." Later, military rule completely replaced the colonial administration of the Marshalls.

Oral history suggests that a weak civilian government remained in most areas for most of the war as a formal buffer between Islanders and the military.[12] Joseph Jibon describes a man named Nakayama in Jaluij, "who loved the Marshallese. . . . He was the fellow who stood in the space between the Japanese and the Marshallese. He traveled around to the various places within Jaluij Atoll and saw whether the way people were living was okay at that time, what problems there were in such-and-such a place." This official also conveyed information about executions of local people. Marshallese repaid his kindness by telling the Americans, "This fellow here, there was not a single bad thing that he did to the Marshallese. He did not fight. The thing that he did was to stay between the Marshallese and watch over them so that the Japanese would not hurt them." The image of remnant civilian officials standing "between" Micronesians and the army is widespread. In Chuuk, Humiko Mori recalls, some civilian officials stayed after the army arrived: "Office workers joined together; they were between soldiers and Chuukese. But their power wasn't what it had been before." When the army came to Chuuk, Toli Jessy recalls, "our administrator also arrived from Japan. I think their ranks were the same, that's why the soldiers didn't give us a hard time. When there were conflicts between us and the Japanese, our administrator would negotiate or smooth things out with the Japanese."

Micronesians' predominant impression was that the influx of Imperial Army personnel overwhelmed and subordinated the civil administration. Lusios Jak describes "big changes" when the soldiers arrived on Kosrae: "There were no governmental rights, only soldiers' rights. The police were just like nothing to them." As Clancy Makroro (Marshalls) says, "The laws of the soldiers were different from the laws of the government, and they were much more severe than the laws of the government."[13] Normal life continued on Pohnpei early in the war, says Marcus Alempia, "but as it progressed, things started to change. Food came to be in short supply and the laws were enforced a lot more strictly. Instead of the government running everything, the soldiers took over everything. . . . The soldiers stopped caring about us. Their concentration and efforts were directed at the war."

Blackton (1946:405) describes the attitude of the military officials who surrendered Chuuk at the end of the war: "The Japanese delegates aboard the U.S.S. *Stack* freely admitted that they had little information to offer regarding civilian matters. The same careless attitude was exhibited with regard to the question of the several thousand Carolinian natives living on many of the smaller islands of Truk Atoll. Little was available beyond the obvious fact that the Japanese considered natives unimportant, and so apparently neither annoyed them nor tried to improve their condition." Given this attitude, anything that was to be done to protect Islanders in an official way would, apart from the efforts of the rare considerate military officer, be the task of the civil administrators who remained.

From Pohnpeian and Chuukese descriptions of wartime activities of Japanese and Islander policemen, it seems that relations between the police organization and military powers were complex. In most areas, police continued to enforce laws, indicating a separation of civilian and military affairs. Anisiro Aninis says some Chuukese on Fefan had a role as translators for the police— "Not to translate to the soldiers; the soldiers ignored what they said." But in Yap, Venitu Gurtmag insisted that "during the war" there were no longer civilian policemen; all authorities were military. In addition, the Japanese army's infamous military police, *kempei tai* (Bateson 1968:40), operated in at least some areas of Micronesia.

Recollections also reveal tensions between the military and civilian legal systems. When, in Chuuk, military accusations of spying caused Magdelena Narrhun's family to be tortured and beaten, the police at Toloas chastised their captors, saying, "And why are you taking the job of civil authorities (*minkan*)?"—trying Chuukese was a civilian task. After trial, all except her father were released. On Pohnpei, Andonio Raidong continued his prewar police job, including enforcing laws against theft. On one occasion, his work brought him up against a soldier: "For example, there was a soldier in Net who stole yams from the chief of police. People saw him. I went to investigate. First I went to see the boss. He took me to the kitchen and there was a bag of yams. The boss said to arrest the guy, throw him in jail and beat him up. I said, 'No, it's OK, now that I know who did it.' I had thought it was someone from outside; I hadn't realized it was a soldier. They gave me the authority to decide what to do with him—scold him, arrest him, or whatever. But I let the guy go." William Prens, a six-year veteran of Pohnpei's police force when war began, confirms that "high Japanese officials" did not permit soldiers to "take things without asking." Yet clearly they did; as Osei Sohram says, "There were police, but they weren't strong. Whatever the soldiers ordered, that's what they did."

While Pohnpeians speak of "policemen" controlling their behavior on the plantations, Chuukese speak of "soldiers" in this role.[14] Military enforcement of food controls on Chuuk used local men, many of them former policemen. Isaac Sakios was a policeman on Udot when the war started: "The military command sent us notice of the incoming war. I was still a policeman; however, I was not doing any civilian work anymore. All of us now worked for the military. I served at that time as a liaison between the Japanese soldiers and the Chuukese. . . . When the military came in, they changed our commander to a military man."

In Palau, once the center of Nan'yō-chō, the Japanese first increased and then essentially abandoned attempts to control Islanders. After Americans controlled Angaur and Peleliu, the Nan'yō government was impotent and the Japanese military "had little time, resources, or inclination to look after the welfare of civilians, Japanese or Micronesian," though they kept up the shadow of patriotism (Peattie 1988:299, citing Bowers 1950:56). By the last year of war, Japanese were too preoccupied with survival to maintain controls on Micronesians' daily lives, and Palauan social organization revived. "Conflicting orders between officials of the South Seas Bureau and the army officers created a situation in which the natives could choose their own course of action" (Useem 1945a:578).

One Japanese officer stands out in Palauan accounts of this period. Yoshiyasu Morikawa was an officer trained in field artillery who had served in Manchuria before being sent to Palau. After the U.S. invasion, with the Japanese worried about civilian unrest, Morikawa was ordered to organize Palauans on Babelthuap and manage relations between Islanders and soldiers. To this end, he organized the Morikawa Corps, a group consisting of Palauan chiefs and elders and Japanese civilian, administrative, and military personnel. This group visited the twelve or thirteen Palauan places of refuge semimonthly to investigate attitudes and living conditions. They heard Palauan complaints against soldiers and encouraged Palauans to support the war. These efforts apparently reduced friction, and many Palauans attribute their survival to Morikawa's efforts. So unusual was his behavior toward Palauans that some have interpreted it as that of an American spy (Higuchi 1986, 1987, 1991).

MILITARY RULE IN DAILY LIFE

The freedom that we used to enjoy came to a sudden halt.

Civil officials' ability to intercede for Islanders and to retain an ever-narrowing domain of decision making diminished and eventually vanished as the front lines passed over the islands. Then, the greater part of Micronesians' life was beyond control of the South Seas Government; their land, their labor, and their safety lay in military hands. Military necessity and security fears imposed increasingly strict rules on daily life. While Islanders had been accustomed to a civil order that called on men to supply a labor quota, children to attend school, and wage workers to adhere to rationalized labor practices, wartime brought restrictions on individual behavior that amounted in some cases to virtual imprisonment.

Travel

Restricted travel caused the greatest problems for atoll people, who relied on interisland transport for supplies, for medical care, to maintain family ties, and to follow current news. Prewar Nan'yō-chō policy had discouraged interisland travel in Micronesian craft, and a deep-sea fishing ban and blackout regulations early in the war further restricted local sailing (Murphy 1949:433, n. 12; Witherspoon 1945). Ijimura Lautoña said that the Japanese "closed the sea" before the invasion of the Marshalls; people had canoes, "but there was no point in us sailing. We were frightened of the Americans." After the U.S. established nearby airbases, boats in the bypassed atolls moved only at night and were then pulled ashore and hidden; the ban on daytime sea travel continued until surrender.

Once U.S. forces established an effective blockade, ocean travel everywhere became very risky. Erwin Leopold, a Japanese-educated Pohnpeian policeman, was evacuated to Tokyo for medical treatment. His surgery was a success, but he recalls a close brush with death on the return trip:

> I came back when the war had already started. I went to Saipan first and then on to Chuuk. We were nearing Chuuk when our ship was torpedoed and sank. I floated around on a lifeboat in the ocean for two nights and one day. . . . The name of the ship was *Kalamaru.* It was a very fast ship, the fastest at the time. Its route of travel was Saipan, Chuuk, Pohnpei, Kosrae, Marshalls, and then back to Japan. The ship was not a military one, it was a cargo ship. It belonged to a company called "Yūsenkaisa."
>
> There were about four hundred of us on the ship, and only sixty of us survived. The torpedoes hit about one o'clock at night. It was a very dark night and I could not see well. An American submarine torpedoed us. It fired two torpedoes. One hit the front of our ship and the other hit the engine room. In less than an hour, our ship was gone out of sight. More than three hundred perished that night. Only sixty of us survived . . . Some of them were headed for Chuuk to work for the admiral there.
>
> Only two lifeboats were saved from the wreckage and it was these boats that we, the sixty survivors, had to use. The one I was in was damaged a little and had a hole in it. We all had to take turns bailing out seawater, day and night. If we had stopped, the boat would have sunk. A Japanese fishing boat happened by and saw us in the wreckage. The people on it saved us. At first, they did not see us because they were busy picking up goods, like onions, that were floating around. In the end, they found us. They took us to Chuuk. . . .
>
> None of us [knew the direction to Chuuk]. We were completely lost. We had no food at all. There were some biscuits in the boats, but they got too wet and could not be eaten. It was impossible [to fish]. We did not even have any fishing gear. . . . [We did not have any drinking water], none at all. We almost died. But we were able to catch rainwater when it rained and that saved us.
>
> [Of the sixty survivors] . . . four of us were Pohnpeian and two of us were Saipanese. The rest were all Japanese. None were soldiers.

Back home, his wife Liwisa Aldis only learned that her husband's ship had been sunk from a friend with a Japanese husband: "They did not let me know. We went to Mass and my mother said, 'Let's go back and make another Mass.'

Every day, I went to Kolonia [from Sokehs] and asked when the ship would come. The day that I did not go to Kolonia was the day he came. He arrived and went down to see me in Palikir. The Japanese did not want people to know any news."

Wartime travel problems trapped Islanders and others far from home, in many cases for the duration. Students were stranded at regional schools in urban centers, the Boston Mission School on Kosrae, and the mandate's vocational schools in Palau. Many of those stranded were workers who had been recruited for the large-scale projects of the first years of war. The Japanese made an effort to get them home; for example, Chuukese and Pohnpeian laborers on Jaluij were returned after the first U.S. attack, but Marshallese from other atolls were unable to leave later in the war. Bwirre Lejmen explains: "Because the word came, 'It is prohibited for [even] a [coconut] husk to move upon the water or it will be shot.' On account of this, no ships could move. Then all of the boats and people were 'jailed.' Nothing could move." Similarly, Chuukese contract workers on Angaur were unable to leave when war threatened, though they stopped working ("And when they came to take us back to Chuuk, we were out of money"). Finally they embarked on a military ship under strict security; when they reached Toloas, they were put to work as stevedores.

Intraisland travel was also restricted. After American invasion, Marshall Islanders were forbidden to move even between the islets of the remaining Japanese-held atolls, where they had been dispersed. The Japanese on Mili were so concerned about Marshallese escaping that they ordered them to stay in bomb shelters ("holes") when U.S. planes or ships appeared; "They said that if you ran off, the rest of your family would be killed."

On Kosrae, Pohnpei, and Chuuk, the military posted armed guards and required written passes or stamped wooden permits for travel. Chuukese needed permits to travel between islands in the lagoon; as the war progressed the Japanese stopped issuing them. Near the end of the war, they destroyed canoes to prevent travel within the lagoon (Hall and Pelzer 1950). On Yap, late in the war, each village was placed under command of a military unit; La'ew remembers people wearing numbered tags around their necks, and U.S. Navy photographs from the western Carolines show people with tattooed identification numbers on their arms. Pohnpeians wore badges to identify their homes: "If your patch was from Sokehs and you entered Net, you would be beaten by the Japanese soldiers." Rosete Hebel, who traveled between Kiti and Madolenihmw on Pohnpei during the war, recalls, "If I had to visit my relatives in Kiti, first I had to get permission and I also had to tell them exactly how many days I would be in Kiti." The regulations and harassment at guard stations reduced even necessary medical trips and encouraged people to walk through the forest. "We didn't want to go near the soldiers. The soldiers guarded the road so that if anyone walked by, they would check whether that person had any dangerous things like knives and so on" (Paulina Aisawa, Pohnpei). Control over travel was also a means of control of the food supply; checkpoint guards confiscated food as well as weapons.

Separation from family during times of danger was perhaps the most trying effect of the travel ban. Jomle Malolo's wife and child went home when the battle for the Marshalls began: "If I had died, I would have died [without seeing them]. . . . And that is why I really thank God. Because I was able to return and meet my family again."[15] During the war, Benjamin Lopez (Pohnpei) says, "I was also thinking that I would be far away when my children might die." Not even a final return home was always possible. "For instance, if you died at one place, you would be buried there though you did not originate from there. That applied to many people who died during the war" (Parang Namono, Chuuk).

Rumors about where bombs had hit and how many had been killed were disturbing accompaniments to the search for news about relatives. Rosete Hebel heard a false story that the Pohnpeians working on Kosrae had been killed by American bombing. For their part, Pohnpeian men on Kosrae could watch the planes "flying overhead on their way to bomb Pohnpei." Sometimes people were close enough to see the attacks that might be killing their families. During the battle for the central Marshalls, people on Lib looked to windward about 30 miles and watched Kwajalein burn. People on Patta, Chuuk, watched the smoke and flames on Toloas when the big oil tanks were ignited in a raid— "and the people on Patta were crying, because they knew their relatives on Toloas would die" (Iteko Bisalen). Tupun Louis, a Losap man who spent the war working on Toloas, thought his people were dead, since he assumed his tiny home atoll was suffering the same devastation. Woleai people who had taken refuge in Ifaluk could see the flashes of light and hear the noise of the bombs as U.S. planes attacked the Woleai air base: "We thought there was nothing left," Matthew Yafimal remembers. Kutu people such as Kenio Ipon sought supernatural contact to learn the fate of relatives: "On my island we had a medium through whom our great spirit communicated. We used to call him Radio; his real name was Retin. When anyone died on any of these Mortlock Islands, no one else knew about it but us Kutu people—that great spirit told us . . . if any Kutuans who had gone away to work in faraway places was dying, the spirit would come and tell us about it."[16]

Military Security

One reason Japanese authorities restricted travel was to control the flow of information. "Almost before the war started," Oska Seiola (Pohnpei) recalls, he was jailed for subversive speech. He had merely opined to a friend that "it would be better if that kind of Japanese who didn't know how to work would go back to Japan." But someone overheard, he was interrogated roughly, and he and his friend ended up in a spartan jail for twenty-one days. During hostilities, it was forbidden to talk about ship movements or anything related to the conflict. "The Japanese didn't allow us to talk about the war. If the Japanese found out you were talking about the war, they would cut your head off " (Ignasio Paulino, Pohnpei). Some Micronesians aided Japanese security work. Bwirre Lejmen recalls a woman on Jabwor who informed on other Marshallese; "On account of her always telling on us, we were always cautious there on Jaluij, for if she knew about you she would report you to the Japanese: 'Watch out for that fellow, he is slandering the Japanese.'"

Rosete Hebel recalls how hearing war news at her father's house on Pohnpei from a soldier "who was very friendly to us" got her in trouble when she passed it on to another woman:

I told her that I heard it from the soldiers, and then I left her. That night my daughter Kasiko and I were at home when the police came and told me to go down to the office. I was walking down the road and the small sticks scratched my face; it seemed as though I couldn't feel anything because I was really afraid. Because the Japanese said that if anyone talked about the war they would be killed.

When I got there the Japanese policeman came; he was a very cruel man. He told me to come along, and asked me if I was Rosete. I said yes. He asked if I came from Kiti. And he asked if I had said that Miyaki was captured, and I said yes. He also asked who had said that, and I told him that it was one of the soldiers. And he said, "A real soldier, or one of those treated like soldiers [military laborers]?" I told him it was a real soldier. . . . He asked, "What did he say?" I told him that his name was Suiisang and that he said that Miyaki was captured at 12:00 and Deniang at 8:00, and the war was almost over. One woman, a sister of Joseph Route's mother, asked him why they didn't beg forgiveness, [i.e., surrender] and he just raised up his hands. And the next day when I left, the man [Japanese policeman] said thanks and that if I heard that again not to tell anyone. He also asked how I knew, and I told him that my father's house was a resting place for soldiers. And he told me if I heard it again not to tell anyone, but to come and tell them in the office. When I left there it felt like something moved away from inside of my stomach. I haven't felt that scared since; that was the first time I had that feeling. My daughter was with me and I said, if they were to kill me, who would take care of her? Because they said that one drop of alcohol is more important than the lives of people [Pohnpeians]. I still remember that man Suiisang.

The Japanese felt the greatest need to control information, and Islander behavior, when invasion was imminent. Yet wartime pressures were sustained in bypassed areas for a year or more, longest in the Marshalls. Marshallese recognized a deterioration in the Japanese attitude toward them as the war continued. Clanton Abija, who lived on Ronglap, recalls: "We knew their thoughts had changed because the law began to change more and they began really to watch us, watch us Marshallese, to see—what? If you came out, then they would say we were spying, or, what? [That we were] an agent, or things like that." Like many Marshallese, Abija thinks that this Japanese concern led to plans for genocide (see next chapter).

In response to security rules, some Marshallese on Jaluij communicated through songs and even developed a form of "whistle speaking." Bwirre Lejmen recalls: "Yes, you could not talk because if you said anything, they beat you. So we used to whistle as a way to signal. Two whistles: 'Is there food with you? Do you have drinking coconuts?' 'What are you eating?' 'What is your life like there?' 'Are there boats that have come?' Those sorts of things, you would just whistle. You could not talk, because if you spoke, well, the soldiers stood right by you and watched what you said. And if you said anything, 'Buuk' [they would shoot you]. Well, the Japanese did not know what the whistles meant, because these things were just whistles."

Religion

Since Japanese Protestant missionaries replaced European clergy in some areas and a few administrators and military men were Christian, some church activity continued, though public services were largely prohibited. But the military in general, as Asako Mateas of Chuuk recalls, presented an intense anti-Christian attitude: "Religion was banned at that time. No one was supposed to go to church or practice anything that had to do with religion. The Japanese soldiers did not allow us to enter those churches because they said no one should worship anything besides their statue which they worshiped. They prayed to their god Tennō Heika." Soldiers, recalls Clanton Abija (Marshalls), enforced Japan's civic religion: "They said, 'Who are you worshiping? You can only worship Tennō Heika.' We had to worship. There were hours when we worshiped. All the time. During the months and times which were important we faced toward the north and bowed down. And then they told us to sing Japanese songs." This was on Ronglap, with fewer than ten Japanese military.

In Chuuk, when bombings started, people did not attend church; the Japanese "said we were to forget about religion and just think about working." In the Mortlocks, people tried to keep services secret, scheduling them late at night—but the Japanese railed against Christian worship; finally "we thought it was better to stop our worship activity" (Koko Suda). Pingelap Atoll was a rare case, where troops attended local services: "The Japanese soldiers didn't worship another God," says Lusiana Sackryas. More often, perhaps, as Parang Namono says happened in Chuuk, Japanese soldiers "could walk into our churches and beat us. They would tell us that our religion is false."

Perhaps because a Japanese missionary headed Pohnpei's Protestant church, those services continued after Catholics were restricted to private prayer, and the Spanish Catholic missionaries were treated less well (Pohnpei has a history of Protestant-Catholic conflict). Catholic missionaries were moved to Net, restricted though not imprisoned. The Catholic school was relocated and limited to catechism classes. Mission personnel were harassed by soldiers. Julie Panuelo, a student at the mission school, saw a Japanese officer physically attack a Spanish nun after she refused his proposition. Ciro Barbosa recalls other harassment:

> I remember one night when Father Quirino was the head priest at the Catholic mission, and some of the Japanese soldiers asked us for help. The Japanese top general got drunk one night and demanded to see the nuns. So we all ran to the mission and helped the nuns escape. But the general and his group caught Father Quirino. The general then asked Father Quirino, "Who is more important, God or the emperor of Japan?" And Father Quirino replied, "God." He would then point his gun at Father Quirino again and demand another answer, but Father Quirino didn't give in. It was some of the soldiers who helped us out that night. So I think they were not all that bad. They took Father Quirino to Yasarin [military headquarters] that night, but released him the next day.

Foreign missionaries were actually expelled from Chuuk and Pohnpei in 1944, but because of the impossibility of transport they remained in place (Dolan 1974:82). Foreign mission personnel were imprisoned or kept under observation, their activities severely restricted (Hezel, n.d.; Kohl 1971). Priests and lay brothers from Saipan and Yap were interned in Palau. Because most missionaries were Europeans, they were often accused of anti-Japanese activity. Even Micronesian church workers suffered such charges. On Ronglap (Marshall Islands), soldiers closed churches, saying the ministers were spies. Church buildings were confiscated for military use on Kosrae, Pohnpei, Chuuk, Yap, and Saipan. Pwelle Church on Tol, Chuuk, was dismantled and the bell carried off to a military headquarters; the robes for Mass helpers were taken to make loincloths and the communion settings for plates. "They came into our churches and took everything on the altar, like the small statues of Jesus and Mary, and threw them outside. Religion was against their law" (Asako Mateas, Chuuk).

Without priests or missionaries, people nonetheless gathered to pray when they could, and they kept private devotions: "All of us were persevering in our religion, trying to pray every day during the war" (Aikichi Samwen, Chuuk). Christian services continued in Pohnpei until air raids scattered people, and even then "People were praying under the trees in the forest," as well as at home and in bomb shelters. On Tol, Chuuk, where people had been displaced to make way for soldiers, local pastors went around to them rather than having them gather for services. Although religious meetings were banned, "there were some people who were steadfast in their Christianity—they'd hide away and hold services, because if the Japanese found you, they'd punish you" (Toli Jessy, Chuuk). Marshallese sustained religious gatherings until the invasion, but then "meeting together and singing and preaching" were "hated" by the Japanese; even so, families were allowed to say grace over their food. It was after the battle for the Marshalls began that the Japanese "did not want us to come and attend church, they would beat you because (they said) there was no God." Marshallese often held services secretly to escape Japanese punishment: "They [Japanese] did not keep us from prayer. Even in the middle of the battle, we held church inside the holes." Low-ranking Japanese and Korean workers urged the Marshallese to pray for them, saying that America was going to win the war, but other Japanese were firm in their patriotism—"This sort, they would never change."

Public services were forbidden because meetings made targets for attack, but also because the military feared subversive activity. Daisey Lojkar (Marshalls) recalls that they "told us not to sing and those sorts of things, and we said, 'Why is that?' 'Because you do not speak Japanese, and we do not know [what you're saying].' We said, 'We do not know how to sing from the book in Japanese. We know only how to sing in Marshallese.' And so then we hid and continued hiding, and then elsewhere in the atoll [Kwajalein], because there were no Japanese there, we went ahead and held church." Living on Pingelap islet, Jaluij, for about two years during the war, Joseph Jibon recalls that Marshallese held church services in their homes but not group meetings. The Japanese feared the Marshallese would exchange ideas about rising up against them. "Plus, they said, 'There is no value to your worshiping God, it is a lie'— this is what the soldiers said."

Religious activities in some areas did in fact serve as an alternative to Japanese military control. Modekngei in Palau, which promoted resistance to Japanese colonialism, had emerged powerfully beginning in 1938 and continued to strengthen despite Japanese attempts to suppress it.[17] By the time of intensive American bombing (beginning March 1944)—with faith in the Japanese gone, but Japanese propaganda presenting Americans as fearsome and dangerous—many Palauans turned to Modekngei, which provided social organization, reassuring prophecies of future well-being, and magical charms to protect individuals from harm and to frighten away American bombers. Modekngei also cured the wounded and advised on participating in the Japanese war effort. At the height of the bombing, when casualties were increasing, Modekngei leadership called a meeting of traditional chiefs to tell them to pray for the end of war. During the worst months of war, Modekngei was "aggressively anti-Japanese," even interfering with labor procurement. As American success weakened Japanese control, Modekngei grew in power, including efforts to control Palau's traditional chiefs. "By September of 1945 [Modekngei head] Rnguul was acting as the undisputed political leader and policy maker for Palau" (Vidich 1980:244–246).

On Kosrae, Japanese soldiers and officials exercised power, leaving King John only a nominal chief. "As deacon, however, he and several other church leaders, in league with missionaries resident at the mission school, apparently controlled the major part of those Kusaiean affairs which the Japanese were either ignorant of or unconcerned with," including judging land and other local disputes (Schaefer 1976:54, citing Lewis 1948a:31–57). In the final days of the war, prophets arose in Kosrae establishing new religious cults, including a woman who predicted that the Japanese would win the war and a man who experienced visions of the struggle between good and evil. These became a catalyst for schism in the powerful Kosraean church (Lewis 1948a:65–68).

On Chuuk, the leaders known as *itang* regained importance during the period of food stress, planning thefts and other deceptions. Though less influential than Modekngei, they led the indigenous moral and social response to the "collapse of the Japanese military and civil administration and the uncertainty as to what was to be expected from the Americans" as the end of war approached (Hall and Pelzer 1950:18).[18]

Social Activities

While the few Europeans who spent the war in the islands were imprisoned and Islanders from Nauru and Kiribati were closely confined, Micronesians also lost much personal freedom wherever Japanese soldiers were stationed in civilian areas. For example, on Kosrae, Osmond Palikun recalls, soldiers were quartered in the villages, "So what I observed at that time was that no one was free to do what they wanted to do."

Blackout regulations came into effect as soon as an island came within the war zone. Lamps and fires were forbidden at night. People cooked in the morning but still worried about visible smoke. On Kosrae, ovens and bright lights at night were banned and people were forbidden to wear white clothes. Instead of lanterns, people lit coconut oil lamps and sheltered the light so that it could not be seen from the ocean. Dobi Kilimete (Pohnpei) recalls that "Funerals were held in the darkness, because we would not light lamps for fear that the planes would see them." On bypassed Maloelap Atoll, Nathan Tartios says: "As soon as the evening (U.S. patrol) plane flew off, you would hurry up and make your food, and then at eating time you would go and sit inside the hole [the bomb shelter you had dug] where you would stay. We told stories during the evenings, mostly, and if there were planes we went off into the holes and remained there."

Pohnpeians had to request permission to hold a feast, to use yams, to kill pigs, dogs, or chickens, or to drink kava—failure to do so was punishable by jail (the *nahnmwarki* was excepted). People explain Japanese control of social gatherings as a desire to protect them from being spotted by attacking planes. An alternative view is that the Japanese "didn't like to waste time" drinking kava and thought it kept Pohnpeians from work, and that constraints on feasting were part of the Japanese effort to ration foodstuffs. "There was a lot of work going on. The Japanese didn't want people always pounding kava, or hung over" (Julio Vallazon). Despite food shortages, even farm work was sometimes constrained by security requirements. On Kwajalein, George Hazard told E. H. Bryan in August 1944 that though they normally burned arrowroot to increase production, the Japanese did not let them burn that year (Bryan n.d. [1944]).

Civilian institutions, such as hospitals and schools, functioned at least until the first air attacks. Before the war, each urban area had a hospital treating immigrants and Islanders (with different fee schedules). Separate military hospitals were established when the region was garrisoned. The war strained medical facilities, with hospitals ruined or evacuated in the bombings. In Chuuk, the large hospital used by Japanese and Chuukese was destroyed, leaving only the military hospital. Some Chuukese recall that it "was the place where the Chuukese went for medical care"; others say, "There was a hospital, but it was only for them [Japanese]. . . . Only those whom they liked could use that hospital." Nathan Tartios recalls three military hospitals (for marines, pilots, and construction workers) and one civilian hospital on the Japanese base at Taroa, Maloelap. Marshallese workers on Taroa could use one of the Japanese facilities, but those living on the other islets of the atoll could not.

The operation of Nan'yō-chō's extensive though elementary schooling program was an index of war's approach. Schools might have to be relocated when soldiers garrisoned an area, as on Kwajalein, but an effort was made to keep them open as long as possible. The Mortlocks' primary school at Oneop operated until near the end of the war (Reafsnyder 1984:103). Canoes would come from other islands at night to take students home for weekends, despite the danger of travel. Tupun Louis from Losap was at school on Toloas when the teacher gathered all the outer islands students and asked them if they had relatives on the island. When Japanese troops arrived two weeks later, those without nearby relatives were shipped to Tol, where they were hosted, with variable enthusiasm, by the local people. Once American attacks began, school closed and the students worked for the military.

Though the war was for the most part a time of limits—"The freedom that we used to enjoy came to a sudden halt" (Mikel Marquez, Pohnpei)—socializing was not completely inhibited. Pohnpeians, Marshallese, Chuukese, and Yapese remember gathering for games, dances, and singing. William Prens says, "When the war was going on, Pohnpeians' life was still good. People still enjoyed themselves, had fun. Pohnpeians held dances for the Japanese soldiers." The first phases of war work produced a host of newly composed songs, which laborers shared. Ignasio Paulino and other Pohnpeians working on Kosrae learned the song later well known as "The Memorial Song of Kosrae," but kept it secret from the Japanese. In the Marshalls, John Ezekiel recalls that during the war, as long as they could, people followed the custom of going from island to island for songfests—partly because they had always done it, but also as "my attempt to stay busy to help distract me from sad thoughts, from my thinking about all sorts of things—suffering and fear and hunger." In fact, the Japanese ordered Marshallese to hold songfests and feasts. While the military strongly discouraged religious activity, in many places it encouraged traditional dancing (which had been opposed by several generations of

Christian effort). On Tol, for example, soldiers called Chuukese to dance for their celebrations. We interviewed Sinino Mateas:

> (Interviewer asks: So the Japanese were different because they didn't like religion but they liked your old dances?)
> That's right.

> (Interviewer: What did the older Chuukese think about that?)
> Oh, they were the ones who did the old dances. They decorated their bodies with paint and leaves, coconut palms before they did those dances. The youngsters did the "march" dancing.

> (Interviewer: When the Japanese stopped religion, was that a reason the people turned to their old dances or old ways?)
> Yes, because religion had no power at that time.

Peleng Kilimete (Pohnpei) recalls that during the war "Everything worked according to the law, even dancing." Paulina Aisawa says that in the midst of fear as Pohnpei was being bombed, "Nobody could be happy; but the soldiers told us to put on a local dance, so we got together and danced for the Japanese. Maybe they were scared and so they told us to do that dance. I thought we did that for them so they could feel better. The war was going on and the Japanese were having a feast or party." Questioned as to whether Chuukese enjoyed being asked to dance at Japanese soldiers' parties, Sinino Mateas replied, "Yes, people enjoyed that because first of all, it was the Japanese government that we were scared of and secondly, there weren't many things we could do with joy, so that was why we enjoyed that a lot."

On Tol, Chuuk, group chanting, traditional dances, sumo wrestling, and parties took place during the war. On Yap, Japanese soldiers would invite the local people to hold traditional and "marching" dances, even during the period of bombings. Such gatherings were permitted only in certain contexts; people might be punished for dancing in other circumstances. The imprisonment and punishment of Magdelena Narrhun's father on Chuuk began when military workers ordered her uncle to bring women to dance for them and he refused, arranging for the women to go fishing instead. The leader then attacked him and accused him of spying.

Alcohol, in some places an enjoyable distraction, was often unavailable to Islanders because only soldiers had the makings. Yet where tight supervision broke down, "The soldiers even let the people drink" (Manuel Hartman, Chuuk). On Uman, Chuukese "had fun" gathering to drink home brew and made it for the Japanese.

Despite all the dangers, there was a kind of freedom in the war years that made for formative experiences in the youth of today's senior generation of Micronesians. The mobilization of labor took young people away from the watchful eyes of family and gave unprecedented opportunities for adventure and romance. Romantic relationships may have been heightened by excitement and danger and the lifting of normal rules. Says Mikel Diana (Pohnpei): "There were songs made about the war, but most were love songs. To me it appeared that while the war was getting worse and the laws tougher, the feeling for love was also getting stronger. A man who was separated from his lover during the war seemed to have developed the feeling of greater affection and love for his lover. That's how it seemed to have happened to people."

Other informants, recalling their own youth, echo his sentiments. "It was increasing in those days. Somehow, when the war was going on, there was also lots of dancing and celebrating [i.e., love affairs] going on" (Ichios Eas, Chuuk). Matsuko Soram suggests that it may have been the scarcity of clothes on the women that gave Chuukese men ideas; people "forgot all about 'being afraid'" but they went on attracting each other's attention." So it is not surprising that love songs are among the most popular songs composed during the war. One, composed by a man from Sapwuahfik working on a plantation on Pohnpei, compares the power of war to the power of love:

> *Planes flying under the heavens—*
> *I am not afraid.*
> *My love for you—*
> *That I fear.*

REALIZING RANK DISTINCTIONS UNDER HARDSHIP

> *At that time, the Japanese no longer respected our chief,*
> *they considered him as just another regular person.*

Wartime reinforced some rank distinctions while it erased other statuses and privileges. It was often Japanese-educated Islander men who supervised

Micronesian labor groups. Benjamin Lopez, a Pohnpeian educated at the advanced Japanese school in Palau, supervised workers on Pohnpei's Nanpohnmal airport construction from 1942 to August 1945. Those who had studied agriculture became bosses on farms, as Milton Timothy did on Kosrae: "I was chosen as one of the Malem leaders. We were the ones who had to tell each person what to do when it was time to send food to the soldiers." Some young men educated in carpentry and agricultural schools worked directly with the Japanese, rather than in local work groups.

Some of these men describe themselves as "lucky," but their position was inherently stressful, balanced between Japanese demands and Micronesian resistance as war pressures mounted. Isaac Sakios, who worked on Udot, Chuuk, for two years as liaison between the Japanese military and local people, says, "I did my job in a way that the Japanese and Chuukese were both satisfied." In contrast, Narian Ropich, a translator for Japanese police on Tol, "started to think about quitting the job" when his kin were punished: "I suffered so much when they beat up my relatives. I felt like walking out." Kun Aaron describes his job on Kosrae as giving "those Malem women and older children some kind of work to do, like collecting copra, bananas, taro, coconuts, and so on, even coconut crabs for the soldiers. This made life hard for them, and they really hated me. They even sang a song criticizing me and their work." The song starts with his nickname, Ankoa:

> *Ankoa is enslaving us,*
> *Forces us to collect copra*
> *For the* Nistai Ompu *soldiers.*
> *We are weary and tired.*
> *A time for picking crabs,*
> *A time for collecting copra,*
> *Ankoa is really enslaving us.*

Sinio Peter, a Mokilese work leader on Pohnpei, says: "Being a boss was not an easy job for me. If I made a mistake, the Japanese would beat me up." The Japanese gave him a nickname: "I didn't want that name but the Japanese wanted all Mokilese and some Japanese to call me Kamsama ("god"). I asked them why they called me Kamsama, and they said, 'We call you Kamsama because when you talk to the Mokilese people they respect you, and also we really like you too.' Kamsama is the one that can talk to the people of the world. The Japanese teased me with the name that they gave me, perhaps, but I was the smartest one among all."

These acculturated young leaders were able to use their language skills and familiarity with Japanese ideology to protect local people. On Tol, Chuuk, a Japanese speaker "usually saved us," Sinino Mateas comments, "by talking to the Japanese when there was a conflict between them and us."

A few families combined wealth with traditional or Japanese-attributed status to influence local conditions. On Pohnpei, the Nahnpei family used their position to assist both the Japanese military and the people of Kiti. One family member, Kaiti Anson, recalls: "We were content during the war because our father had a big business at that time. I do not know anything about laws because there were no laws given to us. The relationship between my family and the Japanese was very good because my father helped them." The Nahnpei family was somewhat insulated from the shock of Japanese occupation and war preparations. Kaiti Anson and some of her relatives—three of them, herself included, married to Japanese—stayed in Kiti during the war: "When the war started, we were already down in Kiti and some soldiers went down there and stayed where we were because my father had many houses and they [soldiers] stayed in some of those houses. One big gun was near our house but the soldiers did not do anything to us. . . . The soldiers were being faithful to my father, because my father helped them well. My father gave them coconuts, pigs, and cows. He gave them these things to eat or as food. We did not have problems with food. Like others, we did not get any help from the Japanese." At war's end, she recalls, the soldiers went to Nahnpei "and said thanks to my father; there were some who cried. They said that my father had helped them really well."

Similar privileges protected elite families on Chuuk, especially the descendants of the famous South Seas entrepreneur Koben Mori (see Peattie 1988). Though married into Chuukese families, the Mori affiliation at that time was primarily Japanese, and Mori men, as Japanese citizens, served in the military. This background enabled the family to protect resources and retainers during the war. Echen Nakamura reports the Japanese did not take food from the Mori farms at the family home in Tol: "If they took something, they chased them [soldiers] and beat them. That's why they couldn't do that to us [confiscate food]. But on those islands like here, on Weno, when a coconut fell down, or a breadfruit, they just took it and ate it, because they treated people here like animals, not like at Tol. Because they were scared of those Moris."

Chuuk had many families of mixed Japanese-Chuukese heritage, such as that of Naboyuki Suzuki of Tol, whose father was Japanese. Mr. Suzuki's brother worked as a houseboy for the local commander and was treated in the Japanese hospital when he became ill. Even for those like himself, identified as Japanese, Mr. Suzuki recalls that life during the war was hard: he and his friends traded fish caught with dynamite for farm produce with Okinawan and Japanese neighbors and boiled saltwater into salt. The Japanese would come to his father for advice on what plants were safe to eat and how to prepare local food.

Some Chuukese leaders established mutual aid links with the military. A chief on Fefan was often visited by military personnel early in the war. His daughter Humiko Mori recalls: "We were friends, acquaintances. . . . They gave us rides from the mountain downtown and from downtown to the mountain. At that time, we were comfortable/peaceful. They would come and bring their dirty clothes and the other women and I would wash them. And they brought their torn clothes, and my mother sewed them."

Traditional leaders' power had already been circumscribed as immigration, economic development, and military preparations encroached on Islander autonomy. The shift to military control of land and labor marked another re-duction in chiefly rights, though island and village-level officials appointed by the Japanese retained a role in most areas. Sachuo Siwi's father, chief of Toloas in Chuuk, used his position to gather information about events and Japanese plans and insisted on staying on Toloas during the bombing. After the first air raid he "begged" the Japanese to leave Chuuk, in a vain attempt to protect the Chuukese people. But he was ill and bedridden as the war progressed and was less able to intercede for them. On Weno, Petrus Mailo (then chief of Weno) and Pwenni (chief of Penia) "really took care of us," asking the military to send home Weno people working on Toloas and elsewhere: "They asked them to bring them back so they could do their work here with the Japanese and not work far away from Weno. That was how powerful those two chiefs were" (Finas Bossin).

On Udot, one of the least fortified of lagoon Chuuk's islands, local officials retained some privileges. When Japanese soldiers tried to take some potatoes from Nusi Niekik, "I told them, 'Those are mine, because I'm the daughter of the chief [or mayor; *sosonchō*].' And they said, 'Oh, sorry—take them.'" Japanese on Udot treated local people better than on other lagoon islands "because they were afraid of the chief." Udot chiefs arranged for official breadfruit distribution, improving the food situation there. In general, Ichios Eas speaks well of Chuukese administrative and traditional leaders: "They took very good care of us. They brought us together. Wherever we went, they were with us, and they were always encouraging us."

On Kosrae, Likiak Benjamin became secretary of Melak in Utwe in 1939 and was still secretary for his father (who was *sonchō*) in July 1942 when Utwe people relocated to Koasr. However, "At that time, the governor was no longer in office, because when the soldiers came we started working for them." Mr. Benjamin and his father filed weekly reports and, at war's end, *sonchō* and secretaries were called to military headquarters to hear the announcement of Japan's defeat.

But as Clanton Abija (Marshalls) observes, special status for either traditional or appointed elites became precarious as conditions worsened: "At first they very much knew how to watch over people and elevate the chiefs. Then when the battle became stronger it is as if there was nothing belonging to the chiefs. Chiefs and people were almost the same in their thinking." On Tol, the military confiscated land and goods regardless of status: "I did not see anyone who mattered to the Japanese, even the chiefs. We were fully 100 percent under control of the Japanese" (Kame Rapun, Chuuk). Linter Hebel says war preparations brought many changes to Pohnpei, "But especially to the *nahnmwarki;* people have stopped obeying them, ever since the war." One factor that reduced traditional status was the disconcerting Japanese treatment of chiefs in the same terms as commoners, brought home shockingly in disciplinary actions. Clancy Makroro (Marshalls) describes the treatment of a chief accused of stealing rice from Japanese storage bunkers: "They tied his feet and his head and strung him up with a rope and beat him. They beat him and asked him if he was the one, and if he said he was the one [who stole the rice] they would then stop but, in truth, it was not him. They wanted him to say it was him, and they tried this thing so that he would beg them to stop beating him. The Japanese themselves stole [the rice] and they lied about the chief so that he would be hurt." This chief, Lankein, was permanently injured by the beating. Makroro names another man who was beaten when accused of stealing from the Japanese, and adds, "There are also many Marshallese people whom the Japanese hurt, and these were not simple people, but were the leaders of the Marshallese during this period."

Less traditional Chuukese "chiefs" were appointees of the Japanese government. Even so, their power decreased as the military gained ascendancy. In most of the lagoon islands, after a time "even the chief worked. Because at that time, the Japanese no longer respected our chief, they considered him as just another regular person" (Okaichy Sapwo). In some places, village and island chiefs "worked like their people worked. . . . The chiefs also worked because the soldiers didn't like anyone to sit at home. So when we were to dig dirt, the chiefs also helped us after the soldiers came "(Finas Bossin, Weno). But this may not have been true everywhere; in some areas of Chuuk lagoon, Micronesians appointed to chiefly roles did office work rather than hard labor. On Yap, Peter Ianguchel said that Chamorros—who had been the local economic elite before the war—"were treated like the Yapese" during the war. There seemed, then, to be no group sufficiently privileged to intercede with the Japanese military in the later phases of the war.

Despite the waning of Micronesian leaders' power under military rule, people did turn to them for advice and assistance. When Eperiam Agripa of Kiti, Pohnpei, was on Ant Atoll at the beginning of the war, the group waved at what turned out to be an American plane. Suddenly afraid, they hid, then asked Nahnpei about it when they returned home. Their leader "told us not to be afraid because the Americans were only going to shoot at the Japanese soldiers and not at us." And some, maybe most, leaders responded as actively as they could to protect their people. Melsor Panuelo describes how the *nahnmwarki* and *nahnken* of Net on Pohnpei ordered that Net people should work for themselves for an hour before they went to work for the Japanese; "Those who obeyed this rule were fortunate."

The one place where traditional chiefs clearly gained power during the war was Palau, where slackening Japanese control late in the war left Palauans to their own devices. Both Modekngei and traditional leaders moved into this vacuum. Describing Angaur before American invasion, John Useem writes that traditional leaders there resumed former duties, clans and families took up old activities and ceremonies, and people began to wear necklaces of

ancient money indicating status in the traditional social hierarchy. They held
church services regularly in secret and restored old dances.

> These activities did not reflect overt opposition to Japan but merely a
> growing sense that in their own social order they found comfort. The An-
> gaurese felt that death was imminent, and so, like any social group in up-
> heaval, they felt more secure in relying on their traditional modes of be-
> havior than in trusting their fate to the newer ways of action. The American
> invasion of Angaur quickened this process. When the islanders were or-
> dered to the hills for safety the chiefs directed the evacuation. Individualis-
> tic activities were completely replaced by cooperative programs organized
> along traditional lines. During the American siege of the hills, the *merreder-*
> *a-talungalak* gave orders to their sisters' families. The *rubak* organized par-
> ties of the men's *abai* to search for food and water. The acting chief and
> senior members of the several *kebliil* assumed active leadership over the
> entire group and made the final decision to surrender to the Americans,
> and thereafter represented their people in all dealings with the newcomers.
> (Useem 1945b:579; author's emphasis)

In remembering the acts of chiefs and other leaders during the war, nearly
all our informants either applauded their efforts to assist or admitted their im-
potence in the face of Japanese power. Describing Marshallese fear when given
Japanese demands, Clanton Abija says, "The thing was [they were able to do]
whatever they desired, because we were afraid. And not a single land head or
chief was there, so they could not even speak with them."

But leaders' wartime activities do not go completely uncriticized. For example, Pohnpeians today comment on the fact that it was nearly all Kiti men
who were sent to work on Kosrae. Was it because Kiti leaders wanted to help
the Japanese by volunteering Kiti men? Or, as one man suggests: "The Japanese tried to get people from the other municipalities, but their leaders didn't
let them. This is the reason why only people from Kiti went to Kosrae. Our
leaders were the ones who let the Japanese take us. There were people from
Salapwuk who hid from the draft." In reflecting on the war, other Pohnpeians
comment, "Everyone was afraid. *Nahnmwarki*s and *nahnken*s were not brave
during that time."

With the Japanese, it was not all of them who were
bad and it was not all of them who were good.

Micronesians had become knowledgeable about Japanese during twenty years
of colonial rule, but during the war familiarity was replaced by estrangement
and personal and political relationships were rethought. Despite mistreatment by the military, a sense of affiliation persisted. As William Prens says,
"Pohnpeians are kind, helpful people. They are similar to the Japanese. They
are also helpful, respectful, and this made relations between us easy." This is
part of the truth.

In reviewing their experiences with Japanese, Micronesians distinguish
between prewar and wartime, and when speaking of the war, they distinguish
civilian from military Japanese and navy from army personnel. And when
speaking of the Japanese military, Micronesians call attention to individual
differences, explicitly acknowledging the kindness of friends, while affirming
frequent harshness. "With the Japanese, it was not all of them who were bad
and it was not all of them who were good. But there were some who were bad,
while most were good" (John Ezekiel, Marshalls).

Some local commanders ensured that Micronesians were treated well and
that necessarily strict food exactions were conducted fairly. Despite serious
shortages for the battalion that arrived on Lukunor in May 1944, "the commander requested rather than demanded food from the people of Lukunor,
and he punished any of his men who took food without permission" (Borthwick 1977:58). On Yap, with adequate resources, Islanders report that Japanese
soldiers were nice; they "came and asked for food" and "begged" for food late
in the war. As Mitag recalled, "A few were friendly because they were asking
for food. They did that at the very end." Micronesians have affectionate memories of some Japanese military men. Isaac Aisaw found "kindly" bosses where
he worked on Pohnpei, but "I heard that in other places they were very tough."
Clanton Abija described a high-ranking soldier on Ronglap as kind, adding:
"I do not think it was only there. For I have spoken with some others and they
say on their atolls there were if not one, two [kind Japanese]." Ronglap does
seem to have had a relatively idyllic time. John Anjain recalls friendships
and exchanges of handicrafts and shells with the Japanese there. Yet even

Life on the Bypassed Islands   **215**

though they were kind, "nonetheless, you did things the moment they moved their hand because if you made a mistake . . . they would bring a board and beat you."

At times, security restricted Micronesians' interaction with Japanese military personnel. In Takio William's part of Pohnpei, soldiers were not permitted in Pohnpeians' houses: "I was the one who asked the chief to permit them to visit me." At other times and places, personal relationships were possible. Joseph Jibon describes his friendship with a Japanese artilleryman stationed on Imiej, Jaluij, before the first U.S. attack. Mr. Jibon lived on Jabwor islet, where the soldier visited him on weekends, exchanging clothes, rice, and dried fish for gifts of shells and a sleeping mat. "That fellow really cared for me," Mr. Jibon comments. Kija Edison shares a sweet memory of a Japanese man in the small garrison on Pingelap islet (Jaluij) who was his "friend" when he was a little boy, perhaps four years old: "That fellow used to come and inform me about things, and me, I knew what it was that he was saying if he commanded, 'Oh, my friend, you bring this thing here,' and he would send me off. I could do the things that he asked me in Japanese."

Those who had no friends among the soldiers realized the vital difference. Describing how he was beaten for collecting breadfruit without permission, Melsor Panuelo says, "They were not concerned with Pohnpeians. If I had a friend, I could have a breadfruit, if not, never mind." And not everyone had friends. When we asked Akeisuk Mokok if anyone working for the Japanese on Weno (Chuuk) had friends among the soldiers, he said, "Nobody. There was nobody who was friends with them. . . . They [Japanese] only talked to our bosses, and the bosses spoke to us. But nobody was friends with them." Finas Bossin was also on Weno: "We'd just work, work, work, and go home. We never associated with any of the Japanese." Chuukese who spoke Japanese had an advantage, but "the rest of us didn't know how to speak Japanese; we were just crazy/beside ourselves, because we didn't know what they were saying."

Those who did have Japanese friends found that they shared food, cloth, tobacco, soap, news, and advice—sometimes risking their own safety. "If you had a Japanese friend, you could ask him for food. If their leader found out, they would kill both of you." Takio William (Pohnpei) says, "The soldiers took care of me and my family, because I worked for them. They built my house and everything." Leon Gargathog gave fish to army friends on Yap, who checked on his family when he was away from home. The strongest friendships survived the hardest years. Ichios Eas, who worked closely with Japanese military on Chuuk and was a supervisor by the end of the war, received a gift of pigs and chickens when his officer left after the surrender, when Japanese gave away their belongings to special Chuukese friends. People on Toloas had more opportunity to become familiar to Japanese than those elsewhere in Chuuk, James Sellem realizes, so many Japanese soldiers "liked" them—and, in both civilian and military regimes, "if you were liked by your boss, you had it easy. If not, then you most likely would be treated harshly."

Besides friendship, romantic, sexual, and kin ties connected Micronesians with Japanese. In all areas except perhaps Yap, some women married soldiers, or lived with them, as Micronesian women had occasionally married foreign civilians before the war. It is only on Chuuk, where food scarcity reached extremes, that reports of Japanese soldiers forcing local women into sex, or trading food for sex, are common. In parts of Chuuk, "they [Japanese soldiers] just came in the house anytime they wanted to sleep with any woman who lived in the house." In some people's minds, desperate times excused such measures. "The love and care toward my spouse was less [important] than the food." "The hunger made people blind and shut their mouths." "Because of the starvation, husbands started to sell their wives to the Japanese in order to get food"; women would "sell themselves for ripe coconut." "It was an agreement between the husband and his wife to sell herself for food. There was still love between them, but the starvation was so bad that they had to give up their wives." Some even encouraged a daughter to sleep with Japanese "so she would come back with some food."

Such brutally direct transactions were unfamiliar on Yap or Pohnpei, though everywhere in the islands friendly or romantic relations with Japanese civilians and soldiers inevitably involved economic transactions in time of scarcity.[19] One Pohnpeian woman describes how she survived those years: "But for me, I lived by dancing and becoming engaged to a Japanese." Later in the interview she said, "I was hungry, that's why I danced and became engaged to a Japanese man—so they would feed me." The situation on Chuuk seems to have been more public—and more threatening. "Some girls, when they saw soldiers coming to their house, they hid from them." (Elsewhere in Chuuk, such as parts of Tol, soldiers were kept under strict discipline and separated from Micronesians.) Although we heard suggestions that soldiers or high-ranking officials "would come and take whom they liked," beating up husbands or relatives who opposed them, there is no evidence even on Chuuk of large numbers of Micronesian women being involved in or forced into regular prostitution for the military.

In reflecting on Japanese behavior, Islanders realize that winning the war — and later, merely surviving it — dominated their attention, and that the soldiers, like themselves, were subject to the exigencies of the times. "Before the war, (the Japanese soldiers) were okay and not so cruel but when the war had started, they became cruel and forced us to do things. They stopped caring about us. It seemed like we did not exist" (Ines Etnol, Pohnpei). Others do not accept war as an excuse. Describing how the Japanese bombed one of their own torpedoed ships, killing thousands of Japanese soldiers who might otherwise have survived, one Marshallese man asked rhetorically, "And you say, how did we know that the Japanese were really [inherently] bad?"

Certainly Islanders recognized that the tragedy of war touched Japanese soldiers also. Ciro Barbosa of Pohnpei recalls: "I was more afraid of the Japanese soldiers than of the war itself. They became rougher and started to act strange. If I didn't show up for work, they would call me an enemy the next day I showed up. They became more suspicious. This may be because some of them lost their families in Chuuk. They were put on ships to be taken to Japan, but the American bombers found them in Chuuk and sank all the ships and all the families perished. My boss at work also lost his family and it affected the way he acted and thought; he kind of became crazy."

Although they themselves were suffering, Micronesians were aware of the equal and, in several places, much greater suffering of Japanese. When American planes attacked the small Japanese installation on Kapingamarangi, "Kapinga men helped to bury the dead and nurse the injured. They hid the survivors on other islets and fed them until they finally left the atoll in 1945" (Lieber 1968:32). Japanese soldiers suffered large losses to privation and illness in the bypassed garrisons, and Islanders responded with sympathy to soldiers even closer to starvation than themselves. Piara Esirom (Chuuk) says: "We would give them some food, because we felt sorry for them. They were very hungry. . . . And when the cargo ships no longer arrived, then some of the Japanese were very hungry. They would lie down in their house and cry out for their mama and papa. Because they were too weak, because this was the time when food was scarce, they would bury them alive."

On Kosrae, Anna Brightly recalls that when they made coconut oil, "we gave the oil and even the waste flakes to the soldiers to eat." Soldiers stole taro from Kosraeans' gardens, and Pohnpeians on Kosrae fished for incapacitated soldiers.[20] Says Austin Albert: "Perhaps the Japanese officers had good food, but the common soldiers did not. There was a house in Lelu used for recuperation. Every day some of the soldiers came to the beach to take some sun. Perhaps they needed vitamin D. Some were just skeletons—just skin and bone." Masataka Mori, who had been a soldier on Chuuk, reflects on how odd it is that young men today volunteer for the army: "'Apply' to be a soldier? Me, I couldn't do it. Because we starved, we ate potato leaves, that's why I wouldn't want a second term as a soldier. It's really hard for soldiers."[21]

Some Micronesians, like Iosep Salvador, can speak in one breath of resentment of and compassion and affection for the Japanese military: "The Japanese helped the Pohnpeians after the Japanese soldiers came to the island. They were kind. If I arrived while they were eating, they asked me to join them. The laws during the war were hard. No one ate anything because everything was for the Japanese." Austin Albert (Kosrae) adds: "Some Japanese soldiers were good; some were not. We had no liberty to get things from our own land. If people didn't obey orders, they were beaten. But I felt sorry for the soldiers; they were malnourished, and many died."

Chuukese saw dramatic evidence of the suffering of blockaded Japanese when the starved soldiers of the Enderby islet garrison were brought from Puluwat to the lagoon. Piriska Nukunukar worked as a nurse when these walking skeletons arrived: "I also felt really bad and sick when I saw those people who came from the island called 'Entabi.' They were very sick, skinny, hungry. They came to the hospital because they were sick. They were hungry, too. They caught lizards and cooked them to eat. The local people couldn't believe what they were seeing." Echen Nakamura vividly remembers groups of starving, skinny, sick workers who gathered near the Mori household on Tol. These poor men were covered with flies and ate lizards and garbage from the Mori cooking shed. Without adequate medical supplies or shelter, what was to be done with the incapacitated and dying? Parang Namono (Chuuk) elaborates:

In the evening I went and watched some Japanese with broken legs who were brought to the mountain above Fanip [village]. They were *kunjoku*, Japanese laborers who came before the soldiers. There were many of them. These people were put on the mountain named Senia. If the grass there were burned off, you could see the skulls of those Japanese. . . . They were still breathing, but would not survive, so they were put there until they died. Only the officers were buried. If those with only half legs said they were still fine, the soldiers would say they were worthless. Those with skin rashes or diseases who could not work were also put in this same place . . . they didn't [build any houses for these people]. Those who were still strong enough would hide under the shade of the coconut trees, bananas, and other trees, but with flies all over their bodies. Others would just sit with the dead beside them. . . . We could watch them, but we could not do anything. Sometimes, when we visited them, they would ask us to bring them sea cucumbers, sea shells, so they could have some, but we wouldn't because we were scared of the war.

"The Customs of War"

In speaking of the worst period of the war, most Pohnpeians and Chuukese say they were treated "just like machines," "like carabao," "like chickens," "like animals," "like slaves," like the Israelites in Egypt. New elites such as Erwin Leopold, whose careers rested with the Japanese, are more measured in their evaluation: "During the war here [Pohnpei], our relationships with the Japanese soldiers were okay, almost normal. Both Pohnpeians and Japanese suffered because of the shortage of food. What they did was make the Pohnpeians work more, with and without pay. They also started to steal food from us because of the food shortage. They did not treat us badly—only made us work more every day from morning until dark in the evening."

A few, because of their unique circumstances, have no harsh recollections of the Japanese at all. Iwate John of Toloas, when asked whether there was cooperation between Chuukese and the Japanese soldiers, answers: "Let me use myself as an example. As for me, when I was there with the soldiers, I was satisfied with whatever they did to me."

Whatever one's circumstances, people recognized that war called for a new attitude. Thaddeus Sampson (Marshalls) speaks of the special way of life that exists during wartime, what he calls "the customs of war," which ran counter to the normal prewar Japanese "kindness and truth and honesty in terms of love—all of these things remained with our friends [the Japanese]":

There is a certain type of custom that appeared in the midst of the war. . . . There are some sorts of customs, warfare, traditions, because during those times, we were very frightened. And we ran off to the windward and leeward and knew nothing about peacefulness. And everyone was afraid on occasion. And we also knew how to be cautious [take care of one another] so they would not kill us if we had done something in error. These are the Japanese I'm talking about. And I was saying, during the times of the battle, the Japanese were very bad. The soldiers, if you erred in the least, they would cut off your head. But before the battle, everything that was good was available to you.

(Interviewer asks: Is it appropriate for them [youth] to know about the differences between the Japanese and the American eras?)

Well, yes, during the times of the battle, well, it was battle. And they need to know how to take care of one another. But during the time when there was no battle, they need to be happy. Because good fortune will appear and everything will be fine. And so in Japanese custom, during the time of war, things are bad. And I think that other nations are similar.

For Micronesians, the keys to survival during the war were self-sufficiency and a keen eye for opportunity. Informants can now reflect on the tactics that enabled them to deal with the military. Sinio Peter (a man from Mokil who worked on Pohnpei) says, "The best way to work for the Japanese was if they told you to do anything, you just said yes." Some informants speculate about how cultural differences shaped relations between the two groups. Nehdo Vicky (Kapingamarangi) says Pohnpeians and Japanese did not get along well, "because the Pohnpeians did not like to hear what the Japanese told them to do and the Japanese did not give in to the Pohnpeians either. It was the outer islanders who got along with the Japanese because they always obeyed them. The Pohnpeians did not agree with and like the laws made by the Japanese." But Japanese-Kapinga relations were good, "because what Japanese liked and wanted, we always did it. We always heeded what Japanese wanted us to do because we were under and controlled by them."

Another way people describe the relationship is that fear prevented friction: "Relations with the Japanese during the war were good, because people were afraid." Nathan Tartios, who worked on the Japanese base at Taroa, Maloelap, answered a question about family life during the war by saying, "Well, life was different than previously, because staying alive depended on your being attentive to the things that the soldiers said. It was a bit more difficult than when you were living in the era when there were no soldiers." Survival, according to Andohn Jemes (Pohnpei), depended on knowing how to follow orders: "If you didn't work or follow what they said, you were beaten up. The Japanese soldiers never beat me up, because if you were a good man, for sure God would help you. If you didn't follow orders, sometimes you couldn't survive. Also important was adherence to Japanese rules." Adds Elson Ebel (Marshalls): "And if you saw them coming toward you, when you saw them, you should bow down. You did not say, just say 'hello' to them, when you saw them you would stand up straight and bow down and say 'hello, *iokwe.*' This method had to be followed precisely."

Attitude counted. On Tol, Anton Chipwe recalls that people did not show their anger toward the Japanese "because whenever the Japanese saw a Chuukese who didn't look happy toward them [who showed signs of dissatisfaction], they beat him. Whenever they saw that a Chuukese had stopped working, they beat him." Survival called for alertness, studied obedience, attention to cultural differences, interpersonal psychology—and, if necessary, magic, as Joseph Jibon (Marshalls) relates: "Do you see, if the Japanese were upset with them, well there were people who made magic on them so that their thoughts would turn around and they would love them. Well, they did this sort of [magic] during the war. They made it so that they would not hate us and kill us."

Even while they evaluated ideas about how to deal with the circumstances of strict military occupation, Micronesians had to confront evidence that individual fates varied widely when it came to Japanese-Micronesian interactions. As Rosete Hebel remembers, "Relations between Pohnpeians and the Japanese soldiers were good. If I was kind to them and fed them, they would be good to me. But if I was not, they would not be good either. Soldiers were cruel." This philosophy implies that Islanders' own behavior shaped Japanese response. Of Pohnpeian workers on Kosrae, Klemente Actouka says, "The Japanese didn't hit the Pohnpeians for no reason. They were beaten for something they had done." And Sinio Peter adds: "Working with Japanese depended on what you could do. If you were obedient, you were fortunate, but if you were disobedient, you would be sad all of the time. The Japanese beat people until they almost died." A few, like Iosep Salvador, even internalized the brutality: "The Japanese were cruel people. But no—I am the one who made them cruel, because I told a lie and that's why they hit me." Bwirre Lejmen recalls the feeling of powerlessness that came when the invasion of the Marshalls began and "everything was difficult. It did not matter that I was a real man who watched over others, it had no value. If I made a mistake, I would be punished."

Resisting Military Rule

As suffering increased and the military repeatedly showed its lack of concern with civilian welfare, Micronesians began to turn away—if not from individual Japanese friends, certainly from the nationalism that had once inspired them to volunteer for military service, work at *kinrōhōshi* labor projects early in the war, or feel themselves a part of the empire. Melsor Panuelo recalls: "Some Pohnpeians started saying that if the Americans came they would help them steal things (guns and so on) from the Japanese. Because of the punishment that was inflicted on them, they said they would help the Americans and kill the Japanese."

As Islanders sensed the turn in Japan's military fortunes, they altered their response to demands for help. On Ulithi, "when it began to seem certain that Japan would lose the war, an about-face was made. The natives, who in the early days of the conflict had signified that they would be willing to fight against the Americans, now began to recoil because of mistreatment and realization of the fact that the Japanese had grossly misrepresented the war and its progress" (Lessa 1950:15). Peattie (1988:300–301) attributes Micronesian disaffection to three causes: "the insensitivity and, eventually, the brutality of the Japanese armed forces toward the Islanders; the miseries brought to the island communities by the war itself; and the recognition among many Micronesians by 1945 that the Japanese could not or would not effectively protect or govern them."

Since repressive Japanese security efforts also increased as the war went on, only very rarely did this antipathy turn into action. An effort by airfield workers on Chuuk to strike was put down quickly by officials and police (Fischer

1961:87–88). Certain sorts of quiet resistance seen earlier in the war continued—Modekgnei on Palau, for example, and the Kosraean use of church organization to mask community affairs from Japanese eyes. Kosraeans did not accede to Japanese claims of social supremacy, though they "bowed to officials and gave Japanese the tokens of respect they required, but as Christians, they could not respect the Japanese or grant them even social equality," and the church forbade marriage with Japanese (Lewis 1948a:96). Chuukese kept communications secret by speaking Chuukese, since few Japanese understood it, and the Marshallese whistle code let workers communicate even within sight of soldiers.

But the predominant form of resistance was individual, and in Micronesian style it is encoded in stories of individual acts that expressed resentment at harsh treatment, took revenge, fought for personal liberty in the face of oppression, and defiantly expressed Micronesian interests at the expense of Japanese military goals. In their mildest form, these were tricks played on the Japanese or insults in satiric song. Stories of duping Japanese soldiers are still told, now as humorous folklore—for example, how a Pohnpeian man working on the Nanpil airstrip tricked supervisors by reversing the drums he was to load with rock and "filling" only the few inches on the bottom. Pensile Lawrence (Pohnpei) recounts how he and another man on Kosrae sneaked stolen bananas through a military guard by hiding them under leaves and taro. Chuukese used their songwriting talent to insult the Japanese—"But the Japanese laughed about it. They did not know that it meant something about them."

Personal resistance took the form of words or blows that even the harshest discipline could not completely restrain, as related by Mary Jane Jemes (Pohnpei):

> I was beaten up by the police master because my daughter was sick and I told my police master that I would take off that day, but he said no, then I said "pakero" to him. He came and beat me up. The word pakero means stupid. The police master didn't hear the word I said, but a man from Madolenihmw told him.
>
> Two days after that, my husband went to Madolenihmw and told my boss that the word I said was not meant for him (police master), but for the Pohnpeian. Working for the Japanese was the worst.

Biloris Samor (Chuuk) remembers how she felt when she was beaten by Japanese: "I just thought, because you beat me up, I have to beat you up, too—in any way I could. Sometimes when they hit me with their sticks, I'd pick up stones and throw them at them. Those local chiefs and men told me not to fight back, but I said that was why those Japanese beat us up all the time, because we never fought back."

Islanders did fight back at times. In another story from Pohnpei, Moses Saimon recalls: "When the war was still going on, I was making salt [boiling salt water] with a soldier at Mesiseu, Madolenihmw. That soldier and I got into a fight and I told him, man-to-man, they wanted me to throw you in the hot water. The soldier told me that he was going to beat me and I told him that Pohnpeian men were different from Japanese men. The soldier apologized and left. He went and told the other soldiers about our argument and they returned, planning to kill me." Stories from Chuuk and the Marshalls also describe encounters in which Micronesian men beat and occasionally killed Japanese civilians or soldiers in self-defense or in contests over food or personal affairs.[22] When a man he considered his brother was executed for stealing tobacco on Chuuk, Kiman Phymon sharpened his knife and went to the place he'd been killed looking for a soldier: "I did not care for my life; I was going to cut someone [Japanese] with my machete." (He didn't see anyone.) A Chuukese woman, Deruko Shirai, reflects on the feelings of the time:

We were crazy. Chuukese are dumb. They [Japanese] talked badly to us, but we didn't dare answer back because we were afraid they might shoot us. So we just kept quiet.

(Chuukese interviewer: You mean you never answered back or fought back at the Japanese all your life?)

No, we were afraid of them.

(Interviewer: Is that why there wasn't any crime?)

They would beat us up. Because we were afraid of them, that they would shoot us or hurt us.

(Interviewer: Did you ever get into fights with them?)

No. They would scold us about the coconuts and breadfruit; they would say it's theirs. And we would say among ourselves, "Why is it yours? You never brought it from Japan." We would tell them that, and sometimes they'd say, "That's true."

Some took much greater risks. Lewis (1948a:93) states that some Kosraeans sabotaged military fortifications where they labored. Pohnpeians working on Kosrae sometimes beat up Japanese soldiers encountered in the forest. If the soldiers reported it to their superiors, they were beaten again, since the Japanese "didn't want their soldiers to be afraid."

The only organized rebellion to Japanese military rule in Micronesia took place at Mili Atoll, where Marshallese and Korean laborers collaborated following the execution of four Koreans found stealing. Elson Ebel tells the story:

> Now it was the Marshallese and the Koreans together, because their low social level was not the equal of the Japanese. After those fellows were shot and died, the Marshallese and the Koreans met together and said, "Is it a good thing if we just start a war?" and they met together and said, "Good." . . . Next they said, "Well, next week we will begin the battle." A week in advance they talked it over. Next, all of the men prepared red pieces of cloth for the night that they were going to fight. And then afterward, precisely that night at one and two o'clock in the middle of the night, they began to move. There were 101 Japanese on the islet, but 59 Marshallese— and Koreans, 400-some, I do not know precisely how many. The Japanese were asleep and they went and entered into their houses and they began fighting. They shot many of them; some few of them were manning the cannon, there were seven men, and they called to them and got them drunk on coconut toddy. Well then, this was fine with those fellows and so they went ahead and drank and became inebriated, and when they were drunk they killed them. They went into the houses of the Japanese and killed them. The Japanese, Tailo, they killed, but you see, his cook escaped. They shot him and he was injured, but he ran off and dove into the water and swam to Lukonwor, and there he reported, "There are no Japanese. All of the soldiers have died, all of the Japanese are dead."

Two Marshallese also died; their headbands had fallen off and they were mistakenly knifed by Koreans.

> Now there were some small islets to the west, and their error was that the Marshallese did not run to those islets. Instead, they remained on the lagoon side of the islet, Jelbon. And that fellow ran off to Lukonwor where there were a thousand Japanese, there and on the other islets between there

and Enejet. He said, "There are no Japanese left, they are dead, the Marshal-lese and Koreans have killed them." Well, there were many small boats that traveled back and forth among those islets. So some three hundred soldiers went off that day. They took machine guns and smaller guns and traveled to windward, during the low tide that morning. The islet is like this on the lagoon side [a high flat reef], and I do not know how the other group came onshore and landed because it was a totally dry reef flat at low tide, but some of them ran up on the ocean side. Then they started shooting one an-other. Some shot toward them, some shot away, and on and on things went until the Marshallese ammunition was exhausted. Then the group came up that had run up along the ocean side and shot them, the Marshallese and the Koreans. Some of the Koreans escaped while they were fighting. That day they escaped across the tide flats where water comes into the lagoon, to the small islets and remained on one of the small islets there. [None of the Marshallese ran off with them] . . . because they were occupied with the group who was fighting. All of the Marshallese died. After the war when we went there, it was filled with skulls, a hundred some skulls—we did not know which were Marshallese and which were Koreans and which were Japanese. They were all mixed together. . . . There were several Marshallese women. . . . They died also—there was no one who lived though this. Eighty-four Marshallese, if we include children with the adults who died.

Elson Ebel also recounts the execution of Marshallese men and women whose family members had participated in the rebellion:

They took sixteen people and tied them together in one fenced enclosure. They took them out of the holes. Those whose family members had es-caped [during the insurrection]. And they dug a hole 12 feet long, and they took them out and tied black strips of cloth over their eyes. And then they shouted, the taijo shouted: "Men!" ["Do this, now!"—i.e., "Kill this one, now!"] The fellow who cut heads off jumped forward and cut the person's throat, and another man came and dropped the corpse into the hole. "Men! Men! Men!" There was a man known as Laimroj—the executioner was short of him [slicing off his head], but he fell down and they went on and killed the others after him. On and on it went, and the wife of Laimroj, they did not kill—they did not kill the two of them. Well, this was not magic. It was the Bible, a Bible that they stitched by hand inside their collar. When they heard that they were going to cut people's heads off, the Japanese who understood the hearts of the Marshallese came and said: "Tomorrow, they are going to kill these friends of ours." Afterward, these two "made" their Bibles. They followed God and then, when it was over, the two of them only, the two of them were alive. [They had a seven-year-old son.] . . . He stayed inside the hole and they did not take him. They took only his mother and father. Then, after the two elders returned, the Japanese took us all out of the hole. They said, "Look to the leeward, look to the windward, those you no longer see around you, you will never see again. They are gone." Then people cried continuously, but they had cut their heads off. . . . Thirteen died [in addition to those who had staged the insurrection].

Most resistance in the bypassed garrisons of the Marshalls took the form of escape to the American lines. Although some sympathetic Japanese allowed Islanders to get out of harm's way, escapes posed a danger both to morale and to military security, and Japanese sought to reduce them through anti-American propaganda as well as security measures. Joseph Jibon describes Japanese on Jabwor displaying pictures of interrogations, threats that if they supported the Americans they would "slice you up . . . and then salt the wounds. . . . But if you said that you believed the Japanese—they would win— well then, they would never harm you or be upset with you. Nonetheless, you stayed with them, as if in jail, and [you] worked."

Marshallese, says Elson Ebel, were ordered to stay inside bomb shelters when American planes or boats appeared, a rule that became even more strict after the rebellion on Mili: "It was much more difficult, and those who came out of the holes would be jailed. Previously, things had been somewhat okay, but after Jelbon then they hung the shell casings of bullets at the openings to the holes, there where we lived, and when someone came out and moved the shell casings they would hear the sound and knew that there were people coming outdoors."

Lele Ram tells the story of some five hundred Marshallese men, women, and children who were gathered on one of Wotje's islets by about twenty Japanese who intended to kill them:

At that time when they were going to kill us, all of the women and men gathered in one location, but they [the Japanese] were few in number, and they encircled all of the Japanese. And if they had begun [to kill people], they [we Marshallese] would have begun beating people and slicing them up. So then the Japanese said, "Well, we are going to go off and return later." Perhaps they were going to go and take on board the real soldiers. There were twenty-some Japanese at that time, but we Marshallese were five hundred-some, for all of the northern atolls met together and talked things over there. Now, when the corral [of Islanders] was constructed around those fellows they had no path to follow [no way to go get the soldiers]. So at that point, when they said they were going to leave and come back, we began shuttling people to escape.

The increasing tension, as Japanese began to lose control and Micronesian resentment grew, made the final months of war the most dangerous in terms of relations between the two groups.

Chapter 7

THE END OF WAR

We give thanks that the war has finally ended.
Now people can gather together from near or far.
Now passenger ships can come again.
Now every kind of boat can come and go from the islands,
And now we can meet with our loved ones. . . .

What should we say about our islands?
We look up at the coconut trees and the breadfruit trees—
They were felled, and have not yet regrown.
Everything was completely destroyed during that evil war.

—From a song of Nama Island

UNLIKE their Japanese and German predecessors, the Americans took Micronesia "at the point of a spear." Not since the first appearance of Europeans had the military might of foreigners been so manifest. Islanders' experiences of the war's end were far from uniform. On invaded islands—Enewetak, Kwajalein, Guam, Saipan—the transfer of power was marked by a boundary of blood and fire. But for people on isolated central Caroline atolls, the end of war was as diffuse as its beginning, and the simple cessation of contact with Japanese provided the best evidence that Americans had won.

The arrival of U.S. troops, whether in an invasion or as part of a mopping-up operation after the surrender of Japan, led Micronesians to contrast sharply their "before" and "after" ways of life—before and after war, and also before and after American rule. And in every locale, the period immediately preceding American occupation marked the climax of tension between Islanders and the Japanese military.

TARGETING ISLANDERS AS ENEMIES

He made up a lie . . . so the Japanese came looking for us.

The threat of rebellion by Islanders and Asian laborers haunted the Japanese. The strict control of civilians that produced resistance and violent reprisals created a climate of mistrust. Micronesians suspected of affiliation with the enemy, either because of ancestry or past association, were under particular scrutiny. The Japanese also watched Islanders heard speaking English or found with American goods (acquired when freight washed ashore, or in rare encounters with U.S. ships or submarines). Japanese with Micronesian family or friends or who seemed sympathetic to Islanders also came under suspicion. For example, a Japanese man on Mili was executed after another Japanese heard him speaking Marshallese to local people and accused him of revealing military secrets. Europeans were also targets of espionage accusations. Even German and Spanish missionaries (citizens of countries offically allied with Japan) were confined and mistreated; some were executed.[1]

Several prominent families in the Marshall Islands and Chuuk suffered because of European ties. One well-known case is that of Claude and Carl Heine, half-American brothers in the Marshalls, who were well educated and spoke fluent English. Claude Heine headed the mission school on Jaluij. The brothers conveyed war news to other Marshallese. Suspected as spies, they, along with Claude's wife, were jailed on Jaluij, then taken to Imiej. They never returned, and though there were no witnesses, Marshallese believe they were killed. Alek Milne, also accused of working with Americans, was brought from Majuro to Taroa islet, Maloelap, and executed.

Manuel Hartman, of German descent, believes that his family came to be accused of spying when another Chuukese invented the charge to protect himself:

He made up a lie on Uman, so the Japanese came looking for us. Me, and my father, the Nauruans, the priests. There were priests also, one French-

man and one Swede. We were the ones who were dragged to Toloas. . . .
they dragged me out and beat me up until my skull broke. Then my father,
they took him and tied him up.

. . . we were in bed. We were not awake yet, because it wasn't yet morning. We were still sleeping, and we were under mosquito nets . . . they
walked in and just pulled the nets down. Then they grabbed us and started
beating us, me and my father. They took my father and hung him up in a
tree. And then I was beaten until I passed out. Then they went and took
[the accuser] and brought him over, and they went back to Toloas.

Then it was night. The next day, they came back again. When they came,
our bodies were swollen from being beaten up. They told us they were taking us to the beach . . . to execute us. Then they tied our hands, and [when
they got there] they tied us to coconut trees. The soldiers who lived there
came by [and saw us] and said, "Just tell the truth. Because we've never
seen you do anything bad—we never even see you going places; you were
with us in our company working all the time. So we testify that you are good
guys." And the officer also told them that we didn't do anything wrong.

So they took us on a boat to Toloas. We got to Toloas and walked the
street with tied hands, until we came to the office, where they separated us,
but kept our hands tied. When it was time to eat, the police gave us one rice
ball each. And then, the second night, they told us to go: "You are free to
go back."

Members of the Narrhun family in Chuuk were also accused of spying
and suffered imprisonment and torture. Mieko Nipuk recounts that her step-
father and a priest were beaten, and the women tied up, when an entire group
of Chuukese was accused of spying for the Americans—"but I don't know
how, when we couldn't even speak English!"

Nauruans, British subjects removed to Chuuk, were also suspected. At first
they enjoyed friendly relations with Chuukese, who exchanged food and visited them for traditional dances. But after bombing began, such visits were
banned. Some Chuukese think the Nauruans were spies and tell stories of hidden radios or signals; they believe that the Japanese executed several of them.
Some also speculate that Chuuk was saved from destruction by Americans because of the Nauruan presence.

More widely told spy stories feature Japanese who are now seen as folk heroes, whose wartime activities have been reinterpreted as efforts to help the Americans—and, at the same time, the Islanders. An example of this genre is the story of a Japanese man on Pohnpei who seemed before and during the war to be a crazy man, but after the war was revealed—it is said—to have been an American officer. Behavior of Japanese who helped Micronesians, such as the high-ranking Japanese officer "Ito" on Yap, were later explained as the actions of an American spy. Captain Yoshiyasu Morikawa, so helpful to Palauans during the war, is remembered as an American agent who saved them from mass execution in a song written by Buikispis entitled "Merciless War of the *Rubak*" (Higuchi 1991:151):

> *Hiding in the woods we were unaware that*
> *They [Japanese] were preparing a bokugo [air raid shelter] at Ngatbang*
> *In an effort to exterminate us all.*
> *Were it not for the rescue of Morikawa, spy of Roosevelt,*
> *We should have perished at Ngatbang.*

Captain Morikawa himself insists that he was never a U.S. agent. In an interview with Wakako Higuchi, Mr. Morikawa said: "That I was a military officer might be a reason why the Islanders paid special attention to me. Because of my officer education and training, I was naturally different from the nonprofessional soldiers with respect to behavior and language" (1991:155).

We have found no firm evidence of Japanese or Micronesians spying for American forces (except for Marshallese, Chamorros, and Carolinians serving as U.S. scouts after invasion). But it is true that some Micronesians had links with the United States, and it is also true that some became so angered by harsh treatment that their responses threatened the Japanese.

Added to air raids, fear of invasion, food scarcity, and hard labor, challenges to security at times pushed Japanese to uncontrollable violence in their relations with Micronesians. Toward the end of the war Islanders everywhere suspected that the Japanese planned to exterminate them. Such a threat did not materialize in most areas, though there were several massacres of Islanders in the final period of the war (Peattie 1988:347–348, n.85; Higuchi 1991: 154–155; Mamara and Kaiuea 1979:129–130, 134). But stories throughout Micronesia recount Japanese plans to kill Islanders en masse as the war drew to a close. Usually the rumor was linked with the construction of a large trench, bunker, or bomb shelter (as in the Palauan song about Morikawa, above). On Pohnpei, Chuuk, and Kosrae, people tell of being warned by kind Japanese soldiers that they would be sent to hide in the caves before surrender. Once inside, however, they would be killed. Islanders responded to the rumors with plans for escape—some masked as songs—spread from person to person.

On Chuuk, conditions after months of blockade were extremely bad and, Chuukese thought, about to get worse. They believed the Japanese solution to food shortages would be to kill them (and perhaps eat them), beginning with the old and the weak who could not work. Chuukese worried about extermination from the other side as well—that Americans would resort to extremes to force capitulation. In one account of how the war ended, Chuuk is described as the original target for the atomic bomb:

> It was Providence that made them drop the bomb in Japan, because those three airplanes that flew from Guam were ordered by the U.S. to drop the bomb in Chuuk. When they learned that, number 1 was Japan, number 2, Chuuk [i.e., the Americans learned that Chuuk held the strongest military force, next to Japan itself]. They were to drop the atomic bomb in Chuuk, but when they flew here, a typhoon struck from the south that hit Guam. The answer was, go to Japan and drop the atomic bomb—because the typhoon was coming from the south so they couldn't come to Chuuk. [In this version, the plane changed course after it was in the air, on personal instructions from President Truman.] So they went to Japan and dropped the bomb. Had it not been for the atomic bomb, the war would not have ended. As soon as they dropped the bomb, it was over.

SIGNS OF THE END OF WAR

When this happened, it was a shock to us.

Despite deteriorating conditions, Japanese morale in Micronesia remained high until the loss of Saipan and the first air raids on the home islands in December 1944, and Islanders largely accepted early Japanese assertions of eventual victory. Humiko Mori recalls that, when American ships appeared outside Chuuk's reef during the February 1944 attack, then turned back as planned, Chuuk's defenders hailed a thwarted invasion: "The Japanese told us, 'You see, America didn't win—we won.'"[2]

While Japanese attempted to maintain a flow of positive propaganda throughout the war, Micronesians say (in retrospect) that they eventually began to suspect defeat. Obvious losses under repeated aerial attacks and the military's inability to launch planes to defend important installations made people critical of optimistic Japanese claims. The suffering of the empire's soldiers and the Japanese command's inability to supply their own troops with food and goods also implied defeat. American propaganda leaflets encouraged doubts. Thaddeus Sampson, a Marshallese man who was pro-Japanese in sentiment, recognized the significance of one American propaganda image, a picture of a rooster consuming a cake. Mr. Sampson worked with Japanese officers as an interpreter and cultural advisor; he describes how the Japanese themselves understood the image:

> The cake was Japan and the rooster was America. It would consume the cake and keep going and keep going until it was eaten up. And so he [a Japanese officer] said, "Let us not be like this cake," meaning, let us not be inadequate. He said [to demonstrate American wealth], "If the Americans were unloading a ship full of chickens, well, it would be full of chickens, nothing else. If it were hats, it would be hats solely and they would unload them until dark and then again until morning. And as for clothing, well, we need not say. And if it were eggs, well, it would be eggs only." And this is why he was saying they [Japanese] were inadequate. And then, if we speak of weapons, well, when the [Japanese] guns were fired, they went "buk! buk! buk!" but their [American] guns went "brrrrrr!"

These predictions of plentiful American resources proved all too accurate. As Islanders like Thaddeus Sampson saw U.S. military power firsthand, they found their loyalties and their self-interest at odds: "When they [Marshallese] had seen the Japanese and the kind of strength that they were building and the things that they were doing to ready themselves for war, well, they said that they would side with them. But then when the Americans landed, a difficult time arrived and they did not know what to do. They did not know where their strength and where their best opportunity would be. And those were the ones who thought they would try to assist the [Americans]."

On islands far from invasion sites, Micronesians had no chance to see for themselves the American superiority in materiel. They continued to respond to the military of most immediate concern to them, the Japanese. Yet even on isolated islands, people received some hint of change. In this Ifaluk prayer to Tilitr, the god foretells American victory (Burrows 1963:413):

> *The war will soon be over now,*
> *The end of the fighting is near.*
> *Do not be afraid anymore!*
> *Soon the Americans will come.*
> *All you women and children who have offered me flowers,*
> *Fear no more!*

In the Mortlocks, some months before the end of war, "a shaman from Kutu named Sebas predicted, while in a trance, the eventual American victory as well as the advent of such things as public radio stations and television. His prediction of the Japanese defeat was concealed from the military detachment on the island [Kutu] for fear of retribution but gave hope to the islanders that their time of hardship would soon end" (Reafsnyder 1984:105, n.40). Indeed, in some places the resident Japanese kept the secret of defeat until the very end. Otneil Eddmont recalls that even after American troops arrived on Kosrae it was hard to believe that the Japanese were no longer in control: "Some men and women were carrying food for the Japanese soldiers when they met the Americans walking on the road. They were afraid of them because they didn't know who they were. They [the carriers] came and told us about this, but we didn't believe them, because the Japanese had never told us that Americans would enter the island. They had promised us that we would be working with them as soldiers until all of us died. So when this happened, it was a shock to us. So when everyone heard the news, everyone was happy."

FIRST ENCOUNTERS WITH MICRONESIA'S NEW CHIEFS

> *And so, from that moment forward all of our fears fell*
> *away from us. And all of our worries disappeared.*

Micronesians were not singled out as a distinct population in Allied preinvasion projections; rather they were included in plans for civilians in general. Japanese and Okinawan civilians could be assumed to be pro-Japanese; Koreans were also a somewhat known quantity. But American troops did not know how to predict Micronesian responses to them, to the invasion, or to the Japanese during an attack. They assumed the people of Kiribati were anti-Japanese but were unsure about Marshallese until they stepped ashore at Majuro; from that point on, they considered them as friendly. U.S. Navy historian Dorothy Richard states: "The natives of the islands were not classified as enemy nationals. They were not Japanese subjects but because the mandate definition of nationality was not clear, the United States could assume that they were liberated peoples and therefore base all military government policies and activities on that assumption" (1957a:164–165). Yet as Ballendorf (1984b:2) points out, distinctions were made. Invading Americans treated Marshallese as liberated citizens, but at first treated Chamorros in the Marianas as enemy nationals, both because of the Marianas' crucial strategic position and because more Chamorros held official positions under the Japanese than Micronesians elsewhere.[3]

Wartime stresses, the increasingly obvious Japanese weakness, and rumors of Allied victories created a climate in which Americans were in fact widely welcomed by Micronesians. Apart from official policy, first contacts between American troops and Micronesians depended on local circumstances and personalities. The greatest contrast in the experience of the end of war distinguishes Islanders on invaded territory from those on bypassed sites. Most important is whether the first encounters took place in the heat of battle or in the backwaters of war after Japanese surrender. A less obvious point is that in the early months of the Pacific war, the U.S. military's civil affairs policy was just taking shape; by the end of the war, newly occupied areas came under a well-established system of governance.[4] A final factor was American preconceptions about the nature and loyalty of the Islanders and their first impressions of the people they called the "natives."

Invasion Encounters: Marshalls

American responses to Marshallese were overwhelmingly positive, perceiving them as mild, pro-American Christians.[5] "One account has it that when American soldiers landed on a small island in the Marshalls, they were greeted by the local people with outstretched hands saying, 'Good morning, we are Christians from Boston'" (Ballendorf 1984b:2).

Americans' first experience with civil affairs in the Pacific went well. On each invaded island, small U.S. Navy Military Government ("MilGov") teams assembled Islanders on undamaged islets and provided food, medical supplies, clothing, and other basic goods, often salvaged from Japanese stores. As islands were secured, MilGov officers relieved Marine Corps Civil Affairs officers, and island or atoll commanders took control.[6] One of the first MilGov officers described Marshallese as "ill and dazed, hungry, and in rags" (Cockrum 1970:208–209).

For their part, Marshallese were stunned by the ferocity and overwhelming might of invasion, frightened by Japanese propaganda that American soldiers would kill them all, weary and sick of war. Americans appeared to be powerful enough to protect them from the Japanese military and generous enough to supply all that was so desperately lacking. Nearly everyone in the region remembers their first experiences with American troops as overwhelmingly anxious, yet ultimately positive.

The war ended first for Islanders on Majuro and Kwajalein in the first months of 1944. On Majuro, taken without a fight on January 31, 1944 (west longitude date), the actual experience of encountering Americans quickly dissolved fears, especially when much-needed food and clothing were distributed. Military government was established the day after the invasion ("D+1"), and Majuro people saw immediate changes: Doctors set up dispensaries by day's end, church services soon resumed, and schools reopened by April 1944. Everyone was eventually moved to other islets to segregate them from the military and keep them safe from "the unfamiliar mechanism of modern warfare and from enemy air attacks." Before relocation, Americans met with the "king" and elders to arrange land, water, food, and housing (Richard 1957a: 330–334).

American landings on heavily defended islands were of course much different. On Roi-Namur in Kwajalein, the Marine Corps Civil Affairs unit could find no civilians when they first came ashore on February 1; later that day they located fifty-one Micronesians who signaled to them by waving white flags. The next day, the civil affairs unit brought thirty-two Micronesian laborers to the division command post, where they helped bury the dead. On D+4, marines began concentrating Micronesians on Boked islet as they searched the atoll; in a few days 350 were camped there. Similarly at Kwajalein, civil affairs officers who went ashore on D+2 found no Islanders on Kwajalein islet but a number on Enelapkan (Ennylebagan), where they had fled when Japanese warned them of the imminent invasion. The civil affairs unit fed them and added them to a voluntary burial detail for Kwajalein's dead (which included fifty-five Marshallese). They were treated at the navy hospital and given clothing. When the assault phase ended on D+8, patrols went to all Kwajalein's islets to search for Japanese stragglers, post proclamations, deliver salvaged rice, and assess Islanders' needs. The navy reported that Marshallese appeared friendly and cooperative as MilGov was established (Cockrum 1970:212; Richard 1957a:336–339).

At Enewetak, fifty natives came through American lines on D+1. They were fed and questioned aboard the U.S.S. *Cambria*, then taken to shelter in a huge bomb crater ashore, where two chiefs distributed food. The Navy gathered 117 Islanders from throughout the atoll, moving them first to Enjebi, then into a camp at Aomon, where they were told to stay until the end of the war.[7]

Ato Lañkio, on Namu Atoll next to Kwajalein, gives this account of the American landing on that undefended atoll:

> They were coming toward the islet, firing all the time. The guns did not move downward but continued to point upward. As they came toward us they just kept firing, and kept coming toward the land. While they were firing and moving closer to land, the people could no longer cope, their abilities were exhausted. The fear we carried around at that time was so great that people might faint because of it. Some people were ready to go crazy. It is possible to have people's minds twisted around during such times.
>
> But, while we were frightened of the landing—I had almost forgotten— each soldier was assigned to one of us to greet. When the soldiers came down from the tanks, they took hold of people's hands. They shook their hands and greeted them, and said, "Greetings to you," and "Do not be afraid, do not run off because we are bringing peace." And then the ministers, that is, the foreign preachers who had come along with them, raised their hands and said these words: "Do not be afraid."

After describing the surrender of his Japanese schoolteacher and the Japanese policeman on Namu, Mr. Lañkio continues:

> A short time later some amtracs landed and brought a great deal of food onto the islet. They brought perhaps a thousand dollars worth of food and left it there, including flour, rice, luncheon meat, and beef tongue. There

were many kinds of meats and also cigarettes—all sorts of things. And they then called out to the people and showed them these things. They gave us cigarettes and food: C-rations, the sort of food suitable for soldiers, and also food for ordinary people. And so everyone was quick to change. Their fear disappeared and they remained there in peace.

This was a very difficult time for us on Namu. We had thought that our lives were finished. We saw that we had absolutely no power. It is perhaps true that our only power rested there in the hands of the Americans, the hands of the American soldiers and their teachers [chaplains] and their generals. But from that time onward—the kinds of things that they did when they landed with their vessels and when the food arrived, the food that they had stored on a huge barge, a barge that was so huge that it was taller than a large church—and they fed people, and they each selected a person and they grabbed their hand and shook it, and they greeted them and they made small talk with them, and they spoke to them in English— we did not know what they were saying, but we did know that they spoke to us in a way that was as pure and as light-hearted as possible—and so, from that moment forward all of our fears fell away from us. And all of our worries disappeared. And all of those things that we were thinking about at that time, things we had no understanding of, the things that were going on during the period when they were coming toward us, because we had thought that this was our last moment. And we thought that there would be no other moments to live. And we thought that the lives of the people of Namu were finished. And all of this was in the midst of the battle be- tween the Japanese and the Americans.

Construction of American bases on the conquered islands began immedi- ately. Construction Battalions (Seabees) came ashore on D+1 at Majuro and in twelve days had a coral airstrip ready for emergency landing; by April 15, airfield and base infrastructure were completed. Seabees accompanied the first wave of marines ashore at Roi-Namur to start an airstrip, then rebuilt Japanese facilities. The Enewetak base was also underway immediately after D-day.[8] On these atolls, Islanders saw overwhelming evidence of American military might and economic wealth.

Undefended Marshall islands quickly came under American control. A unit from Majuro landed on Aur on April 17, on Arno April 25, and on Erikub June 4; these were administered from Majuro. Remaining atolls and islands were reconnoitered by the 22d Marines and army units between March 9 and April 23, 1944 (where there was a small Japanese unit, they usually committed suicide or fought until killed). Occupied islands were organized into the Department for Military Government on Non-Garrisoned Atolls (Richard 1957a: 343–344).[9] Patrols assessing the Marshallese reported yaws, ulcers, sores, cataracts, blindness, and a flu epidemic on Namorik that had killed nearly half the population—the poor health conditions reflected the stress and isolation of war. On Ailinglablab (Ailinglapalap), Ebon, Ronglap, and Utirik, bombardment had destroyed villages and food trees. People were living "as refugees" in uninhabited areas along the reef (Cockrum 1970:215–216).

The construction of American bases at Majuro, Kwajalein, and Enewetak and the occupation of unfortified atolls reshaped the circumstances of the remaining Japanese bases. During the last year and a half of war, U.S. planes used the new bases to bomb Jaluij, Mili, Maloelap, and Wotje regularly, often twice a day. With U.S. bases launching air and sea patrols, Micronesians on the bypassed atolls began to escape, and Marshallese scouts ventured in to gather intelligence for the U.S. Navy. In May 1944, a thirty-six-hour visit by scouts set ashore by outrigger canoe at each bypassed atoll gleaned information about air targets and Japanese strength. As Japanese stockpiles ran out in the second half of 1944, Americans sought more aggressively to remove Marshallese, while planes dropped propaganda leaflets to encourage desertion and surrender by Japanese troops.[10]

Meanwhile, U.S. MilGov moved quickly to establish basic services throughout conquered areas, beginning with food, health, education, and commerce. The navy set up a trading post with confiscated Japanese supplies at Roi-Namur. The navy's own trade goods had been lost in the landing, but ships' stores provided some items. Business flourished, especially after Islanders began getting pay chits for working for the Americans. Labor camps were established on Majuro and the islets of Kwajalein and Roi-Namur in Kwajalein Atoll in February and March of 1944. Those not hired were returned to their own islands as soon as possible, even if those islands were badly damaged. Displaying the strong commitment to their land that would cause such problems for the American nuclear testing program in years to come, Mar-

Photo 9. Marshallese escaping Japanese-held Mili are evacuated by U.S. Navy LCI to Arno Atoll, March 1945. (U.S. Navy photo, National Archives photo no. 80-G-316739)

shallese "resisted every suggestion to permanent resettlement even for valid economic reasons" (Cockrum 1970:219).

At this point, the United States seemed little interested in close involvement with indigenous life, preferring to administer what it regarded as the basic elements of good order through local chiefs or "kings."[11] In the first days after invasion, Marshallese and U.S. troops gathered in the evening to sing (Marshallese had learned American hymns and folk songs from missionaries), but stricter rules controlling interaction and forbidding troops to visit Marshallese settlements were soon in place. The navy established a twelve-week interpreter school on Ebeye (Kwajalein) and schools in labor camps at Kwajalein and Majuro; by March 15, 1945, schools operated on fourteen atolls.[12]

Marshallese leaders responded quickly to American overtures. Tomeing was paramount chief of the Ratak (eastern) island chain. Weakened by illness contracted during the war, he died in October 1946, but before his death he planned tirelessly for rehabilitation of those islands. He moved his capital from Maloelap to the more centrally located Wotje. He spoke for Marshallese in official contexts (to the Americans as he had to the Japanese), taught school until Americans could provide better instruction, and stimulated handicraft production. His people gave as well as taking, offering $10 to the American Red Cross and "$60 and a box of handicraft to the Military Governor of the Marshalls in memory of the naval evacuation of Marshallese from the Japanese-occupied atoll of Wotje in 1944" (Mason 1946:91).

Despite such Marshallese efforts to return tangible thanks for American generosity, most of the giving was one-sided. Officially, U.S. MilGov was to supply "enemy populations" with only sufficient food, clothing, and housing to prevent disease and "unrest prejudicial to military operations," but the directive was "interpreted liberally in the Mandated Islands because they were not indigenous Japanese territory" (Richard 1957a:183). MilGov fed civilians during the fighting, then gave them salvaged Japanese supplies. (The intention was to give free supplies only until basic needs were met, then only until currency was available; after that, supplies were sold. Relief issues ceased in the Marshalls by July 1944.) Initial food supplies for civilians were limited to rice, flour, beans, fats/oils, canned or dried fish and meat, salt, sugar, evaporated or powdered milk, and tea.[13] These, plus standard naval supplies, confiscated local stocks, salvaged materials, purchases of local food, and the American Red Cross, made up what the navy had to work with. It was more than Marshallese had seen in years.

It is not surprising that many stories of the invasion dwell on the distribution of food in great quantity and variety, reflecting both the privation of war and the important symbolism of food in Marshallese culture. Asked to describe any positive reminiscences of the war, Leban Jorju, who spent those years on Kwajalein and Ronglap, said:

Well, I remember with fondness the foods of the Americans. We could throw them away because there was no cost, and one corned beef, *iiyeo!* (He indicates the length of his forearm, and laughs.) A single corned beef [and of such a size]!

Photo 10. American supplies and equipment on Kwajalein, March 1944. Marshall Islanders were impressed with the seemingly endless flow of American goods. (U.S. Navy photo, National Archives photo no. 80-G-400941)

(Marshallese interviewer: Nearly all the respected elders say this in their re-membrances, they say: "You see, during the battle, they came and brought corned beef, iiyeo *[the length of your forearm]!)*

Long ones! The males of the species!

(Interviewer: If you opened one, fifty people would be replete with meat. Well, that is one of the memories the Marshallese will never forget.)

Yes, we young boys did not know how to open those things at the time. These things were inside cases. We would take a case and throw it down on the ground so that one of them would break open. Then we would eat the corned beef, along with scraped coconut.

While Americans undoubtedly thought, correctly, that their gifts were signs of good will and gestures of friendship, they were less aware that Marshallese

Photo 11. Religious services after American occupation of the Marshall Islands, February 1944. (U.S. Navy photo, National Archives photo no. 80-G-213606)

also interpreted them as the customary distributions of chiefs—very powerful chiefs with a seemingly unlimited source of goods. Joined with the invasion's overwhelming display of military might, Americans came to be seen as "the parallel of traditional conquerors writ large—that is, as sacred (and foreign) chiefs" (for Enewetak and Ujelang, Carucci 1989:85). The political implications of this abundant initial generosity would emerge later in the American administration.[14]

Invasion Encounters: Western Micronesia

Marshallese experienced the U.S. Navy's first efforts at governing Micronesians in the Pacific war context. Those in the western islands, invaded later, encountered a more fully organized civil affairs program. A dance song composed by Letaweriur celebrates the American arrival on Ifaluk (Bates and Abbott 1958:94–95; Burrows 1963:414–420):

> *Now all our women rejoice;*
> *Now the Americans have come.*
> *This is pleasing to the chiefs.*
> *They have given us a paper.*
> *This place is to rise;*
> *This island is to be lifted up.*
> *The chiefs say we are to dance.*
> *We will dance, we will rejoice!*
> *This very month, for this is a good year! Ei!*
> *The Japanese are gone.*
> *We did not like their rough ways.*
> *The gods have been good to us;*
> *Now our crops are safe.*
> *The Americans talk kindly.*

Despite similar good relations, the people of Ulithi, which was taken in mid-September 1944, faced great changes. The atoll's largest garden was destroyed to put an airstrip on Falalop; Sorlen islet was razed for a ferry base; Mogmog became a recreation center visited by several hundred thousand troops during the war; a LORAN station was set up on Potangeras. Restricted to Fasserai islet, Ulithians were visited by a chaplain, a physician (whom they converted to Catholicism), a pharmacist's mate, and officials on tour. Though houses were bulldozed for the runway on Falalop, Mogmog village was preserved as a tropical resort for navy rest and recreation: "The native huts, on their neat platforms of coral gravel, were repaired, their sides opened up to the breeze, and their interiors furnished with chairs and tables. In these improvised cabanas, small groups could establish themselves for a day's swimming and loafing, with cards, beer, and assorted delicacies from home. . . . Working parties policed the island every morning, so that it always had a pristine look—white sand and green verdure, with neat, shady paths between . . . a banner proclaimed, 'Welcome to Mogmog, Paradise of the Pacific'" (Meredith 1956:152–153).[15]

MilGov had faced the opposite of paradise on the invaded Marianas. While

Photo 12. Outrigger canoes near American installations at Ulithi Atoll, August 1945. (U.S. Navy photo, National Archives photo no. 80-G-347511)

mass suicides on Saipan evoked shock and sympathy, Americans viewed the large (and largely Japanese) civilian population in the Marianas with caution, and civil affairs units found their preparation and logistical support inadequate to the challenge (Hough 1947:195–198, 227). MilGov on Saipan began with marines gathering civilians met during the fighting of June 15–July 9, 1944, into ethnically segregated camps. Within a few hours of battle, small numbers of them, "homeless, starving, naked, wounded, and in most cases terror-stricken by the savage fighting taking place but a few hundred yards away, suddenly appeared and clamored for assistance" (Richard 1957a:435–438). Combat troops gathered refugees into stockades on the already crowded beach, in miserable conditions. Civil affairs marines came ashore on the third day of the invasion and navy MilGov three days later; on D+5, refugees at last moved to an internment camp at Lake Susupe. More refugees flooded in: on June 16 (D+1) there had been 1,000 civilians in American hands; by July 8, there were 8,130; by August 1, 15,000.

All the civilians faced great danger getting through the lines of battle and identifying themselves for surrender. In addition, they had heard that capture by Americans meant torture, and many fell back toward the north of the island with the Japanese troops. Chamorro and Carolinian Saipanese, who had been dispersed to their farms prior to the invasion, were skeptical of the propaganda but still sought to survive the invasion by sheltering in caves or frequently moving, avoiding Japanese troops who were certain to end up in combat: "For every Chamorro and Carolinian family, the invasion was a harrowing experience. Apart from the danger, they soon ran out of food and water, and their clothing was shredded to rags; they were in wretched condition when they finally reached the safety of internment camps. Many were wounded; over 300 were killed" (Spoehr 1954:92). Saipan's size entailed a lengthy "mopping-up" phase, in which stragglers were gathered in from caves and fields for months after the devastated island was declared secure in early July.

> After battle had passed over Saipan and Tinian, little remained but ruin. The towns, the villages, and most of the farm houses had been used by the Japanese as defense points as they retreated into more and more restricted areas. Gutted buildings, burned houses, piles of rubble and twisted sheet roofing marked the former settlement sites. Fields were burned, communications entirely disrupted, and all industries completely eradicated. All the functions which had provided the islands with the necessities of life were at a standstill, and the social and economic structure which had energized these functions was destroyed. The civilians, who had sought shelter in the hills and caves during the conflict, were gradually captured or coaxed with megaphones to cross to the American lines. Many were ill, wounded, and suffering from shell shock, the strain of constant uncertainty and the lack of food and water. (Bowers 1950:49)

With the rainy season starting, rough and crowded shelter was improvised at Camp Susupe for the five or six hundred civilians—Japanese, Okinawan, Korean, Chamorro, Carolinian—who came in each day.

Caring for internees was a secondary concern for the United States. On Sai-

Photo 13. Chamorro internment camp on Saipan, early 1945. (U.S. Navy photo, National Archives photo no. 80-G-307661)

pan as in the invaded Marshalls, the first job once the island was secure was to build military bases. Whereas Japanese Saipan had been largely a supply depot, under American control it became a huge offensive base from which to attack Japan itself. Saipan held two huge B-29 fields, an extension of Aslito airstrip, small fields at Marpi and Kagman Points, and the naval base at Tanapag with improved harbor, seaplane base, boat repair facilities, supply and ammunition depot, and support facilities. The first raids on Tokyo flew from Saipan on November 24, 1944.[16]

Until the end of war, Saipan, Tinian, and Guam were under "a strict Military Government" with daily air and sea patrols in the region and close control of civilians (Taylor 1945:21). On Saipan in September 1945, MilGov was feeding 13,954 Japanese, 1,411 Koreans, 2,966 Chamorros, and 1,025 Carolinians with Japanese and American supplies. As the first weeks and months passed, basic economic organization reemerged. Farming and fishing resumed; the

United States supplied food, clothing, housing, and medical care. The population's physical condition—very bad at invasion, when in the first weeks most deaths were from dysentery, malnutrition, and diarrhea—began to improve. Medical facilities and schools were set up, cooperatives took over the MilGov trade stores, and civilians started private enterprises, producing for local needs and souvenirs for U.S. troops. In November 1944, Chamorros and Carolinians moved from Camp Susupe to the town of Chalan Kanoa, using Japanese homes still standing and others that had been repaired. They received preference in consumer goods, housing, and personal liberty over Japanese civilians left in the camps, and they elected their own leader in December 1944 (they chose Juan Ada, who had served as *sonchō* before the war). But Saipanese did not regain freedom of movement until the Japanese were repatriated in mid-1946.[17]

While Japanese and Korean civilians were regarded as prisoners, Chamorro camps were self-administered under MilGov supervision. Saipanese were treated like "liberated peoples," though still under military control. MilGov hired 119 Chamorros as guards. They kept an eye on visitors and GIs, checked passes of inmates leaving or entering for work, and created some resentment by their treatment of Japanese and Korean civilians. Forty-five Chamorros and Carolinians became American scouts for security work on Saipan and islands to the north.[18] Within months, Chamorros had established themselves not only as a liberated people (rather than Japanese allies), but in fact as aides to the American military government.

Peleliu and Angaur, also invaded in "Operation Stalemate," involved much smaller Micronesian populations. U.S. MilGov personnel assigned to the Peleliu invasion landed on D-day (September 15, 1944), but found no Islanders to help, since most had been evacuated before the invasion. Angaur was secured on September 20, but not until ten days later did captured Japanese indicate that Islanders had been evacuated from their homes just before invasion and were hiding in caves at the northwest tip of the island where Japanese troops were making their last stand. U.S. Army Civil Affairs officers used a public address system to try to persuade them to leave the caves, fearing they would be killed either by the Japanese or by American bombs. Early in October, troops "uncovered" fifteen Micronesians, originally from Sonsorol (Richard 1957a:611–612). One of them wrote a letter to people still in caves, which eventually brought out 177 more, many suffering from thirst, malnu-

Photo 14. War refugees "on the day they came out of caves" on Angaur, late 1944. (U.S. Navy photo, National Archives photo no. 80-G-291698)

trition, wounds, and diseases. They were housed under tarpaulins next to the POW camp: 147 Angaurese, 11 Chamorros, 16 Yapese, and 8 Woleai men. At the end of the assault, custody of these people was transferred to a U.S. Navy Mil-Gov unit.[19]

Although Guam was in a different legal and psychological state from the Japanese mandate, with Guamanians welcoming and actively aiding the return of American rule, the government installed after the invasion was nonetheless patterned after MilGov units in Kiribati and the Marshall islands (Carano and Sanchez 1964:309). The first civil affairs officers came ashore with the attacking troops and began work as Guamanians found their way to American lines. Unlike Micronesians elsewhere, Guamanians knew what to expect and were eager to get into American hands. The reunion of American military and Guamanians was more unequivocal and emotional than American arrivals in former Japanese colonies. When the 77th Infantry found the Chamorro camp at Yona, the two thousand people were "cheering, weeping, laughing. . . .

They had had little food, no medical care. They were clothed in rags. They were weak, racked by continual coughing fits—victims of malnutrition, malaria and tuberculosis. Their bodies were sticks of bones and their olive skin was drawn drum-tight. But this thirty-first of July was the day they had awaited for nearly three years. When they saw the American soldiers coming through the trees they hobbled to their feet with glad cries" (Leckie 1962:381). Leckie relates that the Guamanians sang "The Marines Hymn" and then "a song of their own underground, composed especially for this date and memorized in face of every threat of reprisal." The refrain of this popular resistance song had been fulfilled (Carano and Sanchez 1964:289):

> *Oh, Mr. Sam, Sam, my dear Uncle Sam,*
> *Won't you please come back to Guam?*

As American troops moved across Guam through the end of July, they gathered refugees into camps run by U.S. Navy Civil Affairs units (those in relatively intact southern Guam were encouraged to remain at home). A concentration camp was set up for several hundred Japanese soldier and civilian POWs, plus Saipanese, Rotanese, and a few local Chamorros suspected of Japanese sympathies. As on Saipan, the civil affairs section was understaffed for the job it faced in the first days after invasion. Its low priority for transport and supplies meant that these arrived after the fifteen thousand civilians were within American lines. Camps lacked equipment and supplies and suffered the misery of the rainy season.

Seabees came ashore behind the marines. As on Saipan and Tinian, the invasion of Guam was followed by massive development of airfields, highways, and harbors, and Guam's people realized that their lives would not return to prewar quietness. Guam became a major U.S. Navy staging, supply, and training base, with thousands of Chamorros employed as laborers and clerical workers and a mid-1945 military and civilian population of over 220,000.[20]

Bypassed Islands Surrender

In contrast to the experiences of immediate, overwhelming American military might and wealth on invaded islands, the end of the war came much more quietly to bypassed locales and was hardly noticeable where there were no major Japanese bases. After the destruction of Hiroshima and Nagasaki on

Photo 15. Initial American proclamation to Japanese and Micronesians on Chuuk, November 1945. (U.S. Navy photo, National Archives photo no. 80-G-356816)

August 6 and 8, 1945, U.S. forces dropped leaflets urging surrender on the remaining Japanese-held islands in Micronesia. "The immediate reaction varied from antiaircraft fire reported in the Bonins to a hurried agreement from badly battered Rota in the Marianas" (Blackton 1946:401). The hard-pressed Japanese bases in the Marshalls were among the first to seek relief, with Mili airstrip displaying a white cross on August 18 and making its formal capitulation the next day; Jaluij, Wotje, and Maloelap soon followed (Richard 1957b:8). Japan's official surrender came on September 2, 1945. Many of the bypassed Micronesian islands, however, saw a delay between the end of war and active American occupation.

The surrender of the uninvaded islands of the Marshalls, Carolines, and Marianas was negotiated with Japanese military commanders on Chuuk. The initial American mission arrived in Chuuk on August 30, 1945, consisting only of a destroyer and a destroyer escort carrying a dozen surrender team members, accompanied by B-24s. The Japanese agreed to cease military action at once while awaiting formal surrender. The Americans flew home that same day.

Vice Admiral George D. Murray, commander of the Marianas, formally received the unconditional surrender of Chuuk on September 2, 1945, aboard the USS *Portland*.[21] But the first American inspection of the Chuuk area did not come until October 2–5; U.S. occupation not until November 24. And it was many months before American units visited all the islands of the region. The long delay between surrender and the start of American rule put Chuukese in an uncertain position. Some might have seen the American planes flying over at the end of August, but they did not learn that the visit signaled Japanese surrender for several weeks. Despite the intermingling of Japanese troops and Chuukese laborers and tight control of Micronesian activities, the Japanese made no public announcement of the surrender. A few residents heard privately from Japanese friends that the war had ended and even fewer learned that the Japanese had lost. This news was transmitted in confidence, however, and the message was not to be openly discussed. Most Chuukese simply noticed changes in routine that signaled the war's end: "I knew that the war was over when American planes came in and flew very low, but no one shot at them."

Dolan (1974:107) interviewed several Chuukese about their recollections of this time: "In Truk, Mr. [Keigo] Ezra remembers that the Japanese 'took aside the Trukese workers and told them that the Emperor would talk over the radio. The Japanese got dressed up in their uniforms and the Trukese who worked for them were very quiet during the ceremony. "We were astonished at the Japanese crying." Most of the older Japanese were crying, but the young ones went off by themselves and were glad that they didn't have to die. The Trukese went home and were so happy, having a thanksgiving service.'"

To Chuukese in rural areas, with no Japanese contacts, the withdrawal of local troops, when it came, was unexplained and dramatic: "One morning the Japanese were gone. They left all their things behind." Americans did nothing to clarify this message, leaving the Japanese in control of surrendered Chuuk for more than two months. Micronesians continued to labor for the Japanese military, farming and clearing bomb damage. U.S. officials were aware of conditions on Chuuk but must have felt that they did not call for immediate action. (In contrast, information obtained at the surrender led the U.S. Navy to evacuate Woleai, where the Japanese garrison was near starvation [Blackton 1946:408]).

When the first U.S. Navy Civil Affairs party did arrive at Chuuk, Japanese silence about the war's outcome and Chuukese fear of Americans made the initial encounters tense. Tupun Louis describes the arrival of U.S. troops:

We didn't know that it was going to be *kaijo* [the end of the war]. During that time before the *kaijo,* we worked really hard, night and day. Most of our work was cleaning up the bomb craters and dead bodies. And then they said, the war is over, *kaijo.* The Japanese did not tell us that it was *kaijo.* We were hiding in the caves, and we didn't know that the noise of airplanes and ships were the Americans. The Americans came on the island. We saw the navy, Americans. We didn't come out; we were scared of them. The leaders said, "Okay, we remain here. If they spray us with poison gas, just stay here. We will die together." And we prayed. Prayed, prayed, and looked out—all the Americans were around. We looked out from inside, and the Americans looked in. And I was thinking, "Maybe the Americans were also afraid that we might hurt them." The Americans spoke to us: We didn't know what they were saying. We were thinking, "Maybe they won't hurt us." That's the time we knew the Americans had won the war. They won—and we lost.

Among the group in that cave were two of the oldest men: one old man from Neme named Damin and one from Losap named Sana. There were women and children. The old man from Neme went out. "If they kill me, then you will know that all of us will die." He went out and stood amongst them. They were all looking at him/studying him and shaking his hand, taking out cigarettes, giving him cigarettes, lighting one for him. They put a shirt on him and a pair of pants. "Wow, lucky guy!"—we were looking out; the Americans actually dressed him. He came back in: "Now we will get out, because Japan lost." Maybe he knew some English because since German times, this old man had been with foreigners. "We will get out and line up, and I'll teach you a greeting, how to greet these people." And someone inside said, "Why are we going to go out?" The old man said, "Japan lost, and they're taking all the Japanese soldiers, without shirts, wearing only pants. They lost. They gathered all the Japanese officers in Rerre." At that time, we didn't know the war was over. We were confused, without information, we were not informed.

We got out, the old man lined us up. He taught us how to say "hello" to the Americans. Before we greeted these Americans, we would bow down, and as we rose, we would say our greetings. Everyone would line up— women and children.

(Interviewer asks: Do you still remember what that greeting was, how you said hello?)

Yes. The old man told us—every one of us, one by one—the word we would say. We would bow down, and then as we came up we would say, "How do you do, sir!" [in English] That was the greeting word: "How d'ye do, sir!" He went away from me, and I just repeated the words, "How d'ye do sir, How d'you do sir," to memorize the words. We were wearing torn clothes.

"Okay, get ready—face them now! Then, give the word." We bowed, and then we said the greeting. And the Americans were laughing. They gave us clothes, one by one, they gave us clothes. For the ladies, they gave them coats [*kappa*, raincoats], because there were no dresses. They gave us cigarettes, until everyone had everything. And then they distributed biscuits and candies. They had four trucks; they got up on their trucks and they left. And we saw Chuukese people riding with these Americans, going around. As we were looking around, we saw these Chuukese on the American trucks, and we said, "What's up?" And they said, "*Kaijo!* The Japanese are on the American ships, going back." And that was the end of the war.

The United States focused occupation efforts in urban centers. In Chuuk, Americans chose Weno as their center of operations because of its airfields. (Chuuk's MilGov unit encompassed the lagoon islands and the central Caroline atolls.) Toloas, the Japanese capital, had been nearly destroyed by years of bombing, and thousands of Japanese "disarmed military personnel" remained at large there (Trumbull 1959:90). Seabees arrived on Weno in late November 1945 to repair airfields and build ramps for ships and the buildings, roads, and water and electrical systems needed by MilGov. The first U.S. plane landed in April 1946.[22]

The navy's "to-do" list on Chuuk shows the range of postsurrender occupation tasks: repatriate Japanese, clear ammunition dumps and debris, build administrative facilities and base camps, provide aid to Micronesians. The navy also arrested forty-two possible war criminals,[23] removed Japanese and

Photo 16. Chuukese on Weno line up for American inspection tour, October 1945. (U.S. Navy photo, National Archives photo no. 80-G-353879)

Allied bodies, conducted a medical survey, and set up a leper colony, two hospitals, and a beach recreation center. Americans used Japanese and Korean labor in the demilitarization and cleanup of Chuuk. As a result, though repatriation began in October 1945, the last Japanese troops did not leave until December 26, 1946—and civilian repatriation went on well after that (Denfeld 1981a:53–59). On Chuuk as elsewhere, occupation forces also had the job of fostering postwar recovery. Artie Moses of Uman was named the first chief of Chuuk lagoon in December 1945 in what became a complex interaction of American officials and Chuukese chiefs (see chapter 8).

Though Chuuk's logistics were the most daunting, MilGov's tasks and priorities were roughly the same on the other high islands occupied after Japan's surrender. U.S. officials accepted Pohnpei's surrender in mid-September 1945, over a year and a half after the intensive bombing of Kolonia had begun. At surrender, Kolonia was "utterly destroyed" save for some sheds at the base of a pier and two churches (Spoehr 1949b:377). Incoming Americans contacted

Photo 17. U.S. Navy personnel occupying Pohnpei greet Spanish Catholic
sisters and priests, Carlos Etscheit, and Pohnpeians, September 11, 1945. There
are few official photos of the American occupation of Pohnpei, Kosrae, or Chuuk.
(U.S. Navy photo, National Archives photo no. 80-G-352092)

the Etscheits, Belgian citizens interned by the Japanese, and Henry Nanpei,
who had learned English at the Kamehameha Schools in Hawai'i. The U.S.
Navy set up at Yasarin, the Etscheit property, which the Japanese navy had
used as headquarters early in the war. They held a simple ceremony, lowering
the Japanese flag and raising the American. A few small celebrations in Uh and
Palikir marked neither American victory nor Japanese defeat, but simply the
end of the war. Most Pohnpeians, however, were relatively unaffected by the
occupation; food and other shortages had not created hardship that required
large-scale American action to remedy.

Kosraeans felt considerable affiliation with Americans, having hosted a
center for American missionary work in the late nineteenth century, and were
confident in welcoming them back. One minister later recounted with pride
that the Japanese military had put his name at the head of the list of Kosraeans
to be executed near the end of the war, because they regarded him "as practi-

Photo 18. The U.S. flag is raised on Kosrae while Japanese and American troops watch, September 8, 1945. (U.S. Navy photo, National Archives photo no. 80-G-352102)

cally an American" (Lewis 1948a: 85). (The U.S. Navy's *Civil Affairs Handbook* named "numerous" Kosraeans as "trustworthy" or "pro-American" [1944b: 32–33]). When Kosrae was surrendered on September 8, people walked long distances to attend the American flag raising, and one man recalls the admiral saying that people were now free from the "red eye" (life under the Japanese flag). Now, they could "sleep in and use two pillows." Most important, those who had been relocated by the Japanese military could return home.

Japanese Lieutenant General Sadae Inoue surrendered forces under his command, including those on Palau and Yap, on September 2, 1945, aboard the USS *Amick*. American forces then occupied remaining Japanese-held territory in western Micronesia. Japanese secrecy kept most Palauans uninformed about the end of the war until "American pilots overhead finally waved back instead of dropping bombs" (Nero 1989: 131). Emerging from a year of near-starvation, Palauans were overwhelmed by American donations of food, willingness to signal equality by sitting down to eat with Palauans, and news of the massive construction on Peleliu and Angaur. "We were no longer frightened of the Americans," said one man. "We looked at them as an easy source of food, of abundance" (Nero 1989:133).

American troops arriving on Yap found a garrison of 6,500 Japanese troops, about 4,000 Yapese, and 300 Chamorros. The troops showed signs of malnutrition, though Yapese did not. On Yap, as on Chuuk, those who had regular contact with the Japanese, like Peter Ianguchel, were the first to know of war's end:[24] "Word came from Okaw through the telephone and we were able to understand Japanese. There was a Japanese high-ranking officer who had befriended us who came and told us: 'Have you heard the news?' The Yapese said, 'No.' He said, 'Do not tell anyone, or I will be in big trouble. The war has ended and Japan has lost.' He said, 'Even the subway in Japan is damaged. A big and great bomb has been dropped on Japan.'"

Here too, a first clue came when American planes flew low without dropping bombs. Raphael Gisog, who worked for the Japanese commander Ito, recalls that when Ito and other officers were summoned to a U.S. ship, they returned with American cigarettes: "That evening he [Gisog] had finished working, so he went home. There was a family he visited in Okaw village; the Yapese man who had gone with Ito came back and stopped at that family's home and gave away cigarettes, those Lucky Strikes and Chesterfields. And in the morning when he went to work he was given cigarettes by the Japanese. You must understand that at that time cigarettes were very, very scarce. And when he went to work in the morning, Ito also gave him cigarettes." A few days later, Ito hosted Japanese officers from throughout Yap at a party, where Gisog again heard that the war had ended, but without learning who had won ("and before the ship arrived, maybe they themselves didn't know").

Venitu Gurtmag also recalls a party, the evening of the day that he and others lined up for roll call at Japanese army headquarters on Yap had heard the news—not that the Japanese had lost, but that the war was going to stop for a while at American request: "Then, in the evening, they [Yapese working at headquarters] were told to go to the house of the military officers for a party. That evening, they had a party and they were invited. And here they had brewed wine, out of coconut tuba, for the soldiers. So they had that, they all took it and some little food they had, and had a very big party—all the officers, soldiers, and those who were here, including [Gurtmag]."

The next afternoon American soldiers landed, armed only with K-rations for the Japanese soldiers (which they shared with some Yapese). They called the people together with the bell the Japanese army had used for roll call: "And they sent word to Ito for a translator, a Japanese who speaks English, to come here and translate for the American officer, who told the people, 'No war, no war.' But the Yapese did not understand what was said. It is only now, you know, that we understand 'no war' [in English] means 'no more fighting.'"

On invaded islands, Micronesians had been sequestered in camps and provided with necessities but at first insulated from easy contact with American troops.[25] But on the bypassed islands that received their first Americans after Japanese capitulation, it was Japanese who were rounded up and removed, while Islanders for the most part stayed in place. Here Micronesians viewed a most impressive spectacle of Japanese defeat. In some places, they were stripped of arms and even uniforms, lined up on shore, and marched off under armed guard or pushed into landing craft. Relief was widespread. Yet the departure of the Japanese—after thirty years of government by them— left Micronesians facing an administrative void. And on most islands, there was no American presence to address that void.

Where news of the surrender was not followed by effective American security, those seeking revenge had an opportunity to act. When asked whether Yapese felt sorry for the Japanese soldiers, Raphael Gisog laughed. He really couldn't say, he responded: "Maybe they were on a personal, person-to-person basis, but on the whole—in general I think there was no grief for the Japanese, because there were instances where Yapese were killed. We also had some very bad people here who took revenge on the Japanese." There are stories of Yapese killing Japanese, and of people greeting an abusive Yapese policeman, who had aided the Japanese, with the taunt, "Where are the Japanese?" (Poyer 1995; similarly on Palau, Nero 1989:133). Este Puri recalls that the Japanese on Chuuk gathered together in large groups after surrender, to prevent Chuukese from taking revenge: "That was the only thing that kept them from getting hurt, because when they were in a bigger group, it was harder for us to get at them. We despised them, because they had treated us badly, as if we were slaves."

In the occupied islands, surrendered Japanese troops began the massive postwar cleanup. In Yap, they repaired bridges and roads in Colonia. The U.S. Navy handed out supplies for a time, then opened stores in Colonia, but the rest of Yap was left on its own. The countryside suddenly seemed emptier. When troops left the villages, says Peter Ianguchel, people used what was left: "The chiefs of Yap said that those things left behind by the Japanese became the property of the Yapese on whose land they were located. Historically, war is like a typhoon. After a typhoon, whatever you find on your property becomes yours." Aside from some construction, little that was left behind could benefit the Yapese. As Martina La'ew says: "They couldn't leave anything. The clothes they wore were ragged. The soldiers' uniforms were all ragged. They used Japanese cooking pots. Even their pillows were made of dried banana leaves stuffed into cloth bags. So they couldn't leave anything usable to the Yapese."

War's end came last to more distant atolls. The thousand-man garrison of the Mortlocks surrendered in October 1945. The Lukunor garrison moved to Satawan for repatriation and, by November 1945, navy LSTs had removed them to Chuuk. As the weeks passed, the U.S. Navy made its way to the many other islands of the Carolines.[26] A small MilGov group sent to survey the ungarrisoned central Carolines went fully armed, unsure of what they would meet. Their job was to search for traces of allied personnel, "find out what the natives thought of us," and evaluate local needs (Kneubuhl 1946:3). They took three Japanese to translate:

> The presence of these three men was necessitated by the fact that many if not all of the islanders we were to visit were still, we thought, ignorant of the war's end and would sooner believe the news from a Japanese colonel than they would from us. Moreover, we were a bit worried of ambush by Japanese soldiers on any of the atolls. . . . But! The colonel as a bearer of news that the war had ended found that the news had preceded us in most of the atolls. When the war ended, Truk, already without food for over a year, sent out small parties of soldiers into the nearby atolls for the purpose of restocking their empty supply tents; they stole the colonel's thunder. (Kneubuhl 1946:4–5)[27]

Wherever Americans landed and Japanese embarked, the contrast was striking: healthy, victorious, rich American soldiers sent off starved and destitute Japanese troops. Even those who had no previous experience with Americans, like the people of Lukunor, felt their optimism rise as the first encounters proved positive:

Photo 19. Woleai man provides information to U.S. Marine Corps and Japanese officers, September 1945. (U.S. Navy photo, National Archives photo no. 80-G-495724)

For years the Japanese had boasted to the Micronesians of their invincibility, but now they were seen scrambling for cigarette butts tossed on the ground by American sailors. Instead of undertaking the wholesale slaughter of the Lukunor people as the Japanese had claimed they would, American sailors disembarked merely to trade for handicraft and play baseball with Lukunor's team. The obvious friendliness of the Americans and their egalitarian attitudes, along with the fact that the land was back in the hands

Photo 20. U.S. Marines and Japanese translator confer with people on Satawal, late 1945. (U.S. Navy photo, National Archives photo no. 80-G-358224)

of its proper owners, appears to have produced a great sense of relief among the people of Lukunor. (Borthwick 1977:59–60)

THE U.S. NAVY: CHIEFS AND FATHERS

> *We were very happy because they were*
> *unloading food all over the dock.*

U.S. strategic interests, which were to produce strikingly different outcomes for island populations, are evident even in the first postsurrender encounters between Americans and local people. In early 1944, the United States needed the Marshalls—at least Kwajalein, Enewetak, and Majuro—as bases from which to prosecute the war. On these atolls, the U.S. Navy worked hard to promote good relations to facilitate plans for use of the atolls as bases. American attention to Marshallese on the invaded atolls eased their transition to the new rulers. Members of Marshallese-European families were listed as potential contacts in military briefing materials, and many worked as military scouts. These and others who had learned English in mission schools became important resources in the first weeks and months after invasion. With their assistance, a strong Christian Church that formed immediate ties of sentiment with the American invaders, and an effective chiefly hierarchy that facilitated indirect rule, the U.S. Navy's Civil Affairs people were able to implement programs rapidly. And Marshallese returned the favor, offering "'Marshallese hospitality' that has come to be a legend among American servicemen who have had a chance to visit a Marshall Island village" (Mason 1946:26).

In contrast, by the time Japanese on bypassed islands farther west surrendered, the war was over. The U.S. Navy's aim was no longer to support the Allied advance but to repatriate Japanese troops and govern the region. Less effort was expended on local people who, in any case, were less preadapted to getting along with Americans. The handful of Caroline Islanders familiar with English were far too few to reach the entire population, even with the help of Japanese-speaking Chamorros and Americans. The navy soon found that its inability to communicate with Caroline Islanders, coupled with the rapid decline in logistical and financial support for the new American responsibilities in Micronesia, made it impossible to provide for or feel comfortable with central and western Micronesians as they had, in the first years of occupation, with Marshallese.

Another factor was the occupiers' lack of information. In the previous transfer of colonial power over Micronesia, Germans had smoothed the transition to Japanese rule, but Americans had little help. Nan'yō civil officials had been evacuated before invasion or killed. None were captured, nor did Americans get useful information from Japanese on bypassed islands. Bombing or invasion destroyed most records. U.S. MilGov started from scratch, with little colonial experience and little knowledge of the territory. The first administrators promulgated conflicting rules; civil affairs staff showed sharp differences in their views, ranging from welfare oriented to police oriented.[28] "The only official policy from Washington was—do not undertake any activity which would necessarily commit the United States to any post-war position." A congressional committee recommended a paradox that prefigured the next decades of American rule: "Teach the American way of life but do not disturb native institutions" (Useem 1946b:9).

New Chiefs for Old

Even before their arrival, the U.S. military represented themselves as providers, elder brothers, or friends of Micronesians as they prepared for the Marshalls invasion. Propaganda leaflets seen on Jaluij portrayed American soldiers shaking hands with Islanders and sharing abundant food. In areas of strategic importance to the United States, the navy's actions during and after invasion reinforced these messages. On Kwajalein and Enewetak, where local people could not escape invasion battles, the might of U.S. forces in comparison to the Japanese and the helplessness of Islanders emphasized the strength and unlimited wealth of Americans. These images of power were reinforced when Majuro, Kwajalein, and Enewetak became supply bases and transshipment locations for the front lines to the west.

While the navy's goal was to establish security and then work toward normalizing local life, Micronesians saw the shift from Japanese to American rule as, in a way, a transfer of power between a defeated and a victorious chief. As Americans had driven Japanese from the islands, they had come, like Marshallese conquering chiefs of old, to take their place as the protectors and rulers of the people and places of Micronesia (Carucci 1989).

The first and least problematic action taken by the navy confirmed the impression of American power and goodwill: the long-awaited return of Islanders displaced by relocation or war labor. Some were repatriated immediately, as navy officers took Micronesians on board during postsurrender inspection trips. In most cases, homecomings had to wait until Japanese were removed, areas were cleared of munitions, or hard-pressed transport vessels were available. Jaluij, Maloelap, Wotje, and Mili were cleaned up and hundreds of Marshallese returned to their home atolls during October and November 1945.[29] Over the next years, the U.S. Navy repatriated Islanders throughout the region. Some had a long road back. From Kosrae, 407 Kiribati people, 250 Banabans, and 114 Tuvalu people went home. The nearly 800 (of an original 1,200) Nauruans who survived confinement on Chuuk were repatriated. Survivors of the group of Kiti men sent to Kosrae were returned to Pohnpei, and four Palauans found on Borneo finally got home in 1947 (Richard 1957b: 48–50).

Every relocation had its poignant story. A group of Enewetak school children had spent the war on Pohnpei, dispersed among families with distant ties to Enewetak and Ujelang. Obet David recalls that the children heard rumors that the people back home had all been slaughtered during the war. He vividly recalls their relief when they finally received letters from home through "Mr. Rooney," the American in charge of their repatriation.

Each relocation gave Islanders a chance to meet American sailors face to face and to view U.S. equipment, food supplies, wealth, and willingness to go out of their way—literally—to help Micronesians. Welcome and impressive at the end of a long period of distress and deprivation, American offers to help and resources to do so (such as sending large ships to very small, distant islands) confirmed Islanders' view of their chieflike power. This belief created confusion and some resentment when the resources of the U.S. administration in Micronesia dropped precipitately after the war.

Cornucopia

The navy faced a formidable job in freeing the islands from the immediate consequences of war. Conditions at surrender ranged from simple shortages of food and medical care on isolated atolls to almost complete destruction of living areas and economic infrastructure on invaded islands: "When the people of Lukunor returned to their island from Piafa in the final weeks of 1945, they found nearly half the trees gone, their cathedral in rubble, houses moved or dismantled, and much of their taro destroyed. In addition, the fish supply in the lagoon had been badly depleted by the Japanese practice of dynamiting and it would be years before the best fishing areas would recover" (Borthwick 1977:150). Andohn Jemes (Pohnpei) speaks of the general exhaustion on the bypassed islands at the end of the war: It was "just like you were under the house—starving, tired, and couldn't take a rest." Despite the concern of facing new, unknown rulers, Micronesians were desperate for relief. U.S. ships that accepted the surrender of Japanese forces brought the first glimpse of it. As Martina La'ew (Yap) says, "When they gave food to the people, I stopped being afraid. I had been starving for a long time."

Throughout the islands, the fact that precious goods were not only used, but wasted, by American soldiers and sailors, contributed to Islanders' assessment of boundless American wealth.[30] On Majuro Atoll, Manutil Lokwot remembers that nearly a hundred Marshallese worked for the Navy: "They made things around here, unloaded and loaded food from ships. They would unload food from ships until there was no longer any place to put it. The island was smaller than the [supply of] food. From those locations where they unloaded food, the stacks of food would be even with the highest coconut trees. The lagoon waters were filled with reflected light from cans [of food] and all kinds of things that they threw away from the ships, for there was no place to store the food on the island; all of the large warehouses were full— [yet] the supply ships did not cease to arrive."

Marshallese removed from invaded islands into camps were given food, clothing, and other supplies. Unlike Marshallese chiefs, the new American rulers only gave, never demanding tribute in return. In fact, Enewetak people said that the Americans accepted their gifts of coconuts, pigs, chickens, fish, or rice with thanks, only to discard them later on the beach; "such is their strength, they do not need them" (Carucci 1989:87).

Farther west in the bypassed islands, some reminiscences of American arrival faintly echo Marshallese appreciation of their wealth and generosity. For example, when she first saw the Americans arrive in Chuuk, Echen Nakamura recalls: "We were very happy because they were unloading food all over the dock, [so much that it was spilling] along the shore, in the water—like pork, chicken, all kinds of meat." Toli Jessy (Chuuk) also remembers excess: "Those American soldiers were dumping used clothes, shoes, in the garbage drums. They also dumped food everywhere and the local people were very thankful to them." Even islands without large Japanese garrisons saw evidence of plenty, as when the navy left "a mountain of C-rations" on Tobi, southwest of Palau (Black 1977:27). When bomb disposal and survey teams came through the Mortlocks in 1946 to destroy weaponry and munitions at Satawan, they visited other islands en route and provided supplies on the spot or made a note for the next trip. "From 1945 to 1947 emergency relief goods were supplied to the islands, including food (rice, flour, dried fish, sugar, salt, soybeans, oil), soap, tobacco, medical supplies, agricultural tools, clothing, and miscellaneous items. Etal received several shipments, which navy manuals said were to 'prevent disease and unrest'" (Nason 1970:276, n.2).

Yet the bypassed islands rarely saw the sort of largesse celebrated on the invaded Marshalls or western Carolines. The immediate needs of Micronesians living near bypassed garrisons at war's end were met by taking over houses and gardens left behind by Japanese troops. This quickly reduced threats of starvation in Yap, Chuuk, and Pohnpei. But consuming leftover Japanese stores carries a far different message than the Marshallese experience of being overwhelmed with the generosity of invaders offering a handshake, campfire sing-alongs, and mountains of "corned beef as long as your arm."

U.S. MilGov moved steadily to provide for basic needs throughout the region. By the end of 1947, the navy had reintroduced many of the services the Japanese had provided: mail, local government, trade, and health care were available in some degree throughout the region. Health care by navy medical teams visiting small islands "helped establish the nurturant 'father' role that the Americans were to play" (Borthwick 1977:150). American willingness to bring care to the outer islands was striking because in Japanese times, medical treatment had been available only by traveling to urban centers.

Access to imported goods and opportunities for wage labor formed nodes of plenty at the new American bases or in the urban centers of bypassed islands at U.S. MilGov headquarters. Peter Ianguchel recalls that, when working for the navy on Yap, "Those who were not paid in money were told to go to the Quonsets where supplies were kept and take all they wanted. If one liked to have food, take all of the food you want. If one wanted tools, take all the tools you want." Clanton Abija, who worked on Kwajalein, was asked whether he was paid for his work with the Americans:

Yes, you were paid and the food was free. Free clothing; there was no cost for clothing or various things; shoes, all variety of things there was no cost. And also, food and housing was free.

(Interviewer asks: And how much did you get paid?)

Well, at first, it tended to be a small amount, but because we did not need anything and we did not use money during those times [it was enough]. So it was about $12, but all of these things they gave us along with the work. And so you see, those fellows who were older than me, they would go off to drink and take $1 with them and they would go off and come back and have 50 cents change. That is how inexpensive it was, because a beer was 10 cents,

5 cents for a package of cigarettes. . . . And so during the navy times it was "a free life."

For societies in which chiefly shows of generosity were expected, the U.S. Navy displayed itself as the greatest of chiefs. Geographical inconsistency in distributing largesse, however, had far-reaching results for local perceptions of the new rulers. For example, Pohnpeians received only intermittent and rarely free access to badly needed goods. Pohnpei's desperate clothing shortage, for example, did not improve with the arrival of Americans; "Nine months after the American occupation, there were fifty to one hundred women in one district alone who were still hiding out on their farms because they had no clothing" (Bascom 1950:147).

Differences in how islands benefited from American generosity played a critical role in the development both of American policies toward various Micronesian populations and of Micronesian attitudes. While all Islanders recognized American wealth and power, communities varied in their willingness to grant legitimacy to the new rulers and in how they evaluated their performance as Micronesia's new chiefs.

WORKING FOR THE AMERICANS

We said: "Okay, let's go to Enewetak, take our money,
and purchase . . . some pants or shirts."

Efforts to help Micronesia recover were dramatically inhibited by the repatriation of not only Japanese soldiers, but also civilians: the fishermen, skilled laborers, and small businessmen who for thirty years had built the colonial economy. The economic implications of this policy are explored further in the next chapter. But by choosing complete repatriation, the U.S. Navy created an immediate labor shortage for itself. In a few places, despite quick recruiting of Islanders, U.S. military labor needs were so great as to delay repatriation of Japanese military personnel until major jobs were done.

As during Japan's war preparations, Micronesians found their greatest employment opportunities in the U.S. era near military installations: first Kwajalein and Majuro, then Guam, Saipan, and Tinian.[31] Shortly after victory in Kwajalein, the navy hired Marshallese to clear war debris, stevedore, and collect garbage (Alexander 1978:38).[32] Though work conditions were improved by American wealth and generosity, and Micronesians had to adjust to culturally and linguistically alien supervisors, the organization of work for the American military was not that much different from prewar and early wartime work for the Japanese. In the Marshalls, Islanders worked an eight-hour day and a six-day week, mostly at construction and maintenance. Pay was slightly higher than under the Japanese: initially, unskilled men got 40 cents/day, skilled men 60 cents. (There was a special fishing unit at Ebeye, and military scouts were paid 89 cents/day.)[33] Workers were fed, and some were assigned quarters.

Like Marshallese, the people of the Marianas were drawn into the economy ancillary to major military bases. Saipan's large population and rapid development as an American base pushed the reestablishment of local economy for the duration of the war. Judging by contemporary documents, working relationships between Americans and Chamorros on Saipan were more tense than between Americans and Marshallese. The first months of navy employment went well. While Japanese civilians in the internment camps were in effect forced to work on farming and other tasks, labor for Chamorros in Chalan Kanoa was probably voluntary. Also, Chamorros held relatively pleasant jobs—men doing police work, women waiting tables in the Officers' Wardroom, for example (Embree 1946a:13–15).[34] Difficulties arose after the war as it became clear that the U.S. Navy and local people had disparate visions of how their economy should develop—a difference of opinion that reverberated through every decision about economic matters made by either side (see chapter 8). Americans also attributed problems interacting with Chamorros to the Japanese policy of discouraging Islander initiative and to war-related reductions in physical and psychological health (Bowers 1950:66–69).

One reason the navy immediately hired local people in areas where it had installations was to push cash into the economy; for this reason too, it set itself up as the purchaser of handicrafts and encouraged fishing, agriculture, and copra production. Throughout the Marshall Islands, where the souvenir trade with servicemen lasted longest, Islanders were surprised, even shocked, by how much Americans were willing to pay before handicrafts were regulated under the Island Trading Company.[35] Henry Moses, for example, recalls selling small red shells found in abundance only on Ebon. Each tiny shell was worth 10 cents, and Henry collected a great number each day. Apinar Edward (Marshalls) recalls how Americans set prices:

(Interviewer asks: So, then, right after the battle, what did you do?)

Well, we fished some and then when they said "make handicrafts," we made them. We made a living from handicrafts. There were people who came and took necklaces and such and gave us money. . . . The soldiers came and took necklaces and shells and they themselves set the price of these things, and then, they paid us. We did not reveal the price. Only they did. They said, "Well, the cost of a shell [cowrie]: $2.00." "Oh, okay [we would say, and give it in exchange]." Well, it was okay [a nice arrangement] for us to make a living from these things. There were many times when we said: "Okay, let's go to Enewetak, take our money, and purchase . . . some pants or shirts."

But islands not occupied until after Japanese surrender did not have major U.S. bases demanding large labor forces and bestowing free room, board, and clothing, nor did they have souvenir-hungry troops with money to burn. In the first year of U.S. occupation, Islanders seeking jobs migrated to U.S. bases. But after the work of war ended, so did most wage-labor opportunities. On islands without military bases, women very seldom worked for money under the Americans, and only a small number of men were able to do so. The small U.S. Navy administration did not require much labor; language difficulties interfered with Islanders' asking to work; and American use of machines reduced the need for unskilled labor. Paid employment was scarce on Chuuk, Pohnpei, and Kosrae and nonexistent on most outer islands. Ichios Eas of Chuuk marvels at American technology, yet he recognizes the inequalities of work opportunity that accompanied American approaches to labor:

Well, it is true, when we started working for the Americans, for example, fixing their road, not everybody worked on it—one guy only could work on it with a bulldozer. And we did work for them when they came here during navy times, but not many were working for the navy government. And, in my own opinion, the Chuukese in Japanese times were better off, as far as earning their own living. . . . in Japanese times, to fix the road, everybody worked on the road, using hoes and shovels. And then, the Japanese paid us. The wages were low [but costs were also low]. . . . And in those days, you didn't feel the difference among the Chuukese as to who was richer and who was very poor. Everyone dressed the same.

Unpaid work, roughly in the same spirit as Japanese prewar labor requirements, did bring Islanders far from military bases into the orbit of American work ideas. The navy established a male poll tax and license fees for business, requiring men at least to find access to some cash. Pohnpeians did public work to pay for taxes in 1946; and males between the ages of seventeen and fifty-five gave a quota of free days of labor to the military government (Bascom 1965:151; Nason 1970:235).

Where people were able to work for the U.S. Navy in the first period of occupation, memories are overwhelmingly positive, as for Toli Jessy of Chuuk: "If I got sick and could not work, I would tell them so and I'd be excused. When they told me to go take food for the prisoners—I was a cook at the jail— they told me I could take anything I wanted from the food storage building, which I thought was very nice."

Islanders from many locations worked side-by-side with U.S. enlisted men and became their friends. Officers remained separate from all but the most privileged Micronesians, but no restraints prohibited Islanders from entering movie theaters or drinking alcohol (social segregation became more noticeable later in the U.S. Navy administration; see chapter 8). Equality with the common U.S. soldier and sailor sharply contrasted with the Japanese ethnic hierarchy. Islanders also appreciated the chance to learn to drive trucks, jeeps, and heavy equipment, something the Japanese had not allowed. "The Ponapeans say that the Japanese were reluctant to teach them useful trades and that even when they were employed by the Japanese they were taught only the essentials necessary to perform the work assigned to them. This is confirmed by the Belgians, who say that the Japanese deliberately tried to keep Ponapeans from acquiring practical skills because they were so quick to learn that they were regarded as an economic threat" (Bascom 1965:125).[36]

Everywhere except Guam, the lack of a common language proved the major problem for Americans seeking to govern and Islanders seeking to find their feet under the new dispensation. As the navy's Japanese translators were demobilized, the islands were left with few communication links between local people and the new rulers.[37] Chuukese recall that a Chamorro man from

Guam was put "in charge" of the Faichuk area (the western lagoon), though his knowledge of English and Chamorro did little to help him communicate with local people. Communication struggled through Japanese, or even German (spoken by a few elderly Yapese or Chuukese). Belarmino Hathey recalls being a translator in Yap: "We sailed from Ulithi to Yap and notified the outer islands people who worked in Yap that the fighting was over, there was no more war. At that time, there was a Hawaiian-Japanese among the Americans on the ship, and I spoke good Japanese. So I would speak Japanese to him, and he would [answer]. And then when somebody told me something [in Yapese], I would speak Japanese to that Hawaiian, and that Hawaiian would translate [into English]."

Raphael Gisog remembers the challenge of communicating with the first Americans on Yap:

Much to everyone's distress, we had a communication problem. We wanted to establish friendships but could not due to the communication barrier between Americans and Yapese. It was really apparent that people yearned for the relationship, as opposed to Japanese times and during the war. Any way that Yapese could avoid the Japanese, they would. Because it was unavoidable, they came to be sociable, because of the harsh treatment [i.e., if they were not friendly]. Whereas in this case [with the Americans], there is no harsh treatment, but you could readily see that people were struggling along, because we had communication problems.

Martina La'ew remembers American soldiers on Yap communicating through hand gestures ("I did not like that"). Bernard and Yasio Behnis (Pohnpei) recall such challenges with humor:

The Americans treated Pohnpeians very well. Americans gave gifts to the elderly Pohnpeians. At first, we went to Enewetak [to work], and it was funny. We used sign language in order to communicate. I was lucky because I had learned English at Ohwa [mission] school, so I used to communicate or talk to them. After six months, we were free [the labor stints had been completed, and we could return home].

Sometimes, however, they [Pohnpeians] mixed salt with coffee because we couldn't read the words [on packages].

But communication problems also meant that most people, like Asako Mateas (Chuuk), did not have the chance to work for the Americans:

(Interviewer asks: So what did you do for money?)
We didn't have any money—our chiefs got all the money because people could not understand; only the chiefs could understand what was being said between them and the navy.

Their linguistic deficiency radically distinguished the Americans from the Japanese. While communication difficulties during the war itself were to be expected (since some American officers and most younger Micronesians spoke Japanese, a "modified pidgin" was improvised [Useem 1945a:99]), they continued throughout the navy era. Americans soon set up schools to teach Micronesians English, but did not seek with the same diligence to teach themselves Chuukese or Yapese. Micronesians worked hard to master the new language, says Palagi Mitag (Yap): "At that time, befriending the Americans was one way of learning the language fast. Having jobs with the Americans was also another. You know, Talley, he was one person who did translation for the Yapese at that time, worked for the Americans—that was [also] a way of learning the language."

In the prewar period, many Japanese had learned Micronesian languages and become local residents. In the postwar period, only a few Americans showed interest in following this important precedent. In American Micronesia, English not only served as a channel of empowerment for a select few Islanders, it also helped maintain the foreignness and distance that allowed Islanders to view Americans as chiefs.

Chapter 8

INAUGURATING AMERICAN RULE

THE FIRST objectives of U.S. Navy Civil Affairs units, and Military Government in particular, were "to assist the military operations and to fulfill the obligations of armed forces under international law" (Richard 1957a:6–7). Until Japanese surrender, MilGov policy focused on maintaining public order in occupied islands, protecting American forces from sabotage, and interning captured personnel. At the conclusion of war, it was occupied with disarming and repatriating thousands of Japanese troops and Korean and Okinawan workers. MilGov's third and most problematic objective was "restoring civilian living conditions to normal" (Richard 1957a:164–165).

Initial MilGov activities in some islands were badly hampered by lack of supplies, unskilled staff, and the navy's reluctance to make long-range investments in infrastructure until the islands' political future was settled. By agreement of the United Nations Security Council and the U.S. Congress, the United States took control of the former Japanese mandate in July 1947, as a *strategic trust* (a term uniquely designed for the Micronesian case), the Trust Territory of the Pacific Islands. The navy's MilGov units officially became Civil Administration ("CivAd") units.[1] The navy administered Micronesia for six or in some places seven years (first under MilGov, then under CivAd) before turning it over to the Department of the Interior in July 1951.

Whereas the needs of navy MilGov units had been subordinated to military necessity, the primary mission of the CivAd units that supplanted them was governing Micronesians. As American administration became regularized, Micronesians adopted modes of interaction familiar from experience with previous colonial governments and developed new strategies suited to Amer-

Photo 21. A U.S. Navy enlisted man visits a home on Pohnpei during a U.S. Navy inspection trip, July 1947. (U.S. Navy photo, National Archives photo no. 80-G-497521)

ican rule. The most enduringly complex encounters, emerging directly from the juxtaposition of prewar life, wartime experiences, and postwar policy, were generated by the interplay of American and local ideas of "freedom" and by economic policy.

FREEDOM, DEMOCRACY, AND STRATEGY

The first years of the U.S. Navy era gave Islanders an opportunity to assess their new colonizers, to measure the United States against past experiences with Japan and Germany. American rule initially presented Micronesians with a sort of "antistructure": not the chaos in which people had lived during the war, but the absence of a coherent plan for the islands. The United States retained the islands for strategic reasons, diverging substantially from Japan's use of Micronesia as a building block of empire. Much of the difficulty faced by both Islanders and navy officials in the first postwar years arose from this change in Micronesia's geopolitical role. Micronesians sought to recover their prewar standard of living but found the resource-rich United States unconcerned with the economic potential of the area that had been so useful to Japan (Embree 1946b:63).

The first contrast in how Micronesians experienced navy rule followed the east-to-west Allied offensive, with islands hosting military bases sustaining the most contact. The Marshalls, with wartime bases on Majuro, Enewetak, and Kwajalein (two bases), experienced much more interaction with Americans than islands farther west. Also, U.S. military plans placed Kosrae and Pohnpei under the Kiribati/Marshalls regional command, reversing the colonial precedent that had privileged high islands over atolls. And, while Japanese forces were removed from the Marshalls, Kiribati, and Kosrae in 1945, those farther west remained for rehabilitation work. The delay blurred the boundaries marking war's end and those separating American rulers from Japanese.[2]

Residents of the central and western Carolines saw the greatest change in their geopolitical role. The largest U.S. military base was on tiny Ulithi Atoll (of no previous political importance), the islands were administered from the Marianas, and Japanese troops stayed longest in this area to assist with cleanup. The eventual equitable assignment of trained officers partly redressed this imbalance (Richard 1957a:168). But in comparison to the Japanese colonial order (which had valued the islands from Palau eastward and the Mariana Islands southward), people in the central and western Carolines felt relatively overlooked by the new government and experienced disproportionate postwar administrative disorganization.

Although in the heat of battle there had been a lack of clarity about the status of some Micronesians, with the end of war American belief was that U.S. troops had liberated the Islanders from Japanese rule.[3] Navy personnel arriving at each formerly Japanese possession made initial proclamations of the principles of democracy. The message came through less than clearly—and for years (some would say decades), what remained unelaborated was how democracy would operate in the Micronesian context and how it differed from prior forms of government. The complex linkages among Japanese colonial institutions, wartime disarray, American rhetoric of freedom and equality, and American strategic, economic, and political policies produced simultaneous distress and opportunity during the navy's tenure in Micronesia.

Freedom

These things were unheard of in Japanese times.

Freedom is a key symbol in Micronesian discourse about the postwar transition—and a complex one. Micronesians recall that the first U.S. officers they saw proclaimed the arrival of "freedom," but they had little context in which to interpret that announcement. Yet in a sense close to that originally intended by the Americans, *freedom* has come to be the word most often used to describe the change in governance. Whereas Japanese had strictly controlled Micronesians as third-rank subjects, Americans proclaimed "freedom" and acted in ways that opened new options in work, leisure, and status relations.

One of the first officers to arrive after the Japanese surrender on Pohnpei proclaimed that Pohnpeians had been liberated by the Americans and were now free to do as they wished.

> This announcement was given many interpretations. Having resumed subsistence farming, some interpreted it as a blessing upon a return to feasting, kava drinking, and relaxation after the period of forced labor, which had been widely resented. Others interpreted it as meaning they had no more obligations to their own chiefs, and the question of the ultimate position of Ponapean chiefs was unnecessarily aggravated. Later they were to learn that these ringing phrases had not meant all the things they had understood. Those who had expected to move into Colonia [Kolonia] and rebuild the city there were told that they could not do so. Those who had expected to return to the farms appropriated from them by the Japanese, or to work the Japanese coconut plantations, were given only temporary rights to part of this land, with no assurance of permanent tenure. They were told that, as former Japanese property, this land now belonged to the American government and that final disposal had to await the conclusion of peace negotiations with Japan. (Bascom 1950:148–149)[4]

Yet despite such problems, individuals were more at liberty under the initially small and lightly rooted American governing force than they had been even under the peacetime Japanese order. Relations with indigenous populations were, for the initial U.S. MilGov, a secondary matter once their most pressing needs had been met. As a result, many Islanders found themselves able to follow their own inclinations in the first months after invasion or surrender—an amazing burst of autonomy after the constraint of Japanese civil-era regulation and then strict military rule.

Some forms of the new liberty were exactly in line with American intentions. On Kosrae, people discussed the idea of personal freedom and began to bring their concerns to local magistrates, who were under the supervision of administrators on Pohnpei, rather than to the previously hegemonic church (Lewis 1948a:62). Others took the liberators by surprise, as when one of the first American-appointed chiefs on Chuuk was so influenced by American films that he "announced on his own initiative to the people that the Americans favored youthful love and that this should be the deciding factor in any marriage" (the belief persisted, though disclaimed as official policy; Gladwin and Sarason 1953:122).[5]

Much that followed in the wake of "freedom," though, combined with delay in filling the vacuum in local governance left by the departed Japanese, seemed more like disorder. Older Micronesians seldom mention the freedom of postwar life without adding cautions about its dangers. Relief from wartime strictures was welcomed, and the early period of navy rule is evaluated very positively, even by those who were pro-Japanese. But American promotion of liberty was, elderly people now say, wrongly interpreted to mean unconstrained, self-willed behavior.

A freedom that became a key marker of the difference between American and Japanese governance was the use of alcohol. Since the arrival of missionaries, alcohol had been prohibited to Islanders (Marshall and Marshall 1976). Before the war, Islanders in most of the mandate needed a special permit to drink it. Men vividly recall the occasional privilege of alcohol consumption bestowed by Japanese or Okinawan friends or employers; others drank secretly despite severe sanctions. With the arrival of Americans, all this changed. Navy enlisted men taught young Islanders how to brew alcohol from baker's yeast and sugar and shared their own alcohol with them.

Young Micronesian men, freed from the burdens of wartime labor and enchanted with new opportunities, responded to the friendliness of equally young Americans who also sought excitement and diversion in their unfamiliar situation. Drinking is just one of the pleasures that Clanton Abija recalls Marshallese sharing with American enlisted men on Kwajalein:

> They were fine, they were kind. As I think of these fellows, (laughing) their lives were really off course. Everything was the same to them. They had no worries. The only thing they were worried about was their day of departure.
>
> *(Interviewer asks: Were there times that you held parties for one another and sang for one another, or drank together?)*
> Well, during those times I did not drink. But, I tended to go with them, and they would drink with those other young men, the sort who were a little older than I was. They would drink and party and play together.
>
> *(Interviewer: And what about you?)*
> Well, I would tell light-hearted stories when I was with them. And play games. Play games. What was the name of that game? Horseshoes! And also billiards.
>
> *(Interviewer: And were there movie theaters on this atoll then?)*
> Movies? Yes, there were many movie theaters that belonged to the navy. And, as for this islet, we could go and observe. We did not have to pay. We just went all the time and watched.

Yet alcohol, the symbol of personal freedom, is also an emblem of license. People complained of drunkenness, thefts, the disobedience of youth. This lack of order contrasted with the prewar years when custom functioned properly and colonial discipline kept domestic peace. Echen Nakamura (Chuuk) explains: "When the Americans came it was very peaceful. Life was easy again, at least we were not suffering as much. Who in Chuuk can say [he or she] did not suffer during the previous government [Japan]? I'll use liquor as an example. If anybody was caught drunk, the soldiers would beat him with swords, and after that he'd be sent to jail. So, during that time, we did not have this liquor problem we're now having today, because alcohol drinkers back then did not make trouble; they hid themselves when they drank."

"In Japanese times," Andonio Raidong of Pohnpei says, "if you drank liquor, you were locked up, so people didn't consume it. Today, nothing is done about the consumption of liquor, drugs, or marijuana. These things were unheard of in Japanese times." Many people remarked that while the Japanese laws were tough, even cruel, and were not always impartially enforced, they were better for Islanders than American freedom. In the words of Reverend Kanki Amlej of the Marshall Islands, "We took the American freedoms and twisted them around until they were not 'correct' freedoms, but totally incorrect freedoms."

In the decades since, Micronesians—especially older people who experienced both Japanese and American philosophies—have thought a great deal about the idea of liberty in the Micronesian context. Some conclude that it is incompatible with an indigenous way of life that flourished in the prewar era. Reverend Kanki Amlej elaborates:

> And so this thing, [freedom], why is it like this? Well, it is possible for us to say that it has come from the changing tides of time, and from changes in custom, and the other things that they [Marshallese] have taken. Do you see, for example, that one thing, alcoholic beverages? Well, we become drunk and then destroy Marshallese customs because we say we are free to get drunk and then we do improper things, right there next to our loved ones, and we are only "free" improperly. These are the sorts of things that I am saying. This word *anemkwôj* [freedom], to a great extent Marshallese have become inebriated with it, and do not know how to use it and then, that is the result: everything is confused within the atoll and customs have been destroyed. . . . Well, in truth, this is *not* the real meaning of freedom, not of "freedom" and "liberty" [in English], that is. [Instead, it has become] freedom in terms of those things that are improper and wrong.

Reverend Amlej and others of his generation are not naively harking back to an untrammeled golden age, but rather to a way of life local people remember as "real" Marshallese, or Pohnpeian, or Chuukese custom. Respect for elders and elder siblings is one example. Today's reminiscence condenses what is known of "ancient" tradition and the Japanese colonial era, constructing a consolidated image of "custom." There is some evidence that ranking by age and generation was part of nineteenth-century life in the Marshalls and elsewhere, and it was reinforced by Japanese values—but then strikingly inverted by American preferences for dealing with the young. Nowadays, younger people are said to "think as though they are old" and openly contradict those of higher rank. Another example is modern women's clothing—wearing blue jeans or dresses that do not cover the thighs, much less calves or ankles. Of course, covering thighs and ankles is a mission-inspired fashion without ancient standing (as seen in early nineteenth-century drawings of Ratak islanders), but nonetheless, it is a symbol of traditional culture that has been compromised under the ideology of freedom associated with Americans.

While Micronesian concerns about freedom focused on what Americans would call individual rights or personal liberty, one of the core meanings of freedom for Americans is linked with democratic forms of government. The U.S. Navy at first thought that its challenge in the islands would be contrasting democracy with Japanese tyranny, but in fact the Japanese colonial order had included local election of leaders in some instances. The challenge came instead when U.S. officials found their desire to instill democracy into Micronesia confronting their desire to respect Micronesian "custom." In promoting democracy in chiefly societies, the new rulers of Micronesia fully awakened to the distinctive qualities of culture shock, Pacific style.

Chiefs and Democracy

Micronesian politics entered a turbulent period. Local governments mixed traditional lineage and clan leadership with Japanese appointees chosen for their complicity with colonial rule. People were recovering from a lengthy war in which those who could hustle were those who survived. Now they faced an unknown set of resources and threats in the form of an administration that first overwhelmed with its wealth and might, then pleaded poverty and manifested its ignorance of local culture.

In governing Micronesia, U.S. Navy MilGov strove to orchestrate policies for the entire region, but it was clear at every turn that such generalizations were useless. As more attention was paid to specific local circumstances, however, administrators fell on the other horn of the dilemma. In any local contest, Islanders were the only ones who knew what was what and who was whom. As outsiders lacking linguistic and cultural competence, American officials were at the mercy of whatever they were told by those they chose as their advisors. Efforts to attend to local customs, then, created as many difficulties as bureaucracy's penchant for promulgating overgeneralizing rules.

The case of the Chuukese chiefs was a publicly argued example of the problem. Because Americans could not speak directly with local leaders, every island experienced a window of opportunity for the ambitious who could make themselves useful before Americans began training their own helpers or learning the local political ropes. In Chuuk, indigenous chieftainship had been largely local and not very hierarchical. Germans and Japanese set up administrative chiefs to organize taxes, labor, and civil obedience—not "traditional" leaders, but men appointed and deposed by colonial supervisors. Preoccupied with securing the islands and removing Japanese troops, MilGov continued the Japanese system, but their first appointments were of interpreters, the few people in the region with whom they could communicate. They then named chiefs, assistant chiefs, secretaries, and other officials for each lagoon island— at one point dealing with an unwieldy seven-level hierarchy.

"These were times of confusion and temptation," anthropologist Thomas Gladwin later wrote (1964:46–47). The United States was pumping in money, American troops were trading black-market cigarettes and cash for Japanese souvenirs. Despite the lack of wage labor, cash from high taxes and uninvested U.S. Commercial Company (USCC) funds filled island treasuries. (The USCC replaced the Foreign Economic Agency as the civilian economic agency for the region in November 1945.) Chuukese appointees took advantage of the opportunities, local people had no way to complain to navy officials, and the navy had no way to check up on those they appointed or confirmed as "chiefs." "In some cases it was found that certain island chiefs paid little or no attention to our military government except to use it as a means for exploiting their own people, by diverting to their own use labor, money and supplies poured into their islands by the U.S. Government" (Hall 1950:27). The distressing situation in Chuuk became of more than local concern when anthropologists working there published their evaluations of navy rule.[6]

Navy officials throughout Micronesia operated at first through existing Japanese structures, with two immediate changes. First, they self-consciously attended to traditional leaders (even when, as with Chuuk's chiefs, what appeared to be tradition was a recent development). As Toli Jessy (Chuuk) recalls, "They [the navy] never bothered us or our chiefs. When our chiefs had meetings, there was a representative from the navy. Also, when the navy had a meeting, they called on our local chiefs to attend the meeting." Second, the navy promoted democratic elections as soon as possible, with a directive to create electoral municipalities in May 1947, and 118 municipalities actually formed in 1948. These contradictory actions—supporting chiefs while instituting elective offices—gave impetus to existing tensions between traditional and colonial governing structures, a tension that continues to reverberate throughout Micronesia.[7] In describing ambiguous attitudes held by U.S. officials on Pohnpei, anthropologist John Fischer (1974:169–170) wrote that some thought Americans had liberated Pohnpeians from Japanese in order to allow them to resume traditional ways, while others opposed the chiefly system, thinking they should "Americanize" Pohnpeians, and viewed chiefs as undemocratic.

American policy was to let elections determine the extent to which traditional leaders would rule (by giving people the option of electing their chiefs), but it also selectively encouraged chiefly rights.[8] On Pohnpei and in the Marshalls, the navy helped resolve contested chiefly successions. The navy lifted limits on honor feasts for Pohnpeian chiefs imposed by German and Japanese law, resulting in a renewal of feast custom and expansion of the traditional title system. Yet in action, navy officials largely ignored Pohnpei's traditional political system, dealing mostly with the highest-ranking chiefs, the *nahnmwarki*.[9]

In the Marshalls, while some American decisions undercut chiefly power, the overall trend was to increase it. Marshallese recall that Americans buying copra for the Island Trading Company told local people to disregard allotting the chief's usual share of the income. But Americans, also eager to demonstrate noninterference with local custom, did not follow the Japanese system of placing a trader on virtually every island and atoll. This left chiefs and their representatives to handle much of the copra trade, at times to their own benefit. And high-ranking Marshallese strengthened their land rights for decades after the war, as American officials formally recognized them as key negotiators between landowning groups and the government.[10] Certainly in its early encounters with Marshallese chiefs, the navy was taken with the idea of "native kings" and "queens." American attention in the form of official events and publicity opportunities gave some traditional leaders a head start in gaining influence in the new order.

Yap and Palau—at opposite ends of the acculturation spectrum—both experienced intergenerational conflict as a result of democratic innovations. On Yap, after an initial snafu in which the U.S. request to meet with the "chief of Yap" was met by a man misrepresenting himself as exactly that,[11] the navy began by working through the existing Japanese-appointed chiefs. In initial elections (July 1946), five of the ten Japanese-appointed acting chiefs lost to

Photo 22. Dinner party at Majuro Naval Air Base, celebrating "the recoronation of the Native King and Queen," February 1944. (U.S. Navy photo, National Archives photo no. 80-G-230614)

higher-ranking traditional chiefs in their districts. This seemed a renewal of chiefly power on an island famous for its traditionalism, and the navy expected chiefs to act accordingly. But in fact, "The chiefs were unable to enforce navy orders because of lack of local support and lack of an effective police force. The local police did not have the power or the courage to arrest their friends and relatives. The naval administrators then became quite angry at the chiefs because they could not control the fighting, drinking, and other social problems" (Lingenfelter 1975:189).

While Yap's district chiefs did not wield enough authority to help the navy rule, they were able to revive feasting and exchange customs that had been abandoned under the Japanese (Labby 1976; Lingenfelter 1972, 1975). In part, Yapese renewal of tradition expressed a strongly held sense of their culture's value: unlike Palauans or Chamorros, Yapese did not quickly adopt elements of American culture. But it also marked tension between generations and social strata. Yap's chiefs responded with alacrity to the American "hands-off" approach that gave them scope to recover control of arenas of life lost under Japanese policies. But those disenfranchised by Yap's stratified society found much to attract them in the egalitarian American style. "The younger lower class men have found an escape from local bonds through Military Government jobs which take them to Yaptown [Colonia] where they are 'free to ride a bicycle'—which means being free of all social pressures" (Useem 1946a:23). And the generation then coming of age, which looked to the new American rulers for new opportunities, saw their expanding horizons threatened by their elders' conservatism. A group of young men officially protested against being held back while Micronesians in other islands progressed (Hunt et al. 1949:171–173).

In Palau, American moves to return power to traditional leaders reordered competing factions in Palauan society. MilGov's initial goal, here as elsewhere, was indirect rule; "the first question put to the Palau people by the American naval administrator was, 'who is the chief?'" (Vidich 1949:122). After thirty years of aggressive Japanese acculturation, however, Palau's traditional leaders no longer ruled. The Japanese had deposed uncooperative chiefs and nurtured a new generation of leaders. During the first year of U.S. rule, ambitious men of different backgrounds jockeyed for position, including chiefs, Modekngei leaders, and Japanese appointees.

But Palau's traditional leaders found their desire for more authority soon gratified. (Vidich 1980 details how chiefs regained power after the war.) Modekngei's influence dwindled as that of chiefs increased and young people turned from Modekgnei's emphasis on Palauan tradition to take American culture as their model. As American indirect rule gave chiefs a role in selecting personnel, they turned to relatives and peers; by 1948 many official positions were held by members of high-status clans. Elected municipal governments, the Palau High Court, and the Palau Congress (which first met in July 1947) were dominated by high-status Palauans. This marked a distinct change from the Japanese effort to reward ambitious men of any background who performed well in the colonial system. In the best cases, chiefs regarded their renewed responsibilities as an appropriate balance between foreign control and Palauan culture. At worst, it allowed exploitation, like the situation in Chuuk, as some chiefs took advantage of American favor to gain prestige and wealth.[12]

Photo 23. Navy officials (including Trust Territory High Commissioner Admiral D. C. Ramsey) confer with "Yap chiefs," July 1948. (U.S. Navy photo, National Archives photo no. 80-G-498964)

The navy saw its plan for municipal government as training, in which the political process would slowly evolve while existing governance was still respected.[13] "In reality," Carl Heine (1974:7) wrote almost three decades later, "the establishment of local municipalities has been more a government sanction of the remnants of the traditional systems than it has been the establishment of the Western system of local government." Broader democratic institutions emerged slowly. Only the Marshalls and Palau (two out of the five districts) had functioning regional congresses at the end of the navy period. The navy's own historian, Dorothy Richard, recognized the essential ambivalence of U.S. policy (it is also acknowledged in the 1948 U.S. Trust Territory *Handbook* [U.S. Navy 1948:45 and *passim*]). While the stated goal was self-sufficiency, local governments had to answer to the American administration; while declaring that they did not necessarily want Islanders to choose a democratic government, all legal and political entities organized by U.S. officials followed American models and were affected by the need to maintain control over the islands (Richard 1957c:388–393).

The dramatically enhanced position of the United States in the post–World War II world created the conditions for this ambivalence. The United States had become, reluctantly, a neocolonial power. The military felt it should not give up lands won by the sacrifice of American lives. The islands were vital to security, as the West sought a strategic position against Communist China and the Soviet Union, and would be kept to maintain peace rather than for national gain. Americans sought a new discourse of protecting Islanders that sat uneasily atop pragmatic military needs. (Lazarus Salii [1972] wrote of Americans' often-contradictory roles of "liberator" and "conquerer" of the islands.) This complex agenda encouraged political development but discouraged economic programs that might have aided Micronesians, because such work may have been perceived (particularly by the Soviet Union) as exploitation. Choices about Micronesian development had to show that the United States was not benefiting economically from its strategic trust. The question remained: Were Micronesians benefiting from American rule?

POSTWAR MICRONESIAN ECONOMIES

As the excitement of the first months of peace and the start of American rule died down, Islanders began to recognize that their economic lives had changed forever. The immediate sense of relief in receiving emergency supplies and seeing that their new rulers were wealthy and powerful soon gave way to unease as people realized that the Japanese economic order had been replaced by—well, by what? The few islands chosen for U.S. military use saw a renewal and even expansion of the prosperity they had known under the Japanese prewar boom. But islands without bases were nearly ignored. It became clear to those living in what had been thriving Japanese-led communities that their towns were now backwaters; that time and the economic tide had moved on. Perhaps most frustrating was that many of the new administrators seemed not to comprehend the major adjustments Micronesians were expected to make.

As time passed, it seemed that Americans thought of the devastated conditions at war's end as the norm for Micronesians, overlooking the busy economy of the 1930s in which even the most far-flung atoll had engaged.

Soon after Japanese surrender, the U.S. Navy's Pacific Command asked the U.S. Commercial Company for an economic survey of Guam and the former mandate. This was done in spring and summer of 1946 (Oliver 1951:v–vi). The first of many surveys and planning reports, it revealed a devastated economy that could only regain prewar affluence with major rehabilitation assistance. The USCC reports, along with later Co-ordinated Investigation of Micronesian Anthropology (CIMA) studies, confirm Micronesian memories of a prolonged and difficult recovery from the wartime economic nadir.

Postwar Economic Conditions

To be sure, the immediate outlook was dim. From the neglect and isolation of the war years and the destruction of Japanese military occupation and battle, the island economies inherited by American administrators were moribund. In the Marshalls, the economy was at "an all-time low" by the time of invasion (Bryan 1972:220) due to curtailed travel, separated families, dispossession, lack of a market for copra and handicrafts, scarce trade goods, and dilapidated houses and canoes. Savings from the boom years of the 1930s had been spent during the war or became useless as the United States allowed only limited, disadvantageous money exchange (Pollock n.d.:44–45). But because the Marshalls hosted U.S. bases in the last period of war, conditions soon improved.

Admiral Richmond Kelly Turner remembers the "Flintlock" operations in the Marshalls as "the perfect campaign" (Dyer 1972:733), despite inevitable problems. In like manner, perhaps, the Marshallese recall the first years after the war as the perfect colonial experience. They enjoyed respite from threats of annihilation, unlimited work opportunities, low prices, and an endless supply of goods. The benefits of the American idea of freedom seemed immediately apparent; its drawbacks in the Micronesian social order had not yet become manifest.

But conditions elsewhere (and eventually in the Marshalls as well) were less sanguine. The first postwar years saw "an appreciable drop in the standard of living for most Micronesians" (Hezel 1995:265). The primary economic ac-

Photo 24. Women on Majuro Atoll, Marshall Islands, celebrate the Fourth of July, 1944, with American sailors and marines. (U.S. Navy photo, National Archives photo no. 80-G-240490)

tivities throughout the region were day labor at military installations and making handicrafts for sale in the PX. Prices and wages were set at a scale that made goods in USCC stores unaffordable. While military wage labor and troops buying handicrafts were plentiful in the Marshalls, the situation in islands without bases was much different.

Apart from initial American generosity to Angaur and Peleliu, Palau's early experience with U.S. occupation was dramatically negative when bomb-damaged Koror was razed on American orders. Once the war was won, the U.S. presence on Palau dropped precipitately. There was only a small U.S. base at Peleliu, Palau's Civil Affairs unit consisted of twelve officers and fifty enlisted men, and Palau's MilGov officers lacked enthusiasm for a posting that they considered a career dead-end (Abe 1986:191). Palau also saw many shifts in administration, with four military governors from 1945–1948. Palauans found the navy's fiscal policies distressing: Japanese currency was exchanged at a low rate, savings accounts were not honored (though bank funds were found intact), wages were low, and the rare consumer goods expensive. Like every island, postwar Palau needed infrastructure, but Palau missed paved roads, banks, and newspapers more because it had had such a good supply of them before the war. "In the words of the senior USCC field representative on Palau, 'We have destroyed a twentieth century economy in Palau, and we are now trying to put it back with baling wire and splintered boards" (Useem 1946a:83). On Angaur: "To take an extreme case, a formerly wealthy native owned $2,450.00 in postal savings and $750.00 in cash. After the exchange he had $10.00. In former times he earned the equivalent of $1.10 a day and now his wage is 25 cents a day. He must now work eight days to earn a sufficient sum to buy a pair of trousers" (Useem 1945b:583–584). Palauans' total annual income fell to less than one-fourth that of the immediate prewar years.

Chuukese, too, ended the war in poverty, though of an odd sort—with plenty to eat and nothing to work with or wear. Though breadfruit trees and taro gardens had been destroyed, Chuukese harvested the vast fields of sweet potato, cassava, papayas, and bananas left behind by the Japanese. Once over the rush of repatriating Japanese troops, Chuuk was staffed by a skeleton crew: by December 1945 there were only about 30 U.S. officers and 150 enlisted men. The occupying force was cut to 55 men in early 1946 and stayed at this level through 1947 (Nason 1970:231). This small military contingent, a copra press, and a soap factory provided wage labor for only a few Chuukese, and those wages bought little. Furthermore, the USCC store offered shelves of useless goods, seldom having in stock badly needed cloth, tools, lamps, kerosene, kettles, and water barrels.[14]

While overall conditions were better than they had been during the war, they were much worse than vivid Chuukese memories of prewar life. During January–July 1946, Chuukese were paid $20,460, compared with $386,129 they had earned in the first half of 1937. Without U.S. action, stated one report, Chuukese will "revert to a status comparable to that prevailing prior to the German period of 1899–1914" (Hall and Pelzer 1946:vii–viii). Ichios Eas does not have good memories of these years:

(Interviewer asks: How did Americans and Chuukese get along? Were they good to Chuukese?)

Photo 25. Children in sweet potato fields in Chuuk, October 1945. (U.S. Navy photo, National Archives photo no. 80-G-353876)

What can I say in response to that question? By what can we really tell whether the Americans liked us or not? They did not continue to distribute food or materials. And there were not enough jobs to go around. Only a few worked for the government, taking care of those at home who had no other source of income. On the other hand, during the Japanese time, there were more paid jobs than there were workers. In fact, many actually got tired of having too many jobs. As for this government, only a few hundred people are working.

(Interviewer: How about the exchange of things between Americans and Chuukese? How was it?)

That I am not fully aware of. When they came, they brought corned beef and distributed it to the people for a few months. After that, it stopped. I do not know. There were still people in need, but the assistance stopped.

USCC analysts prescribed immediate remedies: add interisland boats, import oil suitable for Japanese engines, expand the postal service to serve Chuukese and restart postal savings, reduce the price and increase availability of consumer goods (a can of fish sold for 45–55 cents; the daily wage for men was 40 cents). While missions and schools resumed operation, most community meeting houses had been destroyed in the war, and unlike Pohnpei where monthly track meets were held, Chuukese had no activities to compare with the busy prewar schedule of sports and games. Finally, Chuuk needed legal help for claims against Japan for lost savings and war damage (Hall and Pelzer 1946).

Despite their track meets, Pohnpeians had the same concerns as Chuukese and Palauans in 1946. William Bascom, an anthropologist on the USCC economic survey team, wrote, "A rapid restoration of the prewar economic conditions, by itself, would have insured Pohnpeian loyalty and gratitude to the new American rulers. During the first year of occupation, however, the record was most disappointing" (Bascom 1950:147). Indeed, Bascom's 1950 article is an indictment of the American failure to restore even a basic operating economy to Pohnpei.

As on all islands, Pohnpei's initial occupying force set up a base of operations, disposed of ammunition stores, collected yen, and evacuated Japanese military and civilians; "They had little time for concern with native personnel" (Bascom 1950:149). Then the force was so reduced it could barely maintain itself. There was, almost literally, no source of income on Pohnpei: no wages, no exports, no local market. Pohnpei's tiny MilGov unit spent $236.35 in February 1946, and only $12.28 in April; the payroll similarly declined. The rest of the population had for income only cash exchanged for Japanese yen, which MilGov called in, but since no one could receive more than $50 — regardless of how many yen they turned in — most kept their Japanese currency.

Pohnpei's population in June 1946 was 5,462, plus about 40 Europeans and 10 Americans in the navy and USCC. In August, the navy garrison increased to 50. Obviously, the small American contingent provided little market for handicrafts or wage labor. What was worse, the enlisted men did not even make a good first impression: "Their versatility in practical skills was not questioned, but they were criticized for appearing at work and in the movies without shirts, and for drunkenness and obscenities in the presence of Ponapean women. The problems of the commanding officers were not decreased by the assignment of troublemakers and enlisted men who had broken regulations elsewhere for duty on Ponape" (Bascom 1950:149).[15] Qualified MilGov personnel did not arrive on Pohnpei until ten months after occupation. The bright spot was a free navy hospital and dispensary. Pohnpeians were grateful also to be able to return to their farms and liked the innovation of monthly islandwide meetings. And they refrained from condemning too quickly: "In the face of shortages which would have caused violent protests in any American community, Ponapeans have withheld final judgment of their new rulers" (Bascom 1950:150).

A MilGov report of 1946 implied that copra production was very low because Pohnpeians were unwilling to work (having seized on the notion of "freedom"). Bascom's response indicates the lack of information, or comprehension, that kept American officials on Pohnpei from effectively addressing economic problems: "Ponapeans were urged to resume production when there were no knives with which to produce it, when no agency existed to purchase it, when there were no warehouses in which it could be stored, and when inter- and intraisland shipping was inadequate to export it. At the same time there were no imported goods to be purchased with money received for copra" (1950:148).

While Bascom thought the immediate object of U.S. occupation of Pohnpei should have been to restore the Islanders' prewar standard of living, in fact, "Since the end of the war, the standard of living on Ponape has been so far below prewar conditions . . . that there is no point in making comparisons . . . only the most foolhardy could claim that the American occupation has meant an improvement over conditions under the Japanese before the war" (Bascom 1965:101–102).[16]

"If the [economic] situation was bad on Ponape, it was incomparably worse on the smaller outlying islands" (Bascom 1950:148). The initial American view saw outer island exports as limited to copra, handicrafts, and a few laborers—but even these were hampered by the lack of shipping, a persistent problem.[17] In addition to a well-developed transport system, the Japanese had encouraged a variety of outer island exports. Recall that by the late 1930s, many outer islands had had "a standard of living at least comparable and in some ways superior to that of a rural Japanese community" (referring to Lukunor, Mortlock Islands [Tolerton and Rauch 1949:88–89]; the most distant atolls, however, saw minimal economic development). Under American rule, enterprising leaders organized handicraft sales enabling Lukunor to import cigarettes, food, and clothing (in that order). But that market soon dried up; by March 1948, Lukunor was exporting only copra and mats, with a little cash coming in from men working for the navy on Pohnpei. People responded with concern to devastating shifts in American economic policies:

> The attitude of most of the people to a lowered volume of trade and consequently of the standard of living was one of unhappy resignation. When men mentioned the price of copra, "8 cents a kilo," they were likely to laugh scornfully and hopelessly. On public announcement of the second drastic cut in the price of mats, there was an involuntary and explosive sigh from the women. They spent much of the remainder of the day in informal protest meetings, in which they expressed themselves quite plainly. For three weeks so far as we could observe not one woman made a mat, but they gave in under the urging of their husbands and brothers and the weekly admonitions of the chief. (Tolerton and Rauch 1949:169)

When CIMA researcher Raymond Murphy visited Mokil in mid-1947, he commented that Mokilese are "likely to judge their new rulers chiefly on an economic basis." The real test would be "how well off the people are in things considered essential" (Murphy 1950:83). In this regard, supplies sent in the summer of 1947 were a failure, with the USCC store stocking a surplus of unwanted items but not the badly needed clothes, irons, sailcloth, sewing machines, and kerosene lanterns.[18]

Although postwar economic conditions were poor, Micronesians agree on two areas in which U.S. naval administration was more successful than the Japanese colonial order: health and education. Health care was widely recognized as more readily available to Islanders under the U.S. Navy than under Japan. With the eager assistance of Micronesian communities, the U.S. Navy set up local elementary schools to begin teaching English as soon as possible in every locale. Limited secondary schooling and a teacher training school joined the local primary schools, which by 1947 were established even on many outer islands. By June 1951 (despite budget cutbacks accompanying the shift from MilGov to CivAd), there were 138 elementary schools attended by 6,609

Photo 26. U.S medical team treating people on Losap, Caroline Islands, around January 1946. (U.S. Navy photo, National Archives photo no. 80-G-358165)

students.[19] Yet success in health care and schooling did not compensate for the "economic impasse" (Converse 1949:282).

Restoration or Subsistence?

To the Americans organizing MilGov, who had first seen the islands after four years of war—isolated from shipping, destroyed by bombs, neglected by labor impressed for military needs—it may well have seemed that Islanders would be doing well to get even the basics of economic life operating again. Researchers who worked directly with Micronesians disagreed: "One often meets the thinking that it will be sufficient to restore the economy at a subsistence level. Such a view does not recognize that this would 'set the clock back'" (Hall and Pelzer 1946:58).

Chuukese, Hall and Pelzer reminded Americans, "are no longer 'primitive natives' with very few wants which they can fulfill by relying on their own resources and skills"; in fact, they expected that the American era would improve on the Japanese era (as the Japanese had improved on the German) in education and material welfare. The USCC survey recommended that the navy commit to restoring Micronesia's economy (Hezel 1995:266), and reports for each island made clear how satisfactory that economy had been for Micronesians. William Bascom (1950:149) emphasized the strength of Pohnpei's prewar economy by saying that the two Belgian families living there, in European style, had not had to import supplies, "since everything they needed could be purchased locally; and even before Pearl Harbor, most Ponapeans had worn better clothes, lived in better houses, and eaten better food than the Okinawan immigrants. The picturesque era of the grass skirt and the grass shack had ended." He concluded, "Having assumed responsibility for Ponape in the name of our own safety, we cannot honorably ask the Ponapeans to accept a standard of living lower than that which they enjoyed under the Japanese."

Yet this, in the end, is what happened. The distressingly weak postwar economy was not due only to American sensitivity to criticism about colonial exploitation, limited resources, self-serving actions of local people, or the loss of labor due to repatriation (discussed below). It was also in part attributable to MilGov's lack of knowledge about and continuing misperception of Micronesians as "primitive" people who should be happy with a small-scale subsistence economy. Thus, as months and years passed, even as the prewar era began to glow more golden for Micronesians, knowledge of how Islanders had lived under Japanese rule faded rapidly from American memory, replaced by an image of subsistence-level "traditional" life. Chave (1950:66) quoted one official: "In the May 3, 1947 Saturday Evening Post, Admiral Carlton Hubert Wright, U.S.N., who is much interested in Military Government and a power in making policy, asks, 'What shall we do with or for them?' (The natives of the former Japanese Mandate.) 'And I say, for mercy's sake let them alone in their happiness. . . . Let's give them doctors, nails, tools, corrugated roofing, sail cloth, but teach them not to want radios, juke boxes, button shoes. . . . Teach them basic English and support the schools to perfect their own culture, not to impose an alien one.'"

Before Admiral Wright made the ideology of primitivism explicit, it had appeared in policies across the region.[20] The CIMA interim report for Chuuk dated October 1947 recommends that U.S. Navy officers stop discouraging Chuukese from wearing clothes—officers were even restricting imports of clothing, assuming that the Chuukese desire for them was due to missionary pressure. CIMA and USCC reports repeat the refrain of contrast between prewar and postwar material conditions, urging administrators to recognize the level of services and consumer goods to which Micronesians had become accustomed in the Japanese era. Like John Useem, who was among the first civil affairs officers on Angaur, they argued against "the preconceived American notion of 'primitiveness'" (Useem 1945b:580).

> It would be an irresponsible policy to assume that the Palau people were primitives prior to the war and that their simple life may be spoiled by the introduction of a modern standard of living. This point of view has permeated some of the thinking on the economic life of Palau. When the writer submitted to CincPac [U.S. Navy Commander in Chief, Pacific] the list of supplies needed for Ngeaur [Angaur] prior to the invasion of that island, he was informed that the native had no use for dishes, western style clothes, spoons, blankets, and the like. Two years later, the requisitions of the USCC representative on Palau have been subjected to similar decisions in Guam. It is vital that the guidance on supplies be based on a realistic conception of the standards of living prevailing in Palau. (Useem 1946a:84–85)

Teaching Micronesians not to want the products of industrial civilization, as Admiral Wright recommended, meant teaching them to forget what they had had before the war.

If their new rulers quickly lost sight of conditions in Japanese Micronesia, Micronesians did not. Older people remembered clearly what life had been like, especially in the towns, in the booming 1930s. And young people, educated with American books and movies and talking with American visitors, gained a new standpoint for comparison. As the Japanese era faded into the background, foreign observers began to remark that it was exposure to American culture that stimulated Micronesians' desire for material goods that could not reasonably be fulfilled (e.g., Richard 1957c:619). In fact, it was both the memory of the past and distant but ungratified glimpses of the American present that fueled Micronesian visions of a desirable economy. "A proposal to build thatched houses elicited the reaction that they were not as healthy or as comfortable as the modern wooden type. There was no interest in returning to the earlier type of dress or sanitary practices and rice plus canned goods was regarded as the only completely satisfying food. Children were more interested in learning American than in hearing about the former customs. The attempts of the older women to teach the ancient dances were soon abandoned for lack of interest; youth wanted to do Western dances. Moving pictures were far more popular than native festivals" (Useem 1945b:581).

After years of deprivation, starvation, fear, and hard labor, Islanders, like Americans, were looking to the postwar years for relief, for compensation for all they had suffered, for comfort and pleasure. Americans—showy with wealth, confidence, and novelty—suggested unlimited new choices. Some Micronesians, like Yapese, responded by observing the novelty and turning aside from most of it. Others wanted as much of it as they could grasp. A postwar researcher on Kosrae decried this attitude: "They would like diversions and amusements to make existence more enjoyable and material objects to make it more American. Men want houses like American houses and such things as tables, chairs, dishes, and all the equipment that go with them. In their own words they want to live like Americans. The impracticality of such an existence even if it were possible does not occur to them" (Lewis 1948a:87). But many Micronesians had already experienced elements of such an "impractical" existence in the Japanese colonial economy of the 1930s. So, from generation to generation, the knowledge of a materially more comfortable life was visible to Micronesians, but the means for achieving it remained elusive.

Although wartime destruction had caused much of the loss of infrastructure that plunged Micronesia into an economic slough, the explanation for why no viable new economy arose lies in decisions made—or avoided—on the American side. The first fateful ruling was to repatriate Japanese and Okinawan civilians. As late as July 1945 a MilGov pamphlet assumed that some would stay in the Marianas: "Many people will probably return to Japan, others will become fishermen, farmers, mechanics, ship repairmen, office workers, teachers, cooks, gardeners and servants" (Taylor 1945:23). But within a year of war's end, nearly all foreign civilians had gone. "These had been the people who formed the total managerial force in the Territory. They were the businessmen, the shopkeepers, the civil administrators, the educators, the police forces; in short, they represented that group which is essential for day-to-day societal functioning. As could be expected, this move, together with the destruction resulting from the war, caused the Micronesian economy to collapse entirely" (Ballendorf 1984b:3). The evacuation created an "economic vacuum," and by depopulating urban centers such as those in Pohnpei and Palau, it also created cultural vacuums.[21]

Repatriation was devastating emotionally as well as economically. Hall (1950) castigated the navy for its disregard for civilians, exemplified by the roundup and embarkation of Okinawans—some of whom had Chuukese families—on three hours' notice one day in May 1946. While Micronesians had seen Japanese troops leave with relief, they bid farewell to civilian bosses, neighbors, and relatives with tears and sentimental songs. After repatriation, there was "great concern among the inhabitants of Chuuk as to just what the United States is going to do about re-establishing the native economy on a pre-war basis" (Hall and Pelzer 1946:vii–viii). But by this point U.S. officials had embarked on a course that made such an outcome impossible. "Any chance of restoring the artificial, capitalistic type of pre-war economy was definitely obliterated by the decision of the Joint Chiefs of Staff to repatriate all aliens. Their removal, accomplished by the end of 1946, took both the artisans and the majority of unskilled labor from the islands, and left only a small, un-trained native labor supply. . . . The problem, therefore, was to determine the 'normal' degree of self sufficiency of the islands and aim for its restoration" (Richard 1957b:406).[22]

For islands that had been under colonial rule for one hundred to several hundred years, "normal self-sufficiency" was a relative concept. Isolated atolls were able to reconstruct their subsistence economy fairly quickly despite wartime destruction.[23] But consider the Marianas. Not only had these islands been part of Spain's global empire in the sixteenth century, they had been a productive source of exports for Japan. Their population was fully accus-tomed to being enmeshed in a global capitalist economy. Under what terms could "self-sufficiency" make sense for Saipan or Tinian? And why should Chamorros (any more than French or Japanese) accept this as the goal for postwar rehabilitation of their economy?

On Saipan and Palau, memories of the first years of U.S. rule contrast sharply with the positive tone of accounts of this era by Marshallese and Amer-icans. Both Saipan and Palau had been prewar centers of Japanese activity; both lost prominence under the new rulers. Moreover, the Japanese defeat on Saipan and Peleliu had come at great cost in American lives; victory was not so clearly decisive as on Kwajalein or Enewetak. It is not surprising that indigenous portrayals of Americans and of life during the postwar era is more equivocal for Chamorros and Palauans than for Micronesians farther east.

The history of handicraft production (Mason n.d.) suggests how this contrast was manifested in economic policy. In many senses, handicraft production epitomized the American image of what Pacific Islanders should be doing. In most locales, it was the first productive activity supported by the U.S. Navy. In the Marshalls, sales of handicrafts made for positive encounters with Americans, and Marshallese recall being paid exorbitant sums for shells and handicrafts, even if in indigenous eyes the quality was substandard. Reinforcing the image of Americans as high chiefs with inexhaustible wealth, Marshallese like Clanton Abija recall that sometimes handicrafts were purchased and then dumped in the sea: "Well, then, it was the navy people by themselves who sought out handicrafts. And I do not know why they took them, because it did not matter if they were worthless. But it was a dollar for a belt or a fan. And some of them, they paid five or fifteen or twenty-five dollars for. And it did not matter if they were bad or if I did not know how to make them. When they sought them out it would be five dollars. Perhaps they just took them and disposed of them over there [in the lagoon]. But this is the way they helped out. Perhaps it was just their way of helping out during that time."

In the opinion of the first American administrators, Marshallese handicraft was of the highest quality.[24] Saipanese work was seen as substandard in comparison, and Marshallese examples were sent to Saipan to improve quality. This effort never proved successful and, by 1948, Saipan's handicraft cooperative was moribund. While Americans regretted the co-op's demise, they seemed oblivious to its cause. In this center of prewar Japanese economic activity, where sugar production had provided the bulk of the wealth, handicraft production would have represented economic regression. Not only did it yield little profit, but the negative comparison with Marshallese must have sat poorly with the people of Saipan.

Chamorros on Saipan consistently disagreed with American plans for their economic future. The first postwar economic report on Saipan (Gallahue 1946), like those for Chuuk and Pohnpei, explained the need to renew the import-export economy that had supported the region for decades. The living conditions American officials observed in mid-1946 were "not normal" compared to before the war and should not be taken as the style of life to which Chamorros were accustomed. (Similarly, Hall and Pelzer [1946] pointed out

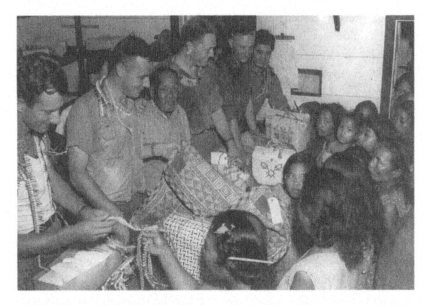

Photo 27. Marshallese at Arno Atoll selling handicrafts to U.S. Navy Civil Affairs officers in navy store, April 1945. (U.S. Navy photo, National Archives photo no. 80-G-313599)

that the spartan households seen on Chuuk in 1945 were not the prewar norm.)[25] Chamorros were refugees, living in internment camps or new settlements. Lives, homes, and property had been lost, land taken for military or other uses, relocated wartime laborers not yet returned. People were in great need of consumer and capital goods. Because imports were not arriving through government channels, Guamanians were using mail order catalogs, and Chamorros on Saipan who could afford it were beginning to do this too. Gallahue's report takes it as a "fundamental principle" that "Mariana islanders have a right to expect as high a standard of living during the post war period as they had prior to the war" (Gallahue 1946:41–42) and concludes optimistically that local people can revive their economy if given a chance, guidance, and material assistance.

But American policy decided otherwise, and the next economic survey of the Marianas reflects the altered vision for the islands' future. Neal Bowers' CIMA report (1950:62) concludes that after repatriation of the Japanese, the Mariana Islanders lacked the "background and experience" needed to restore the high prewar standard of life. His task was to examine how existing resources could meet the goal of "reestablishment of the former level of living on as self-supporting a basis as the local resources will permit" (1). Of course, the task was quixotic. Only in Guam, Kwajalein, and Majuro was Micronesia's prewar standard of living soon met, then exceeded—and those cases were not based on a policy of self-sufficiency.[26]

In Nan'yō times, Carolinians on Saipan had worked mostly as stevedores, Chamorros at a wide range of crafts and skilled work (nurses, teachers, policemen, mechanics, carpenters). Employment and leasing land to Japanese commercial interests were the principal economic activities. After the war, and after Okinawans, Japanese, and Koreans were evacuated in early 1946, the U.S. Navy in effect tried to turn Chamorros on Saipan and Tinian into farmers. This "back-to-the-farm program," according to Farrell (1991:485), "would create a subsistence economy similar to that which existed during the German administration, but certainly not comparable to that which the people of the Northern Mariana Islands had enjoyed under the Japanese." Chamorros esteemed land for its commercial value but were not attracted to farming. "One hears, 'If the NKK came back tomorrow, many people would be very happy to lease their land and if possible work for wages'" (Spoehr 1954:145–146). Yet farming seemed, to American administrators, the only thing for them to do. War and repatriation had left the land underpopulated and unused (Bowers 1950). MilGov provided extravagant support for farming—land, oxen, plows, seed, fertilizers, insecticide, marketing help, and co-op associations. Despite the aid, by 1951 co-ops were no longer functioning, and out of a total population of 4,700, Saipan had somewhat more than two hundred farmers (Taylor 1951).

Most people took advantage of a different opportunity: demobilization of U.S. troops in the summer of 1946 produced a labor crisis at Saipan's military bases. The sudden need for labor overturned the pro-farming policy. Demand was so great that school age was lowered, women were urged to take wage work, and some nurses in training were directed to jobs as domestic servants for newly arrived American officials. Despite a desire to work, some felt they were again facing forced labor, aggravated by what some saw as an inadequate wage scale and poor living conditions in Chalan Kanoa.[27] Saipan soon looked prosperous, as retail stores appeared in response to wages of base workers, who spent their income on familiar and much-desired imported foods and goods. But its economy was desperately vulnerable. When bases closed in the spring of 1950, leaving only the small navy unit, half the stores begun in 1947 shut down. Chamorros continued to acquire wage-work skills, but had no way to earn a living with them. Several hundred took jobs in Guam, but their immigration status was uncertain, and travel to Guam was restricted in 1952.[28]

While Chamorros had limited success in redirecting American development efforts to paths they preferred, they did gain a favorable position relative to other Micronesians. Americans found Chamorros to be, as they themselves claimed, more acculturated to Western ways. Chamorros had shifted their model from Japan to the United States, but they remained resolutely cosmopolitan. After several foreign rulers, Chamorros' greater westernization, literacy, borrowings, and intermarriage had given them "a preferred position" (Spoehr 1954:27–28). In the Marianas, this meant continuing the relatively privileged status of Chamorros in education and employment.[29] What was to have long-term implications for the political trajectory of the Trust Territory was the decision to hire Chamorros—rather than local people—for work in the Caroline Islands.

Chamorros learned English speedily, adopted American fashions, and petitioned for U.S. citizenship to a visiting U.N. mission in 1950. "Looking back" on his trip, a mid-1950s visitor to Micronesia commented, "I find that Saipan was the only island whose citizens expressed any interest at all in being absorbed by the United States" (Trumbull 1959:21–22). Eighteen months after the July 1951 transfer of control of Micronesia to the U.S. Department of the Interior, Saipan and Tinian were returned to the navy for security reasons (the rest of the Northern Marianas, except for Rota, followed in July 1953). Until 1962, when these islands were reintegrated with the Trust Territory (and territory headquarters was moved to Saipan), Saipan hosted Naval Technical Training Units, which trained Chinese Nationalists in anticommunist efforts (Farrell 1991:505; Gale 1979:84–86). The navy presence allowed a level of material wealth and familiarity with Americans unmatched in the other islands. But there was no long-range plan for economic stability, and people in the Northern Marianas knew that their well-being was fragile.

Palauans had, perhaps, the worst of both worlds. Like people on Saipan, they were accustomed to a wage economy and links with metropolitan culture. Unlike Saipan, Palau saw no sizeable American presence after the war and no effort to stimulate the economy—not even in unwelcome directions.

As the prewar Japanese capital, Palau was particularly hard hit by demotion to the fringes of the new order. Palauan life in the immediate postwar years was shaped by the U.S. policy of "restoring" what officials envisioned as pre-Japanese economy and polity. Like the people of Saipan, many Palauans had to struggle to develop (not "return to") an agrarian economy; if taro was to replace rice, gardens had to be dug. Ironically, it was the women's clubs organized in the context of prewar society that took the lead in urging women to care for the taro gardens. Palauan men, who had run construction firms and worked in Japanese offices, "have been encouraged to take up the practice of old crafts such as fish-net construction and old methods of carpentry which do not require the use of manufactured tools" (Vidich 1980:271–272).

Yet so strong was the association of progress with foreign administration that many Palauans persisted in the belief that Americans would eventually restore Palau's devastated economy. Entrepreneurs sought business licenses, believing "that there would be an American era of prosperity based on economic development and colonization which would surpass the Japanese period" (Vidich 1980:289–291). Trained in Japanese crafts schools and veterans of Japanese businesses, Palauans set up in carpentry, fishing, chicken farms, bakeries, and wholesale and interisland trade. The link in Palauan culture between wealth and prestige stimulated these efforts. As soon as CivAd replaced the economically regimented MilGov, Palauans pushed business as far as they could. But those who sought to renew Palau's business sector found that CivAd limited licenses to businesses it thought could succeed using only local supplies; development that diverged from the policy of self-sufficiency was discouraged. "By 1948 it was becoming apparent even to these 'bullish' Palauans that Palau was to return to an agrarian economy with the consequent devaluation of their business and trade skills" (Vidich 1980:309). To ambitious Palauans, "the American [economic development] efforts seemed not only feeble, but deliberately regressive and counterproductive" (Ballendorf 1988b:61).[30]

Palau's capitalists brought into relief the dilemma of "freedom" in postwar life, for what Americans saw as "self-sufficiency," Micronesians could just as well interpret as a failure of Americans to accept their obligations. John Useem (1946b) made the point that after decades of colonial subordination, Micronesians could not respond readily to demands that they rule themselves (see also Heine 1974:20). Nor was it enough for the United States to declare that freedom would somehow be equivalent to the restoration of a pre-Japanese mode of life; in fact, "There is deep concern that self-government may be a guise for Americans to abandon the natives rather than help them restore their way of life" (Useem 1946a:91–92).

If Chamorros and Palauans could not convince navy decision makers that they had no desire for a subsistence lifestyle, Islanders farther east had even less of a chance to do so. Perhaps it was the romance of the Pacific isles, perhaps it was preexisting racist notions of how Islanders should live abetted by the lack of current English-language information about the region,[31] perhaps it was simply making a virtue of the necessity of a limited budget for the new territory, but as the months passed it became clear that Islanders were not going to see the level of engagement in the global market that they had experienced under the Japanese for a long time—if ever.[32]

The honeymoon, such as it had been, was over. American prestige in Micronesia had waned a good deal by 1947. U.S. rule had not met the Mokilese test; demand for goods in the late 1940s still far exceeded supply. The vision of a subsistence economy worked in tandem with other navy policies that soon reaped more critical attention. With few ships, few personnel, a limited budget, and no clear marching orders, the naval administration was by the end of the decade chastised for managing Micronesia as a "zoo," with some officials opposed to all outside influences. Even the pro-navy author John P. Marquand, invited to visit the islands, wrote in his 1947 essay: "From the point of view of health and general economy, war has left this ocean world in such a bad condition that it is not nice to admit, though it is the truth, that most of its people were better off under Japan than they are so far under the United States" (164).[33] Living conditions and the appearance of American outposts were poor; the navy maintained tight security and resisted capital investment by either Americans or Japanese. As navy rule switched to CivAd and pulled military resources out of Micronesia, no new resources replaced them. CivAd undertook public works projects and requested additional funds, but never got as much as it needed. Once the war was won, the new American obligations dropped suddenly and dramatically on the list of funding priorities.

The first United Nations Visiting Mission in 1950 reported that Micronesians in every district asked for help in remedying the inadequate cash economy. The Trusteeship Council and the Visiting Mission agreed with the American intention not to exploit Micronesia, but saw that people needed more

Photo 28. Island Trading Company store on Yap, July 1948. (U.S. Navy photo, National Archives photo no. 80-G-498970)

income, more wage labor opportunities, and new exports (this was difficult, since the U.S. levied import taxes on island products). Lack of shipping was still a major problem. The territory tried numerous unsuccessful economic development projects: a chicken farm in Chuuk, a duck farm on Majuro, a marine railway in Chuuk, coir fiber production on Pohnpei, ramie fiber and coffee on Saipan, a cacao plantation in Palau, a fruit and vegetable farm to supply military camps on Guam. The navy decided not to revive the Japanese sugarcane business on Tinian, Saipan, and Rota. Attempts to establish locally run fishing enterprises failed; the territory was opened to Japanese fishing in May 1950. In brief, throughout the islands cash remained in short supply, and imports were equally scarce. In 1952, the Trust Territory was still asking whether or not Americans should be "civilizing" natives (Sherrod 1952:110).[34]

In later decades, after a Kennedy-era shift in American policy gave Micronesia in abundance the consumer goods and cash income it had so longed for in the postwar years, the context and the evaluation of American motives was quite different. When Micronesians were again linked with the global economy in the 1960s and 1970s, a new generation seeking its own definition of freedom argued that integration into a metropolitan economy was undesirable dependence. That later generation decried economic integration in favor of a self-supporting economy for the islands—an elusive goal that Micronesians still seek.

But it would be many years before Micronesians began explicitly evaluating the challenge of American individualism and publicly shaping their own definitions of freedom and self-sufficiency. During the final years of navy rule and as the transition to the Department of the Interior began, senior Islanders' attention remained focused on the dramatic change in their material lives and how they could both adjust to it and press the United States to increase support for Micronesian economies. At the same time, they were exploring what new opportunities the postwar order could provide for themselves and their children.

MICRONESIAN-AMERICAN RELATIONS

The economic issues that preoccupied Islanders and administrators in the first years after the war were entangled with racial stereotypes as the notion of a subsistence economy became policy. Americans also found themselves ill at ease in the colonial role, especially since they had taken it on through what was perceived as a war of liberation. Micronesians thus had to deal not only with new rulers—but with rulers who had not yet decided how, or to what end, they would rule.

In the first months and years of occupation, the encounter of indigenous and American cultures created mutual misperceptions that took decades to untangle. Anthropologist John Useem, who spent three years in the Civil Affairs Division of MilGov during the war (and was also a USCC and CIMA researcher), analyzed the early interactions of Americans and Micronesians. Americans were sympathetic to the devastation of Micronesians' homelands but did not fully appreciate the dimensions of the changes Islanders faced. Micronesians appreciated Americans' goodwill but found them "beyond understanding and unpredictable." To Islanders, the best response in the early period of occupation seemed to be the familiar one of showing submission to the foreigner while shielding their own ways of life. Useem (1947:1, n.9) reported attending meetings at which chiefs explicitly discussed how to present their society to Americans. Elsewhere he wrote:

> Each group [Americans and Micronesians] seems to the other a mystery compounded of idealization mixed with suspicion. Americans regard natives through the focus of the Hollywood movie projector and feel let down when this does not correspond to reality. They are unduly anxious that the natives like them, and like them better than their former rulers. Americans expect sexual drama and are unhappy when confronted with the complications of the marital patterns which prevail. They admire independence as a social attribute yet resent natives who are aggressive. Native institutions are respected, but the mores evoke emotional reactions—as when the native class-caste system calls for inequalities, or when indirection or silent acquiescence are the reactions to proposals made instead of the natives "speaking their minds."
>
> Micronesians, in turn, feel endless admiration for the technological skill and equipment displayed and seem eager to emulate American ways of doing things. Yet these same natives fear our attitudes on the race question, wonder what our real motives are, are upset by the ambivalence of American personalties, are confused by the constantly changing orders, the frequent turnover in administrative personnel and the contradictory activities undertaken. (Useem 1946c:22)

Americans relied on personal interaction to create good impressions, a policy that generally succeeded, yet affability was no substitute for recognizing that Micronesian cultures had their own rules. Cross-cultural faux pas on the part of American personnel built an image of cultural incompetence and provoked complaints. So did American habits of efficiency and speed (even when the situation did not require them) and constant change in search of improvement.[35]

In April 1946, the U.S. Navy opened the School of Naval Administration (SONA) at Stanford University to prepare administrators for Micronesia and Samoa.[36] Before special training was in place, officers had only their own instincts and outdated information in official handbooks to guide them. Some administrators succeeded admirably, dedicating their careers to Micronesian service and receiving good reviews from visitors and local people (Murrill 1948b:100; Trumbull 1959:174).

Over the years of MilGov and CivAd governance, the interactions of Micronesians and Americans (administrators, anthropologists, and visitors) created a quasi-official body of literature that became, in some sense, "traditional Micronesian culture." One element shaping this emerging body of ideas about Micronesian culture was the identification of the nonnegotiable elements of American culture—for example, freedom of religion.[37] Another was the impact of the early USCC and CIMA reports, which were in part designed to familiarize American officials with the variety of peoples in their new domain, but also had the effect of establishing some old and some new stereotypes.[38] The combination of genuine cultural distinctions and official ethnic categories became an important element of regional politics and was key to the eventual dismantling of the Trust Territory in the 1980s.

Significant in the institutionalization of custom and ethnic groupings in the islands was the racism that permeated American culture at this time. Micronesians were anxious to learn how American racial ideas compared with Japanese. To existing Japanese categories of Chamorros and Carolinians as third-class peoples—*tōmin*—with Carolinians also called *kanaka*, they added their developing understanding of American classifications such as "native" and "Black." Aware of the connotations of inferiority in colonialists' use of these and other terms, Islanders noticed and resented them. Anthropologist Edward Hall arrived at Chuuk in May 1946 and observed that the majority of navy and civilian personnel classed Chuukese as Negro because of their dark skins: "The irrational nature of this bias is difficult enough to deal with in the United States; it constitutes an almost insuperable barrier to successful military government" (Hall 1950:29–30).[39] The use of ethnic insults by the first cohort of occupation forces was soon superseded; the arrival of SONA graduates on Chuuk, for example, caused the demise of the term *gook*, the usual word enlisted personnel had been using for Chuukese (Gladwin 1950:18).

But American officials referred to and wrote about "natives," with some of the colonial distancing that term implied, though they were always affected as well by their country's explicitly anticolonial stance. Micronesians, John Useem wrote, were "in principle" equal to Americans, but practice differed. "'Equality' implied to some administrators that Micronesians were of the same quality as *white* Americans" (author's emphasis). Others interpreted it to mean natives were equal to "ordinary" Americans and should associate only with enlisted men. "Most common was the belief that basically the natives were a 'lower class of people' who were innately inferior. . . . Surprise was general when natives readily learned to speak English, operate electric generators, moving picture projectors and the like" (Useem 1946b:5).

The most obvious racial distinction in American Micronesia was that between expatriate and native. Though seldom analyzed in the endless reports generated by the navy and Trust Territory administrations (Spoehr 1954 is an exception in his discussion of Saipan; see Poyer 1999), the gap was manifest in pay rates, housing location and quality, separate schools for American children, and access to expatriate enclaves and services. While invading American troops in Kiribati and the Marshalls had sung around the campfire with "natives," the situation changed once occupation forces were in place. In Saipan, the American military lived and worked mostly in reserves separate from local people (though Saipan's small scale allowed some interaction). Employment as office workers, household servants, and base labor gave Chamorros especially the chance to learn new skills, practice English, and get to know American culture. Yet American authorities purposely limited off-the-job contacts between military personnel and Chamorros, and the number of civil administrators was quite small (Spoehr 1954:98–100).

Micronesians everywhere noted the social distance of Americans. In comparing Americans and Japanese on Chuuk:

Although all such statements began with general praise for the "politeness" of Americans, which meant that unlike the Japanese they did not flog, slap, and insult the Trukese, there were two important reservations sometimes expressed. In the first place, those who were old enough to remember the pre-war period often said that economically they were much better off under the Japanese because there was more money in circulation and more jobs to be had. Secondly, although the Americans are more polite than the Japanese, the Japanese "loved" the Trukese more. The last means, for the most part, that many Japanese learned to speak Trukese whereas only American anthropologists, never government officials, do, and many of the Japanese lived in Trukese villages before the war whereas the American officials and their families live in a settlement far removed from the natives. (Swartz 1961:78)

The policy of segregation continued through the first years of the Trust Territory. Until the Peace Corps arrived—with the exception of a few missionaries and anthropologists—Americans in Micronesia lived lives quite separate from those they governed and did not usually learn the local language.

The U.S. Navy also brought its own culture's notions about gender and age to the islands. In large part, it was young men who were given new routes to power under MilGov and CivAd, especially through training as teachers or administration employees. Many girls also took new opportunities for schooling, but the postwar association linking women and domesticity in the United States was reflected in the Trust Territory. Women's education translated into important government positions far more slowly and to a lesser degree than that of men. For the first decades of American rule, women's work may well have become significantly more restricted than under the Japanese.[40]

AFTER THE NAVY YEARS

While the strategic value of Micronesia was undisputed throughout the postwar years, as the Korean War and Cold War replaced World War II defense concerns, the discussion of American obligations to the people of Micronesia turned into a long and ultimately unresolved one. Despite the navy's fairly clear intentions, one of which was "to win the good will, cooperation, and loyalty of the native peoples" (Richard 1957a:164–165), neither civilian critics, Micronesians, nor the navy itself was satisfied with conditions during those years. John Useem listed U.S. problems in Micronesia as insufficient personnel, incoherent foreign policy, disjuncture between official policy and strategic need, inexperience in governing foreign peoples, and "the inapplicability of traditional American concepts and attitudes to the area" (Useem 1946c:21; Richard 1957b:279). Some of these were distinctive of navy administration; others were problems of all colonial governments and remained unchanged under civilian rule.

After an acrimonious public debate over navy rule, responsibility for the Trust Territory was transferred to the U.S. Department of the Interior on July 1, 1951. As the navy CivAd era closed, the hope of a restoration of prewar economy faded. Micronesians outside Guam adjusted to diminished material expectations (though not without great concern) and put their efforts into education, political development, and increasing their familiarity with all things American. Mahony (1969:9–10) comments that under U.S. control, economic development in Chuuk was stagnant for two decades, but "social development was stepped up." Micronesians rewove the texture of community life, with renewed church activities, sports events, and new holidays such as United Nations Day.

Like navy CivAd, the U.S. Department of the Interior was criticized for its "anthropological zoo" philosophy, with visitors, outside investment, and social change discouraged. The Trust Territory maintained—but limited budgets prevented it from expanding—much-praised navy programs in basic health, education, and sanitation. Economic development remained piecemeal and generally not successful. Robert Trumbull's oft-quoted comment in *Paradise in Trust* elicits rueful agreement from those familiar with Micronesia's postwar experience: "No country, I thought many times while I was in the islands, could govern the Trust Territory better than it was being done, except perhaps the United States" (Trumbull 1959:214).

Department of Interior administration continued political development, with the emphasis on representative democracy. But political advances did not stop the 1961 U.N. Visiting Mission from criticizing the U.S. for failing to settle war damage claims or compensate Micronesians adequately for land used by its military. Public criticism (e.g., Price 1966) and a change in government produced a course adjustment during the Kennedy administration. The budget jumped from some $6 million in 1962 to $15 million in 1963—with other increases to follow. Changes in schooling, a vast expansion of bureaucracy, increases in tourism and other business, and the Peace Corps soon followed.

Chapter 9

THE LEGACY OF WAR

THE FUTURE of the islands of Micronesia was irrevocably altered by the transformations that swept through them during the wartime years: first, militarization and initial Japanese war preparations; second, the defensive buildup beginning in 1943; and finally American bombing, blockading, and invasion. These successive waves of change profoundly affected Micronesia's physical and social environment. Landscapes, oceanscapes, agricultural and marine resources, and economic and communication infrastructure were altered, expanded, and destroyed. The transformations also reshaped Micronesian societies and cultures in terms of landownership, gender relations, familiar and novel forms of leadership, and interaction with other societies. During the few years of war in the islands, certain changes took place that could never be undone, certain losses that could never be made good.

In August 1945, John Embree (1946a:2) wrote, "The only thing left of prewar Saipan is a steady damp oppressive heat." The landscape was littered with pillboxes, bomb shelters, and the abandoned farmhouses and sugar fields of Okinawan settlers. Much of it was also veneered with the dilapidated remains of American installations: row on row of Quonsets, warehouses, and service buildings falling into ruin (Spoehr 1954:18). The destruction, transformation, and abandonment of Saipan's prewar economy and landscape was seen throughout Micronesia.[1] While areas destroyed in World War II were rebuilt in Europe, Japan, China, and Southeast Asia, the war-devastated terrain of Micronesia became instead the de facto starting point of American planning for the region. Restoration, reconstruction, rebuilding—these words, with their implication of a status quo ante, soon left the vocabulary of Micronesia's new rulers, or were transmuted to mean something else. But the prewar condition of their island homes did not so soon leave the memories of Micronesians themselves.

WARTIME DESTRUCTION OF RESOURCES

In 1966, E. J. Kahn wrote: "Wherever there was ground fighting, the destruction was very nearly total. The pride of Saipan, for example, was the Japanese-built city of Garapan, which on the eve of the war had a population of twenty-nine thousand and amenities comparable to those of Koror and Dublon. After the invasion of Saipan, there was nothing left of Garapan. There still is nothing left" (1966a:46).[2] Every prewar urban area in the islands suffered the same fate as invaded Garapan. Kolonia (Pohnpei) was completely destroyed by bombing; Toloas (Chuuk) and Jabwor (Jaluij, Marshall Islands) were largely destroyed. Agana's Guamanian population fell from over ten thousand to under a thousand. Koror (Palau), somewhat damaged by bombing, was demolished after the war.[3]

The war destroyed more than towns, of course. It took out the transportation infrastructure that had been essential to the Japanese colonial economy. Airstrips throughout Micronesia were judged too difficult to rehabilitate, leaving nothing gained after the loss of freshwater lenses and taro swamps entailed by their construction. It was impossible to replace the fleet of vessels destroyed in the war or to rebuild Japanese shipping networks, communication systems, electric-generating plants, or roads. Capital goods that would have been needed to restore the prewar economy were destroyed, along with those needed for subsistence.[4] Where destruction was not deliberate, postwar neglect took its toll. On Kosrae, improvements such as a dock, dam, and roads made during Japanese war preparations were useless within two decades (Peoples 1977:154–158).

The war seriously and in some cases permanently altered Micronesia's natural resources. Revegetation was a major concern; in many islands the greatest need was to restore coconut palms for copra. Experts expected the damage would depress copra production for eight to ten years. In Palau, wartime felling of thousands of trees produced ideal breeding grounds for the destructive rhinoceros beetle. Copra eventually made a postwar comeback but never reached prewar levels since global demand for coconut oil had fallen.[5]

The impact of Japanese military occupation on Chuuk's agricultural resources can stand for that on other islands with large garrisons: land taken for defense installations, coconut and breadfruit trees felled for lumber or cleared for crops, taro swamps drained and filled in for planting fast-growing vegetables, flood gates installed in drainage ditches, and the loss of nearly all cattle and 90 percent of hogs. Most of Chuuk's war-damaged taro swamps remained idle in 1946. Intensive sweet potato cultivation had ruined much gardening land. All but the highest peaks of the lagoon islands had been cleared, so that by the 1950s secondary growth covered the ground and little natural forest remained.[6]

While some elements of a subsistence economy could recover from the effects of war, others could not. Airbases caused major losses of agricultural land on small islands. When the U.S. airstrip was built on Falalop islet, Ulithi's primary source of plant food was permanently lost. Satawan had the second largest taro swamp in Nomoi until Japanese made an airfield of it. The Parem (Chuuk) and Puluwat airstrips also buried taro gardens. Woleai was short of breadfruit for years because of the loss of trees to Japanese construction and American bombing.[7]

The war also compromised marine resources. Early postwar visitors reported fish scarcities in several locations. Chuuk's postwar protein shortage was caused by depleted fishing in the lagoon and loss of the fishing industry, which had been a source of food for Islanders. The lack of canoes curbed fishing. Breadfruit trees needed to build them had been felled; sailboats, equipment, and tools were lost in the war. Overfishing in Chuuk and Palau, especially the use of explosives, along with bombing and mines, caused long-term harm to marine resources. The damage continues today, as fishermen still use dynamite despite the danger and despite laws and policing effort.[8]

American occupation left its own distinctive legacy. While Islanders continue into the twenty-first century to use Japanese-era buildings, U.S. wartime construction was not built to last. Even in 1945 and 1946, "Airstrips and roadways were washing away under tropical rains, Quonset huts loose from their foundations, piles of materials for buildings not even begun molding near the docksides" (Pomeroy 1947:689). Where they did build permanent installations, the U.S. Navy's choices of sites reshaped local geography, society, and economy (Hezel 1995:250–253). Heavily damaged Kolonia (Pohnpei), Colonia (Yap), and Koror (Palau) continued as administrative centers, but Toloas

Photo 29. The runway on Enewetak islet, built by American troops in 1944 and expanded during the nuclear testing era, now consumes nearly half the crop land on one of the major residence islets of the atoll. (Photo by L. M. Carucci)

Photo 30. Ms. Matsuko Soram standing in the ruins of her childhood home on Toloas (Dublon), Chuuk, 1991. (Photo by L. Poyer)

and Jabwor were bypassed in favor of new sites for navy headquarters. Activity in the Marshall Islands shifted to Laura islet on Majuro, where the navy established its branch government office, a hospital, and a teacher training school. By 1947 there was only a small navy unit on Majuro, but that atoll remained the center of information and power; the islet names "Laura" and "Rita" seem to have become permanent replacements for the Marshallese names (Spoehr 1949a:28–30). In the year 2000, Majuro remains the center of government and economy, and major lines of tension in the modern Republic of the Marshall Islands can be traced to this shift in the locus of power. The transfer of administrative influence from Toloas to Weno in Chuuk lagoon likewise altered local politics. In Palau, invaded Peleliu and Angaur benefited from earlier and more generous relations with Americans compared to Babelthuap, creating tension until the traditional power center regained its role (Useem 1946a:83, 69).

The fight across Micronesia's lands and seas left a junkyard of Japanese and American war materiel which, despite repeated efforts, has not yet been fully cleared. Salvage companies moved in to retrieve what was readily salable soon

Photo 31. Repainted Japanese tank outside tourist office in Kolonia, Pohnpei. (Photo by L. Poyer)

after the war, but the massive amount of equipment, weaponry, and construction entailed years of cleanup. The 1948 Trust Territory *Handbook* warned that only South Pass was a safe entrance to Chuuk lagoon, since minesweeping had not yet cleared the other entrances. In the mid-1970s, Carl Heine (1974:146) wrote that Micronesia's largest export was copra; the second largest was "still" scrap metal from World War II. Today, though, while most of the debris is dangerous (unstable old shells and ammunition) or troublesome (concreted areas useless for agriculture), a few war relics are seen as potential economic assets through tourism (Poyer 1992).

LAND TENURE PROBLEMS

Legal wrangles over landownership remain one of the most enduring legacies of war in Micronesia. Of course, records were lost in the destruction of urban centers. But the problems began earlier, as Japanese military requirements led to partially paid, unpaid, quasi-voluntary, and forced acquisition of land from Micronesians. During the war, invaded islands lost all landmarks in battle-scarred areas and where Japanese work crews or American bulldozers cleared large tracts for airstrips or bases. In some places the land itself was gone, or so reshaped as to stymie efforts to assign ownership, as Eten Island was leveled. After the war, American land needs led to new, confused, and quasi-legal arrangements, some of which created lasting problems. Furthermore, with the disappearance of the Japanese—and, often, all their records—old land feuds could be revived, giving the new administration the headache of conflicting claims.

In Chuuk, for example, since Weno was to be the new American headquarters—which meant land was needed—the navy sought to resolve disputes there first, starting with the Land Claims Commission in October 1946. This and the subsequent Land Titles Investigating Commission seem to have worked through island chiefs and elected magistrates. Not only did this approach produce a mass of conflicting data (since they simply recorded land claims, not indicating disputes), it gave these men information in a society where information is power. "The more the magistrate, who later became Mayor, learned about land in the twelve villages of Moen, the more powerful he became" (Parker 1985:283). Thus the American habit of relying on the few people with whom they could communicate shaped local politics and land use for decades.

Pohnpeians found their land tenure situation complicated less by American than by Japanese policies. Government appropriation of all land not covered by individual title (common throughout the mandate) was compounded by later purchases for military sites. The government rented land to Islanders; in some cases only an initial survey fee and perhaps a year's rent were collected before war intervened, leaving some people with the impression that the land was theirs. Also, refugees moved during the war had been given temporary use permits to raise food on public land. The war destroyed official records of leases and permits. The U.S. Navy inherited this confusion when it took control of Japanese government land, which included large areas of contested ownership. It is said that the initial U.S. MilGov team gave verbal permission to anyone asking to use government land, sometimes to more than one person for the same parcel. The U.S. initiated public land distributions several times before June 1951, but the project was never carried out (McGrath and Wilson 1971:185; Fischer 1958a). Ioana Tipen captures the sense of disarray, still evident in legal proceedings, when she says, "Some of the Pohnpeians had problems on their lands because the Japanese took away their lands during the Japanese era, and they are still looking for them now."

In some areas problems could be left unresolved for years, even decades, before events pressed for settlement. Japan had begun changing Palau's land laws in 1927 and continued for a decade to expropriate interior land, which it opened to immigrants and public works, while defining land in and near Koror as private property. After Japanese were repatriated, Palauans were invited to reoccupy their former lands in the Koror area, and other Palauans were attracted to the district center. Then the United States set aside land disputes for other priorities, so cases languished in court in Dickensian *Great Expectations* style. The 1950s saw intermittent but inconclusive efforts to deal with land claims. In time, the desire to rent out land led people to want individual (not clan or lineage) registration of ownership. In the 1970s and 1980s, when a tourist boom raised the price of land in Koror, there was a concerted effort to regain title to lands confiscated by the Japanese government or sold to immigrants. Thus came a series of land tenure hearings (not resolutions), which themselves gave rise to new claims.[9] Goh Abe (1986:239–241) describes the case of a Palauan chief who in 1945 began a court battle to regain land confiscated during the Japanese era. When his claim was finally approved in 1971, he sold the land for development as a resort area.

While land tenure concerns in some areas could be left (from the navy's point of view) to make their way gradually through commissions and courts, quick resolutions were called for where the United States needed to build installations to prosecute the war. On well-populated Saipan, where 40 percent of the land was in use by the U.S. military before the end of the war, resolving land tenure was vital. Japan had completed a prewar cadastral survey, and officials had set up concrete boundary markers and kept good records. But the invasion changed all that: "Almost all land records were destroyed during the American assault, property markers were obliterated, and normal lines of inheritance were broken. Extensive areas were occupied by the military, native families were displaced from rural and urban holdings. . . . In no cases have the islanders been paid for their land by either rental or purchase. Property exchanges have been made, but titles have not yet been cleared" (Bowers 1950:77). Not only did the military need resolution in order to proceed with construction; any hope of setting Saipanese to work as farmers depended on clear titles.[10]

MilGov's first effort to examine land ownership on Saipan came in October 1944–February 1945. Before repatriation, 776 land-ownership hearings were held involving Saipanese, Japanese, and Koreans. In 1947–1948, 1,587 hearings were held. But by the end of 1948, only nineteen cases had been settled (Bowers 1950:80–82). Meanwhile, the U.S. military was using private land without compensating the owners or confirming local property rights (Spoehr 1954:129–130). Experts thought rebuilding Micronesia's economy "could be speeded up greatly" if the United States would determine its land needs and settle financial claims (Oliver 1951:11). According to the 1944–1945 investigation, Chamorros and Carolinians may have owned more than 20 percent of Saipan's arable land, concentrated in the productive western coastal strip, much of it leased; the rest of the arable land was public domain leased to NKK. Since the parameters of former Japanese government land on Saipan were unclear, the United States allowed a person to use land unless someone else claimed it. But Saipan people, preferring wage labor, did not hurry to get use permits until military bases began to close in 1950; by then the administration had let a few people hold large tracts. The principal Saipanese interest in land was in its rental potential, rather than farming. This has continued to be the case, and land tenure cases on Saipan recognize the potential commercial value of parcels.[11]

Guam's land situation was also dramatically affected by military needs in the final stages of the war. After American reoccupation in July 1944, 58 percent of Guam was taken for military use, with residents moved into camps as their farms became airfields and supply dumps. Guamanians felt that the navy had in too many cases taken the best areas, leaving them inaccessible land that only the navy had resources to develop. As elsewhere, records and landmarks were destroyed in the invasion, and boundaries were ignored during military construction. Also, people had often conveyed rights informally before the war, leaving no written records. "As a consequence, the land-title situation on Guam was in extraordinary confusion" and problems "multiplied out of all proportion to the area involved" (Souder 1971:105–106). As elsewhere, the legal niceties were dealt with after the military fact, and perceived injustices in compensation and military control of land continue to be contested in federal courts.[12]

As civilian concerns gained importance throughout the region in 1946 and 1947, the administration laid out a policy on land claims and established commissions to sift through claims and resolve problems. USCC and CIMA reports commented on other cases (in addition to the Marianas) where U.S. military uses of land interfered with civilian rehabilitation. For example, on Peleliu after the war: "The American armed forces occupy much of the best land—more than appears justified by their number and military requirements—and have shunted the population into less desirable districts. The population is prevented from growing its staple crop, since the armed forces claim the only remaining taro lands on the island" (Oliver 1951:11). But most obvious abuses of native land rights were corrected by 1949, and administrative machinery protecting local land rights was set up.[13]

Bowers (1950:91–92) explained that "the guiding principle of [Trust Territory] land policy is to safeguard native land rights and land ownership, and so far as possible to provide each family with land sufficient for adequate subsistence." While this did happen, and Micronesians found much formerly foreign-controlled land returned to them, it took a long time for people to feel confident in their possession of land (if indeed they yet do). Decades after the war, an anthropologist who lived on Woleai wrote, "Even though the U.S. administration returned all of the land of the atoll to Woleaians at the end of the war, there is still a fear in the minds of some of the islanders that the Americans may someday attempt to reclaim land originally expropriated by the Japanese as government land" (Alkire 1974:68). In the Marianas and the Marshalls, the fear was more pervasive and long lasting because of the scale and apparent longevity of American military landholdings, extending into the postwar years (and, in some cases, into the present).

The problem of eminent domain continued throughout the Trust Territory era, and persists in the independent nations of Micronesia. Since much of what is now public land became so through actions of the German or Japanese administrations, which Micronesians consider illegitimate or unjust, Trust Territory or (now) state or national rights to these lands are challenged (McGrath and Wilson 1971:187). Land tenure disputes continue to be a drag on Micronesian economic and social life.

In addition to obtaining land for its own use, the U.S. Navy also affected land tenure by relocating Islanders. For the most part, Micronesians moved to return home or as temporary laborers in the first years of American rule, but there were several cases of involuntary relocation. The first U.S. MilGov, in the Marshall Islands, followed a policy of not displacing people except for medical care, labor, or where people lived too far for easy administration (e.g., Richard 1957a:364; but these were significant exceptions). Yet the Marshalls became the site of the most contested, infamous, and long-lasting cases of relocation for another purpose entirely: the removal of Marshallese from Bikini (in 1946) and Enewetak (in 1947) for U.S. nuclear tests at those sites. The removal of Kwajalein people for military facilities has also been a matter of long-standing negotiation between the U.S. government and Marshallese.[14] While shifts in the geopolitical arena have now created special considerations for the residents of the atolls involved in nuclear testing, the CivAd era and much of the Trust Territory era is remembered as a time of suffering by residents of these atolls who feared the United States had abused or disowned them.

Other wartime and postwar relocations received less than worldwide publicity. Enewetak, Kwajalein, Majuro, Guam, and Saipan, of course, saw much relocation for the development of American bases. The five hundred people living on the small islands of the Northern Marianas (Pagan, Agrihan, Asuncion, and Alamagan) were moved to Saipan in September 1945 for access to food and medical supplies. Ten villages in the Marianas were resettled or newly established in the first postwar years. Peleliu people were resettled into a single village to make way for airfield development. On Weno, Chuuk, the navy moved people from Mechitiw village, initial U.S. headquarters, and did not allow their return even after that land was no longer needed for American installations. The navy then displaced inhabitants of nearby Fano islet to make it a military recreation area. In 1946, people from both villages were crowded together with the people of Tunnuk. The people of Iras on Weno, who had been repeatedly relocated first by Japanese, then by American orders, finally returned home by 1948. The navy decided to retain the airstrip built on their coastal land, so they settled inland on swamps and mountain slopes. Iras people and the U.S. government then began a long-term legal engagement that remains unresolved despite repeated attempts at settlement.[15]

Voluntary migration also resumed, at first on the small scale that Micronesians had known before the war. In the Marshalls, Arno and Majuro had been relocation centers for refugees from bypassed atolls, some of whom stayed after the war. People from Chuuk lagoon and central Caroline Islands moved to Weno when that became the district administrative center. On Pohnpei, U.S. officials used public land (i.e., land that had been claimed by the Japanese government) for homesteaders from Kapingamarangi, Pingelap, and Losap. After travel became freer in the 1960s, internal migration (especially to and from Guam) became a major vehicle of social change in Micronesia.[16]

A LOST GENERATION OF LEADERS

Economic infrastructure was lost, clear property titles were lost, and in some cases the use of land itself was lost to Islanders. Another toll of war is less tangible but equally important in understanding the difficulty Micronesians encountered in rebuilding their lives after the war. This is the loss—in a sense—of a portion of one generation of leaders: the young men and women who were, at the start of war, ready to step into their future. Prepared in Japanese elementary schools for Islanders, anticipating lives of personal achievement and service to their lineage, community, and island, those who came of age in 1940 looked forward to participating in a thriving economy and a global network as part of the Japanese empire. By 1945, forced to abandon their plans for the future, enervated by bearing the brunt of labor and caring for those older and younger during the war years, many discovered that they were too old to participate in the new order: too old to learn English in the new schools, too old to be selected for the programs the U.S. Navy set up to train leaders who would identify with American interests and turn to American culture as a guide to how they wanted to live.

It was a difficult time for these mature and ambitious men and women who were approaching the peak of their productive years. Though occupying positions of power before or during the war, they were often overlooked by the Americans. Indeed, the very nature of the U.S. Navy's attempt to set themselves apart from the Japanese sometimes meant the renunciation of Japanese-trained individuals. One of the most poignant legacies of war is the lives of men who devoted their youthful energy and capacity to learning Japanese and accepting Japanese ideals, and then saw their bright future dim around them in the shadows of war. Asked if any Pohnpeians felt sorry for the Japanese when they left, Pretrick Ringlen replies: "I felt sorry, but what could I do, because this era was not going to be the same. What I have to say is that if the Japanese were still in Pohnpei, maybe I would have become a high person in the Japanese era because I used to be a foreman [for road construction in Madolenihmw]."

Thaddeus Sampson (Marshalls), describing his work as an interpreter for high-ranking Japanese officials, said, "If it had not been for the start of the war, I would have been one of those selected to go to Japan and go to school. They had already gathered us all up, those that were going to be there in the school. And then the war broke out; but if it had not been for the war, well, we would have gone to Japan." Fifty years later, regret for lost opportunities can still be heard. The Micronesian of this generation, John Embree wrote, is a man without a country. "After twenty years of Japanese education, he suddenly finds the Japanese language, like the Japanese yen, at a discount against the English language and the American dollar. Those who achieved educational and economic status under the Japanese must begin all over again and, in some cases, their success under Japanese rule is considered a demerit in the eyes of the new regime" (Embree 1946b:62).

The generational conflict on Yap described earlier shows that the situation was more complex than the simple shift from Japanese to American control. On Yap, postwar conflict was between youth in general and elders who were chiefs, and also between low-status people and all chiefs: "a fundamental fight between those who want to retain old ways and those who want to change to Western ways" (Hunt et al. 1949:188). Younger men, especially those of lower-status families, saw in American ideas of personal liberty and equality—and in American wage labor—a chance to rewrite the social charter. By presenting a well-organized argument to CivAd officials, they gained a hearing. Senior men of rank responded by pressuring Americans to respect Yapese custom (and, not incidentally, shore up their power) by enforcing rules about clothing, eating habits, and chiefly economic prerogatives.

As we have seen, American policy altered the balance of political and economic power in Palau. While the Japanese had rewarded individuals on the basis of skill and willingness to acculturate, the U.S. favored those whose ideas aligned with postwar policy—agrarianism, self-sufficiency, minimal administration—and allowed traditional chiefs to gain power. The result was "the creation of dissident factions whose broken hopes and loss of skill-value contributed to their feelings of resentment" toward chiefs and rulers (Vidich 1980:340–341).[17]

The difficulties in administering Chuuk, described in chapter 8, are another example of how newly empowered groups gained a position in the first period of American rule at the expense of those who had expected to lead. U.S. MilGov in Chuuk lacked interpreters, so any local person who knew some English got a foothold in the bureaucracy: "They were, in effect, at the top of the native administrative hierarchy, a position which was later formalized by titles of Atoll Chief, Assistant Atoll Chief, etc. They were the ones who were told to get things done, and they got them done, rapidly and effectively, acquiring in the process considerable personal property and a great deal of power" (Gladwin 1950:16). The situation would resolve itself, as navy schools produced English speakers, but meanwhile two things had happened: A few individuals and families had greatly benefited, and those who had come of age under the Japanese, expecting to take their place on the stage of local life, had learned a bitter lesson.[18]

Not all members of this generation of well-trained Japanese speakers lost the war in a personal way. There were also those who gained from it. In some cases, it was the same individuals and families who had done well before the war, who were able to transfer their political skills and business savvy to new resources in the American administration. Some traditional and Japanese-appointed leaders were confirmed in their positions by American officials; limited and indirect U.S. rule gave these men more power than they had had under the Japanese colonial order. On Pohnpei, though the Japanese military had regarded Carlos and Leo Etscheit as spies and interned them with their families, they began their "slow climb back to prosperity" by working for U.S. MilGov as interpreters and advisors (Kahn 1966b:60). American officials also began to develop ties with a newly emerging group of intermediaries. In some areas such as Palau, these were the younger generation of chiefly families; elsewhere, English-speaking individuals and those with foreign parentage; and, in the east, those connected with the American Protestant mission (Mason 1946:38–39, U.S. Navy 1948:66).

Many Micronesians moved rapidly to take advantage of opportunities to succeed in the new order. They had valued education under the Japanese and, if anything, they expected their children to be better educated under the American system. Mikel Marquez of Pohnpei recalls how academics, rather than the skilled trades familiar to an earlier generation, became the key to employment for him:

> The navy administration didn't try to build up the island's economy. They provided jobs like in carpentry, etc.; they were building houses and getting other things ready for occupation. Maybe they did not have time yet to

make plans for economic development. They paid Pohnpeians then about $7.00 biweekly. Later on the pay increased. When I started to work as an assistant to an anthropologist, I was paid $34.00 biweekly. I started working right after I completed my schooling. The Americans built schools and educated us. The guys who were older, like Lenet Santos, Pensile Lawrence, and their peers were the first to be educated. I did not attend the government schools; I attended the mission school run by the Catholic priests. Most of my work was doing translations for the anthropologist, because by then I could speak and understand a little English.

As everywhere in the world, the experience of the Second World War separated old and young. Japanese defeat at first undercut the confidence of the young, who had hitched their wagon to the star of Japan. "Their standards shattered, they became more submissive to leadership of the older generation, turned back to traditional ways" (Useem 1945b:586). But as they became familiar with American culture, youth developed an alternative vision of success, and the spread of Americanisms on Palau, for example, foreshadowed a future of passionate argument and anguished consultation about the virtues and evils of acculturation. "When I was a child, I cried when my mother forced me to put on a pair of shoes," one elder commented after the U.S. occupation of Angaur, "now my children cry when they have no shoes to put on" (Useem 1945b:586).

MODES OF REMEMBRANCE

For people reaching maturity in the late 1930s, especially men, the battles that ended the war were also personal rites of passage that crucially determined their own futures. Those who were graduates of Japanese schools and held positions of power during the Japanese era and those who were the first to complete their schooling under the Americans and who gained in rank as a result of their youth and accomplishment have strongly contrasting images of the Japanese and American eras. Likewise, those who were in positions to become powerful people, either through chiefly right or by specialized training, and who failed to do so under the new administration, see the war as a turning point and view their own life under Japanese rule as potentially more rewarding. Accounts of the past, in other words, convey information about the war at the same moment they tell many other stories about events, about others, and about one's own identity, both past and present. All of these are important messages not only because they enrich our understanding of the way Micronesia has come to be remembered at the time of U.S. occupation, but also because they continue to fashion the way people live today.

The Typhoon of War

One of the most striking characteristics of Micronesian recollections of the Pacific war is a sense of the impersonality of the conflict. In our conversations with people, it was not harsh Japanese soldiers nor American bomber crews but the war itself that was the enemy. The war happened without warning, in people's memories; it happened without adequate preparation, with previously unknown weapons and equipment; it happened for no reason known to Islanders, with no connection to their own actions or will. War, with its hard times, is spoken of as an active agent, while Islanders are represented as unfortunate bystanders. The war, they say, "came looking for" the Japanese, who happened to be on the islands where Micronesians lived. Peleng Kilimete, remembering when she hid from Japanese soldiers on Pohnpei, comments, "That was very hard because I wasn't fighting the war, but I was suffering from it." Jomle Malolo (Marshalls) adds: "Do you know about *Ailiñ in torlañ?* The meaning of this is a typhoon island, and the outcome of the typhoon (of war) is that which you see today. As you know, there are typhoons which create damage, but there are also typhoons like this one, and America is today's typhoon. They are the ones who have seized the position of speaker today, and so this is not of great concern; rather, as you can see, things have been turned around and good fortune has appeared." [19]

While some Micronesians began the war as Japanese loyalists, many were excited by the patriotic fervor that surrounded them, and a few had a mission-inspired sympathy for the United States, most felt no emotional commitment to the outcome. "Viewed objectively," John Useem commented (1946a:23), "the war meant to many natives merely the loss of their wealth and a change in the governing class"—not a dramatic release from oppression, other than the oppression of war itself. "The Micronesians do not regard the Americans as liberators who saved them from an awful fate; they know that, had the invasion not taken place, their lives would not now be so disorganized. But there is no resentment against Americans for having come and destroyed their way of living. The war is accepted as given and the accompanying chaos as inevitable" (Useem 1945a:100).

Americans visiting the islands in the first postwar years often noted the absence of active allegiance to Japan. Marines who conducted the first reconnaissance of the atolls south and west of Chuuk lagoon in October 1945 reported that the people had suffered relatively little from the war and cautioned Americans not to expect Islanders to cooperate out of anti-Japanese feelings: "The war, to most of them, was a foreign and unrelated episode. They developed no prejudices or ideologies concerning it" (Witherspoon 1945:12–13). American observers on Ulithi and elsewhere also commented on the absence of partisanship.[20]

One reason for the sense of the impersonal violence of the war was the Allied strategy of neutralization bombing and blockade, which kept Americans at a distance until surrender. Another was the professional role of the soldier. From their own history, Micronesians like Clanton Abija (Marshalls) recognize the actions and attitudes of military men on both sides as those of warriors, focused on getting what they needed for survival and victory, unconcerned with the human qualities valued in peacetime: "Because they came in a certain atmosphere, because they needed to use [Ronglap]—my belief is that if they had come in kindness it would have been different, but instead they came in their ferocity, and we were frightened at that time. When they asked us things, no one would respond and say 'good' or 'bad,' but we just bowed down, that is all, we would not say no. This is how things were; so they got whatever they desired, because we were afraid."

As Peleng Kilimete comments, "The Japanese were suffering, so they made the Pohnpeians suffer, too." Acknowledging the Japanese equally as victims of the war is common; rarely are they—or the Americans—blamed for it.[21] Even where a few people had been killed by American strafing or bombing, there was "no sign of hostility or distrust." Witherspoon (1945:12) noted: "Their attitude on this matter is best summed up by quoting the reaction of the Nukoror [Nukuoro] native constable: 'We wondered only *why* they bombed and strafed [an] unfortified island.' The possibility that their cement cisterns may have been mistaken for gun emplacements and their fishing boats for radio-equipped craft seemed to them a logical suggestion which they received with sincere good grace" (author's emphasis).

In our interviews about wartime experiences nearly fifty years later, we found that Micronesians were fairly ready to criticize Japanese and American governance, but did not lay blame for the conflict. Their attitude recalled that of Ifaluk people who spoke with American visitors a few years after the war: "A few Ifaluk men were killed by American bombs and bullets [when working on Yap]; this too is accepted without bitterness. I think they realized clearly that they were pigmy bystanders, trapped on a battlefield where careless giants fought. The idea of wars they could understand, for Ifaluk has fought its own bloody battles in the past, and the warrior chief Mailias was its greatest hero in traditional song. The scope and power of the war, the reason for it—these were beyond them, incomprehensible. Doubtless many of our own [American] fighting men never saw the war in full perspective, either" (Bates and Abbott 1958:208; also 65–66).

Indeed, very few Micronesians we interviewed expressed any idea of the origin or motive for the conflict, and those who did used personalistic explanations (e.g., a personal competition between a Japanese and American military leader) rather than geopolitical ones. In part, as Bates and Abbott suggest, the concept of a war of conquest for territorial acquisition was perfectly familiar to Micronesians from their own history. Just as they understood what it meant to be a warrior, motivated by the sole desire to use all means to the end of victory, so they understood that those who were not warriors could only watch the contest to see who their new chiefs would be. As Robino Amusten of Pohnpei says: "For me, I was only thinking about when I was going to die, when the planes would shoot me. The Pohnpeians didn't take sides in the war. They just stood aside and waited for the end of the war."

Memories of War

The physical, economic, social, and political changes we have described combine to form the legacy of the Pacific war in Micronesia. They set the tune for the last half-century's tense dance of dependence and self-sufficiency in economy, of indigenous form and imported model in political structure. The changes form a vital part of Micronesian historical and cultural memories— memories that are another important legacy of the wartime era. The memories are personally powerful, embodying such profound experiences that

Micronesians feel they should be valued and remembered for their own sake. Further, these memories serve as a source of knowledge and wisdom for the development of local and national memories and for charting Micronesia's economic, social, and political future.

Viewing World War II as an impersonal destructive force may be part of a broader perspective on human action. John Useem (1945b:583) suggests a Micronesian attitude "that comprehends events as shaping the course of life as much as any purposive action," and this attitude—sometimes mischaracterized as "fatalism" or "passivity"—is expressed in Micronesian understandings of the war. But most individuals do not struggle with philosophical implications of war as human fate. Instead, they continue to engage with the war as a part of their own personal and family history and to add to its construction as a useful community memory with which to understand current events.

Our own interest in this topic as anthropologists was inspired by Micronesian elders who impressed us with the fact that the war remains important in Micronesia today. The older generation wishes to ensure that their experiences do not fade from collective memory, and they were eager to help us explore and record them. Apart from any formal effort, however, the war is in a sense relived daily, encoded and recounted in traditional genres. Wartime events are still the important stuff of Micronesian stories—told as jokes, anecdotes, or personal histories—shared with family and friends. War paraphernalia and photographs are cherished memorabilia. As stories are retold in extended family households or at community gatherings, they reinforce strong links among members of the wartime generation. While most Micronesian indigenous history is treated as intellectual property, carefully guarded and transmitted only under restricted conditions, stories of the war are largely free of these constraints—though, like all history, war recollections are often edited and arranged to make a particular point (e.g., King and Carucci 1984: 505; Parker 1985:30). A few war stories have achieved near legendary status; they are crossing over into the Micronesian category of important history, told in the manner of the old lore. First as parents, now as grandparents and great-grandparents, the wartime generation recounts their stories and songs to children, "so they will know about war and the hardships it brings." Rare is the Micronesian youth who cannot recount sufferings under Japanese military rule, name a suspected American spy, or hum a few bars of a war song. The war, in truncated and stereotyped form, then, lives on in the younger generation as well.

Song is of great importance in maintaining Micronesian historical memory, and songs originally composed and sung during the war remain popular today. They are sung in traditional style, as hymns, or to tunes inspired by Japanese music. They are composed in the local language, in Japanese, or often in a combination of both. Some are composed for dance performance. A women's sitting dance from Gagil, Yap, displays wartime events: "The forces of the United States and Japan are symbolized by dance movements, as huge whales at sea and immense eagles in the sky. Bombs are characterized as exploding coconuts. The harsh years of Japanese occupation are recorded in the dance, as is the defeat of the Imperial Japanese occupation troops by the American marines" (Montvel-Cohen 1982:234). Songs tell of the new people and new things that arrived on their islands during the war years. Some mourn forced relocations or laud valorous deeds. Others describe work on a wartime project or recount a personal experience. Some lament the misery of war; others are teasing, self-deprecating, bawdy. In whatever form they are sung, they often include the names of actors and places. Thus heroes are made and events transformed into collective memory. The formal structure of a war song, furthermore, serves to codify, preserve, and authenticate this history.[22]

War stories and songs have been readily transferred to modern technology and used in new social contexts. The best of the old songs have been recorded on cassettes, circulated among friends, and become local favorites on island radio, the most important means of communication in modern Micronesia. Some war songs are now more widely sung than ever, with interesting results. For example, one of Pohnpei's best-known war songs, the "Memorial Song of Kosrae," which recounts the experiences of Kiti men working on Kosrae, was recently recorded by a popular singing group from the chiefdom of Uh. While this has resulted in more intraisland and intergenerational understanding of history and even contributed to feelings of national pride among Pohnpeians, it also raises the question of who has rights to the historical knowledge encoded in the song. Not only are Kiti and Uh traditional rivals, but some report that the Uh group took the liberty of making minor changes to the original tune (Falgout 1995b).

While old songs are revived, new songs, dances, and dramatic skits about the war continue to be composed and choreographed. The ongoing intellectual importance of the war is revealed in the context in which these are presented, as when the Yapese performed a "unity dance" at the 1989 opening of the Federated States of Micronesia capital in Pohnpei (Pinsker 1992:44–47). Composed by dance master Goofalan of Maap, the dance was introduced by former Yap State governor John Mangafel, who addressed the diverse audience in English: "This dance is newly composed, composed by an old man from Yap and it's based on what happened in World War II and on forward to times when we had a good agreement with the United States and word was spread and all the states look at it, read it, discuss it, and like it and finally, they say it's good. And then finally, they sign it" (Pinsker 1992:45). Thus the war is presented as the starting point for a unified history of the new nation.

Oral history is not the only—or even the primary—reminder of the war in the islands. Physical signs of the war abound. Postwar American restoration efforts repaired some of the worst damage. Yet even with the continued sale of war remains as scrap, a survey of World War II sites in Micronesia estimated that there are more relics of war in Micronesia than in all of Europe (Denfeld 1981b). Many remain as they were left: bomb shelters, barracks, mess kitchens, coastal defense guns standing vigil on ammunition-littered beaches. They decay under the tropical sun, reclaimed by the surrounding vegetation or, rarely, are removed and displayed for tourists. Physical changes wrought by the war remain etched in the landscape—deforested hills, lines of basalt rocks cleared from the Japanese army's sweet potato fields, bomb craters now serving as taro gardens or water catchments (Denfield 1981a; King and Carucci 1984:495, 504). The most famous remains of the war are the Japanese ships sunk in Chuuk lagoon. Over the years this ships' graveyard has created a new lagoon ecosystem, of interest to people ranging from Jacques Cousteau in his 1970 documentary "Lagoon of Lost Ships" to tourists who enjoy scuba diving the wrecks.[23]

To add to these original relics of war, Japanese, Koreans, and Americans have erected war memorials and peace memorials throughout the area. Some Islanders work in historic preservation or tourist activity related to war sites (e.g., diver Kimuo Aisek of Chuuk, well known for his work on the wartime wrecks of Chuuk lagoon [Lindemann 1987]). Saipan has emphasized the war as an element of tourism, especially for Japanese. "The souvenir postcards

Photo 32. War debris remains plentiful on Toloas, Chuuk, 1991. (Photo by L. Poyer)

on sale feature photographs not of beaches or palm trees or sunsets but of a ruined Japanese hospital, a rusty tank, and the Japanese jail where Amelia Earhart was said to have been held captive before she disappeared" (Kahn 1971:112).

Physical mementos of war hold little historical interest for most Micronesians, who may use them for their practical value—narrow-gauge rails as roof beams, caves and tunnels as typhoon shelters, propellers as decorations, a seaplane runway as a playground and road (Poyer 1992; Young et al. 1997:39–41). Micronesian nations, however, have recognized the cultural importance of the Pacific war by sponsoring locally produced videos, using documentary materials and interviews with elders. Such videos, along with Hollywood's versions of the Pacific war stocked on shelves at video rental stores, are popular family viewing in urban households throughout Micronesia today. (Interest in war movies is long-standing. The favorite film at the Truk Trading Company movie theater in the mid-1950s was the documentary "The Bombing of Truk," which was shown "once a month, every month, by popular demand" [Trumbull 1959:91].) Graphic artists, too, use war themes, as in Palau

Photo 33. Mr. Stem Salle in front of a cave in Weno, Chuuk, 1991. Excavated during the war years as a bomb shelter, the cave is now used for storage and as a typhoon shelter. (Photo by L. Poyer)

on storyboards on *bai* (community centers) and at tourist sites and hotels (e.g., Nakano 1983:197).

Our project is one of the most recent to benefit from Micronesians' concern about the war and perpetuation of its memory. We received wholehearted assistance from every level of government and from the people we interviewed. They want to preserve this history and to correct the imbalance that makes Islanders nearly invisible in American and Japanese accounts of the Pacific war. Their desire to assume a more visible role in the history of the war is expressed in musings about construction of their own war memorials, though only Guam and Saipan now preserve memorials and historical parks devoted to Micronesian experiences. Chamorros on Guam, and to a lesser extent Saipan, have long made something of a memory industry of the war. These populations are more interested in writing as a means of communication, and so more publications are to be expected here. Like many areas in Micronesia, Guam sees a moral tale in the war and uses war memories as important public retellings of its own story (e.g., Lotz 1988; the Memorial Wall at the War in the Pacific National Historical Park [Underwood 1994]; see Diaz 1994).

Photo 34. Use of war debris as decoration at a resort hotel in Weno, Chuuk.
(Photo by L. Poyer)

Even though the war and subsequent military construction destroyed many
of Guam's archaeological sites, World War II sites there had already been given
historical markers and monuments by 1952 (Reed 1952).

While physical memorials are absent elsewhere, most islands quickly instituted commemorative holidays marking the local end of war. Encouraged
by American administrators, these celebrations combine elements of American, Japanese, and local Micronesian notions of holidaymaking and variously
mark the war's beginning, people's survival, or the arrival of Americans. Arno's
Liberation Day on February 16 celebrates the day Americans came ashore,
peacefully (Rynkiewich 1972:30–32; similarly, for Yap, Moore 1952). Saipan's
Liberation Day on July 4 marks release from civilian internment camps (Stewart 1989:28). In some places, the holidays have begun to lose their explicit
historical content, and young people may be unaware of their origin. But elsewhere, as on Kosrae, events are deliberately scripted so as to teach war history.
There, the near-starvation of wartime "is largely responsible for the annual re-

Photo 35. Antiaircraft guns at Taroa islet, Maloelap Atoll, which has been surveyed as a possible historic and tourism site for its Pacific war remains. (Photo by L. Poyer)

membrance of the anniversary of the American occupying force on September 8, 1945, a holiday second only to Christmas in importance in modern Kusaie" (Peoples 1977:151). On Enewetak and Ujelang, the "Day to Be Thankful" on the second Sunday of March every year commemorates "the day we came out of the holes" after the invasion of Enewetak, to find the island destroyed and many dead. In a church service, an elder war survivor recounts the battle, other survivors weep, hymns are sung, and the rest of the day is spent in visiting and talking about the past: "[The Day to be Thankful] has a group of survivors to create vocal and visual enactments of the event. Their stories concentrate on warfare, helplessness, and death. They transport listeners back to a time of terror, when the very existence of Enewetak was tenuous and community survival was miraculous" (Carucci 1989:79).

Modern memories of war continue to develop as Japanese veterans of the war in Micronesia (both colonial civilian and military) hold reunion events, stimulating such activities in the islands. Publications, friendship societies, letters, tourism, and pilgrimages reestablish Japanese links to Micronesia. Older Japanese come to hold memorial services and search for remains of war dead. Mostly, they return to look for their Micronesian buddies, or even their adversaries, from the past. They wish to reconnect—to reminisce about shared experiences, to see what has changed on the island and in their lives, to right old wrongs.[24] Sometimes Japanese visitors seek out Micronesians who are part of their own family, left behind in postwar repatriation. A few who return to their prewar homes even choose to remain in the islands (Young et al. 1997:33 reports continued links between Chuukese men and their Japanese fathers). Younger Japanese come as vacationers, especially to Guam, Saipan, and Palau. Some American veterans, too, make pilgrimages, coming to view memorials and to walk the beaches where they offered their lives; a few write about it (Bahrenburg 1971:187–188; Barnard 1974; Bronemann 1982; Manchester 1979). But when American Pacific war veterans reunite, they usually do so only with each other and usually in the United States. The war in Micronesia has left them with few longstanding personal links to the islands.

Finally, Micronesians continue to seek war claims from both Americans and Japanese. The hope for compensation, a pragmatic economic interest, thus helps family memories of wartime events persist to the next generation. In Pohnpei, the "Sunshine" group led by Jose Cruz was formed to lobby Washington for additional funding and also served as a watchdog to ensure proper disbursement of received monies. Weekly meetings in Kolonia in the 1980s provided a context for a wider group of Islanders to share their memories and feelings about the war and to build consensus about its import today.[25]

COMPARING JAPANESE AND AMERICAN RULE

As the century closes, historians identify World War II as a turning point in the trajectories of American, European, and Asian societies. This is no less true for Pacific Islanders. The war, when two foreign peoples came into conflict in the Micronesian homelands, forms the background to the story of the similarities and differences of Japanese and American relations with Micronesians—a story with implications that pervade current politics and economics in the islands. For some individuals, the powerful sense of peace after the experience of war makes differences between American and Japanese rule seem slight by comparison. The years of preparing for war and the battle for the islands sharply contrast with the continuous flow of peacetime experiences under either colonial administration. But for most—and for younger generations whose knowledge of the war comes from oral history rather than personal experience—the passage from Japanese to American eras epitomizes the rift between a former way of life and the present.[26]

Micronesians think of Japanese society as consisting of inherent differences of rank, not unlike the rankings that exist in many Micronesian cultures. In the Japanese empire's social order, Micronesians occupied the lowest level. Thaddeus Sampson, who spent much of the Japanese era on Jaluij Atoll, thought that—had the Japanese won the war—Micronesians would have been raised to the "second rank" in the Japanese ethnic hierarchy. Micronesians like Mr. Sampson, allied with Japanese culture, valued the chance to demonstrate their loyalty during the war and so earn the reward of an increased level of Japanese citizenship. Others, at least in retrospect and in contrast with their understanding of American culture, reject the ethnic discrimination that characterized the Japanese colonial order. Although (as chapters 7 and 8 indicated) American rule imposed its own status hierarchy and limits on Micronesian aspirations, Islanders living through the end of the war immediately recognized the contrast with Japanese philosophy and social organization. While Islanders recall that postwar jobs were distressingly few and often menial in character ("we just cleaned up for a while"), their relations with American supervisors were markedly different from the status-consciousness of Japanese interactions. Clanton Abija (Marshalls) recalls:

In my work with the Americans, that is, those of us who worked with them, with the navy people, there were no spaces between people in their reckoning. When you did something, it was the same as what they did. With the navy, if you wanted to do the heavy work, they did not want that. They wanted you to do the same things they did. They did things in the proper manner [like those who are church people]. And, in my view of it, there were no differences among people in their eyes. So when we went and worked together, there was a single type of work. As for the Japanese, they separated people, and they worked by themselves. But their [the Americans'] workers, everyone was the same. Their work was one. It did not differ.

(Interviewer asks: And the Japanese?)

Well, they did not work.

(He laughs.)

Yes, it is true. They only yelled. They yelled out and said to do this thing. And so then, you stopped and you went and did it.

It is ironic that the first generation of American administrators, who consciously sought to "return" Micronesians to a subsistence lifestyle, are recalled as the rulers who provided opportunity for individuals to achieve to the full extent of their capacity. The Japanese, who offered a wide range of consumer products and work options, are also remembered for the limits they put on Islanders. Micronesians of the 1930s accepted and appreciated much of the modernization program of the South Seas Bureau (though not all—not the heavy-handed acculturation). But they resented the constraints put on their participation in it, and they feared the end result of the massive immigration that was transforming their islands. In contrast to Japanese ethnic barriers, Micronesians felt that under the American system, one could "grab hold of that of which one is capable," with no formal barriers to attainment, whatever practical difficulties might arise. Americans offered unlimited achievement, at least in theory; and it took a number of years before Islanders (or Americans) appreciated the price of this offer: that in the American system, success was open to all but could be achieved only by a few, and that the elite who held rank, money, or access to powerful friends were the most likely to succeed.

Micronesians distinguish, however, between the American economic and political system that increased their options and broader American cultural patterns. The more overtly egalitarian style of interaction, the presence of African-American troops who ate, worked with, and possessed the same wealth and knowledge as white Americans, the willingness of troops to share their food, cigarettes, alcohol, and songs, all impressed Micronesians with the distinctiveness of these new rulers. But, though Americans may have expected that their casual and generous cultural style would encourage Micronesians to regard them with the eye of fellowship, it may have had the opposite effect.

In many senses, the Japanese way of life is thought to be more suited to Islanders than the American. Looking back on colonial history, some Islanders see the various lifestyles as a series of stages from less to more advanced, much like nineteenth-century social evolutionists. They say that the Japanese way of life was perhaps less advanced than the American but was nonetheless better suited to Islanders. Even the language was easier to learn, due to perceived similarities with local languages. In the Marshalls, American power, wealth, and behavior (giving gifts without expecting return, limiting personal contact between Americans of rank and Islanders) made them incommensurate with commoners—and thus perfectly comprehensible in the role of chiefs (who are by nature different from commoners). But Japanese policies had been explicit and strict and very clear about what Micronesians had to do in order to become more like the colonials; thus on Enewetak, Japanese are spoken of as "being like us," "thinking more like us." "In contrast, Americans are said to be 'gods or chiefs [iroij ro] of the earth,' 'another kind than [are] we,' and 'smart, but their intelligence is different from our own'" (Carucci 1989:87).[27]

Similarly, Japanese are remembered as being better companions. Particularly in eastern Micronesia, Americans are seen as extraordinarily friendly, but this friendliness, for Marshall Islanders, masks a hollow core, an attitude that in local terms is "sly" or "trickster-like." In other words, the overt guise of American friendliness did not result in long-lasting, dependable friendships. Long-term personal connections with military or, later, civilian American administrators were rare. This view makes sense in contrast to the Japanese, who are remembered as being of two sorts: high-ranking people who were off limits and common people who were "just like us." For example, when asked about jokes, Reverend Kanki Amlej says: "Certainly there were jokes. We tended to make jokes with them [Japanese] as well, with those Japanese whom we had befriended for some time, those who were kind. But, as for those other folks who were in the offices, well, we never made jokes with them, that is, not with that group that was high ranked." The unranked group is remembered as really living in the island style, loving local people and treating their island friends in the proper indigenous manner. These Japanese and Okinawans were true friends, and their friendships endured, as in Istor Billimont's reminiscences:

We worked together in the village called Sapuun, Toloas (Chuuk). At that time we used to transport gasoline to Eten Island and transport back the empty drums to Sapuun. At that time we were friends, because he was the only one among the Japanese who was very nice to Chuukese. When he came back from Japan to visit me, he told me that all the Japanese were dead because they were bad during the war.

(Interviewer asks: When was the last time he came to Chuuk to visit you? What year?)
1990, in either September or February.

(Interviewer: How many times did he come to visit you?)
Four times. The first time he came out here, he had trouble finding me. He asked a man named Osiem ... about me. When we met, we did not recognize each other. I recognized him after he mentioned some of the names of Chuukese we used to work with: Nipwech, Kota, Kotaro, Moniok, and the names of the people from Siis.

(Interviewer: When he came back to visit you, did he still speak and understand Chuukese?)
Yes, he still knew some.

Religion complicates comparisons of Japanese and Americans. In the Marshall Islands and on Kosrae, some people claim that they knew that the Americans would inevitably win the war, even before the fighting began. Missionaries had told them of American goodness and superiority. In contrast, the unfamiliar religions of the Japanese placed them as outsiders, and the perception of them as anti-Christian—and therefore evil—became more apparent as the Japanese military restricted religious activities. In Ato Lañkio's account of the Americans' arrival on Namu, near Kwajalein, clergymen mediate the relationship between soldiers and local people. The sense of a history shared with Americans is noted by Labwinmij Laelôñeo of Arno Atoll: "If it had not been for the Americans coming and bringing these things, we would never have been alive. They brought the gospel in 1860 and 1870; then the war ... appeared in the 1870s when the Spaniards left the Marshalls. Then they [Germans, also *dri belle* (white people)] began building up these atolls during the time of Admiral Dewey, if it was not slightly before that. . . . and then again during the Second World War, the soldiers arrived, and they [Americans] have remained up until the current day."

Memories of the Japanese era took on new meanings as the harshness of the war years receded into the background and the economic strictures of the postwar American era came to the fore. The Japanese period came to be represented as a golden age of sorts.[28] Historians have begun to render judgment on the quality of Japanese colonial administration of its Micronesian mandate (e.g., Peattie 1988; Hatanaka 1973–1974, 1967:66). The overall conclusion at present is that Japan excelled at basic education, health, and public order, its economic development policy benefited Micronesians both directly and indirectly, and many Micronesians enjoyed participating in an urban, even global, society. On the negative side, Japan's economic goals were primarily for the benefit of the empire and its citizens, not for Islanders; immigration and possession of land threatened Micronesian communities; racial policies limited Micronesian achievement; heavy-handed acculturation policies harmed local artistic and cultural practice; and strict political control did little for the development of internal community governance. But in telling their stories of the war, Islanders are not concerned with rendering a global judgment on Japan as a colonial power. Rather they are responding to their own experiences and to accounts they have heard to evaluate where they stand—as individuals and communities—in their own histories, and to judge where their best future lies.

The degree of contrast between prewar and postwar standards of living predicts the intensity with which Islanders present a glowing vision of the prewar world. Palauans, not surprisingly, continued throughout the postwar years critically to contrast American with Japanese management, and also actively maintained cultural and personal links with Japan. A Japanese scholar visiting Palau in the 1970s wrote, "Even today, the ways of communication, business, social behavior and even attitudes and pace of work are almost indistinguishable from those in Japan" (Hatanaka 1973–1974:17). Palauans cited the pluses and minuses of that era for Japanese researcher Goh Abe (1986:181–196): a comfortable life due to cheap goods and controlled prices, much money and many stores, low crime and good civic order, only rare sales of land. They recall good relations with Japanese—but also educational segregation and limits on Micronesians. Palauans credit their reputation as hard-working entrepreneurs to what they learned from watching Japanese business success (Ballendorf 1988b:60). Japanese Koror was an exciting place, with an active port, marine industries and research, a commercial center, an administrative center hosting visiting dignitaries, shops, theaters, a roller-skating rink, and geishas. "These are the things Palauans remember most, or perhaps learn from their parents—especially when they enjoy baiting American listeners with the observation that 'things were better' under the Japanese'" (McKnight 1978:9; Nishi 1968:2).

Similarly, Saipan—which saw a significant drop in the postwar standard of living and whose people did not agree with American agrarian policy for their island—continued to feel nostalgia for prewar life. In the 1970s, as the U.S. military withdrew from Vietnam and Okinawa and as Japan reached out again to the Pacific Islands, American visitors saw in Palau and Saipan at least that the Japanese economic and even political presence could readily be revived (e.g., Bahrenburg 1971:188, 219). When Federated States of Micronesia president Tosiwo Nakayama went to Japan to locate his father, who had been unwillingly repatriated from Micronesia in 1946, "he came back so impressed by Japanese kindness he felt that a person with his heritage should look to Japan for help after independence" (Nakano 1983:279–280). Even on Yap, where people had opposed Japan's acculturative policies, positive memories of the prewar economy played a role in postwar life (Allen 1953:54). But Caroline Islanders in general felt less nostalgic about those old days. On Pohnpei, "there is less loyalty and devotion to the Japanese than one might have expected from their long period of rule and the compulsory education in Japanese. Certainly, when the Americans returned as the new rulers of Pohnpei, they found a situation quite different from that on Palau, where the people remember the period of Japanese administration as the 'golden years' of their history" (Bascom 1950:145).

Japan had, in twenty-seven years of peaceful civilian rule, made an enormous impact on Micronesians and forged many positive ties. The question was whether the harshness of the far briefer period of war destroyed those links. Observers immediately after the war thought it had:

> Any loyalty to Japan developed over the preceding two decades was largely neutralized by the authoritarian treatment by the Japanese military. After 1941, material goods ceased to arrive for the people and there was no one to buy their products; so their standard of living, which had been gradually changing for the better since 1919, sharply declined. Priority for medical supplies went to the Japanese army and navy so that few, if any, reached the natives after 1941. And finally, in 1943, as Japan began to retreat, Microne-

sian respect for Japanese as conquerors changed to disdain for them as defeated men. As a chief in Pohnpei remarked to the writer, the Japanese were stupid to think they could defeat America. (Embree 1946b:62)[29]

But the passage of time changes the meaning of memories. Americans visiting the region today are more likely to hear of the golden age as a separate topic from the hard times of war. Both memories of Japan's rule coexist—but the Micronesian understanding of the war separates the two and evaluates them differently. Japanese colonial rule in Micronesia is judged in terms of the distinctive qualities of Japanese culture, the personal actions of individual officials and immigrants, and economic and political results. The question of war lies on a separate plane. Japan was involved in war not because it was Japan but because it was a world power. One of the characteristics of powerful nations is their tendency to engage in war. Thus, Micronesians cannot feel safe in the hands of any world power—regardless of the quality of their personal interactions with the nationals of these powers.

THE PACIFIC WAR IN MODERN MICRONESIAN GEOPOLITICS

After demonstrating their capacity to endure the extreme conditions of modern war and their resilience in managing the impositions and opportunities of yet another in a succession of colonial regimes, Micronesians are, for the first time in a hundred years (three hundred years in the Marianas) in political control of their own future. What role does the memory of World War II experiences play as Micronesians chart the decades ahead? What do Micronesians take as the lasting lessons of the Pacific war?

As we have seen, Micronesian reflections on the war are openly ambivalent, especially when they speak of their relations with the combatant powers. Colonial demands could be tolerated in the past because their rather limited administrations offered certain material advantages and because foreign rule was backed with the threat of force. But the scales in which Micronesians weigh their twin desires for sovereignty and economic growth were certainly tipped by the experiences of war. Righting the balance dominates Micronesian politics today.

Micronesian participation in global economy and society is accepted as a given. Micronesians have no desire to return to an entirely "traditional lifestyle," however that might be imagined. Their dual goal is to assure a more comfortable economic future and to retain their valued cultural practices. The worldwide problem of reconciling cultural integrity with economic growth is compounded in Micronesia today by the diversity of languages and cultures and by generational differences exacerbated by growing up in two such divergent colonial contexts. Clearly, much of the change in Micronesia's future will be in the direction of the American cultural model that has become familiar during the past half-century—in terms of physical setting, consumer goods, education, jobs, and government. However, Micronesians hold serious reservations about aspects of the American model that directly contradict Micronesian values, such as American-introduced yet uniquely Micronesian-interpreted ideas and practices of freedom, democracy, individualism, and social control.

In seeking to balance cultural values with economic growth, Micronesians have plenty of company. They are limited, however, in having so little to offer global trading partners. After years of general neglect and the repeated failures of economic schemes, the Micronesian islands remain, to varying degrees, unsuccessful in developing their economic potential. But then, strong economic growth was never a real goal of either American administrators or of Micronesians themselves (see discussion in Hanlon 1998). While complete independence remains an ideal for most Micronesians, they know their tiny islands cannot make it on their own. Links of dependence with metropolitan states, in some form and to some degree, seem a necessary condition of life.

It is Micronesia's wartime experience that indicated the outlines of current and future political and economic strategy. The memory of the war, linked with an understanding of international postwar politics, has given Micronesians a clear sense of the strategic value of their islands. Negotiations at the close of the Trust Territory era ended in a juggling act in which Micronesians bargained with their strategic geographical position to provide for their economic needs (Firth 1989; Hezel 1995:325–367). Here, global politics is local economics. International security issues are the financial underpinning of modern Micronesia.

The potential military significance of each island region to the United States—and the different levels of autonomy each hopes to achieve—explains the separation of these islands into new political entities. From the outset it was evident that some areas were more strategically located or more militarily developed—and therefore in better bargaining positions—than others. Those with more to offer split from the remaining islands early in the negotiating process as the Trust Territory of the Pacific Islands came to an end. The Northern Marianas, located closest to Asia and the former Soviet Union and with a population that had become highly acculturated during the Japanese and American periods, sought aggressive modernization. They did not wish to be politically joined with "backward" Micronesia or, as the most developed area in Micronesia, to see their tax revenues spread out among the other islands (Liebowitz 1989). At first, the Northern Marianas asked to be joined with the American territory of Guam, but that initiative was rebuffed by continuing bitterness over World War II experiences (Rogers 1995:249–250). In 1975–1976, the Northern Marianas entered a commonwealth agreement that grants the United States authority over foreign affairs and defense, while allowing considerable local autonomy. The monetary and trade arrangements between the United States and the Commonwealth of the Northern Mariana Islands (CNMI) are often the envy of the rest of Micronesia. Since the signing of the commonwealth agreement, the CNMI has undergone a comparatively dramatic economic boom.

As in the case of the CNMI, U.S. military needs in the Marshalls allowed for negotiation of a separate Republic of the Marshall Islands (RMI). Agreements included reparations for Marshallese affected by nuclear testing and limits on contracts for existing bases. This has translated into higher U.S. funding levels for the RMI. The RMI government has also aggressively pursued foreign investment and begun its own development projects, including a fishing fleet, an airline, two luxury hotels, a foreign ship registry, and sales of RMI citizenship (Johnson 1990; Ogden 1994; Dahl 1996 on the modern Marshallese economy).

Palau, in the extreme western part of Micronesia, also holds special strategic value for the United States. Close to American bases in Guam and with deep water channels, Palau could be developed as a naval port and is a potential rollback site, along with Guam and the Marianas, for U.S. forces in Asia. But the rest of the Caroline Islands, comprising approximately 75 percent of the area of Micronesia, have no distinct strategic value to the United States. In the end, while Palau established itself as a separate political entity (the Republic of Palau), the rest of the Carolines acceded to the American negotiators' wish for them to band together in the Federated States of Micronesia.

Photo 36. A Japanese bunker now protects golfers in mid-fairway on the Kwajalein U.S. Army facility. The dual-edged blessing and curse of a multifaceted military legacy continues to follow Kwajalein residents to the current day. (Photo by L. M. Carucci)

The Republic of the Marshall Islands, the Republic of Palau, and the Federated States of Micronesia take part in a political innovation called free association (a status reviewed in Michal 1993). Under this agreement, Micronesians are members of independent nations, with their own constitutions and sovereignty over internal and external affairs (the compact of free association went into effect for the RMI and the FSM in 1986; for the Republic of Palau, after a long political struggle, in 1994; see Liebowitz 1996; Shuster 1994). In large measure, then, these are self-governing states. Free association grants the U.S. special powers, including control over national security. The new states do have the right unilaterally to end their relationship with the United States, but this is unlikely given current economic realities. In exchange for arrangements securing American defense interests in the islands, the freely associated states receive money and services from the United States, part of the continuing effort to balance autonomy with the need to support a desirable standard of living.

Though recognized as necessary, the decision to maintain formal association with the United States and to form new ties with other Pacific powers is not an easy one for Micronesians to make. While prewar Micronesia was economically integrated into the Japanese empire, its global value since the late 1930s has been solely strategic and therefore, in part, dependent. During the war, it was alternately a shield and a stepping-stone to Japan. After the war, it became a buffer for the United States against the threat of Communist expansion, a location for strategic bases, for air support and troop staging for Vietnam, for secret CIA activities, for advanced missile warning systems, and for testing weapons systems including nuclear devices. From the first bombs and shells that hit the invasion beaches of Kwajalein to today's negotiations over the future of American bases in the Marshalls and base closings on Guam, Micronesians' lives have been transformed by the ongoing presence of the U.S. military.[30]

In the half-century since they have been ruled by Americans, Micronesians have worried about whether the U.S. presence, and particularly the existence of military bases in Micronesia, will bring another war to their islands. They worry about American weapons testing in the Marshalls, about damage from Pacific nuclear testing (formerly in the Marshalls, and until recently in French Polynesia) and nuclear ships. Every interaction with the American military, however innocuous, calls up the specter of wartime suffering: relocation, hard labor, military occupation, bombing, starvation. When a thirteen-member U.S. Navy Seabee team arrived on Chuuk in the 1960s, using impressive heavy construction equipment for civic projects and showing movies to two or three hundred Chuukese every night, Tosiwo Nakayama (then a senator in the Congress of Micronesia) commented: "You know some of the older people talk about the time when the Japanese came (after World War I). They say there was sort of a Japanese peace corps that came first, then military civic action teams, and finally the troops. Now they wonder about the Americans" (Griffin 1969:6; also Kahn 1971:110).

In an analysis of Enewetak people's view of the Pacific war and its consequences, Carucci describes how they see "Japanese and American militarization" as a process that began in 1939 and "has never ended; it has only moved from place to place. . . . All conflicts (Korea, Cuba, Vietnam, Middle East) are viewed as a continuation of the war" (Carucci 1989:76–77). Carucci quotes an Enewetak explanation: "These battles, there are many even today, and the war, it still goes on. Like the fighting on Enewetak. It began on Hawaii and then grew. They moved to Kiribati and then to the Marshalls, then they came to Enewetak and ruined it, and then moved onward to Pohnpei and Saipan and those places. And after Japan they moved onward to that place they call Korea and afterward to Vietnam. You see that, they haven't finished fighting [or haven't finished the war], they only move around from place to place; . . . and all the time they [the warriors] have to remain ready."

Many Micronesians serve in the U.S. armed forces, and Micronesians follow world news. Micronesians know that their islands are potential bases for American action in any part of the world, particularly Asia. Their responses, which to outsiders may seem excessively anxious, are, we think, reasonably informed by vivid and emotional memories of suffering conveyed by their elders. These fears began immediately after the war and continue to the present. When William Lessa was on Ulithi in 1949, people still ran for shelter when a plane flew overhead: "They have come to associate any airplane whatsoever with destruction and death. After the passage of several years since the war, some people still have bad dreams in which they see themselves being machine-gunned" (Lessa 1950a:16). In 1950, Alexander Spoehr watched Chamorros and Carolinians on Saipan respond to the outbreak of the Korean War:

> The community became extremely jittery. Stocks of rice in the stores were bought up as families attempted to lay in food; rumors of every sort ran through the island. The people did not calm down until it became apparent that Saipan was not under imminent attack.
>
> The anxiety over war is seldom expressed by these people but occasionally it comes out. I was talking with a Chamorro friend about his corn crop. Suddenly he said, "I tell you, señor, I am afraid. I never say anything, but in my stomach I am afraid of war. We have seen it once and many people are anxious. When we hear talk of war, there is fear in us. We wonder whether it is worth-while to clear the land and plant our crops. Yes, we are anxious and afraid." (Spoehr 1954:94)

We conducted part of our study in Micronesia during "Operation Desert Storm." The war in the Persian Gulf (which involved U.S. bases on Guam) renewed for Micronesians—especially the younger ones—the importance of knowledge about the Pacific war. While this new war strengthened local images of U.S. power and American ability to protect Micronesians, it simultaneously gave immediacy and salience to community memories of wartime suffering. At the beginning of the conflict with Iraq, some Micronesian public schools were closed, and parents insisted that their children return home (even from college in Guam). "Desert Storm" produced nothing less than an overnight communications revolution in parts of rural Micronesia, where international news suddenly had local value. People were glued to unprecedented "Voice of America" radio broadcasts and news updates. The occasional videotaped CNN reports sent from the Marianas were at a premium, and community leaders arranged video equipment for rural villagers who gathered in the evening to follow the news. Special church services for Micronesians serving in the U.S. military were held throughout the islands. Although no statistics were available, some local officials believed that Micronesian enlistees were overrepresented in the troops sent to Iraq.[31]

Each of the authors of this study was approached with questions and concerns about the war. In the Marshall Islands, Carucci attempted to assuage frequently expressed fears of an imminent Iraqi missile attack on U.S. military facilities at Kwajalein Missile Range. In Falgout's Pohnpeian family, the mother read the Bible for days and wept at the thought that she would experience another war in her lifetime. Members of the community half-jokingly asked if the visit of this American researcher would bring the war into their household. Rumors spread that an Iraqi spy had been spotted at the Pohnpei airport. For a time, the Federated States of Micronesia post office refused to handle packages—part of a general bomb scare. News of an attempted Iraqi bombing of the U.S. Embassy in Manila seemed to confirm everyone's worst fears. On Chuuk, where Poyer was working, the radio regularly carried BBC news broadcasts—for the first time ever—and people eagerly inquired about the naval capabilities of Middle Eastern countries. Families checked the readiness of their bomb shelters—the war-era caves and dugouts usually used for storage and typhoon refuge—and asked the old people to recall the rules for safety in case of bombing. One American-educated Chuukese woman, driving with her elderly mother, turned off the radio when a Gulf War news bulletin came on.

"No, turn that on—I want to hear it," her mother said.

"Why, Mom? That war has nothing to do with us."

Her mother's reply silenced her. "That is what they said about the last one."

EPILOGUE

In thinking and talking about the Pacific war, Micronesians have transformed memories of suffering into lessons for the future. Clanton Abija (Marshalls) spoke of how he will never forget "the way we learned how to care for ourselves" and for others during the war, how people learned to be observant and to live through whatever happened. Nathan Tartios (Marshalls) was asked whether any good came out of the war years. He said no at first, then added:

> Well, it is true that we knew about one another before the war, we knew a lot about one another.
>
> *(Interviewer asks: But did you become even more closely bound together during the war?)*
>
> Yes. So great was your knowledge of who others were and your closeness to others within this thing, this knowledge. We consulted one another and shared in all things.

The younger generation has a much simplified, overwhelmingly negative view of the war and all its participants. Nevertheless, younger Micronesians have grown up in a time of peace and have benefited from modern, global education, in many cases completed in the United States or Japan, and from exposure to American and Japanese tourists and businessmen. In talking to Micronesians of all ages today, visitors recognize that they have long ago sorted out the virtues and handicaps of Japanese and Americans, two major Pacific powers. Now, they wish to benefit from what each of these nations can offer.

Today Micronesians perceive the Americans as the most powerful military presence in the world; although a potential source of trouble, it is, nevertheless, good to have them on your side. The Japanese, during the civilian administration of Micronesia, proved themselves to be good businessmen and to be much more personally involved than most Americans in their dealings with Islanders. Since Micronesian independence, and especially during the 1980s, Japanese reenergized old ties and developed new ones with the political leaders and entrepreneurs of the islands. In a review of Japanese tourism and trade throughout the Pacific, Shuster (1982c:37) wrote, "what was lost to the gun has been won by the yen." But Micronesians are not unreservedly enthusiastic about Japanese investment, having learned the lesson of exploitation from their Nan'yō experience.

Micronesians recognize that their wartime experience has given them a sophisticated appreciation for some of the main players in today's global game. They realize that major powers set their goals with little regard for consequences to lesser states, but they also understand that their long history of experience with colonial rulers give them insight that can be translated into political strategy.

The inconspicuousness of life in this part of the world, marginalized in the eyes of large nations by the small population and scant landmass of the islands, is contradicted by strategic location and powerful memories of a time when global history was decided here. Despite their position as bystanders and victims of the conflict, "the War" in Micronesian eyes is a tale of self-discovery, a story in which Islanders' lives became closely interwoven as they cared for each other, and a time when indigenous identities that otherwise might have been unnoticed by the world were linked inextricably to those of peoples from large and powerful lands. The future of those world powers was contested and, in part, constructed on these tiny sand spits and secluded islands that both Japan and the United States found so attractive yet that each, in its own way, worked so hard to destroy. In remembrance of a war fought by foreigners for foreign purposes, Micronesians have found sources of meaning and strategy in their own struggle for an honorable place in the company of peaceful nations.

APPENDIX A

List of Participants in Oral History Interviews, 1990–1991

REPUBLIC OF THE MARSHALL ISLANDS

Clanton Abija

Klenere Abner

John Abraham

Aili Albios

Ledre Alek

Winnie Amja

Kanki Amlej

John Anjain

Ruth Arelōñ

Limkij Beolu

Anko Billy

Makbi Bokin

Maine Briand

Moody Briand

Kemro Buotwōt

Tibon Buti

Obet David

Onil David

Elson Ebel

Kija Edison

Apinar Edward

Emty Edwin

Jobi Elija

Welli Elija

Joseph Ernej

John Ezekiel

Tira George

Benjamin Gideon

Nataniel Henry

Kileon Ijo

Lojan Isaac

Tonki Jabba

Elmina Jahnol

Carl Jelkan

Bellam Jello

Joseph Jibōn

Helena Jitbōn

Median Job

Hertes John

Lajiko Jor

Tamar Jordan

Leban Jorju

Kottar Kamram

Aneo Keju

Bobo Keju

Raitu Keju

Labwinmij Laelōñeo

Kobeta Laijek

Taiwel Laimroj

Joraur Lainlij

Aneab Laitak

Tibierke Lakbel

Kilinik Lañejo

Atonej Lang

Keja Laniep

Ato Lañkio

Luke Lantir

Ijimura Lautoña

Yoseph Leban

Ken Lebo

Thomas Lejer

Bwirre Lejmen

Jamba Likinen

Lirio

Bonni Lodrenni

Daisey Lojkar

Manutil Lokwōt

Jabue Lorak

Alowina Lukas

Clancy Makroro

Jomle Malolo

Lombwe Mark

Jacob Maun
Kinoj Mawilōñ
Jimen Mejbon
Don Melōñ
Akji Menwa
Henry Moses
Arelōñ Nadrik

Balik Paul
Neimon Philippo
Renton Pita
Lele Ram
Thaddeus Sampson
Ateniel Tarki
Nathan Tartios

Jabi Tenjue
Edward Toluwi
Eolōt Torelañ
Kaname Yamamura
Katzan Zion

FEDERATED STATES OF MICRONESIA

Pohnpei State

Carmihter Abraham
Suhlet Abraham
Klemente Actouka
Katarihna Adalpret
Demaunis Adolf
Eperiam Agripa
Isao Aisawa
Paulina Aisawa
Clara Albert
Iosep Aldis
Liwisa Aldis
Marcus Alempia
Isiro Alex
Alfonso Alexander
Ludwik Alik
Alwihs Amida
Manuel Amor
Robino Amusten
Sother Andon
Kaiti Anson
Ciro Barbosa
Alter Bedley
Bernard Behris
Yasio Behris
David David
Eliaser David
Janet David

Keropin David
Mikel Diana
Anastasio Dosoliwa
Emensio Eperiam
Regina Esiel
Yvette Etscheit
Ines Etnol
Victor Edwin
Imanuel Gallen
Mihna Gallen
Robert Gallen
Swingley Gallen
Melsor Gilmete
Wendolin Gomez
Dione Hatchkarawi
Linter Hebel
Rosette Hebel
Etson Henly
Dopias Ilon
Francisco Iriarte
Senoleen Iriarte
Lusios Jak
Andohn Jemes
Mary Jane Jemes
Ainrick Joshua
Masako Luhk Karen
Dobi Kilimete

Peleng Kilimete
Melpirihte Konsaka
Carl Kohler
Iens Lainos
Pernardo Lainos
Lihna Lawrence
Pensile Lawrence
Pelsina Lipai
Erwin Leopold
Benjamin Lopez
Solomon Lorrin
Johna Luda
Ariko Luhk
Hill Manuel
Niemwe Mark
Mikel Marquez
Augustine Mauricio
Johna Melia
Carmen Miguel
Yosko Miguel
Eneriko Pablo
Melsor Panuelo
Julie Panuelo
Phillip Patterson
Ignasio Paulino
Elper Penias
Sinio Peter

William Prens
Danis Pretrick
Damian Primo
Andonio Raidong
Pretrick Ringlen
Ela Ringlen
Ruben Rudolph
Lusiana Sackryas
Moses Saimon
Iosep Salvador

Edgar Santos
Tadasy Santos
Okin Sarapio
Sekismwindo Sarapio
Kristina Sehna
Lotis Seneres
Oska Seiola
Misko Shed
Konsepsion Silbanus
Pedrus Silbanus

Osei Sohram
Merlusi Stephenson
Ioana Tipen
Julio Vallazon
Nehdo Vicky
Meruse William
Norman William
Takio William

Kosrae State

Kun Aaron
Austin Albert
Palikun Andrew
Likiak Benjamin
Anna Brightly

Otinel Eddmont
Tulpe A. Jackson
Tolenna Kilafwasru
Kilafwa Likiak
Lupalik Nithan

Osmond Palikun
Milton Timothy
Tulenkun Waguk

Chuuk State

Achanto (of Fason)
Kan Achew
Anisiro Aninis
Estefania Aunu
Litong Aunu
Aknes Bier
Marusina Bier
Adenis Bilimon
Istor Billimont
Aitel Bisalen
Iteko Bisalen
Nekuun Boone
Finas Bossin
Anton Chipwe
Ichios Eas
Nifereta Eas
Ikeichy Edwin
Sumier Elias

Konstantin Enik
Leon Episom
Masaichi Erimas
Piara Esirom
Eter (of Losap)
Filipos (of Neue)
Sisko Harper
Manuel Hartman
Urur Inek
Kinio Ipon
Antonio Isaias
Umiko Isaias
Topias Isam
Toli Jessy
Iwate John
Simako Joseph
Nikapwut Kachupin
Sontak Kansou

Take Katiw
Kalifin Kofak
Chipun Kom
Litia Kosam
Akki Lorin
Tupun Louis
Kariti Luther
Menas Makimi
Iowanes Manuere
Auchun Marar
Machiko Marcus
Teruo Marcus
Marwin (of Mwaan)
Lucia Masawer
Pius Masawer
Asako Mateas
Sinino Mateas
Mine (of Neue)

Misasi (of Nama)
Akeisuk Mokok
Mine Mokok
Humiko Mori
Masataka Mori
Rokuro Mori
Darshy Nabamura
Echen Nakamura
Parang Namono
Sr. Magdelina Narruhn
Aten Niesik
Nusi Niesik
Miso Nifinifin
Este Puri Nipuk
Mieko Nipuk
Kisiuou Nua
Piriska Nukunukar
Ikefai Onopey
Simako Onusun
Tarup Ounuwa
Anumi Partonome
Faste Petter
Kimon Phymon
Piana (of Nama)
Este Puri
Andon Quela

Kintin Raphael
Akelina Rapun
Kame Rapun
Julio Repwech
Netek Rewein
Saito Rewein
Simon Rewie
Narian Robich
Ropat Romano
Resen (of Mwaan)
Rutok Ruben
Sachiko Ruben
Liwiena Rudolph
Isaac Sakios
Stem Salle
Yuniko Salle
Esperansa Samo
Biloris E. Samor
Anang Samwel
Aikichi Samwen
John Sandy
Okaichi Sapwo
Norimasa Selet
Osong Seleti
James Sellem
Deruko Shirai

Liaf Sigra
Limperta Simmy
Sachuo Siwi
Emwene Sopo
Matsuko Soram
Tomuo Soram
Emilio Sota
Pilar Soumwei
Kristo Souwas
Koko Suda
Ikiuo Sulluk
Weresi Suta
Mori Suzuki
Nobiyuki Suzuki
Keke Tawe
Takis Taylor
Naris Teitas
Soino Tokochee
Nifang Tommy
Saikichi Tommy
Iofina Topich
Likur Uruo
Akena Victus
Wangko Wasan

Yap State

Buthung
Mike Faraguy
Leon Gargathog
Gilipin
Vicente Gilwrol
Raphael Gisog
Joseph-Mary Goofalaan

Alvera Guro
Venitu E. Gurtmag
Patrick Hachigelior
Belarmino Hathey
Peter Ianguchel
Ikefai
Martina La'ew

Maria Leemed
Ignasio Letalim
Palagia Mitag
Santiago Sathau
Matthew Yafimal
Francis Yow

In addition to our informants, who shared with us the stories of their wartime experiences, we thank the family members who aided our interviews and people who directed or introduced us to knowledgeable elders. Although we cannot name everyone who helped us, we especially thank the interviewers, translators, and local officials and others who helped with the project. We have listed each person's title at the time of our project (1990–1991).

IN THE REPUBLIC OF THE MARSHALL ISLANDS

Carmen Bigler, Historic Preservation Officer, RMI
Alfred Capelle, Assistant Historic Preservation Officer, RMI
Hilda Heine Jetnil, President, College of the Marshall Islands
Oscar Debrum, Chief Secretary of the Marshall Islands
Naptali Peter, Mayor, Enewetak Atoll
Relang Lamari, Chief Secretary's Representative to Ebeye
Alvin Jacklick, Mayor, Kwajalein Atoll
Aeto Bantol and Noda Lojkar, Kwajalein Atoll Local Government
Thomas Keene, Office of Host Nations on Kwajalein Atoll
Enewetak / Ujelang Local Government Council
Interviews/assistants for the Marshall Islands: Henry Moses, Susan Heine
Translation assistance: Neimon, Titus, Joemy

IN THE FEDERATED STATES OF MICRONESIA

Baily Olter, President, FSM
Teddy John, FSM Historic Preservation Officer
Jones George, FSM Archives and History

Pohnpei and Kosrae States:

Emensio Eperiam, Pohnpei Historic Preservation Officer
Berlin Sigrah, Kosrae Historic Preservation Officer
Paul Gallen, President, Community College of Micronesia
Tony and Julie Ovello
Assistants for Pohnpei: Lerleen David, Ersina David, Eltes Sehd, Wendolin Lainos,
Antolin Gomes
Assistant for Kosrae: Kerrick Benjamin

Chuuk State:

Office of the Governor
Elvis Killion Osonis, State Historic Preservation Officer
Kaio Noket, Assistant Historic Preservation Officer
Francis X. Hezel, SJ, the Tunuuk Catholic Mission, and the Tol Mission
Graceful Enlet, President, Community College of Micronesia-Chuuk
The Mori Family
George Hartman
Grace Serious
Linda Smith
John Wendel
Richard and Betty Benson
Camy Akapito
Mensi Ifanuk
Kimuo Aisik
Itios Eas
Interviewers and translators: K. M. Mefy, Jasinto Howard, Nancy Moufa, Frannie Oneitom, Kaio Noket, Linda Mori, Sidro, Matsuko Soram, Ino Oneisom, Francis X. Hezel, SJ, Nick Isaac, Aaron Suzuki, Philip Mwangin, Rosalinda Walter, Miako Hengio, Desder Johnny, Floren Akkin, John Sandy, Minda Oneisom, Basilio Dilipy, Graceful Enlet, Elvis Osonis, Johnson Elimwo, Ioanes Martin, Narcisso Sebastien, Kerio Walliby, Grace Serious, Dersy Erwin, Dolores Roskow, Akiosy Aniol

Yap State:

Andrew Kugfas, State Historic Preservation Officer
Belermino Hathey, Chief of the Outer Island Council
Lewis Taramweiche, Outer Island Council
Interviewers and translators: John Chodad, Dolores Dinagpitin, Moche'en, Fidelia Adgil, Robert Kelly, Lewis Taramweiche, Sabino Sauchomal, Tony Marliol, Corinne Mogon, Lina Ruan, Andrew Kugfas

HISTORICAL CONSULTANTS

David Purcell, University of Hawai'i–Hilo
Francis X. Hezel, SJ, Micronesian Seminar

FOR OTHER ASSISTANCE

In Micronesia: Scott Russell, Sam McPhetres, Dirk Ballendorf, Wakako Higuchi, Don Shuster, the Micronesian Area Research Center, Sr. Alaina Talu, Don Rubinstein, Micronesian Seminar
In the United States and Japan: Geoffrey White, Lamont Lindstrom, Gregory Trifano-vitch, the East-West Center, Mac Marshall, David Hanlon, Karen Peacock (Pacific Collection, Hamilton Library, University of Hawai'i), Hisafumi Saito, Len Mason, Lela Goodell, Mary H. Maifeld, James West Turner, Robert Kelly, Betty Kam (Bishop Museum Archives, Honolulu), Sandy Ives (Northeast Archives of Folklore and Oral History, University of Maine), Colby College, University of Cincinnati, Taft Memorial Fund (University of Cincinnati), University of Wyoming, University of Hawai'i–West Oahu, Montana State University, National Archives, Navy Historical Center, U.S. Naval Institute, U.S. Army Military History Institute, National Anthropological Archives (Smithsonian Institution).

Lin Poyer thanks these graduate students at the University of Cincinnati for assistance with the bibliography and chronology: Lora Anderson, Shawn Barrick, David Conrad, Lori Lamarre, Cay Mateyko, Laura Moll-Collopy, Jennifer Reiter, and Matt Van Pelt. Laurence Carucci thanks students at Montana State University for help with data entry and cataloging, particularly Jocelyn DeHaas, Dory Allard, Angela McDunn, Kate Maxfield, and Sara Mansikka. The College of Letters and Science at Montana State University graciously provided funding for Carucci's research assistants.

APPENDIX B

Chronology of World War II in Micronesia
(West Longitude Dates)

1922   • Japan established a civilian administration, the South Seas Government (Nan'yō-chō), for governance of League of Nations mandate of Micronesia. Nan'yō-chō established schools, hospitals, civil administration, and economic infrastructure throughout the 1920s and 1930s. October 1930 census of Nan'yō: Japanese: 19,825; Islanders: 49,695; Foreigners: 96 (Higuchi 1987).

1931   • Japanese citizens allowed to purchase land from Islanders with government permission. By 1932, all government and foreign-owned land was surveyed and registered; survey of private land followed. After official surveys, the Japanese government began to take possession of unoccupied land for lease to Japanese settlers or companies (McGrath and Wilson 1971; Peattie 1988:97–100; Spoehr 1954:87).

   • **SEPTEMBER** Japanese forces marched into Manchuria.

1932   • **APRIL** Independent budget established for Nan'yō-chō, by this time financially self-supporting (Hatanaka 1973–1974:2; Higuchi 1987).

1933   • **MAY** Japan gave notice of intent to withdraw from the League of Nations; actual withdrawal was in 1935.

1930–1934 • Japanese government undertook infrastructure improvements: navigational aids and harbor improvements in Saipan and Palau; construction of airfields at Pagan Island and Aslito, Saipan, and a seaplane ramp on Koror, Palau; Punton Flores seaplane base on

Saipan (completed 1935). The Japanese navy conducted surveys throughout Micronesia.

1934–1939 · Japanese navy cooperated with Nan'yō-chō on airfield construction in the Marianas and Carolines: expansion of Aslito field on Saipan, seaplane ramps at Arakabesan (Palau), and an airfield on Eten (Chuuk) were first projects undertaken.

1935
· Attendance at mission schools no longer permitted to substitute for government schooling (Peattie 1988:91).

· Additional land on Kosrae purchased by Japanese agricultural company. At this point, the Japanese population of Kosrae numbered 25, with 1,189 Kosraeans (Peoples 1977:142). After this date the Japanese population increased rapidly.

· Construction of airfield began on Eten, Chuuk (some sources give a later date) (Dolan 1974:85–86; Denfeld 1981a:125; Hezel 1995:215).

· Japanese immigrants outnumbered Micronesians. October 1935 census: Japanese (including Korean and Taiwanese): 51,861; Islanders: 50,573; foreigners: 103 (Higuchi 1987). Economic development continued: fish-drying operation on Lukunor, a fishery and ice plant built by South Seas Marine Company (Nambō) on Toloas (Chuuk), a fishing company in Koror (Palau).

· **MARCH** Japan withdrew from the League of Nations, continuing to claim Micronesia as part of empire.

1936
· Government immigration and economic development policy implemented. Nan'yō Takushoku ("Nantaku," South Seas Colonization Corporation) formed; "Ten Years Development Planning for the South Seas Islands" commenced (Higuchi 1987: 18; Peattie 1988:133; Hezel 1995:198–199).

1937
· Japan's last report to the League of Nations on its Micronesian mandate clearly denied the existence of military forces, bases, fortifications, or military training of Islanders in the region.

· **JULY** Japan invaded China. Explicit military preparations began in several areas of Micronesia. Civilians on Saipan were ordered to build air-raid shelters (Sheeks 1945). The Japanese navy took charge of infrastructure construction projects in the region. Military personnel supplemented Japanese colonists on Pohnpei (Bascom 1950). Some

commercial activity altered as certain Japanese returned home; for
example, copra trader on Lukunor recalled to Japan (Borthwick
1977:5).

1937–1939 · Gradually increasing restrictions on movements of foreign
missionaries. By 1938 or 1939, replacements not allowed to enter.

1938 · Island and settlement names officially changed from local language
to Japanese names, at least in Chuuk and areas of Palau (e.g., Peattie
1988:173).

· Agricultural development program begun on Kosrae; Nambō
established stations at Malem, Tafunsak, and Lelu (Peoples 1977).

1938–1939 · Construction of seaplane base in Arakabesan Island adjacent to Koror
Airfield begun on Peleliu; oil pumps and storage constructed in Palau.

1939 · Regular commercial air flights initiated from Yokohama to Palau,
extended in 1940 through Yap, Chuuk, and Pohnpei to Jaluij (Peattie
1988:149–150).

· Militarization of Micronesia began. Military Manpower Mobilization
Law began drafts of Micronesians and importation of Korean workers
and Japanese convicts for construction labor (Peattie 1988:250).

Marshall Islands: Japanese navy surveyed Marshall Islands, decided
on rapid construction of airfields on Roi (Kwajalein Atoll), Taroa
(Maloelap) and Wotje (Peattie 1988:250–251).

Chuuk: Korean workers and Japanese prisoners arrived on Chuuk
to build airstrip on Weno and other military installations. Late in the
year, new regulations required Islanders to devote time to service
of the empire, primarily for initial round of military construction.
Nonmilitarized areas also saw intensification of local community
labor obligations. Lukunor coral stone seawall and dock built by
about 150 regular workers in 1939–1940 (Borthwick 1977:57). Initial
relocation of Iras village on Weno for airfield construction between
1937 and 1941; work on final airfield began December 1941 (Denfeld
1981a:78; King and Carucci 1984:475, 478; King and Parker 1984:106).

Yap (1939–1940): Japanese established *kumiai,* co-op farms for
pineapple, sweet potatoes, sugarcane, papayas, and pumpkins, worked
by women (Useem 1946a).

· **APRIL** Development of civilian infrastructure continued: Saipan
Girls' High School, Young Men's School established in Koror
(Higuchi 1987).

- **NOVEMBER** Japan's navy organized Fourth Fleet, headquartered at Chuuk, which took as its first job military construction throughout Micronesia.

1940
- German raiders shelled Nauru and sank several ships offshore.

- France fell; its Pacific island territories aligned themselves with the Free French Movement (M. Keesing 1944:13–14).

- U.S. built seaplane base on Johnston Atoll.

- Japanese navy organized militarization of Micronesia, dividing it into four sectors, establishing "Base Force" headquarters at Saipan, Koror, Chuuk, and Kwajalein (Peattie 1988:252).

- Marshallese relocated as areas on Jaluij, Kwajalein, Wotje, Maloelap, and Mili were cleared for military construction. Labor drafts and relocations by end of year separated families, curtailed travel, and interfered with cash economy (Bryan 1972:220). Christian missions came under increasing constraints—property seized, foreign missionaries encouraged to leave.

- Chuuk fortifications started.

- Construction of military installations begun in Saipan (Russell 1984:79).

- **SEPTEMBER** Japan signed Tripartite Act of mutual assistance with Germany and Italy.

- **NOVEMBER** Major Shinto shrine at Koror established.

- **DECEMBER** Twice-monthly flights connecting Japan, Saipan, and Palau initiated (Higuchi 1987).

1941
- After this date, local standard of living sharply declined as shipments of consumer goods such as textiles ceased and market for local goods disappeared; military priority for medical supplies limited Micronesians' access to these (Embree 1946a:162; Hall and Pelzer 1946:62).

- As militarization and military construction proceeded, Japanese navy confiscated private and civil government land and buildings. Compulsory military drill for Micronesians initiated in some areas.

- American missionaries left Kosrae and the Marshall Islands.

- Chuukese began large-scale labor conscription for military construction and military agricultural work. Toloas' circulating road, 7,000 meters long, was laid (Denfeld 1981a:116; Dolan 1974:42).

- Palau extensively fortified, especially Peleliu (with residents evacuated to Babelthuap). Palau used as a staging and replacement center; Babelthuap as main base for land forces; air base under construction; Koror had seaplane facilities and AA defenses (Yarbrough 1971:188).

- **JANUARY** Construction began on U.S. air and submarine base at Wake Island.

- **FEBRUARY** Warships and shore defense units entered Saipan, Palau, Chuuk, Pohnpei, and key Marshalls atolls; martial law in effect on larger atolls when navy arrived (Peattie 1988:253, 297; Russell 1984:82).

- Fourth Fleet headquarters established at Chuuk; barracks built; Toloas athletic field became navy drill area; tunnels blasted for guns; planes flown into Chuuk from Rabaul (Hezel 1995:220).

- **APRIL** Palau Kōtō Jogakkō (high school for Japanese girls) established (Higuchi 1987).

- **JUNE** AA guns for naval batteries arrived at Chuuk, installed on Toloas and Eten (Lindemann 1982:114).

- U.S. defensive troops arrived at Wake (Morison 1948:225–227).

- **SEPTEMBER** Funding allocated for military construction on Saipan (Russell 1984:82).

- **OCTOBER** By mid-October, all American women and children evacuated from Guam in preparation for Japanese invasion (Morison 1948:184).

- **DECEMBER** Chuuk-based naval air organization—known as the 902nd Naval Air Corps *(Kokutai)*—established (Bailey 1989:51).

- Catholic priests in Chuuk region imprisoned on Toloas.

- Army prostitutes from Japan arrived on Guam, stayed through 1944 (Apple 1980:28).

- **DECEMBER 8** Pearl Harbor attacked. Japanese attacks conducted from seaborne strike force, the Bonin Islands, and Micronesian sites

(Palau, Saipan, Jaluij, Majuro, and Kwajalein) hit Hawaiʻi, the Philippines, Guam, Wake, Kiribati, Howland Island, Nauru, and Banaba (Peattie 1988:257).

- **DECEMBER 8–9** Marine headquarters and other areas of Guam bombed and strafed by virtually unopposed Japanese air attack from Saipan. Saipanese Chamorros landed on northern cape of Guam to aid Japanese invasion (Morison 1948; Apple 1980:23; Beardsley 1964:211–212).

- **DECEMBER 8–11** First Japanese attack on Wake, successfully defended by U.S. forces.

- **DECEMBER 9** Japanese banned public acts of religion (D. F. Smith 1946:8).

- **DECEMBER 9–10** Japanese forces seized Kiribati, began to fortify Tarawa, Makin, then Banaba and Nauru as patrol bases and outer defenses.

- **DECEMBER 10** After two days of bombing, Japanese forces occupied Guam.

- **DECEMBER 23** After air strikes and second major attack, U.S. forces surrendered Wake to Japan.

1942
- Moen #1 airfield in Iras (Weno, Chuuk) became operational (date approximate) (Parker 1985).

- Construction of Japanese bases in Kiribati; Japanese bases strengthened at Kwajalein, Jaluij, Wotje and Maloelap; Mili built into major base. Japanese navy built small airstrip on Woleai.

- **JANUARY** Royal Australian Air Force from Kavieng conducted first Allied reconnaissance flights over Chuuk. Japanese planes flying from Chuuk attacked Rabaul (Denfeld 1981a:22–26; Anonymous 1944; Bailey 1989:3–4).

- American POWs from Guam shipped to the island of Honshu, Japan; 250 Guam POWs put on work release (Apple 1980:30; Beardsley 1964:213).

- South Seas Detachment departed Guam, leaving around four hundred Japanese navy guard forces; everything American banned.

- **JANUARY 15** First Allied raid on Chuuk; six Australian Catalinas respond to planes from Chuuk attacking Rabaul with attempt on Chuuk (four reached the target, one dropped bombs) (Denfeld 1981a:22–26).

- **JANUARY/FEBRUARY** American naval task force raid on Marshalls bases.

- **APRIL** Palau Chūgakkō (lower secondary school) established in Koror (Higuchi 1987).

- Change in government gave navy more authority; civilian governor of Nan'yō-chō and heads of newly designated districts were navy officers.

- First U.S. air attack on Japan, the Doolittle raid on Tokyo.

- **MAY** Twenty Pohnpeian men recruited to go to Rabaul to serve Japanese military (Hezel 1995:223–224). Throughout 1942–1943, Micronesians served with colonial government volunteer units (*teishintai*) as noncombatants with Japanese army in New Guinea theater (Peattie 1988:301).

- Battle of the Coral Sea ended Japanese expansion in the Southwest Pacific.

- **JUNE** Battle of Midway, a major defeat for the Japanese navy.

- **JULY** Combined Fleet arrived at Chuuk, including battleships *Yamato* and *Musashi*, headed by Admiral Yamamoto—remained at ease through November 1943 (Morison 1951; Peattie 1988:260–262; Agawa 1979:326–342).

- **AUGUST** U.S. landing on Guadalcanal; Japanese sent only one reinforcement battalion of five hundred men from Chuuk (USSBS 1975).

- U.S. Marines, Carlson's Raiders, landed on Makin, Kiribati, from submarines in a limited attack; Japanese then strengthened Makin and Tarawa.

- Japanese began military and mining buildup on Nauru (Pollock 1991:93).

- **NOVEMBER** Nan'yō-chō transferred to jurisdiction of the Greater East Asian Ministry, established to administer conquered regions (Grahlfs 1955:21; Bryan 1972:208; U.S. Navy 1943:44).

- **AUTUMN 1942–AUTUMN 1943** Beginning of U.S. offensive in Southwest Pacific; no active fighting in Micronesia except increasing U.S. submarine attacks on Japanese shipping.

1942–1943 · Japanese naval construction crews built undefended airstrip on Enjebi in Enewetak (Peattie 1988:268).

1943

- Satawan and Lukunor in the Mortlock Islands garrisoned; work on airstrip on Satawan began immediately. Satawan and Ta people relocated to Kutu; Lower Mortlocks men heavily conscripted for airfield and provisioning work.

- Intensive conscription for military labor on Kosrae (Peoples 1977:150).

- Small Japanese navy garrison assigned to Woleai.

- Two of twenty Pohnpeians drafted by Japanese for army duty at Rabaul returned to Pohnpei (twelve killed, five captured by Allies) (Cockrum 1970:334).

- Palauans contributed 130,000 yen to Japanese war fund campaign (Hezel 1995:223).

- Young Palauan men volunteered to aid Japanese troops in Melanesia (Hezel 1995:223).

- **JANUARY** Casablanca Conference of British and Americans established Allied plan for war against Japan.

- **FEBRUARY** Headquarters of Japan's Combined Fleet transferred to flagship *Musashi* at Chuuk (Agawa 1979).

- **MARCH** U.S. began bombing airstrips at Nauru; after destroyer bombardment in November 1943, bombing continued almost daily from December 1943 to January 1945 (Pollock 1991:99).

- **APRIL** Yamamoto traveled from Chuuk to Rabaul, where he was killed.

- **MAY** Catholic missionaries in Mortlocks ordered to Toloas (Hezel n.d.).

- **JUNE** Trident Conference in Washington, D.C. planned two-pronged Allied offensive against Japan, one through Southwest Pacific toward the Philippines (led by MacArthur); one through the Central Pacific (under Nimitz).

- Construction of Parem airfield in Chuuk begun; completed January 1944 (Denfeld 1981a:34).

- **JUNE–AUGUST** Japanese brought 1,203 Nauruans to Chuuk (reducing Nauru's population to 591); final deportation canceled when ship sank before loading, September 1944) (Richard 1957b:49; Denfeld 1981a:30; Pollock 1991:93).

- **JULY** Radio station, weather station and aircraft spotter post at Kapingamarangi destroyed by U.S. bombing (Witherspoon 1945).

- **SUMMER** A contingent of 179 Pohnpeian men sent to Kosrae to work on Japanese army installations.

- **JULY–AUGUST** Allies developed plan for Central Pacific campaign.

- **AUTUMN** Evacuation from Micronesia began for Japanese women, children, and old men (despite danger of U.S. submarine attacks); successful in Marshalls and Carolines, leaving mostly single men, but many Japanese families were trapped in Marianas by time of U.S. invasion (Peattie 1988:298).

- **SEPTEMBER–JANUARY 1944** Japanese built three airstrips on Nauru, using local and imported labor (Pollock 1991:96).

- **SEPTEMBER** Japanese strategy shifted from offensive to defensive: Tokyo high command adopted "A-Go" strategy to delay Allied drive in Southwest and Central Pacific while seeking to destroy U.S. fleet in a decisive battle. New strategy was to consolidate smaller defensive perimeter, an absolute national defense sphere running from Kuriles to Bonins, Marianas, western and central Carolines; Marshalls and Kiribati to be rapidly strengthened to delay enemy. Relocations of Islanders to make way for troops and defensive construction: Koror, Angaur, Peleliu, Majuro, Kosrae, Chuuk.

- U.S. fast carrier strikes against Marcus Island.

- **SEPTEMBER 18–19** U.S. carrier air strikes on Tarawa and Makin.

- **OCTOBER 5–6** U.S. carrier planes struck Wake.

- **NOVEMBER** Nan'yō-chō bureaucracy reorganized. Branch governments reduced from six districts (Saipan, Palau, Yap, Chuuk, Pohnpei, and Jaluij) to three: a north district with Saipan as its HQ; a south district with Chuuk as its HQ; and a west district with Palau as its HQ.

- Mistreatment at Chuuk of forty-two U.S. POWs from submarine *Sculpin,* as charged in war crimes trials (Denfeld 1981a:63).

- Allies began offensive to retake Pacific.

- "Operation Galvanic," Allied invasion of Kiribati, and occupation of Makin, Tarawa, and Abemama. By end of 1943, British had set up colonial HQ in Tarawa (Maude and Doran 1966:286).

- Three hundred officers and men of Japanese army 52nd Division arrived in Chuuk; this was the only army force on Chuuk until January 1944 (Denfeld 1981a:5). At the end of 1943, the Japanese planned evacuation of Islanders and nonessential Japanese on Chuuk, but air attacks beginning February 1944 and the Allied blockade prevented implementing the plan (Hall and Pelzer 1946:6).

- **MID-NOVEMBER** Air strikes on Marshalls accompanied invasion of Kiribati, continued through December by carrier planes and land-based B-24 bombers.

- **AUTUMN** Japanese army units from Asia and Philippines reorganized and sent to Micronesia to strengthen defense in central and eastern Carolines and Marshalls. Attention turned to fortifying Central Pacific bases.

- **NOVEMBER–FEBRUARY 1944** Nearly fifty thousand Imperial Japanese Army troops deployed in Carolines and Marshalls (Hezel 1995:225).

- **NOVEMBER–MARCH 1944** Four massive turreted guns removed from cruisers and emplaced on the hill at Sapwuk, Weno, in Chuuk. Difficult gun emplacements also accomplished at Pohnpei (Denfeld 1981a:97; Peattie 1988:264).

- **DECEMBER** Probable completion of Eten airfield, Chuuk (Denfeld 1981a:25).

- Cairo Declaration stated U.S. intention to gain no territory as a result of war, but to strip Japan of its Pacific Island possessions.

- Supply of consumer goods steadily decreased throughout Micronesia. This and other evidence of weakening Japanese position, along with harsh military rule, produced shift in Micronesian attitude toward Japanese.

1943–1944 · By 1943, military personnel were being moved into Pohnpei; that year and next, Japanese weathermen, soldiers, and air force pilots moved to Kapingamarangi to establish a weather station, sea plane base, AA gun emplacements; about fifty military personnel on Kapinga by 1945 (Lieber 1968).

1944

- By the beginning of 1944 throughout Micronesia, public schools closed, mining discontinued, most industries closed (Hezel 1995:226).

- **JANUARY** After U.S. attacked Tarawa, Japanese reorganized army's 52nd Division on Saipan and sent half to Chuuk. They began to arrive in January 1944, building to fourteen thousand troops. With arrival of army came confiscation of local buildings and land and construction of fortifications. Parem airfield completed (Denfeld 1981a:5–17, 134; Morison 1951; Vogel 1948).

- Continual U.S. bombings since mid-November destroyed airbases at Taroa and Mili by the end of January 1944, leaving them with no aircraft and feeble defenses. Installations at Kwajalein, Wotje, and Maloelap devastated.

- **JANUARY 29–FEBRUARY 7** U.S. aerial and surface bombardment, then invasion of Kwajalein Atoll (Kwajalein and Roi-Namur islets) and Majuro Atoll. Simultaneous air attacks on other Marshalls bases.

- **JANUARY–FEBRUARY** During U.S. assault on Marshalls, Japanese rushed defensive construction and deployed troops at Enewetak. U.S. bombed Enewetak constantly from January 31 in preparation for invasion February 19.

- **FEBRUARY** Following U.S. attack, a second large Japanese army detachment arrived at Chuuk. Troops spread over Toloas, Weno, Fefan, Uman, and Tol, confiscating housing and food. Supplies from Japan virtually ceased by early 1944. Air raids continued throughout

1944 and 1945. Vice Admiral Hara arrived at Chuuk a week after
February attack, began rebuilding defenses. Army built tunnels for
living and duty quarters, ammo, airplane bunkers, shelters. Eventual
Chuuk fortifications in 1944: 191 army guns in 86 positions, 85 navy
(AA and coastal defense), 302 automatic weapons (Bartlett 1970:52;
Denfeld 1981a:7, 135; Vogel 1948; USSBS 1947b; Lindemann 1982:115,
123; Vogel 1948).

- American POWs killed in Chuuk in incidents in January (six prisoners), February (two), and July (two), as dealt with in Pacific war
crimes trials (Denfeld 1981a:61; Piccigallo 1979:79).

- **FEBRUARY–APRIL** After U.S. capture of Kwajalein, Majuro, and
Enewetak, remaining Marshalls left isolated; Wotje, Jaluij, Mili, and
Maloelap regularly bombed; ungarrisoned islets taken by Americans
in mop-up through April 1944.

- Shortly after taking Kwajalein, U.S. recruited Marshallese from outer
islands for military work there (Alexander 1978:36).

- **FEBRUARY 4** First U.S. high-altitude photo reconnaissance flight
over Chuuk. Flight alerted Japanese fleet to leave area.

- **FEBRUARY 10** Warships dispersed from Chuuk lagoon, most to
Singapore, some to Palau or Japan. Combined Fleet moved from
Chuuk to Palau.

- **FEBRUARY 10–15** First U.S. air raids on Pohnpei.

- **FEBRUARY 12** Twelve to fourteen Japanese seaplanes sortied from
Pohnpei for effective night raid on new U.S. base at Roi-Namur in
Kwajalein.

- **FEBRUARY 16–26** U.S. retaliated with B-24 raids on Pohnpei from
Tarawa, destroying Kolonia waterfront and town; bombings
continued throughout spring.

- **FEBRUARY 17–18** "Operation Hailstone," air attack on Chuuk,
lasting two days and one night; major losses to Japanese navy and
merchant marine and damage to base.

- **FEBRUARY 16** Arno Atoll (Marshalls) taken peacefully by U.S.
forces.

- **FEBRUARY 17** Bombing of Kosrae began. At some point, Kosraeans abandoned villages and moved to hills.

- **MID-FEBRUARY** Lukunor people relocated to Piafa. Japanese prepared Lukunor for combat, felling trees and eventually dynamiting the cathedral. Satawan developed as an airfield and garrison.

- **FEBRUARY 17–22** American invasion and capture of Enewetak Atoll.

- **FEBRUARY 22** U.S. carrier raid on Marianas. Air raids crippled Japanese air power on Saipan, Tinian, and Rota. Following first U.S. bombings, residents hastened to improve shelter and participate in defense activities.

- **MID-FEBRUARY** All able males drafted to work on defense projects.

- **MID-FEBRUARY–MARCH** Second Japanese airfield built on Pohnpei.

- **FEBRUARY–MARCH** Fall of Marshalls spurred defensive preparations in Marianas. Garapan residents ordered to their farms, and the town taken over by military. Virtually all civilian work stopped, as effort shifted to war preparations. First major troop influx in February 1944; reinforcements continued until a few weeks before invasion. Work on Guam airfields escalated.

- **FEBRUARY–AUGUST 1945** Pohnpei hit with about 250 air strikes.

- **FEBRUARY AND APRIL** Japanese installations on Lukunor and Satawan shelled by Allied destroyers and attacked by air; then bypassed and cut off from resupply.

- **MARCH** Isolated Japanese garrison at Mili received some supplies by submarine; these submarines sunk later that month trying to resupply Wotje.

- Three groups of planes from Mitscher's Task Force 58 struck Koror, Babelthuap, Peleliu, Yap, Woleai, and garrisoned Marshalls on return to Majuro anchorage, extensively damaging Babelthuap.

- Three American fliers killed on Jaluij Atoll (Piccigallo 1979:77).

- Japanese armed forces began to use and destroy Palauan property, beginning on a large scale from March 1944 through surrender, contracting with Palau chiefs to repay at end of war (Useem 1946a).

- **MARCH 4** Japanese army returned to Guam in force.

- **MARCH 8** More army troops arrived at Chuuk, placed in western lagoon.

- **MARCH 15–SEPTEMBER 15** Continual aerial bombardment of Chuuk by 7th and 13th AAF, targeting Toloas, Eten, Weno, Parem. First attack was night mission with twenty-two planes; large fuel tank on Toloas exploded. Then intensive day and night raids through March 29. B-24s from 7th and 13th AAF hit Chuuk regularly to October 1944. From February to September 1944, more than 4,000 tons of bombs dropped on Chuuk (Craven 1950; Denfeld 1981a: 37–41; USSBS 1947b).

- **MARCH 26** Undefended Pulusuk bombed when U.S. planes flying to support March 30 raid on Palau had too little gas to reach intended targets on Chuuk.

- **MARCH 31–APRIL 1** Two-day carrier air raid on Palau destroyed airport under construction at Airai; also, attacks on Yap, Woleai, and Ulithi.

- **APRIL** Palau reinforced; defensive preparations begun. Chuuk cut off from Japan due to bombing and U.S. attack on Marianas.

- **APRIL 6–7** Major B-24 raids on Chuuk destroyed aircraft and Toloas town; carrier raid destroyed additional planes; night attacks continued through June; almost without a break during April, 7th AF bombers hit Chuuk from Kwajalein, coordinating with Liberators from Solomons, dropping 160 tons of bombs on Weno, Parem, and Toloas April 5–12 (Howard and Whitley 1946:20; Peattie 1988:276–277).

- **APRIL 13–14** Second major air attack on Chuuk lagoon; two night waves and predawn formation of 7th and 13th AF bombers from Kwajalein (Howard and Whitley 1946:207).

- **SPRING–SUMMER** Concentrated American bombing of garrisoned islands of Micronesia.

- **APRIL–MAY** Last chance for some old men, women, and children to leave Saipan; more than three thousand left before mid-June, risking U.S. attack en route (Sheeks 1945:110).

- **APRIL–JUNE** Woleai garrisoned with seven thousand troops and developed as major base in April; at same time, U.S. carrier and land-based bombing attacks began; daily B-24 raids for fifteen months. By mid-June garrison's supplies were already stressed; mortality began to climb (Boyer 1967:727–728; Peattie 1988:306).

- **APRIL 30–MAY 1** Two-day U.S. Navy carrier air raid on Chuuk, followed by naval bombardment of Pohnpei.

- **APRIL–JUNE** U.S. Marines took control of ungarrisoned Marshall Islands.

- **MAY** Air strikes on Chuuk declined, letting Japanese repair airfields as Allies concentrated on Marianas. Japanese transferred seventy-one Chuuk aircraft to Yap and Guam. Air raids on Chuuk on May 10 (Toloas, Eten) and 21 (Parem, Weno) by 13th AAF; less frequent attacks by 7th AAF (no missions May 13–31); Allies resumed bombing Chuuk at end of month (Denfeld 1981a:36,43; Lindemann 1982:116).

- Japanese army company on Lukunor moved to Satawan; replaced on Lukunor by five-hundred-man battalion and one hundred navy men, coming from lagoon with no food (Borthwick 1977:58).

- Last ship to Palau from Japan, the *Osaka-maru,* was torpedoed.

- U.S. battleships shelled Pohnpei for over an hour (target practice) (Peattie 1988:279).

- **MAY 30** Puluwat bombed by U.S. planes.

- **MAY–AUGUST** Last Japanese supply ships reached Chuuk.

- Blockaded Japanese garrisons began to suffer as food stocks ran out. Rationing of food and fuel began in early 1944 on Chuuk; by late 1944, troops on Mili faced starvation.

- In the American-occupied Marshall Islands, U.S. Military Government established some thirty trading outlets (Mason 1946:31; Chave 1950:66).

- **JUNE OR JULY** Incendiary bomb dropped on Murilo, destroying part of aircraft spotter station and killing two Micronesians (Witherspoon 1945).

- **JUNE** Renewed intensive bombing of Chuuk lagoon daily throughout June; 1,813 tons of bombs total (Denfeld 1981a:43; USSBS 1947b).

Chronology of World War II in Micronesia **379**

- Chuuk airfields not neutralized; used in attacks on Saipan Harbor in mid-June and early July (Denfeld 1981a:45).

- **JUNE 18–19** Battle of the Philippine Sea destroyed most of remaining Japanese air power.

- **MID-JUNE** Japanese troops relocated from Mortlocks to smaller Chuuk islands (USSBS 1947b).

- On Guam, labor gangs of local people no longer dismissed at night but moved together to temporary camps inland (Apple 1980:40).

- **JUNE 10–15** Total of 727 Micronesians escaped from Wotje Atoll, evacuated to Arno by U.S. Navy (Cockrum 1970:218).

- **JUNE 15** Invasion of Saipan (after bombardment beginning June 11). Beachhead secured by June 17, and on July 9 Saipan was declared secure, though many Japanese troops remained.

- **JULY** U.S. attacks on Chuuk at rate of three to five times/week (Denfeld 1981a:45).

- **AROUND JULY** By summer 1944, foodstuffs and medicine in perilously low supply on bypassed island garrisons (Peattie 1988:303–304). Officers, men, and civilians formed into groups, given land to grow their own food.

- **JULY 18** Tojo and his cabinet replaced.

- **JULY 21** U.S. invasion of Guam (preinvasion bombardment began July 8). Fighting continued through August 10. Seabees and Navy Civil Affairs unit came ashore on the heels of Marines. Guam turned into U.S. Navy base.

- **JULY 24** U.S. invasion of Tinian; organized resistence ended July 31.

- **JULY 24–27** U.S. attack on Ulithi.

- **LATE SUMMER** Japan decided to pull back to Philippines, making Palau expendable. After July 1944, Palau received no supplies or reinforcements.

- **AUGUST–OCTOBER** Chuuk hit by B-24 bombing raids about twice a week in August (Denfeld 1981a:45). Japanese army began day and night work to dig caves and tunnels. Troops moved to live in or near caves and tunnels.

- **AUGUST 10** Japanese forces on Guam surrendered. Later that month, Guamanians in refugee camps (eighteen thousand at peak) began to move to ranches (Apple 1980:63).

- **AUGUST 18** U.S. reconnaissance mission search team landed at Gagil-Tamil area of Yap (Denfeld 1988:6).

- **LATE AUGUST–SEPTEMBER** Regular B-24 attacks on Koror and Babelthuap.

- **SEPTEMBER** U.S. attacked Chuuk irregularly as it appeared to be neutralized (Denfeld 1981a:45).

- After U.S. took Palau, the Nan'yō-chō administrative center moved back to Chuuk.

- **SUMMER–FALL** Bypassed Japanese bases continued to be bombed by U.S. Army Air Force: Jaluij, Mili, Wotje, Maloelap, Pohnpei, Chuuk, Kosrae, Woleai, Puluwat, Satawan.

- **SEPTEMBER 16–NOVEMBER** American invasion of Peleliu and Angaur. Battle on Angaur lasted approximately three days; Peleliu battle until November 25. Palau remained split between Japanese and American rule until September 1945.

- **SEPTEMBER 20–21** Unopposed occupation of Ulithi by American troops.

- **OCTOBER** High-altitude B-29s began bombing raids from U.S. airfields in Marianas, including experimental and training raids on Chuuk through July 1945.

- **AUTUMN** Food stress on bypassed high islands; little livestock, indigenous food became scarce; malnutrition began, starvation in some places (Peattie 1988:300).

- **OCTOBER 23–27** Japanese navy fought its last major battle near Leyte in the central Philippines.

- **NOVEMBER** Japanese troops on Lukunor left for Chuuk lagoon; people briefly returned to Lukunor until March 1945 (Borthwick 1977:59).

- U.S. Military Government units set up on Pula Anna and Kayangel (PCAA 1978:446).

- B-29s from U.S. base in Saipan conducted first mass bombing raids over Japan.

- Chamorros and Carolinians on Saipan moved to village built at Chalan Kanoa, where they remained until July 4, 1946.

- U.S. established camp at Angaur for Peleliu and Angaur people and escapees from Babelthuap.

- **DECEMBER** U.S. asked Japanese on Maloelap for truce to remove Marshallese, but received no answer (Cockrum 1970:219).

- Group of 116 Chamorros escaped from Babelthuap, describing near-starvation conditions there. Joseph Tellei, highest-ranking Palauan in Japanese government, paddled to American lines. Japanese began to patrol beaches to keep Palauans from fleeing. Captain Yoshiyasu Morikawa assigned to relate to Palauans; organized Patriotic Shock Troops of eighty Palauan men. By late 1944 nearly all Palauans evacuated to Babelthuap (Cockrum 1970:284; Hezel 1995:238–239; Vidich 1980:261; Nero 1989:120–122).

1945
- Supervision of trading outlets in the Marshalls was turned over to USCC, which began to turn stores into co-ops. USCC was given business monopoly in the territory (Mason 1946:31; Hezel 1995:266–267).

- By end of the year, commissioned MilGov units were in place on Koror, Saipan, Tinian, Yap, and Chuuk. Others soon followed on Pohnpei, Kwajalein (for the northern Marshalls), and Majuro (for the southern Marshalls) (PCAA 1978:449–450).

- **JANUARY** Emaciated Japanese troops from Puluwat (Enderby) arrived at Chuuk.

- Last Japanese garrison in Micronesia to go down fighting—eight navy men killed defending Fais Island, southeast of Ulithi (Peattie 1988:297).

- **JANUARY 11** U.S. fleet conducted maneuvers off Maloelap and in next four days, 462 (all but 20) Marshallese escaped to LCIs (Cockrum 1970:219).

- **FEBRUARY 19** U.S. invasion of Iwo Jima, staged from Saipan.

- **MARCH** Japanese army troops numbering 150 landed on Lukunor, again forcing people back to Piafa and to producing food for Japanese (Borthwick 1977:59).

- **APRIL** Marshallese evacuated from Mili Atoll.

- **APRIL 8** U.S. invaded Okinawa.

- **APRIL–MAY** Two weeks of B-24 bombings in April–May 1945 by 7th AF. This was the last major raid on Chuuk, though B-29 runs continued (Denfeld 1981a:49–51).

- **APRIL–OCTOBER** Civilian and military workers in the Mortlocks sent 10 tons of taro to Satawan garrison every three weeks (Borthwick 1977:59).

- **MAY** Pulo Anna residents relocated to Angaur camp (Yarbrough 1971:190).

- **JUNE 14–15, 16–17** Final attack on Chuuk was training mission for British Pacific fleet; day and night air attacks plus naval bombardment. Little damage, but destroyed records and caused Japanese (fearing invasion) to burn remaining files (Denfeld 1981a:46–48; Lindemann 1987).

- **JUNE 26** United Nations Charter signed; first meeting January 10, 1946.

- **AUGUST 6** *Enola Gay* took off from U.S. base in Tinian to drop atomic bomb on Hiroshima.

- **AUGUST 9** Atomic bomb dropped on Nagasaki.

- **AUGUST 15** Cease-fire, as Japan accepted surrender.

- **AUGUST 22** Mili first bypassed area to surrender.

- **AUGUST 30** Americans arrived at Chuuk to accept Japanese cease-fire; formal surrender delayed until after imperial surrender September 2, 1945.

- **SEPTEMBER** Northern Marianas Chamorros moved to Saipan for food and medical care; fifty-seven Guamanians and thirty-one Rotanese sent home (Cockrum 1970:336).

- SCAP HQ in Tokyo established as the principal U.S. war crimes agency in the Far East (Piccigallo 1979:40).

- Americans entered Koror, Palau, and began demobilizing and repatriating Japanese (Vidich 1980:268).

- **SEPTEMBER 2** General MacArthur accepted surrender of all Japanese forces on USS *Missouri*.

- **SEPTEMBER 2** Surrender of Japanese forces in Micronesia, including surrender of nearly forty-five thousand Japanese military in Palau area on U.s. ship off Airai; surrender of all remaining Japanese forces in Micronesia at Chuuk. U.S. Navy MilGov established control of Micronesia (Higuchi 1987:15; Blackton 1946; Nero 1989:122; Richard 1957b; Cockrum 1971:317; Bailey 1989:59).

- **SEPTEMBER 2** U.S. Navy MilGov moved onto Chuuk. At time of surrender, Chuuk held 38,354 Japanese: 14,294 army, 9,841 navy, 14,219 naval construction workers, 1,590 civilians; also 9,082 Chuukese, 791 Nauruans, 8 Germans, 7 Spanish, 6 Chinese (Denfeld 1981a:53, Pillsbury 1948:854).

- **SEPTEMBER 6** Jaluij, Wotje, and Maloelap surrendered.

- **SEPTEMBER 6** Japanese on Pohnpei received instructions for surrender proceedings aboard the USS *Hyman;* surrender was September 11, with Americans landing September 17 (Denfeld 1979:36; Cockrum 1971:316; Higuchi 1987).

- **SEPTEMBER 8** Kosrae surrendered.

- **SEPTEMBER 16 and 17** Lamotrek, western Carolines, and Namoluk, central Carolines, surrendered.

- **SEPTEMBER–OCTOBER** U.S. Navy units visited small eastern, central, and western Caroline Islands, leaving Guam September 18 with three Japanese, to announce surrender and assess conditions (Witherspoon 1945; Kneubuhl 1946).

- **SEPTEMBER 19** Woleai, western Carolines, surrendered. Some 1,600 desperate survivors of 7,000-man garrison were first Japanese repatriated from Micronesia (Peattie 1988:305–306).

- **OCTOBER** Repatriation of Japanese, Okinawans, and Koreans began on Chuuk with 2,500 prisoners kept for labor; final repatriation was December 27, 1947 (Denfeld 1981a:54).

- U.S. Navy returned displaced Marshallese: 292 returned to Maloelap; 330 to Wotje; 90 to Ailinglablab; 121 to Mili (Cockrum 1971:333–334).

- **OCTOBER 2–5** USS *Columbia* arrived for first U.S. landing and official inspection of Chuuk (Toloas and Weno) (Denfeld 1981a:54; Richard 1957b:6–17).

- **OCTOBER 6–21** Surrenders of small islands: Tobi, Sonsorol, Merir in western Carolines; Puluwat and Nomoi in central Carolines.

- **OCTOBER 9** Group of Pohnpeians sent to work on Kosrae returned home (Cockrum 1971).

- **OCTOBER–NOVEMBER** Evacuation of Japanese from Pohnpei, Chuuk, and Palau began. Japanese removed from Pagan, Puluwat, Nomoi, Namoluk, Tobi, Sonsorol. Repatriation of Micronesians throughout region, such as 76 Chamorros sent home to Saipan from Pohnpei. U.S. evacuated 14,066 Japanese from Pohnpei (nearly 8,000 military) (Bascom 1950; Murrill 1950:186; Cockrum 1971:323; Peattie 1988:309).

- **NOVEMBER** Japanese military personnel on Lukunor moved to Satawan where they surrendered and were repatriated; Lukunor people returned from Piafa to find island much destroyed (Borthwick 1977:59, 150).

- Further repatriation in the Marshalls, as displaced Islanders were moved to and from newly surrendered atolls; all Marshallese repatriated by fall 1945 (Cockrum 1971:333–334).

- U.S. Navy Seabees arrived at Weno (Chuuk), began airstrip, administrative area, roads, camp, electrical and water systems, with Japanese military doing much of work (Denfeld 1981a:55).

- USSBS on Chuuk for twelve-day visit (Bartlett 1970:49).

- **NOVEMBER 5** First evacuation ships from Kosrae left with Japanese. Kosrae's 1945 population was 7,041; 4,523 were Japanese or Korean and 976 were other Pacific Islanders (Cockrum 1971:323).

- **NOVEMBER 24–25** Official U.S. occupation of Chuuk, with flag raising on Weno (Denfeld 1981a:54; Richard 1957b:7; Cockrum 1971:317)

- **NOVEMBER 25** Eight hundred Kiribati, Tuvalu, and Banaba people on Kosrae sent to Tarawa on British ship; four hundred Mokilese and Pingelapese on Pohnpei repatriated (Hezel 1995:249; Cockrum 1971).

- **DECEMBER** Official representatives presented Palauans' claim for property destruction to Japanese military governor of Palau, who acknowledged the debt (Useem 1946a).

- First evacuation ships left Yap with Japanese (Cockrum 1971:323).

- Fano islet off Weno (Chuuk) cleared of residents; became site of U.S. recreation center (Denfeld 1981a:58).

- Artie Moses of Uman became first chief of Chuuk lagoon under American rule (Denfeld 1981a:59).

- By the end of December, all Japanese had been removed from Marshalls-Kiribati area (Cockrum 1971:324).

- **DECEMBER 1** Holdouts on Saipan surrendered—the last Japanese fighting men in the Nan'yō to lay down their arms (Peattie 1988:310).

1946
- U.S. Commercial Company research project, surveying Micronesian postwar economic status.

- Guam's wartime military government reverted to naval government much like prewar. Civilian economy expanded. Agana rebuilt.

- First migration of Chamorros from Yap back to Marianas (Spoehr 1951:18).

- **JANUARY** Palauan official native representatives resubmitted war claims to Japanese and were told to return at end of February; then told to file with U.S. MilGov (Useem 1946a:03).

- U.S. Navy MilGov hospital and training center established; young Micronesians began training as nurses and health aides (Hezel 1995:261).

- Civilian repatriation continues: A few Marshallese on Chuuk returned home; about a hundred Chuukese repatriated from Pohnpei and Kosrae, ten from Palau; Yapese returned from Pohnpei, Kosrae, and

Saipan; Ulithi and Ifaluk people from Yap; two hundred Woleai people who had escaped bombing by fleeing to Ifaluk (Richard 1957b:49; Cockrum 1971; Cockrum 1970:336).

- Nauruan survivors on Chuuk boarded MV *Trienza* for trip home (Denfeld 1981a:30; Richard 1957b:50).

- **JANUARY 24** Joint Chiefs of Staff announced selection of Bikini Atoll as the site for the experimental explosion of atomic bombs (Baron 1973:178). By 1958 sixty-six atomic and hydrogen bombs detonated in Marshalls (Hezel 1995: 273).

- **MARCH 6** At request of U.S. atomic weapons testing program, Marshallese left Bikini Atoll for Rongrik.

- **EARLY 1946** Palau's district chiefs met to discuss return to indigenous feasting and dance customs and use of traditional currency (Hezel 1995:277).

- **APRIL** First U.S. plane landed at Moen #1 airport (Weno, Chuuk) (King and Carucci 1984:473).

- School of Naval Administration opened at Hoover Institute, Stanford University.

- **SPRING** Atoll commands instituted on Palau and Chuuk after American occupation forces were removed. Pohnpei and Kosrae remained under the Chuuk commander (PCAA 1978:454; Richard 1957b:99).

- **MAY** U.S. authorized repatriation of all Okinawans.

- **SPRING AND SUMMER** Japanese, Koreans, and Okinawans repatriated from the Marianas.

- **JULY** Two atomic bombs exploded at Bikini.

- Leper colony opened on Sala Island, Chuuk (Denfeld 1981a:58).

- Plans for a representative form of government discussed in a meeting of Palauan chiefs (Vidich 1980:278).

- **JULY 4** Populations released from civilian camps in the Marianas.

- **AUGUST** U.S. Navy lifted ban on foreign (U.S.) missionaries, and they began to return to the islands.

- **SEPTEMBER** USS *Orca* visited Mokil Atoll to proclaim U.S. MilGov and leave supplies (Bentzen 1949:35–36).

- **OCTOBER** MilGov unit in Chuuk established first of several Land Claims Commissions.

- Tomeing, Radak *iroij* (chief) during war, died in Marshalls (Mason 1946:91).

- **FALL** Ulithi Atoll command dissolved and the U.S. Coast Guard took over (PCAA 1978:454).

- **DECEMBER** After delays to allow them to aid in rehabilitation and cleanup work, last of Japanese troops left for home from Palau, Yap, and Chuuk (Hezel 1995:249).

1947
- Four Palauans and one Chamorro repatriated from Borneo (Cockrum 1971:336).

- Island constabulary established (Hezel 1995:261).

- Co-ordinated Investigation of Micronesian Anthropology (CIMA) research project began, ran through 1949.

- Marianas Area Teacher Training School opened in Guam (Hezel 1995:261).

- **APRIL** United Nations approved strategic Trust Territory of the Pacific Islands, administered by the United States.

- **MAY** Washington officials issued directive to establish municipalities, urging elections before end of year; set head taxes and business license fees.

- **MAY 1** Repatriation at U.S. expense until this date (Cockrum 1970:336).

- **JULY** Palauans established district-wide government (Hezel 1995:280).

- **JULY 18** U.S. Military Government ends, and U.S. Navy Civil Administration begins (runs until June 30, 1951), as, by the agreement of the U.N. Security Council and the U.S. Congress, the United States officially takes control of the new Trust Territory of the Pacific Islands (TTPI).

- **OCTOBER** First elections held under U.S. rule: results confirmed traditional leaders, but let people eliminate Japanese-appointed chiefs (Hezel 1995:278–279).

- **DECEMBER** Last Japanese repatriated from Micronesia (POWs held to work for occupation authorities on Saipan) (Peattie 1988:310).

- **DECEMBER 2** U.S. government closed Enewetak for security reasons, to use it as nuclear test site (Baron 1973:202).

- U.S. reorganized hierarchy of Chuukese officials and introduced secret elections for chiefs (Gladwin and Sarason 1953:67–68).

1948
- Token U.S. forces left Tarawa and Butaritari (Maude and Doran 1966:287).

- Bikinians relocated again, this time to Kili; resettled Bikinians and Enewetak people (now on Ujelang) began negotiations with U.S. government and Marshallese government that continue to present.

- U.S. Atomic Energy Commission began nuclear weapons test series at Enewetak, continued through 1952 (Baron 1973:202).

- **JANUARY** The Island Trading Company, under navy direction, took over from the U.S. Commercial Company (Moore 1948:78). Regional trading companies replaced USCC: Chuuk Trading Company (January 1948); Pohnpei Cooperative Company and Western Carolines Trading Company (1948), Kwajalein Importing and Trading Company and Majuro Trading Association (1950), Marshall Islands Importing and Exporting Company and Yap Trading Company (1951): "These . . . became the backbone of island commerce for the next twenty years"(Hezel 1995:268).

- **AUGUST** Navy moved district center of Marshall Islands from Kwajalein to Majuro (Hezel 1995:275).

- **APRIL** A second group of Chamorros moved from Yap to Tinian.

1949
- Scientific Investigation of Micronesia (SIM) research project.

- **MAY 21** Pacific war crimes trials ended (Piccigallo 1979:82).

- **OCTOBER** Native Trading Company goes out of business (Richard 1957c).

- Administrative headquarters for Micronesia moved from Guam to Hawai'i.

1949–1950 • Dangerous explosives in Micronesia resurveyed (Cockrum 1971:393).

- U.S. administration called for creation of district congresses; Marshalls Congress begins; others several years later.

1950 • **JUNE** Field headquarters of high commissioner of the Trust Territory moved to Chuuk (Richard 1957c:19).

- **AUGUST 1** Organic Act made Guam a territory of the United States and shifted its administration from the navy to the Department of the Interior; Guamanians became U.S. citizens. Navy retained security clearance system controlling civilian travel. Organic Act took effect retroactively on July 21, Liberation Day.

1951 • Marshallese on Kwajalein islet relocated to Ebeye islet, beginning decades of tension between Marshallese people and the U.S. Army over compensation and treatment of local workers and landowners.

- **JULY 1** Administration of Trust Territory shifted from the navy to the Department of the Interior. Navy CivAd ended.

1953 • **JANUARY** Jurisdiction over Saipan and Tinian transferred from Department of the Interior back to the navy for strategic reasons; other Northern Marianas except Rota added to navy governance in July 1953.

1954 • Trust Territory government moved from Honolulu to Guam.

- Hydrogen bomb testing at Ronglap.

1959 • Kwajalein became part of the Pacific Missile Range.

1962 • Under Kennedy administration, new activist policy in Micronesia: Congress doubled appropriations; Peace Corps brought the first non-Micronesians to live locally since the Japanese era; revisions in education system; faster movement toward elective democratic structures; travel permitted throughout islands.

- **JULY** Those Marianas under navy control returned to Interior Department; Trust Territory headquarters moved to Saipan.

1965 • **JULY** Territory-wide Congress of Micronesia met for first time.

1969
- First settlement of World War II financial compensation claims (Cockrum 1971: 437–522).

- Micronesian congressmen began negotiations that eventually led to end of TTPI (Hezel 1995: 331–363).

1978
- Congress of Micronesia dissolved itself; next several years saw creation of governments of new nations and territories of Micronesia.

NOTES

CHAPTER 1. WAR IN THE JAPANESE MANDATED ISLANDS OF MICRONESIA: AN INTRODUCTION

1. This translates the Pohnpeian phrase, *"keieu apwal."* Similar terms reflecting the hardship and suffering of the war years are found throughout Micronesia. The image of war as a typhoon is less often explicit, but it reflects the common representation of war as an impersonal destructive force. Like a typhoon, war arises, it covers the islands, devastating land, people, and crops, and passes on, leaving a distressed population to rebuild their lives from the wreckage.

2. We use modern spellings of names for islands and new nations, which more accurately reflect local pronunciation and meaning. The list of "Island Names" correlates text spellings with those common in English-language documents of the World War II era. It also identifies current official names.

3. Researchers who have explored the war era include Dirk Ballendorf, Don Farrell, Francis X. Hezel, SJ, Wakako Higuchi, Mark Peattie, David Purcell, and Don Shuster; their work and that of others is cited throughout this book. Those working with World War II materials elsewhere in the Pacific include Geoffrey White and Lamont Lindstrom (cited in the Preface), as well as Islander and Australian researchers in the Central and Southwest Pacific (cited in the text).

4. We used the same set of open-ended questions for each interview, with two modifications. Wartime experiences for each region required some additional specific inquiries (for example, about U.S. invasion in Kwajalein or Enewetak), and the order and phrasing of questions was tailored to each speaker in the course of the interview. Interviews were conducted in the local language (with the exception of a small set of interviews with Micronesians fluent in English), by us or by Micronesian assistants, with subsequent translation by local translators or one of the authors. Carucci trans-

lated most of the Marshall Islands interviews; Falgout and assistants (listed in Appendix A) translated the Pohnpei interviews; those from Kosrae, Chuuk, Yap, and other Caroline Islands were translated by assistants listed under the appropriate area.

5. Hezel (1983, 1995) provides the most comprehensive history of the Caroline and Marshall Islands. For Northern Mariana Islands history, see Farrell (1991); for Guam, Carano and Sanchez (1964), and Rogers (1995). Hiery (1995) discusses the transition from German to Japanese rule in Micronesia. Peattie (1988) is a comprehensive study of the Japanese administration of Micronesia.

6. A growing body of literature by historians and anthropologists describes Melanesian experiences in World War II. White and Lindstrom (1989) and White (1991) include articles on the war in Melanesia (as well as Micronesia and Polynesia) and are good starting points for exploring the literature; Lindstrom and White (1990) discusses impacts of the war throughout the Pacific.

CHAPTER 2. BEFORE THE WAR: ISLANDER LIFE IN THE JAPANESE MANDATE

1. The invaluable resource for Japanese colonial rule in Micronesia is Mark Peattie's *Nan'yō: The Rise and Fall of the Japanese in Micronesia, 1885–1945* (1988; esp. pp. 62–229; pp. 64–68 describe the initial period of naval administration). See also Hatanaka (1973–1974, 1977), Hezel (1995), Hiery (1995:130–153; 252–254), Peattie (1984a), and Purcell (1976) on prewar life in the mandate. Articles in Myers and Peattie (1984) describe the broader context of the Japanese empire. U.S. Navy Civil Affairs Handbooks (U.S. Navy 1943, 1944a, b, c) and Co-ordinated Investigation of Micronesian Anthropology (CIMA) reports provide detailed descriptions for each area of Micronesia. Here, we focus on aspects of prewar life that were to prove significant during wartime. We follow Peattie's (1988:xvii–xviii) use of the term *Nan'yō* ("South Seas") as shorthand for the Japanese mandated territories.

2. See Peattie (1988:73–74) on Nan'yō-chō colonial police. Chen (1984) describes the role of police throughout the Japanese Empire and in particular notes the degree of their involvement in low-level administrative work. In 1936, Nan'yō police spent more than 13 percent of their time on general administrative tasks. In decreasing order of time spent, these were road building, taxation, harbor survey, animal husbandry, training and supervision of youth corps, forestry, labor supply, and agricultural matters (Chen 1984:234–235).

3. On Nan'yō policy toward traditional leaders, see Peattie (1988:75–76); on 1922 separation of chief's functions, Hatanaka (1973–1974); on Pohnpei honor feasts, Bas-

com (1948:212); on Palau, Force (1960:72–73) and Vidich (1980:196–198); on the Mortlocks, Nason (1970:220); on Namoluk, Marshall (1972:36, n.22); on linking leadership to wealth, Hatanaka (1967).

4. For details on Japanese economic development of the mandate, see Peattie (1988: 153–197), Nakajima (1990), Nishi (1968), and Purcell (1976); also U.S. Navy and Trust Territory Handbooks and CIMA and United States Commercial Company (USCC) reports for each region.

5. See Kodama (n.d.) on immigrants. Okinawans were thought of as "well-adapted to the South Seas island life"—which was just as well; since agricultural laborers had to pay their own way back, many brought their families and stayed (9, 12). Of the immigrants, it seems that Okinawans settled in most firmly; they predominated among those who wanted to stay in the islands after the war (Cockrum 1970:327).

6. On these 1930s developments in Saipan, Tinian, and Rota, see Bowers (1950:45, 83–84), Gallahue (1946), Peattie (1988:161–169), Spoehr (1954:86–87), and U.S. Navy (1944a). Tinian's native inhabitants—numbering about ninety-five—had been moved to Saipan after Japan took control in 1914 (Bowers 1950:84).

7. On the problems of rural Japanese immigration to Palau, see Peattie (1988:170–174). On Palau's prewar economy, see Abe (1986), Barnett (1949), Bowers (1950:96), Ehrlich (1984), Peattie (1988:170–176), Useem (1946a:13–16), and Vidich (1980).

8. Details on Pohnpei's prewar economy and life are found in Bascom (1949, 1965), Fischer (1957:59–62), Hanlon (1981), Murphy (1949:434), Peattie (1988:176–180), and Peoples (1977:146).

9. Population figures are from Bascom (1950:144, 1965:12). On exhausting Pohnpeians' land, see Bascom (1965:131). Bascom suspected a Japanese effort to subdue or even supplant the indigenous population on Pohnpei (Bascom 1950:144–145). Postwar American researchers took a similar charge seriously enough to investigate it on Yap. Hunt et al. (1949) concluded that Japanese health care makes it unlikely that they were trying to wipe out the Yapese (but see Labby 1973:33). Several of our interviews mentioned fear of Japanese intentions to take Micronesia from Islanders.

10. Information on Kosrae is from Peoples (1977:142–147; 1985:55–58) and Kodama (n.d.:17).

11. On Chuuk, see Peattie (1988:182–184), Gladwin and Sarason (1953:43), and Young et al. (1997:27–34).

12. These points about Yap's prewar economy are found in Labby (1973:32, 1976), Lingenfelter (1975:186), Peattie (1988:180–182), and Useem (1946a:27–28, 36–40).

13. Information on the prewar Marshalls is from Bryan (1972:210–211), Mason (1946:89, 95–98), Pollock (n.d.:37), Poyer (1997:22–25), and Tobin (1970).

14. On Satawan, see Nason (1970:210); on Kapinga people on Pohnpei, Lieber

(1968:29). A single energetic Japanese official could have a great impact on an atoll, as in the case of Mokil's permanent Japanese resident, who served as "schoolteacher, trader, and dentist" (Murphy 1949:433); or Yoshino, a Japanese commercial agent on Tobi in the 1920s, who "exerted a great deal of influence in the affairs of the island" (Black 1977:113–114). For descriptions of prewar life on small islands, see Lessa (1950:15) on Ulithi Atoll, Tolerton and Rauch (1949:21–22) on the Nomoi Islands, and Kneubuhl (1946:18) and Borthwick (1977:52–53) on Lukunor and Satawan, which became small regional centers with schools, stores, a court, and a jail. Atolls also felt the impact of land tenure changes experienced on large islands, where foreign control of land accompanied economic development, as described by Nason (1970:375) for Etal in the Mortlock Islands.

15. Other sources describing contract labor include Yanaihara (1938); for Yap, Useem (1946a:45); for the Chuuk area, Borthwick (1977:152), Dolan (1974:71–72), King and Parker (1984:103), Nason (1970:217), Reafsnyder (1984:102), and Tolerton and Rauch (1949:163).

16. On *kumi* in Kosrae, see Lewis (1948a:70–71), Peoples (1977:152–153); on Yap, Useem (1946a:7, 72–73). The Kumiai Association (Producers' Union) established by pro-Japanese Palauans in 1935 to increase agricultural production and marketing was used during the war to ensure that produce came onto the market—so what had been started to aid producers later came to be resented by them (Vidich 1980:260–261). In other areas of Micronesia such as Kosrae and Pohnpei, cooperative work groups stimulated during Japanese times persisted into the American era (Fischer 1957:156).

17. Goh Abe found that former Japanese colonial officials whom he interviewed in the 1970s and 1980s "showed a prevalent bias or prejudice toward Micronesians, feeling that they were incapable of advancing toward 'civilization' because of 'innate inferiority,'" as the interviewees said (Abe 1986:24, 151).

18. In Kodama's view (n.d.:37), much of prewar Japanese impact is better thought of as a continuation of an ongoing process of "Westernization" rather than as "Japanization."

19. Peattie (1988:90–96) explains "practical education" and the segregated Japanese colonial education system. Descriptions of Japanese education in Micronesia are also found in Anttila (1965), Ballendorf, Peck, and Anderson (1986), Ballendorf, Shuster, and Higuchi (1986), Heath (1975), Hezel (1995:153, 172–173), Ramarui (1976), Shuster (1979, 1982a), and Yanaihara (1938). Fischer (1961) explores the intersection of Chuukese values and Japanese schooling, including how educated Chuukese formed ties with Japanese.

20. On patriotic schooling, see Peattie (1988:105, 1984b) and sources on Japanese education. Despite a consistent educational policy, schools in urban areas got more at-

tention than those on isolated islands. John Kneubuhl, who visited Etal at war's end, comments: "In most of the atolls, neglect is a better way to describe Japanese-native relations than saying that the Japanese wisely let the natives run their own affairs"; "The Japanese in Etal as well as elsewhere did surprisingly little propagandizing; even the school at Lukunor seemed to have been free from any political policy" (Kneubuhl 1949:20).

21. On Lukunor, see Borthwick (1977:49–50); on Yap, Labby (1976) and Lingenfelter (1975).

22. On Islanders participating at Shinto temples, see D. F. Smith (1946) and Peattie (1988:106). Keesing (1945:289) indicates that in Palau about five hundred became Buddhists and one hundred Tenrikyo Shintoists. Shuster (1982a:85) gives a figure of some six hundred Palauan Buddhists from government records, but "the conversion was superficial" (87). Shuster (1982b) is a thorough discussion of religion, especially the penetration of State Shinto in Japanese Micronesia.

23. On Modekngei, see in addition Abe (1986), Aoyagi (1978), Shuster (1982a, b), and Yarbrough (1971).

24. The Japanese in charge also recalled good personal relations. Former colonial officials interviewed by Goh Abe spoke warmly of Micronesians, were welcomed back when they returned thirty years later, and said that "We administered with affection beyond the formalized rules of the administration" (Abe 1986:179)—for example, providing liquor when a project was done, although that was illegal.

CHAPTER 3. THE FIRST PHASE OF WAR PREPARATIONS: SPRINGBOARDS FOR JAPANESE EXPANSION

1. Most of the islands of Micronesia lie west of the international date line, which explains the December 8 date for the Pearl Harbor attack.

2. We treat events in Kiribati, Nauru, and Banaba only briefly here. Standard military sources cover Japanese and American strategy and actions. Information about Micronesian impacts and responses can be found in Crowl and Love (1955), Garrett (1996), Highland (1991), Howard and Whitley (1946), Lundstrom (1976:141–159), Mamara and Kaiuea (1979:128–146), Maude and Doran (1966:286–287), Morison (1950: 235–241, 1951:76–77, 83), Petit-Skinner (1981:25–28), Pollock (1991), and Viviani (1970: 77–87). Allied response to the Japanese fortification of Kiribati was occupation of Funafuti Atoll in Tuvalu (Ellice Islands) in October 1942, preparing an anchorage in the lagoon and building an airfield. Nanumea and Nukufetau also held Allied airfields (Morison 1951:73, map 78–79).

3. A description of the raid—by the 2d Marine Raider Battalion led by Lt. Col. E. F. Carlson—from the Kiribati viewpoint is in Mamara and Kaiuea (1979:132–133); this source indicates that Japanese retaliation bombing aimed at Butaritari village mistakenly hit Keuea, killing forty-one Kiribati people and injuring twelve.

4. We include here only a very brief summary of wartime events on Guam. For detailed descriptions of the Japanese invasion and occupation of Guam, including recollections of survivors, see Apple (1980), Beardsley (1964), Carano and Sanchez (1964), Eads (1978), Hough (1947), Owings (1981), Palomo (1984), Rogers (1995), Sanchez (1983), and Sullivan (1957:150–178).

5. On Ellis' trip and intelligence efforts, see Ballendorf (1983, 1984a), Gailey (1983:5), Peattie (1988:237–247), and Ronck (1983). Levi (1948) and Pomeroy (1948) review U.S. military policy in response to Japanese takeover of the area after World War I. Western visitors' observations about the region varied. R. V. C. Bodley (1934) insisted that there were no signs of war preparation during his visits. Paul Clyde traveled throughout the region in 1934 as a guest of the Japanese government and discusses international politics and the question of fortifications with conclusions favorable to Japan (1935:155–224). Compare Willard Price's 1936 description of his prewar visit, which is rather laudatory of the Japanese colonial order, with his later book based on the same trip (1944a), and with Price (1944b), an anti-Japanese view of the Bonins and Saipan based on the same prewar visit (Stephen n.d.:6).

6. On protomilitary and military construction in western Micronesia, see Ehrlich (1984), Farrell (1991), Gailey (1983:6), Peattie (1988:248–249), Russell (1984:79), Wilds (1955), and Yarbrough (1971). For Chuuk and the central Carolines, see Ballendorf (1987, 1988a), Denfeld (1981a:25), Dolan (1974:87), Hezel (n.d.:20), Peattie (1988:248–249), Reafsnyder (1984:104), and Young et al. (1997).

7. On Marshall Islands base construction, see Peattie (1988:250–256); also Bryan (1972:209–210), Forrestel (1966), Mason (1946), Poyer (1997:25–26), Rynkiewich (1981), and United States Strategic Bombing Survey (USSBS) (1947a:1–24).

8. Land was purchased, though in some cases payment was never made, or was limited to the cost of trees and buildings (not land), or was obligatorily invested in Japanese enterprises or government stock. There was a degree of coercion or confiscation in how land for these bases was obtained; see Bryan (1972:210), Mason (1946), Oliver (1951:14), and Poyer (1997:25).

9. For military preparations in the Marianas, see Bowers (1950), Peattie (1988:248–253), Russell (1984), and Sheeks (1945). For Palau and nearby islands, see Black (1977:26), Ehrlich (1984), Gailey (1983:6), Kaneshiro (1958:310–311), Peattie (1988:176), Smith (1953:460–463), and Yarbrough (1971:188, 196).

10. Bascom (1965:18) says that Pohnpeians refer to two events as "the beginning of

the war"—the opening of Japanese aggression against China in July 1937 and the U.S. incendiary raids that destroyed Kolonia in mid-February 1944. For military preparations on Pohnpei, see Bascom (1950), Denfeld (1979), and Peattie (1988:253).

11. Sources on the fortification of Chuuk include Bailey (1989:51), Denfeld (1981a: 22–26), Dolan (1974:161–162, 170), King and Carucci (1984:475–478), King and Parker (1984:106), Parker (1985), USSBS (1947b), and Vogel (1948). Agawa (1979:326–342) describes Admiral Yamamoto's pleasant life there aboard the *Yamato* in August 1942; see also Peattie (1988:250–262).

12. The experiences of these exiles are told in King and Parker (1984), Parker (1985); also King and Carucci (1984:475) and Denfeld (1981a:78). King and Carucci (1984:478) discuss the difficulty in dating the construction of Moen #1 airfield and conclude that initial construction in a swampy area may have relocated some Chuukese in the late 1930s; the site was switched to Iras in 1941 when those villagers were moved. Young et al. (1997:37) indicate that some Chuukese moved into caves as early as 1942 because of military confiscation.

13. "Gunzoku-koin or laborers, skilled and unskilled, wearing military uniform and attached to the armed forces" worked on roads and defense installations and at truck farms—Blackton calls them "semi-military laborers" (1946:404 n.11).

14. Like Losap in the central Carolines, Mokil had only a single Japanese resident throughout the war (Kneubuhl 1946; Murphy 1949:433). Other relatively unaffected atolls were Pingelap, Sapwuahfik, Nukuoro, and some of the Mortlocks (Nason 1970: 229 for Etal; Severance 1976 for Pis islet, Losap). The first effects of war on Ifaluk were "slight"—the resident Japanese agriculturalist left, and canoe travel was banned. Later, planes from Woleai flew over occasionally; Japanese visits grew scarcer and finally stopped, with "many of the younger men" taken to Yap on the final trip (Bates and Abbott 1958:207–208).

15. This two-day attack (sailing from Samoa) by carrier- and cruiser-based planes and bombardment hit Roi and Kwajalein, with additional strikes on Wotje, Jaluij, Maloelap, and Mili (USSBS 1947a:26). The attack is also described in Bailey (1989:3), Broadwater (1971:2), and Lundstrom (1976:30–32). A second early raid into Micronesia was an Australian air attack on Chuuk, January 15, 1942, with six Catalinas (four reached the target) responding to attacks on Rabaul by planes from Chuuk (Denfeld 1981a:22–26).

16. It was after this bombing—which Maloelap people identify as "when the war started" or "when the war became strong"—that most Taroa people, including all the women and children, left that fortified islet (Poyer 1997:25).

17. For these constraints on Saipan, see Price (1944b:404–405) and D. F. Smith (1946:7–8).

18. Information about limits on missionary work during this period comes from Hezel (n.d.) and Battle (n.d.) for Chuuk, Nason (1970:374:n.2) for Lukunor, Cockrum (1970) and Mason (1946:34) for the Marshalls, and Schaefer (1976:37) and U.S. Navy (1944b) for Kosrae. Hezel (1995:221) summarizes the situation.

19. Sheeks (1945:109) describes *kinrōhōshi* on Saipan as "a patriotic labor group which worked at stevedoring, road-building, airfield construction, and other manual labor 'without pay for the Emperor'," whose work began months before the first U.S. attack on Saipan and greatly increased after it.

20. The clearest evidence of the distances covered and the numbers who moved during this period comes from U.S. Navy reports of Islanders repatriated after the surrender. The navy was kept busy for months repatriating not only Japanese, Okinawans, and Koreans, but also Islanders far from home at war's end. Those from the western islands followed labor needs to Palau or the Marianas; central Carolinians from outlying atolls were brought to work in lagoon Chuuk; eastern Caroline atoll dwellers and Kosraeans worked on Pohnpei; Marshallese men were brought to sites of base construction. Some Micronesians, including ten Yapese, spent the war years in Japan (Richard 1957c).

21. According to survivors, six died of illness on Kosrae, two returned to Pohnpei earlier due to illness, and two returned to Pohnpei to face criminal charges.

22. The "open sea of selfishness" refers to the tradition that, in times of danger, a Pohnpeian man's first responsibility was to his brother-in-law, next to his close matrilineal kinsman; he was to think of himself last. On the open seas, however—a place that land-hugging Pohnpeians consider dangerous and unpredictable—each man was advised to think of his own life first. In the final lines, "authority" translates *manaman* (legitimate power). A brave Pohnpeian man should enter battle in service of his *nahnmwarki* without regard for his own life. The singer doubts whether there was genuine authority for sacrificing one's life in this context; though indirectly, the song questions Japanese wartime *mana*.

A memorial song is an important Pohnpeian song genre, usually composed following a significant event such as the death of a notable person. This song, composed by Linter Hebel and Salpa, is often sung over kava on Pohnpei, particularly when Kiti people are gathered. Today it has been recorded by a group from another chiefdom, Uh, and is often broadcast over the local radio station. The song and its new recorded version have stimulated discussion of Kiti's Kosrae labor group and the war years in general.

23. A survey of Japanese nationals imprisoned during the war in Saipan revealed that most of the imported laborers there were Okinawan. There were differences in "educational and economic level" between the Okinawan laborers and "homeland

Japanese," and the Japanese regarded them as the equivalent of the derogatory American term "hillbillies" (Bosse 1945:177–178).

24. These were workers for NKK and the military (Peoples 1977:148–150; Lewis 1948a:46; Murphy 1949:431). Kosraeans recall 600–700 hundred Banabans brought in 1942 and 1943 for NKK plantation labor and fishing. Osmond Palikun describes a census before the arrival of troops, listing 780 Japanese civilians (including Japanese and Okinawan contractors), 700 Banabans, and 2 Americans.

25. On the experiences of Nauruans brought to Chuuk in July–August 1943, see Pollock (1991), which includes several personal accounts; also Cockrum (1970), Denfeld (1981a:30), Garrett (1996), Petit-Skinner (1981:25–28), and Underwood (1989:11). Pollock (1991) and Cockrum (1970) say they were taken to Tol and Fefan. Our interviews in Chuuk mention Nauruans at Weno, Tatiw, and Tol. Blackton (1946:405), who accompanied the American team accepting the Japanese surrender at Chuuk, did not refer to these Nauruans as prisoners and in fact stated that "Detailed and persistent questioning revealed no evidence of the presence of allied prisoners-of-war or interned civilians, living or dead." He writes of "some seven hundred natives from Nauru who had been imported as laborers," along with a Swiss missionary. Survivors returned to Nauru in January 1946. Graves remain in two graveyards on Tol, and Nauruans have come to Tol to visit the village site (Denfeld 1981a:30). Petit-Skinner (1981:26–28) suggests that the experience of wartime exile encouraged Nauruan leader Timothy Detudamo to pursue Nauru's political and economic independence after the war.

26. Some exceptions include the following: Kun Aaron (Kosrae) says he and others learned "how to use guns"; Pretrick Ringland (Pohnpei) notes, "They gave me a gun to carry" when he was leader of a work crew in the Madolenihmw mountains. The Marshallese who joined an armed revolt against the Japanese garrison on Mili were not very skilled in the use of firearms, limiting their success (see chapter 6).

27. Mariul's and Eungel's recollections are in Higuchi (1991). On the Palauan volunteers, see also Nero (1989) and Shuster (1982b:77). Tellei (1991) describes his recruitment and service to the Japanese military in Irian Jaya and elsewhere. Depending on the outcomes, the Japanese recruitment of Islander volunteers is remembered in very different ways. In the Marshall Islands, the Japanese recruited promising young men for a proposed conquest of Fiji and Hawai'i at the beginning of the war. Yet John Ezekiel, who filled out a recruitment application, remembers the event with ambivalence. After filling out the form, he reported to the recruitment office, where they told him that his application was good enough to get him to Hawai'i. Nevertheless, they asked him if he would like to go to Rabaul. In telling the story, Mr. Ezekiel describes the Japanese as "two–faced," since he feels they deceived Islanders by recruiting them but never drafting them into service.

28. It is hard to say how clearly the recruits understood what their job would be (or whether the assignment changed when they reached New Guinea). Mikel Diana says of them, "They were treated more like slaves than like soldiers." Benjamin Lopez, at first chosen to be one of the group, recognized that the volunteers suffered from "a big deception." When he was chosen, "They didn't tell me I would be with the soldiers; they told me I was going to be the boss"; he was happy at the prospect of higher pay as a work supervisor. Only after the recruits had been gone for two or three months did they learn that they were "among the soldiers." Yet survivor Ludwik Alik claims the group did know that they would be working with the Japanese soldiers. See also Peattie (1988:301).

29. Not all were Pohnpeians. Watakabe's list of names differs slightly from that given by Ludwik Alik in 1990–1991.

CHAPTER 4. DEFENSIVE PREPARATIONS: THE JAPANESE MILITARY TAKES CHARGE

1. The figure is from Peattie (1988:263). The first Japanese navy forces arrived at Maloelap in November 1941; the first army forces in September 1942. The first American attack came in November 1943, and Maloelap received its last ship in mid-January 1944. The first Japanese military arrived on Mili in June 1943; army units arrived in December 1943. The first troop ship attempting to land at Jaluij was sunk by U.S. submarine attack on May 20, 1943, seaside of Jabwor, with the first successful reinforcement probably in November 1943 (USSBS 1947a). Enewetak was fortified more slowly. Its runway was completed mid-1943, but Enewetak did not see large numbers of troops until January 1944, followed by a rapid effort to fortify (Shaw, Nalty, and Turnbladh 1966:191–192).

2. Information about the late phase of war preparations on Pohnpei is found in Denfeld (1979, esp. 21–27, 118), Morison (1951:156), and Bascom (1950:145). Denfeld (1981b) describes the physical structuring of Japanese fortifications in the Central Pacific.

3. There were several incidents of relocation on Kosrae. Malem and Utwe people moved in June 1942. Later in the war, pressure from the arrival of army troops and the need to seek safety from bombing raids caused additional relocations.

4. Information about this phase of war preparations on Chuuk is found in Bailey (1989:51), Denfeld (1981a:5, 17), Dolan (1974:165–166), Vogel (1948:1270–1272), and Young et al. (1997:34). The 52nd division, originally mobilized in Japan in late 1943 for service in the eastern Carolines, had been reorganized on Saipan, with half sent to Chuuk in response to the U.S. attack on Tarawa. A large army detachment arrived in

January 1944, taking quarters in schools and any other housing they could find, since no army barracks had been provided; then a second large group arrived shortly after the U.S. carrier strike in February, having lost its equipment to an American submarine attack en route (Vogel 1948:1270–1272).

5. On Chuuk lagoon's defenses, see Denfeld (1981a), Dolan (1974:171–173), and USSBS (1947b). The withdrawal of most of the fleet in February 1944 left Japanese bases in the Central Pacific with only garrisons and a decimated air force for protection (USSBS 1946:194). Weno Island's defenses are described in King and Carucci (1984: 481–495).

6. In our interviews, people who were forced from their homes spoke of the generosity of those who hosted them. But John Fischer mentions that, while Chuukese displaced in aboriginal warfare had sometimes received gifts of land, those displaced by the Japanese military "were resented by the people on whose land they were temporarily resettled" (1958b:81).

7. The fortification of Yap is described in Labby (1973, 1976:5–6) and Useem (1946a:20); see also Poyer (1995).

8. Information on the fortification of Woleai is in Boyer (1967:727) and Morison (1951:19, 33, 156). The move to Ifaluk is described in Burrows and Spiro (1957:31) and Cockrum (1970:336). Alkire writes that military activities had "typhoonlike effects on some areas of the Woleai." Four islets of Woleai Atoll (an airfield was built on Falalap islet) and parts of Lamotrek were occupied by Japanese troops. Woleai people first moved onto Falalus islet, then to Ifaluk; only a few remained to ensure postwar claims to the atoll's land (Alkire 1974:67; see also Burrows 1949; Burrows and Spiro 1957).

9. On Lukunor, see Borthwick (1977) and Tolerton and Rauch (1949). On Satawan, Borthwick (1977), Craven and Cate (1950:602), and Morison (1951:38). Borthwick (1977:59) says Satawan and Ta people were relocated from those islets to others in Satawan Atoll in the summer of 1942.

10. Regional effects of the Satawan base are described in Borthwick (1977) and, for Kutu, Reafsnyder (1984:104–105).

11. Nukuoro, Sapwuahfik, and Mokil held no military. Pingelap Atoll held a few Japanese soldiers in two "bases"—one for civilians and one for soldiers—few enough that they left by submarine before the Americans arrived. In the central Carolines, the Japanese used sites in the Hall Islands and Namonuito as aircraft spotter stations and weather-radio stations in support of Chuuk's defenses (there had been a weather observation station on Ulul islet in Namonuito since the 1930s [Thomas 1978:33]). Nama's only construction was bomb shelters made of coconut logs dragged over ditches; the few Japanese on Nama had a radio. Japanese military directly enforced work regulations and the liquor ban throughout the lower Mortlocks, traveling from Chuuk and

later from Satawan to islands such as Etal; no military were stationed on Etal itself (Nason 1970). In the western Carolines, Japanese on Fais built bomb shelters and large, fake guns but evacuated all but a handful of soldiers; the "company people" continued to run the phospate mines (Santiago Sathau, Fais; Morison 1958:47–52). Neither Ulithi nor Ifaluk was defended.

12. Sources for Palau include Cockrum (1970:284), Hezel (1995:235–239), Gailey (1983:7–8, 47), McKnight (1978:11–12), Nero (1989), Palau Community Action Agency (PCAA) (1978), R.R. Smith (1953), and Yarbrough (1971).

13. Sources for Saipan's preparation for war include Bowers (1950), Embree (1946a), Morison (1963), Peattie (1988:280–283), Russell (1984), Sheeks (1945), and Spoehr (1954). Bowers lists Japanese force strength as 29,000 on Saipan, 10,000 on Tinian, fewer on Rota. Dyer (1972) gives a 1959 army historian's estimate of 31,629 Japanese military personnel on Saipan, 8,039 on Tinian, and 18,500 on Guam.

14. Anko Billy expresses an unusual perspective of appreciation for the Japanese ability to use people's skills appropriately. After explaining how Japanese leaders, once they learned that Kosraean women wove mats, told local men "to ask the women of the house to make them sleeping mats," he says, "All of the people who were alive during the battle took some responsibility for the Japanese, in accord with their 'talents' or the special knowledge they had."

15. Michael Lieber (1968:59) writes that Kapingamarangi people feel that Japanese rather favored them "because they were good fishermen and good workers," especially during the period when supplies were cut off and Kapinga fishermen provided vital protein to Japanese soldiers in Madolenihmw on Pohnpei.

CHAPTER 5. THE SECOND ROAD TO TOKYO

1. On Kiribati experiences during the recapture, see Highland (1991), Morison (1951:177–181), Mamara and Kaiuea (1979:141–143), Maude and Doran (1966:286), and Shaw, Nalty, and Turnbladh (1966:106). Mamara and Kaiuea indicate that two local people were killed on Betio during the preliminary bombardment (before all could seek safety on a nearby islet), four on Butaritari, and "a few" at Abemama. The many military histories of "Operation Galvanic" contain little information about Islander experiences. U.S. Navy, Bureau of Yards and Docks (1947:314–318) describes U.S. base construction in Kiribati, including stevedoring and construction assistance by up to 426 local workers. *Among Those Present* (Great Britain Colonial Office 1946:82–95) is the official colonial history of these islands during the war years.

As part of the attack on Kiribati, two U.S. warships attacked Nauru in November 1943; aerial bombardment continued for six weeks (Morison 1951). Nauru had already been subjected to Allied air raids from Funafuti in April 1943. Many Islanders on Nauru died, including some forty Nauruans; many more were injured. Nauru's Japanese surrendered on August 21, 1945, and the island was occupied by an Australian force (Pollock 1991; Viviani 1970).

Aerial support for early Allied operations in the Pacific relied on bases in Tuvalu (Ellice Islands) on Funafuti, Nukufetau, and Nanumea, as well as Canton and Baker. The experiences of Tuvalu people are not discussed here.

2. See also Wheeler (1983:208) on campfire songfests in Kiribati. In describing the Islanders whose homes served as bases to support the Allied counteroffensive, Morison (1951:208) writes: "The simple natives of Funafuti were astonished in January to see two of the largest and newest United States battleships steam through Te Buabua Passage into the lagoon." The phrase, "The simple natives . . . were astonished" summarizes the treatment of Islanders in most military histories. Morison's footnote 13 on p. 214 reads: "Funafuti, Nanomea and Nukufetau were still going strong when this writer visited them in early July 1944; but Abemama had seen its best days as an air base. Only transport planes passed through, the garrison was reduced, and the natives, having reclothed themselves and acquired a valuable collection of canned goods and miscellaneous gadgets by working for the U.S. Navy at a shilling a day plus rations, were beginning to move back to their own villages and resume life as lived in the days of R.L.S." The idea that Islanders had lived a simple life unchanged in the century preceding the war was common; it bore significant implications for American policy in Micronesia (see chapter 7). For comparison, see discussions of American and Japanese views of Melanesians in Zelenietz (1991) and Saito (1991).

3. Sources for the invasion of the Marshall Islands include Bailey (1989), Broadwater (1971), Craven and Cate (1950:304–307), Crowl and Love (1955), Morison (1951), Richard (1957a), Shaw, Nalty, and Turnbladh (1966), and USSBS (1947a). Peattie (1988: 265–274) provides a summary integrating Japanese and American military sources.

4. On the Enewetak invasion, see Morison (1951), Peattie (1988:270–271), Crowl and Love (1955:341–343), Shaw, Nalty, and Turnbladh (1966:191–219), and Richard (1957a).

5. This account is discussed in Carucci (1989). See Carucci (1997a) for other recollections of the invasion of Enewetak and a detailed examination of the modern meaning of Enewetak memories of the war.

6. "These [reconnaissances] afforded much gratification to junior naval officers who had the pleasure of reading Admiral Nimitz's proclamation and assuming a paternal and benevolent sway over the Micronesians, while the Marines who formed the 'expeditionary forces' found virgin fields for souvenir collecting. The natives were uniformly friendly, joyfully assisting the Marines in hunting down stray Japanese and in providing souvenirs" (Morison 1951:310).

7. The U.S. Seventh Air Force used Kiribati bases to attack Mili, Jaluij, Roi, Wotje, Maloelap, Kwajalein, and Kosrae during the invasion of Kwajalein and Majuro ("Operation Flintlock"); it continued neutralization bombings of the bypassed Marshalls bases and also attacked Pohnpei and Wake during the invasion of Enewetak ("Catchpole"). When the U.S. Army Air Force moved from Kiribati-Tuvalu bases to forward bases in support of the Marianas campaign, the Fourth Marine Aircraft Wing took over regular bombing of the bypassed Marshalls bases ("much to its disgust" because of the lack of action) (Morison 1951:309; Craven and Cate 1950:305–310). USSBS (1947a) reviews U.S. air attacks on the bypassed Marshalls—as well as the invaded islands—in detail. Pilots assigned to these "milk runs" rather than to more exciting frontline action sometimes took a playful and frightening approach to air attacks on civilians (e.g., buzzing a woman in a latrine, Olds 1944:119).

8. Despite heroic efforts by the Japanese and their workers to maintain minimal air facilities, the military potential of the bypassed bases evaporated. Loss of planes in air raids and evacuation of flight personnel left Japanese with no air power in the Marshalls by the beginning of February 1944; after that the bases struggled to maintain at least one runway in usable condition, but even that effort had to be abandoned later that year as bomb damage never ceased and repair crews grew few and feeble (USSBS 1947a). Masataki Okumiya (Okumiya et al. 1956:281–290) describes what must have been his very similar experiences at Buin on Bougainville in the Southwest Pacific in mid-1943, when growing American air superiority meant constant air raids, as exhausted Japanese personnel struggled to repair the airstrip and send aloft a dwindling number of planes.

9. See Richard (1957a:360–363). John Heine (1991) describes hiding out for eleven months on a Japanese-controlled islet before escaping, then serving as an American scout.

10. Morison (1951:310 n.9) dates the first escape from Wotje to September 1944, when Marshallese working for the U.S. Navy helped 700 Marshallese ("together with poultry and pigs") escape; another evacuation in March 1945 brought out 452 Marshallese. Mamara and Kaiuea (1979:130–131) describe how a group of young men sought to escape from Banaba to Kiribati in April 1944. Only one survived—Nabetar of Nikunau—coming ashore at Papua New Guinea after seven months at sea.

11. Mr. Tartios recalls that only six of the thirty-two people on board lived to reach their destination. Of the entire attempt to escape from Maloelap, Richard (1957a:362) reports that eighty people made it to Aur on January 11; thirty-one others attempting to escape were lost at sea.

12. Detail on these escapes is in Richard (1957a:362).

13. On Pohnpei bombings, see Peattie (1988:278–279), Craven and Cate (1950:307),

Denfeld (1979), Howard and Whitley (1946:106), and Morison (1953:40–41). The endless series of predictable raids tested new weapons and trained U.S. aircrews: "The [Pohnpei] raids demonstrated for the first time in the Central Pacific, the deadly effectiveness of incendiaries. They gave a preview of what might be expected later when [Japanese] mainland cities were brought within effective bombing range. . . . This was actually the first time that Seventh AF bombers engaged in strategic bombing, and the results obtained point the way to even greater destruction of the enemy as more important and densely populated areas come within our range" (Howard and Whitley 1946:197).

14. For details of the air war on Chuuk and related background, see Bailey (1989), Denfeld (1981a), Lindemann (1982, 1987), Morison (1951:320–329), Peattie (1988:274–277), Shaw, Nalty, and Turnbladh (1966), Stewart (1985), Tillman (1977), and USSBS (1946:206, 1947b). The initial fighter attack was followed by bombing airfields on Weno, Eten, and Parem with fragmentation clusters and incendiaries. Throughout the day, dive-bombers and torpedo-bombers hit the lagoon repeatedly; an experimental night bombing attack on shipping followed. Aircraft carriers launched new attacks the next day, aiming at airfield installations and fuel and ammunition storage.

"Operation Hailstone" fascinates military historians because it meant destruction of the Combined Fleet headquarters, because the dozens of ships sunk in Chuuk's tropical lagoon constitute a dramatic permanent monument to the event, and because it marked innovations in the use of carrier air (Denfeld 1981a:27–34). The raid also was the first in a series of heavy blows to Japanese shipping and contributed to limiting the Japanese fleet's oil supply (USSBS 1946:380). The 1944 attack was not the first Allied attempt on Chuuk. Australians conducted an early reconnaissance flight in January 1942, followed by two attempts at air attacks (Bailey 1989; Anonymous 1944:50, 166; Denfeld 1981a:22–26).

15. USSBS (1946:208–209) summarizes the second carrier air attack on Chuuk (April 29–30, 1944): "The plan provided for a daily initial fighter sweep by approximately 84 planes followed by the usual staggered launchings of subsequent bombing attacks. . . . In excess of 2,200 sorties were flown against land installations after air control had been achieved [by eliminating virtually all airborne opposition by midmorning]. Hangars, ammunition dumps, oil in storage, and a large number of miscellaneous structures were destroyed" along with small vessels.

16. Information on the ongoing "neutralization" bombing of Chuuk is in Craven and Cate (1950:678–690), Denfeld (1981a:35–48), Lindemann (1987), Peattie (1988:274–277), and USSBS (1947b). Throughout this period, when bad weather or bad navigation caused U.S. planes to miss Chuuk, they bombed alternate targets such as Kolonia on Pohnpei or Oroluk.

17. Lindstrom and White (1990:163–171) discuss wartime use of traditional religion and Christianity throughout the Pacific. Chuukese, at least, also used traditional medicine to treat war wounds. A Fano (Chuuk) man working as a sailor on a Japanese diesel boat was a survivor of an American bombing and strafing attack on it; he was wounded in his upper arm and treated by a practitioner of "Stinger" medicine—traditional medicine for wounds suffered in battle. He survived, but the two Japanese sailors also wounded later died, despite treatment by a Japanese physician; "Trukese on Fano still point to this wartime incident as a good example of the power and effectiveness of their own medicine" (Mahony 1969:175).

18. A very different, but also strong, memory of the war is that of the dramatic spectacle. Este Nipuk of Chuuk relates this view:

During the war, when I was in Tatiw [an unfortified small island near Parem airstrip], it was beautiful. If I had had a camera, I would have taken pictures, because of the many planes . . . it was a clear view. It was a beautiful sight, to see them come. We could see the pilots in the planes. The American planes would come by way of Tatiw to stay out of the way of the big [anti-aircraft] guns. The planes would come toward Parem, then they would come down to Tatiw, trying to get out of range. [The Japanese were not shooting] because they were flying so low, down near the cement [of the airstrip]. Then they would go back to their aircraft carrier.

The recollection of agile aerial dogfights and spectacular attacks on ships in blue waters is especially vivid for those who saw the war in the natural theater of Chuuk lagoon. But people everywhere recalled that it was always a struggle to keep children (and some adults) inside bomb shelters; they longed to watch the planes.

19. The first major bombing of Chuuk was February 17, 1944. The date in the song may refer to the small Australian raid in mid-January 1942.

20. On attacks on Yap, see Craven and Cate (1950:603–604, 687–688), Poyer (1995), and Spoehr (1951). A U.S. reconnaissance mission landed a five-man search team in the Gagil-Tomil (Gagil Tamil) area of Yap on the night of August 18, 1944; only two survivors returned to the submarine offshore (Denfeld 1988:6).

21. On Woleai, see Boyer (1967) and USSBS (1946:206). Ifaluk suffered only a single strafing run, "by an American Navy pilot who probably thought he was shooting at Woleai" (Bates and Abbott 1958:207); no one was hurt. Ifaluk was mislabeled on some American aerial photographs as Woleai (Burrows and Spiro 1957:204).

22. In summarizing the use of air power against the "bypassed" islands, USSBS (1946:206) states: "A standard pattern of almost daily strikes was evolved, using Army medium bombers and Navy 'Venturas,' and Navy and Marine fighter-bombers and dive-bombers. Neutralization of runways, and destruction of gun emplacements, trucks and a variety of small boats were the objectives."

23. Shuster (1982b:73) describes two "guerilla training centers" at Nelekeok and Ngardmau on Babelthuap, where young Palauans learned martial arts, signals, and the use of weapons.

24. Saipan was secured by August 10, though small groups of Japanese continued to fight until the end of the war. The Marianas invasion is described in Crowl (1960), Garard and Strobridge (1971), Morison (1953), Peattie (1988:280–290), Shaw, Nalty, and Turnbladh (1966:231–428), Sheeks 1945, and USSBS (1946:209–272). Local accounts can be found in interviews archived at the Micronesian Area Research Center at the University of Guam (Owings 1981); see also Farrell (1991) and Sullivan (1957:180–182).

25. The events surrounding the invasion of Guam are treated only briefly here. For detailed description, including local accounts, see Apple (1980), Beardsley (1964), Carano and Sanchez (1964), Hough (1947), Josephy (1946), Palomo (1984, 1991), Rogers (1995), Sanchez (1983), Shaw, Nalty, and Turnbladh (1966), and Sullivan (1957: 150–178).

26. On summer 1944 air attacks on Palau, see Peattie (1988:279); Craven and Cate (1950), Morison (1951), and USSBS (1946:273–274). On preinvasion Palau, see Bronemann (1982), Gailey (1983:47), and Richard (1957a:623). Peattie (1988:290–297) summarizes the battles for Peleliu and Angaur from Japanese and American military sources. See also Ballendorf, Kluge, and Carson (n.d.), Denfeld (1988), Richard (1957a: 51–157), and USSBS (1946:207). The numerous military histories of the battle of Peleliu contain little or no information about Palauans. Palauan accounts of this period are found in collections at the Micronesian Area Research Center, including Ballendorf et al. (1986) and Higuchi (n.d., 1986, 1991). Karen Nero (1989:117–147) provides a detailed description of Palauan life during the war, including individual recollections.

27. On escapes to American lines, see Cockrum (1970:284) and Higuchi (1987, 1991).

CHAPTER 6. LIFE ON THE BYPASSED ISLANDS

1. On Japanese shipping losses, see USSBS (1975) and USSBS (1946:378–389).

2. For conditions on the bypassed Marshalls bases, see Morison (1951) and USSBS (1947a). Using Japanese sources, Peattie (1988:305) states that, of the 4,700 in the Japanese garrison on Mili, 900 were killed in bombing raids and over 1,000 died of starvation and disease. On Maloelap, only 1,000 of the 3,300-man garrison survived; on Wotje, 1,000 of nearly 3,000 survived.

3. Vice Admiral Chuichi Hara was in charge at Chuuk. When the USSBS team visiting Chuuk in November 1945 asked him, "Which of the hostile forces operating against you caused you the most concern?" Admiral Hara answered, "Rats. They made dry storage almost impossible. Then comes potato bugs. Aside from that, any air attack

that was sustained beyond a single bombing raid was always troublesome" (Bartlett 1970:52).

4. Most military men and civilian laborers suffered equally. Peattie (1988:344n.54) describes the fate of a hundred Japanese prison laborers on Weno: "Only ten survived the bombing, starvation and disease of the war," including Kubota Kiyoshi, who wrote a noted war book about his experiences. Post-surrender U.S. Navy photographs show the degree of malnutrition of some Japanese military.

5. Peattie (1988:304) states that three hundred of the Kosrae garrison died.

6. See Falgout (1989:279–297) on Pohnpeian experiences of wartime scarcity. As an indication of stress but not desperation on Pohnpei, Bascom (1948:217) reports that Pohnpeians maintained traditional values, such as the secrecy surrounding yam cultivation, despite food scarcity: "The two Belgian families [interned] on Ponape found that, in spite of the urgency of their need for food, they could not get their servant to grow yams in the yard because he did not want them to see how it was done."

7. See Reafsnyder (1984:105). On Lukunor, see Borthwick (1977:59); on Etal, Nason (1970:219).

8. The U.S. Navy (1944c) reports that Japanese had instituted rationing (including sugar, rice, meat, and fish) in this area in June 1940.

9. She did recover her baby; a grown man, he was listening as we recorded this interview.

10. When John Kneubuhl accompanied the first U.S. military survey team to Kapingamarangi after the war, they found people in tattered but precious apparel: "Despite the shredded condition of the loin-cloths, G-strings, and dresses, the natives clung to each garment tenaciously; their immediate need, they told me, was for clothes. Soap ranked next, but clothes was the overwhelming demand. The two chiefs wore white suits, silk shirts, detachable collars, neckties, socks, and good leather shoes" (Kneubuhl 1946:11).

11. The South Seas Bureau, which had been responsible to the Japanese minister of Overseas Affairs since 1924, shifted after November 1942 to the purview of the recently established Greater East Asia Ministry, "an emergency organization, formed to administer 'conquered regions'" (Grahlfs 1955:20; also Bryan 1972:208). In November 1943 control of civilians shifted to the navy, with the appointment of Vice Admiral Ishiro Heosokaya as governor. After the U.S. invasion of Palau, the Nan'yō-chō's administrative center was moved to Chuuk; at some point it was replaced by direct military government (Peattie 1988:344–345, n.7; Blackton 1946:405, n.13; Grahlfs 1955:21).

12. The official status of relations between military and civilian rulers as decreed by Tokyo was beside the point once communication ceased; local military and Nan'yō-chō officials managed their own relations. Writing of Palau, for example, Goh Abe as-

signs the years 1922–1944 to South Seas Bureau control but adds, "The years between 1940 and 1944 witnessed an overlapping of Bureau and military control" (1986:108). This seems to have been the case throughout the region. Since Micronesians speaking of the war not infrequently use current terms to refer to similar roles or activities during the Japanese era, informants' discussions do not clearly distinguish military, military police, and civilian police functions.

13. Islanders perceived the Japanese army as much more harsh than the navy. In addition, a structural pattern of dual command made army-navy conflict nearly inevitable anywhere there were sizeable numbers of each. It does not seem from interviews that most Islanders recognized this problem in Japanese military bureaucracy, but it certainly played a role in the conditions of their lives (Peattie 1988:345, n.8). Near the end of the war, Japanese leaders were aware of a lack of discipline on the part of the army even in respect to Japanese civilians in the home islands (Hayashi and Coox 1959:151).

14. Yvette Etscheit describes her family living as prisoners of war guarded by policemen from December 1941 until the bombing of Pohnpei began, when they were moved to the new prison camp where Japanese, Koreans, Pohnpeians, Marshallese, and Chuukese arrested for civil crimes were kept. Even here the Etscheits seem not to have been directly under military supervision, for Yvette Etscheit speaks of a Japanese policeman who had long known the family arranging separate quarters for them. Again, when in December 1944 "the police told us they had orders to move the prisoners to Madolenihmw to help work in the fields" because of a manpower shortage, "the police wouldn't take us there" but sent them to another camp. Though by this time their captors were strict and food was limited, it was only now that the policemen guarding them were armed. See Meredith (1995:27) for Mrs. Carlos Etscheit's 1953 comments on her wartime experiences.

15. When his boss told him the war was imminent, Andon Quele (Chuuk) went through a great deal of trouble to get himself and his companions back home to the Mortlocks, despite the official ban on workers leaving. Julio Vallazon (Pohnpei) remembers thinking about his family in the Philippines and in Japan during the war years. Meruse William and her husband worked separately on different Japanese agricultural projects on Pohnpei. After he was imprisoned and beaten for missing work, he escaped to tell her to go to Mokil (she was pregnant) to wait for him to finish. Later, her husband's father came to Mokil to get her because her husband had been beaten again by Japanese soldiers and was in a coma. She didn't see him again until after the war.

16. More than bombing was going on back home, while war workers were away. Once reunited with family after the war, some would discover much that was not to

their liking. When the 179 Kiti men returned to Pohnpei from their work on Kosrae, Tadasy Santos recalls, the Americans did not let them go home to Kiti until all the Japanese had left—a good plan, he says, because the men "were mad as hell and ready to kill the Japanese" when they found wives and other relatives made pregnant by them: "The big discussion on the ship on our way to Pohnpei [from Kosrae] was to beat up the Japanese if we found that they had harmed or abused our relatives. They were lucky to have left when we got to our homes." When Pensile Lawrence returned from his stint of work on Kosrae, he did not recognize his younger brother: "Just two years and two or three months, and I had forgotten the face of my younger brother. Hard times."

17. On Modekgnei, see Aoyagi (1978), Shuster (1982a:71–79, 1982b:34–36), Useem (1946b, 1947:6), and Vidich (1980:228–244).

18. Of Chuuk, Kosrae, and Pohnpei, John Fischer (1957:64) wrote:

Perhaps a more common reaction [than violent resistance] to the troubles of the war was a reversion to certain aspects of the old pagan religion. While there was apparently no outright abandonment of Christianity, on all three high island groups certain individuals went into trances and came forth with alleged visions or possession by spirits of the dead. One of the activities of these mediums was to prophesy the outcome of the war and the fate of individuals whom the Japanese had transported to other islands. These activities were directly related to the tension of the war and blockade and later sank into insignificance following the American occupation.

19. Writing of the time after Pohnpei was blockaded and the military was effectively in control, Bascom states: "Ponapean girls as young as thirteen or fourteen were taken away to serve as domestic servants and, as a matter of course, as mistresses to the Japanese men. . . . As the number of half-castes today indicates, this practice was too widespread to be dismissed lightly by the older people" (1950:145).

20. At the end of the war, Micronesians commented on the shock of learning that Japanese commanders had kept back some food reserves. Tulenkun Waguk recalls going to a warehouse on Kosrae with a Japanese soldier when the war was over, where he was given some leftover rice and canned foods—"They still had some food supplies," he comments, "but many of their soldiers had died of hunger." Japanese military leaders on Chuuk stated during surrender inquiries that they held in reserve thirty days' full rations for every fighting man "to be broken out in the event of an assault" and that "Summer uniforms for the entire garrison were stored so that the men might be able to go into final battle in a clean and soldierly condition" (Blackton 1946:404).

21. Mr. Mori joined because that was the law and strove to force himself to be a soldier because of that obligation. He was struck by young men *wanting* to join the (U.S.) Army—now a common choice for Micronesian youth.

22. Of the eastern Carolines, John Fischer (1957:64) wrote:

It is unclear how much resistance the islanders made to the Japanese military. Most of the islanders were certainly not enthusiastic workers, yet the Japanese were present in such great numbers that open resistance of the type which had occurred a generation or two earlier in Ponape [the Sokehs rebellion during the German colonial era] was unthinkable. The senior Ponapean policeman under the Japanese has said that there were a few mysterious deaths of military personnel on Ponape during the war which may have been due to the actions of islanders. If so it is probable that personal grudges for beatings, insults, or stolen wives were responsible rather than political convictions.

CHAPTER 7. THE END OF WAR

1. Accused of being pro-American, the German missionary on Palau was tried as a spy (Useem 1946a). Six Catholic missionaries and four Chamorros were executed by Japanese as alleged spies on Palau in September 1944, after the invasion of Peleliu (Shuster 1982b:82–83). A Chamorro priest, Father Jesus Baza Duenas, was executed just before the U.S. invasion of Guam (Rogers 1995:178). Spoehr (1949a:33) mentions at least two native pastors of mixed Marshallese and European descent (see below) and one German/Australian resident missionary executed in the Marshall Islands. European missionaries in Kiribati who were not evacuated were harassed, and several were executed (Mamara and Kaiuea 1979).

2. This probably refers to seeing eight American warships, detached from the carrier force for "Operation Hailstone," assigned to hunt ships seeking to escape from the aerial attack on Chuuk lagoon (Jones 1944). The United States did not plan to invade.

3. In a pamphlet on the Marianas issued by the U.S. Military Government Education Office in mid-July 1945, Chamorros, Carolinians, and Koreans are classed as "Japanese subjects," who, like the Japanese nationals, "are held for safekeeping by the American government." Guamanians, in contrast, as U.S. nationals, were fairly free, since by that date most Japanese on Guam had been sent to Tinian or Saipan (Taylor 1945:20, 1951:344).

4. That Japan would lose its Pacific possessions at the conclusion of war had been determined by the Cairo Declaration of December 1, 1943, affirmed at Potsdam in July 1945, and incorporated into surrender terms for Japanese (Bowers 1950:60). After being taken by the United States, islands were ruled by the U.S. Navy under military government as occupied regions. Until "U.S. title to the area was resolved," governance followed international laws of war and Admiral Spruance's directive in early 1945 out-

lining military government (Ballendorf 1984b:2; Hezel 1995:257). U.S. Military Government of the newly conquered region was first headquartered on retaken Guam.

5. American predispositions toward Micronesians, and especially Marshallese, had been shaped by the U.S. military's experience with Pacific Islanders throughout the region and throughout the war, most immediately by the strong impression made on American troops in Kiribati (see also chapter 3). Leckie (1962), for example, presents a romantic image of Kiribati people, perhaps close to that experienced by American troops: "There were smiling young men, strong and athletic; eager youngsters more than willing to shinny up trees and throw coconuts to the Marines; young girls with round bare breasts and straight black hair.... The Marines looked away.... It was ... as though they had blundered into some Eden which had not known the serpent.... It was, of course, a romantic notion" (Leckie 1962:227). Some of these same troops were soon involved in the Marshalls invasion. Kennett (1987:149–171) offers a general comparison of GI experiences in European and Pacific theaters (of course, a great many more army troops served in Melanesia than in Micronesia). Also enlightening is comparison of the U.S. military in Micronesia with the wartime American occupation of Vanuatu, then the New Hebrides (Lindstrom 1996).

6. See Richard (1957a:84). Though American military eyes focused on the mandate early in the Pacific war, a separate office for military government at CincPac/CinCPOA headquarters, the civil affairs section, was only established in December 1943, less than two months before the Marshalls invasion (Ballendorf 1984b; Bowers 1950:49, 60; Cockrum 1970:203; Richard 1957a:73). Beginning with the Marshalls invasion, a small civil affairs unit went ashore with military invasion teams to establish the basics of dealing with civilians, later turning most matters over to some form of local government. Islands used as U.S. bases remained under direct military control for the rest of the war. By the end of 1944, use of the term *civil affairs* was dropped, replaced by *military government* or *MilGov* (Richard 1957a:88). PCAA (1978:432–446) describes planning for U.S. Military Government in the region.

7. On Enewetak people during and immediately after invasion, see Carucci (1989), Richard (1957a:341–343), and Cockrum (1970:210–214).

8. Descriptions of construction of the first U.S. bases in the Marshalls are in Richard (1957a:28–131) and U.S. Navy, Bureau of Yards and Docks (1947:318–326).

9. Richard (1957a:26) lists unfortified atolls and islands taken by marines (west longitude dates):

March 9, Wotho	March 22, Ailinglablab
March 11, Ujae	March 24, Ebon, Namu
March 12, Lib	March 26, Namorik
March 13, Lae	March 27, Kili

March 29, Bikini   April 17, Aur
March 31, Ronglap, Ailuk   April 23, Ujelang
April 2, Mejit   April 25, Arno
April 3, Likiep   June 4, Erikub
April 5, Utirik

10. See Cockrum (1970:218–219), Howard and Whitley (1946:194–195), and Richard (1957a:360). In all, about 2,500 Marshallese left Japanese-held atolls before the end of the war; another estimated 1,000 remained. Marshallese experiences on the bypassed atolls, and escapes from them, are described in chapters 5 and 6.

11. See Cockrum (1970:221–222). U.S. administrators immediately faced questions of the legitimacy of the traditional leaders with whom they dealt. During the invasion of Majuro, some Marshallese told the Americans that the atoll had two chiefs; others, one. The navy handled the local dispute by recognizing the two as independent paramount chiefs during ceremonies at the new U.S. air base in early 1944, but factional problems continued (Mason 1946:93–94). The American administration became involved in conflicts over rights to chieftainship in several areas of the Marshalls, as well as property disputes such as a sponge farm planted in Ailinglablab lagoon about 1938, which the U.S. held as captured Japanese property (Mason 1946:95–98). Journalist W. Robert Moore (1945a) describes the Marshalls soon after U.S. occupation.

12. On the first U.S. stores in the Marshalls, see Cockrum (1970:211–212). On labor camps, see Richard (1957a:403–405). Cockrum describes the first U.S. schools in the Marshalls, but also see later citations on American-era education in Micronesia.

13. On relief supplies, see Cockrum (1970:223) and Richard (1957a:96–197, 258). In 1945, Foreign Economic Administration resources for civilians became available, including agricultural tools, seeds, fertilizers, insecticides, fishing kits, and trade goods.

14. The generous habits of invading Americans were also noted elsewhere in the world. "The lavishness with which American troops were supplied impressed anyone who came in contact with them" (Kennett 1987:96). In Europe, historians of wartime Napoli comment that local people preferred to work for the American army rather than the British—Americans were less severe disciplinarians, more comradely, more generous with gifts and bonuses (Kennett 1987:204). On Melanesia, see Lindstrom and White (1989:11–13, 1990:14–23).

15. Ulithi during its time as an American base is described in Cusenbery (1946: 8–9, 14), Divine (1950), Hynes (1988), Lessa (1950), and Wees (1950). U.S. Navy, Bureau of Yards and Docks (1947:332–335) describes the extensive construction.

16. On U.S. construction on Saipan, see Bowers (1950:56), Denfeld and Russell (1984), Embree (1946a), Richard (1957a:41), and U.S. Navy, Bureau of Yards and Docks (1947:340–343). Cook and Cook (1992:281–292) recounts a Japanese soldier's descrip-

tion of the battle for Saipan. Most of Tinian's Chamorros had been relocated to Rota and Yap, leaving only 26 Chamorros out of a population of 17,900 Japanese and Korean civilians (and none of the Chamorros was reported on the island at the time of invasion in mid-July 1944). Declared secured August 1, 1944, Tinian soon held 50,000 U.S. troops and the largest B-29 base in the world. On August 6, 1945, the first atom bomb to be used in war was loaded into a B-29 there. Rota, Pagan, and the smaller islands were not invaded but were bombed and subjected to a tight blockade, suffering from hunger and disease until the Japanese surrender. Nearly 900 Chamorros remained on Rota, some of whom had worked as translators or in intelligence for the Japanese on Guam. Rota was occupied by Americans on September 4, 1945. On Tinian, Rota, and Pagan, see Bowers (1950), Peattie (1988:288–290, 304), Richard (1957a:44–148), and U.S. Navy, Bureau of Yards and Docks (1947:358–370).

17. Conditions for Chamorros and Carolinians on Saipan during the invasion and its aftermath are in Bowers (1950:50–55), Embree (1946a), Farrell (1991), Richard (1957a:435–491), Russell (1983), Sheeks (1945:111–113), Solenberger (1964), Spoehr (1954:94), U.S. Navy, Military Government Section (n.d.), and Williams (1946). The poet John Ciardi's war diary of November 1944–March 1945 describes life for American bomber crews on Saipan, including a description of Carolinian and Chamorro dances staged for American troops (Ciardi 1988:52–55).

18. On Chamorro guards and Chamorro and Carolinian scouts, see Embree (1946a: 6–8), Farrell (1991:426), and Sheeks (1945:113).

19. On Islanders at Angaur, see Moore (1945b:474), Richard (1957a:611–613), Useem (1945b:579–580), and R. R. Smith (1953:529).

20. Rogers (1995:194–210) describes the far-reaching impact of U.S. military actions on Guam in 1944–1945. See citations for the invasion of Guam in chapter 5. Information about the immediate postinvasion period in Guam is also found in Apple (1980:61), Carano and Sanchez (1964:311–312), Hough (1947:284–285), James (1946), Josephy (1946), Sanchez (1984:110–121), and Shaw, Nalty, and Turnbladh (1966:544, 570). U.S. Navy, Bureau of Yards and Docks (1947:343–358) describes wartime navy construction work on Guam. In October 1944 the civil affairs unit became the Military Government of Guam; in April 1945 it changed again to U.S. Naval-Military Government.

21. Blackton (1946) and USSBS (1947b) differ in their description of the surrender at Chuuk. Denfeld (1981a:53–59) summarizes the surrender process and describes it as the largest in the Pacific, comprising 14,294 Japanese army troops, 8,841 navy, 14,219 naval construction workers, 1,590 civilians, and 9,082 Chuukese, along with 791 Nauruans, 8 Germans, 7 Spanish, and 6 Chinese. Statistics prepared by the Japanese command for the initial surrender meeting summarized conditions at the end of August

1945. Chuuk's ground defenses were well equipped, but air and sea operations were nil; interisland transport was barely possible because small craft were falling apart and fuel was very scarce. Water, housing, and communication were adequate, but food "desperately" short. Military and civilians lived on sweet potatoes with occasional bits of vegetables or fish (Blackton 1946:404–405).

22. On the initial U.S. occupation of Chuuk, see Denfeld (1981a:53–59), King and Carucci (1984:473–474), Parker (1985:276–277), Richard (1957b:7, 257), and U.S. Navy, Bureau of Yards and Docks (1947:415–416). The U.S. flag was raised over Mechitew on Weno, where the U.S. Navy established its first headquarters, and a navy tent camp was set up on Moen #1 airfield. Later, the administrative center moved to Nantaku and the airfield was repaired for use (King and Carucci 1984:473–474, King and Parker 1984:108).

23. In Chuuk, the Marshalls, and several areas of western Micronesia, Islanders provided information useful in war crimes prosecutions, as well as other information about the fate of U.S. servicemen and Japanese treatment of prisoners of war. See Denfeld (1981a:60–64) on trials for alleged war crimes on Chuuk and Piccigallo (1979:74–83) on the U.S. Navy's Pacific war crimes trials.

24. On the U.S. occupation of Palau, see Frank and Shaw (1968:440–450), Nero (1989), Richard (1957b:7), and U.S. Navy, Bureau of Yards and Docks (1947:326–332). Duncan (1946) describes Yap at the time of occupation; the end of the war on Yap is described in more detail in Poyer (1995).

25. Richard (1957a:64–165) writes: "The landing forces were thoroughly indoctrinated as to their treatment of the people and their contacts with the natives were regulated. Service personnel were ordered to show the islanders all possible consideration, to refrain insofar as possible from disturbing their normal existence, and not to intermingle with them. All native areas were out of bounds to military personnel except those whose duties made visits to the villages and camps necessary."

26. On the Mortlocks removal, see Nason (1970:230) and Borthwick (1977:59). Richard (1957b:6) gives the following (west longitude) surrender dates:

Aug 22	Mili, Marshall Islands
Sept 2	Rota and Pagan, Marianas
	Chuuk, Central Carolines
	Palau and Yap, Western Carolines
Sept 4	Aguijan, Marianas
Sept 5	Jaluij, Marshalls
Sept 6	Wotje and Maloelap, Marshalls
Sept 8	Kosrae, Eastern Carolines

Sept 11	Pohnpei
Sept 16	Lamotrek, Western Carolines
Sept 17	Namoluk, Central Carolines
Sept 19	Woleai, Western Carolines
Oct 6	Tobi, Sonsorol and Merir, Western Carolines
Oct 16	Puluwat, Central Carolines
Oct 21	Nomoi, Central Carolines

Local people say there were no Japanese on Namoluk when Americans came ashore (despite Richard 1957b:7; Mac Marshall, pers. comm.).

27. Witherspoon (1945) is a detailed report of the U.S. Marine Landing Force sent on reconnaissance to the atolls south of Chuuk.

28. Then-Lt. John Useem (1945a) described the difficulties facing initial MilGov personnel, remarking, "No two islands are being administered in the same way" (Useem 1945a:96–97). American civil affairs officers held attitudes ranging from "regard[ing] the native population as enemy nationals who were to be given the minimum aid necessary for survival" to "view[ing] the islanders as friendly neutrals who should be restored as soon as possible to a working society." While MilGov administrators began with the intention of "restoring" indigenous society, he wrote, the question of what that meant persisted: "Hence each governor arbitrarily constructed his own frame of reference; to some, native society meant the disorganized social order operative at the time of the island's capture; to others, the ancestral social structure of the pre-colonial era; and to still others, the style of life found among 'primitives' elsewhere" (1946b:2).

29. By early October 1945, Mili had been sufficiently cleared for people on Arno and Majuro to return. Later that month, 292 were returned to Maloelap and 330 to Wotje. In mid-October, 90 Ailinglablab people went home from Jaluij. In November, 90 were repatriated from Wotje to Ailuk, Mejit, and Utirik; 524 Marshallese returned to Jaluij and 531 were taken from Jaluij back to their homelands (Richard 1957b:48).

Repatriation was also important to Islanders farther west. Sixty-four Yapese had been taken to Kosrae and Pohnpei; 8 to Saipan; 319 Ulithians and 88 Ifaluk people had been moved to Yap; 300 from Woleai were living on Ifaluk—the navy returned all these to their homes in 1946. Chamorros who had been living on Pohnpei, Yap, and Palau were returned to Saipan. Fifty-seven Guamanians and 31 Rotanese returned from Saipan. In mid-October 1945, 76 Chamorros left Pohnpei for Saipan. At the beginning of March 1946, 226 Chamorros and 8 Carolinians returned to Saipan from Yap. Thirty-nine Saipan people returned from Palau later the same year. In 1947, a single Chamorro from Saipan was returned home from Borneo (Richard 1957b:48–52).

30. The same was true in Europe. Captured German soldiers were "cocky and confident that their country would win the war; after they were transported to the rear and saw the masses of supplies stocked there, that confidence vanished" (Kennett 1987:96). The U.S. Army's Eastern Base Section in Tunis had a supply dump covering 3 square miles (Kennett 1987: 96–97). "Here was perhaps the most graphic impression the Americans made on those who fought against them or beside them: In the sophistication and the lavishness of means and material put at their disposal, the G.I.s were truly 'the rich Americans'" (Kennett 1987:109).

31. The navy's most pressing need for labor was in Guam (Richard 1957b:487), where military labor needs were always greater than the supply of local workers. Guamanian women began to take employment beyond the domestic, nursing, or teaching jobs they had known before the war, becoming clerks, telephone operators, and stenographers. The demand for construction workers was so great that a separate Labor Department was established in October 1944 (Carano and Sanchez 1964:313).

32. Recruitment of Marshallese to work on Kwajalein began with 300 workers, then fluctuated between 175 and 160 from 1951 to 1959. Kwajalein became a long-term American base. In the early 1950s, Kwajalein's military activity related to bomb tests at Bikini and Enewetak; in 1959 it became part of the Pacific Missile Range to test missiles and was renamed "Kwajalein Missile Range." In 1951, Marshallese workers were moved off Kwajalein islet to live on Ebeye. Until 1950 most Americans on Kwajalein were military; since then, civilian contractors have handled many functions, including managing Marshallese laborers (Alexander 1978:36–39). For additional information on Kwajalein, including battle sites and locations of value to Kwajalein people, see Carucci (1997b) and Panamerican Consultants, Inc. (1994).

33. American pay scales for Islanders varied. The lowest was in the Carolines, at up to $10 to $20 a month for administrative and professional workers. Pay increased over time and also reflected costs of living on different islands and gender distinctions (Richard 1957b:489). Embree (1949:208, n.1) notes the irony that pay for POWs was regulated by treaty: thus, POWS on Saipan at one point received 70 cents per day, while civilian Japanese and Chamorro workers received 40 cents.

34. Chamorros and Carolinians in the Marianas came to their postwar labor experiences with different work histories. Of 333 Saipanese classed as "artisans" (skilled labor) early in the American period, only 45 were Carolinians (Bowers 1950:66).

35. American soldiers were similarly free-spending in Europe, where attempts were made to reduce the impact of their purchasing power by paying in local currency and at a rate that overvalued it (this was apparently not a policy in Micronesia). Soldiers nevertheless spent freely, bartered or sold cigarette and candy rations, and bought scarce local supplies. In France—as in Micronesia—this gave the impression that

Americans were going to be the ones taking care of them in the future (Kennett 1987:196–197).

36. Ken Reightler (pers. comm.), an American serviceman stationed on Kwajalein in 1946, recalls that there was nothing unusual in Islanders driving, but one enterprising resident was memorable: a Pohnpeian who set up a prostitution ring on Kwajalein and purchased his own jeep.

37. American occupiers knew of only five people who spoke English in Chuuk, four in Yap, and five in Palau: "Of necessity the Americans had to use them as interpreters and to channel through them almost all verbal contacts. . . . This situation has not been a healthy one for many obvious reasons." A November 1947 directive of the deputy high commissioner urged navy personnel to acquire a "working knowledge of the local language to measure up to his job" (U.S. Navy 1948:47–48), but in fact the burden of language learning was put largely on Micronesians.

CHAPTER 8. INAUGURATING AMERICAN RULE

1. See Dorothy Richard (1957a, b, c) for the official history of U.S. Navy MilGov and CivAd administrations; Yarbrough (1971:193–194), Embree (1949), and Useem (1945c) for initial problems. The form of U.S. Navy Civil Administration is described in Richard and in U.S. Navy (1948:99–114). We have deliberately limited our discussion of postwar Micronesia to a few topics linked with the experience of war. A comprehensive review of the history of the Trust Territory of the Pacific Islands and its dissolution is Hezel (1995:242–367). Gale (1979) discusses some of the political and strategic issues involved in postwar decisions about governing Micronesia. Hanlon (1998) provides a critical evaluation of economic and development issues. Articles in Kiste and Marshall (1999) review American anthropology's role in a variety of topics in Micronesian studies.

2. By fall of 1945, commissioned U.S. Navy MilGov units operated on Koror, Saipan, Tinian, Yap, and Chuuk, with others soon in place on Pohnpei, Kwajalein (for the northern Marshall Islands), and Majuro (southern Marshalls). During the last year of fighting, Allies split the occupied region into the Marshalls-Gilberts Area and the Marianas Area. By the beginning of 1946, Kiribati returned to British rule and the Marshalls were put under the Marianas Area commander. Over the next year, as occupation forces were removed, command boundaries shifted; by the end of 1946, five districts had been defined (PCAA 1978:450–455; U.S. Navy 1948:93–99). Some boundary changes had greater local significance than others. For example, Ujelang, which we identify as part of the Marshall Islands—the district in which it was placed by U.S. MilGov—had been administered from Pohnpei during the Japanese era.

3. But there was not agreement about the legal status of the islands or the standing of its inhabitants in American constitutional terms. Even after the establishment of U.N. trusteeship, these issues remained unclear. See, for example, Gale (1979:47–96) and U.S. Navy (1948:85–91). Pomeroy (1947) discusses postwar strategic issues and American attitudes toward Islanders.

4. As anthropologists who spoke with Islanders immediately after the war pointed out, the term *liberation* did not suit, since Micronesians did not regard the Japanese civilian government as having been tyrannical—and for some, the souvenir gathering or racial intolerance of American troops was more oppressive than actions of the South Seas Bureau (e.g., Useem 1946c:23). And, despite proclamations of freedom, military needs required that "affairs had to be regulated in all the major concerns of life, far more stringently than they had been under the Japanese South Seas Bureau" (Useem 1946b:4–5). Even when military security was no longer threatened, MilGov maintained controls on public life. Thompson (1947a:275–277, 303–304) explicitly criticized the long-standing contradiction on Guam between "authoritarian military rule" and "the American democratic ideal."

5. Other Chuukese leaders used the postwar vacuum in colonial administration to press moral agendas. Murdock et al. (1948:118) report area chiefs imposing alimony and discouraging divorce, despite Governor Huxley's explicit statement that they were not to impose any church policy (see also Hall 1992).

6. Problems of navy administration in Chuuk are described in Gladwin (1950, 1964), Hall (1950), Hall and Pelzer (1946), Murdock and Goodenough (1947), and in the Co-ordinated Investigation of Micronesian Anthropology interim reports for Chuuk (Goodenough and LeBar 1948; Murdock et al. 1948). The complicated role of anthropologists in American Micronesia—engaged as culture brokers—is discussed in Falgout (1995a), Gale (1979:73–79), and chapters in Kiste and Marshall (1999). Anthropologists' work during the navy era included the Co-ordinated Investigation of Micronesian Anthropology (CIMA), Scientific Investigations in Micronesia (SIM), and the U.S. Commercial Company (USCC) economic survey (see Mason 1953a).

7. One use for American criticism of traditional institutions (despite de facto support of chiefs) was to demonstrate the superiority of democracy. The "inadequately developed" nature of a government vested in chiefs was one marker of Class "C" League of Nations mandated territories that, in Western eyes, were unprepared for political autonomy. The United States, as trustee, thus took on the obligation of developing local governance. On establishing municipalities, see Abe (1986:195–197), Richard (1957c:388–406), and U.S. Navy (1948:101–126).

8. And, at times, American policy confirmed the role of Japanese-appointed leaders, as U.S. MilGov at first confirmed Japanese-era leaders in their offices on Saipan in

1945 (Solenberger 1964:57). On islands with no resident MilGov officer, inertia supported existing leaders. The "king" of Mokil had complete freedom in assessing fines for infractions of the naval penal code (this is in 1947); "There is no appeal from the king's sentence except to the Native Affairs Officer [on Pohnpei] who almost invariably supports the king" (Weckler 1949:31).

9. For U.S. Navy treatment of traditional leaders on Pohnpei, see Bascom (1950:149–150), Dahlquist (1972:59), Fischer (1974:169–170), Murrill (1948a:57), and Riesenberg (1948).

10. On U.S. Navy dealings with Marshallese chiefs, see Fischer (1974:175), Heine (1974), and McGrath and Wilson (1971:186–187).

11. When Americans first landed on Yap, "there was an immediate demand to see the chief. Having become somewhat accustomed to this sort of request, a couple of the more astute elders framed it so that one would say he was chief of all Yap and have the other men confirm this fact for the Americans. His reward for this would be the chieftainship of the district in which he lived. This trick worked beautifully, and was only upset when an investigation disclosed that these two men, in terms of old Yap customs, were not the rightful chiefs. Indeed, there was no chief of all Yap at all but a relative equality of the top three" (Hunt et al. 1949:183).

12. Vidich (1980) details postwar conditions and politics in Palau; see also Force (1960), McKnight (1960, 1974), and Useem (1946a).

13. While altering the interplay of traditional and new leaders in the islands, the navy also introduced novel institutions (Lingenfelter 1975:190). Referring to "our government's obsession with the need to 'bring democracy to the Trukese,'" Edward Hall (1992:162–164) describes weekly meetings that Chuuk's military governor held with the fifty to sixty island and village chiefs. (Though the chiefs were eager to cooperate, the governor was frustrated by their unwillingness to engage in open discussion—Chuukese had not altered their cultural belief that advice should be conveyed indirectly and privately.) On small atolls, where chiefs continued as political leaders, the most important innovations were that of elected municipal magistrate and the island meeting held during each field trip ship visit (focused on the magistrate and navy directives), an "enduring alteration of native political affairs" that developed at this time (Nason 1970:242–243, 250–251).

Many writings describe the development of local, regional, and national political structures in Micronesia. General coverage for the postwar decades, including discussion and critique of the navy's approach to political change, is found in Heine (1974), Gale (1979), Hezel (1995), Meller (1969), articles in Hughes and Lingenfelter (1974), and Petersen (1999) and citations therein.

14. MilGov handled all trade goods for Islander purchase until May 1945, when the Foreign Economic Administration took over (Richard 1957b: 471; PCAA 1978: 425). By July 1945, Islanders and Japanese in occupied areas were paying for their own food, clothes, and goods. The USCC replaced the FEA in November 1945; it was in turn replaced in December 1947 by the Island Trading Company. Problems of supply remained constant, with goods limited in quantity and variety. When reporter Robert Trumbull visited Micronesia in 1946, "all the women were wearing dresses of the same color" because it was cheapest for the government to import large quantities of a single kind of cloth. "So there was nothing but purple for the women to buy, on island after island, for many months" (Trumbull 1959: 95).

15. On Kapingamarangi, "A few women remarked that Japanese soldiers were much more polite and considerate in approaching them than the American naval personnel, who were loud and 'rough' with them." Kapinga people call American curse words *nherekhai neipi*—"navy talk" (Lieber 1968: 32). These sailors may have had a reputation similar to the European theater GIs. Kennett (1987: 208–209) describes U.S. Army troops' irritating habits in Europe: loud and belligerent when drunk, generous but "casual about property rights," and crudely blunt in approaching women.

16. On the other hand, although Yapese at war's end were equally in want of repaired roads and supplies of kerosene, nails, lamps, mosquito nets, blankets, and lumber for replacing destroyed boats and canoes (Lingenfelter 1972: 273–274), they had no problem with the desultory American rule. People felt they had suffered a lot under the Japanese; "Against this background, the initial American neglect of the area seemed simply like noninterference, a promising change from previous colonial administrations" (Labby 1973: 33).

17. As late as 1948, Ifaluk people were unable to resume copra production since they could not predict the arrival of ships (Burrows and Spiro 1957: 173). Islands nearer administrative centers—such as most of the Mortlocks and Mokil—saw a ship every three to four weeks after transport was regularized, but at the beginning of American occupation shipping was erratic (U.S. Navy 1948: 24). The first navy ship at Mokil and Pingelap collected Japanese yen, but then the lack of vessels prevented a return to distribute dollars: "Ironically, the first American visit to these islands reduced them to barter. They remained without a medium of exchange until the chief of Mokil and some of his people traveled the ninety miles to Ponape in a twenty-foot native-made whaleboat, using mats as sail, and returned with their money and some trade goods. Their party arrived on Ponape just in time to join the Fourth of July celebration of American independence" (Bascom 1950: 148). Military and medical personnel never made it to outlying islands again in that first year of U.S. occupation (Bascom 1965: 26).

18. Postwar Mokil is described in Bentzen (1948, 1949), Murphy (1950), and Weckler (1949).

19. See Richard (1957c:993). On U.S. Navy educational policies, see Fink (1948). After the Department of the Interior took over, the emphasis in Micronesia's schools shifted from learning English to supporting local languages and cultures. Teaching English—the navy's first educational goal—was nearly eliminated in 1952–1955 to preserve local cultures. On the history of education in Micronesia, see Coletta (1980), Peacock (1990), Ramarui (1976), and Shuster (1982a).

20. Carlton C. Wright was first deputy high commissioner of the U.S. Trust Territory. In February 1947, he was deputy commander Marianas Area and deputy governor of Guam, with the task of coordinating and assisting with rehabilitation in education, health, and agriculture using resources available on Guam (PCAA 1978:458).

Although Admiral Wright's statement is strikingly frank, "primitivism" had been an official policy option earlier. In evaluating wartime MilGov, Useem (1946c:22–23) states that MilGov staff were handicapped by military needs and attitudes and by severe supply shortages, caused both by lack of shipping space and "reluctance to grant anything but bare essentials to civilians, on the theory that they were primitive in their standards of living, [which] sharply limited all rehabilitation efforts." A U.S. Congress report recommending placement of U.S. bases throughout the Pacific gave as the economic goal "native" self-subsistence—agriculture and crafts—and encouraging indoctrination of Islanders as Americans for future independence or affiliation with the U.S. (Johnstone 1945:196–197; see Hezel 1995:262–270). Walter Karig, author of *The Fortunate Islands*, suggests the way to keep them fortunate is to "leave one corner of the earth uncontaminated by tin-can civilization," in a view of the islands from the (unofficial) perspective of early navy administrators (1948:226). Seeing changes in Pacific Island life as despoliation has a long history in Western representations of the area.

21. In Palau, the departure of some 16,000 Japanese, Koreans, Okinawans, and Chinese left 5,634 Palauans in a suddenly empty land (Embree 1946b:63–164; Fischer 1957:65; Useem 1946a:635). Repatriation began October 1945; the last foreigners and POWs were deported from the islands (Guam and Saipan) late in December of 1947. About 4,500 Asians stayed after initial repatriation to work on cleanup—2,500 on Chuuk and 2,000 on Palau. Europeans and Americans in the islands during the war did not have to leave unless they had been involved in anti-American activities (PCAA 1978:426–427).

Peattie (1988:308) gives a total figure of 147,000 Japanese, Koreans, Okinawans, and Taiwanese repatriated from the South Pacific, of whom 52,000 were civilians. See also Hezel (1995:249–250) on civilian repatriation.

22. Hezel (1995:264–270) reviews the economic history of this period in a section headed "A Reservation Economy." There are many parallels and links—both conceptual and historical—between U.S. government policy on Native American reservations and in Micronesia. See also Hanlon (1998), a close and critical study of American development efforts and discourse in Micronesia.

23. A navy CivAd team visiting Woleai in March–April 1947 reported that "a native subsistence economy . . . exists and is flourishing" despite extensive damage to the islands by Japanese construction and U.S. air raids. Chiefs had organized coconut replanting; Gagil on Yap (historically in a tribute/assistance relationship with Woleai) provided seed taro and banana slips. Fais people also had replanted coconuts and were covering the areas stripped by phosphate mining with carted-in soil (U.S. Navy 1948:133).

24. Americans inherited the results of years of Japanese work with this product. The Japanese had organized Marshallese women's handicrafts extensively, identifying saleable items and placing orders for delivery by the atoll magistrate. The Japanese chose a craftswoman on each atoll to maintain standards and encourage production; they rewarded those who worked well with prizes. "Much of the present handicraft manufacture goes back to encouragement given during the Japanese period" (Bryan 1972:211).

25. Douglas Oliver also, in the USCC survey report, reminded his audience of American administrators, "The temporary camps built during the war . . . should not be set as the model of what natives want, were accustomed to before the war, or need for permanent living," though they had been useful during the war and were handy for administrators (1951:6).

26. In 1946, Guam's military government reverted to a naval government much like that before the war. Though the occasional appearance of Japanese army stragglers always made news, the significant military presence was American, with rapid military construction pushing an economic boom and close navy control of the economy. Unlike the Chamorros of Saipan, Guam's people had been farmers before the war, and the wartime scarcity of food made them keenly aware of the importance of a reserve of land for agriculture (Gallahue 1946:16). Loss of land to the military—much of it prime farmland—became a critical concern in U.S.–Guam relations. It was not economic growth, but labor, land, and the legal status of Guamanians that became major issues. Guam's distinctive position as a U.S. possession made its postwar course as different from the rest of the Marianas as its prewar life had been.

27. Chamorros on Saipan received 50 cents/day, with about $1/family/day of rations, compared with 30 cents/hour on Guam—where Guamanians criticized setting the wage at one-fourth to one-third the U.S. mainland rate (Gallahue 1946:74).

28. Spoehr (1954) gives a detailed account of postwar Saipan; in addition to the reports cited, see also Farrell (1991:504) and Taylor (1945, 1951).

29. On Chamorros' postwar status, particularly vis-à-vis Carolinians in the Marianas and elsewhere, see Alkire (1984), Oliver (1951:8), Poyer (1999), and U.S. Navy (1948:50–51). It was partly this special relationship that resulted in the resettlement of Tinian. Chamorros living on Yap as copra traders, skilled laborers, and Japanese colonial employees were also used by U.S. MilGov, which hired and promoted them disproportionately. Yapese objections, and the fact that the war destroyed Chamorros' niche in Yap's Japanese-era trading economy, led to a less-than-successful plan to relocate a group of them to Tinian in 1948. They supported themselves adequately by wage labor until spring of 1950. But when the navy presence dwindled that year, so did income. Tinian had good land, no complicated landownership problems, and a market for produce on Guam. But the settlers were unfamiliar with and uncommitted to farming; as on Saipan, they did not see an agricultural future for themselves (Emerick 1958; Lingenfelter 1975:187; Spoehr 1951; Useem 1946b).

30. For these points and descriptions of postwar Palau, see Ballendorf (1988b), Barnett (1949), Force (1960:85, 113), McKnight (1959), Trumbull (1959:168), Useem (1946a:89; 1949:107–110; 1952), Vidich (1980:268–269, 285–290), and Yarbrough (1971:193–194).

31. "The civil-affairs planners had been misled by the anthropological literature perused prior to invasion; it presented an antiquated picture of native life at the level of the German era, and was permeated with propagandistic stereotypes of Japanese actions. As a result, supplies were taken for an aboriginal people, whereas in reality what was needed were items of the same type as would be brought to a South Dakota rural community" (Useem 1945b:580). See also, for example, Vidich (1980:275, n.11).

32. In a further ironic twist, as Micronesians came to acknowledge the unlikelihood of economic development under American rule, some sought to make a virtue of the necessity of traditionalism. In the eastern Caroline Islands, John Fischer (1957:67) wrote more than a decade after the war: "The low economic value of the islands to the United States makes it seem unlikely that the real income of the islanders will easily regain its heights of the Japanese period. A certain amount of disillusionment of the islanders with the idea of economic progress has been inevitable under the Americans. Economic progress is still held to be desirable but conceived to be nearly impossible to attain. A return of interest in the old ways has resulted in some places, especially where the economic decline has been greatest."

33. John Fischer (1957:59) said much the same thing of the eastern Caroline Islands a decade later: Japanese economic development "raised the income and standard of living of the islanders to a new high which has yet to be attained under American rule."

34. See Pillsbury (1948) for an official and optimistic view of Chuuk under U.S. Navy rule. But it was not only navy public relations officers who saw benefits in the status quo. Anthropologist Sir Peter Buck, visiting Kapingamarangi in 1947, wrote that Kapinga people need only "a simple system of education in English, which they earnestly desire," some medical attention and a few items of trade, both available from the navy; "they have nothing to gain from the outside world" (1950:285). Farrell (1991:502) points out that delayed economic development had the virtue of preparing local people with education and political experience. Rapid development by outside economic interests immediately after the war might have meant loss of local control. On navy and Trust Territory commercial activities, see Bowers (1950:143, 184), James (1949:16), Nason (1970:237), Richard (1957c:621, 681–697, 704–715), Tolerton and Rauch (1945:175). Farrell (1991:487) adds that, on Saipan, business experience gained in operating trade stores was the only navy-era economic development initiative of lasting value. A creative Chuukese response to the tight economy was district savings systems, started by Petrus Mailo (Mahony 1960).

35. On Micronesian-American attitudes during the navy era, see U.S. Navy (1948:67–68) and Useem (1946b:6–7). Baseball games, which Americans like Japanese took as a significant form of cross-cultural interaction, are described in Murdock (1948b:70) and Tolerton and Rauch (1949:19).

36. On SONA, see Kiste and Falgout (1999), PCAA (1978:456–459), and Richard (1957a:37–171). The five-month training course covered cross-cultural awareness and skills, cultural anthropology, and Pacific topics. For a description of wartime training for the first generation of MilGov officers, see Embree (1949).

37. The trusteeship agreement guaranteed freedoms similar to those in the U.S. Constitution, including a Bill of Rights (Baron 1973:74). This was inevitably problematic when set against the variety of Micronesian customs. On smaller islands, unity in religion is valued and the introduction of new missions strongly opposed (e.g., in 1949 the Catholic Church was established on Namoluk despite a "great deal of opposition" from Protestants [Marshall 1972:34]). On Kosrae, the prewar theocracy was finally dismantled under the pressure of administrators from Pohnpei (Lewis 1948a:61–62, 1948b:42; Schaefer 1976:54).

38. For example, Murdock (1948a:424–425) gives a thumbnail sketch of each population: "The Palauans are progressive and eager to adopt Western ways. The Yapese are ultra-conservative and deeply suspicious of foreigners. The Chuukese desire material advantages but are satisfied with their traditional social structure"; see Poyer (1999). See Petersen (1999) on anthropology and postwar politics in Micronesia.

39. For other examples, see Barnett (1948), Embree (1949), Gladwin (1964:57–58), Spoehr (1954:88), and Useem (1945a). "When it was proposed to send Black marines

to American Samoa, Marine General C.F.B. Price warned of the danger of contact between Blacks and 'primitively romantic' Polynesian women. Mixture of the Polynesian with the white race and the Chinese had produced desirable results, said Price, but the union of Blacks and Polynesians had to be guarded against. He recommended stationing Black troops 'in Micronesia where they can do no racial harm'" (MacGregor 1981:92, cited in Spector 1985:390).

40. Kapingamarangi women on Pohnpei, for example, had sold handicrafts and local food to Japanese women and worked in factories before the war, but during the first part of the American era, their only wage work was as domestic help (Lieber 1968:29). Marshallese women were employed only as nurses and nurses' aides (Cockrum 1970:232). And navy-set wage scales were significantly higher for men—40 cents/hour compared to 25 cents/hour for women. In the mid-1950s, "most" Americans working for the Trust Territory employed "one Micronesian servant girl [*sic;* often a mature woman] for cleaning, babysitting, and general housework" at a maximum of $30/month, "frequently much less," for an eight-hour day (Trumbull 1959:202).

CHAPTER 9. THE LEGACY OF WAR

1. Micronesia does not often figure in American fictional literature, but Charlie Smith explores the physical landscape of Tinian's ruins—decades after the war—in his novella *Tinian* (1991). Joseph Meredith (1995) describes the ruins and debris of war throughout the islands seen when he commanded a destroyer escort on navy duty in Micronesia in 1953–1954.

2. Garapan came back to life as a few people began to move back in the late 1960s, and by the mid-1970s it had become a focus of Japanese tourism development on Saipan; in another decade it had "regained its position as the most important settlement in the Northern Marianas" (Russell 1987:26).

3. On Agana's population, see Useem (1948:22). Thompson (1947b) criticizes the navy's delay in rebuilding Agana, leaving people still in temporary housing more than two years after the war. On the destruction of Koror, see McKnight (1978:12), Sherrod (1952:113), and U.S. Congress (1970:49). Quonsets and other structures were set up on the bulldozed ruins to serve as U.S. government headquarters, and in 1946 about 1,100 Palauans were living there (U.S. Navy 1948:180). The 3,500 Palauans and 60 Americans on Koror in the mid-1950s still lived in the midst of the ruins.

4. American troops did a share of the damage, destroying captured food stocks, looting stores, and scattering civilian goods taken as souvenirs: "Bulldozer operators have a psychology all their own. In clearing an area, any obstacle in the neighborhood is a challenge and must be knocked down. Native buildings not destroyed in the fight-

ing suddenly disappeared. These practices were rationalized on the grounds that 'it's all Jap stuff anyway.' No appeal by the military government officers to the combat forces that such activities were unwarranted had any effect" (Useem 1945a:97). On Koror, the first MilGov commander "ordered sufficient goods burnt or thrown into the sea to have started the population on the road back to recovery" (Useem 1946a:83).

5. On natural resource effects of war damage, see Baker (1946), Brower (1974), Fischer (1957:77), Hall and Pelzer (1946), Mason (1953b), Richard (1957a:416), Rynkiewich (1972:30–32), Tolerton and Rauch (1949:13), and Trumbull (1959:144–145).

6. Damage to Chuuk is described in Hall and Pelzer (1946:53), Pelzer (1947:80–81), Gladwin (1952), and Gladwin and Sarason (1953:31).

7. On Ulithi, see Lessa (1950:16); on Satawan, Tolerton and Rauch (1949:13); on Parem and Puluwat, Hall and Pelzer (1946); on Woleai, Alkire (1974:67–68) and Burrows and Spiro (1957:174). Postwar American policies essentially ended rice cultivation in the Marianas (Solenberger 1967).

8. On damage to fisheries, see Gladwin (1952), Hall and Pelzer (1946:53, 58), and Johannes (1981:4, 30).

9. Attempts to resolve land tenure problems in Palau during the early American era are described in Kaneshiro (1958), D. R. Smith (1983:128–131), Vidich (1980:202–203), and Yarbrough (1971:203–204).

10. On the need for clear titles for farming in Saipan, see Spoehr (1954:104). All of Tinian had been owned by the Japanese government. Rota (occupied after Japanese surrender) had only limited American military construction. Rota had problems similar to Saipan; the Japanese had relocated people repeatedly since 1925, making for a complex land tenure situation (Bowers 1950:79; Gallahue 1946).

11. On Saipan's land situation, see Bowers (1950:79), Emerick (1958), and Spoehr (1954:85, 131–132).

12. For these points about Guam, see Apple (1980:62), Oliver (1951:11), Reed (1952: 80–82), and Souder (1971:105–106).

13. See Oliver (1951:27, n.1,3). By June 30, 1951, Micronesians owned 250 square miles of Trust Territory land, mostly under clan or lineage ownership. At the close of the navy era, the Trust Territory owned about 434 square miles of land (Richard 1957c: 505). On Peleliu, see also Bronemann (1982:176). Some Palauans returned to Peleliu from Babelthuap in 1946; others in 1947–1949; only about 200–250 people lived there in the 1970s, with others on Saipan or on Koror or Babelthuap "where they can make a living." On their return, they found property lines no longer evident, and controversy remains (Bronemann 1982:176).

14. There is a large literature on these removals. See, for example, Baron (1973), Carucci (1997a), Kiste (1968), Mason (1954), and Richard (1957c:511–556).

15. On relocation in the Marianas, see Bowers (1950:98–116), Emerick (1958), Farrell (1991:469), and Richard (1957b:52, 1957c:565); on Peleliu people, Kaneshiro (1958: 326–327); on Weno, Hall and Pelzer (1950), King and Parker (1984:108), Gladwin (1964:49), and Parker (1985:287).

16. On Arno, see Rynkiewich (1972:30–32); on Weno, King and Parker (1984:109); on Pohnpei, Trumbull (1959) and Emerick (1960). On internal migration in Micronesia, see Gorenflo and Levin (1995) and Hezel and Levin (1996) and sources cited therein.

17. In addition to reshuffling the distribution of rewards, wartime destruction had the overall effect of reducing the severity of distinctions of wealth. On Saipan, the complete loss of material possessions leveled all to bare subsistence; not until 1950 did modest differences in housing emerge, and status differences due to wealth remained muted for years (Spoehr 1954:110–111, 221, 305). On Palau, where tangible wealth is culturally linked with prestige, chiefs found themselves too old or too high in status to do the manual work that would bring American currency (Force 1960:85, 113).

18. This shift in leadership was less true on atolls, where few choices were available to American administrators (e.g., Etal men educated at Japanese schools became American-era leaders; Nason 1970:374, n.3).

19. While the analogy of war and typhoon was only rarely voiced in our interviews, the compelling image matches local perceptions of war's effects. For example, low islanders traditionally turn to high islands for aid after a typhoon, and they did so also after the war—as when Yap assisted Woleai and Chuuk assisted Puluwat with replanting and food shortages in the aftermath of war (U.S. Navy 1948:133; Hall and Pelzer 1946:3). Recall also the Yapese comment that goods left by departing Japanese troops are like the debris remaining after a typhoon.

20. On Ulithi, see Lessa (1950a:6). As John Fischer (1957:64) wrote of the eastern Carolines: "While individual islanders undoubtedly had preferences for one side or the other they did not consider the war to be their own or within their ability to affect the outcome." Responding to emotional American claims that the islands were "purchased" by American blood shed in taking them from Japan, Lazarus Salii (1972:37) wrote clearly, "the blood which was spilled . . . was not spilled at the request, or for the benefit of the Micronesian people."

21. Vidich (1980) mentions Palauan resentment at the Japanese for bringing down American attacks, but this attitude was either not widespread in the islands or did not long outlast the war. American visitors to Yap in 1947–1948 commented: "It was quite impossible to get an exact picture of the native reaction to the war. In some moods, the people reacted strongly against Japanese injustices. If this opinion was not accepted, informants would complain about the hard and stingy Americans, and picture the Japanese as kindly and paternalistic" (Hunt et al. 1949:111).

22. Lindstrom and White (1989) discuss the form and meaning of World War II stories throughout the Pacific Islands.

23. On the Chuuk lagoon wrecks, see Stewart (1985), Bailey (1982), and Lindemann (1987). On Kwajalein's World War II remains, see Carucci (1997b) and Panamerican Consultants (1994). On those of Taroa islet, Maloelap, see Adams (1997).

24. For example, on Japanese veterans visiting Woleai, see Boyer (1967); on the 1978 installation of a monument to the 9th Regiment of the Japanese Imperial Army on Saipan, Oxborrow (1979); on a suicide submarine veteran visiting western Micronesia, Cook and Cook (1992:312). Some Japanese memorial efforts to recover war dead actually destroy other historical materials. Ward and Pickering (1985) document illegal excavation, use of earth-moving equipment, destruction of prehistoric sites, and recovery of prehistoric Chamorro remains as well as wartime Japanese remains by a group of war veterans and others who came to the Commonwealth of the Northern Mariana Islands in 1985. Mcintyre (1985:78) describes and pictures Japanese collection efforts of war remains and ceremonies on Saipan. The Korean government has also arranged for the return of the remains of war dead (Denfeld 1984:13).

25. Micronesians began filing claims, first against Japan, immediately after the war (e.g., Richard 1957c:505). Claims against Japan included not only war damages but also postal savings, war bonds, and other items that in some cases were initially to have been compensated by Japanese funds seized by American forces (e.g. Useem 1946a:102–103). Claims against Japan filed through the United States, as well as direct claims for damages by American forces, have been ongoing since the war. The Department of the Interior conducted a 1961 survey of war claims, which interviewed Micronesians and examined claim documents filed in 1944 and 1945 (U.S. Congress 1970:26). The U.S. government negotiated Japanese contributions to a Micronesian claims fund, established a Micronesian Claims Commission, and appropriated money for claims for wartime and postwar damages in 1971 (with subsequent amendments; see U.S. Congress 1970; 1971a, b; 1973a, b). On Guam's continuing efforts for restitution, see Underwood (1994:117–118). This is entirely separate from the question of compensation for the victims of postwar American nuclear testing in the Marshall Islands.

26. A useful comparison is Hiery's (1995) study of the impact on Pacific Islanders of the transition from German to Japanese rule consequent upon World War I.

27. But there may be significant differences among Micronesians in this regard. In discussing Chuukese attitudes toward cultural differences, Marc Swartz writes that Chuukese believe that they and Americans are fundamentally alike, not completely different cultures, so any differences in fact are of a specific and limited nature, not wholesale differences that disvalue Chuukese culture (Swartz 1966:79–80).

28. But Micronesian political leader Lazarus Salii (1972:37) rejected a sentimental

view of Japan that ignored its intent to force cultural assimilation: "Whatever its usefulness for rhetorical purposes this is not a nostalgia in which I, or most other Micronesian leaders, choose to participate." Early American visitors to the area found that the Spanish and German eras had been similarly idealized by the previous generation (U.S. Navy 1948:67).

29. The 1948 *Handbook of the Trust Territory* draws a similar conclusion (U.S. Navy 1948:67).

30. A 1996 U.S. Congress Joint Hearing on *U.S. Interests in the South Pacific: The Freely Associated States* explores both economic issues (including a discussion of whether and how the FAS can become "self-sufficient") and the role of Micronesia in U.S. strategic interests at the end of the twentieth century. Emerging Micronesian leaders in the 1970s spoke actively about how an understanding of American military activities in the Pacific should guide political status negotiations (e.g., Salii 1972; Uludong 1969).

31. Citizens of the freely associated states may join the U.S. military. Heine (1991: 120) describes an active recruitment program in the Marshall Islands: "Maybe that's another result of the war," he comments.

REFERENCES CITED

Abe, Goh

1986   "An Ethnohistory of Palau under the Japanese Administration." Ph.D. dissertation, University of Kansas.

Adams, William Hampton, ed.

1997   *The Japanese Airbase on Taroa Island, Republic of the Marshall Islands, 1937–45: An Evaluation of the World War II Remains.* San Francisco: National Park Service, Pacific Great Basin Support Office.

Agawa, Hiroyuki

1979   *The Reluctant Admiral: Yamamoto and the Imperial Navy.* Tokyo: Kodansha International.

Alexander, William J.

1978   "Wage Labor, Urbanization and Culture Change in the Marshall Islands: The Ebeye Case." Ph.D. dissertation, New School for Social Research.

Alkire, William H.

1974   "Land Tenure in Woleai." In *Land Tenure in Oceania,* ed. by H. P. Lundsgaarde, 34–69. Honolulu: University Press of Hawai'i.

1984   "The Carolinians of Saipan and the Commonwealth of the Northern Mariana Islands." *Pacific Affairs* 57(2):270–283.

Allen, Riley H.

1953   *Journey to the Trust Territory: Uncle Sam's Wards in the Pacific.* Pamphlet published by Honolulu Star-Bulletin Press.

Anonymous

1944   "Truk Reconnaissance." *Flying* (May):50, 166.

Anttila, Elizabeth K.

1965 "A History of the People of the Trust Territory of the Pacific Islands and Their Education." Ph.D. dissertation, University of Texas.

Aoyagi, Machiko

1978 "Gods of the Modekngei Religion in Belau." In *Cultural Uniformity and Diversity in Micronesia,* ed. by I. Ushijima and K. Sudo, 339–361. Osaka: National Museum of Ethnology.

Apple, R. A.

1980 *Guam: Two Invasions and Three Military Occupations: A Historical Summary of War in the Pacific National Historical Park, Guam.* MARC Miscellaneous Series, no. 3. Guam: Micronesian Area Research Center.

Bahrenburg, Bruce

1971 *The Pacific: Then and Now, A Revisiting of the Great Pacific Battlefields of World War II.* New York: Putnam.

Bailey, Dan E.

1989 *World War II Wrecks of the Kwajalein and Truk Lagoons* (rev. ed.). Redding, Ca: North Valley Diver Pubs.

Baker, Rollin H.

1946 "Some Effects of the War on the Wildlife of Micronesia." Transactions of the 11th North American Wildlife Conference, March 11–13, 1946, New York, ed. by Ethel M. Quee, 205–213. Washington, D.C.: American Wildlife Institute.

Ballendorf, Dirk A.

1983 "Earl Hancock Ellis: The Man and His Mission." *U.S. Naval Institute Proceedings* 109:53–60.

1984a "Secrets without Substance: U.S. Intelligence in the Japanese Mandates, 1915–1935." *Journal of Pacific History* 19(1/2):87–99.

1984b "American Administration in the Trust Territory of the Pacific Islands, 1944–1968." *Asian Culture Quarterly* 12(1):1–10.

1987 "Japanese Fortifications in Micronesia." Part 1. *Glimpses of Micronesia and the Western Pacific* 27(4):28–31.

1988a "Japanese Fortifications in Micronesia." Part 2. *Glimpses of Micronesia and the Western Pacific* 28(1):32–37.

1988b "The Japanese and the Americans: Contrasting Historical Periods of Economic and Social Development in Palau." *Asian Culture Quarterly* 16(4):55–63.

Ballendorf, Dirk, P. F. Kluge, and Meredith Carson

n.d. "Peleliu: Yesterday and Today." Manuscript seen at Micronesian Seminar, Chuuk (now in Kolonia, Pohnpei).

Ballendorf, Dirk, William M. Peck, and G. Geiyer Anderson

1986 *Oral History of the Japanese Schooling Experience of Chamorros at Saipan and Rota in the Commonwealth of the Northern Mariana Islands.* American Association for State and Local History, 1986. (Copy available at Micronesian Area Research Center, University of Guam.)

Ballendorf, Dirk, Donald M. Shuster, and Wakako Higuchi

1986 *An Oral Historiography of the Japanese Administration in Palau.* Final Report submitted to the Japan Foundation Institutional Project Support Program. Agana, Guam; Micronesian Area Research Center, University of Guam.

Barnard, Charles N.

1974 "Room with a View of World War II: Going Back to Micronesia." *Signature* 9(4):24–30, 50.

Barnett, Homer G.

1948 "CIMA Project Report, Palau Islands." In *Interim Reports: Co-ordinated Investigation of Micronesian Anthropology 1947–1948,* 151–153. Pacific Science Board, National Research Council.

1949 *Palauan Society: A Study of Contemporary Native Life in the Palau Islands.* CIMA Report No. 20. Washington, D.C.: Pacific Science Board. Reprinted (n.d.), Eugene: Department of Anthropology, University of Oregon.

Baron, Dona Gene

1973 "Policy for 'Paradise': A Study of United States Decisionmaking Processes Respecting the Trust Territory of the Pacific Islands and the Impact Thereupon of United Nations Oversight." Ph.D. dissertation, Columbia University.

Bartlett, Donald

1970 "Vice Admiral Chuichi Hara: Unforgettable Foe." *U.S. Naval Institute Proceedings* 96(10):49–55.

Bascom, William R.

1948 "Ponapean Prestige Economy." *Southwestern Journal of Anthropology* (now *Journal of Anthropological Research*) 4(3):211–221.

1949 "Subsistence Farming on Ponape." *New Zealand Geographer* 5(2):115–129.

1950 "Ponape, The Cycle of Empire." *The Scientific Monthly* 70(3):141–150.

1965 "Ponape: A Pacific Economy in Transition." Anthropological Records no. 22. Berkeley: University of California Press. (Reprinted from: Economic Survey of Micronesia, Report No. 8, Honolulu: U.S. Commercial Company, 1946.)

Bates, Marston, and Donald P. Abbott

1958 *Ifaluk: Portrait of a Coral Island.* London: Museum Press.

Bateson, Charles

1968 *The War with Japan: A Concise History.* East Lansing: Michigan State University Press.

Battle, Fr. Santiago [probable author]

n.d. "Diary of a Jesuit Priest in Truk from 13 Dec. 1941 to 3 May 1943." Translated from Spanish by R. Levesque. Part of Document BV 3680 T6 H4 at Micronesian Area Research Center, University of Guam.

Beardsley, Charles

1964 *Guam: Past and Present.* Tokyo: Charles E. Tuttle.

Bentzen, Conrad

1948 "Interim Report." In *Interim Reports: Co-ordinated Investigation of Micronesian Anthropology 1947–1948*, 43–44. Pacific Science Board, National Research Council.

1949 *Land and Livelihood on Mokil, an Atoll in the Eastern Carolines.* Co-ordinated Investigation of Micronesian Anthropology (CIMA) Report No. 25, part 2. Washington, D.C.: Pacific Science Board.

Black, Peter

1977 "Neo-Tobian Culture: Modern Life on a Micronesian Atoll." Ph.D. dissertation, University of California at San Diego.

Blackton, Charles S.

1946 "The Surrender of the Fortress of Truk." *Pacific Historical Review* 15(4): 400–408.

Bodley, R. V. C.

1934 *The Drama of the Pacific: Being a Treatise on the Immediate Problems Which Face Japan in the Pacific.* Tokyo: The Hokuseido Press.

Borthwick, Mark

1977 "Aging and Social Change on Lukunor Atoll." Ph.D. dissertation, University of Iowa.

Bosse, Paul C.

1945 "Polling Civilian Japanese on Saipan." *Public Opinion Quarterly* 9:176–182.

Bowers, Neal M.

1950 *Problems of Resettlement on Saipan, Tinian, and Rota, Mariana Islands.* Co-ordinated Investigation of Micronesian Anthropology (CIMA) Report No. 31. Washington, D.C.: Pacific Science Board. (Also: Ph.D. dissertation, University of Michigan, 1950.)

Boyer, David S.

1967 "Micronesia: The Americanization of Eden." *National Geographic* (May): 702–744.

Broadwater, John D.

1971 *Kwajalein, Lagoon of Found Ships.* Kwajalein: n.p.

Bronemann, Leroy B.

1982 *Once Upon a Tide: Tales from a Foxhole in the South Pacific.* Pennsylvania: Dorrance.

Brower, Kenneth

1974 "Wings of the Rhinoceros." *Atlantic* (July): 47–59.

Bryan, E. H., Jr.

1972 *Life in the Marshall Islands.* Honolulu: Bernice P. Bishop Museum (Pacific Scientific Information Center).

n.d. Field notebook [1944]. Bernice P. Bishop Museum.

Buck, Peter H.

1950 *Material Culture of Kapingamarangi.* Bernice P. Bishop Museum Bulletin no. 200. Honolulu: Bishop Museum Press.

Burns, Richard D.

1968 "Inspection of the Mandates, 1919–1941." *Pacific Historical Review* 37(4): 445–462.

Burrows, Edwin G.

1949 *The People of Ifalik: A Little-Disturbed Atoll Culture.* Co-ordinated Investigation of Micronesian Anthropology (CIMA) Report No. 16. Washington, D.C.: Pacific Science Board.

1963 *Flower in My Ear: Arts and Ethos of Ifaluk Atoll.* Seattle: University of Washington Press.

Burrows, Edwin G., and M. E. Spiro

1957 *An Atoll Culture: Ethnography of Ifaluk in the Central Carolines.* New Haven, CT: Human Relations Area Files.

Carano, Paul, and Pedro C. Sanchez

1964 *A Complete History of Guam.* Rutland, VT: Tuttle.

Carucci, Laurence Marshall

1989 "The Source of the Force in Marshallese Cosmology." In *The Pacific Theater,* ed. by G. White and L. Lindstrom, 73–96. Honolulu: University of Hawai'i Press.

1995 "From the Spaces to the Holes: Ralik-Ratak Remembrances of World War II." *Isla: A Journal of Micronesian Studies* 3(20):279–312.

1997a *Nuclear Nativity: Rituals of Renewal and Empowerment in the Marshall Islands.* DeKalb, IL: Northern Illinois University Press.

1997b *In Anxious Anticipation of the Uneven Fruits of Kwajalein Atoll: A Survey of Locations and Resources of Value to the People of Kwajalein Atoll.* Huntsville, AL: U.S. Army Space and Missile Defense Command.

Chave, Margaret E.

1950 *The Changing Position of Mixed-Bloods in the Marshall Islands.* Co-ordinated Investigation of Micronesian Anthropology (CIMA) Report No. 7 [1948]. Washington, D.C.: Pacific Science Board.

Chen, I-te

1984 "The Attempt to Integrate the Empire: Legal Perspectives." In R. H. Myers and M. R. Peattie, eds., *The Japanese Colonial Empire, 1895–1945,* 240–275. Princeton: Princeton University Press.

Ciardi, John

1988 *Saipan: The War Diary of John Ciardi.* Fayetteville: University of Arkansas Press.

Clyde, Paul H.

1935 *Japan's Pacific Mandate.* New York: Macmillan.

Cockrum, Emmett E.

1970 "The Emergence of Modern Micronesia." Ph.D. dissertation, University of Colorado.

Coletta, Nat J.

1980 *American Schools for the Natives of Ponape.* Honolulu: East-West Center.

Converse, Elizabeth

1949 "The United States as Trustee-II." *Far Eastern Survey* 18(24):277–283.

Cook, Haruko Taya, and Theodore F. Cook

1992 *Japan at War: An Oral History.* New York: New Press.

Costello, John

1981   *The Pacific War.* New York: Rawson, Wade.

Craven, Wesley Frank, and James Lea Cate, eds.

1950   *The Army Air Forces in World War II.* Vol. 4: *The Pacific: Guadalcanal to Saipan, August 1942 to July 1944.* Chicago: University of Chicago Press.

Crowl, Philip A.

1960   *The War in the Pacific: Campaign in the Marianas. The U.S. Army in World War II.* Washington, D.C.: Office of the Chief of Military History, Department of the Army.

Crowl, Philip A., and Edmund G. Love

1955   *Seizure of the Gilberts and Marshalls.* Washington, D.C.: Office of the Chief of Military History, Department of the Army.

Cusenbery, J. Donald

1946   "The 'Ulithi' Encyclopedia." Pamphlet.

Dahl, Christopher

1996   "Economic Development in Two Atoll States." *Isla: A Journal of Micronesian Studies* 4(2):289–316.

Dahlquist, Paul A.

1972   "Kohdo Mwenge: The Food Complex in a Changing Ponapean Community." Ph.D. dissertation, Ohio State University.

Denfeld, D. Colt

1979   *Field Survey of Ponape: World War II Features.* Micronesia Archaeological Survey Report, no. 2. Saipan: Historic Preservation Office, Trust Territory of the Pacific Islands.

1981a   *Field Survey of Truk: World War II Features.* Micronesian Archaeological Survey Report, no. 6. Saipan: Historic Preservation Office, Trust Territory of the Pacific Islands.

1981b   *Japanese Fortifications and Other Military Structures in the Central Pacific.* Micronesian Archaeological Survey Report, no. 9. Saipan: Historic Preservation Office, Trust Territory of the Pacific Islands.

1984   "Korean Laborers in Micronesia During World War II." *Korea Observer* 15(1):3–17.

1988   *Peleliu Revisited: An Historical and Archaeological Survey of World War II Sites on Peleliu Island.* Micronesian Archaeological Survey Report, no. 24. Saipan: Historic Preservation Office, Trust Territory of the Pacific Islands.

Denfeld, D. Colt, and Scott Russell

1984   *Home of the Superfort: An Historical and Archaeological Survey of Isely Field.* Micronesian Archaeological Survey Report, no. 21. Saipan: Historic Preservation Office, Trust Territory of the Pacific Islands.

Diaz, Vicente M.

1994   "Simply Chamorro: Telling Tales of Demise and Survival in Guam." *The Contemporary Pacific* 6(1):29–58.

Divine, Arthur D. [pseud. David Divine]

1950   *The King of Fassarai.* New York: Macmillan.

Dolan, Susan

1974   "Truk: The Lagoon Area in the Japan Years, 1941–1945." M.A. thesis, University of Hawai'i.

Dower, John

1986   *War without Mercy: Race and Power in the Pacific War.* New York: Pantheon.

Duncan, David D.

1945   "Yap Meets the Yanks." *National Geographic* 89(3):364–372.

Dyer, George C.

1972   *The Amphibians Came to Conquer: The Story of Admiral Richmond Kelly Turner.* Washington, D.C.: U.S. Department of the Navy.

Eads, Lyle W.

1978   *Survival Amidst the Ashes.* New York: Carlton Press.

Ehrlich, Paul

1984   *Koror: A Center of Power, Commerce and Colonial Administration.* Micronesian Archaeological Survey Report, no. 11. Saipan: Historic Preservation Office, Trust Territory of the Pacific Islands.

Embree, John F.

1946a   "Military Government in Saipan and Tinian. A Report on the Organization of Susupe and Churo, together with Notes on the Attitudes of the People Involved." *Applied Anthropology* 5(1):1–39.

1946b   "Micronesia: The Navy and Democracy." *Far Eastern Survey* 15(11):161–165.

1949   "American Military Government." In *Social Structure: Essays Presented to A. R. Radcliffe-Brown,* ed. by Meyer Fortes, 207–225. London: Oxford University Press.

Emerick, Richard

1958   "Land Tenure in the Marianas." In *Land Tenure Patterns in the Trust Territory of the Pacific Islands,* 216–250. Guam: Office of the Staff Anthropologist, Trust Territory of the Pacific Islands.

1960   "Homesteading on Ponape: A Study and Analysis of a Resettlement Program of the United States Trust Territory Government of Micronesia." Ph.D. dissertation, University of Pennsylvania.

Emory, Kenneth P.

1949   "Myths and Tales from Kapingamarangi: A Polynesian Inhabited Island in Micronesia." *Journal of American Folklore* 62(245):230–246.

Falgout, Suzanne

1984   "Persons and Knowledge in Ponape." Ph.D. dissertation, Anthropology Department, University of Oregon.

1989   "From Passive Pawns to Political Strategists: Wartime Lessons for the People of Pohnpei." In *The Pacific Theater*, ed. by G. White and L. Lindstrom, 279–297. Honolulu: University of Hawai'i Press.

1995a   "Americans in Paradise: Anthropologists, Custom, and Democracy in Postwar Micronesia." *Ethnology* 34(2):99–111.

1995b   "The Importance of World War II in Pohnpei." Paper presented at Association for Social Anthropology in Oceania, Tampa, Florida.

Farrell, Don A.

1991   *History of the Northern Mariana Islands.* Saipan: Public School System, Commonwealth of the Northern Mariana Islands.

Fink, T. Ross

1948   "United States Naval Policy on Education in Dependent Areas." Ph.D. dissertation, University of North Carolina.

Firth, Stewart

1989   "Sovereignty and Independence in the Contemporary Pacific." *The Contemporary Pacific* 1(1/2):75–96.

Fischer, John L.

1957   (with Ann M. Fischer) *The Eastern Carolines.* HRAF Behavior Science Monograph. New Haven: HRAF Press.

1958a   "Contemporary Ponape Island Land Tenure." In *Land Tenure Patterns in the Trust Territory of the Pacific islands,* ed. by J. E. deYoung, 77–160. Guam: Office of the Staff Anthropologist, Trust Territory of the Pacific Islands.

1958b   "Native Land Tenure in the Truk District." In *Land Tenure Patterns in the Trust Territory of the Pacific Islands,* ed. by J. E. deYoung, 161–215. Guam: Office of the Staff Anthropologist, Trust Territory of the Pacific Islands.

1961   "The Japanese Schools for the Natives of Truk, Caroline Islands." *Human Organization* 20(2):83–88.

1974   "The Role of the Traditional Chiefs on Ponape in the American Period." In *Political Development in Micronesia,* ed. by Daniel T. Hughes and Sherwood G. Lingenfelter, 166–177. Columbus: Ohio State University Press.

Flinn, Juliana B.

1982   "Migration and Inter-Island Ties: A Case Study of Pulap, Caroline Islands." Ph.D. dissertation, Stanford University.

Force, Roland W.

1960   *Leadership and Culture Change in Palau.* Fieldiana: Anthropology, vol. 50. Chicago: Chicago Natural History Museum.

Forrestel, Emmet P.

1966   *Admiral Raymond A. Spruance, USN: A Study in Command.* Washington, D.C.: U.S. Government Printing Office.

Frank, Benis M., and Henry I. Shaw Jr.

1968   *Victory and Occupation: History of U.S. Marine Corps Operations in World War II.* Vol. 5. Washington, D.C.: U.S. Marine Corps, Historical Branch.

Gailey, Harry A.

1983   *Peleliu 1944.* Maryland: Nautical and Aviation Publ. Co. of America.

Gale, Roger W.

1979   *The Americanization of Micronesia: A Study of the Consolidation of U.S. Rule in the Pacific.* Washington, DC: University Press of America.

Gallahue, Edward E.

1946   *The Economy of the Mariana Islands.* USCC Economic Survey of Micronesia, Report No. 5. Honolulu: U.S. Commercial Company.

Garard, George W., and Truman R. Strobridge

1971   *Western Pacific Operations: History of U.S. Marine Corps Operations in World War II.* Vol. 4. Washington, D.C.: U.S. Government Printing Office.

Garrett, Jemima

1996   *Island Exiles.* Australian Broadcasting Corporation.

Gladwin, Thomas

1950   "Civil Administration on Truk: A Rejoinder." *Human Organization* 9(4): 15–24.

1952   "Personality and Development on Truk." Ph.D. dissertation, Yale University.

1964   "Petrus Mailo, Chief of Moen (Truk)." In *In the Company of Man,* ed. by J. Casagrande, 41–62. New York: Harper & Row.

Gladwin, Thomas, and Seymour B. Sarason

1953   *Truk: Man in Paradise.* Viking Fund Publications in Anthropology No. 20. New York: Wenner-Gren Foundation for Anthropological Research.

Goodenough, Ward H., and Frank LeBar

1948   "Second Interim Report of CIMA Field Work on Truk." In *Interim Reports: Co-ordinated Investigation of Micronesian Anthropology 1947–1948,* 127–132. Washington, D.C.: Pacific Science Board, National Research Council.

Goodenough, Ward H., and Hiroshi Sugita

1980   *Trukese-English Dictionary.* Memoirs of the American Philosophical Society, Volume 141. Philadelphia: American Philosophical Society.

Gorenflo, L. J., and Michael J. Levin

1995   "Changing Migration Patterns in the Federated States of Micronesia." *Isla: A Journal of Micronesian Studies* 3(1):29–71.

Grahlfs, Francis L.

1955   "The Effects of Japanese Administration in Micronesia (An Example of Culture Contact)." M.A. thesis, Columbia University.

Great Britain Colonial Office

1946   *Among Those Present: The Official Story of the Pacific Islands at War.* London: His Majesty's Stationery Office. (Printed by the Government Printing Office, Honiara, 1967.)

Griffin, John

1969   "Micronesia: The Truk-Ponape Decompression." *The Alice Patterson Fund* [Newsletter]:JG-8.

Hall, Edward T.

1950   "Military Government on Truk." *Human Organization* 9(2):25–30.

1992   *An Anthropology of Everyday Life: An Autobiography.* New York: Doubleday.

Hall, Edward T., and Karl J. Pelzer

1946   *The Economy of the Truk Islands: An Anthropological and Economic Survey.* USCC Economic Survey of Micronesia, Report No. 17. Honolulu: U.S. Commercial Company. Mimeo.

Hanlon, David

1981   *From Mesenieng to Kolonia: An Archaeological Survey of Historic Kolonia, Ponape, Eastern Caroline Islands.* Micronesian Archaelogical Survey Report, no. 5. Saipan: Historic Preservation Office, Trust Territory of the Pacific Islands.

1998 *Remaking Micronesia: Discourses over Development in a Pacific Territory.* Honolulu: University of Hawai'i Press.

Hatanaka, Sachiko

1967 "The Process of Cultural Change in Micronesia under the Japanese Mandate." In *Bunka Jinruigaku,* ed. by M. Gamo, T. Okayashi, and S. Muratake, 65–124. Tokyo: Kadokawa Shoten.

1973–1974 *Culture Change in Micronesia under the Japanese Administration.* Programme of Participation, No. 4, UNESCO.

1977 *A Bibliography of Micronesia Compiled from Japanese Publication 1915–1945.* Occasional Papers no. 8, Research Institute for Oriental Cultures, Gakushuin University, Tokyo.

Hayashi, Saburo, and Alvin D. Coox

1959 *Kogun: The Japanese Army in the Pacific War.* Quantico, Va: Marine Corps Association.

Heath, Laurel

1975 "Education for Confusion: A Study of Education in the Mariana Islands 1688–1941." *Journal of Pacific History* 10(2):20–37.

Heine, Carl

1974 *Micronesia at the Crossroads: A Reappraisal of the Micronesian Political Dilemma.* Honolulu: University Press of Hawai'i.

Heine, John

1991 "Marshall Islanders' Experiences in World War II." In *Remembering the Pacific War,* ed. by G. White. Occasional Paper 36, Center for Pacific Islands Studies, University of Hawai'i, 113–121.

Hezel, Francis X., S.J.

n.d. "The Catholic Church on Truk." Manuscript seen at Micronesian Seminar, Chuuk (now in Kolonia, Pohnpei).

1983 *The First Taint of Civilization: A History of the Caroline and Marshall Islands in Pre-Colonial Days, 1521–1885.* Pacific Islands Monograph Series 1. Honolulu: University of Hawai'i Press.

1995 *Strangers in Their Own Land: A Century of Colonial Rule in the Caroline and Marshall Islands.* Honolulu: University of Hawai'i Press.

Hezel, Francis X., S.J., and Michael J. Levin

1996 "New Trends in Micronesian Migration: FSM Migration to Guam and the Marianas, 1990–1993." *Pacific Studies* 19(1):91–114.

Hiery, Hermann Joseph

1995 *The Neglected War: The German South Pacific and the Influence of World War I.* Honolulu: University of Hawai'i Press.

Highland, Sam

1991 "World War II in Kiribati." In *Remembering the Pacific War*, ed. by G. White. Occasional Paper 36, Center for Pacific Islands Studies, University of Hawai'i, 109–121.

Higuchi, Wakako

1986 "Micronesians in the Pacific War: The Palauans." Typescript. Micronesian Area Research Center, University of Guam.

1987 *Micronesia under the Japanese Administration: Interviews with Former South Seas Bureau and Military Officials.* Guam: University of Guam, Micronesian Area Research Center.

1991 "War in Palau: Morikawa and the Palauans." In *Remembering the Pacific War*, ed. by G. White. Occasional Paper 36, Center for Pacific Islands Studies, University of Hawai'i, 145–156.

n.d. Interviews on file at Micronesian Area Research Center, University of Guam.

Hough, Frank O.

1947 *The Island War: The United States Marine Corps in the Pacific.* Philadelphia: Lippincott.

Howard, Clive, and Joe Whitley

1946 *One Damned Island after Another: The Seventh Air Force from Pearl Harbor to the End of the War.* Chapel Hill, NC: University of North Carolina Press.

Hughes, Daniel T., and Sherwood G. Lingenfelter, eds.

1974 *Political Development in Micronesia.* Columbus: Ohio State University Press.

Hunt, Edward E., Jr., Nathaniel R. Kidder, David M. Schneider, and William D. Stevens

1949 *The Micronesians of Yap and their Depopulation.* Report of the Peabody Museum Expedition to Yap Island, Micronesia 1947–1948. Cambridge MA: Peabody Museum, Harvard University. (Also published as Co-ordinated Investigation of Micronesian Anthropology [CIMA] Report No. 24, Washington, D.C.: Pacific Science Board.)

Hynes, Samuel

1988 *Flights of Passage.* New York and Annapolis: Frederick C. Bell and Naval Institute Press.

Iriye, Akira

1981 *Power and Culture: The Japanese-American War, 1941–1945.* Cambridge MA: Harvard University Press.

James, Roy E.

1946   "Military Government: Guam." *Far Eastern Quarterly* 15(18):273–277.

1949   "The Trust Territory of the Pacific Islands." In *America's Pacific Dependencies,* ed. by R. Emerson, L. Finkelstein, E. Bartlett, G. McLane, and R. James, 109–126. New York: American Institute of Pacific Relations.

Johannes, Robert E.

1981   *Words of the Lagoon: Fishing and Marine Lore in the Palau District of Micronesia.* Berkeley: University of California Press.

Johnson, Giff

1990   "Marshall Islands." In "Micronesia in Review: Issues and Events. 1 July 1990 to 30 June 1991." *The Contemporary Pacific* 4(1):83–185.

Johnstone, William C.

1945   "Future of the Japanese Mandated Islands." *Foreign Policy Reports* 21: 190–207.

Jones, George E.

1944   "Airpower and Gunnery: The Battle of Truk." *Harper's* June:36–44.

Josephy, Alvin M., Jr.

1946   *The Long and the Short and the Tall: The Story of a Marine Combat Unit in the Pacific.* New York: Alfred A. Knopf. (Reprinted by Zenger, Washington, D.C.)

Kahn, E. J., Jr.

1966a   "A Reporter at Large: Micronesia, I, The American Period." *The New Yorker* (June 11):42–112.

1966b   "A Reporter at Large: Micronesia, II, from U to Kapingamarangi." *The New Yorker* (June 18):42–109.

1971   "A Reporter at Large: Micronesia Revisited." *The New Yorker* (December 18): 98–113.

Kaneshiro, Shigeru

1958   "Land Tenure in the Palau Islands." In *Land Tenure Patterns in the Trust Territory of the Pacific Islands,* ed. by J. E. de Young, 288–336. Office of the Staff Anthropologist, Trust Territory of the Pacific Islands.

Karig, Walter

1948   *The Fortunate Islands: A Pacific Interlude.* New York: Rinehart.

Keesing, Felix M.

1945   "People of the Mandates." *Far Eastern Survey* 14(20):288–291.

Keesing, Marie M.

1944   *Pacific Islands in War and Peace.* New York: Institute of Pacific Relations.

Kennett, Lee

1987   *G.I.: The American Soldier in World War II.* New York: Charles Scribner's Sons.

King, Thomas F., and J. Carucci

1984   "The Guns of Tonaachaw: World War II Archaeology." In *Pisekin Noomw Noon Tonaachaw,* ed. by T. King and P. Parker, 467–507. Carbondale: Center for Archaeological Investigation, Southern Illinois University.

King, Thomas, and Patricia Parker

1984   *Pisekin Noomw Noon Tonaachaw.* Carbondale: Center for Archaeological Investigation, Southern Illinois University.

Kiste, Robert C.

1968   *Kili Island: A Study of the Relocation of the Ex-Bikini Marshallese.* Eugene: Department of Anthropology, University of Oregon.

Kiste, Robert C., and Suzanne Falgout

1999   "Anthropology and Micronesia: The Context." In *Anthropology in Micronesia: Assessing Fifty Years of American Involvement,* ed. by Robert C. Kiste and Mac Marshall, 11–51. Honolulu: University of Hawai'i Press.

Kiste, Robert C., and Mac Marshall, eds.

1999   *Anthropology in Micronesia: Assessing Fifty Years of American Involvement.* Honolulu: University of Hawai'i Press.

Kneubuhl, John

1946   "Life in the Lesser Carolines." A talk given to the Hawaiian Anthropological Society, March 27, 1946. Manuscript seen at Micronesian Seminar, Chuuk (now in Kolonia, Pohnpei).

Kodama, Michiko

n.d.   "Japanese in Micronesia (1922–1937): Impact on the Native Population." B.A. thesis, University of Hawai'i [1975]. Manuscript seen at Micronesian Seminar, Chuuk, and University of Hawai'i Pacific Collection.

Kohl, Manfred W.

1971   *Lagoon in the Pacific: The Story of Truk.* Schooley's Mountain, NJ: Liebenzell Mission.

Labby, David

1973   "Old Glory and the New Yap." *Natural History* 82:26–37.

1976   *The Demystification of Yap: Dialectics of Culture on a Micronesian Island.* Chicago: University of Chicago Press.

Leckie, Robert

1962   *Strong Men Armed: The United States Marines against Japan.* New York: Bonanza Books.

Lessa, William A.

1950   *The Ethnography of Ulithi Atoll.* Co-ordinated Investigation of Micronesian Anthropology (CIMA) Report No. 28. Washington, D.C.: Pacific Science Board.

Levi, Warner

1948   "American Attitudes toward Pacific Islands, 1914–1919." *Pacific Historical Review* 17:55–64.

Lewis, J. L.

1948a   *Kusaien Acculturation.* Co-ordinated Investigation of Micronesian Anthropology (CIMA) Report No. 17. Washington, D.C.: Pacific Science Board. (Reprinted 1967 as *Kusaiean Acculturation 1824–1948,* Saipan: Division of Land Management, Resources and Development, U.S. Trust Territory of the Pacific Islands.)

1948b   "Second Interim Report on Kusaie CIMA Project—Anthropological Research." In *Interim Reports: Co-ordinated Investigation of Micronesian Anthropology 1947–1948,* 37–42. Washington, D.C.: Pacific Science Board, National Research Council.

Lieber, Michael D.

1968   *Porakiet: A Kapingamarangi Colony on Ponape.* Eugene: Department of Anthropology, University of Oregon.

Liebowitz, Arnold H.

1996   *Embattled Island: Palau's Struggle for Independence.* Westport: Praeger.

Lindemann, Klaus

1982   *Hailstorm over Truk Lagoon.* Singapore: Maruzen Asia.

1987   "Beneath the Waters of Truk." *After the Battle* 57:21–36.

Lindstrom, Lamont

1996   *The American Occupation of the New Hebrides (Vanuatu).* MacMillan Brown Working Paper Series, no. 5. Christchurch, New Zealand: Macmillan Brown Centre for Pacific Studies, University of Canterbury.

Lindstrom, Lamont, and Geoffrey M. White

1989　"War Stories." In *The Pacific Theater,* ed. by G. White and L. Lindstrom, 3–40. Honolulu: University of Hawai'i Press.

1990　*Island Encounters: Black and White Memories of the Pacific War.* Washington, DC: Smithsonian Institution Press.

Lingenfelter, Sherwood G.

1972　"Political Leadership and Culture Change in Yap." Ph.D. dissertation, University of Pittsburgh.

1975　*Yap: Political Leadership and Culture Change in an Island Society.* Honolulu: University Press of Hawai'i.

Lotz, David

1988　"Roaming the Skies: Orote Field Plays Host to the Great Marianas Turkey Shoot." *Islander* (Sunday extra of the *Pacific Daily News*), June 19:5–9.

Lundstrom, John B.

1976　*The First South Pacific Campaign: Pacific Fleet Strategy, December 1941–June 1942.* Annapolis: Naval Institute Press.

MacGregor, Morris J., Jr.

1981　*The Integration of the Armed Forces 1940–1965.* Defense Studies Series. Washington, D.C.: U.S. Army Center of Military History.

Mahony, Frank J.

1960　"The Innovation of Savings Systems in Truk." *American Anthropologist* 62(3):465–482.

1969　"A Trukese Theory of Medicine." Ph.D. dissertation, Stanford University.

Mamara, Biritake, and Sister Tiura Kaiuea

1979　"Awakening: The Gods at War in the Atolls." In *Kiribati: Aspects of History,* by Sister Alaima Talu et al., 128–146. Tarawa: University of the South Pacific and Ministry of Education, Training and Culture, Kiribati Government.

Manchester, William

1979　*Goodbye, Darkness: A Memoir of the Pacific War.* New York: Little, Brown.

Marquand, John P.

1947　"Why the Navy Needs Aspirin." *Harper's Magazine* 195:160–169.

Marshall, Mac (Keith)

1972　"The Structure of Solidarity and Alliance on Namoluk Atoll." Ph.D. dissertation, University of Washington.

Marshall, Mac, and Leslie Marshall

1976   "Holy and Unholy Spirits." *Journal of Pacific History* 11(3):135–166.

Mason, Leonard

n.d.   Note cards; personal communication.

1946   *Economic and Human Resources, Marshall Islands.* USCC Economic Survey of Micronesia, Report No. 8. Honolulu: U.S. Commercial Company.

1953a   "Anthropology in American Micronesia: A Progress Report." *Clearinghouse Bulletin of Research in Human Organization* 2(3):1–5.

1953b   "Re-establishment of a Copra Industry in the Marshall Islands." In *Proceedings of the 7th Pacific Science Congress,* 7:159–162.

1954   "Relocation of the Bikini Marshallese: A Study in Group Migration." Ph.D. dissertation, Yale University.

Maude, H. E. and Edwin Doran Jr.

1966   "The Precedence of Tarawa Atoll." *Annals of the Association of American Geographers* 56(2):269–289.

McGrath, William A., and W. Scott Wilson

1971   "The Marshall, Caroline and Mariana Islands: Too Many Foreign Precedents." In *Land Tenure in Oceania,* ed. by R. Crocombe, 172–191. Melbourne: Oxford University Press.

Mcintyre, Michael

1985   *The New Pacific.* Collins BBC.

McKnight, Robert

1959   "The Oyabun-Kobun in Palau: A Master-Apprentice System." Anthropological Working Papers No. 5. Guam: Office of the Staff Anthropologist, Trust Territory of the Pacific Islands.

1960   "Competition in Palau." Ph.D. dissertation, Ohio State University.

1974   "Rigid Models and Ridiculous Boundaries: Political Development and Practice in Palau, ca. 1955–1964." In *Political Development in Micronesia,* ed. by D.T. Hughes and S. G. Lingenfelter, 37–53. Columbus: Ohio State University Press.

1978   "Nanyo Paradaisu: Images of Life in the Western Carolines." In *Catalog of Toshi Maruki Exhibition: Island Ways: Impressions from the Micronesia, Palau and Yap Islands,* 7–12. Koror: Palau Museum.

Meller, Norman

1969   *The Congress of Micronesia: Development of the Legislative Process in the Trust Territory of the Pacific Islands.* Honolulu: University of Hawai'i Press.

Meredith, J. C.
1956 "Mogmog Revisited." *U.S. Naval Institute Proceedings* 82(2):152–155.
1995 *A Handful of Emeralds: On Patrol with the Hanna in the Postwar Pacific.* Annapolis: Naval Institute Press.

Michal, Edward J.
1993 "Protected States: The Political Status of the Federated States of Micronesia and the Republic of the Marshall Islands." *Contemporary Pacific* 5(2):303–332.

Montvel-Cohen, Marvin
1982 "Craft and Context on Yap (Caroline Islands)." Ph.D. dissertation, Southern Illinois University, Carbondale.

Moore, W. Robert
1945a "Our New Military Wards: The Marshalls." *National Geographic Magazine* 88(3):325–360.
1945b "South from Saipan." *National Geographic Magazine* 87(4):441–474.
1948 "Pacific Wards of Uncle Sam." *National Geographic Magazine* 94(1):73–104.
1952 "Grass-Skirted Yap." *National Geographic Magazine* 102(6):805–826.

Morison, Samuel Eliot
1948 *A History of United States Naval Operations in World War II.* Vol. 3: *The Rising Sun in the Pacific: 1931–April 1942.* Boston: Atlantic, Little, Brown.
1950 *A History of United States Naval Operations in World War II.* Vol. 4: *Coral Sea, Midway and Submarine Actions, May 1942–August 1942.* Boston: Atlantic, Little, Brown.
1951 *A History of United States Naval Operations in World War II.* Vol. 7: *Aleutians, Gilberts, and Marshalls: June 1942–April 1944.* Boston: Atlantic, Little, Brown.
1953 *A History of United States Naval Operations in World War II.* Vol. 8: *New Guinea and the Marianas: March 1944–August 1944.* Boston: Atlantic, Little, Brown.
1958 *A History of United States Naval Operations in World War II.* Vol. 12: *Leyte, June 1944–January 1945.* Boston: Atlantic, Little, Brown.
1963 *The Two-Ocean War: A Short History of the United States Navy in World War II.* Boston: Little, Brown.

Murdock, George P.
1948a "New Light on the Peoples of Micronesia." *Science* 108(2808):423–425.
1948b "Waging Baseball in Truk." *Newsweek* 32(9):69–70. (Reprinted in G. P. Murdock, 1965, *Culture and Society*, Pittsburgh: University of Pittsburgh Press, 291–293.)

Murdock, George P., Thomas F. Gladwin, Ward H. Goodenough, and Frank M. LeBar

1948 "CIMA, Truk: Interim Report (October 1, 1947)." In *Interim Reports: Co-ordinated Investigation of Micronesian Anthropology 1947–1948*, 105–125. Washington, D.C.: Pacific Science Board, National Research Council.

Murdock, George P., and Ward H. Goodenough

1947 "Social Organization of Truk." *Southwestern Journal of Anthropology* [now *Journal of Anthropological Research*] 3(4):331–343.

Murphy, Raymond E.

1949 "'High' and 'Low' Islands in the Eastern Carolines." *The Geographical Review* 39(3):425–439.

1950 "The Economic Geography of a Micronesian Atoll." *Annals of the Association of American Geographers* 40(1):58–83.

Murrill, Rupert I.

1948a "Ponape: A Micronesian Culture of the Caroline Islands." *Transactions of the New York Academy of Science*, Series II, 10(4):154–158.

1948b "Interim Report." In *Interim Reports: Co-ordinated Investigation of Micronesian Anthropology 1947–1948*, 99–100. Washington, D.C.: Pacific Science Board, National Research Council.

1950 "Vital Statistics of Ponape Island, Eastern Carolines." *American Journal of Physical Anthropology*, n.s., 8(2):185–194.

Myers, Ramon H., and Mark R. Peattie, eds.

1984 *The Japanese Colonial Empire, 1895–1945*. Princeton: Princeton University Press.

Nakajima, Hiroshi, ed.

1990 "History of Nantaku." *Journal of the Pacific Society* 13(2):11–18.

Nakano, Ann

1983 *Broken Canoe: Conversations and Observations in Micronesia*. St. Lucia: University of Queensland Press.

Nason, James D.

1970 "Clan and Copra: Modernization on Etal Island." Ph.D. dissertation, University of Washington.

Nero, Karen L.

1989 "Time of Famine, Time of Transformation: Hell in the Pacific, Palau." In *The Pacific Theater*, ed. by Geoffrey M. White and Lamont Lindstrom, 117–147. Honolulu: University of Hawai'i Press.

Nishi, Midori

1968 "An Evaluation of Japanese Agricultural and Fishery Developments in Micronesia during the Japanese Mandate, 1914–1941." *Micronesica* 4(1):1–18.

Ochs, Peter, and Toarus

n.d. "Talk of the Sea: Oral Navigational Lore on Puluwat." Manuscript seen at Micronesian Seminar, Chuuk.

Ogden, Michael R.

1994 "MIRAB and the Marshall Islands." *Isla: A Journal of Micronesian Studies* 2(20):237–272.

Okumiya, Masatake

1968 "For Sugar Boats or Submarines?" *U.S. Naval Institute Proceedings* 94(8): 66–73.

Okumiya, Masataki, and Kiro Horikoshi, with Martin Caidin

1956 *Zero: The Air War in the Pacific from the Japanese Viewpoint.* New York: Dutton.

Olds, Robert

1944 *Helldiver Squadron: The Story of Carrier Bombing Squadron 17 with Task Force 58.* New York: Dodd, Mead.

Oliver, Douglas L., ed.

1951 *Planning Micronesia's Future: A Summary of the United States Commercial Company's Economic Survey of Micronesia, 1946.* Cambridge, MA: Harvard University Press. (Reprinted 1971, Honolulu: University of Hawai'i Press.)

Owings, Cathleen R.W., ed.

1981 *The War Years on Guam: Narratives of the Chamorro Experience.* 2 vols. Micronesian Area Research Center, University of Guam, Misc. Pub. #5. Agana, Guam: MARC.

Oxborrow, Ted

1979 "Saipan: The War, the Survivors, and the Monument." *New Pacific* 4(1): 20–21, 52.

Palau Community Action Agency

1978 *A History of Palau.* Vol. 3: *Japanese Administration–U.S. Naval Military Government.* Guam: Navy Printing Office.

Palomo, Tony

1984 *An Island in Agony.* Agana, Guam: Privately published.

1991   "Island in Agony: The War in Guam." In *Remembering the Pacific War,* ed. by G. White. Occasional Paper 36, Center for Pacific Islands Studies, University of Hawaiʻi, 133–144.

Panamerican Consultants

1994   *Comprehensive Resource Inventory and Preservation Planning Study for World War II Cultural Resources at the United States Army Kwajalein Atoll.* Prepared by Panamerican Consultants under contract to EARTH TECH. Huntsville, AL: U.S. Army Space and Strategic Defense Command.

Parker, Patricia L.

1985   "Land Tenure in Trukese Society: 1850–1980." Ph.D. dissertation, University of Pennsylvania.

Peacock, Karen

1990   "Maze of Schools: Education in Micronesia, 1951–64, 'The Gibson Years.'" Ph.D. dissertation, University of Hawaiʻi.

Peattie, Mark

1984a   "The Nan'yō: Japan in the South Pacific, 1885–1945." In R. H. Myers and M. R. Peattie, *The Japanese Colonial Empire, 1895–1945,* 172–210. Princeton: Princeton University Press.

1984b   "Japanese Attitudes toward Colonialism, 1894–1945." In R. H. Myers and M. R. Peattie, *The Japanese Colonial Empire, 1895–1945,* 80–127. Princeton: Princeton University Press.

1988   *Nan'yō: The Rise and Fall of the Japanese in Micronesia, 1885–1945.* Honolulu: University of Hawaiʻi Press.

Pelzer, Karl J.

1947   "Agriculture in the Truk Islands." *Foreign Agriculture* 11(6):74–81.

Peoples, James G.

1977   "Deculturation and Dependence in a Micronesian Community." Ph.D. dissertation, University of California–Davis.

1985   *Island in Trust: Culture Change and Dependence in a Micronesian Economy.* Boulder: Westview Press.

Petersen, Glenn

1999   "Politics in Postwar Micronesia." In *American Anthropology and Micronesia,* ed. by Robert Kiste and Mac Marshall, 145–195. Honolulu: University of Hawaiʻi Press.

Petit-Skinner, Soulange

1981   *The Nauruans.* San Francisco: Macduff Press.

Piccigallo, Philip

1979   *The Japanese on Trial: Allied War Crimes Operations in the East, 1945–1951.* Austin: University of Texas Press.

Pillsbury, John D.

1948   "Truk: A 'Tourist' Attraction." *U.S. Naval Institute Proceedings* 74:853–861.

Pinsker, Eve C.

1992   "Celebrations of Government: Dance Performance and Legitimacy in the Federated States of Micronesia." *Pacific Studies* 15(4):29–56.

Pollock, Nancy

n.d.   "A Schema of Growth Applied to the Economic History of the Marshall Islands." Manuscript seen at Micronesian Seminar, Chuuk (now in Kolonia, Pohnpei).

1991   "Nauruans during World War II." In *Remembering the Pacific War,* ed. by G. White. Occasional Paper 36, Center for Pacific Islands Studies, University of Hawai'i, 91–107.

Pomeroy, Earl S.

1947   "The Problem of American Overseas Bases: Some Reflections on Naval History." *U.S. Naval Institute Proceedings* 73(6):688–700.

1948   "American Policy Respecting the Marshalls, Carolines, and Marianas, 1898–1941." *The Pacific Historical Review* 17(1):43–53.

Poyer, Lin

1989   "Echoes of Massacre: Recollections of World War II on Sapwuahfik (Ngatik Atoll)." In *The Pacific Theater,* ed. by Geoffrey M. White and Lamont Lindstrom, 97–115. Honolulu: University of Hawai'i Press.

1992   "Defining History across Cultures: Insider and Outsider Contrasts." *Isla: A Journal of Micronesian Studies.* 1(1):73–89.

1995   "Yapese Experiences of the Pacific War." *Isla: A Journal of Micronesian Studies* 3(2):223–255.

1997   *Ethnography and Ethnohistory of Taroa Island, Republic of the Marshall Islands.* Micronesian Resources Study: Marshall Islands Ethnography. San Francisco: Micronesian Endowment for Historic Preservation, Republic of the Marshall Islands, U.S. National Park Service.

1999   "Ethnicity and Identity in Micronesia." In *American Anthropology and Micronesia,* ed. by Robert Kiste and Mac Marshall, 197–223. Honolulu: University of Hawai'i Press.

Price, Willard

1936   *Pacific Adventure.* New York: John Day.

1944a   *Japan's Islands of Mystery.* New York: John Day.

1944b   "Springboards to Tokyo." *National Geographic Magazine* 86(4):385–406.

1966   *America's Paradise Lost.* New York: John Day.

Purcell, David C.

1976   "The Economics of Exploitation: The Japanese in the Marianas, Caroline and Marshall Islands, 1915–1940." *Journal of Pacific History* 11(3):189–211.

Ramarui, David

1976   "Education in Micronesia: Its Past, Present and Future." *Micronesian Reporter* 24(1):9–20.

Reafsnyder, Charles B.

1984   "Emergent Ethnic Identity in an Urban Migrant Community in Truk State, FSM." Ph.D. dissertation, Indiana University.

Reed, Erik K.

1952   *General Report on Archaeology and History of Guam.* Santa Fe, NM: National Park Service.

Richard, Dorothy E.

1957a   *United States Naval Administration of the Trust Territory of the Pacific Islands.* Vol. 1. Washington, D.C.: Office of the Chief of Naval Operations.

1957b   *United States Naval Administration of the Trust Territory of the Pacific Islands.* Vol. 2. Washington, D.C.: Office of the Chief of Naval Operations.

1957c   *United States Naval Administration of the Trust Territory of the Pacific Islands.* Vol. 3. Washington, D.C.: Office of the Chief of Naval Operations.

Riesenberg, S. H.

1948   "Interim Report, CIMA Project." In *Interim Reports: Co-ordinated Investigation of Micronesian Anthropology 1947–1948,* 101–104. Washington, D.C.: Pacific Science Board, National Research Council.

Rogers, Robert F.

1995   *Destiny's Landfall: A History of Guam.* Honolulu: University of Hawai'i Press.

Ronck, Ron

1983   "Pete Ellis: A Spy in the Rock Islands." *Glimpses of Micronesia and the Western Pacific* 23(1):22–27.

Russell, Scott

1983   "Camp Susupe: Postwar Internment on Saipan." *Pacific Magazine* (May–June):21–23.

1984　*From Arabwal to Ashes: A Brief History of Garapan Village: 1818 to 1945.* Micronesian Archaeological Survey Report no. 19. Saipan: Historic Preservation Office, Trust Territory of the Pacific Islands.

1987　"Garapan: The Rebirth of a City." *Glimpses of Micronesia and the Western Pacific* 27(1):20–26.

Rynkiewich, Michael A.

1972　"Land Tenure among the Arno Marshallese." Ph.D. dissertation, University of Minnesota.

1981　*Traders, Teachers and Soldiers: An Anthropological Survey of Colonial Era Sites on Majuro Atoll, Marshall Islands.* Saipan: Micronesian Archaeological Survey.

Saito, Hisafumi

1991　"Barefoot Benefactors: A Study of Japanese Views of Melanesians." In *Remembering the Pacific War,* ed. by G. White. Occasional Paper 36, Center for Pacific Islands Studies, University of Hawai'i, 207–222.

Salii, Lazarus E.

1972　"Liberation and Conquest in Micronesia." *Pacific Islands Monthly* 43(6): 37–40, 123.

Sanchez, Pedro C.

1983　*Guam 1941–1945: Wartime Occupation and Liberation.* Tamuning, Guam: P.C. Sanchez Publishing House.

Schaefer, Paul D.

1976　"Confess Therefore Your Sins: Status and Sin on Kusaie." Ph.D. dissertation, University of Minnesota.

Severance, Craig J.

1976　"Land, Food and Fish: Strategy and Transaction on a Micronesian Atoll." Ph.D. dissertation, University of Oregon.

Shaw, Henry, Bernard C. Nalty, and Edwin Turnbladh

1966　*Central Pacific Drive: History of U.S. Marine Corps Operations in World War II.* Vol. 3. Washington, D.C.: Historical Branch, G-3 Division Headquarters, U.S. Marine Corps.

Sheeks, Robert B.

1945　"Civilians on Saipan." *Far Eastern Survey* (May 9, 1945):109–113.

Sherrod, Robert

1952　"Two Thousand Islands, and We're Stuck with Them." *Saturday Evening Post* (Nov. 8, 1952):36–37, 110, 112–113.

Shuster, Donald R.

1979 "Schooling in Micronesia during Japanese Mandate Rule." *Educational Perspectives* 18(2):20–26.

1982a "Islands of Change in Palau: Church, School, and Elected Government." Ed.D. dissertation, University of Hawai'i.

1982b "State Shinto in Micronesia during Japanese Rule, 1914–1945." *Pacific Studies* 5(2):20–43.

1982c "The Sweep of the Yen." *Far Eastern Economic Review* (July 2):36–37.

1994 "Palau's Compact: Controversy, Conflict, and Compromise." *Isla: A Journal of Micronesian Studies* 2(2):207–236.

Smith, Charlie

1991 *Tinian.* In *Crystal River: Three Novellas.* New York: Linden Press.

Smith, D. F.

1946 "Saipan Historical Notes for the Personnel of the Naval Operating Base." Mimeo, Washington, D.C. Copy seen at Micronesian Seminar, Chuuk (now in Kolonia, Pohnpei).

Smith, DeVerne R.

1983 *Palauan Social Structure.* New Brunswick, NJ: Rutgers University Press.

Smith, Robert R.

1953 *The War in the Pacific: The Approach to the Philippines. The U.S. Army in World War II.* Washington, D.C.: Department of the Army, Office of the Chief of Military History.

Solenberger, Robert R.

1964 "Continuity of Local Political Institutions in the Marianas." *Human Organization* 23(1):53–60.

1967 "The Changing Role of Rice in the Marianas Islands." *Micronesica* 3(2): 97–103.

Souder, Paul B.

1971 "Guam: Land Tenure in a Fortress." In *Land Tenure in Oceania,* ed. by R. Crocombe, 192–205. Melbourne: Oxford University Press.

Spector, Ronald H.

1985 *Eagle against the Sun: The American War with Japan.* New York: Free Press.

Spoehr, Alexander

1949a *Majuro: A Village in the Marshall Islands.* Fieldiana: Anthropology, vol. 39. Chicago: Natural History Museum.

1949b   "Surrender at Ponape." *The Pacific Spectator* (Autumn):376–383.

1951   "The Tinian Chamorros." *Human Organization* 10(4):16–20.

1954   *Saipan: The Ethnology of a War-Devastated Island.* Fieldiana: Anthropology, vol. 41. Chicago: Natural History Museum.

Stephen, John J.

n.d.   "Japan's Economic Development of Micronesia: A Re-evaluation." Manuscript seen at University of Hawai'i.

Stewart, William H.

1985   *Ghost Fleet of the Truk Lagoon: An Account of "Operation Hailstone," February 1944.* Montana: Pictorial Histories.

1989   "Chronology of the Pacific War and the Battle for Saipan." *Guam-Pacific Sports Leisure Magazine* 3(4):26–30.

Sullivan, Julius

1957   *The Phoenix Rises: A Mission History of Guam.* New York: Seraphic Mass Assn.

Swartz, Marc J.

1961   "Negative Ethnocentrism." *Journal of Conflict Resolution* 5(1):75–81.

Taylor, John L.

1945   "History of the Marianas." Mimeo pamphlet. Camp Susupe, Saipan: Education Office, Military Government Section.

1951   "Saipan: A Study in Land Utilization." *Economic Geography* 27(4):340–347.

Tellei, Ubal

1991   "Palauans and the Japanese Military Experience." In *Remembering the Pacific War,* ed. by G. White. Occasional Paper 36, Center for Pacific Islands Studies, University of Hawai'i, 157–160.

Thomas, Mary D.

1978   "Transmitting Culture to Children on Namonuito Atoll, Caroline Islands." Ph.D. dissertation, University of Hawai'i.

Thompson, Laura

1947a   *Guam and Its People.* 3rd revised ed. Princeton, NJ: Princeton University Press.

1947b   "Guam's Bombed-Out Capital." *Far Eastern Survey* 16(6):66–69.

Tillman, Barrett

1977   "Hellcats over Truk." *U.S. Naval Institute Proceedings* 103:63–71.

Tobin, Jack A.

1970 "Jabwor: Former Capital of the Marshall Islands." *Micronesian Reporter* 18(4):20–30.

Tolerton, Burt, and Jerome Rauch

1949 *Social Organization, Land Tenure and Subsistence Economy of Lukunor, Nomoi Islands.* Co-ordinated Investigation of Micronesian Anthropology (CIMA) Report No. 26. Washington, D.C.: Pacific Science Board.

Trumbull, Robert

1959 *Paradise in Trust: A Report on Americans in Micronesia, 1946–58.* New York: William Sloane Associates.

Uludong, Francisco T.

1969 "A Review of Some Aspects of American-Micronesian Relations." In *Political Modernization in Micronesia: A Symposium.* Santa Cruz, CA: Center for South Pacific Studies.

Underwood, Jane H.

1989 "Population History of Nauru: A Cautionary Tale." *Micronesica* 22(1):3–22.

Underwood, Robert A.

1994 "The State of Guam's Agenda in Washington." Speech by Honorable Robert A. Underwood, delivered November 13, 1995, in chamber of Guam Legislature. *Isla: A Journal of Micronesian Studies* 4(1):109–130.

United States Congress

1970 *Micronesian Claims.* Hearings before the Subcommittee on International Organizations and Movements of the Committee on Foreign Affairs, House of Representatives. 91st Congress, 2nd session, June 16, 23, September 16, 1970.

1971a *Micronesian Economic Development and Claims.* Hearing before the Subcommittee on Territories and Insular Affairs of the Committee on Interior and Insular Affairs, United States Senate. 92nd Congress, 1st Session, March 30, 1971.

1971b *Micronesian Claims Act of 1971.* Hearings before the Subcommittee on International Organizations and Movements of the Committee on Foreign Affairs, House of Representatives. 92nd Congress, 1st Session, April 22, 1971.

1973a *To Amend the Micronesian Claims Act of 1971.* Hearing before the Subcommittee on International Organizations and Movements of the Committee on Foreign Affairs, House of Representatives. 93rd Congress, 1st session, April 3, 1973.

1973b *To Amend the Micronesian Claims Act of 1971.* Hearing before the Subcommittee on Territories and Insular Affairs of the Committee on Interior and Insular Affairs, United States Senate. 93rd Congress, 1st session, August 3, 1973.

1996   *U.S. Interests in the South Pacific: The Freely Associated States.* Joint hearing before the Subcommittee on Asia and the Pacific of the Committee on International Relations and the Subcommittee on Native American and Insular Affairs of the Committee on Resources, House of Representatives. 104th Congress, 2nd session, September 25, 1996.

United States Navy

1943   *Civil Affairs Handbook: Marshall Islands.* OPNAV 50E-1. Washington, D.C.: Navy Department, Office of the Chief of Naval Operations.

1944a   *Civil Affairs Handbook: Mandated Marianas Islands.* OPNAV P22–8 (formerly OPNAV 50E-8). Washington, D.C.: Navy Department, Office of the Chief of Naval Operations.

1944b   *Civil Affairs Handbook: East Caroline Islands.* OPNAV P22–5 (formerly OPNAV 50E-5). Washington, D.C.: Navy Department, Office of the Chief of Naval Operations.

1944c   *Civil Affairs Handbook: West Caroline Islands.* OPNAV P22–7 (formerly OPNAV 50E-7). Washington, D.C.: Navy Department, Office of the Chief of Naval Operations.

1948   *Handbook of the Trust Territory of the Pacific Islands.* Washington, D.C.: Navy Department, Office of the Chief of Naval Operations.

United States Navy, Bureau of Yards and Docks

1947   *Building the Navy's Bases in World War II: The History of the Bureau of Yards and Docks and the Civil Engineering Corps, 1940–1946.* Vol. 2. Washington, D.C.: Government Printing Office.

United States Navy, Military Government Section

n.d.   *Camp Susupe: A Photographic Record of the Operation of Military Government on Saipan.* San Francisco: U.S. Navy, Military Government Section.

United States Strategic Bombing Survey (USSBS)

1946   *The Campaigns of the Pacific War.* Washington, D.C.: U.S. Strategic Bombing Survey (Pacific), Naval Analysis Division.

1947a   *The American Campaign against Wotje, Maloelap, Mille and Jaluit.* Washington, D.C.: U.S. Navy, Naval Analysis Division.

1947b   *The Reduction of Truk.* Washington, D.C.: U.S. Navy, Naval Analysis Division.

1975   *United States Strategic Bombing Survey, Summary Report.* Reel 18, Microfilm 500940, National Archives Microfilm Publications, U.S. National Archives, Washington, D.C.

Useem, John

1945a "The American Pattern of Military Government in Micronesia." *American Journal of Sociology* 51(2):93–102.

1945b "The Changing Structure of a Micronesian Society." *American Anthropologist* 47(4):567–588.

1945c "Governing the Occupied Areas of the South Pacific: Wartime Lessons and Peacetime Proposals. *Applied Anthropology* [now *Human Organization*] 4(3):1–10.

1946a *Report on Yap and Palau.* USCC Economic Survey of Micronesia, Report No. 6. Honolulu: U.S. Commercial Company. Mimeo.

1946b "Americans as Governors of Natives in the Pacific." *Journal of Social Issues* 2(3):39–49.

1946c "Social Reconstruction in Micronesia." *Far Eastern Survey* 15:21–24.

1947 "Applied Anthropology in Micronesia." *Applied Anthropology* [now *Human Organization*] 6(4):1–14.

1948 "Institutions of Micronesia." *Far Eastern Survey* 17(2):22–25.

1949 "Report on Palau." Co-ordinated Investigation of Micronesian Anthropology (CIMA) Report No. 21. Washington, D.C.: Pacific Science Board.

1952 "South Sea Island Strike: Labor Management Relations in the Caroline Islands, Micronesia [Angaur]." In *Human Problems in Technological Change: A Casebook,* ed. by Edward H. Spicer, 149–164. New York: Russell Sage Foundation.

Vidich, Arthur J.

1949 *Political Factionalism in Palau: Its Rise and Development.* Co-ordinated Investigation of Micronesian Anthropology (CIMA) Report No. 23. Washington, D.C.: Pacific Science Board.

1980 *The Political Impact of Colonial Administration.* New York: Arno Press. (Reprint of "The Political Impact of Colonial Administration." Ph.D. dissertation, Harvard University, 1952.)

Viviani, Nancy

1970 *Nauru: Phosphate and Political Progress.* Honolulu: University of Hawai'i Press.

Vogel, Bertram

1948 "Truk—South Sea Mystery Base." *U.S. Naval Institute Proceedings* 74: 1269–1275.

Ward, Graeme K., and Michael Pickering

1985 "The Japanese Bone Collecting Expedition on Tinian, Mariana Islands, March 1985: Its Impact upon Historic Resources. *Bulletin of the Indo-Pacific Prehistory Association* 6:116–122.

Watakabe, Mitsuo

1972 *Deserted Ponapean Death Band.* Ube, Japan: Privately published.

Weckler, Joseph E.

1949 *Land and Livelihood on Mokil, An Atoll in the Eastern Carolines.* Co-ordinated Investigation of Micronesian Anthropology (CIMA) Report No. 11, Part 1. Washington, D.C.: Pacific Science Board.

Wees, Marshall P.

1950 *King-Doctor of Ulithi.* New York: Macmillan.

Wheeler, Richard

1983 *A Special Valor: The U.S. Marines and the Pacific War.* New York: Harper & Row.

White, Geoffrey M.

1991 *Remembering the Pacific War.* Occasional Paper 36. Honolulu: Center for Pacific Islands Studies, University of Hawai'i.

**White, Geoffrey M., David Gegeo, David Akin,
and Karen Watson-Gegeo, eds.**

1988 *The Big Death: Solomon Islanders Remember World War II.* Suva: Institute of Pacific Studies.

White, Geoffrey M., and Lamont Lindstrom

1989 *The Pacific Theater: Island Representations of World War II.* Honolulu: University of Hawai'i Press.

Wilds, Thomas

1955 "How Japan Fortified the Mandated Islands." *U.S. Naval Institute Proceedings* 81(4):401–407.

Williams, John Z.

1946 "Administration of the Natives of Saipan." *Foreign Service Journal* 23(4): 7–10.

Witherspoon, Jack A.

1945 "Report of Reconnaissance of Islands in Area V." Moen, Truk: U.S. Commercial Company, Pacific Ocean Division, Economic Survey.

Yanaihara, Tadao

1938 *Pacific Islands under Japanese Mandate.* London: Oxford University Press.

Yarbrough, Michael

1971 "The History of Palau." Typescript seen at Micronesian Seminar.

Young, John A., Nancy R. Rosenberger, and Joe R. Harding

1997   *Ethnography of Truk, Federated States of Micronesia.* Micronesian Resources Study: Truk Ethnography. San Francisco: Micronesian Endowment for Historic Preservation, Federated States of Micronesia, U.S. National Park Service.

Zelenietz, Marty

1991   "Villages without People: A Preliminary Analysis of American Views of Melanesians during World War II as Seen through Popular Histories." In *Remembering the Pacific War,* ed. by G. White. Occasional Paper 36, Center for Pacific Islands Studies, University of Hawai'i, 187–205.

Zelenietz, Marty, and Hisafumi Saito

1986   "Both Sides Now: Anthropological Reflections on Kilenge Reminiscences of the Second World War." *Man and Culture in Oceania* 2:101–114.

1989   "The Kilenge and the War: An Observer Effect on Stories of the Past." In *The Pacific Theater,* ed. by Geoffrey M. White and Lamont Lindstrom, 167–184. Honolulu: University of Hawai'i Press.

INDEX

Page numbers in italics refer to illustrations.

egy, 7, 8, 9. *See also* Pacific War strategy; United States military operations

Americans: as Christian, 237, 265, 330, 344; encounter in Chuuk, 255–256; encounters in Guam, 251–252; encounters in Lukunor, 262–264; encounters in Marshall Islands, 119–120, 123–124, 237–240; encounter in Palau, 167–168; fear of, 123–124, 203–204, 239–240, 255, 260; Japanese, compared to, 340–347; image as powerful, 119–120, 240, 266; image as symbolic chiefs, 245, 266–267, 270, 275, 343; image as wealthy, 118, 235, 239–240, 243–245, 256, 267–270, 415n. 14, 419nn. 30, 35. *See also* Images; Micronesian-American relations

Amida, Alwihs (Kapingamarangi), 90

Amlej, Reverend Kanki (Marshalls), 282, 343

Amor, Manuel (Pohnpei), 190

Amusten, Robino (Pohnpei), 332

Andrew, Palikun (Kosrae), 80–81

Angaur Island (Palau) phosphate mining, 19, 26; U.S. invasion and occupation, 171, 250–251, 251, 260, 319, 416n. 19; during war, 165, 197, 213–214, 409n. 26

Aninis, Anisiro (Chuuk), 179, 193

Anjain, John (Marshalls), 76–77, 98, 99–100, 215

Anson, Kaiti (Pohnpei), 210

Anthropology: role in U.S. era, 284, 311, 421n. 6, 426n. 31, 427nn. 36, 38

Apple, R. A., 38, 40, 163, 434

Arno (Marshall Islands), 76, 131, 135, *242, 303,* 325, 338, 415n. 9, 418n. 29, 430n. 16

Aur (Marshall Islands), 57, 76, 133, 135, 241, 415n. 9

Babelthuap (Palau): during war, 165, 167, 185, 194, 319. *See also* Palau

Bahrenburg, Bruce, 340, 346, 434

Ballendorf, Dirk, xii, 237, 301, 306, 434, 435

Banaba (Ocean Island), 9, 37, 406n. 10; Banabans relocated by Japanese, 38, 47, 57, 60, 266, 401n. 24

Barbosa, Ciro (physician, Pohnpei), 97, 102, 112, 202, 218

Bascom, William R., 17, 20, 42, 78, 153, 182, 189, 270, 273, 279, 294, 295, 298, 346, 435

Bates, Marston, and Donald P. Abbott, 246, 332, 436

Bedley, Alter (Pohnpei), 110, 111, 113, 153, 160

Behris, Bernard (Pohnpei), 274

Behris, Yasio (Pohnpei), 78, 110, 170, 274

Benjamin, Likiak (Kosrae), 100, 114, 212

Bentzen, Conrad, 155–156, 436

Bier, Aknes (Chuuk), 187

Bier, Marusina (Chuuk), 106, 109

Bikar (Marshall Islands), 76

Bikini (Marshall Islands), 14, 325, 415n. 9

Billimont, Istor (Chuuk), 177, 343–344

Billy, Anko (Marshalls), 34, 100, 116, 170

Bisalen, Aitel (Chuuk), 161

Bisalen, Iteko (Chuuk), 95–96, 116, 152, 198

Black, Peter, 157, 268, 436

Blackton, Charles S., 193, 253, 254, 436

Bombings: effect on daily life, 10, 145–158, 195–197, 198–199, 202–203, 205, 206. *See also* Neutralization strategy; *and the specific names of individual islands*

Bonin Islands, 44, 253

Borthwick, Mark, 26, 49, 88, 215, 264, 267, 269, 436

Bossin, Finas (Chuuk), 101–102, 211, 213, 216

Bowers, Neal M., 171, 194, 248, 271, 303, 304, 322–323, 324, 437

Brightly, Anna (Kosrae), 53, 79–80, 98, 181, 188, 218–219

Bryan, E. H., Jr., 205, 290, 437

Buddhism, 29–30, 35–36, 397n. 22. *See also* religion

Burns, Richard D., 41, 246, 437

Burrows, Edwin G., and M. E. Spiro, 115, 236, 437

Bypassed islands: bombing of Carolines, 144–158; life during Allied offensive, 169–229; Marshallese on, 127–135; surrender of, 252–264. *See also* Escapes from Japanese-held islands; Neutralization strategy; *and the specific names of individual islands*

Cannibalism, 171, 174, 179

Carano, Paul, and Pedro C. Sanchez, 39, 163, 251, 252, 438

Caroline Islands: attacks on, 135–144, 154–156; strategic role, 13, 135; wartime conditions, 175–185. *See also* Neutralization strategy; *and the specific names of individual islands*

Carolinians in the Marianas: relations with Americans, 416n. 17, 419n. 34;

postwar repatriation from Yap, 304, 418n. 29, 426n. 29; on Rota, 21; on Saipan during US invasion, 92–93, 162, 248, 249, 413n. 3, 416n. 17; as US military scouts, 250, 416n. 18. *See also* Mariana Islands; Rota Island; Saipan

Carucci, Laurence Marshall, 245, 266, 268, 339, 343, 351–352, 353, 438, 447

Casualties from military action: Chuuk, 140–144, 146, 147, 149, 196; Guam, 163–164; Kiribati, 37, 398n. 3, 404n. 1; Kosrae, 136, 147; Marshalls, 51, 121, 123, 239; Micronesian, 69, 147, 332; Nauru, 405n. 1; Palau, 204; Pohnpei, 96, 146, 147, 153; Pulusuk, 158; Ulithi, 168; Yap, 155, 332. *See also* Deaths of Micronesians

Catholic Church. *See* Christianity

Chamorros (Guamanian): postwar American attitudes towards, 413n. 3; during battle for Guam, 163–165, 413n. 1; under Japanese occupation, 38–40, 162–163; memories of war, 337–338, 349

Chamorros (northern Marianas): on Angaur, 251; economic development under US, 271, 301–305, *308*, 346; Japanese military service in Guam, 39; prewar life, 21–22, 27; memories of war, 335–336, 337; in Palau, 167; postwar repatriation of, 418n. 29; during US invasion, 92–93, 162–163, 246–250, 416n. 17; US policy towards, 237, 250, 271, 413n. 3; working for Americans, 250, 271, 273–274, 305, 416n. 18; in Yap, 24, 64, 87, 155, 213, 260, 426n. 29. *See also* Guam, Mariana Islands; Rota Island; Saipan; Tinian

Chiefs: Americans as symbolic chiefs, 245, 266–267, 270, 275, 343; occupied and postwar Marshalls, 119–120, 238, 242–243, 265, 285, 286, 415n. 11, 422n. 10; postwar Chuuk, 280, 283–284, 327–328; postwar outer Carolines, 422nn. 8, 13; postwar Palau, 285, 287, 327, 328, 422n. 12, 430n. 17; postwar Pohnpei, 279, 285, 422n. 9; postwar Yap, 285–287, 327, 422n. 11; in prewar Nan'yo, 18–19, 25, 64, 394n. 3; under US rule, 283–289, 286, 327–328, 422nn. 8, 13; during war, 63–66, 191, 208–214; wartime Chuuk, 55, 116, 140, 176, 211–212; wartime Kosrae, 204; wartime Marshalls, 44, 45, 212–213; wartime outer Carolines, 88, 89, 103; wartime Palau, 194, 204, 213–214; wartime Pohnpei, 58, 205, 210, 212, 213. *See also* Elites; Leaders

Children: childhood memories of war, 74, 81, 111, 113, 154; prewar experiences, 27–29, 35–36; wartime experiences, 52, 133, 140–141, 145–146, 147, 148, 149, 166, 176, 178, 184, 187, 408n. 18; wartime labor, 53, 85, 86, 100, 108–110, 206

Chipwe, Anton (Chuuk), 222

Christianity: constraints during war, 52–53, 201–204; as link with Americans, 237, 245, 265, 330, 344; Nan'yo policy towards, 29–30; role during war for Micronesians, 53, 116, 148–149, 154, 168, 177, 196, 201, 203, 231, 413n. 1. *See also* Churches; Missions; Missionaries; Religion

Chronology of World War II in Micronesia, 365–391

Churches: confiscated or destroyed by Japanese military, 52–53, 77, 99, 202

Chuuk: bombing of, 138–146, 399n. 15, 407n. 14, 408n. 19; conditions at end of war, 292, 293, 317, 429n. 6; defensive fortification, 81–84, 94–95; initial fortification, 34, 42, 44, 48–49, 398n. 6, 399n. 11; headquarters of Combined Fleet, Fourth Fleet, 48, 138, 399n. 11, 403n. 5; Islanders serving in Japanese military, 67–68; *itang* role during war, 177, 204; Japanese Army arrives, 81–82; prewar life, 17, 23–24, 42, 395n. 11, 396n. 19; problem of chiefs under US rule, 257, 275, 283–284, 321, 327–328, 422n. 13; strategic role, 13, 42, 48, 126, 135, 138; surrender and US occupation, 253–257, 253, 257, 261, 268, 416nn. 21, 22, 420n. 37; under US Navy rule, 272, 298–299, 420n. 2, 424n. 21, 427n. 34; war remains on, 335–336, 292–294, 431n. 23; wartime conditions, 81–84, 98, 99, 138–143, 150–154, 175–179, 194, 201–202, 208, 217–218, 410n. 4. *See also* Eten Island, Tol Island, Toloas Island, Weno Island

Cities: prewar, 17, 20, 31, 396n. 20; during war, 112, 114, *164*, 170, 188, 205, 316, 320. *See also the specific names of individual cities and towns*

Clothing: postwar scarcity, 269, 270, 299, 423n. 14; scarcity during war, 78, 100, 157, 170, 188–190, 191, 216, 255, 261, 410n. 10

Cockrum, Emmet E., 110, 238, 241, 242, 438

Colonia (Yap), 24, 155, 170, 261, 317. *See also* Yap

Comparison of Japanese and American eras: 272, 275, 281–282, 340–347; economic conditions, 289–290, 292–293, 295–296, 345–346; social relations, 312–313

Confiscation: of crops and food sources by Japanese military, 170, 173, 175–177, 180–184, 198, 225; of land for Japanese military bases, 41, 44–45, 47, 74, 77, 82–83, 90, 98–99, 320, 398n. 8, 399n. 12; of land by US military, 321, 322, 323–324, 325, 430n. 15; of property by Japanese military, 37, 38, 52–53, 74, 78, 83–84, 86, 90, 93, 153, 170, 202. *See also* Food production, organization of during war; Micronesian relations with Japanese military; *and the specific names of individual islands*

Conscription. *See* labor

Construction of bases. *See* Military bases, construction of Japanese; Military bases, construction of US/Allied

Consumer goods. *See* Imported goods

Craven, Wesley Frank, and James Lea Cate, 145, 158, 439

Cross-cultural interactions: among Micronesians, 54–55, 60–64, 56, 102–103, 110; between Micronesians and Americans, 309–313, 341–342, 427nn. 35, 36, 37, 431n. 27; between Micronesians and Japanese, 221–222, 342–344. *See also* Micronesian relations with Americans; Micronesian relations with Japanese

Daily life: on bypassed islands, 169–228; prewar, 16–19; wartime regulation of, 49, 52–53, 90–91

Dan (*nahnmwarki* of Pingelap), 103

Dances: during war, 52, 67, 206–207, 217, 232, 416n. 17

David, Keropin (Pohnpei), 78

David, Obet (Pohnpei), 267

Deaths of Micronesians: from disease and malnutrition, 69, 155, 173–174, 176, 185, 186, 409n. 2, 410n. 4, 422n. 21; executions by Japanese military, 163–164, 129, 130, 163–164, 178, 190, 192, 227–229, 231, 413n. 1; from fishing with dynamite, 95–96, 159–160; from other causes, 95, 133, 160; themes of, 111, 114, 115, 129, 133, 139, 140–144, 151, 152–153, 160, 198. *See also* casualties from military action

Debris. *See* War: physical remains

Democracy: US policy in Micronesia, 278, 283–289, 348, 421n. 7

Denfeld, D. Colt, 145, 147, 257, 335, 439; and Scott Russell, 44, 46, 145, 158, 439, 440

Dengoki, Kyota (Palau), 185

Destruction: due to military operations, 117, 135–154, 164, 172, 205, 241, 248, 256, 257, 267, 315, 316–320, 428n. 1, 429nn. 5–8; of property by American military, 291, 421n. 4, 428n. 3, 429n. 4; of property by Japanese military, 37, 38, 47, 83–84, 86, 89, 181–184. *See also* the specific names of individual islands

Diana, Mikel (Pohnpei), 79, 189, 208

Disease. *See* Health

Displacement. *See* Evacuation, Relocation

Dolan, Susan, 42, 63, 66, 67, 202, 254, 440

Dosilua, Valentine (Pohnpei), 69

Dublon (Chuuk). *See* Toloas Island

Eas, Ichios (Chuuk), 8, 83, 151, 160, 176–177, 187, 208, 212, 217, 272–273, 292–293

Ebel, Elson (Marshalls), 94, 122, 127, 129–130, 173, 222, 227, 228

Ebon (Marshall Islands), 45, 57, 113–114, 115, 241, 414n. 9

Economic development: destruction of economy in war, 170–171, 316–324; prewar intensification of, 34–35, 39–42; Nan'yo programs of, 15, 17, 19–25, 34–35; "primitivism" in US Navy policies, 297–300, 301–304, 306–307, 308, 342, 424n. 20, 426nn. 31, 32, 427n. 34; initial US efforts in occupied islands, 241–243, 249–250, 268–273, 415nn. 12, 13; under US Navy administration, 278, 289–309, 320, 328–329, 423nn. 14, 17, 425n. 22, 426nn. 32, 33, 427nn. 34, 35. *See also the specific names of individual islands*

Eddmont, Otinel (Kosrae), 79, 136, 236

Edison, Kija (Marshalls), 186–187, 216

Education: in Nan'yo, 17, 28–29, 35, 53, 64–66, 396nn. 19, 20; under US Navy, 250, 296–297, 313, 326, 328–329, 415n. 12, 424n. 19; during war, 35, 161–162, 206. *See also* Schools

Edward, Apinar (Marshalls), 272

Edwin, Ikiechy (Chuuk), 103

Edwin, Victor (Pohnpei/Sapwuahfik), 157

Elections: municipal, under US Navy administration, 284–285, 287, 421n. 7, 422n. 13, 423n. 14; postwar Saipan, 250

Elites: change in status of Japanese-educated, 287, 326–328, 430n. 17; Japanese-educated, 64–66, 208–210; postwar, 265, 328; prewar, 64–66; during war, 97, 109–110, 208–214. *See also* Chiefs; Leaders; Micronesian-European families; Micronesian-Japanese families; Police, Japanese

Ellice Islands. *See* Tuvalu

Ellis, Earl "Pete" (U.S. intelligence), 41, 398n. 5

Embree, John F. 170, 271, 278, 315, 327, 347, 440

Emotions: anger/resentment, 224–225, 411n. 16, 413n. 22; at beginning of war, 112–113; at end of war, 267, 300, 301, 251–252; greed/selfishness, 185–186; grief/pity, 124, 129, 140, 198; love/compassion, 186–187, 208; pity for Japanese troops, 184–185, 218–221; pride in war work, 58, 104–105, 404n. 15; sadness/homesickness, 44–45; in recounting war stories, 5, 326–327; during war, 152–153, 206. *See also* Fear, Micronesian feelings of

Employment by Americans, 269–275; in Chuuk, 293; in Guam, 252, 270, 304–305, 419n. 31, 425n. 26; in Marshalls, 241, 242, 270–271, 291, 415n. 12, 419n. 32, 428n. 40; in Pohnpei, 428n. 40; in Saipan, 270, 419nn. 33, 34, 425n. 26; Tinian, 270

Gomez, Wendolin (Pohnpei), 65, 110, 136–137, 146–147

Goodenough, Ward H., and Hiroshi Sugita, 113, 443, 452

Goofalaan, Joseph-Mary (dance master of Yap), 335

Guam: battle for, 162–165, 164, 251–252, 404n. 13, 409n. 25; Japanese invasion and occupation, 38–40, 398n. 4; memories of war, 337–338, 349, 431n. 25; US MilGov, 251, 416n. 20, 421n. 4, 425n. 26; postwar conditions, 304, 323, 326, 340, 323, 425nn. 26, 27, 429n. 12; prewar preparations, 38; US bases, 92, 252, 270, 325, 416n. 20, 419n. 31, 425n. 26; US reoccupation, 245, 251–252, 415n. 3, 416n. 20. See also Agana

Gurtmag, Venitu (Yap), 86, 193, 260, 261

Hall, Edward T., 177, 284, 301, 311, 443; and Karl J. Peltzer, 151, 197, 204, 292, 294, 297–298, 301, 302–303, 443

Handicrafts: clothing manufacture, 188, 189, 190; in postwar economy, 243, 290, 291, 296, 302–303; in prewar economy, 20, 24–25, 105, 425n. 24; for US servicemen, 118, 157, 263, 271–272, 291; during war, 91, 100, 107, 157, 184, 215, 216; weaving as wartime labor, 79–80, 107, 404n. 14

"Hardships" of war. See War, threat of recent and future

Hartman, Manuel (Chuuk), 61, 84, 208, 231–232

Hatanaka Sachiko, 19, 26, 30–31, 53, 67–68, 345, 444

Hatchkarawi, Dione (Kapingamarani), 90

Hathey, Belarmino (Yap), 274

Hazard, George (Kwajalein), 205

Health: hospitals, 65, 97, 107, 110, 136–137, 146, 150, 180, 188, 205–206, 319; impact of war on, 107, 162, 170, 180, 184, 195–196, 198, 205–206, 218–220, 241, 247, 248, 250, 251, 252, 410n. 4; in Nan'yo, 24, 65, 395n. 9; traditional practices, 408n. 17; under US Navy administration, 126, 250, 257, 269, 296–297

Hebel, Linter (Pohnpei), 212

Hebel, Rosete (Pohnpei), 55, 107, 198, 199–200, 222

Heine, Carl, 128, 231, 288, 306, 320, 444

Heine, Claude (Marshalls), 231

Hezel, Fr. Francis X., xi, 34, 53, 202, 290, 298, 317, 348, 444

Highland, Sam (Kiribati), 37, 445

Higuchi, Wakako, xii, 66–67, 68, 69, 161, 162, 168, 185, 195, 233, 435, 445

History: Micronesian, prewar, 6–7; oral, 4; Pacific War summary, 7–8; place of war memories in Micronesian, 1–6, 344; war memories as genres of, 332–340

Hough, Frank O., 39, 164, 247, 445

Howard, Clive, and Joe Whitley, 128, 136, 142, 445

Hunt, Edward E., Jr., Nathaniel R. Kidder, David M. Schneider, and William D. Stevens, 87, 287, 327, 445

Ianguchel, Peter (Yap), 213, 260, 262, 269

Ifaluk (Caroline Islands): postwar, 423n. 17; prewar, 50, 64; during war, 88, 115,

157, 184, 198, 246, 399n. 14, 403n. 8,
408n. 21, 418n. 29
Ikefai (Puluwat), 89
Images: of Americans by Micronesians,
8, 12, 65, 161, 168, 203–204, 309–310,
340–342; of Japanese by Micronesians, 8, 30, 64, 215–223, 340–344,
395n. 9; of Micronesians by Japanese,
24, 27, 31–32, 397n. 24; of Pacific Islanders by Americans, 12, 118–119,
168, 237, 237, 298–301, 309–310,
405nn. 2, 6, 414n. 5, 418n. 28, 424n.
20, 427n. 35; "primitivism" in US
Navy policies, 297–300, 301–304,
306–307, 308, 342, 424n. 20, 426nn.
31, 32, 427n. 34. *See also* Americans;
Japanese
Immigration of Japanese and Okinawans: Chuuk, 23; Guam, 39; Kosrae, 23; Marianas, 21–22, 400n. 23;
Marshalls, 24–25; Micronesian relations, 16–17, 31–32, 35; Palau, 22,
395n. 7; Pohnpei, 22–23, 395nn. 8,
9; prewar, 19–20, 21–25, 31, 35,
74, 395n. 5. *See also* Micronesian-
Japanese relations
Imported goods: prewar, 17, 23, 298;
postwar shortages, 292–293, 296,
298–300, 303, 423n. 14; shortages
during war, 78, 169, 170, 171, 184,
187–191, 262; abundant supplies
from Americans, 118, 267–270, 415n.
13. *See also* Clothing; Economic
development
Interned non-Micronesian civilians,
46–47, 204, 411n. 14, 416n. 21. *See also*
Etscheit (Belgian family on Pohnpei);
Missionaries

Internment camps: Japanese, on Guam,
163–164, 252; US, on Saipan, 163,
247–248, 249, 250, 271
Invasion. *See the specific names of individual islands*
Ipon, Kenio (Mortlocks), 60, 184,
198–199

Jackson, Tulpe (Kosrae), 106, 107
Jabwor (Jaluij Atoll, Marshall Islands):
postwar, 316, 319; prewar, 25, 45; during war, 36, 128, 216. *See also* Jaluij
Jak, Lusios (Pohnpei), 112, 180, 192
Jaluij (Marshall Islands): escapes from,
131–132, *134*, 135, 159; fortification, 45,
63, 402n. 1; postwar, 266, 418n. 29;
prewar, 17, 25, 45; strategic role, 44,
45; surrender, 253, 417n. 26; US air
attacks, 50–51, 119, 126, 127, 399n. 15,
406n. 7; wartime conditions, 62, 128,
172, 173, 174, 200–201, 203. *See also*
Escapes from Japanese-held islands,
Marshall Islands
Japan: Micronesian travel to, 28, 33, 64,
196, 326; postwar links with, 339–340,
345–346
Japanese: evaluations of behavior, 215–
223; as generous and kind, 99–100,
105, 215–217, 220, 222; as powerful,
62–63, 120, 127; as powerless, 235,
261, 262–264; as similar to Micronesians, 32, 64, 215, 341, 342–343;
as strict, 8, 18, 28, 30, 32, 56, 101–
105, 221–222. *See also* Micronesian-
Japanese relations
Japanese convict laborers: 44, 45, 48, 49,
53–54; Chuuk, 48, 410n. 4; Kosrae, 53,
80; Marshalls, 45, 55

Japanese emperor (Tenno Heika), 30, 65, 66, 67, 101, 160, 201

Japanese military: Army-Navy differences, 73–75, 215, 411n. 13; Micronesian service in, 33, 39, 67–72; prewar Navy role, 15; relations with civil government, 41, 42, 45, 101, 150, 191–195; repatriation of troops after surrender, 261–264, 270. *See also* military bases, construction of Japanese Micronesian relations with Japanese military; *and the specific names of individual islands*

Jelkan, Carl (Marshalls), 130

Jemes, Andohn (Pohnpei), 106, 114, 222, 267

Jemes, Mary Jane (Pohnpei), 53, 106, 224

Jessy, Toli (Chuuk), 83, 105, 148, 192, 203, 268, 273, 284

Jibon, Joseph (Marshalls), 36, 51, 103–104, 115, 159, 192, 203, 216, 222, 228

John, Iwate (Chuuk), 220

Jorju, Leban (Marshalls), 66, 113, 120–121, 243–244

Kahn, E. J., Jr., 316, 328, 336, 351, 446

Kansou, Sontak (Chuuk), 66, 100, 102, 149, 152, 170, 186

Kapingamarangi (Caroline Islands): Kapinga people on Pohnpei, 25, 77–78, 96, 110, 157, 395n. 14, 404n. 15; postwar, 325, 423n. 15; during war, 90, 218, 221

Karen, Masako Luhk (Pohnpei), 79, 108, 170, 189

Kava (sakau): on Pohnpei, 153, 205

Kilafwasru, Tolenna (Kosrae), 79, 110

Kili (Marshall Islands), 76, 414n. 9

Kilimete, Dobi (Pohnpei), 61, 181, 189, 205

Kilimete, Peleng (Pohnpei), 207, 330, 331

King, Thomas, and Patricia Parker, 95, 147, 447

King, Thomas F., and J. Carucci, 95, 177, 333, 335, 447

kinrohoshi (public labor). *See* Labor

Kinship: altered by labor, 26, 54, 69–70, 98, 99, 105, 106, 107, 113–114, 209, 411nn. 15, 16; assistance among kin, 60, 88, 150, 161, 171, 177, 184, 186–187; Japanese executing kin in Marshall Islands, 129, 131, 197, 227–228; separation of Micronesian-Japanese families, 74–75, 301; use of shaming before kin on Chuuk, 152, 179; ties weakened under stress, 153–154, 177, 217; worry while separated, 91, 168, 185–186, 196–197, 198–199, 411nn. 15, 16. *See also* Micronesian-Japanese families

Kiribati: Allied bases in, 135, 278, 406n. 7, 420n. 2; Allied invasion of, 74, 76, 114, 117–118, 127, 237, 414n. 5; Japanese seizure and occupation, 9, 36–37, 38, 50, 397n. 2; people moved to Kosrae, 57, 60, 180, 204, 266, 401n. 24; people moved to Nauru, 38; US marine raid on, 37, 398n. 3

Kiti (Pohnpei). *See* Pohnpei

Kofak, Kalifin (Chuuk), 96, 97, 159–160, 170

Kohatsu. *See Nan'yo Kohatsu Kaisha*

Kolonia (Pohnpei): bombing of, 135–138, 145, 150, 257, 316, 407n. 16; postwar, 279, 317, 320, 340; prewar, 22; during

ism, 67, 159–162; privileged, 97; shift to unpaid, 100–101, 170; and social disruption, 91, 98, 108; Sundays, 53, 93, 98; types of, 94–97; while under attack, 128, 129–130, 148, 151–152, 170, 172–173, 223; by women, 79–80, 87, 105–108; negative memories of, 93; positive memories of, 104–105. *See also* Children, Wartime labor; Women

Labor during initial phase of military construction, 42, 44, 47, 53–60; Chuuk, 48, 49; Marshalls, 45, 51–52, 55, 56; movement of, 50, 54, 56–60, 60–62, 400n. 20; and social disruption, 26, 57; types of, 45, 49, 56; volunteer (*kinrohoshi*), 54–55, 400n. 19. *See also the specific names of individual islands*

Labor for US military. *See* employment by Americans *the specific names of individual islands*

Laborers: Chuuk, 48, 94, 257; foreign military construction: 44, 47, 53, 60, 169, 236, 333n. 13; Guam, 40, 163; Kosrae, 47, 53, 80, 180, 401n. 24; Marshalls, 45, 55, 134, 173, 174, 203, 226–228; Micronesian relations with, 35, 44, 60, 65, 163, 203; Micronesians working with, 45, 49, 53–54, 55, 65, 180; US military policy towards, 236, 248, 250, 257, 413n. 3; Palau, 185; Pohnpei, 65, 77, 411n. 14; repatriation, 276, 300–301, 424n 21; Saipan, 163, 248, 249, 400n. 23; Yap, 85, 87, 94, 100; *See also* Japanese convict laborers; Koreans; Okinawans

Lae (Marshall Islands), 414n. 9

Laelôñeo, Labwinmij (Marshalls), 344

La'ew, Martina (Yap), 74, 87, 262, 267, 274

Laimroj (Marshalls), 227

Lainlan (chief, Majuro), 120

Lainos, Pernardo (Pohnpei), 60–61

Lamotrek (Caroline Islands), 148, 418n. 26

Land ownership: on Chuuk, 321; Japanese seizure for military bases, 41, 44–45, 46, 47, 74, 77, 82–83, 90, 98–99, 320, 398n. 6, 399n. 12; on Palau, 322; on Pohnpei, 321–322; postwar problems, 279, 320–326, 415n. 11, 425n. 26, 429nn. 9–13; prewar, 21–25, 29, 395nn. 8, 9, 396n. 14; on Saipan, 322–323; US seizure for military bases, 321, 322, 323–324, 325, 430n. 15

Language: Micronesians' knowledge of English, 119, 156–157, 231, 237, 255–256, 258, 261, 265, 272, 273–275, 296, 312, 313, 326, 327, 328, 420n. 37, 424n. 19, 427n. 34; Micronesians' knowledge of Japanese, 25, 28, 31, 32, 64, 193, 209–210, 216, 260; and military security, 61, 200–201, 203, 224, 231; translators for Americans, 242, 273–274, 275, 284, 327, 329, 420n. 37

Lankein (chief, Marshalls), 212–213

Lankio, Ato (Marshalls), 239–240

Lantir, Luke (Marshalls), 62

Lautona, Ijimura, 76, 121, 195

Lawrence, Lihna (Pohnpei), 78, 108

Lawrence, Pensile, 47, 57–58, 61, 112–113, 224, 329

Leaders: change in status, 326–330, 430n. 18; effective Japanese military,

Mauricio, Augustine (Pohnpei), 62–63

McGrath, William, and W. Scott Wilson, 21, 25, 321, 324, 450

McKnight, Robert, 22, 32, 346, 450

Medical care. *See* Health

Mejit (Marshall Islands), 415n. 9, 418n. 29

Melanesia: comparison of war experiences, 11–12, 394n. 6, 405n. 2, 406n. 8, 414n. 5, 415n. 14

Melia, Johna (Pohnpei), 97

Memories of war, 1–6, 10, 93, 104, 116, 145, 155, 185, 186–187, 215, 220, 221, 230–231, 329–330; generational differences, 329, 341, 353–354, 354–355; genres of war memory, 332–340; recollections of Nan'yo era, 16–17, 28–32; impact of recollections of Nan'yo on modern life, 300, 332–333, 347–355, 432n. 31; recollections of the start of war, 40, 43, 46, 49, 50, 110, 112–116, 398n. 10, 399n. 16; retrospective comparisons of Japanese and American rule, 340–347; role of in modern Micronesian geopolitics, 347–354; war as impersonal "typhoon," 10, 330–332

Mendiola, Felipe Camancho (mayor of Tinian), 39

Micronesia: geography, 6, 13, 75, 114; strategic position in Pacific War, 7–8, 75

Micronesian-American relations: contact and occupation by US forces, 230–231, 236–237; contact and occupation in western Micronesia, 191, 245–264; cross-cultural interaction during Navy era, 309–313, 420n. 36;

under Department of the Interior, 313–314; economic development under Navy, 289–309; geo-strategic differences in US occupation, 13–14, 264–265, 268–269, 270, 272, 278, 290–291, 301–302; labor relations, 270–275; Micronesians' retrospective on Americans and the war, 10, 330–333, 430nn. 20, 21, 431n. 27; Micronesians' views on US military, 348–354; occupation in Marshall Islands, 119–127, 237–245; political development under Navy, 273–289; under US Navy CivAd, 276–313; under US Navy MilGov, 264–270, 276

Micronesian Area Research Center, xi–xii

Micronesian-European families, 231–232

Micronesian-Japanese families (includes Micronesian-Okinawan families), 33, 64, 67, 74–75, 97, 109, 112, 210–211, 217, 231, 301, 340, 346. *See also* Mori family

Micronesian relations with Japanese civilians: comparison of prewar and wartime, 220–223; postwar, 183, 322, 323, 340, 343, 354–355; prewar, 7, 10, 16–19, 23, 25–32, 140, 220, 395n. 8; at repatriation, 301; in retrospect, 342–343, 432n. 28; during war, 63–72, 77, 79, 91, 92, 112, 113–114, 116, 176, 182–183, 191–195, 215–220. *See also* Friendship; Kinship; Sexual relations between Micronesians and Japanese

Micronesian relations with Japanese military: aid to suffering, 184, 218–219; fears of intention to kill Micronesians, 126, 131, 132, 163–164, 171,

Tinian (Mariana Islands): postwar, 304–305, 426n. 29, 428n. 1, 429n. 10; prewar, 21, 395n. 6; strategic role, 13; US base, 270, 416n. 16, 420n. 2; during war, 39, 45, 165, 249, 404n. 13, 416n. 16. *See also* Mariana Islands

Tipen, Ioana (Pohnpei), 321–322

Tobacco: cigarettes as gifts, 99, 260; plantation on Pohnpei, 22; shortages, 171, 190, 260; use during war, 101, 105, 128, 157, 171, 183, 240, 255

Tobi (Caroline Islands), 46, 157, 268, 395n. 14

Tol Island (Chuuk): Nauruans on, 61–62, 401n. 25; prewar, 24; during war, 83, 84, 96, 99, 109, 116, 145, 150, 176, 187, 202, 203, 206, 207, 210, 212, 217. *See also* Chuuk

Tolerton, Burt, and Jerome Rauch, 26, 54, 55, 108, 296, 460

Toloas Island (Chuuk): postwar, 256, 316, 317–318, *319, 336;* prewar, 24, 256; US bombing of, 138–144, *143,* 148, 151, 198, 211, 217, 316, 407n. 14; during war, 48, 81–82, 83, 97, 98, 109, 113, 114–115, 150–153, 170–171, 176, 188, 193, 206, 211, 217, 399n. 11. *See also* Chuuk

Tomeing (chief, Marshalls), 45, 242–243

Tommy, Saikichi (Chuuk), 84

Tourism: war-related, 320, 335–336, 340

Trade: informal, during war, 90, 170, 176, 177, 184, 188, 189, 191, 211, 215–217, 232

Traders: Japanese on outer islands, 20, 49, 396n. 14

Training of Micronesians: civil defense, 53, 110–111, 114–115; military, 68, 161–162, 409n. 23

Translators: for Americans, 242, 273–274, 275, 284, 327, 329, 420n. 37; for Japanese, 193, 208, 326

Travel: for contract labor, 25, 26, 42, 50, 54, 56–57, 61, 400n. 20; Micronesians to Japan, 28, 33, 64, 196, 326; postwar restrictions, 305; restricted during war, 53, 56–57, 88, 90, 91, 109, 128, 195–199, 206, 417n. 21

Truk. *See* Chuuk

Trumbull, Robert, 68, 256, 305, 311, 314, 336, 460

Trust Territory of the Pacific Islands: dissolution of, 349–351; establishment of, 276, 420n. 1, 421nn. 3, 7, 424n. 20, 427n. 37; later years, 313–314

Turner, Richmond Kelly (Admiral), 290

Tuvalu: Allied bases in, 118, 397n. 2, 404n. 1, 405n. 2; people on Kosrae, 60, 266, 401n. 24; people on Nauru, 38

"Typhoon" of war: image, 262, 330–332, 393n. 1, 430n. 19

Typhoon Society on Pohnpei, 16

Ujae (Marshall Islands), 45, 414n. 9

Ujelang (Marshall Islands), 45, 245, 267, 339, 415n. 9, 420n. 2

Ulithi (Caroline Islands): postwar repatriation, 352, 418n. 29, 430n. 20; prewar, 64, 396n. 14; during war, 50, 91, 165, 168, 171, 223, 404n. 11; US base, 155, *156,* 168, 246, *247,* 274, 317, 415n. 15, 429n. 7

Uludong, Francisco, T., 460

Underwood, Robert A., 337, 460

United Nations Visiting Mission, 307–308, 314

ABOUT THE AUTHORS

All three authors are anthropologists with many years of Pacific experience. Lin Poyer, of the University of Wyoming, has conducted field research with the people of Sapwuahfik and is the author of *The Ngatik Massacre* (1993). Suzanne Falgout, at the University of Hawai'i, West Oahu, has published on Pohnpei and the history of anthropology in Micronesia. Laurence Marshall Carucci's research has long focused on the Marshall Islands. He is a professor at Montana State University and the author of *Nuclear Nativity*.

CPSIA information can be obtained
at www.ICGtesting.com
Printed in the USA
LVOW01*2017150316

479297LV00007B/28/P